Teaching Physical Education

FOR LEARNING

SIXTH EDITION

Teaching Physical Education
FOR LEARNING

Judith E. Rink

University of South Carolina

Mc Graw Hill **Higher Education**

Boston   Burr Ridge, IL   Dubuque, IA   New York   San Francisco   St. Louis
Bangkok   Bogotá   Caracas   Kuala Lumpur   Lisbon   London   Madrid   Mexico City
Milan   Montreal   New Delhi   Santiago   Seoul   Singapore   Sydney   Taipei   Toronto

A Division of The McGraw-Hill Companies

Published by McGraw-Hill, an imprint of The McGraw-Hill Companies, Inc., 1221 Avenue of the Americas, New York, NY 10020. Copyright © 2010, 2006, 2002, 1998, 1993, 1985 The McGraw-Hill Companies, Inc. All rights reserved. No part of this publication may be reproduced or distributed in any form or by any means, or stored in a database or retrieval system, without the prior written consent of The McGraw-Hill Companies, Inc., including, but not limited to, in any network or other electronic storage or transmission, or broadcast for distance learning.

This book is printed on acid-free paper.

1 2 3 4 5 6 7 8 9 0 FGR/FGR 0 9

ISBN: 978-0-07-337652-3
MHID: 0-07-337652-3

Editor in Chief: *Michael Ryan*
Publisher: *William R. Glass*
Senior Sponsoring Editor: *Christopher Johnson*
Executive Marketing Manager: *Pamela Cooper*
Development Editor: *Phil Butcher*
Editorial Coordinator: *Marley Magaziner*
Production Editors: *Melissa Williams/Les Chappell, Macmillan Publishing Solutions*
Manuscript Editor: *Jillian West*
Cover Designer: *Margarite Reynolds/Carole Lawson*
Production Supervisor: *Louis Swaim*
Composition: This text was set in 10/12 Times Roman by Macmillan Publishing Solutions
Printing: Printed on 45# New Era Matte Plus by Quebecor World, Inc.

Library of Congress Cataloging-in-Publication Data

Rink, Judith.
    Teaching physical education for learning / Judith E. Rink.—6th ed.
        p. cm.
    ISBN 0-07-337652-3
    1. Physical education and training—Study and teaching. 2. Physical education for children—Study and teaching. I. Title.
    GV363.R55 2010
    613.7'07—dc22

                                                                                                        2009002183

For my mother, Eleanor

Brief Contents

Preface   xv

PART I
Understanding the Teaching-Learning Process

1   Teaching Physical Education:
     An Orientation   1

2   Factors That Influence Learning   21

PART II
Effective Teaching Skills

3   Designing Learning Experiences
     and Tasks   41

4   Task Presentation   62

5   Content Analysis and Development   82

6   Developing and Maintaining a Learning
     Environment   107

7   Teacher Functions During Activity   130

8   Teaching Strategies   151

9   Student Motivation, Personal Growth,
     and Inclusion   181

10   Planning   209

11   Assessment in the Instructional Process   239

PART III
Context and Reflection

12   Content-Specific Pedagogy   269

13   The Professional Teacher and the
      Continuous Learner   304

14   Observation Techniques and Tools   322

Glossary   352

Index   357

Contents

Preface   xv

PART I
Understanding the Teaching-Learning Process

1 **Teaching Physical Education: An Orientation   1**

Teaching as a Goal-Oriented Activity   2
  Types of Goals   3
  Establishing Realistic Goals   5
  Choosing Instructional Processes to Meet Goals   6
  Achieving Goals Through Processes   6
Criteria for a Learning Experience   7
  Criterion One   9
  Criterion Two   10
  Criterion Three   11
  Criterion Four   11
Understanding the Instructional Process   12
  Prelesson and Postlesson Routines   12
  Movement Task–Student Response Unit of Analysis   13
  Teaching Functions   14
  Management and Content Behavior   15
Looking to the Future: Becoming a Professional Teacher   16
  Value Positions and Beliefs in Teaching   16
  Personal Characteristics of a Teacher   17
  Developing Commitment   18

Summary   19
Checking Your Understanding   19

2 **Factors That Influence Learning   21**

What Is Learning?   22
How Do People Learn Motor Skills?   23
Understanding the Control of Movement   24
Stages of Motor Learning   25
Requirements for Learning a Motor Skill   26
  Prerequisites   27
  Clear Idea of the Task   27
  Motivational/Attentional Disposition to the Skill   28
  Practice   28
  Feedback   28
The Nature of Motor Skill Goals   29
  Open and Closed Skills   29
  Discrete, Serial, and Continuous Skills   31
Issues of Appropriateness in Skill Development and Learning   31
  Environmental Conditions   31
  Learner Abilities   32
Practice Profiles and Success Rates   33
  Whole or Part   33
  Practice Variability   33
  Massed and Distributed Practice   35
Motivation and Goal Setting   35
Transfer of Learning   36
  Bilateral Transfer   36
  Intertask Transfer   36
  Intratask Transfer   37

Learner Characteristics   37
    Motor Ability   37
    Intelligence and Cognitive Development   38
Summary   39
Checking Your Understanding   39

PART II
Effective Teaching Skills

3 Designing Learning Experiences and Tasks   41

Criteria for a Learning Experience   42
Designing the Movement Task   42
    Content Dimension of Movement Tasks   43
    Goal-Setting Dimension of the Task   44
    Organizational Arrangements for Tasks   46
Transitions from One Organization to
    Another   52
Designing Learning Experiences That Are Safe   52
Teacher Legal Liability for Student Safety   53
Student Decision Making in Environmental
    Arrangements   54
The Influence of the Nature of Motor Content
    on the Design of a Learning Experience   55
    Closed Skills   57
    Open Skills   58
Summary   59
Checking Your Understanding   60

4 Task Presentation   62

Getting the Attention of the Learner   63
    Establishing Signals and Procedures   64
    Student Preoccupation with Other
        Environmental Factors   65
    Inability to Hear or See   65
    Inefficient Use of Time   65
Sequencing the Content and Organizational
    Aspects of Tasks   66
Improving the Clarity of Communication   67
    Orient the Learner (Set Induction)   67
    Sequence the Presentation in Logical Order   68
    Give Examples and Nonexamples   68
    Personalize the Presentation   68
    Repeat Things Difficult to Understand   68
    Draw on the Personal Experience of
        Students   68
    Check for Understanding   68
    Present Material Dynamically   69
Choosing a Way to Communicate   69
    Verbal Communication   69
    Demonstration   69
    Media Materials   72
Selecting and Organizing Learning Cues   72
    Good Cues Are Accurate   73
    Good Cues Are Brief and Critical to the Skill
        Being Performed   73
    Good Cues Are Appropriate to the Learner's
        Skill Level and Age   75
    Good Cues Are Appropriate for Different
        Types of Content   77
    Cues Are More Effective If They Are
        Sequentially Organized and Learners Have
        the Opportunity to Rehearse Them   79
Summary   81
Checking Your Understanding   81

5 Content Analysis and Development   82

The Process of Content Development—
    Overview   83
    Establish a Progression (Extension)   83
    Demonstrate a Concern for Quality
        of Performance (Refinement)   84
    Give Students an Opportunity to Apply/Assess
        Their Skills (Application)   85
Planning for Content Development: The
    Developmental Analysis   86
    Developing Extension Tasks—The Teacher's
        Progression   88
    Adding the Qualities of Refinement   92
    Designing Application/Assessment Experiences
        for Content   93
    What Content Development Looks Like
        in a Real Lesson   95
Guidelines for Developing Different Types
    of Content   95
    Developing Closed Skills   96

Developing Closed Skills Performed in Different
Environments 98
Developing Open Skills 98
Summary 105
Checking Your Understanding 105

6 Developing and Maintaining a Learning Environment 107

The Ecology of the Gymnasium 108
Establishing and Maintaining a Management
System 109
Establishing Routines 109
Establishing Class Rules 113
Gaining and Maintaining the Cooperation of
Students 114
Strategies for Developing Student Self-Control
and Responsibility 117
Hellison's Levels of Responsibility 118
Behavior Modification 118
Authoritative Orientations to
Management 122
Group Process Strategies for Developing
Self-Direction 122
Conflict Resolution 123
Discipline: What to Do If It Does Not
Work 123
Deterring Problems Before They
Become Problems 124
Continued Inappropriate Behavior 124
Handling Students Who Continually
Misbehave 126
Summary 128
Checking Your Understanding 128

7 Teacher Functions During Activity 130

I've Sent the Students Off to Practice—Now
What? 131
Setting Priorities of What to Do First 133
Maintaining a Safe Learning Environment 134
Clarifying and Reinforcing Tasks
for Learners 134
Maintaining a Productive Learning
Environment 135

Observing and Analyzing Student
Responses 136
Positioning of the Teacher 137
Determining a Plan for Observing Large
Groups 137
Knowing What to Look For 138
Providing Feedback to Learners 139
Evaluative and Corrective Feedback 140
Congruency of Feedback 140
General versus Specific Feedback 141
Negative versus Positive Feedback 142
The Target of Feedback 143
Timing of Feedback 144
Use of Feedback to Promote Student
Understanding 144
Changing and Modifying Tasks for Individuals
and Small Groups 144
Extending the Task for Individuals 145
Designing Applying/Assessment Task
for Individuals 145
Changing the Task Completely
for Individuals 146
Refining the Task for Individuals 146
Indirectly Contributing Behaviors 146
Attending to Injured Students 146
Engaging in Off-Topic Discussions 147
Dealing with the Personal Needs
of Students 147
Participating with Students and
Officiating 148
Noncontributing Behaviors 148
Summary 148
Checking Your Understanding 149

8 Teaching Strategies 151

Direct and Indirect Instruction 152
The Teaching Strategy as a Delivery
System 155
Selection of Content 156
Communication of Tasks 156
Progression of Content 156
Provision for Feedback and Evaluation 156
The Teaching Strategies Described 156
Interactive Teaching 157

Station Teaching   160
Peer Teaching   162
Cooperative Learning   166
Self-Instructional Strategies   169
Cognitive Strategies   172
Team Teaching   175
Selecting a Teaching Strategy   179
Summary   179
Checking Your Understanding   179

9   Student Motivation, Personal Growth, and Inclusion   181

Motivation in Learning   183
Theories of Motivation—The Why of
    Behavior   183
    Behaviorism   183
    Social Learning Theory   183
    Self-Determination Theory   183
    *Achievement Goal and Social Goals
        Theory*   184
    Interest Theories   185
    *Designing Experiences to Develop Personal
        and Situational Interest*   186
    Implications of Theories of Motivation   186
Promoting Personal Growth Through Personal
    Interaction   190
Motivation and Personal Growth Through
    Instructional Decision Making   192
    Planning   192
    *Selection of Tasks and Design of Learning
        Experiences*   193
    Presentation of Units and Tasks   194
    Organizational Arrangements   195
    Teacher Functions During Activity   195
    Pacing of Lessons   196
    *Assessment of Tasks, Units, and
        Lessons*   196
Teaching Affective Goals as a Lesson
    Focus   196
    *The Unique and Shared Affective Goals
        of Physical Education*   197
    *Instructional Strategies for Teaching
        Affect*   197
Physical Education for Inclusion   199

Becoming Aware   200
Developing a Climate for Inclusion   201
Building Equity   202
    Gender Equity   202
    Ethnic and Cultural Differences   203
    Disadvantaged Students   203
    Students with Disabilities   204
Discussion of Affective Goals for Physical
    Education   206
Summary   207
Checking Your Understanding   207

10   Planning   209

Establishing Goals and Objectives
    for Learning   211
    *Writing Objectives in Terms of What Students
        Will Learn*   211
    *Levels of Specificity in Educational
        Objectives*   213
    *Objectives in the Three Learning
        Domains*   215
Writing Objectives Consistent with Content
    Standards   215
Planning Physical Education Experiences   217
Planning the Lesson   217
    Beginning the Lesson   218
    Developing the Lesson   218
    Ending the Lesson—Closure   219
    Format for Lesson Planning   219
    Planning the Curriculum   225
    *Developing Curriculum from a Set of
        Standards*   226
    Planning for Units of Instruction   226
    Considerations in Planning Units   229
    Developing the Unit   231
    The Unit Plan   232
Summary   238
Checking Your Understanding   238

11   Assessment in the Instructional Process   239

The Role of Assessment in Physical Education
    Programs   240

Formative and Summative Assessment   241
  Formative Assessment   241
  Summative Assessment   242
Validity and Reliability Issues of
  Assessment   243
  Validity of Assessment Measures   243
  Reliability of Assessment Measures   244
Collecting Information: Formal and Informal
  Evaluation   245
Alternative Assessment   246
  Checklists   246
  Rating Scales   247
  Scoring Rubrics   247
Types of Student Assessment   248
  Observation   248
  Event Tasks   250
  Student Journals   255
  Portfolio   256
  Written Test   256
  Skill Tests   257
  Student/Group Projects and Reports   258
  Student Logs   258
  *Student Interviews, Surveys, and
    Questionnaires   258*
  Parental Reports   260
Making Assessment a Practical and Important
  Part of Your Program   260
  Establish Criteria   260
  Use Self-Testing Tasks Frequently   262
  *Use Simple Check Sheets and Rating
    Scales   262*
  Use Peer Assessment   263
  Use Thirty-Second Wonders   263
  Use DVD/Computers   263
  Sample Student Behavior   264
  Get Comfortable with Technology   264
Preparing for Formal and High-Stakes
  Assessment   264
Student Grading   266
  Student Achievement   266
  Student Improvement   266
  Student Effort   266
  Student Conduct   266
Summary   267
Checking Your Understanding   267

PART III
Context and Reflection

12 **Content-Specific Pedagogy   269**

Teaching Lifetime Physical Activity and
  Fitness   270
  Teaching Lifetime Physical Activity   271
  *Teaching Fitness Concepts in the
    Classroom   272*
Curricular Alternatives to Teaching
  Fitness   272
Teaching Games and Sports   275
  The Games Stages   276
  Considerations Using the Games Stages   284
  *Tactical and Skill Approaches to Teaching
    Games and Sports   284*
  Sport Education   286
  Dance   287
  Gymnastics   287
  Outdoor Pursuits   287
Movement Concepts—Teaching for
  Transfer   289
  *Learning Theory Associated with the Transfer
    of Learning   290*
  *Important Concepts in Physical
    Education   291*
  Teaching Movement Concepts   295
Summary   301
Checking Your Understanding   302

13 **The Professional Teacher and the Continuous
    Learner   304**

Teaching as a Profession   305
What Does It Mean to Act Professionally?   305
  *Professional Teachers Acquire the Skills
    for Best Practice   305*
  *Professional Teachers Are Continuous
    Learners   307*
Collecting Information on Your Teaching   312
  Maintaining a Teaching Portfolio   312
  *Collecting Data on the Products and Processes
    of Teaching   312*

Observing and Analyzing Your Teaching   313
  Deciding What to Look For   313
  *Choosing an Observational Method or Tool
    to Collect Information   315*
  Collecting Data   318
  *Analyzing and Interpreting the Meaning
    of Data   319*
  *Making Changes in the Instructional
    Process   319*
  Monitoring Change in Teaching   320
Summary   320
Checking Your Understanding   320

14 Observation Techniques and Tools   322

Observational Methods   323
  Intuitive Observation   323
  Anecdotal Records   325
  Rating Scales   327

  Scoring Rubric   329
  Event Recording   329
  Duration Recording   331
  Time Sampling   332
Observational Tools for the Analysis of
  Teaching   335
  Student Motor Activity: ALT-PE   335
  Student Use of Time   337
  Content Development: OSCD-PE   338
  Teacher Feedback   339
  Student Conduct   341
  *Qualitative Measures of Teaching Performance
    Scale (QMTPS)   343*
  Teacher Movement   347
Summary   350
Checking Your Understanding   350

Glossary   352

Index   357

Preface

The recent obesity epidemic in this country has given physical education programs an opportunity to demonstrate that we can achieve what we say we can do. In order to do this, teachers are going to have to have the skills to teach effectively to outcomes. Teaching is a process that is both interactive and context specific. Teachers need the technical skills of teaching, but they also need to be able to apply them situationally.

The focus of this book is on the basic skills of teaching that are appropriate to teaching all content areas. Without these skills teachers cannot be effective.

■ CHANGES IN THIS NEW EDITION

In this new edition, the beginning teaching standards (NASPE, 2008) are woven into each chapter's introduction and are used as a framework for the introductory chapter. The research chapter has been removed, primarily because other, more inclusive sources for this information are now available and most beginning methods classes have not used the chapter. The chapter including motivation has been rewritten to include a more comprehensive discussion of newer motivation theories as the basis for teacher decision making and teacher efforts to increase student motivation. New and revised sections on Mosston's teaching styles, organizational transitions, legal liability, Bloom's taxonomy, diversity, and writing objectives using standards have all been added to this addition. Additional examples and clarifications of material occur throughout.

■ ORGANIZATION

The text is organized to begin with an orientation chapter that sets the stage for student learning as the primary goal of the teaching process. This chapter is a key to developing student understanding of the importance of chapters to follow. It is followed by a chapter on factors that influence student learning. Although many programs have course work in motor learning and development, the essential concepts from these areas are presented with their implications for teaching.

Part II of the text presents chapters on the critical teaching skills for teaching physical education. Although there is a rationale for the order in which they are presented, it is expected that instructors use order flexibly according to the specific needs of a program. Part III of the text presents a chapter on content-specific pedagogy. This chapter is not intended to be inclusive of what a teacher needs to know to teach fitness, games/sports, or movement concepts, but rather begins to identify pedagogical issues specific to a content area. The Rink Games Stages, a model found useful by many programs to help learners understand progressions in teaching games, is described in this chapter. Chapters on the professional teacher and observational techniques and tools are included in Part III of the text, as well. Many instructors want to begin course work in pedagogy with the chapter on the professional teacher to set the stage for that course work. The chapter on observation is designed as a reference tool for systematic observation of teaching to facilitate instructor feedback on the teaching skills described in the text.

■ SUCCESSFUL FEATURES AND SUPPLEMENTS

Each chapter begins with an overview that sets the stage for the importance of the chapter, followed by an outline of the major topics presented in the chapter. Chapters conclude with a summary of key ideas of the chapter, questions designed to check student understanding of the materials, references, and suggested reading. The website that accompanies *Teaching Physical Education for Learning* includes a test bank of short-answer questions for the instructor, as well as PowerPoint presentations for each of the chapters.

The latest edition of *Moving into the Future: National Content Standards for Physical Education* can be packaged with *Teaching Physical Education for Learning* at the instructor's request. This resource is an ideal accompaniment for the text, as the standards define learning outcomes for effective teaching.

■ ACADEMIC REVIEWERS

I am indebted to the many friends, colleagues, and students with whom I have worked over the years. They are a continuous source of support and challenge for me and have played a major role in the development and growth of this text over the years. I am grateful to the reviewers who have challenged me to continue to make this text a better source for new generations of teachers.

Reviewers for this edition include:

Thomas Fuchs
State University of New York Cortland

Deborah A. Garrahy
Illinois State University

Betsy A. McKinley
Slippery Rock University

Joan Neide
California State University Sacramento

Teaching Physical Education: *An Orientation*

1

OVERVIEW

Teaching can be viewed from many perspectives. The perspective teachers take when they look at the teaching-learning process determines what they will look at in that process and how they will look at it. Perspectives are important because they cause the teacher to see things in certain ways. This chapter establishes a perspective for this text. It is an overview on instruction from which other chapters in the text are developed.

OUTLINE

- **Teaching as a goal-oriented activity**
  Types of goals
  Establishing realistic goals
  Choosing instructional processes
    to meet goals
  Achieving goals through processes
- **Criteria for a learning experience**
  Criterion One
  Criterion Two
  Criterion Three
  Criterion Four

- **Understanding the instructional process**
  Prelesson and postlesson routines
  Movement task–student response unit of
    analysis
  Teaching functions
  Management and content behavior
- **Looking to the future: Becoming a
  professional teacher**
  Value positions and beliefs in teaching
  Personal characteristics of a teacher
  Developing commitment

Most people who decide to teach physical education do so because they are good at it, have enjoyed their past experiences with sport and physical education, and like to work with people. These are good reasons to choose a profession. Because engaging in sport and physical activity is fun for most people, a misconception often exists that teaching physical education is easy, or at least easier than teaching any other content. Teaching physical education can be exciting, rewarding, and fun, but to do it effectively is not easy.

Teaching is a complex activity. Its goal is student learning. The teacher has primary responsibility for directing the teaching-learning process. This is why teaching can become difficult. If a student is not learning, the teacher must find an effective way to reach this student. There are many types of students and many types of skills, knowledges, and values that teachers will want to teach. Finding ways to reach objectives for learning with all students is a real challenge. Teaching is not an exact science. Teachers need to design and redesign experiences for their students based on their pedagogic goals and their knowledge of the learner, the lesson content, and the teaching-learning process.

Teaching Physical Education for Learning is primarily a text on instructional processes and the teaching skills required to execute those processes effectively; that is, what teachers can do to help students learn what teachers want them to learn. Several key ideas will be reinforced throughout this text. The first is that instruction is a *goal-oriented activity*. This means that the process is meaningless unless it is designed with a clear goal regarding what the student will learn. You will be asked to articulate what you want learners to learn as a result of what you do as a teacher. The second key idea is that *instructional processes are specific to an intent*. This means that you select an instructional process to best accomplish a specific purpose.

For instance, a teacher may decide to lead students through a problem-solving experience while teaching balance to help them understand principles related to base of support. The teacher selects *problem solving* as the instructional process rather than *telling* because the teacher's intent is not only that students know the information but that they are able to use this information in their balance activities. If you want students to lead a physically active lifestyle outside of your class and as adults, you will teach differently than if you want them only to know that physical activity is good for them.

It is important for teachers to choose instructional processes appropriate to their goals. To do this, teachers must have a clear idea of what they want students to be able to do and be able to implement instructional processes effectively for a given activity and group of students. This chapter explains the basic framework of the instructional process in physical education and identifies the skills needed to operate successfully within this framework.

■ TEACHING AS A GOAL-ORIENTED ACTIVITY

Instruction is guided by a long-term plan for student outcomes called the *curriculum*. When curricular decisions are not made or used to guide instruction, the instructional process is like a moving car without a driver. For this reason curriculum and instruction are integrally related. Teaching as a goal-oriented activity begins at the curricular level. Many curricular decisions in today's educational climate are being determined by content standards at the national, state, and local level that clearly prescribe what students should know and be able to do in physical education. The consensus in the field is that the purpose of physical education is the development of a physically active lifestyle. The national standards for physical education were developed and published by the National Association for Sport and Physical Education in 1995, revised in 2004, and have been used extensively by states and local districts to articulate program goals related to this purpose. The six standards describe the skills, abilities, and dispositions students will need to lead a physically active lifestyle. These standards are listed in box 1.1. In the publication *Moving into the Future: National Standards for Physical Education* (NASPE, 2004), each of the standards is broken down by grade level so teachers can identify what students at each age should know and be able to do.

National Content Standards for Physical Education Programs

Standard 1: Demonstrates competency in motor skills and movement patterns to perform a variety of physical activities.

Standard 2: Demonstrates understanding of movement concepts, principles, strategies, and tactics as they apply to the learning and performance of physical activities.

Standard 3: Participates regularly in physical activity.

Standard 4: Achieves and maintains a health-enhancing level of physical fitness.

Standard 5: Exhibits responsible personal and social behavior that respects self and others in physical activity settings.

Standard 6: Values physical activity for health, enjoyment, challenge, self-expression, and/or social interaction.

Reprinted from *Moving into the Future: National Standards for Physical Education* (2nd ed., 2004).

Physical educators must explain and defend their role and program in the schools. Physical education programs are expensive in the facilities, equipment, and personnel they require. Growing opportunities for students to participate in sport activities outside the schools have caused educators, administrators, and taxpayers to view with uncertainty the contributions of physical education programs to the overall educational picture. Research done by physical educators on the attitudes of secondary students toward physical education (and the products and processes of physical education programs) largely confirms the discrepancy between what physical educators promise and what they produce. Many physical education programs are not defensible. Lack of accountability for program goals in the schools has resulted in many poor programs of physical education: those without identifiable or defensible goals and programs that bear no relation to their stated goals. If physical education is to attain credibility as a truly educational program, the relationship between curriculum and instruction must be clearly defined and programs must be oriented toward clearly stated goals. The contrast between two elementary and secondary programs is made clear in box 1.2 (see p. 4), which describes two different programs, one defensible and one not defensible. Read the example and see if you can identify what it is that makes a program defensible.

Types of Goals

Educational program outcomes are commonly called **goals** when they refer to broad outcomes and **objectives** when they refer to more specific outcomes. Whereas curriculum objectives and, more recently, student performance standards usually define what the student should achieve as result of an entire program, instructional objectives usually describe what the student should achieve as a result of a single lesson or unit of instruction. Educational goals and objectives are used for both curriculum and instruction. They are usually classified under one of three interrelated categories according to the domain of learning that characterizes that particular goal or objective: psychomotor, cognitive, or affective. As you review the national standards, you should be able to identify which of the standards address which domain (figure 1.1).

Psychomotor Domain	Affective Domain
Motor Skills Fitness Outcomes	Feelings Values Social Behavior Attitudes

Cognitive Domain
Knowledge Strategies Cognitive Abilities

FIGURE 1.1
Physical education has responsibility for all domains of learning.

Defensible and Not Defensible Programs

Elementary—Defensible

The teacher has planned the day's lesson with psychomotor, cognitive, and affective objectives from a written plan that describes what the learning objectives for the day will be and how the lesson will proceed. The second-grade class will be working on combining locomotor patterns. Opportunities to practice the skills separately and then combine them are provided. The teacher also has planned to have each student develop a personal routine that will be shared with a partner and assessed using peer review.

Elementary—Not defensible

The teacher decides on the way to work that the second-grade class really likes to play with the parachute so that is what the class will do today. The teacher thinks of all the fun things that the students like to do with parachutes and writes them down when he/she gets to work.

Secondary—Defensible

The teacher is teaching a unit on volleyball. The teacher has carefully planned the unit so that each day students work on some aspect of their skill development they have decided with the teacher is a weakness. Each part of every day is also devoted to some gamelike or game play. At the end of each class the teacher and the students assess their play and skill and make a decision about what needs the most attention. The teacher plans the next lesson to work on those aspects of play that need attention.

Secondary—Not defensible

The teacher has been working on a unit in volleyball. The first day of the unit the teacher presented all of the skills of volleyball and is running a tournament for the rest of the unit. Some students are better than others, but the students really don't like to practice the skills. The teacher has decided that his/her role is primarily to keep the peace during play and to help the students deal with conflict that emerges on an individual basis.

Goals and objectives that deal with motor and physical abilities are termed **psychomotor objectives.** Standards 1 and 4 (box 1.1) are directly related to the psychomotor content of physical education. Psychomotor outcomes are the unique contribution of physical education to the education of the students. No other educational program emphasizes psychomotor objectives the way physical education does. Psychomotor objectives include motor skill objectives such as teaching fundamental skills (e.g., skipping, throwing, or rolling) or the complex skills required for sports (e.g., the basketball layup or back handspring). Psychomotor objectives also include fitness outcomes (e.g., arm strength, cardiorespiratory endurance, and flexibility). A psychomotor goal might be to play basketball at an intermediate level of ability or to reach a particular level of ability on a fitness test.

Cognitive objectives describe knowledge or ability levels in processing information. The national standard that is related to this outcome is primarily standard 2: Demonstrates understanding of movement concepts, principles, strategies, and tactics as they apply to the learning and performance of physical activities. Many aspects of performance in the psychomotor and affective domains (discussed next) are related to cognitive abilities that must be developed as well. In other words, you have to know how to achieve fitness in order to design a program to achieve and maintain a fitness level. Cognitive goals and objectives are intellectual and thinking related. They include outcomes related to knowledge students should have (e.g., how to develop joint flexibility) and outcomes related to problem solving and creativity or the transfer of knowledge from one situation to another (e.g., how to apply zone defense to a six-on-six soccer game).

Affective objectives describe student feelings, attitudes, values, and social behaviors. The national standards directly related to affective outcomes are 5 and 6. Standard 5 deals with personal and social behavior, standard 6 with values related to the benefits of participation in physical activity. The desire to have students value fitness and engage in activity on a regular basis (standard 3) is mostly an affective goal

Physical education should prepare students for a life of physical activity.

that needs skill and knowledge. Objectives teachers have related to student feelings, attitudes, values, and social behaviors are affective objectives. A major goal of physical education is to prepare students for a lifetime of physical activity. Unless teachers address affective goals in their programs, students may be skilled and may even be knowledgeable but may choose not to participate.

Unlike sport programs outside the school, physical education also shares many cognitive and affective goals with all educational programs within a school. The teacher in physical education often has psychomotor, cognitive, and affective objectives in one lesson. Physical educators should help students to be thinking, caring, and sharing individuals. Lessons that in part teach working productively with a partner, fair play, independent learning skills, and positive self-regard have objectives classified as affective.

Chapter 10, "Planning," describes in detail how teachers can write goals and objectives for different purposes when planning both curriculum and instruction. At this point it is important to recognize that educational goals are concerned with each dimension of human development.

Establishing Realistic Goals

If the relationship between curriculum and instruction is to be maintained, the curriculum goals and objectives established must be appropriate to the instructional situation. Instructional programs cannot be conducted in a manner consistent with established goals if the goals set are hopelessly unattainable. Selecting realistic goals for a program is difficult in physical education. The field has the potential to contribute in many ways to educational goals and objectives. Physical educators can use active learning and physical activity to make major contributions to all domains of learning, and that makes it difficult to define our responsibility. Designating realistic goals has been a major problem for many programs. Physical educators for the most part have tried to be all things to all people. As a result, they have tended to accomplish little. For example, a representative high school curriculum guide for the ninth grade might list the following goals:

- Develop and maintain fitness.
- Develop skills for participation in six team sports, four individual sports, gymnastics, and dance.
- Teach students how to value themselves and interact with others in positive ways.
- Teach students how to be independent learners and problem solvers.
- Develop skills, attitudes, and knowledge related to participation in physical activity that will transfer to new skills and encourage lifetime participation.

If students in this ninth grade have physical education class two times a week, it should be apparent that even the first goal of fitness is not attainable within the confines of the assigned class time. If the sport, gymnastics, and dance objectives are divided by the time normally available in a school year, the extent of the problem becomes apparent. Each sport would have less than two weeks of program time. Enough time is not available to successfully complete even the simplest of the stated goals. The goals listed in this curriculum are worthwhile. Teachers should be setting their goals high. However, had the designers of this curriculum considered the instructional process needed to reach their goals, they would have realized that the goals stated were not attainable in the time allotted.

To attempt to meet all of these goals in one program can result only in accomplishing none of them, because the students need adequate time to experience any degree of success. The goals established for any program must be realistic to their setting, which often means that the teacher must choose between many worthwhile goals.

More realistic skill and fitness goals for this ninth-grade setting might have included the following:

- Students should be able to design personal goals for fitness with the help of the instructor and meet those goals by the end of the school year through a personal fitness program.
- Students should be able to attain a participant level of competency in one team sport and one individual sport of their choice.
- Students should be able to design and safely conduct a personal weight-training program.

Choosing Instructional Processes to Meet Goals

Once the teacher has chosen goals and has translated those goals into objectives for instruction, the teacher must choose instructional processes that can reach a specific objective. Instructional experiences and processes are chosen intentionally to reach specific goals. Although more occurs in classes than is intended, teaching processes are designed to be specific to their desired learning outcomes. It is impossible to discuss what to do or what is good instruction without discussing what the teacher hopes to accomplish.

One of the best examples of the specificity of teaching processes to desired outcomes occurs in the area of fitness. Fitness is developed only when certain criteria for workload, duration of activity, and intensity are met. The type of exercise is specific to the type of fitness desired (e.g., strength, muscular endurance, flexibility, or cardiorespiratory endurance). Most activities that develop strength do not also develop flexibility. The type of fitness is specific not only to the type of exercise but also to a muscle group.

Criteria for teaching processes involved in learning motor skills objectives are not as neatly defined as those for fitness, but they are beginning to emerge in the literature. Open motor skills (those that take place in changing environments, such as the basketball

layup shot) require different processes from closed skills (those that take place in more stable environments, such as archery). Teaching for transfer of learning from one skill to another requires a different process from teaching that does not intend transfer. All motor skill learning involves processes that require consideration of certain prerequisites for learning, such as the amount and type of information, practice, and feedback that learners at different levels of development need.

Processes and criteria for meeting affective and cognitive objectives in physical education are not neatly packaged but are as specific as those for other areas. Physical educators have traditionally assumed that if learners are engaged in creative experiences, creative learning is occurring. They have assumed that learners engaged in social interaction with others are developing positive social interaction skills and that learners engaged in team sports will develop sportsmanship and self-discipline. Teachers have come to realize that merely engaging in an experience that has the potential to make a positive contribution to affective or cognitive goals does not ensure that these goals are met. Learning experiences must be designed and developed for specific outcomes: *What is not taught often is not learned.* Fair play, independent learning skills, problem solving, positive social interaction, and the development of positive self-concepts require specific conditions and processes. These goals should be designated, planned for, taught, and assessed, as with other kinds of content goals.

Achieving Goals Through Processes

Teachers can achieve psychomotor goals and objectives directly by teaching movement content. Physical educators can teach basketball, jumping, dance, or swimming by providing carefully planned and conducted experiences in basketball, jumping, dance, or swimming. A more difficult question concerns how the educator teaches creativity, positive self-concept, positive social interaction skills, love of activity, or fair play.

Sometimes a teacher might put the primary emphasis of a lesson on developing student cooperative behavior or creativity through physical activity. A

Instilling a love of activity in students is a primary objective of the physical education program.

teacher might also plan an entire lesson using physical education content to teach a moral value or to positively contribute to the self-concept of students. Most often these affective concerns are taught in conjunction with psychomotor or fitness skill development. The teacher chooses a way to develop the lesson with students so that more than a psychomotor emphasis becomes the focus of the lesson. This means that although the primary content might be the basketball layup shot (and we design experiences to best teach the basketball layup shot), how the teacher goes about teaching this skill contributes a great deal to affective and cognitive goals. How students feel about basketball, themselves, and others; their knowledge of

basketball; and their abilities to work independently, think creatively, and problem solve are all affected by the process the teacher chooses to teach the layup shot. If teaching the basketball layup were the only objective, teaching would be easy, or at least easier.

A teacher's goals must be more inclusive. Although no teacher would intentionally teach for negative affect in class, in many classes affective goals and cognitive goals related to learning activity are ignored. Teacher decision making in the instructional process is affected by the complex interrelationship between what to teach (content) and how to teach it (process). The two are not easily separated. The teaching process a teacher uses results in products many times not intended. Effective teachers choose processes because they are aware of the potential contributions of those processes to their comprehensive goals.

Little research has been done that links different pedagogic processes to specific affective and cognitive outcomes because of the difficulty of measuring such elusive and long-term products of instruction. Teachers, however, should be objective in assessing all the outcomes of their teaching. This necessarily includes affective and cognitive goals. Until teachers have a better understanding of the contribution of different instructional processes to these important outcomes, they must make informed decisions regarding teaching and carefully observe the products of these processes. In the next section, criteria for designing learning experiences with students are established.

■ CRITERIA FOR A LEARNING EXPERIENCE

To teach motor skills or concepts to learners, teachers must design learning experiences that lead the learners from where they are to the desired objectives and goals. One of the most critical functions a teacher performs in an instructional setting is the design of learning experiences and the movement tasks that constitute them. The learning experience delivers the content to the learner. It structures and gives focus to student responses. It is at the level of the learning experience that the teacher determines the student's role in the process of learning.

Teachers have many options in the design of learning experiences and movement tasks. For example, the questions in box 1.3 only begin to sort out the alternatives for teaching the headstand. Which approach would you take and why? Learning experiences can be designed to individualize the content for the learner, to give learners a decision-making role, or to focus student responses on a psychomotor, affective, or cognitive process. Teachers choose one way of designing a learning experience over others, based on the specific nature of the content, their objectives for a lesson, their broader program goals, the characteristics of their students, and the facilities and equipment of their specific environment.

A learning experience is that part of an instructional lesson used to develop a particular set of student outcomes. In this text the term **learning experience** is defined as *a set of instructional conditions and events that gives structure to student experience and is related to a particular set of teacher objectives.*

BOX 1·3

Content Decisions—The Headstand

Should the teacher demonstrate the skill, walk the students through the skill one step at a time, or teach concepts about base of support and have students apply those concepts to a balance using the head and the hands?

Should all students be doing a headstand? What other arrangements for ability levels can and should be made?

What kind of learning environment does the teacher want for practice? Should the practice be fun, task oriented, or relaxed?

Should the student focus be maintaining balance? Showing extension and a clear body shape? Both?

Should the students know why the head and hands are placed the way that they are?

How should students be grouped for practice of the headstand? Should they practice in small groups, individually, or with a partner? Who chooses the groups and with what criteria?

How will student performance be assessed? Self-assessment? Partner assessment? Teacher assessment?

If the teacher is trying to teach partners how to dribble a soccer ball against a defensive player, the teacher might have several tasks related to this learning objective, including the following:

- Two offensive players and one defensive player without a goal
  Half speed without a goal
  Full speed without a goal
  Using the fake in the above
- Focusing on the player without the ball
  Full speed—count number of passes
  Full speed—with a goal

The teacher would design more than one task to reach the learning goal related to passing against a defensive player. How to develop the content to establish viable progressions of tasks is discussed in chapter 5. Each of the tasks related to the learning experience of passing against a defensive player can be described in many ways, including the following:

- What the nature of the content was for the task
- What the nature of the goal was for each of the tasks
- How students were organized for the activity
- How the space was arranged
- What kind and how much equipment was used
- What the teacher did during activity
- How much time the class and each student spent in activity

The decisions teachers make in regard to these questions and others determine the potential of the learning experience to contribute to reaching learning objectives, as well as the potential of the experience to contribute to different domains of learning.

In this section, four essential criteria for the design of a learning experience are presented. These criteria should act as a first screen in sifting out instructional experiences that have the potential to facilitate learning from those that do not. The criteria are a blend of professional knowledge, beliefs, and attitudes concerning what is important in what teachers do with their students in physical education.

Teachers are guided in what they do by their knowledge, beliefs, and attitudes. The answers to such questions as "Would the teacher consider checkers appropriate content?" "Would the teacher line up half the class in front of one basket for a task?" "Does the teacher consider the role of the student merely to duplicate what the teacher shows?" and "Does the teacher consider student ability levels in teaching?" are determined by the teacher's knowledge of, beliefs about, and attitudes toward the content of physical education and learning. Although it may not be possible for every learning experience the teacher designs to meet each of these criteria, it is desirable that the teacher strive to meet these criteria. Teachers who are effective and provide well-rounded educational programs for students meet these criteria more often than not.

Criterion One

The first criterion is that *the learning experience must have the potential to improve the motor performance/activity skills of students.* This criterion makes clear a commitment to provide students with skills for a physically active lifestyle as the unique purpose of the instructional physical education program. It is not meant to exclude from physical education those activities that contribute to developing an active lifestyle but may not require complex motor skills. It is meant to exclude from programs experiences that do nothing but engage students in activity or play activities with no learning goal. Teachers must design experiences for students with the intent to provide a legitimate learning experience. Unless an experience has the potential to contribute to student learning and development in this way, it is not considered a valid physical education instructional experience.

Support for this criterion comes from the idea that adults who are physically active were those who were active as youths in organized sport.

The implications of this criterion should be clear. The teacher does not play games just because they are fun. The teacher does not teach reading through the use of movement experiences during time designated for physical education unless the psychomotor objective is an equally valid learning experience. The teacher does not plan lessons merely to engage students in motor activity or to provide a social experience. The criterion is not merely that students be engaged in an activity that involves balls or balance or coordination,

but that the activity has the potential to improve performance in these areas.

Interrelated variables. The following Real World box presents some of the problems we have when teachers at all levels do not see a responsibility to produce learning in psychomotor skills. There are times when teachers will want to focus on affective or cognitive goals in the design of learning experiences. Cooperative games are examples of a content area specifically designed to use activity to focus on affective concerns. Also, much has been written about physical education experiences integrated with other academic subjects, as well as developing cognitive goals in physical education. The position taken in this text is that these goals are important but it is possible to use the

---

THE REAL WORLD

Criterion One: The Learning Experience Must Have the Potential to Improve the Motor Performance/Activity Skills of Students

In my experiences in the public schools, I have had many opportunities to discuss this criterion with practicing teachers. I have talked to elementary teachers who feel their job is merely to expose students to skills that they are not yet ready to learn. I have spoken with middle-school and junior high school teachers who feel their main responsibility is to introduce and expose students to as many skills as they can. Finally, I have encountered many senior high school teachers who believe their job is simply to let students play. The following questions then remain:

- Who has the responsibility to teach motor and activity skills to students?
- Who has the responsibility to improve the physical potential of students?

To say that students suffer from overexposure to skills is an understatement. Rather than only expose students to skills, the physical education curriculum and the instructional process should be designed to make students skillful. This may mean spending more time on fewer skills.

content of physical education to develop these goals without having to create content that has no potential to contribute to physical education's unique goal.

Criterion Two

The second criterion for the design of a learning experience is that *the learning experience must provide maximal activity or practice time for all students at an appropriate level of ability.* This criterion is not only a managerial concern, but a content decision as well. There is a direct relationship between opportunity to learn and learning. For physical skills and ability, this relationship is related to practice time. If the teacher's objective is manipulative skills (throwing, catching, and striking), then circle games in the elementary school, relay or squad formations in the high school, and many other so-called lead-up activities would not provide maximal potential for practice time. Most throwing, catching, and striking skill development requires practice by no more than one or two people.

Practice time is perhaps the single most critical element in the learning of a motor skill or the development of fitness. Maximal practice time can be obtained by identifying the minimal number of students in an organizational arrangement necessary to develop a psychomotor skill or ability and then designing experiences using the smallest number of students possible.

Designing learning tasks that allow students to progress at their own rate is a major challenge in teaching.

Maximizing practice time should be a primary concern in the design of a learning experience.

Interrelated variables. A teacher may choose to design a learning experience that does not maximize activity for several valid reasons, including the following:

- Limited equipment or space
- Lack of independent working skills of students
- Need to limit the observational field (to what the teacher has to attend) to provide more accurate feedback
- A primary objective intended to develop social interactive skills

Limited equipment and limited space for an activity are valid reasons for restricting practice time if the activity is deemed critical to a program and no alternative organizational arrangements or equipment is available. However, in many instances, teachers who value maximal participation can find alternatives to students waiting for opportunities to practice.

Another valid reason a teacher may choose not to maximize practice time is the students' inability to work independent of direct teacher supervision and to remain active at the same time. Unfortunately, this is often used as an excuse for a teacher's failure to help students work in a more self-paced manner. Nevertheless, when all students are not active at the same time, the experience becomes more structured and may be easier for some teachers to handle. A word of caution: Idle students are a primary cause of behavior problems in a gymnasium, and many times arrangements that decrease activity also increase management and student behavior problems.

The third reason a teacher may not want to maximize practice time is so that the teacher can minimize the observational field (i.e., to what the teacher must attend) to provide more accurate feedback. If only a few students are moving at a time, the teacher can attend to those students better and therefore provide more accurate feedback. This situation may also cause students to think more carefully about what they are doing and to be performers in front of their peers. Teachers should carefully consider whether students are advanced enough to be affected positively rather than negatively by performance in front of others.

Criterion Three

The third criterion for designing learning experiences is that *the learning experience must be appropriate for the experiential level of all students.* Students profit from a learning experience when it is appropriate to their level of ability. Students who cannot take weight on their hands can practice handstands for a full instructional period and still not be able to do a handstand. Teachers thus must design learning experiences that challenge students yet are within reach of all students in a class.

Error rate is a useful concept in determining whether the level of an experience is appropriate for students. If students are successful every time they try a movement, the task is probably not challenging to the students. On the other hand, if students are never successful with a task, the task is probably beyond the ability of the students. In classroom research, an 80 percent **success rate** is deemed appropriate. For many physical education activities, a very high rate of success is probably not appropriate for the teacher to aim for. In some activities, 80 percent success is too high (e.g., basketball free throw shooting). The teacher must consider the nature of the activity and what a skilled person would consider successful and then adjust this downward for a beginning learner.

The idea that students should be allowed to progress at their own rate is also included in the concept of appropriate level of ability. Even a task initially appropriate for all students quickly becomes inappropriate for everyone, because students learn at different rates (e.g., when learning a new skill, students initially may start at the same level of ability, but some learn more quickly than others). By moving on regardless of the needs of students who have not accomplished previous goals or by holding students back because other students are not ready, teachers make the task inappropriate for some students.

One of the most challenging teaching skills is to design a learning experience that permits each student to function at an appropriate level. This concept is sometimes called *individualization.* When individualization is taken to the point where the specific needs of each individual are considered in the design of an experience, this concept is often called *personalization* and is often accomplished by giving different students different tasks.

Criterion Four

The fourth criterion is that *the learning experience should have the potential to integrate psychomotor, affective, and cognitive educational goals whenever possible.* Students are people, and each person functions as a whole. In one sense it is impossible to perform an intended motor skill without an affective or cognitive component, because people feel, think, act, and relate at all times in some way. People tend to repeat those activities at which they are successful and to avoid those at which they are not. The goals of physical education cannot be attained unless students are ultimately successful at what they are asked to do.

Physical educators also share affective and cognitive concerns for development with all other curricular programs. Students should be developing positive self-concepts. They should be learning how to relate to others in positive ways, how to exercise good judgment when making decisions, how to learn, how to express feelings, how to set personal goals and work toward their completion, and how to function in a democratically oriented society. Probably many more affective and cognitive goals should be part of this list. It is important to recognize that a physical educator must be concerned with more than the development of physical skills.

In physical education, the teacher's unique contribution is psychomotor development, but experiences can be designed to contribute to all areas of development without lessening the psychomotor intent. The following examples illustrate this point:

Psychomotor experience only. The teacher tells students to work on moving under a volleyball to get height on the hit.

Cognitive and psychomotor experience. The teacher asks students to find out what they have to do to get a high arch on a volleyball hit.

Affective, cognitive, and psychomotor experience. The teacher asks students to observe each other hitting and to decide together what must be done to get a high arch on the ball.

The last experience in this series is a richer experience than the other two because it involves students in affective and cognitive, as well as psychomotor, ways. Teachers do not want to and cannot make everything they do with students a rich experience. Nevertheless, the total learning experience should reflect a concern for affective and cognitive development. Careful thought should be given to ways in which each task can be made richer in its potential to contribute to all phases of development.

These four criteria should serve as a guide for the teacher in selecting and designing appropriate learning experiences. Although the criteria are easy to state and define, they are difficult to apply. As shown in the next section, the teacher can manipulate different dimensions of the task to meet these criteria.

■ UNDERSTANDING THE INSTRUCTIONAL PROCESS

It is helpful in designing and implementing successful instructional programs to understand instruction as a process that involves both teacher and students in a highly interrelated set of events. If someone asked what happened in gym class today, how would what the teacher and students did be described? An example of a high school class described in observable events is shown in box 1.4. Many of you will find this example consistent with your own experiences.

Not all physical education lessons fit the description given. However, many physical education lessons share aspects of this record. First, "getting ready" and "ending" routines frequently stand apart from the lesson of the day. There are identifiable times when the lesson begins in earnest and ends. Second, there is usually a recurring series of events in which the teacher presents a movement task to the students, the students respond to that task, and the teacher observes and tries to improve performance. Third, two kinds of behavior and/or events are commonly present: (1) those that arrange or manage

---

BOX 1·4

Sample Secondary Lesson

- A bell rings. Students go to the locker room and gradually come into the gym after changing clothes.
- Some students remain on the fringes of the gym, talking with each other. Others begin playing with the balls.
- After a few minutes the teacher asks the students to form squads. One student from each squad checks attendance and preparation for class and then gives the squad card to the teacher.
- The teacher asks for student attention and gives an overview of the day's lesson. After the overview the teacher describes and demonstrates a new skill with another student. The teacher explains how the skill will be practiced and asks that students go to their area of the gym to practice. Students begin practicing.
- While students are practicing, the teacher observes the students' work, provides help to individuals, and occasionally stops the whole class to offer help on performance.
- The teacher asks one student to stop fooling around and get serious about the task.
- After students have had sufficient time for practice, the teacher calls the group together and asks the students to begin practicing the skill with a partner.
- The class puts the extra balls away, organizes into partners, and begins practicing the new task.
- The teacher resumes helping students with the task—sometimes individually and sometimes as a class.

---

the environment in which the lesson is taught; and (2) those that work directly on the lesson content. Each of these aspects of instruction is described in the following pages.

Prelesson and Postlesson Routines

In most elementary classes, **prelesson** and **postlesson routines** are not as elaborate as in the secondary school. Elementary children usually do not change clothes for class, and taking attendance is sometimes not necessary. Lessons begin almost immediately. In instructional classes at the secondary level, however, teachers are required to perform tasks before class, such as checking attendance and determining whether the students are prepared for class. Usually this time is used also for announcements concerning after-school programs and events. In some cases, after-class routines include such duties as checking showers. Prelesson and postlesson routines should be accomplished in the least possible amount of time. Time used for these routines is time taken away from the lesson. If dressing and showering are necessary, time must be allotted for students to accomplish these tasks. If the tasks for a lesson do not require dressing before or a shower after, teachers can cut down or eliminate locker room time. Having something attractive for students to do when they get out of the locker room is another way to reduce time students spend in the locker room.

Movement Task–Student Response Unit of Analysis

Instruction in physical education technically begins when "getting ready" routines end. After the **set induction** of a class in which the teacher orients the class to what is to happen in the class for the day and why, an identifiable series of events revolves about the interaction unit called the *movement task–student response*. This cycle of events is described in figure 1.2.

The movement task. At the heart of the instructional process in physical education is the **movement task.** Movement tasks are motor activities assigned to the student that are related to the content of the lesson. The teacher directive to "practice the volleyball set to yourself until you can do it three times in a row without moving out of your place" is a movement task. "We're going to play keep-it-up in groups of six to see how long you can keep the volleyball up in the air using sets only" is also a movement task. Movement tasks are content. They are learning activities defined by the teacher either in an explicit (direct) or implicit (indirect) way. An observer should be able to watch a physical education lesson and identify "what

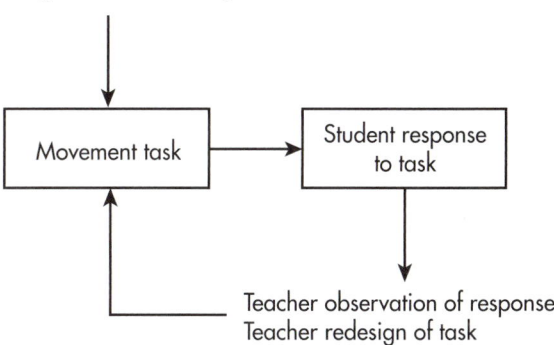

FIGURE 1.2
Movement task–student response to task.

the teacher asked students to do." In lessons taught by effective teachers, students should be able to identify rather specifically what they should be working on at any point in the lesson.

Teachers design movement tasks as a progression of experiences to meet their objectives. Movement tasks do not necessarily have to be communicated directly by the teacher, although they usually are. Task cards, other students, media, or all three can communicate tasks.

Organizational arrangements. In group instruction, not only must tasks be communicated, but the arrangements for practicing the tasks must be communicated. Teachers must organize people, space, time (for practice), and equipment (when appropriate). They also should establish procedures for these organizational arrangements—how students will get equipment, how they will organize into groups, and how the space will be divided among students for practice. This is discussed in greater depth in chapter 3.

Student response. After the teacher has given students the signal to begin working on a task, student practice or work with the task begins. Once the students have begun to practice the movement task, a major responsibility of the teacher is to observe and provide feedback to students on their performance, either individually or as a group. Initially when work begins on a task, the teacher is observing to see that the environment is safe, that students are working on the task, and that students have interpreted the task correctly. The teacher then must assess the responses of the student to the task to determine an appropriate next teaching move.

Many teachers may find that as a result of their observations of student responses, they must restate or clarify the task, handle organizational or safety problems, motivate the students, and maintain on-task behavior during student response time. Teachers select the next step in the lesson after assessing student performance on the previous task. Sometimes the next step is an entirely unrelated task (e.g., moving from the volleyball set to the serve), but most often the appropriate next step is to provide the students with additional information and an additional task focus to help them (1) improve the performance of the tasks they are currently working on, (2) increase the level of complexity or difficulty of the task, or (3) assess their ability in a self-testing or competitive situation. If a task with a new focus is assigned, the movement task–student response cycle begins again. This process is called **content development** and is discussed in chapter 5.

Teaching Functions

Each instructional event in the sample secondary lesson (see box 1.4, p. 12) can be described in terms of its contribution to the movement task (box 1.5).

Because the movement tasks and the events (both direct and indirect) associated with them are so critical to the instructional process, many teaching skills are associated with this unit of interaction. We can begin to describe teaching behavior in terms of the function that teacher behavior performs in the teaching-learning process (box 1.6).

The chapters of this text are organized primarily by the concept of **teaching functions.** Many of the chapters are designed to consider each of these teaching functions separately. The concept of teaching functions is a useful concept because it allows us to focus on the purpose of a teaching behavior rather than on the specific behavior. Teachers can effectively perform a teaching function in many appropriate ways. We cannot prescribe the specific way in which teachers should perform a function. Teachers must choose how they will implement a lesson based on their pedagogic intent, their knowledge of the student, and their own skills and characteristics. Although specific behaviors are not prescribed, criteria for these functions that are general principles can be established (e.g., a good task presentation lets the students understand task requirements, practice arrangements, and goals). Guidelines can also be established for specific situations (e.g., beginning learners are not able to use specific information on motor skills and must be provided with more holistic descriptions of the tasks to be performed). Guidelines and general principles are

---

BOX 1·5

Contribution of Instructional Events to Movement Tasks

Teacher behavior	**Contribution to the task**
Gives an overview of the lesson	Develops a learning set and motivation for students to engage in the movement tasks of the lesson
Describes a new skill	Helps students get a clear idea of the task and what they will be trying to do
Describes how students will be practicing the skill	Arranges the environment for task (equipment, space, and people)
Moves from student to student	Provides information on performance of the movement task and makes suggestions on how to improve performance
Asks a student to stop fooling around	Maintains on-task behavior

Teacher Functions in the Teaching-Learning Process

Identifying outcomes: Identify learning goals and objectives.

Planning: Design and sequence appropriate learning experiences and tasks to meet the identified goals.

Presenting tasks: Present and communicate these tasks effectively so that students have a clear idea of what they are being asked to do and are motivated to do it.

Organizing and managing the learning environment: Arrange and maintain the learning environment that maximally motivates student practice of the task.

Monitoring the learning environment: Provide students with feedback on their performance through accurate assessment of student performance in relation to the task.

Developing the content: Modify and develop the task further based on student responses to the task.

Assessing student performance: Determine the extent to which students meet objectives.

Evaluating: Evaluate the effectiveness of the instructional process.

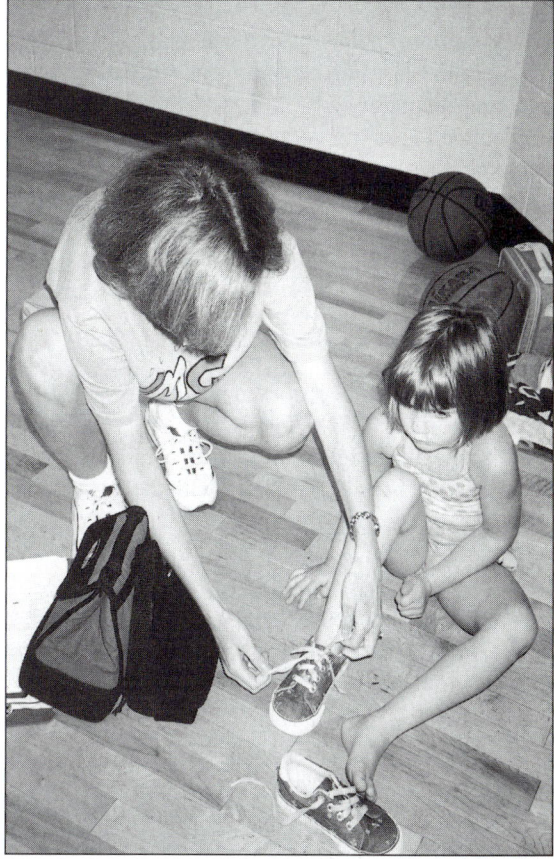

Teachers play many different roles.

used appropriately when they are adapted to the specific context in which they are used.

When teachers perform teaching functions, they exhibit specific behaviors and employ specific methods. For example, a teacher might use demonstration, explanation, task cards, video, or other media to present a task to learners. Even though specific methods of presenting task behaviors or methods for individual teachers cannot be prescribed, the competency and appropriateness of teacher performance in using any of these methods of task presentation can be evaluated. Did the teacher describe or demonstrate the skill accurately? Was the level of presentation appropriate to the age and ability level of the students? Was the media selected appropriate and accurate? At the level of specific behavior, guidelines of appropriateness and competency can again be established.

In summary, teachers must perform particular functions essential for effective instruction. They can perform these functions in many ways and still be effective. We can evaluate the extent to which teachers adequately perform a function and, to some extent, the adequacy and appropriateness of their choice. Teachers decide what and how they will teach based on what they know, what they believe, and their unique personality, skills, and interests. This text is designed to increase the teacher's awareness of the factors involved (and the criteria that need to be considered) in performing teacher functions appropriately and competently.

Management and Content Behavior

Some of the teacher functions just described are directly related to the content of the lesson; the purpose of others is to arrange and maintain a learning environment in which the content may be learned.

Transactions directly related to lesson content are called **content behaviors;** those that arrange and maintain the learning environment are called **management behaviors.**

Content behavior contributes directly to the movement task. Management behavior contributes to the task only indirectly by creating the conditions for learning. Examples of both content and management behaviors from our sample secondary lesson (box 1.4) follow:

Content Behaviors

- The teacher describes how the task is to be performed.
- Students engage in the task.
- The teacher helps students with the task.
- The teacher modifies and develops the original task.

Management Behaviors

- The teacher gives directions for arranging the equipment, people, and space before practice of the task begins.
- The students get the equipment and organize themselves into partners.
- The teacher asks a single student to stop fooling around.

Content behaviors are important because they directly address the essence of the physical education lesson—the content—and contribute directly to the intended lesson outcome. If the lesson content is a cartwheel, the teacher communicates information on the cartwheel, directs students to do tasks related to the cartwheel, gives students information on how they have performed the cartwheel, and makes suggestions to them on how to improve their performance.

Management behaviors are concerned with two types of problems: conduct and organization. Teachers manage when they structure, direct, or reinforce the appropriate behavior of students, such as taking turns, following directions, or being supportive of their classmates. They also manage when they structure, direct, or reinforce arrangements for people, time, space, and equipment for the practice of a movement task. One kind of management deals with the conduct of students

and another with the organizational arrangements for the class. The teacher who says "Walk, don't run" or "You're working very hard today" is dealing with conduct. The teacher who says "Get your rackets and go to a court" or "Everybody stop what they are doing" is dealing with the organization of the class.

Management behaviors are important because they create the learning environment. Teachers want a learning environment that will support the learning of lesson content. They also want a learning environment that contributes in a positive way to how the students feel about themselves, others, and the content of the lesson. No matter how good a teacher is at selecting appropriate tasks, explaining tasks, or providing appropriate feedback, it is all for nothing if the environment does not support the lesson's short- and long-term goals.

Directing content-related experiences and establishing and maintaining a learning environment (both with an eye to the student successfully achieving intended lesson outcomes) are the two most important functions of a teacher in the instructional process.

■ LOOKING TO THE FUTURE: BECOMING A PROFESSIONAL TEACHER

Your professional preparation program has been designed to give you the skills you will need to be a competent teacher. Box 1.7 lists the skills that the National Association for Sport and Physical Education (NASPE, 2008) has identified as those critical for the beginning teacher of physical education. Professional preparation programs all over the country are assessed on the extent to which they meet these standards.

Value Positions and Beliefs in Teaching

The first part of this chapter introduced you to a lot of ideas related to the teaching-learning process, which will be developed throughout this text. You are taking your first steps to becoming a professional teacher.

Different teachers have different beliefs about teaching that affect how they teach. Beliefs in teaching commonly have their roots in theories of learning in psychology and philosophy and are concerned with

B O X   1 · 7

National Association for Sport and Physical Education Beginning Teaching Standards (2008)

Standard 1: Scientific and Theoretical Knowledge

Physical education teacher candidates know and apply discipline-specific scientific and theoretical concepts critical to the development of physically educated individuals.

Standard 2: Skill and Fitness Based Competence

Physical education teacher candidates are physically educated individuals with the knowledge and skills necessary to demonstrate competent movement performance and health enhancing fitness as delineated in the NASPE K–12 Standards.

Standard 3: Planning and Implementation

Physical education teacher candidates plan and implement a variety of developmentally appropriate learning experiences and content aligned with local, state, and national standards to develop physically educated individuals.

Standard 4: Instructional Delivery and Management

Physical education teacher candidates use effective communication and pedagogical skills and strategies to enhance student engagement and learning.

Standard 5: Impact on Student Learning

Physical education teacher candidates utilize assessments and reflection to foster student learning and inform instructional decisions.

Standard 6: Professionalism

Physical education teacher candidates demonstrate dispositions essential to becoming effective professionals.

issues related to what is most important for schools to teach and how people best learn. These theories of learning and the teaching methodologies spawned from their roots are explored throughout the text but particularly in Chapter 2. Although national standards and state and local standards establish guidelines for program objectives, as a physical education teacher, you will have to decide how much of your program you want to devote to teaching students higher-level thinking skills, personal interaction skills, fitness, or movement skills. You will have to decide whether your

job is to make learners fit or to give them the skills to make themselves fit, or a combination of these ideas. These decisions and many more are related to the idea of what is most important for schools to teach. They are largely curriculum decisions but are also related to learning theory and how you think people best learn. Inherent in these views of teaching is a continual tension between beliefs that characterize the teaching process as manipulative and teacher directed and those that emphasize a more student-centered orientation to teaching. Research is not likely to prove one of these views right and the other wrong, because at the heart of the question are the long-term products of education and the values of the teacher.

Contrasting ideologies are often helpful when discussing theories but may do the practitioner a disservice. The practicing teacher has many kinds of goals that require different approaches for different students. Most teachers find themselves at different times using procedures borrowed from many different theories. The important thing is that teachers choose procedures with an eye to their effect on both long- and short-term teaching goals.

Sometimes contrasting theoretic positions make it difficult for teachers to get beyond the "I believe" stage. Beliefs are important in determining behavior. Beliefs uninformed by experience can inhibit growth. Teachers must be careful not to defend what they do (what processes they employ) solely in terms of a set of beliefs and must be willing to discard beliefs that are no longer useful when evidence to the contrary is present.

Personal Characteristics of a Teacher

Each teacher is an individual with his or her abilities, personality traits, and likes and dislikes. Educators that people think of as good teachers in their own experience are often very different individuals. Some are quiet and reserved, and others are more aggressive; some display their feelings clearly, and others are more subtle.

Personality and individual teacher characteristics influence the way teachers perform instructional functions. What is common to good teaching is that good teachers perform teaching functions in ways

Teachers must be willing to learn new skills.

consistent with their goals, particular students, and teaching environments. As a general principle, learners need accurate, appropriate information on how to perform the task required. Some teachers use student demonstration, some demonstrate themselves, some walk their students through a task, and some use media or verbal description effectively. The selection of how to give students this information is not as important as the appropriateness and accuracy of the information and the effectiveness of the communication.

Teachers will likewise motivate students in different ways. Some teachers write poems about how enjoyable the activity will be, some show films that show the end product, and some are so enthusiastic about what they are teaching that their enthusiasm infects the students. How the teacher chooses to motivate his

or her students is less important than that the students have been successfully motivated.

Teachers are free to be themselves within the structure of required instructional functions. Teachers are not free to say, "It's just not me to try to motivate students or provide feedback, to take time to communicate clearly, or to establish a productive learning environment." Other teachers may be able to tolerate high levels of off-task behavior or noise in their gymnasiums, but successful learning cannot occur under these conditions. The instructional functions described in box 1.6 (p. 15) provide the minimal structure necessary for successful learning to occur.

Within the structure of these functions, teachers are free to use behaviors that satisfy personal concerns (e.g., a preference for a particular approach to learning) as long as these concerns facilitate the goal of education, which is successful learning. The effective delivery of instructional functions is not optional. These functions are necessary for successful learning and cannot be set aside for personal reasons. Attention to the psychomotor, affective, and cognitive goals of a lesson will facilitate the selection of techniques appropriate to the student and the situation, whatever the pedagogic orientation or personality the teacher chooses to use to enhance the learning process.

The chapters that follow in this part of the text are designed to fully explore the teacher functions described. Criteria are developed in terms of how the function must be performed if learning is to occur.

Developing Commitment

Teaching is an exciting and rewarding profession. Few jobs afford the opportunity to influence the lives of so many in as significant a way as does teaching. Teaching is most of all a moral activity. Because you are a teacher and are in a position of power over children, sometimes what seems to you to be an insignificant interaction with a child can have significant consequences for that child. As a teacher you will be making decisions about what is important for people to learn and how they should learn it. These decisions will influence others either positively or negatively.

Teaching is a profession, which means that in your preparation you should acquire the skills, attitudes, and values of those people who are successful teachers. Because teaching is a profession, you will have much freedom to function in your role. It is primarily your values and your willingness to continue to grow that will determine your ability to be a successful teacher and contribute to the lives of others.

Your growth as a teacher will be determined largely by the extent to which you profit from your experiences, as a teacher and as a student learning to be a teacher. The effective teacher and the teacher who continues to grow is most of all a reflective teacher. The reflective teacher does not just act. Reflective teachers ask many questions about what they are doing and why they are doing it. The reflective teacher chooses what to do based on information gathering about what is going on in a teaching-learning situation. The reflective teacher bases decisions of what to do on goals, values, knowledge, and accurate information about learners. The more experienced you become as a teacher, the more information you will be able to use in your decision making and the more accurate you will be in identifying what is important.

You never stop growing as a teacher. There is always more to learn and more to do. As soon as you think you have it figured out, you will have an experience that lets you know that you have not. As a professional, you will be expected to continue to learn through your experiences and by keeping up with what is going on in your field through workshops, conventions, and additional course work. Teaching is not a job, in the sense that you can leave it when the bell rings or school closes. Teaching is a commitment. Professionals are guided by a desire to serve and contribute to society, and to do this well often requires that teachers work at becoming good at what they do and take advantage of all the opportunities they have to be the best they can be.

5. Instructional processes are selected to meet specific instructional goals and objectives—they are specific to an intent.

6. Many teaching outcomes are the result of not only what is taught (content), but how it is taught (process).

7. Good learning experiences meet four criteria:
   - Have the potential to improve motor performance/activity skills of the students
   - Provide maximal activity or practice time for all students at an appropriate level of ability
   - Are appropriate for the experiential level of all students
   - Have the potential to integrate psychomotor, affective, and cognitive educational goals whenever possible

8. Physical education lessons revolve about an interaction unit called the movement task–student response.

9. Two types of events—content behaviors and management behaviors—occur in large-group instruction. Content behaviors are those directly related to lesson content. Management behaviors arrange and maintain the learning environment.

10. The instructional functions teachers perform in a physical education setting are the following:
   - Identifying outcomes
   - Planning
   - Presenting tasks
   - Organizing and managing the learning environment
   - Monitoring the learning environment
   - Developing the content
   - Evaluating

SUMMARY

1. The goal of teaching is student learning.
2. Instruction is guided by curricular goals.
3. Goals and objectives are designed in three learning domains: psychomotor, cognitive, and affective.
4. Goals should be set realistically if they are to be useful.

CHECKING YOUR UNDERSTANDING

1. What is meant by the idea that teaching is a goal-oriented activity?
2. Into what categories are outcomes or goals in education usually divided?
3. What is meant by the idea that goals should be realistic?

4. Why is the process that teachers choose to use to teach content important?

5. Why is the movement task–student response unit of analysis so important in physical education?

6. What is the difference between management and content behavior? List three things teachers do that fall under each category.

7. What is the relationship between teaching functions and teaching skills? List two teaching functions teachers must perform, and describe two alternative behaviors teachers can choose to perform these functions.

8. What role do teacher value positions and beliefs play in what and how a teacher teaches?

9. What role does teacher personality play in teaching?

10. How does teaching differ from other occupations?

REFERENCE

NASPE. (2004). *Moving into the future: National standards for physical education* (2nd ed.). Reston, VA: NASPE.

SUGGESTED READINGS

Corbin, C., Dale, D., & Pangrazi, R. (1999). Promoting physically active lifestyles among youths. *JOPERD 70*(6), 26–28.

Lambert, L. (2003). Standards-based program design: Crafting a congruent guide for student learning. In S. Silverman and C. Ennis (Eds.), *Student learning in physical education.* Champaign, IL: Human Kinetics.

Lee, A. (2004). Promoting lifelong physical activity through quality physical education. *JOPERD, 75*(5), 21–24.

Masuurier, G., & Corbin, C. (2006). Top 10 reasons for quality physical education. *JOPERD, 77*(6), 44–53.

Prusak, K., & Vincent, S. (2006). Is your class about something? *JOPERD, 76*(6), 25–28.

Young J. (1996). Current trends and issues in physical education. In B. Hennessey (Ed.), *Physical education sourcebook* (pp. 3–11). Champaign, IL: Human Kinetics.

Factors That Influence Learning

2

O V E R V I E W

To design educational experiences for students that result in learning, teachers must understand the nature of learning and the factors that influence learning. Although a comprehensive theory is not available that would predict or explain learning (or the lack of it) in all situations, information is available that can provide direction for educators in working with students toward learning goals. General principles of learning are modified by characteristics of the learner, the context in which teaching occurs, and the content to be taught.

  This chapter discusses the factors related to the nature and process of learning, the nature of the content to be taught, and the nature of the learner. Concepts have been selected because they are considered essential to the teaching-learning process in physical education. Most general education course work focuses on general learning principles and emphasizes cognitive learning. For this reason learning motor skills is emphasized in this chapter.

Standard 1: Scientific and Theoretical Knowledge

Physical education teacher candidates know and apply discipline-specific scientific and theoretical concepts critical to the development of physically educated individuals.
NASPE Beginning Teaching Standards, 2008

O U T L I N E

- **What is learning?**
- **How do people learn motor skills?**
- **Understanding the control of movement**
- **Stages of motor learning**
- **Requirements for learning a motor skill**
  Prerequisites
  Clear idea of the task
  Motivational/attentional disposition to the skill
  Practice
  Feedback
- **The nature of motor skill goals**
  Open and closed skills
  Discrete, serial, and continuous skills
- **Issues of appropriateness in skill development and learning**

- Environmental conditions
- Learner abilities
- **Practice profiles and success rates**
  Whole or part
  Practice variability
  Massed and distributed practice
- **Motivation and goal setting**
- **Transfer of learning**
  Bilateral transfer
  Intertask transfer
  Intratask transfer
- **Learner characteristics**
  Motor ability
  Intelligence and cognitive development

■ WHAT IS LEARNING?

Learning is commonly thought to be a relatively permanent change in behavior resulting from experience and training and interacting with biological processes. One of the problems teachers have in directing learning processes and in assessing learning is that learning cannot be directly observed. Learning can only be inferred from a person's behavior or performance. Performance is observable, whereas learning is not. This creates difficulty for teachers, because sometimes students have learned and are not performing according to what they have learned, and sometimes they have not learned but perform as though they have. For example, a student may demonstrate a motor skill when you are observing him or her but may not be able to produce that skill in any consistent way again. Likewise, a student may have learned the skill but may be fatigued and not demonstrate the motor skill. That is why the idea of *consistent observable performance* is important in determining whether learning has taken place. If students cannot demonstrate an ability consistently, they probably have not learned it.

Teachers have another major problem related to learning when they try to design learning experiences for students and then try to assess whether they have learned. Students may be able to identify a rule on a written test and may not be able to apply that rule when they are playing the game. They may be able to demonstrate a motor skill on a skill test, but they may not be able to use that skill in a game situation. On the other hand, they may be able to use a skill in a game but may not be able to demonstrate proficiency in this skill in a test situation. Students may be able to tell you why and how to live a physically active lifestyle, but they do not lead a physically active lifestyle. To help explain this, educators talk about different levels of learning. Learning that takes place at a lower level (performance in a drill) may not be usable in a situation that demands a higher level of learning (performance in a game). Students may know why it is important to lead a physically active lifestyle but may choose not to. In this text you will learn how to specify the level of learning you are trying to teach and how to design experiences that lead learners from lower levels of learning to higher levels of learning.

You will be able to design experiences that have a better chance of influencing student behavior.

■ HOW DO PEOPLE LEARN MOTOR SKILLS?

Although physical education teachers will teach children many cognitive ideas and skills and can also make a major contribution to student attitudes and values as described in the national standards (National Association for Sport and Physical Education [NASPE], 2004), teaching motor skills that contribute to an active lifestyle is the unique contribution of our field. There is sufficient support for the idea that students who are successful at motor skills are the children, youth, and adults who are more likely to lead a physically active lifestyle. Many ideas are generic to all kinds of learning, regardless of whether what is to be learned is motor, cognitive, or attitudes and values, but this chapter focuses primarily on how people learn motor skills.

Motor skills are acquired in many ways. Some skills, such as walking, are developmental skills that all children acquire as the result of a maturational readiness and environmental conditions that encourage their development. By the time children go to school, they can perform a large number of fundamental motor skills, all without the assistance of a physical education teacher. More specialized skills, such as sport skills, and the skillful use of fundamental

Teachers can design the environment to facilitate learning.

patterns (e.g., running a race, catching a ball) develop largely as a result of learning.

Learning can take place independent of an intent to influence its occurrence; that is, a teacher is not necessary for learning to take place. Children learn how to do many things, including developing more advanced motor skills, outside an instructional environment. They learn by interacting with their environment, experimenting, and imitating what they see other people do. Most children, however, will develop their motor skill potential more fully as the result of instruction. Instruction is characterized by a specific intent to influence learning in a particular direction.

Effective instruction in motor skills can take many forms. Most people think of instruction as a "telling" process. The teacher tells and demonstrates to students how to do something, and students try to do it. Direct instruction was alluded to in chapter 1 as an orientation to teaching and has been shown to help people to learn motor skills. Teachers also have a variety of approaches to learning that may not be direct instruction that they can use to help students acquire motor skills. A more recent emphasis, but not a new emphasis, stresses the role of **environmental design.** This means that the teacher can *elicit* motor responses by designing the environment to bring out the skill. If students are ready, they will respond to the conditions of the task with an effective response. The teacher does not have to go through an analysis of the exact way the movement should be performed. The teacher who puts a target area on a mat or floor for people to jump to is encouraging specific movements without using a lengthy description of how that movement should be performed. The teacher who increases the height of the volleyball net encourages students to get under the ball. The teacher who selects equipment appropriate to a particular learner is using environmental design.

Using an environmental design approach to skill learning requires that the teacher have a good grasp of task conditions and requirements and that he or she is able to design conditions appropriate for different learners. Students who learn in this manner do not necessarily process what they are doing at a conscious level. The motor response is a coordinated response of a dynamic system to both external (the environment) and internal (the abilities of the learner) conditions.

Although learning motor skills has many unique aspects, approaches to learning motor skills are, for the most part, consistent with general learning theories. Learning in physical education can be approached from a *behaviorist model,* an *information-processing model,* or a *cognitive strategy model.* Each of these models looks at the process of learning differently and therefore advocates different approaches to teaching.

A **behaviorist orientation** to learning stresses the role that the external environment plays in shaping behavior. The focus is on what the learner does that is observable. Behaviorists suggest that teachers should model good behavior and shape desired behavior by rewarding and positively reinforcing desired responses. Content is usually broken down into small parts the student can handle successfully, and more difficult material is added gradually, building on the success of the student. Most of your formal motor skill learning in your experiences as a student or athlete has probably been conducted by teachers or coaches who at least in part oriented their work with you from a behaviorist orientation.

Information processing stresses the importance of the internal cognitive processing of the learner. Information processors study how learners select, use, interpret, and store information. Information-processing theory suggests ways in which teachers can present information to learners so that learners attend to important ideas, draw meaning from what they attend to, and integrate what they have learned in useful ways. Knowledge of how learners process information helps teachers and coaches to select appropriate cues and to design appropriate feedback for learners.

Cognitive theorists have attended to more holistic perspectives on learning and are interested primarily in how people solve problems, create, learn how to learn, and apply what they have learned. Cognitive strategy approaches to teaching stress problem solving, environmental approaches, and interactive models of teaching. Current classroom teaching strategies emphasize *constructivist* orientations to learning that focus on the role of the learner in mediating instruction

and constructing personal meaning from the learning experience. Constructivists feel that students construct their understanding of what is to be learned by linking their past experiences and understandings with new material and by engaging in creative, goal-oriented problem-solving experiences. Sociocultural constructivists also say that knowledge is socially constructed and therefore educators should emphasize the social interaction of learners and cooperative learning orientation to teaching.

In physical education, teaching strategies that approach instruction from more of a behaviorist or information-processing model are usually referred to as *direct instruction models.* More *indirect* strategies of instruction use principles of learning that have their roots in work being done in cognitive strategies.

The focus of this text is on learning facilitated through both direct instruction and more indirect ways to help students learn. There are times when the teacher wants students to deal with the transfer of learning and higher levels of learning, such as the development of problem-solving abilities. There are times when the teacher wants to attend more carefully to making the learning process more meaningful for the learner. Under these conditions the teacher will choose methods of instruction based on what is known from cognitive strategy about how to facilitate this type of learning. There are also times when the teacher wants the student to master a motor skill in the most efficient way and wants to use direct instruction. The skilled teacher chooses an appropriate approach based on what he or she wants students to learn and the characteristics of the learner. Each of these approaches will be made more clear in chapter 8.

■ UNDERSTANDING THE CONTROL OF MOVEMENT

One of the more popular theories for explaining movement responses is known as dynamical systems. This theory is particularly relevant for teachers. In this theory movement is seen as a complex response that allows us to respond to different conditions and demands. The selection of a response is constrained by organismic, environment, and task constraints. *Organismic constraints* include the maturational level and physical abilities of the learner. *Environmental constraints* would include those factors such as the physical environment (e.g., weather conditions, social environment). *Task constraints* would include factors such as the rules of the game, boundaries, equipment, and what the student thinks the task might be (Haywood & Getchell, 2005). From a teaching perspective, this theory explains why young children who do not have the strength choose a two-handed underhand pattern to shoot a basketball, why students put close to a partner do not choose to use a mature overhand throw pattern, and why high school students may not give it their best effort when placed in an environment where they fear peer criticism. The teacher will learn to identify the constraints that operate in a task and manipulate the constraints to produce good movement responses.

■ STAGES OF MOTOR LEARNING

A useful way to describe how an individual learns a motor skill was developed by Fitts and Posner in 1967 and is still useful today. According to them, an individual goes through three stages before he or she can reproduce a skilled movement (box 2.1).

The first phase is called the **cognitive phase,** because at this stage the learner is heavily focused on processing how the movement should be performed. Beginning learners at this stage have been observed with their tongue to the side of their mouth in intense concentration on what they are doing or completely oblivious to what is happening around them as they try to sort out what they must do to perform a movement. At this beginning level the learner is concentrating on getting the general idea of the skill and sequencing the skill. The responses of the learner at this stage of learning are variable and also characterized by processing errors in performance.

The second phase of the learning process is called the **associative phase.** At this stage, the learner can concentrate more on the dynamics of the skill: getting the timing of the skill and coordinating the movements of different parts of the skill to produce a smooth and refined action. Learners at this level often

---

BOX 2·1

Stages of Motor Learning

Cognitive stage

The learner uses information on how the skill is to be performed to develop an executive/motor plan for a movement skill.

Thought processes are heavily involved as the learner consciously attends to the requirements of the whole idea of the skill and sequencing the pattern.

Student responses are characterized by a high degree of concentration on how to perform the skill. The learner is unable to manage small details of the movement or cope with adapting the movement to environmental changes.

Associative stage

The learner can begin to concentrate on the temporal patterning of the skill and the refinement of the mechanics of the skill.

For most complex skills the learner is in this stage a great deal of time. The learner at this stage can profit from feedback and can begin gradually to cope with external demands of the environment. All the attention of the learner does not have to be on every aspect of the performance.

Automatic stage

The goal of motor learning is for the skill to be performed automatically. At this stage the learner does not have to give cognitive attention to the movement itself. Performance is consistent and can be adapted to the requirements of the environment, such as where to place the ball and defensive players in open skills.

Source: P. M. Fitts and M. I. Posner, *Human Performance,* 1967, Brooks/Cole Publishing, Belmont, CA.

---

find themselves attending to different components of the skill, such as the backswing in a tennis forehand or the hand position in a jump shot in basketball.

The third phase of learning a motor skill is called the **automatic phase.** At this point in the process, the learner does not have to concentrate on the skill. The processing has been relegated to a lower brain center, which frees the individual to concentrate on other things.

The movement response does not require the attention of the learner. Many movements of adults are at an automatic phase. Many of you can ride a bike, shoot a basket, run, or serve a volleyball without even thinking about where the parts of your body are or what they are doing. Skilled basketball players are not concentrating on how to perform the layup shot; they are concentrating on how to get around the defensive players.

The stages of motor learning are significant ideas that should be part of the knowledge base for teachers of motor skills. First, they are important because they alert the teacher to the idea that higher levels of functioning in cognitive learning result in increased cognitive processing, whereas higher levels of learning in motor skill acquisition result in less cognitive processing. The objective of motor skill learning is to have learners not focused on their response. Students who have acquired high levels of ability in motor skills should not have to think about how the skill is being performed. If students cannot get beyond this first phase of the learning process, they cannot concentrate on what is happening around them; this is why skills often fall apart after learners practice in simple conditions and then are expected to use the skill in more complex situations, such as a game. The skill is never developed to the automatic phase.

Second, the stages of motor skill acquisition are important because they help the teacher define the needs of the learner at different stages. The teacher who knows what learners need can better interpret the responses of learners and meet the unique needs of learners through careful selection of an appropriate instructional process.

If you are going to teach a skill directly to learners at the cognitive phase, you have identified that the learners need a clear idea of what they are trying to do. You also know that they are so highly involved cognitively that (1) you must reduce the information you give them to only the essentials to get them started, and (2) you need to sequence the pattern for them. Although it is not always possible to do, beginning learners should be presented with the whole idea of the skill when possible and should practice it as a whole if meaningful work on any of the parts of the skill is to take place at the associative phase. Teachers who provide accurate demonstrations and sequence verbal cues for the learner, such as "get set," "racket back," or "swing through," help the learners to organize their beginning attempts at a skill.

After beginning learners have developed some consistency with the pattern and have moved into the associative phase, they are more able to use additional information from the teacher on refining and coordinating aspects of the movement they are trying to learn. Work on such areas as timing, speed, force levels, direction, follow-through, and hand position becomes meaningful. For more complex skills, learners are in this phase for a long time and often return to it even after high levels of skill have been developed. The learner at this associative phase can work on one aspect or one part of the skill and still be able to perform other parts of the skill without much attention. Also, the learner at this stage can begin to concentrate on other things besides the skill, so the teacher can begin gradually to increase the complexity of the practice conditions, for example, by adding other skills, players, or rules to the practice. Working through this phase requires much practice. Teachers can facilitate the practice by helping learners to focus on what is important in skills and by providing feedback to learners on how to improve.

The student at the automatic stage of learning a motor skill does not have to concentrate on the movement. This learner can focus energy on other areas, such as offensive and defensive situations in sports, the target in activities such as golf and archery, or the aesthetic feeling of the movement in dance. The learner at this point is skilled at that movement.

■ REQUIREMENTS FOR LEARNING A MOTOR SKILL

If you are going to try to teach someone a motor skill directly, you must be alert to the idea of what people need to learn that skill. Most of these ideas will seem like common sense, but they are often violated in practice and are not as easy for a teacher to do as it would seem. These requirements are summarized in box 2.2 and discussed next.

A prerequisite for many skills is strength.

BOX 2·2

Requirements for Learning a Motor Skill

Prerequisites

Prerequisite motor abilities
Prerequisite physical abilities
Developmental readiness
Implication for the teacher: Do a task analysis to determine the prerequisites of the skill.

Clear idea of the task

Students perform according to their cognitive understanding of how to perform a task.

Implication for the teacher

Make sure students have an accurate motor program from your communication.

Motivational/attentional disposition to the skill

Implication for the teacher: Eliminate repetitive drills, design tasks that capture student attention, and require the students to process what they are doing.

Practice

Implication for the teacher: Practice is necessary for students to use information on how to do the skill and to develop consistency of performance.

Feedback

Implication for the teacher: Teachers can help students utilize feedback on knowledge of results and performance inherent in a skill and can use teacher feedback to maintain student focus and motivation to continue practice.

Prerequisites

For learners to learn the motor skill you are trying to teach them, they must have the prerequisites to learn that skill. Prerequisites for motor skills often involve already having mastered some easier related skills or abilities. Prerequisites also often involve having the physical abilities to do that skill, which for young children may only be a maturational ability or something as simple as physical strength or

flexibility. Prerequisite abilities are often not defined for the teacher, which makes it imperative that the teacher do a task analysis of a skill and engage in a consistent process of trying to determine why a student is not able to perform a skill. Learners may not be able to catch a ball with a high trajectory because their eyes have not matured to the point where they have the ability to visually track the ball. Learners who cannot learn a tennis serve may not be able to use an overhand pattern in any sport. Learners who cannot get a serve over a volleyball net or do a hip circle on a bar in gymnastics may not have the physical strength to do so. Practice can only lead to frustration, because the individual does not have the capability to do the skill regardless of the amount of practice. Learners should not be put in situations where they cannot succeed.

Clear Idea of the Task

If learners have the prerequisites to learn a skill, the next concern is whether they have a clear idea of what they are trying to do. Most skill-learning problems occur because the learner is operating with false or incomplete information on what he or she is trying to do. The body can perform the skill, but the mind has not given the body the right directions. Sometimes these directions are called **motor programs** or an executive plan for the skill. Motor programs are a memory representation for a pattern of movement that is rather abstract and usually does not involve a specific movement performed by a specific set of muscles and limbs, but a pattern that is general to a variety of responses. For example, you have a motor program for writing that is usually carried out with your hand holding an instrument such as a pen or pencil. If, however, you were to write your name in the sand with your foot, you would still be able to read what you wrote. The motor program is an important idea because it emphasizes the highly cognitive role in motor skills. Most problems in learning a motor skill come from problems in the motor program the learner has been given or the way he or she has interpreted the motor program. Good instruction facilitates the acquisition of accurate motor programs. Good demonstrations and the careful selection of information given to learners facilitate accurate motor programs.

Motivational/Attentional Disposition to the Skill

If students are to learn motor skills, they must be actively engaged in the learning process. This is facilitated if students are motivated to learn. Motivation usually involves a disposition to engage in a particular behavior. Motivation is a critical aspect of learning because learning is an active process. For learning to occur, the individual must be actively engaged in the process, and to do this learners must find the learning meaningful in some way. The critical component of learning is the active processing by the learner of what is to be learned. Although it is possible to design situations that force the learner to actively process what he or she is doing without the learner being highly motivated to learn a skill, it is easier to design situations that will result in active processing of behavior if the learner is motivated to learn. Chapter 9 will address issues of helping students develop motivation more specifically.

The notion of active processing is directly related to the cognitive aspects of motor skill acquisition. The motor plan is developed and refined by the learners actively processing what they are trying to do. The teacher is trying to get the learners to attend to what is important in the skill, to focus the learners' attention on critical aspects. The teacher designs practice situations that will facilitate the learners

attending to what they are trying to do. Repetitive practice of the same movements in the same way ultimately leads to the learners no longer processing what they are trying to do, which decreases the potential for learning. Success also plays a major role in motivating learners and maintaining attention on learning. Lack of success often decreases motivation, attention to the task, and therefore any potential for learning.

Practice

Once you have learned a cognitive fact, such as the capital of a country, chances are that if you take a test on your knowledge of that fact for ten consecutive days, you will be able to reproduce that piece of information with 100 percent accuracy. After you have learned how to do a basketball free throw and you do ten throws for ten days in a row, chances are that you will not be able to reproduce that skill with 100 percent accuracy. Because motor skills are learned as motor programs that are more general and not specific to muscle groups, you are able to more easily adapt your movements to different situations, as well as perform skills with different muscle groups. But because motor programs are not learned as a specific set of instructions for a particular set of muscles, human motor performance is inconsistent and variable. Practice of motor skills is essential for developing and refining the motor program and reducing the variability. Practice should be designed to facilitate processing of motor information and move the learner to the automatic stage of motor skill learning. Practice increases the consistency of performance. More specific guidelines for practice are addressed in a separate section on practice later in this chapter.

Feedback

Motor learning theorists have often addressed the importance of the role of feedback in learning. **Feedback** is information the learner receives on performance. Feedback has been characterized as **knowledge of results (KR)** and **knowledge of performance (KP).** Knowledge of results is usually associated with information on the outcome of

Knowledge of performance
Was movement executed as planned?

		Yes	No
Knowledge of results Was goal accomplished?	No	Change strategy or plan.	Change everything.
	Yes	Do that again!	Surprise!

FIGURE 2.1
Evaluative feedback.

the movement, such as whether the ball went into the basket. Knowledge of performance is usually information the learner receives on the execution of the movement, how the movement feels, or the form characteristics of the movement. Learners can obtain information on both knowledge of results and knowledge of performance internally from sensory information, such as auditory, visual, or kinesthetic, or through information they receive externally from others. They can hear the results, see its results, or feel the movement. They can also be provided this information from external sources, such as a teacher or observer. Figure 2.1 describes the effect of different types of knowledge of results and knowledge of performance on the learner. The most desirable situation is to have the learner execute a skill correctly and also accomplish the goal of the movement. It is frustrating to the learners when they think they have performed correctly and still have not been effective in accomplishing the goal. It is difficult for the teacher to encourage students to perform correctly if the students accomplish the goal of the movement when they have not performed correctly.

Externally provided feedback by the teacher has been thought of as a source of error detection. It has also been thought of as a source of reinforcement and motivation for the learner. Recognize that in a teaching situation, particularly with large groups of

learners, individual feedback to the learner for error detection may not be as important as the role feedback plays in monitoring group instruction to maintain motivation and reinforce the task focus. The role feedback plays in error detection in group learning situations has not been supported, despite the emphasis it receives as part of the teaching-learning process. Feedback will be discussed as part of the instructional process in chapter 7.

■ THE NATURE OF MOTOR SKILL GOALS

How a teacher goes about teaching motor skill objectives to a class is largely determined by the type of motor skills the teacher is trying to teach. Movement skills have been dichotomized using several different criteria, such as fine or gross motor skills; simple or complex; fundamental or specialized; discrete, serial, or continuous; self-paced or externally paced; and open or closed. These characteristics have implications for what to teach and how to teach it. This section addresses some of these characteristics.

Open and Closed Skills

According to Fitts (1962), skills can be placed on a continuum according to their self-paced or externally paced nature. Self-paced skills, such as a dive, golf swing, gymnastics move, and the archery shot, are performed with the body and the object at rest before the execution of the skill. In other skills, such as a punt in football, batting a ball, and doing a forehand tennis stroke, the body or the object is moving, and these skills are identified as having characteristics of externally paced skills. In skills that are at one of the extreme ends of the self-paced/externally paced continuum, both the body and the object are moving. These ideas are illustrated in figure 2.2.

Gentile (1972) modified Poulton's (1957) designation of open and closed skills for sports skills. **Open skills** are those skills regulated by variable or changing events in the environment. A layup shot in basketball is an open skill, because the environment is rarely the same from one time to another and is unfolding during performance. In basketball, for

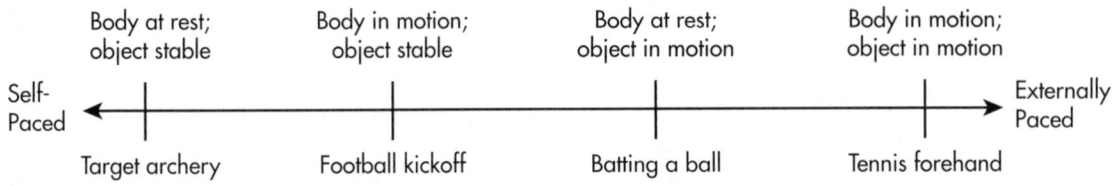

FIGURE 2.2
Continuum of self-paced and externally paced skills.

example, the angle of entry to the goal, the speed, the number of defenders, and the distance from which the shot is initiated change from one time to another. If a skill is closed, the environmental conditions are relatively stable from one situation to another. The basketball free throw is considered more of a **closed skill,** because environmental conditions, such as the distance to the basket, remain stable from one time to another. Figure 2.3 illustrates the nature of open and closed skills.

The ideas of self-paced/externally paced and closed/open skills are similar but represent two different characteristics. Most skills that are self-paced are closed skills, and most skills that are open skills are externally paced. However, a skill such as a golf putt can be self-paced but still have some aspects of open skills, because the golfer does have to adapt performance to such situations as different lies and distances.

The instructional goal of these different types of skills is different. Skills that are self-paced and closed require the development of consistency in stable movement conditions. Skills that are primarily externally paced and open require that the individual be able to perform in complex external environments. Closed skills performed in a variable

environment, such as the golf putt, require that the learner be able to adapt performance to changing external conditions. These different goals are best met by different kinds of progressions and instructional objectives. How the skill is presented, how it is developed, and how it is practiced are affected by the nature of the skill.

Generally speaking, the teacher will not want to practice closed skills in variable environments and will not want to practice open skills for stability. If the skill is self-paced and closed, such as a gymnastics vault or many target activities like bowling, the teacher may initially make the skill easier, but ultimately, practice must take place in the exact environment in which the skill will be used. If the teacher is teaching a layup shot, the teacher may initially reduce the conditions by not using defenders and by slowing down the speed of the movement. Eventually, however, the skill must be practiced in gamelike conditions if it is to be performed in gamelike conditions. This means the teacher may gradually add defenders, other players, skills that precede and follow the layup, and practice doing the layup from different directions and distances from the basket. Open and closed skills are discussed further in chapter 3.

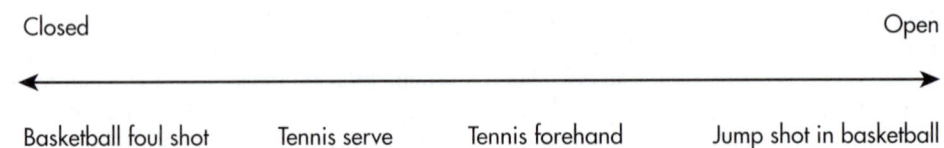

FIGURE 2.3
Nature of open and closed skills.

Discrete, Serial, and Continuous Skills

Another useful framework for teachers when they are thinking about the skills they are teaching describes the discrete, continuous, and serial nature of skills. Skills that are **discrete** are performed once, with a clear beginning and end. Their beginning or end is not governed by any movement preceding or following the skills. A javelin throw or vault in gymnastics is an example of a discrete skill. Different discrete skills that are put together in a series are usually called **serial skills.** Many motor skills, such as fielding a ball and then throwing it or dribbling and then passing a basketball, are serial skills because they are usually performed with other skills. **Continuous skills** have arbitrary beginning and ending points, such as basketball dribbling, swimming, and running. The teacher who wants to teach a discrete skill can focus on the beginning point and ending point of the movement and approach the skill as a closed situation (like the javelin throw). The teacher who wants to teach skills that will eventually be put into a serial relationship with other skills (such as the basketball dribble and pass or catching and then throwing a ball) must combine the skills early in a teaching progression and teach students how to prepare for the next skill during the previous one (transition). For example, if you want students to catch a ground ball and then throw it, they will need to learn

how to place their feet and body so that they can come right up from the fielding situation into the throw.

These categorizations of movement skills used in physical education settings are important ideas that determine the goal of instruction for the teacher. The instructional section of this text will help you to plan instruction appropriate to the type of skill that you want to teach. At this point you will need to be able to characterize skills according to these characteristics.

■ ISSUES OF APPROPRIATENESS IN SKILL DEVELOPMENT AND LEARNING

Most of the professional literature describes skills in terms of what a skill should look like when it is performed by a skilled person. Sport books describe how to dribble a soccer ball. Texts that focus on young children describe what a *mature* throw pattern should look like. This is useful information, but the ideas expressed in these sources are misleading in identifying skill goals to be taught to different learners. What follows are several key ideas to consider when you are thinking about instructional objectives for motor skills.

Environmental Conditions

Environmental conditions, sometimes referred to as task conditions, determine the appropriate process characteristics of most skills. The following Real

Young students sometimes have difficulty understanding the importance of the quality of the toss to their partner's success.

World box describes the problem of task conditions. One of the first problems with using the descriptions of skills that are found in many textbooks as a guide for teaching a skill is that for all but closed skills in self-paced environments, the skill looks different and is adapted differently to different environments. Soccer dribbling looks different depending on whether you are closely guarded. If you are closely guarded, you will want to keep the ball close to you. If you are not closely guarded, you will want to move as fast as you can and therefore will keep the ball farther in front of you. The overhand throw pattern looks like the one shown in the book only when the individual needs maximum force production in the skill and is not performing serial movements (a skill before the throw or after it). If you want to throw a short distance or need to be concerned about getting an object to a target area accurately or quickly, variations of the overhand throw pattern are *appropriate*. The same foot forward as the throwing arm is appropriate for short distances where accuracy is at a premium. If you are fielding a ball before you throw it, the skill looks different. The environmental conditions of a task are critical factors that determine the most appropriate way to perform a skill.

Learner Abilities

Teachers face a second problem when using descriptions of skills found in sport books. Learners adapt the way a skill is performed to their abilities. Sometimes when you are working with young children and even some beginning learners, you will find learners using immature patterns because that is where they are developmentally. They may not have the physical ability to perform differently because of maturational problems or because of physical characteristics. When faced with the task of getting a basketball up to a basket at a standard height, a young child will often use two hands and will perform in an underhand manner. Many 9-year-olds will still misjudge balls in flight because of lack of visual tracking maturity. A student not capable of handling the weight or length of a tennis racket will use two hands, and in fact the two-hand backhand in tennis was developed by an emerging tennis star who did not have the strength to do it the way it was "supposed" to be done. We usually consider these approaches inappropriate skill responses because they do not match the description we have of the way the skill is supposed to be performed. Actually, the responses of these learners are quite appropriate for their abilities. The notion that students should be practicing skills at a mature level of performance is a relevant idea. If, however, the teacher wants the student to practice and learn a mature level of performance, the conditions of practice will have to be adapted for that individual to be able to perform at that level. This means that baskets must be lower, balls smaller and lighter, and rackets shorter and lighter if mature performance is to be developed.

The notion that learners adapt skills to their abilities is also a valid observation for students who have abilities that allow them to reduce the skill to what we used to think was an immature performance. In skills that require much force production, teachers generally encourage the use of a mature pattern, such as differentiated rotation in the volleyball overhand serve. If, however, a student has the strength to get the ball over the net without using rotation, the student may be responding appropriately for the conditions.

The issue of appropriateness is important for teachers. There are many implications of this idea for teaching, such as the following:

1. If a teacher asks a student to demonstrate a particular motor response, the teacher must be sure that the motor response is appropriate for that situation and that learner. It is not appropriate for a teacher to ask learners to use a full overhand throw pattern in a practice situation where students are a short distance from each other. Also, it is not appropriate for a teacher to expect a child who cannot handle the weight of an implement to be able to manipulate that implement in a mature way unless the conditions are changed to facilitate that response.

2. The teacher must design progressions that include combining skills and must focus on helping learners to make the transition from one skill to another. How do you stop the basketball dribble if

you are going to pass? Shoot? How do you place your feet to field a ball if you are immediately going to throw to your right? Left? How do you go from a run into a two-foot takeoff? How do you come out of a forward roll if you are going to go right into an arabesque? These issues are part of progressions that begin to focus on the appropriateness issue.

Many learners will automatically adapt their performance to the conditions of a task, but many will not and will need help. Serial movements, open skills, and externally paced skills all require that the teacher be sensitive to the conditions of the task in terms of what the task requires and the appropriateness of the response to those conditions based on the abilities of the learner.

■ PRACTICE PROFILES AND SUCCESS RATES

Nearly everyone accepts the idea that to learn motor skills, you must practice them. In general, a direct relationship exists between the amount of practice and the amount of learning, assuming the task is an appropriate task. In general, when students in our physical education classes do not learn and they have a clear idea of how to do a skill, it is because they have not had enough practice time. Although motor skill learning is remembered much longer than other kinds of learning, learning motor skills takes time. Effective teaching can facilitate that learning, particularly in the design of practice conditions. What follows are some general principles that teachers must consider when designing practice for motor skills.

Whole or Part

One of the first decisions teachers must make in designing practice for learners is whether it is better to (1) break up a skill into its parts and practice one part at a time or (2) practice a skill as a whole. In general, it is better to practice a skill as a whole. The rhythm and timing of a skill are maintained better when the whole skill is practiced. The more rhythmic the skill, the less appropriate practice of parts becomes. Sometimes, however, it is better to first practice the whole

to give students the general idea of the skill and then break down the skill into parts. When safety is an issue, such as a back handspring in gymnastics, or when the skill is complex, such as the tennis serve, many teachers find that students learn the whole skill better if they have an opportunity to practice the parts. Unless safety is a real issue, learners should always be given an opportunity to get the feel for the whole skill before the skill is practiced in parts. From this framework, then, it can be concluded that there is a whole skill approach and there is a whole/part/whole skill approach. It is not often appropriate to use a part/whole approach.

Practice Variability

The manner in which teachers order and organize what is to be practiced for a given time can affect learning. Practice variability refers to the idea of changing either the environmental conditions of practice or the skills involved in practice. Each of these ideas will be discussed.

Varying practice conditions. The type of skill you want to teach determines to a large extent the amount of variability you want to have in practice. Variability of practice refers to the changing conditions of practice. The opposite of variability is drill and repetition of the same movement for a long period. Practice can be organized so that many conditions are changing, such as changing the speeds, distances, and intent of practice, or so that the same movement is repeated (no variability).

In general, open skills should be practiced in variable conditions and closed skills should be practiced more repetitively in the same conditions (assuming a high level of student processing). Remember that open skills are those in which the learning goal is that the individual be able to adapt the skill to a variety of conditions (the basketball dribble), and the closed skill should be practiced to remove variability (bowling). Variability in practicing catching, for instance, can be added by changing the speed, distance, or direction the ball comes to the catcher or adding serial skills together, such as moving to receive the ball or throwing the ball after you catch it. A certain amount of variability

Practicing with a passive defender increases the difficulty of the skill.

exists in most practice situations, because performers are not consistent to begin with. Adding too much variability, such as too much distance to throw the ball, may change the skill the learner uses (toss to a full overhand throw pattern in the case of throwing) or may make the practice inappropriate for particular learners.

Variability of practice is a critical concept for open skill development. Teachers who practice open skills in closed drill-like practice situations are running the risk that the learner will not be able to adapt his or her

performance. For instance, a student who has practiced the chest pass in basketball from the same distance and from the same position in the center of the body may not be able to pass quickly from other than the chest level.

Teachers may want to reduce conditions of open skills initially for beginning learners to almost closed conditions, such as practicing skills without a ball or with reduced speed or space. This is advisable while the learner is in the cognitive stage of learning the skill. The important idea is that practice in these conditions should not be extensive, and the learners should not be left at this stage of learning and this level of practice if they are to be able to use the skill.

Varying skills. Some work in motor learning (Magill, 2004) suggests that if students practice more than one skill at a time, such as the long serve and short serve in badminton, they are more likely to learn both skills. This idea is based on a theory of *contextual interference,* which says that if you interfere with the rote characteristics of practice, you will encourage the learner to process the information more and therefore learn more. Although the phenomena of contextual interference are beyond the scope of this text, the idea is that practicing one skill and then another skill, such as two different skills in random order, causes the learner to increase the level of processing and therefore increases the chance of learning. Rote repetition of the same skill decreases cognitive processing and therefore the amount of learning. Research is conflicting on how these concepts can best be applied. Other evidence would support the idea that for the complex motor skills taught in most physical education programs, beginning learners are better served by some repetition of practice of the same skill before being asked to practice unselected skills in combination (French, Rink, & Werner, 1990; Herbert, Landin, & Solmon, 1996). Highly skilled learners who may not be highly involved in processing the skill may benefit from more random practice. What this theory does stress is the importance of the learners processing what they are doing. Maintaining learner motivation and attention on what the learners are doing is critical. Unmotivated practice that comes from remaining on the same idea or task for extended periods is not supported.

Massed and Distributed Practice

The physical education teacher often must make decisions related to how long at one time students should practice a skill and how to distribute the practice over a unit of instruction. Although research in this area is limited (Magill, 2004), several ideas are significant for the teacher. Unfortunately, many units of instruction in physical education devote a day to the practice of a particular skill, such as the volleyball forearm pass, and then move on to another skill the next day, never returning to the forearm pass. Learners do not learn motor skills in this way. If the teacher has a twenty- or twenty-five-day unit in a sport, it is better for him or her to distribute practice of a skill over the unit and provide for practice of more than one skill a day after its introduction. This is called **distributed practice,** and although we don't know what the limits of this idea may be for what we do, we do know that distributed practice is better than massing the practice (**massed practice**) of a skill into a short amount of time. If we were to keep track of the number of times a first-grade student added 2 plus 2 over the year, we would find that adding 2 plus 2 would appear on student work sheets throughout the year. Repetition is a basic tenet of learning, and repetition over time ensures the development of skills.

Lessons that vary (1) the skills that are practiced and used and (2) the way in which skills are practiced have more potential to maintain student motivation for practice. Units that distribute the practice of a skill over time have a far greater potential to enhance learning. Yearly programs, particularly with young children whose abilities are changing at rapid rates, have a greater potential to enhance skill development if the teacher revisits skills and ideas throughout the year.

■ MOTIVATION AND GOAL SETTING

Although it is possible for a person to learn motor skills or other types of skills if he or she is not motivated to learn, learning is more likely to occur if the individual is motivated to learn. This is particularly true at the beginning stages of learning a motor skill when cognitive processing of the skill is greater. If students are not motivated to learn, it is likely that they will not process what they are doing to the degree that is needed for learning to occur. Motivated students approach a learning task positively and with great intensity. Unmotivated students spend much of their time avoiding the task.

Motivation is a complex issue in the teaching-learning process. It is enhanced by good decision making on the part of the teacher as to what to teach and how to teach. Learner motivation is also related to the success levels of the students, their experience with the content being taught, the social dynamics of the group they are in, and learner personality and aspiration level.

Every teacher would like to have an entire class of students internally motivated to do well. Students at this level are largely students able to grow and approach new experiences positively. Many students we work with in schools are not able to do this for a variety of reasons. Although it is not always possible to know what all students need to be motivated learners, making the learning environment one that feels safe to individuals both physically and psychologically and having content that is both appropriate and interesting can go a long way in producing motivated learners.

Additional work done in the areas of attribution theory and locus of control can also provide some help for the teacher in understanding students and designing learning environments that encourage growth-producing behaviors and motivated students. One of the more recent efforts of research in teaching physical education has been to try to establish a theoretical understanding of motivation. The more theoretical bases of these ideas are expanded in chapter 9. The major ideas for the practitioner are as follows:

1. Attribution theory is concerned with questions related to what people attribute their success and failure to in a learning situation.
2. When students attribute their success to factors within their own control, they are more likely to be active participants in the learning process

(effort, practice, difficulty of the task). These are primarily internal factors and are associated with a *mastery* orientation to learning.

3. When students attribute their success to factors outside their control (luck, genetics), they are less likely to be active participants in the learning process. These are primarily external factors and are associated with an *ego* orientation to learning.

4. The kinds of experience teachers provide can affect how students interpret their success or failure in learning experiences. Teachers can create a motivational climate that helps students to take a mastery or performance orientation to their learning experiences.

5. Perceived competence of the students (how competent they perceive themselves to be in a given task) also affects participation in a learning experience the teacher designs. Students are more likely to perceive themselves to be competent in a mastery-oriented learning environment and therefore put forth more effort.

■ TRANSFER OF LEARNING

The concept of **transfer of learning** refers to the influence of having learned one skill or ability on learning other skills and abilities. If you are a soccer player, are you more or less likely to do well in lacrosse? If you can throw a football, are you more or less likely to be able to serve a tennis ball? The influence of one activity can be positive, negative, or have no influence on the learning of another activity. Transfer can take many forms. When what you learn with one hand or foot transfers to the other hand or foot, as in the basketball dribble, it is called **bilateral transfer.** When what you learn in one skill or task transfers to another skill or task, it is called **intertask transfer,** as in tennis to racquetball. When what you learn from practice of a skill in one condition transfers to practice of that task in another condition, it is called **intratask transfer,** as in practicing the volleyball set with a trainer ball and then moving to a regulation ball.

Transfer of learning is important to teachers because the way the teacher designs curriculum, the way the teacher sequences the practice of skills, and the way the teacher presents tasks to learners can influence transfer of learning. The teacher will want to maximize the positive transfer of learning and minimize the negative transfer of learning.

Bilateral Transfer

It is commonly accepted that practice with one limb will affect practice with the other; that is, if you learn to dribble a basketball or soccer ball with one hand or foot, learning will transfer to the other hand or foot. Although the limb you practiced with will show the greater gain, both limbs will show improvement. Because physical education teachers deal with the learning of complex motor skills that sometimes need to be performed by both limbs, teachers often ask whether the skill should be learned with both limbs and, if so, should practice with the dominant limb or nondominant limb be first. Most of the research supports the idea that for many reasons, learners should practice first with the dominant limb. Only after a reasonable level of proficiency is acquired should the teacher introduce practice with the nondominant limb.

Intertask Transfer

The influence of learning one skill first before trying to learn another skill is measured by the amount of time it takes to learn the second after having learned the first. If it takes less time to learn the second skill because the first one has already been learned, there is said to be a positive transfer from one skill to another. Although many of our assumptions about the positive transfer of one skill to another are handed down in terms of conventional wisdom rather than research efforts, it is commonly accepted that learning of fundamental skills, such as throwing, kicking, and jumping, should precede learning more specialized and complex sport skills, because there is a positive transfer from one to the other. The effect of transfer is largely determined by the number of component parts in one task that are similar to the other. The tennis serve, for instance, has many characteristics of the overhand throw pattern. The volleyball spike requires the learner to take a few steps into a one- to two-foot vertical jump before striking the ball. If the learner already has become proficient in running and jumping with a one- to two-foot takeoff, you would expect a positive transfer, from having learned these fundamental patterns, to the more specialized skill of the volleyball spike. Physical education curriculum should be based on an easy-to-more-difficult transfer of learning between skills.

Intratask Transfer

When the teacher develops progressions for teaching skills that go from easy to difficult or simple to more complex, the teacher is hoping that there will be a transfer from the practice at one level to the practice at another level. As discussed in the issues related to whether to teach the whole task or to break it down into parts first, there are many times when because of safety, the complex nature of the skill, or the complex nature of the way the skill is used in a game, the teacher will have to design a progression that goes from simple to complex. Teachers can determine if their progressions are successful by determining the extent to which practice in one situation transfers to the other. For instance, if students practice dribbling a soccer ball and shooting the ball into the goal in a practice situation, will they be able to do that in the game situation? If not, there has been no transfer and the teacher will have to either find another way of practicing or add some other kind of practice that more nearly approaches the game situation. If the teacher designs a way to practice the toss in tennis, but when the whole skill is put together, there is no evidence that students can toss the ball correctly and then hit it, there has been no transfer from the practice of the toss to using the toss to serve the tennis ball.

Designing an effective curriculum and progressions for learning depends on the ability of the teacher to monitor carefully their effectiveness in terms of transfer. Transfer can also be facilitated if the teacher keeps in mind some general principles that will facilitate transfer:

1. *The more the practice situation resembles the game situation or the final task, the more likely transfer will occur.* This means that ultimately the

teacher will have to analyze game situations and add components of the game situation to the practice situation. How to do this is discussed in detail in chapters 5 and 11.

2. *The more a skill is learned, the more likely there will be a positive transfer to the game situation.* This means that skills take a long time to learn. The more time devoted to what you want to transfer, the more likely that transfer will occur. Sometimes skills or abilities do not transfer because students have not learned them to begin with.

3. *Transfer can be facilitated by the teacher encouraging students to use information they already know and abilities they already have and making task expectations clear.* This means that the teacher can encourage transfer by making the components of a task clear to learners; cognitively making the connection between skills, such as "this is like . . ."; and giving concrete examples of concepts that the teacher wants students to generalize from one skill to another. These ideas are discussed in detail in chapter 4, where task presentation ideas are developed, and in chapter 12, where the idea of teaching concepts for transfer is developed.

■ LEARNER CHARACTERISTICS
Motor Ability

One of the first observations that a beginning teacher of physical education makes as he or she tries to teach a group of learners a physical task is that any typical physical education class is usually made up of learners with great differences in ability. Unfortunately, too many physical education teachers assume that because a learner cannot do something when it is initially presented, the learner is incapable of learning. Teachers too often take their cue from students who have already done a skill or who do not need instruction. If a student does not learn, often it is because the teacher is not teaching effectively. Although teachers talk about the idea of general motor ability, it is more commonly accepted to consider that there is a set of motor abilities related to specific skills (Thomas & Halliwell, 1976). These specific capacities are related to physical abilities, such as gross body coordination, static and dynamic balance, strength of particular muscle groups, and eye/foot coordination. The importance of each capacity depends on the skill that is to be learned. It is also generally accepted that although the limits of these capacities are most likely set genetically (given at birth), their development is influenced by experience; that is, probably not everyone is capable of being an Olympic performer in a sport, but most people are capable of developing their abilities to the extent that participation in the sport can be both successful and enjoyable. Many people who physical education teachers considered "motor morons" as students are successfully engaged as adults in tennis, golf, racquetball, and other sports.

It is important that teachers do not "tag" students in their classes as being capable or not capable of learning. This is true for many reasons. First, there is not a strong relationship between who learns a skill the fastest and who will ultimately be better at a skill. Second, teachers who communicate either positive or negative feelings to the student about what they are capable of doing can significantly affect learning. A third factor is related to working with children. Children who are older or mature earlier have increased abilities in many motor capacities that do not necessarily represent their potential. It is where they are at the time. Some students may be incapable of learning what teachers present because what teachers present is not appropriate for the students' stage of development. These same children who are developmentally not as mature as their classmates may have more potential than those who are mature. If they are turned off to activities and skills at an early age, they may never reach that potential.

Intelligence and Cognitive Development

Many teachers have wanted to draw relationships between movement abilities and intelligence of the learner. It is not true that students with high academic ability are also good at motor skills or that students with low academic ability are poor at them. Students of low academic ability may not learn in the same way as more academically oriented students and may need to be taught differently, but no direct relationship exists between motor ability and intelligence.

Several developmental factors related to cognitive functioning are critical concepts to teachers choosing how to approach teaching learners at different cognitive levels of development. The first of these is related to Piaget's levels of cognitive development (see box 2.3). Although a complete description of Piaget's levels of functioning is beyond the scope of this text, it is wise to remember that children do not think in

---

BOX 2·3

Piaget's Stages of Cognitive Development

Stage 1: Sensorimotor intelligence

Prelanguage period of development. Prior to the end of this stage objects do not have permanence and motor responses are random. The world exists only as the child acts upon it.

Stage 2: Preoperational intelligence (approximately 2–7 years of age)

Beginning of the use of language and symbols to internally represent ideas and objects. Do not recognize points of view other than their own and are not logical in their reasoning processes.

Stage 3: Concrete operational intelligence (approximately 7–11 years of age)

Can mentally represent objects, see the relationships between parts of an object and the whole, and organize objects by particular characteristics. Remains limited to concrete examples and observations of objects and ideas. Toward the end of this stage can deal with more complex notions of *sameness* and *differentness*.

Stage 4: Formal operational intelligence

Can create and understand hypotheses and "if-then" relationships. Can think scientifically and logically about an idea or problem. Understands other perspectives. Can reflect on their behavior and carry on conversations with self about their behavior.

the same way that adults do. Adults can use scientific thinking. They can deal with "if . . . then" relationships between ideas and can use abstract ideas. The very young child the teacher is likely to encounter in an elementary school (from kindergarten to Grade 2) does not necessarily think in a logical way. Children in this stage of development do not recognize points of view other than their own. I am reminded of an experience with a kindergarten child moving around the gymnasium pushing others out of his way. When the child was asked why he was doing this, he replied, "Because they are in my way."

Children who are 7 to 11 years of age are moving into what is called the *stage of concrete operations*. Children at this level of development can begin to order relationships between things and ideas and begin to reflect on their own behavior. Children at this stage can begin to think logically and handle causal relationships. Some evidence exists that learners with little experience in a content area may operate at a concrete level of operations regardless of their age.

Teachers who work with students of elementary school age and students who have little experience with a content area should keep learning active and concrete. Teachers should limit problem-solving activities and attempts to deal abstractly with ideas with which students have not had a great deal of experience. As students get older and as they become more experienced with content, work that is more abstract is appropriate.

SUMMARY

1. Learning is a relatively permanent change in behavior resulting from experience and training and interacting with biological factors.
2. Common theories of learning describe learning from a behaviorist, an information-processing, or a cognitive theorist perspective.
3. Motor learning is largely consistent with other types of learning, except that the goal of learning is to reduce the level of cognitive processing.
4. Learning takes place in three stages—cognitive, associative, and automatic.

5. To learn a motor skill, learners must have the prerequisites, have a clear idea of the task, be motivated, have opportunity for practice, and have feedback on their performance.
6. Motor skills can be open, closed, discrete, serial, or continuous.
7. An appropriate movement response depends on the conditions of the task and the ability of the learner.
8. Skills that are high in complexity and organization may be better learned if they are taught in parts. In general, it is better to practice skills as a whole if possible.
9. Open skills should be practiced in variable conditions; closed skills, in less variable conditions.
10. In general, practice should be distributed over time for more learning.
11. Motivation increases the potential for learning.
12. In general, skills transfer from one limb to another.
13. Skill-to-skill transfer depends on the similarity between skills: the more similar the skills, the more likely the transfer.
14. Most learners are capable of developing motor skills to the extent that participation is enjoyable and successful.

CHECKING YOUR UNDERSTANDING

1. Describe briefly three different orientations to describing how learning takes place.
2. Describe what a student would look like who is in different stages of learning a motor skill.
3. What are the requirements for learning a motor skill? What do each of these requirements mean for the teacher of motor skills?
4. What is the difference between the way closed skills, open skills, discrete skills, and serial skills should be taught?
5. What is meant by the idea that the student always chooses an appropriate response?
6. Describe how a teacher might elicit the following skills: a standing broad jump, a tight

tuck in a forward roll, and getting under the ball in a volleyball set.

7. Describe three skills that might be better taught as a whole and three that might be better taught in a whole-part progression.

8. Describe how a teacher can facilitate transfer from one skill to a similar skill.

9. What role does cognition play in learning a motor skill?

REFERENCES

Fitts, P. M. (1962). Factors in complex skill training. In R. Glaser (Ed.), *Training research and education*. Pittsburgh: University of Pittsburgh Press.

Fitts, P. M., & Posner, M. I. (1967). *Human performance*. Belmont, CA: Brooks/Cole Publishing.

French, K., Rink, J., & Werner, P. (1990). Effects of contextual interference on retention of three volleyball skills. *Perceptual and Motor Skills, 71,* 179–186.

Gentile, A. M. (1972). A working model of skill acquisition with application to teaching. *Quest, 27,* 3–23.

Haywood, C., & Getchell, N. (2005). *Lifespan motor development*. Champaign, IL: Human kinetics.

Herbert, E., Landin, D., & Solmon, M. (1996). Practice schedule effects on the performance and learning of low- and high-skilled students: An applied study. *Research Quarterly for Exercise and Sport, 67*(3), 52–58.

Magill, R. A. (2004). *Motor learning and control. Concepts and applications* (7th ed.). New York: McGraw-Hill.

NASPE. (2004). *Moving into the future: National standards for physical education* (2nd ed.). Reston, VA: NASPE.

Poulton, E. C. (1957). On prediction in skilled movement. *Psychological Bulletin, 54,* 467–478.

Thomas, J. R., & Halliwell, W. (1976). Individual differences in motor skill *acquisition. Journal of Motor Behavior, 8,* 89–99.

SUGGESTED READINGS

Ackland, B. (2002). Building appropriate student choice through responsibility and trust. *Teaching Elementary Physical Education, 13*(1), 24–26.

Apache, R. (2003). Motor development for the practitioner. *Teaching Elementary Physical Education, 14*(1), 30.

Gagen, L., & Getchall, N. Combining theory and practice in the gymnasium: "Constraints" within an ecological perspective. *Journal of Physical Education, Recreation & Dance, 75*(5), 25–30.

Magill, R. (1994). The influence of augmented feedback on skill learning depends on characteristics of the skill and the learner. *Quest, 46*(3), 314–327.

Rink, J. (2003). Motor learning. In B. Mohnsen (Ed.), *Concepts and principles of physical education: What every student needs to know*. Reston, VA: National Association for Sport and Physical Education.

Schmidt, R. A. (2004). *Motor learning and performance* (3rd ed.). Champaign, IL: Human Kinetics.

Shea, C., & Kohl, R. (1990). Specificity and variability of practice. *Research Quarterly for Exercise and Sport, 67*(2), 169–177.

Ward, P. (2002). A review of behavioral analysis research in physical education. *Journal of Teaching in Physical Education 21,* 241–266.

Designing Learning Experiences and Tasks

3

O V E R V I E W

There is not a direct relationship between the ability to do something and the ability to teach something. A good athlete may not be a good teacher. One of the reasons that this is so is that teachers must be able to translate the content to be taught for the learner. They must know the content in a different way, and they must be able to design learning experiences for the learner that lead the learner to higher levels of ability with that content. This chapter will help you design learning experiences for learners and will help you understand the content of physical education in a different way.

Standard 3: Planning and Implementation

Physical education teacher candidates plan and implement a variety of developmentally appropriate learning experiences and content aligned with local, state, and national standards to develop physically educated individuals.

Standard 4: Instructional Delivery and Management

Physical education teacher candidates use effective communication and pedagogical skills and strategies to enhance student engagement and learning.

NASPE Beginning Teaching Standards, 2008

O U T L I N E

- **Criteria for a learning experience**
- **Designing the movement task**
  Content dimension of movement tasks
  Goal-setting dimension of the task
  Organizational arrangements for tasks
- **Transitions from one organization to another**
- **Designing learning experiences that are safe**

- **Teacher legal liability for student safety**
- **Student decision making in environmental arrangements**
- **The influence of the nature of motor content on the design of a learning experience**
  Closed skills
  Open skills

■ CRITERIA FOR A LEARNING EXPERIENCE

Four criteria for a learning experience were presented in chapter 1 as a guide for teachers to use to determine the educational value of the experiences they provide learners. These criteria are:

- *Criterion One:* The learning experience must have the potential to improve the motor performance/activity skills of students.
- *Criterion Two:* The learning experience must provide maximal activity or practice time for all students at an appropriate level of ability.
- *Criterion Three:* The learning experience must be appropriate for the experiential level of all students.
- *Criterion Four:* The learning experience should have the potential to integrate the psychomotor, affective, and cognitive educational goals whenever possible.

From the previous chapters you should begin to see the importance of and support for these criteria. Opportunity to learn and experiences designed at an appropriate level for all students are critical ideas if students are to profit from physical education. The teacher who designs experiences that include both cognitive and affective concerns of an educational program recognizes the integrated nature of learning. The focus of this chapter is to help you design learning experiences that meet these criteria, as it is not always easy to do.

■ DESIGNING THE MOVEMENT TASK

At the heart of each learning experience is the movement task. *Movement tasks* are the specific movement experiences that constitute learning experiences in physical education. When the teacher says, "Practice giving with the ball until you can't hear the ball hit your foot," the teacher is giving a movement task. Movement tasks are what students do that are related to the content. When students are involved in a movement task, they are involved in content with a specific intent and are organized in some way to engage in the task. There is always a what, a why, and a how to a movement task. Teachers should not just say, "Go practice basketball dribbling." If the teacher does not describe how dribbling will be practiced in a group instructional setting and the intent of that practice, the experience lacks focus.

Movement tasks have a content dimension, a goal orientation, and an organizational dimension that provide the needed focus:

- The *content of the task* is the movement content with which the students are asked to work.
- The *goal orientation of the task* describes the qualitative, or goal, aspect of the movement experience.
- The *organization of the task* is concerned with arrangements of time, space, people, and equipment, all designed to facilitate work on the task.

Consider the examples of movement tasks presented in box 3.1.

Examples of Movement Tasks

Example 1

Practice the overhead set with your partner to see how long you can keep the ball going with your partner at a high level. If the ball falls to a low level, catch it and start again.

Content: Practice overhead set.

Goal orientation: Number of consecutive passes without losing control.

Organization: Practice with a partner (no other arrangements explicit).

Example 2

We are going to play basketball three-on-three but will not be using the baskets. To score you must catch the ball across the end line after three passes are completed. Your group of six will have half the court in which to play your game and you will use the red lines at either end of that space as the end line.

Content: Play three-on-three game with no baskets; pass and move to receive a pass.

Goal orientation: Use quick passes and move into a space to receive a pass.

Organization: Play in groups of six on one-fourth of a basketball court using one ball per group.

In some situations, organizational arrangements for tasks are implicit because of learner previous experience or class established procedures. They are always present in some form, whether they are implicit or made explicit by the teacher. Each of these dimensions of the task is a critical aspect of task design. As important parts of the task, they can be manipulated by the teacher to achieve different goals and different objectives.

Content Dimension of Movement Tasks

The content dimension of the movement task describes for the learner the substance of the task (e.g., pass the ball to a partner, play softball, or self-assess your performance). The choice of content is primarily a curricular decision based on the unit of study and lesson objectives. Teachers decide on a progression of experiences that lead the learners from where they are to where the teachers want them to be with the content. Once these decisions are made, however, teachers must further decide (1) the amount of decision making students will have in the choice of content and (2) the affective and cognitive involvement of the learner in each task. Teachers rarely make these decisions for a whole lesson. Each task is a unique decision for the teacher.

Teachers select the content of a task because they think that having students experience that content is important to a learning goal. As stated in chapter 1, if the teacher has no goals, it does not matter what tasks are provided to learners. The selection of the content of a task is easier if the teacher's goals are clear. As a beginning teacher, the content you are to teach will probably be selected for you. In this case, you will have to determine the best task(s) to use to develop that content with a given set of learners.

Most of the learning experiences teachers present will be related to learning motor skills. The teacher will select a skill to teach and then will develop a learning experience to improve learner performance in that skill. Sequencing content is discussed in chapter 5 on content development. Designing learning experiences to meet other goals is also discussed in chapter 5.

Checking the value of the content you have selected. The content the teacher selects can contribute to or can diminish the value of the learning experience. When you select the content, ask yourself the following questions:

- If students are engaged in this content, will this experience contribute to an objective I have for learning in my program?
- Is the experience valuable for all of these students? Are there some students for whom this experience is not challenging? Are there some students for whom this experience is too difficult for them to experience success?
- Would the experience have more value if I redesigned the task to include both cognitive and affective involvement on the part of the learner?

Box 3.2 (see p. 44) illustrates examples of content that is redesigned to include a concern for the appropriateness of the task for individuals as well as a concern for more inclusive involvement of the learner.

B O X   3 · 2

Making the Content Dimension of the Task More Appropriate

Original content

When I say go, everyone skip.

Revised content

When I give the signal, everyone do either a skip or a gallop. Who can tell me what the difference is between these two skills?

The teacher has decided that not everyone in the class is able to skip yet, but everyone in the class is able to either skip or gallop. When students choose a gallop, they will be working on a skill that will help them to eventually skip.

I have posted the warm-up drill on the wall.

We will spend the first few minutes warming up for today's lesson. Each of our groups for today will be responsible for designing a warm-up exercise for a particular part of the body. We will put each part together, and that will be the warm-up drill we will use for this unit.

The teacher has decided to give students a richer experience by having cooperative groups design exercises that they will bring to the whole class as a group contribution. Students will have to use their knowledge of warm-up exercises and will have to work with each other in cooperative ways to contribute to the whole.

The teacher has explained how to do the overhand volleyball serve and then sends the students off to practice at the service line.

The teacher has explained how to do the overhand volleyball serve and then says, "Some of you may want to start your practice close to the net until you are more successful. You can then move back closer to the service line."

The teacher in this instance recognizes that although students should all be able to do the skill at some level, some of the students may not be able to produce the force necessary to get the ball over the net from the service line. Giving students the option to make that choice helps the teacher individualize for skill level. Giving students the choice also gives students experience with decision making.

Goal-Setting Dimension of the Task

Goal setting involves communicating to the learner the intent of a task and student practice. Most teachers assume the intent, or purpose, is to "learn" a skill or concept, but the perceptions of students about what the intent might be and the intent of the teacher may be different. When teaching motor skills, for instance, most teachers assume that the goal is to improve "form" or how the skill is done. Most of the time students are not working toward this goal; they are more interested in what the skill accomplishes rather than in how the skill is performed. Beginning learners are also likely to be discouraged if they think the goal of the practice is to do the skill perfectly. *The students and the teacher are more likely to have the same goal*

for a movement task if that goal is shared with the students at the beginning of the lesson.

EXAMPLE: *"I am more interested in whether you can use each of these cues in your performance than I am in how hard you can hit the ball."*

Most teachers want students to become more proficient at motor skills, but learners cannot acquire proficiency in short periods of practice for one task. Instead, they acquire proficiency in stages. For instance, an initial goal for students in learning to field a ball might be to get their body situated in the proper fielding position. Later goals might involve the position of the glove or what to do after the ball is in the glove. In chapter 2 the importance of making tasks achievable for students was identified as an important aspect of learning. *Teachers can manipulate the goal orientation of tasks to ensure success by setting short-term goals en route to proficiency.*

Examples:

- *"I don't care where the ball goes right now. I just want you to get the feel of the movement."*
- *"Walk through your sequence until you know what the transitions are going to be. You don't have to do each move until you have it all figured out."*

Teachers often explain a skill and then have the students start to practice or work on a task without the benefit of a goal for practice. For example, assume that the teacher has worked on the toss in a tennis serve and has explained the critical cues involved in the tennis toss. To set a useful goal for practice, the teacher might say, *"Toss the ball until you can get it to land in the same spot consistently."* The practice then has purpose. Teacher

The goal of this task is for the student to receive the teacher's toss and direct it to a partner so that it can be returned.

goals can also be set for practice involving skills that do not have easily identifiable results or that do not result in movement responses that are the same for all students. For example, the teacher can say, *"Practice the backward roll until you don't have to stop the movement to let your head come through"* or *"Find all the ways you can think of to balance using three parts of the body as a base."* These tasks provide a goal rather than just an intent to move.

It is also possible for goals to be both individualized and personalized for the student. When teachers individualize or personalize goals, they are accommodating individual differences in students (e.g., *"Some of you may want to work to get ten in a row and some of you may want to choose to get your pattern smoother"*). Goal setting helps learners focus their work and realistically evaluate their progress. Goal setting also helps the teacher with analysis, observation, and evaluation of student responses in preparation for a new task focus.

The goal orientation of the task cannot be assumed unless stated by the teacher. Teacher responsibilities include not only telling students what task to do but also informing them how to do the task and indicating the goal toward which the task contributes. Statements such as the following help by giving the learner a goal and a qualitative emphasis in practice:

- *"Work to get the transitions smooth."*
- *"Stay at the dribble until you can bounce the ball five times without looking at it."*
- *"Don't worry about accuracy yet, but work toward getting a full swing and hard hit."*
- *"I am also looking to see how you work cooperatively with your group to get their task done."*
- *"Stay with the toss until you get the ball to fall consistently in one spot."*
- *"Choose a specific goal for your practice today so that you can evaluate your work at the end of the period."*

An intent for good performance is communicated in these tasks. The teacher is sharing the purposes for which the tasks are designed, which gives the learners a focus for the learning experience.

More specific and narrower focuses of tasks will make the goal orientation clearer. Follow-up tasks that focus the learner on the quality of the response (e.g., *"Make your body shape much clearer"*) provide a clear goal for students when efficiency of performance is what the teacher has identified as most important. These types of tasks are called refining tasks and will be discussed in chapter 5. More specific and narrower focuses of this type also sequence learning cues for students one at a time. Students, particularly beginning learners, cannot assimilate a lot of information about movement at one time. The teacher can sequence goals for performance so that major ideas of good performance can be handled first and then performance can be polished.

When students are ready to test the effectiveness of their performance, a task with an application/assessment focus provides a clear goal. Application/assessment tasks take the focus of the learner off how to execute the movement and put it on the product of the performance. Application/assessment tasks can be designed as self-testing, assessment experiences or competitive experiences against others. The following examples have been reworded from previous examples to illustrate the design of an application task and to clarify the goal orientation:

- *"See how long it takes you before you can get your roll so smooth that you don't have to stop to let your head through."*
- *"Work until you can hit the ball seven out of ten times in the same spot without losing control."*
- *"Count how many ways you can find to balance on three parts of your body."*
- *"When you are ready, ask your partner to assess your form using the checklist."*

A warning: There is a danger in designing tasks focused on application/assessment too soon. The student focus is taken off the quality of movement in highly competitive tasks, even those of a self-testing nature. Beginning tasks should help the learner focus on the intent of the whole movement and not just on the effectiveness.

Tasks that involve group responses, such as "Design an aerobic dance sequence in groups of four students," also should have a clear goal. In this instance the teacher should establish how students are to work, what a good sequence would look like, and what good group work would look like.

Organizational Arrangements for Tasks

In group instruction, teachers must make decisions about the following:

- Whether students will work on a task alone or with a partner or group (people)
- How long they will practice (time)
- Where students will work on the task (space)
- What equipment they will use (equipment)

These decisions are organizational. They arrange the environment for the content of the task. How the teacher arranges the environment is important, not only to the content of the movement task itself, but also to the potential of that experience to contribute positively to other program goals and objectives. **Organizational arrangements** *are instructional arrangements for people, time, space, and equipment.* Sometimes these arrangements are explicit in a task, and sometimes they are implicit. They should always be purposefully designed. The teacher arranges people, time, space, and equipment to accomplish specific objectives. Teachers should not underestimate the importance of environmental arrangements in the facilitation of learning. Hough et al. (1975) define instruction as "the process of arranging human, material, and temporal resources with the intent of facilitating one's own learning and the learning of others." Arranging environments for learning and instruction is part of if not the same process.

Arranging people. In physical education, arrangements for people include decisions concerned with the number of students in a group, the number of students active within each group, and the criteria the teacher uses to group the students.

Group size. Group size and opportunity for learning are integrally related. It is often useful to consider the following categories when determining how students are functioning within a class:

- Individual
- Partner
- Small group (three to six)
- Large group (seven or more)
- Whole class

In each of the units mentioned, one student or all students within a single group can be active. For example, relays are usually a small-group activity, but only one student is active at a time. The game of *"keep-it-up"* in volleyball is a small-group activity with all students active.

Teachers should base the decision of how many students to include in a group primarily on the answer to the question, *"How many students are necessary to engage in this task?"* Some skills or experiences require more than one or two people to a group (e.g., offensive and defensive game experience cannot be gained by working alone). However, many teachers group students into larger units than necessary to practice a task. As a result, students are forced to share equipment and wait for turns. Sometimes limited space or equipment forces less than total activity. Sometimes students who cannot respond productively in a total activity environment need to be arranged in organizational formats that allow for greater teacher monitoring. And sometimes teachers will want to give students roles in a group other than being physically active, such as observing, assessing each other, or working on a task together in a cooperative way. Again, it should be stressed that teachers should seek out alternatives to inactivity and work toward an environment that permits all students to be active.

Criteria for grouping. Criteria for grouping describe the basis on which students are put in groups. Unfortunately, most physical educators group randomly, using no criteria. Grouping is a powerful tool that a teacher can use to influence the learning process, yet many times teachers fail to take advantage of it. One of the most destructive ways of grouping students is legendary in our profession. We still have teachers choosing captains and having captains battling it out for the best and worst players.

Consider the situation in which twenty-five students are in class at five different levels of ability in a particular activity. Assume that the unit is a basketball unit and that the students at levels one and two are ready for a five-on-five game using regulation rules. The students at levels four and five are able to handle only modified situations. The class is coed, with no more than the usual number of social antagonists in the group. How would you handle this situation?

The immediate response of most beginning teachers to this situation is to create five teams with one student from each ability level. The first criterion for a learning experience, as described at the beginning of this chapter, is that the experience be appropriate for the student. Grouping five different ability levels on one team, regardless of game design, makes the experience inappropriate for a majority of students. The rationale given for such a decision is usually that the less-skilled players will learn from the more-skilled players. The students most likely will learn, but probably not much about basketball. It is sometimes desirable for students with greater skill to be placed in situations where they have to adapt to the abilities of less-skilled students. And in some situations, students with less ability profit from being with students with more ability. There is a new approach to teaching physical education, called sport education, which deliberately places students with different abilities on the same team. The teacher then works with these teams in a deliberate way to make sure that the needs of all students placed on a team are being met. In the basketball situation just described you do not want to put students in a situation where they are continuously criticized for not passing the ball to someone who loses possession every time. What are the alternatives? How can this situation be handled?

Although research findings are mixed on the value of ability grouping, this criterion remains one of the most desirable for skill acquisition. Teachers can ability group for the same or different tasks. Teachers can leave the choice to students, or they can make it themselves. Students will tend to ability group themselves when given the choice. Unless the students' choice is socially nonproductive, teachers should strongly consider this alternative. Heterogeneous (mixed ability level) grouping can work well, especially in peer-teaching situations and cooperative learning (see chapter 8). However, teachers should avoid as much as possible the continuous use of heterogeneous groups for competitive situations with a large range of skill ability. Other alternative criteria for grouping may include the following:

- *Gender.* Grouping by gender within a class is not a desirable choice in today's culture and should be avoided under most circumstances unless contact activities are involved.

- *Ethnicity.* If ethnic problems or an ethnic imbalance occurs in a class, serious consideration should be given to having ethnically balanced groups preestablished by the teacher or an expectation for students who are asked to group themselves.
- *Interest.* When alternative tasks are to be presented, teachers should seriously consider allowing students to choose tasks by interest.
- *Social compatibility.* Many times teachers have to separate students who cannot work together productively and regroup them for productive social relationships.
- *Size.* It is sometimes important for students to work with others of equal or unequal size. Support activities and combative activities are examples of when consideration should be given to size. It is sometimes advisable to use size as a criterion for grouping when height is a decided advantage or disadvantage.
- *Chance.* Sometimes it makes no difference how students are grouped. Clever teachers have found many ways to create random groups other than the time-consuming "count-off" method. Some of these include grouping by colors of clothing, birthdays, or colors of eyes. If teachers want to produce an experience that allows students to work with others with whom they ordinarily might not choose to work, chance may provide a good criterion for grouping. The Real World box describes the efforts of an elementary and a secondary teacher to group students using several criteria.

Arranging time. The time aspect of task design concerns the length of time students will spend in practicing a task and the responsibility for pacing responses to the task. Time is an important aspect of structure and can be used by the teacher to create more productive learning environments.

Task time. Few teachers, even experienced ones, can predict beforehand exactly how much time students will need to work on a movement task before shifting the focus of the task. In some teaching strategies (e.g., station teaching, see chapter 8), the teacher must make

---

THE REAL WORLD

Use of Grouping Strategies in a Real-Life Setting

Elementary

Ms. T noticed that when she gave students the opportunity to choose their own partner there was always one student whom no one ever picked, even if it meant that there were two people without partners after the "choosing" was finished. Ms. T thought about not letting students choose to avoid this issue but decided instead to talk to one of the more popular students before class and ask that student to choose the unpopular child for partner work when it came to that part of the lesson. The popular student was proud to be picked for the job.

Secondary

SP middle school was located in a racially mixed location. The teachers acknowledged that there was little racial tension between the students, but if left to form their own groups, students would group themselves by gender and by race. The teachers created a rule for physical education that all groups had to have at least one member of a different race and at least one member of a different gender than the other members. At first it took the students some time to work this out for their groups. The teachers made it a rule that they would not begin until the groups were organized in this way. Within a short time students were in compliance and it was not uncommon to hear several boys say that they would join the "girls group" that had formed or several African American students volunteer to join the "white" group.

---

this decision ahead of time. Having to make this decision in advance makes time allocation more difficult, particularly because there is no good way to anticipate how much time students will need or can spend productively before the teacher must refocus students.

The decision of when to refocus students on a new task or when to change the task is based largely on what the teacher sees happening with student responses. *Teachers should not let practice deteriorate into unproductive responses.* There is a limit to both the physical capabilities permitting continued practice and the interest of even the most motivated student. However, sufficient time must be provided for a student to gain some consistency of response. Many effective teachers will stop work short of deteriorating responses and provide a short transition period to focus on evaluation. This evaluation may result in continuing the same task or switching to a new focus using the same material.

Pacing responses to tasks. When tasks are student paced, the teacher gives a task, and the students begin and end a task in their own time. When tasks are teacher paced, students begin and usually end each movement on a teacher signal. Sometimes signals are verbal, and sometimes a whistle, drum, or clap of the hands is used. Teachers who count out exercises or a dance or cue or walk students through the practice of a skill are presenting tasks in a teacher-paced manner. When a task is teacher paced, all students are performing the task at the same time and in the same rhythm. Deciding whether a task is to be student paced or teacher paced should be determined by the type of skill the teacher wants the student to develop (open or closed) and the level of difficulty of the task. Teacher pacing of tasks may be more appropriate to skills that are more closed or for the introduction of a skill allowing the teacher to "walk through" the cues with the student.

When teachers pace the task, they can select appropriate cues, and students are more likely to be "with" the teacher and not off task. Teacher pacing allows the teacher to attend to the speed and other dynamics of the movement. For many years, teachers of dance have practiced the use of teacher voice and rhythm instruments to ensure proper dynamics in a response such as "Forward-two-three, Back-two-three, Turn-two-three." Teachers of bowling who walk students through the cues "push out, swing back, bend, and release" are teacher pacing the initial practice of the skill. Some excellent teachers of sports skills have helped students' first attempts at skills by communicating the rhythm and dynamics of the skill through teacher voice and pacing.

Teacher pacing can help the student remember the sequence of cues used for a skill, because the student is using the cues immediately and not waiting until all the information has been given. Because the first stage in learning a motor skill is cognitive (see chapter 2), retention of cues can help the student form an accurate motor plan when teacher pacing is removed. Teacher pacing at the early stages of a complex skill may be of some benefit, particularly if the skill is a closed skill. However, teacher pacing for open skills destroys the desirable quality of unpredictability and should be removed quickly if used at all (Singer, 1980).

Arranging space. The arrangements teachers make for the use of space are important and can determine whether the intent and potential of a task can be fulfilled. These arrangements are determined in part by the answers to the following questions:

- What area is going to be defined as the practice area?
- How is the practice area to be partitioned for students?
- What organization of people in the space will be used?

Defining the practice area. Teachers must initially define the area of the field or gymnasium that will be considered the practice area. Teachers who neglect to establish clear practice areas probably will need to recall students from remote areas of a playing field or from the side of the gymnasium, where the students are leaning against walls or hanging on apparatus. Practice areas can be defined with natural boundaries or with the help of markers.

The selection of a work area is dictated largely by the nature of the movement content. Some skills need a great deal of space, and some need less space. Striking activities, when control is a problem, are better practiced against a wall when inside, because ball retrieval and safety are strong considerations. How much space teachers allow for tasks in many cases determines the way in which the task can be performed and its safety. In manipulative skills, the skill requirements for force production and absorption are determined largely by the size of the space. If a student and a partner have one quarter of a tennis court for their striking work with paddles, their practice of forehand striking skills will be far different from their practice if they have a whole court and is likely to resemble more of a tap. Volleyball is a different game when played on a regulation court than when played on a smaller, modified court.

Experienced teachers of young children learn another space consideration, but they somehow forget to share it with beginning teachers; that is, large open spaces are disconcerting to the very young child. Sometimes a large gymnasium is scary. Partitioning that space into smaller spaces until children feel secure in that environment is sometimes necessary. Psychologically, the smaller space makes the individual feel more secure. It also helps the teacher establish a more productive group learning environment, because group membership is more keenly felt in the smaller space. Chairs, traffic cones, or boxes are useful to divide space when large barriers are not available.

Partitioning practice areas. Partitioning practice areas involves deciding how to break up the play area for the use of students. The teacher's inclination is either to reduce the amount of space available to each student so that all may be active or to reduce the space and minimize the force or speed used in some activities. Sometimes, however, it is necessary to give students some opportunity to experience the effects of a larger space on their movement. This is particularly true in activities where force production and redirection are crucial. It should be considered also in dance and gymnastics tasks. The challenge is to allow some students the opportunity to use larger spaces and at the same time provide meaningful tasks for those who do not have use of the larger space.

The size of the space also is an important organizational decision, because teachers can manipulate the size of the space to reduce or extend the complexity or difficulty of a task, either for the class or for individuals. The need for a large space must be balanced with the need for maximum activity. I once observed a high school floor hockey class of forty students in which twelve students were playing and twenty-eight were sitting out. The value of that experience for any of the students was indeed questionable.

Organizing people in space. The organization of people in space concerns the spatial formation of people in the play area. Figure 3.1 describes some of

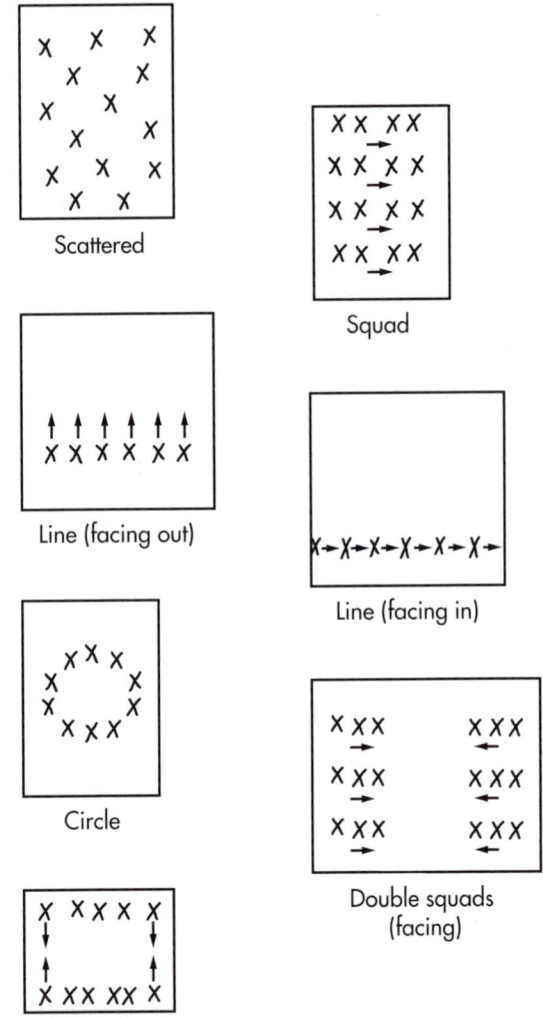

FIGURE 3.1
Organizational arrangements of people in space.

the more popular arrangements for people. The present emphasis on maximal participation in physical education classes has made the use of lines, squads, and circles of people less popular than it once was. Much time is lost getting people into these formations, and many of these formations restrict the number of people active at any one time.

The scattered formation is a useful organizational arrangement of people when all individuals are going to be active at one time and when the task does not require other spatial arrangements. Telling individual students, partners, or small groups to quickly find a place to work readies students for activity without extensive time spent in organization; also, it uses all the play area available. Having other students around them, all working at the same time, is probably less confusing to the students than it is for the teacher. The scattered formation also eliminates the situation where one student watches another perform. This can be an asset when working with all learners, but particularly beginning learners.

The problem with the scattered formation is that the teacher cannot observe students as easily as in formal formations. Students can get "lost" in the crowd easily unless teachers make it a point to be aware of the total group. At times, teachers will want students in more formal organizations. Task presentations that are teacher paced (e.g., initial practice of dance steps) are more successful if everyone is facing the same direction. The practice of striking or throwing skills, either with partners or against a wall, is safer if missed balls do not interfere with other students. Teachers will want to consider front-facing lines for these sorts of activities.

Group games usually have their own organizational formats. Teachers are cautioned to be alert in selecting games that have high rates of student activity. Highly organized formations for skill practice usually require much time to get students organized and often are unnecessary for the skills practiced. It is not uncommon to see a teacher take seven minutes to get students into a practice situation that lasts three minutes.

Arranging equipment. Procurement and arrangement of equipment are also critical determinants of the potential ability of a motor task to accomplish its objectives. For most situations, particularly in the games and sports areas, it is ideal to have one piece of equipment for each student or, in the case of specialized equipment, for every two students. Teachers should try to avoid a situation where the arrangements for people and space are dictated by the amount of equipment available. Few children in an ordinary classroom share texts, papers, or pencils. They should not be expected to share equipment when one piece of equipment for each learner is appropriate.

Included in decisions about equipment is determining whether to provide all students with exactly the same equipment (e.g., the same size, weight, or shape ball; the same rhythm instruments in dance; the same arrangements of apparatus; the same height net). As with decisions regarding space, the arrangement of equipment can change or modify the tasks. Higher nets in volleyball encourage getting under the ball to play it; lower nets make the spike more attainable for shorter or less-skilled players. Some combinations of gymnastics apparatus encourage traveling in one direction, whereas other combinations of equipment encourage a change in direction. The size and weight of manipulative equipment can often determine whether younger and less-skilled students can be successful in performing a skill in an efficient way. Nothing is sacred about regulation-size equipment. If the equipment needs to be modified, teachers should seriously consider modifying it, even on an individual basis. The choice and arrangement of equipment is not just an organizational detail, but a critical factor of task design.

A large part of safety is teaching students how to do a skill or activity correctly.

■ TRANSITIONS FROM ONE ORGANIZATION TO ANOTHER

One of the biggest time wasters in physical education classes is the inefficient transitions teachers make from one organizational design to another. If students are working by themselves and you want them to work in partners or if students are working with one piece of equipment and you want them to use a different piece of equipment, you will want to have a strategy for making the transitions quickly. Some of the following situations will help you think through how to get students from one organization to another.

Changing equipment. Have all the equipment that students will need for the lesson arranged in several small access areas so that everyone can change their equipment at one time. A simple direction such as "Take your small ball and replace it with a big one in one of the hoola hoops and come back to your space and sit" will be efficient for most groups. If students tend to run at the equipment, you may need to have a few start at a time or, better yet, teach them how not to run and get the equipment.

Changing the organization of people. If students are spread out working independently, there are several ways the teacher can regroup students. One of the quickest ways is to have students stop and "walk over to a person near you and stand by them." In this case, the teacher may need to watch that students move toward someone close to them. Or, if you need larger groups, "walk over and stand next to three people close to you." More often than not teachers can say "find a partner" if who the student works with is not an issue.

Moving to a new practice area and more formal organization. There are times when teachers do want a formal organization of students, such as a line facing front, a circle, or a double line. The following guidelines will get you started thinking about how to do this.

- *Circle.* The practice of asking students to hold hands and make a circle usually doesn't work with any age for different reasons. However, because most gyms and outdoor spaces have a basketball circle on the floor, the teacher can quickly get students into a circle by asking

them to stand on the circle and take steps back according to the size of the circle needed.

- *One line facing front.* For dance instruction or while using a wall for striking or throwing activities it is often desirable to have students in a line facing front (or facing the wall). The easiest way to do this is to have students "find a spot on the blue line facing me." If there are no lines, ask students to line up in front of you. You will then have to move and ask them to face you.

- *Two lines facing.* Many times teachers want students across from a partner with all partners throwing, striking, or kicking in the same direction for safety. Two lines facing can be achieved by asking students to get in partners, then have one partner stand on one line and the other partner stand on the other line facing the partner. Then the teacher moves them the distance needed by asking them to step forward or backward. If you don't have two lines painted on the floor, follow the directions for forming one line and then demonstrate to students where you want the other partner to stand.

■ DESIGNING LEARNING EXPERIENCES THAT ARE SAFE

One of the essential characteristics of any arrangements made for a task is the safety of that task. The quality of safety overlaps decisions made regarding the content, the goal-setting dimension of the task, and the organizational arrangements of the task. All of these factors contribute to the safety of the task.

Teachers are legally responsible for keeping students safe. When a teacher asks students to do something, the teacher must be sure that what the teacher asks the student to do will not harm the student in any way. Although some risk is involved in the content of physical education, that risk can be minimized by the following precautions:

1. *Make sure all students have the prerequisites to do a skill.* It is unsafe to ask students to try a skill they have no chance of being successful with. Not all students are ready to do a gymnastics vault or to catch a hard and fast ball at the same time. If you have students in the class who cannot do

what most other students are ready for you must individualize the task (see next section).

2. *Do not let students work "out of control" in any task.* Make control of movement a goal for all experiences. Students who are allowed to swing away recklessly with a bat, stick, or racket or are allowed to fling their bodies at equipment or a mat are dangerous to themselves and others and should not be allowed to function in this manner with any content.

3. *Teach students how to work safely with a task.* Students can be taught to work safely in physical education.

   - They can be helped to be aware of others in their movement and adjust their movement in relation to others.
   - They can be made aware of the danger of flying balls and work with control.
   - They can be taught to return other students' equipment to them without flinging the equipment across the gymnasium.
   - They can be taught what control is on landings from a gymnastic move and taught how to land with control.
   - They can be taught that any kind of "crashing" into students or onto a mat or anything else is not allowed in class.
   - They can be taught not to assist others in their movements unless asked to do so by the teacher.
   - They can be taught to look around and make sure they have enough space before they swing any implement.
   - They can be taught to "rest off equipment not on it" and to not use large equipment unless they have permission so they are not tempted to "fool around" on the equipment.

4. *Arrange the environment for safe participation and practice of the skill.* Each content creates its own potential for being a safety problem, and the teacher must think through the potential problems with each task that is given. Some examples follow:

   - Gymnastics must include mats if students are going to land from great heights.

   - Finish lines for races must be placed well before a wall or other obstruction so that students have time to decelerate.
   - Targets for archery must be staggered at different distances rather than where students line up to shoot at the target.
   - Any sport in which the student is swinging an implement must ensure that there is enough space to do so safely.
   - Objects traveling at great speeds should never come "by accident" to another student.
   - When students are all moving in the same space they must be taught how to do this safely.
   - For activities that require physical contact between students, consider the size and weight of students being asked to work together.

■ TEACHER LEGAL LIABILITY FOR STUDENT SAFETY

Teachers can be held liable for the safety of students. Usually liability suits on behalf of students involve teacher negligence and, in some cases, teacher abuse. The nature of our content makes us particularly vulnerable to potential student injury. School officials and school personnel may have legal liability when a student is injured either by a deliberate action or negligence by a teacher. Courts have found teachers guilty of assault and battery when a teacher's discipline has been cruel, brutal, excessive, or administered with malice, anger, or intent to injure.

Usually student injury suits involve tort claims of negligence. Tort laws are laws that offer compensation to individuals harmed by the unreasonable actions of others. Although tort laws may differ from state to state, they are based on the legal premise that individuals are liable for the consequences of their conduct if it results in injury to others. In order to prove negligence, a student must demonstrate to the court that what happened was not intended and that it was not an expected outcome of the teacher's behavior. Cases for negligence must demonstrate that (1) the teacher's behavior did not protect the student from unreasonable risks, (2) the teacher failed in that duty by not exercising a reasonable standard of care, (3) there is a causal connection between the breach of the duty to care and the resulting injury, and (4) there must be an actual physical or mental injury resulting from the negligence. In a court, all four elements must be proven before damages will be awarded for negligence.

The courts have acknowledged that our content has an inherent risk but they have also acknowledged that teachers must do what is prudent to reduce that risk. Often in physical education cases, expert witnesses are called to determine whether the teacher acted in accordance with "best practice." Specifically, did the teacher do what is expected of a physical education teacher to protect the student? When teachers leave students without supervision, tell students they have to do a skill they are clearly not ready for, allow student horseplay to get out of hand, have students hitting balls into other students, or grab a student in anger, they put themselves in an indefensible position. Methods of teaching texts like this one in a sense define "good practice." When you choose to put students in danger, you also put yourself in danger of legal liability.

■ STUDENT DECISION MAKING IN ENVIRONMENTAL ARRANGEMENTS

A critical concern in the design of movement tasks is the amount of student involvement in the learning process. Students can often be part of the decision-making process when environmental factors are discussed. They may make decisions for themselves or may be helped to make a group decision. Consider the possibilities presented in box 3.3 for student choice relating to environmental arrangements of a task.

When teachers make all the decisions relative to environmental arrangements, task content, and criteria for performance, the task is highly *teacher structured* and teaching becomes very direct teaching. When teachers begin to share these decisions with students, tasks become less teacher structured, and teaching becomes more indirect. Many beginning teachers assume that task structure is an all-or-nothing proposition. This is not true. Teachers need to learn to add

---

BOX 3·3

Possibilities for Student Choice Relating to Environmental Arrangements of Tasks

People

Whom to work with
How to choose whom to work with
How many to work with

Time

When to start a movement
How much time to spend on a selected task before moving to a new task

Space

Where to work
How much space to work in
Where the boundaries are to be placed

Equipment

What kind of equipment to use
How to arrange the equipment
What adjustments to make to the equipment
How much equipment to use
When to change equipment

---

and remove structure as needed in particular learning experiences.

Although it is true that some students cannot and perhaps will not ever work productively in more-unstructured environments, the concept of structure does not solely depend on the developed independent learning skills of students. Any learners inexperienced in an area of work will need more structure until a repertoire of appropriate responses for a situation can be developed. Appropriate decision making is a skill with carryover value from one area of work in the gymnasium to another. However, it is not independent of experience with the content.

The following example illustrates the importance of environmental arrangements in task design.

EXAMPLE: A teacher of third-grade students has worked with students extensively in the games area. During one of her class periods, she has students choose their own partners, move to an area of the gymnasium, choose a ball from within a range of choices, and work on a task involving throwing and catching. The students are able to work in this area without the need for long organizational periods during which they get partners or equipment. The teacher finds it unnecessary to use lines or more formal arrangements for the use of space. However, during the next class period, the teacher introduces some work in creative dance. The teacher introduces the idea of pathways in space with different body parts. She explains what a pathway is and sends the students off into their own space to practice. The students do not work productively. Within a few seconds, little work is taking place that can be described as productive.

The teacher's problem in the second class period is one of structure. The task was a new one to the students and different from any experiences the students had encountered before. The students did not have a complete enough idea of appropriate responses to the task to be able to work independently with the content. The students in this situation could have profited from some initial experiences in which the teacher did the following:

- Chose the body part to be used
- Paced the task with verbal cues or instrument support
- Limited movement to personal space

The teacher could have then gradually removed aspects of the structure before encouraging students to work independently with the task.

The question of whether to highly structure tasks or whether to encourage student decision making is again a curricular decision. Students involved in the process are more likely to learn more than just psychomotor skills than those who are uninvolved in the process. When arrangements show some flexibility, they can potentially be made more appropriate for individuals. Some evidence exists that highly structured, teacher-dominated environments may be more efficient in producing more narrowly defined learning (Good, 1979). Highly structured environments will generally involve much time spent in organizational types of behaviors.

Teachers should operate at all points on this continuum, depending on what is appropriate for their objectives. The need for structure depends on the student's competence and confidence with the task and independent learning skills. Creating a learning environment that will allow you to work with students in less-structured ways is the subject of chapter 6. Students should not be placed in unstructured environments unless they can work productively in those environments. Students learn few skills in decision making when allowed to drift aimlessly in undirected freedom. If students cannot direct themselves, teachers should add structure and gradually remove that structure as students are capable of handling a less-structured environment. Teaching decision making and student independence implies a gradual development of these skills.

■ THE INFLUENCE OF THE NATURE OF MOTOR CONTENT ON THE DESIGN OF A LEARNING EXPERIENCE

The nature of the content you are working with as a teacher has an important influence on the design of learning experiences. Motor skill acquisition is a primary responsibility of the physical educator. Physical educators have the unique responsibility of developing motor skills. The goal in teaching motor skills is the development of skillful performance for participation.

One of the first questions teachers should ask themselves about the motor skill content they want to teach is, "What does it mean to be skilled with this content?" If asked what it means to be a skilled bowler, almost everyone will respond with the same idea: a skilled bowler (1) can knock down all of the pins most of the time with one ball and (2) can knock down any that are missed with the second ball. If asked what a skilled bowler looks like, everyone will respond by describing from a mechanical perspective the action of bowling a strike (i.e., the position of the body and the steps taken at different parts of the action). If a third question is asked about how the bowler has to adjust the skill to the conditions of the game, responses will contain information on strategies for spare bowling.

Each of the responses to these questions will describe only a part of the concept of skillfulness in bowling. Together they form a more complete picture of what is involved in being skilled in bowling. They describe the quality of **effectiveness of skill performance,** the quality of **efficiency of skill performance,** and the quality of **adaptation of skill performance.** All three are part of what is meant by skillfulness.

The quality of effectiveness is the essence of goal-oriented, or objective, movement. A basketball free throw is effective if it goes in the basket. An archer is effective if the arrows hit the center of the target. A defense is effective if the offense is prevented from scoring. Motor skills are effective if they accomplish their purpose.

The quality of efficiency describes the performance. A skill is performed efficiently when the action is mechanically correct for a given performer and situation. There are "best" ways of performing many skills. Sometimes a way becomes the "best" because most people have been consistently successful performing in that way. Changes in styles of performance in some sports substantiate that we are always in search of better ways and that all people (especially children) may not perform efficiently in the same way. The underlying theory regarding the effect of task constraints is that there is more than one mechanically efficient way. These differences are becoming clearer to theorists advocating a dynamical systems approach and constraints approach to understanding movement responses. According to a constraints approach, movement is a response to the task (characteristics of the task itself including intent), organismic (physical abilities), and environmental constraints (contextual factors surrounding performance) (Kugler, Kelso, & Turvey, 1982; Newell, 1986). A good example of this theory would be the small child who uses a two-hand underhand shot to get a basketball in the basket because the ball is too big and the basket too high to do it any other way. What is mechanically efficient can change with the conditions of the task and the characteristics of the learner. Another good example is national level badminton players who are asked to perform a drop shot from a clear. In a game, they would disguise the shot with a preparation looking like a smash. In a testing situation where they are asked to be accurate in doing a smash from a clear with no opponent, they will use

no preparation and keep the arm as stable as possible going into the shot. Although it is possible to be effective performing in a mechanically incorrect way (e.g., stepping with the wrong foot on an overhand throw), it is difficult for most people to be effective consistently using an incorrect action or skill.

The quality of adaptation describes the ability of the performer to adjust to conditions surrounding performance. The quality of adaptation is critical to skills where changes in conditions are continuous during performance (e.g., the basketball layup, the forehand stroke in tennis, the football pass).

If asked what a skilled basketball dribbler looks like, a person might arrive at the responses presented in box 3.4. The responses described for the skill of dribbling a basketball are more complex than those

---

BOX 3·4

Characteristics of a Skilled Basketball Dribbler

Effective

Keeps the ball away from the defense
Uses the dribble to put the team in a better scoring position

Efficient

Uses pads of fingers and wrist action
Keeps ball close and slightly to the side of the dribbling hand when stationary and out in front when traveling with more speed
Keeps knees flexed when stationary

Adaptable

Varies *direction* of dribble appropriately for an offensive or defensive situation
Varies *speed* of dribble appropriately for an offensive or defensive situation
Varies *level* of dribble appropriately for an offensive or defensive situation
Chooses appropriate time to dribble in relation to the pass
Places body between ball and opponent

TABLE 3·1

Classifying Motor Skills

Classification of content	Definition	Examples
Closed skills	The environmental conditions surrounding performance of the skill stay the same during performance.	Tennis serve Bowling for strikes Volleyball serve Basketball free throw
Closed skills in differing environments	The environmental conditions surrounding performance of the skill stay the same during performance, but the performer may be asked to perform in different environments	Bowling for spares Archery Golf Educational gymnastics
Open skills	The skill is performed in changing environments.	Tennis forehand Basketball layup Soccer dribble Baseball fielding

described for bowling. The basketball dribble is very much an open skill because the conditions under which the skill is performed are rarely the same. The responses described for the skill of bowling are less complex, and bowling approaches an almost totally closed skill because conditions remain the same. In bowling, the only adaptation the performer must make is to the pin setup on the second ball.

In some skills, such as swimming and competitive gymnastics, efficient performance is a primary goal and almost always determines effectiveness. Adaptation is not a primary concern. In other skills, adaptation is more important than efficiency. Knowing the intent and nature of the content is essential to make decisions about how that content should be taught. Physical educators teach many different types of skills with different intents and descriptions of skillfulness. These skills can be divided into the categories of closed skills, closed skills used in different environments, and open skills. Table 3.1 defines these areas and gives examples of each. The divisions between these groups are not always clear and there are times when teachers will want to initially teach an open skill in a more closed way, but the divisions help teachers

think about the specific teaching implications inherent in their nature. Each will be discussed separately.

Closed Skills

As identified in chapter 2, Singer (1982) credits Poulton (1957) with the concept of closed and open skills. A closed skill is a skill performed in a fixed environment. A fixed environment means that conditions surrounding the performer during performance do not change. When performing a closed skill, performers can concentrate on self-pacing the skill (doing it in their time) and using feedback from within their bodies to guide their actions. Although theoretic differences probably exist between the terms, closed skills are most often self-paced skills. Examples of more closed skills are bowling, archery, darts, the foul shot in basketball, a dive in swimming, and the serve in volleyball or tennis.

Skilled performance in closed skills requires *efficiency* and *consistency* of response. The skill should be performed in the same way each time. The skilled learner relies on kinesthetic feedback (located in the joints and muscles) to provide information on how the skill is performed. Like all motor skills, closed skills eventually become automatic at highly skilled levels of performance.

Teaching a closed skill requires that the practice conditions and the manner in which the movement is performed be the same each time. Teachers do not want variation or a change in conditions that affect the movement. Although highly skilled athletes want to vary conditions associated with practice, such as sites of practice, speed and direction of wind, floor surfaces, and noise levels, in general, practice conditions that affect the movement should remain the same. Teachers want to develop closed skills through repetition (not rote) practice in consistent environments. They will want to help the learner establish an efficient performance and then gain consistency with that pattern. This does not mean that practice should be organized with endless drill and repetition of a movement. As discussed in chapter 2, the intent is that the learner be highly engaged in practice and process each repetition of the movement. As the learner advances, the teacher will want to help the student focus on developing a kinesthetic awareness of the skill so that it can be self-corrected.

As discussed in chapter 2, much controversy exists over whether closed skills should be taught as a whole action or in parts. If the skill is one that is complex, parts of the skill may be taught separately. Unless safety is an issue, students should first have the opportunity to practice the whole. Teachers should be cautioned that in many instances the rhythm of a movement, particularly a flowing movement, is destroyed when parts are practiced in excess and then combined. The whole movement is different from the parts combined: Preparation for a successive move occurs during the previous move in most complex skills. The practice of parts should not be carried on at great length. Where possible, skills should be taught as a whole. It is easier to insert practice of parts into the whole at a later date than to practice parts and then put them into a whole.

Closed skills require great efficiency of performance to be effective. Closed skills require little or no adaptation of performance, because conditions under which the skill is performed are, for all practical purposes, the same.

Closed skills in different environments. Some basically closed, self-paced skills require performer adaptation to different, but not changing, environments. Spare bowling requires adjustments of a basically closed skill to differing pin setups. Golf requires adjustment to different clubs, distances from the hole, and surfaces. These kinds of skills are referred to as closed skills in different environments.

Skilled performance in closed skills that must be adapted to different environments requires that the skill first be learned under less complex conditions and then practiced in a variety of environments and conditions to which the skill must be applied. The idea of adaptation of performance is added to the idea of consistency of performance as the learner adjusts the skill to differing conditions. Sometimes the ability of adaptation is referred to as *versatility* (Barrett, 1977).

When specific closed skills are used in different environments, they can be taught as a closed skill first. Practice in differing environments is then added. Whether the skill should be practiced in parts again depends on its complexity and flow quality. Successful adaptation of a skill requires opportunity to practice the skill in different environments (e.g., trying for spares in bowling, hitting from sand traps in golf).

Open Skills

An open skill is performed in an environment that is changing during performance. Examples of open skills are hitting the tennis forehand, dribbling a basketball, catching a baseball, and responding to a partner in dance. Open skills are usually externally paced (timing is controlled by the environment) and rely heavily on the ability of the performer to rapidly process perceptual (primarily visual) cues. Skilled performers can interpret the environment and can adjust the skill to changing conditions.

Some disagreement exists as to whether open skills should first be learned as closed skills. Open skills do require that the skill first be learned under the simplest conditions. Sometimes this means reducing the nature of the skill to a more closed and less complex environment (e.g., batting off a tee instead of using a pitched ball, dribbling without a defender in basketball, or practicing a skill without the ball). Because open skills require the performer to attend to perceptual cues (e.g., the oncoming ball or other players), there is no guarantee that the student who can perform a skill in the closed environment will be able to perform the skill in an open environment, but for many skills, it is a first step. Practice conditions for open skills should never be left in closed environments for long periods.

An example from a high school girls' basketball team illustrates the danger of practicing open skills for long periods in a closed environment. In this instance, one of the team's players had a need to bring every ball to a chest pass position before passing it. This allowed defensive players to tie up the ball and severely limited the player's speed in getting off a quick pass. Although it is difficult to establish a cause-and-effect relationship between the player's passing skills and the way in which she learned passing, it is reasonable to conclude that she practiced passing in a relatively closed skill manner (i.e., she always used a chest pass). The player thus did not choose the level or type of pass appropriate to the situation but brought the ball to a chest pass position regardless.

Two factors are involved in the performance of an open skill: (1) The performer must choose the correct response; and (2) the performer must be able to execute that response efficiently and effectively. To do this, practice situations must be variable. The job of the teacher is to reduce the complexity of the perceptual field in early stages of learning and then help students identify how their movement must change as complexity is gradually added.

SUMMARY

1. A learning experience is a set of instructional conditions and events that gives structure to student experience and is related to a particular set of teacher objectives.
2. Four criteria should act as an initial screen in the design of learning experiences: The learning experience must have the potential to improve the motor performance of students; it must provide maximal activity or practice time for all students; it must be appropriate for the experiential level of all students; and it must have the potential to integrate psychomotor, affective, and cognitive educational goals whenever possible.
3. The movement task is what teachers ask students to do that is movement content.
4. Movement tasks have three components: a content dimension (the movement content of the task); a goal orientation (the expected goal of practice or performance); and an organizational dimension (the conditions under which the content will be experienced).
5. Students can be involved in the choice of content. Tasks that provide for little student choice in content are called **limited tasks.** As more student choice is made possible, tasks become more **unlimited.** The teacher's choice of content and student ability largely dictate how and when tasks can be made more unlimited.
6. Affective involvement of students in a movement task is developed through both the design of the task and the appropriateness of the task for the individual learner. A positive affect is achieved through competence and confidence with the content and the social and emotional involvement of the learner in the task.
7. The goal-setting component of the task involves communicating the short-term intent of student practice and should be built into every task.
8. Environmental arrangements are the instructional arrangements for people, time, space, and equipment. Environmental arrangements are purposefully designed to accomplish specific learning outcomes.
9. The arrangements for people include the number of students in a group, the number of students active within a group, and the criteria for grouping.
10. The time aspect of task design has two considerations: how the task will be paced (teacher paced or student paced) and how much

time is allowed for a task before a change in the focus is made.

11. Spatial arrangements include defining the play area and organizing people in the defined play area.

12. Equipment arrangements include decisions concerning how much equipment to provide students, what type of equipment to use, and how to arrange the equipment.

13. Teachers must ensure that a learning environment is safe for students through their selection of content and how they present and arrange the conditions for learning.

14. When teachers make all the decisions relative to environmental arrangements and content, the task is highly structured. When students are permitted to make some of the decisions, the task is less structured. Deciding when to add and remove structure is part of the decision-making process in teaching.

15. Skillfulness in motor activity can be described in terms of the effectiveness of performance, the efficiency of performance, and the adaptive nature of performance.

16. Effective performance accomplishes its goal. Performance is efficient if the action is performed in a mechanically correct form for a given performer and situation. The quality of adaptation is the ability of the performer to adjust to conditions surrounding performance.

17. The motor skill content of physical education can be divided into the categories of closed skills, closed skills in differing environments, and open skills.
    - Closed skills are those in which the environment in which the skill is performed stays the same during performance. Practice conditions and the manner in which the movement is performed should be the same each time.
    - Closed skills in differing environments are performed in predictable environments, but the environment may change from one performance to another. Closed skills in

differing environments are practiced in the least difficult environment first, and then opportunities are provided to teach learners to adapt to different environments (e.g., sand traps, spare bowling).
    - Open skills are performed in environments that are changing during performance. Practice conditions must build complexity and variability of conditions.

CHECKING YOUR UNDERSTANDING

1. For each of the four criteria for a learning experience, give an example and a nonexample from a physical education setting.

2. Write a sequence of related movement tasks for the development of a motor skill. For each task, label the content, organizational dimensions, and goal orientation of the task. When organizational dimensions are implicit in the experience, indicate in brackets what they are.

3. List five tasks in the same content area that move from minimal student content choice to maximal student content choice.

4. Four different ways to involve students in content decisions were presented. List each and provide an example using the same content area.

5. List four affective objectives you might have for a physical education lesson. For each objective, design a movement task that potentially could contribute to the objective.

6. Design a four-on-four basketball experience that includes one of the following concepts: the ability to encourage a teammate in a positive fashion, the ability to settle disputes over calls in a rational way, the ability to win or lose graciously, or the ability to use the ability of all members of the team.

7. On what basis do teachers decide how many students should be in a group?

8. What are the advantages and disadvantages of grouping by skill level?

9. How do teachers decide when to move on to the next task?

10. What is the difference between student-paced responses to tasks and teacher-paced responses? What are the advantages and disadvantages of each?

11. How can the spatial arrangements of a task influence student responses to the task?

12. What are the advantages and disadvantages of the scattered formation? Give an example of movement tasks that might appropriately use lines, circles, facing lines, and double squads as the organization of people in space.

13. On what basis do teachers make the decision to modify equipment?

14. What decisions can students make in the organizational arrangements of an experience? What criterion does the teacher use to transfer these decisions to students?

15. Describe the effectiveness, efficiency, and adaptability aspects of skillfulness for the basketball layup shot or the tennis forehand.

16. Develop a list of twenty physical education skills and classify each as either closed skill, closed skill in different environment, or open skill.

17. What guidelines should a teacher follow when teaching closed skills? Open skills? Closed skills in different environments?

REFERENCES

Barrett, K. (1977). Games teaching: Adaptable skills, versatile players. *Journal of Physical Education and Recreation, 47*(7), 21–24.

Good, T. (1979). Teacher effectiveness in the elementary school. *Journal of Teacher Education, 30*(2), 52–54.

Hough, J. B., et al. (1975). *What is instruction?* Unpublished manuscript, Ohio State University at Columbia, Faculty of Curriculum and Foundations.

Kugler, P., Kelso, J., & Turvey, M. (1982). On the control and coordination of naturally developing systems. In J. Kelso & J. Clark (Eds.), *The development of movement control and coordination.* New York: Wiley.

Newell, K. (1986). Constraints on the development of coordination. In M. Wade & H. Whiting (Eds.), *Motor development in children: Aspects of coordination and control.* Dordrecht, Netherlands: Martinus Nijhoff.

Poulton, E. C. (1957). On prediction in skilled movement. *Psychological Bulletin, 54,* 467–478.

Singer, R. N. (1980). *Motor learning and human performance* (3rd ed.). New York: Macmillan.

Singer, R. N. (1982). *The learning of motor skills.* New York: Macmillan.

SUGGESTED READINGS

Belka, D. (2002). A strategy for improvement of learning-task presentations. *Journal of Physical Education, Recreation and Dance, 73*(6), 32–35.

Byra, M., & Jenkins, J. (2000). Making instructional tasks to learner ability: The inclusion style of teaching. *Journal of Physical Education, Recreation and Dance, 71*(3), 26–30.

Carlton, B., & Henrich, T. (2000). Strategies for enhancing the performance of low-skilled students. *Journal of Physical Education, Recreation and Dance, 71*(2), 29–31.

Christie, B. (2000). Topic teamwork: A collaborative integrative model for increasing student-centered learning in grades K-12. *Journal of Physical Education, Recreation and Dance, 71*(8), 28–32.

Condon, R., & Collier, C. (2002). Student choice makes a difference in physical education. *Journal of Physical Education, Recreation and Dance, 73*(2), 26–30.

Conkell, C., & Pearson, H. (1996). Do you use developmentally appropriate games? *Strategies, 9*(1), 22–25.

Helion, J., & Fry, F. (1995). Modifying activities for developmental appropriateness. *Journal of Physical Education, Recreation and Dance, 66*(7), 57–59.

Humphries, C., & Ahsy, M. (2000). The games students play: Selecting and teaching activities. *Journal of Physical Education, Recreation and Dance, 71*(4).

Johnson, R. (1999). Time-out: Can it control misbehavior? *Journal of Physical Education, Recreation and Dance, 70*(8), 32–34.

Mitchell, M., Barton, G., & Stanne, K. (2000). The role of homework in helping students meet physical education goals. *Journal of Physical Education, Recreation and Dance, 71*(5), 30–34.

Napper-Owen, G. (2003). Individualizing your instruction as appropriate practice. *Strategies, 16*(4), 19–22.

Pellet, T., & Harrison, J. (1996). Individualize to maximize success. *Strategies, 9*(7), 20–22.

Ratcliffe, T., & Lynn, S. (1999). Grouping strategies for physical educators. *Strategies, 12*(3), 13–15.

Schempp, P., & Johnson, S. (2006). Learning to see: Developing the perception of an expert teacher. *JOPERD, 77*(6) 29–33.

Williams, N. (1992). The physical education hall of shame. *Journal of Physical Education, Recreation and Dance, 63*(6), 57–60.

Williams, N. (1994). The physical education hall of shame. (Part II). *Journal of Physical Education, Recreation and Dance, 65*(2), 17–20.

4

Task Presentation

O V E R V I E W

One of the critical teaching functions described in chapter 1 was the presentation of learning tasks. Most learning experiences are delivered to the learner via the presentation of tasks for student engagement with the content. The learning task describes how the teacher intends the learner to be involved with the content. The movement task asks the learner to engage motorically with the content. One of the most important skills a teacher can develop is the ability to present movement tasks to learners in a way that facilitates appropriate learner engagement with the content. This chapter discusses the qualities of a good task presentation. Although managerial and organizational issues relative to task presentation are explored, a major part of the chapter is devoted to developing clear task presentations and selecting and organizing learning cues for motor tasks. Learning cues are considered a major factor in determining the initial success of the learner with the content.

Standard 4: Instructional Delivery and Management

Physical education teacher candidates use effective communication and pedagogical skills and strategies to enhance student engagement and learning.
NASPE Beginning Teaching Standards, 2008

O U T L I N E

- **Getting the attention of the learner**
  Establishing signals and procedures
  Student preoccupation with other
    environmental factors

  Inability to hear or see
  Inefficient use of time
- **Sequencing the content and organizational aspects of tasks**

- **Improving the clarity of communication**
  Orient the learner (set induction)
  Sequence the presentation in logical order
  Give examples and nonexamples
  Personalize the presentation
  Repeat things difficult to understand
  Draw on the personal experience of students
  Check for understanding
  Present material dynamically
- **Choosing a way to communicate**
  Verbal communication
  Demonstration

Media materials
- **Selecting and organizing learning cues**
  Good cues are accurate
  Good cues are brief and critical to the skill
    being performed
  Good cues are appropriate to the learner's
    skill level and age
  Good cues are appropriate for different types
    of content
  Cues are more effective if they are
    sequentially organized and learners have
    the opportunity to rehearse them

Everyone has had opportunities to observe or attend a class in which the teacher was able to elicit good student performance. With good teaching, students are engaged at a high level with the content and are performing skillfully in a short time. Likewise, most people have experienced a class in which the teacher muffed the task presentation and spent the rest of the time correcting communication errors. Sometimes learners do not know what to do because they are not listening, but most of the time students do not know what to do because the teacher is not selective or clear enough in presenting the tasks. When it comes to movement tasks, communication is the name of the game. The ability to present clear tasks that have the potential to facilitate learning requires preparation and practice.

Regardless of the type of content inherent in a task, the presentation of a task is always an exercise in communication. On some occasions, teachers can merely name or quickly describe what they want learners to do and assume that the learners have had experience with tasks that call for similar responses. In most teaching, however, this assumption cannot be made. This chapter, therefore, pays special attention to ideas that relate to the presentation of tasks having some aspect of unfamiliarity to the student. Box 4.1 includes an example of a task presentation.

■ GETTING THE ATTENTION OF THE LEARNER

It seems almost unnecessary to point out that students must be attentive to benefit from any task presentation. Unfortunately, throughout the gymnasiums of this country, teachers are trying to communicate by talking over or outshouting students in an environment that is not supportive of any kind of communication. The best task presentation in the world is worthless unless the teacher has the **attention** of the students.

Many conditions contribute to why students are not attentive when tasks are presented. Although the

Students in back of the teacher probably can't see or hear. Where should the teacher be to present a task?

Example of Task Presentation

Liz is beginning a unit in striking with paddles with her fourth-grade students. When the students walk into the gymnasium, they immediately spy the paddles separated into several piles and spaced throughout the gym. They want to know if they are "going to get to do that today."

Liz has the students gather in the center of the gymnasium as a normal procedure. When the last child has sat down, Liz, in a normal tone of voice, says, "May I have your attention?" She waits a few seconds for everybody's eyes to be on her and begins.

"Today we are going to start a unit on striking with paddles. We will be working on this unit for the next few weeks. What sports do you know that use rackets? (*Students give some examples.*)

"I have a videotape prepared that shows different sports that use rackets. When the sports are shown, I am going to stop the tape and see how many you can recognize the sport.

"(*Teacher shows prepared videotape of tennis, racquetball, badminton, deck tennis, and squash and leads the students to identify the name of the sport.*) How many of you have ever played these sports before? Which ones do you think you would like?

"All of these sports require that you have some control of the paddle and the object—you must make the object go where you want it to go. We are going to start today to get some control of these paddles and foam balls.

"When I say 'go,' I would like for you to pick up a ball and paddle at one of the locations around the gym— find a space you can work in—and show me you are ready to begin. GO. (*Students complete organizational task.*)

"When I say to start practicing, we are going to try to bounce the ball down in our own space. (*Teacher demonstrates bouncing the ball down, attending to keeping a forward stride position, bent knees, and flat racket face in the demonstration.*) What you are trying to do is to maintain enough control of the ball so that you don't have to travel out of your own space and so that you can keep the ball going. (*Teacher demonstrates what "out of control" is.*) Who can show me what control means? (*Teacher asks a student to demonstrate the task.*) Okay, that was pretty good control—the ball kept going, and you didn't have to move too far out of your own space. Everyone stand up and see if you can keep your ball in control in your own space, tapping it downward."

---

teacher may not have control over some of these conditions, the teacher *can* prevent many of the causes of inattention. The following section explores some of the reasons a teacher may not have student attention and discusses some ways a teacher can exert more control over student attention.

Establishing Signals and Procedures

It is easier to get the attention of a learner if you have established signals and procedures with students when you want their attention. Teachers should have routines to begin class so that students know when it is time to begin class. Sometimes students will gather in a place in the gym or in the outside area. A place where students can sit comfortably without having to sit on wet grass or sand is almost a necessity. Maintaining student attention is difficult when

students have to stand for more than a few minutes or sit uncomfortably. When the teacher wants practice to end and wants the attention of learners, it is helpful to have a signal. A whistle is useful in large play areas but should not be relied on as a substitute for a learning environment that is conducive to learning. Many teachers find that the whistle in smaller play areas is unnecessary and creates an undesired atmosphere. Students can be taught to respond to a signal (hand clap, drum beat, or raised hand) or a teacher call for attention.

If you find that you are not easily getting the attention of your students, you may need to take the time to establish a procedure or signal. You will need to make clear your intentions and practice with students responding to a signal until it is clear that the expectation is for quiet and attention. Teachers should not proceed until they have the attention of the students. Students cannot be attentive to teacher presentations if the environment is noisy or distracting. If the noise comes from the class, teachers should not try to compete. Shouting over a noisy class when the teacher has asked for attention may be effective once or perhaps even twice, but it quickly loses its effectiveness.

Distractions over which the teacher has less control are more difficult. In situations in which two classes are sharing a facility, workers are changing lightbulbs, dogs are on the field, or airplanes are flying overhead, the teacher must try to remove the distraction when possible and cope creatively when all else fails. One way in which teachers can minimize the effects of distractions is to bring the students into a smaller group, closer to the teacher, with the students facing away from the distraction. A teacher who says, "I know it's hard to listen when workers are up on the roof, but let's try," is also likely to be successful in soliciting student attention.

Student Preoccupation with Other Environmental Factors

Many times students are not attentive because their attention is engaged by other people or other articles in the environment. Teachers who work with young children have a hard time competing with objects the children may have in their hands (e.g., balls, ropes, beanbags) or with nearby equipment (e.g., mats, bars, nets). Teachers can set up class procedures to eliminate some of these problems by giving students something to do with the objects (e.g., telling the students to place the beanbag on the floor in front of them). When young children have had sufficient time to explore the qualities of these objects, the children can be expected to hold them without trying to get the beans out of the beanbag or picking at the foam of the ball.

Teachers can solve many attention problems by having children rest between tasks away from mats, equipment, and walls as a routine procedure. If students are not working with partners or as a group, they should not be resting near others. Standard procedures

that teachers take time to structure and reinforce will eliminate many problems in the long run.

The attention of older students can be requested. Older students should be expected to be able to ignore distractions in the environment. If the teacher consistently holds the students' attention despite the influence of external factors, a strong chance exists that internal causes of inattention will be controlled as well.

Inability to Hear or See

Many times teachers do not have students' attention because the students cannot hear or see what is going on. Because of the time wasted, many teachers are reluctant to call students in from large play areas to some central point for a task presentation. This is acceptable in situations where all the students can hear, the material is brief, and the concepts with which the students are being asked to work are not new. However, if any of these conditions do *not* exist, teachers can save productive work time by calling students in to a smaller area so that the task can be properly communicated.

Another commonly occurring problem that teachers must address, particularly in outdoor settings, is that students' vision is impaired because of glare from the sun. Sometimes students will complain, but usually they will just struggle with limited vision. Teachers should always position students so that they are sitting with their back to the sun.

Inefficient Use of Time

Teachers may find that they have student attention initially and then gradually lose it. Many times this is because the learning experiences that teachers have designed fail to meet one or more of the criteria for a learning experience discussed in chapter 1. Often attention wanes because teachers take five minutes to do what could be done in one minute or because teachers use verbal discourse rather than activity.

Teachers of young children must recognize that these children have short attention spans to begin with and even shorter attention spans in a gymnasium that invites activity. The secret to effective task presentation is brevity. Young children are motivated to move, and if teachers have much to communicate, they will have better results doing it through activity and short transitions between activity periods.

Older students' longer attention spans do not excuse inefficient task presentation. Older students will tolerate more inefficiency, but that does not mean they are attending. These students may not express their lack of interest overtly but will simply tune out the teacher. The amount of information, particularly new information, that people can attend to at any one time is limited. Teachers of older students must spend more time in communicating material and in motivating students, but long verbal discourses are again to be avoided in favor of shorter, more frequent breaks in activity to communicate what needs to be communicated.

■ SEQUENCING THE CONTENT AND ORGANIZATIONAL ASPECTS OF TASKS

How the teacher orders the content and organizational aspects of the task can determine how successful the student response to the task will be. The presentation of tasks usually involves information concerning (1) what task is to be performed (including the goal orientation) and (2) the organizational arrangements for the way the task will be practiced. Teachers have a tendency to mix these two types of information in their task presentations. This is confusing for the students. Task clarity is enhanced if these two types of information are not confused in the presentation.

EXAMPLE: Problem task presentation
"Today we are going to work on fielding ground balls. We are going to work with partners. When you field a ground ball, you have to make sure that you get your body behind the ball in the proper position. If the ball gets by you, it is going to go over that hill over there."

In this example the teacher started with identifying the skill to be practiced and then gave the organizational arrangements. As soon as the idea of partners was introduced, it is likely that only a few students heard anything else. At that point they would be either shuffling around to find a partner or trying to anticipate how the teacher was going to choose partners.

When tasks have an involved management component, teachers may need to separate the management aspect of the task from the content aspect of the task. Beginning teachers working with students for the first time should not expect students to be able to handle too much too soon. Teachers can structure a complex task by giving the *management directions* first and waiting until the students have complied before giving the *content dimension* of the task, as in the example that follows.

EXAMPLE: Separating the content and organizational aspects of the task
"We are going to work with partners and a ball. When I say 'go,' I want you to sit next to a partner in a good work space." *The teacher waits until students have a partner and are listening.* "One of you will walk over and get a ball and sit back down with your partner." *The teacher waits until students have complied with the organizational task.* "We are going to work on passing a ball to a moving receiver. . . ."

With time, many groups of students can handle both organizational tasks (getting a partner and getting a ball) simultaneously. If they cannot, the teacher must break down the organizational tasks. Organizational directions do not always have to be given before the content is explained. Separating organizational

Setting the stage for class with young children sometimes means taking time to reduce the level of excitement.

directions from the content part of a task presentation is useful if students will anticipate that they will have a choice of partner or equipment.

If the organization for practice is critical to how the task is performed, the organizational arrangements should be described and be part of the demonstration. For example, if partners will be on opposite sides of the volleyball net and will work with hitting the ball from a toss across the net, the student will need to know that the ball is coming over the net from a toss and that the tosser will catch the hit ball when it is returned. In this case the students are practicing a volleyball skill but they are practicing it in specific conditions arranged by the teacher that must be communicated. Few groups of learners can handle having the organizational aspects and content aspects of tasks mixed in the teacher's presentation.

In tasks that involve an extensive management dimension (e.g., getting in groups of three, selecting a ball, and working on passing the ball while moving continuously), the management aspect (getting in groups and selecting a ball) will usually need to be preceded by the cue "When I say go, . . ." to prevent students from beginning the organizational dimension of the task before they have fully comprehended the content dimension. The value of signals or cues to begin should not be underestimated, even with older learners. Teachers' descriptions of what to do are often communicated in language associated with an expected response (e.g., "get a partner"), but teachers do not want that response until they are finished giving their instructions. Young children and people with whom teachers have not worked previously in a learning situation may not be sure when a response is expected. Alerting learners to the idea that a signal will be given ("When I say go, . . .") and using signals ("Go!") makes intention clearer.

When new material is being presented, the directive "Now go and do this" usually involves a summary of the explanation (e.g., "When you get your ball, take it to a wall and begin striking it to the wall with at least four different parts of your body"). The assumption is that the specific details of the skill have already been explained. Thus the teacher is summarizing the directive. This summary is necessary and many times is used in conjunction with the type of summary cues mentioned earlier in this chapter. The summary helps fix in the students' minds exactly what they will be working on and the order in which the parts of the task will be performed. The summary should also include the goal orientation of the task (work to set control of the ball). Teachers who want to check the students' understanding of directives should ask the students what they are going to work on.

■ IMPROVING THE CLARITY OF COMMUNICATION

A teacher has been clear when learner intent in responding to a task is the same as teacher intent. Many factors determine whether the students will do what the teacher expects them to do when they are requested to engage in a learning task. The teacher may have no control of some of these factors. In many cases the teacher can improve the probability that students will engage in the task appropriately if the task is presented with attention to the factors that we know improve attention and communication. The clarity of a presentation is often helped by using some of the following guidelines when presenting material.

Orient the Learner (Set Induction)

People feel more comfortable if they know in advance what they will be doing and, in some cases, why they will be doing it. Educators often refer to this as set induction. Teachers should seriously consider giving learners information in advance on what they will be doing. This allows students to relate parts of lessons to a larger whole.

EXAMPLE: "Today we will be focusing our lesson on the transition from fielding the ball to throwing the ball. This will be important in game play so that you can make a smooth transition to quickly throw the ball where you want it to go. We will work first with a partner at a closer distance and then begin to increase the distance and a target area to throw to."

Sequence the Presentation in Logical Order

Putting material in a logical order facilitates communication. Sometimes in physical education it is logical to present the most important part of an action first. Thus the teacher does not necessarily present the parts of the action in chronological sequence. Examples are (1) teaching the chorus in a folk dance first and (2) teaching the contact phase of a striking action first. Some teachers have been successful in presenting the major part of the action first (e.g., the takeoff and placing the ball against the backboard for the basketball layup before the steps toward the basket; the striking action without the backswing in tennis). This is called **backward chaining** and may be more logical and meaningful than beginning with preparatory aspects of skills. Usually, however, order is sequenced chronologically, with the beginning of a movement presented first. For many complex skills there are preparation, execution, and follow-through stages. Backward chaining is discussed further in chapter 5.

Give Examples and Nonexamples

Many important ideas relating to movement, particularly the qualitative aspects of movement, are more fully understood when both examples and nonexamples are given. For instance, to know what a soft landing is, the learner needs to know what a hard landing is. Similarly, traveling is more fully understood in terms of what traveling is not, and full extension is more easily understood in terms of what full extension is not. The use of both examples and nonexamples in teaching such concepts is helpful.

Personalize the Presentation

Referring to the experience of a student or to the experience of the teacher is helpful in communication. Phrases such as "When I tried to . . ." or "Johnny has had a lot of experience with . . ." help the learner identify with the material being presented. Teachers personalize in a lesson when they refer directly to the experiences of participants.

Repeat Things Difficult to Understand

Many teachers assume that students will understand material after it is explained once. Repetition is useful, particularly repetition that takes a slightly different approach. Planned repetition of essential cues just before students begin work on a task is helpful in effective communication. Repetition of significant information is important also after students have had an opportunity to try new skills or when skills are practiced on more than one day.

Draw on the Personal Experience of Students

Showing students how the activity they are preparing to do is similar to or different from other skills they have learned can help students use the new information more effectively. "The floater serve is like the overhand throw pattern, except there is no follow-through" is an example of drawing on past experience. Transfer of learning is also facilitated through teacher attempts to bridge past experience and new experience, such as, "You remember that last week we worked on including techniques to improve upper arm strength in your warm-up routines. Today we are going to explore ways to develop abdominal strength so that we may add these exercises to your routines. The principles that govern how strength is developed will be the same. Let's review them."

Check for Understanding

Teachers need feedback from students regarding whether students have understood teacher instructions. Many teachers do not discover that students have not understood a set of instructions until the students try to act on the information they were given. Teachers can avoid wasting a great deal of time if, before the students begin work on a task, the teachers ask them questions to determine their understanding or ask them to demonstrate what they learned from the teacher's instructions. When teachers take the time to do this, they generally find that they were not communicating as well as they thought.

Present Material Dynamically

Voice inflection, nonverbal behavior, and timing can do much to enhance communication. Loudness contrasted with softness, high-pitched inflection contrasted with low-pitched inflection, and quick delivery contrasted with slow delivery will catch students' attention. Teachers need not be public speakers, but they should know how to use voice dynamics when needed to make communication clearer.

Box 4.2 summarizes effective methods in improving communication and can be used as a checksheet for a good task presentation.

■ CHOOSING A WAY TO COMMUNICATE

A third critical aspect of task presentation is selecting a means of communication. Teachers may choose to present a task verbally or to use demonstration and/or other visual materials. As with other instructional decisions, the characteristics of the learners and of the content must determine which method will be best.

Verbal Communication

If learners are experienced with a skill or activity and know its language label, verbal directions should be sufficient. Caution should be used, however, because teachers generally assume too much understanding on the part of a learner. Because of their familiarity with the material, teachers who study movement terminology or who use the same terminology in five different class periods a day tend to assume that students understand after they have been "told" something once or twice. Teachers often think they have done a good job of verbal communication, but they need only ask students what was meant by a communication (a *check for understanding*) to gain enormous insight into the difficulty of describing movement in abstract terms. It should be remembered that the younger the student, the more the student is functioning at a concrete level with regard to verbal material. Therefore, a teacher will be less able to rely on verbal communication unaided by demonstration.

BOX 4·2

Improving Communication

Orient the learner (set induction)

Alert the learner to what he or she will be doing, how, and why.

Use a logical sequence

Present material in chronological order unless there is a good reason to do otherwise.

Use examples and nonexamples

Many concepts are best understood if the learner is helped to understand not only what the concept is but also what it is not.

Personalize the presentation

Use students' names and personal experiences of the teacher and students in the class.

Repeat things difficult to understand

Repetition of important ideas during the initial presentation, after students have had an opportunity to engage in the task, and when tasks are continued on other days improves clarity.

Draw on personal experience of learners

Bridge the gap from old experiences to new material by showing the learner how things relate; this improves communication and increases the potential for transfer.

Check for understanding

Ask students what you meant or ask students to demonstrate what they are trying to do.

Present material dynamically

Students are more attentive if voice inflection (volume, pitch, tone, speed of delivery) is not always the same.

Demonstration

In physical education, visual communications most often take the form of demonstrations. Used in conjunction with verbal explanations, they provide the learner with two sources of information. A discussion of guidelines for the use of demonstration in physical education follows.

A good demonstration facilitates learning.

Demonstrations should be accurate. Students will attempt to reproduce the movement they see. No matter how much an important point is emphasized verbally, many students will attend primarily to the visual demonstration for information. The demonstration therefore should be accurate. Teachers tend to only partially go through the action of a movement skill or task or to demonstrate a skill out of the context in which the students will be using it. At some point, students need to see the whole action performed at correct speed and in context. Students will also gain more accurate information from a demonstration if they see it performed at more than one angle.

Use students to demonstrate when appropriate. If students are capable of demonstrating accurately, they should do so rather than the teacher, unless the performance would put students in an undesirable situation with their peers. When students demonstrate, the teacher can focus the attention of the observers on important aspects of the performance.

Demonstrate the organizational format. If the task to be practiced stipulates a specialized organizational format (e.g., standing across a net from a partner or working in groups of three), the demonstration should use the same organizational format that will be required in practice. Many teachers who give good skill demonstrations are still unsuccessful in getting students to understand what is expected because they have failed to include the organizational format for the practice of the task. Good task presentations use demonstrations to communicate both skill and the organizational format of the practice.

Use demonstrations and examples in creative and cognitive problem-solving tasks. Many teachers who set creative responses, expressiveness, group projects, or problem-solving processes as task goals are reluctant to use demonstration in presenting the task. They are concerned that if demonstration is used, the spontaneity of student response will be impaired and students may not go through the desired processing to produce a response. Indeed, spontaneity will be hurt if the teacher demonstrates only one response to a task and asks that it be copied or if a teacher presents a problem having only one solution and then demonstrates that solution. Teachers who use more indirect approaches to learning usually want students to choose from a variety of responses or to respond with a variety of responses. However, tasks that require expressiveness, creative responses, or solutions to movement problems can use demonstration successfully to communicate to the learners the *type* of response expected as well as the procedures used to formulate a response. If a teacher wants expressiveness, the teacher needs to communicate the *concept* with which the students are to work by giving examples of responses within that concept (e.g., "Who can show me one example of a balance?"). If a teacher asks students to solve a movement problem that has only one solution, the principle or idea with which the students are to work can be demonstrated and the criteria for good performance should be communicated. For example, the teacher could demonstrate a few examples of contrasting quick and slow movements with a partner.

Tasks that seek variety, expressiveness, or problem solving should not result in a student's or a group's futile search for the assignment. Beginning learners of all ages depend on visual and concrete cues. The need for demonstration should not be taken lightly. The need for accuracy of demonstration is critical. The clarity of a task is enhanced by demonstration and examples of the concept being developed. The teacher can encourage students to seek responses within a framework clearly understood by all.

Tasks that ask students to generate a cognitive response need to be presented in a manner that makes it clear to the student the type of response requested as well as the process the student should use to arrive at the response. For example, if you want students to discover the best way to get a shuttlecock to the end line in badminton, you need to be clear that you want them to experiment with different ways to generate enough force to get the shuttlecock to the back line and to be prepared to identify and demonstrate what they have determined is the best way. If you want students to identify three different vigorous activities they can participate in outside of class, then you must share with them the criteria. The activity must be vigorous, and the students must identify three that can be done outside of class in their own situation.

Emphasize important information about a task. For students to get the most from a demonstration, the teacher must guide their observations. The critical aspects of a skill or task should be highlighted verbally and, if possible, visually through freezing the action at critical points or verbally overemphasizing important aspects of a task. For example, if a teacher is going to teach a back handspring, three points should be emphasized before the execution of the movement: (1) starting in the sit position with a straight back, (2) subsequently losing balance backward, and (3) thrusting the arms and legs. If a teacher wants students to identify three different ways to develop cardiovascular endurance, the teacher should emphasize that an appropriate response would involve (1) activities that get the heart rate up for a sustained period and (2) three different activities.

Provide information on why a skill is performed a certain way. Some learners will be able to remember the visual and verbal cues of a skill better if they are provided with information regarding why a skill is performed in a certain way. The badminton serve, for instance, is performed with a low backswing and follow-through because the rule says that the shuttlecock cannot be contacted above the waist. The influence of a rule or the principles of movement efficiency on an action often help learners pay attention to important cues. This kind of information is useful but should not turn an efficient task presentation into a lecture on the skill. Information should be provided only where it is critical to understanding the skill.

Demonstrate the skill at a slower speed. Many ballistic movements occur so fast that it is not easy, even for experienced observers, to see what is happening. A teacher can demonstrate the skill at a slower speed if the student also sees it several times at the appropriate speed.

Check student understanding after a demonstration. Before teachers have students practice a skill, teachers should check the students' understanding of what they have observed. This can be done by asking questions after an observation or by asking students to demonstrate what they are trying to do. It can be done also by asking students to look for particularly important points during the observation and checking their understanding afterward. Box 4.3 summarizes the qualities of a good demonstration.

BOX 4·3

Qualities of a Good Demonstration

- Information is accurate.
- Demonstration is performed by student if possible.
- Teacher uses organizational format students will use for practice.
- Important information is emphasized.
- Information is provided on why a skill is performed in a certain way.
- Student understanding is checked.
- The demonstration is repeated more than one time.

Teachers can use audiovisual resources to emphasize important information about a skill.

Media Materials

Because the CD/DVD, recorder/player, and computer are standard equipment in many homes and are becoming a more essential part of gymnasium equipment, teachers have access to a wide variety of visual media in their content area. These materials can be used to motivate students and give students a perspective on the "whole." Knowing what games look like when they are played well helps students to know what they are working toward and therefore makes practice more meaningful.

An increasing supply of commercially produced computer programs, pictures, films, charts, and DVDs, as well as Web-accessed materials, are available to physical educators relatively inexpensively. As visual aids to communicating a skill, these materials have the advantage of being professionally produced. In addition, the teacher has some assurance that the models provided are good ones. Most of the materials can also be repeated in slow motion if desired. Such materials tend to motivate a computer- and television-age audience and allow the teacher to observe both the demonstration and the student response.

One disadvantage of using commercially produced visual materials that attempt to show how a skill is performed is that the materials may not be appropriate for the particular group of learners with whom a teacher is working. Material above or below a learner's ability

may not be valuable. Much commercially produced material with dialogue gives learners more information than they need for one skill. The sound tracks of such material will probably be more valuable if they are not used in the initial presentation of a movement skill or idea but are saved until the learners can make better use of more specific information.

To use visual materials well, the teacher should preview these materials, use them for a specific purpose, and set up the equipment for their use in advance. Student time should not be consumed with teacher preparations. Teachers should not abandon their role as teachers to be projectionists or instructors on how to use a computer program. Setting up and taking down the equipment should occur outside the instructional period. These materials are useful instructional tools, and teachers should seriously consider using them and adapting their use to the specific needs of their learners.

■ SELECTING AND ORGANIZING LEARNING CUES

A final aspect of task presentation is the teacher's selection and organization of learning cues. A **learning cue** is a word or phrase that identifies and communicates to a performer the *critical features of a movement skill or task.* If the teacher is going to teach the floater serve to a volleyball class that has learned the regular overhead serve, the following information might be useful in helping the students understand the skill:

- The action of the floater serve starts like the regular overhead serve.
- Contact is made with an open hand straight through the ball.
- The action used is a punching action with little or no follow-through.

Each point would be considered a critical feature of the skill. Teachers can facilitate the cognitive process needed to establish an accurate motor plan for a skill by determining critical features (sometimes called "essential elements") of that skill and then selecting a learning cue that can be used to represent that critical feature (see box 4.4).

BOX 4·4

Identifying Learning Cues

Definition of a learning cue

A word or phrase that efficiently communicates as much information about a critical feature as possible.

Example

Critical features of a tennis overhead smash

- Position yourself where the ball will be coming down (the ball should be in front and slightly to the right).
- Bend your knees.
- Position the racket head behind you at about head level.
- Shift your weight to the back foot.
- Point your hand or finger at the ball.
- Swing the racket upward and forward with an extended arm at contact.

Learning cue for critical features

- Get set.
- Point and shift.
- Swing up and forward.

In designing the learning cues for the badminton smash, the teacher decided that the "get set" cue could be taught as a package. The first four critical features have to do with the "get set" position, which can be practiced apart from the execution and follow-through.

Selecting good cues is important for all learners but is absolutely essential for the beginning learner. This is because motor performance and cognition are interdependent, especially in the early stages of learning. Cues presented to learners should be reduced to key words and organized with the specific learner in mind. What the teacher focuses the learner on is critical and largely determines the ability of the task to elicit the desired outcome.

Good cues have several characteristics. They are (1) accurate, (2) critical to the task being presented, (3) few in number, and (4) appropriate to the learner's age and stage of learning.

Good Cues Are Accurate

Teachers must know their subject matter to select accurate cues, and good teachers spend a lot of planning time selecting good cues. What the teacher focuses the learner on can make the difference between student success and student failure in performance. Physical educators are often called on to teach activities with which they have no experience. Resources are available to help familiarize teachers with almost any activity they may be asked to teach. If you will make a list of the critical features of a skill from a textbook or website, you will then be able to reduce those critical features to important learning cues. Many inexperienced teachers remain ignorant because they fail to consult appropriate resources and prepare themselves to teach the lesson.

A research team at the University of South Carolina asked four physical education specialists to teach jumping and landing skills to one of their second-grade classes. The ability of the students was tested before and after six lessons taught by each teacher. Only one of the four teachers had accurately identified the learning cues for the skills involved. The performance of the students reflected this accuracy. The more effective teacher had used reference material to correctly identify what was important in the skill being taught (Werner & Rink, 1989).

The ability to select critical cues that are accurate and can elicit the desired response from students is developed through preparation and practice. With experience, teachers will become selective in choosing critical cues for a movement skill or concept.

Good Cues Are Brief and Critical to the Skill Being Performed

Learners cannot use a great deal of information on the specifics of a movement response. In some cases, it is beneficial to get students doing a skill and then come back and present the skill more formally. The cues the teacher selects should be chosen because they are critical to the performance. For the overhand serve, the following description might be written by a beginning teacher:

- The performer stands in an open stride position with his or her side to the intended direction

Teachers will need to identify specific cues for how a skill is done.

of the object being thrown. The foot forward should be opposite to the throwing arm.

- The backswing of the throw is initiated by rotating back at the hips and shoulders. The arm movement is led with the elbow, which is about shoulder level. The hand drops back at the close of the backswing as the weight is transferred to the back foot.
- The forward motion of the throw is initiated with an elbow lead and trunk rotation forward. The momentum of the throw is released sequentially through the shoulder, elbow, and wrist with a quick, sudden action leading to weight transfer onto the forward foot and a follow-through in front of the body.

How much do students need to know? Few students initially would gain much from all that information. It would be better to assume the ready position for the skill and then select only three cues for the action as follows:

1. "Keep your elbow high and lean forward."
2. "Step to the opposite foot."
3. "Put your hand out and snap your wrist on the throw."

Selecting critical cues is important to giving learners good, accurate pictures of what they are trying to do. One teacher asked an 8-year-old to tell the rest of the class how to throw a ball. The youngster replied, "I just l-e-a-n back and let 'er fly." Physical educators might all take a lesson from that child.

For complex skills, some cues are especially important. Most of the time these cues involve locating the body in space at critical points in the action. The stance, the backswing release or contact, and the follow-through are usually critical points for manipulative tasks. Breaking down most body actions into preparation, execution, and follow-through helps divide actions into manageable parts. Picture these three phases for the cartwheel, the bowling approach and release, and the forward roll.

Words that help students understand the type of action desired (e.g., *snap, punch, push, press*) often are useful in designing cues. Sometimes these words are referred to as **summary cues** because they are single words that capture a quality or critical feature of the movement. These types of words give the learner a description of the time quality (e.g., quick or sustained) and weight quality (e.g., strong or light) of the action. In skills such as the basketball layup, it is important to know that the ball is placed up to the basket and not thrown up. Striking activities are primarily quick actions requiring muscular tension just before contact. In sports such as field hockey, some actions are hits (with a backswing) and some are pushes (no backswing). In gymnastics, a walkover is a continuous application of force, whereas a round-off is an explosive action. Cues that describe the action can help the learner get a more accurate picture of what to do.

The selection of cues is just as critical for task presentations that use an environmental design approach.

EXAMPLES:
- The teacher is teaching the overhand throw pattern and has decided to use a high target and the cue "hit the wall above the line as hard as you can" without giving the learners any more information on how the overhand throw is performed.
- The teacher has decided to encourage students to get under the ball when using a volleyball overhead pass by having them set the ball into a basket or large hoop placed at least ten feet high. The teacher uses the cue "get the ball into the basket" or "use a high arc to get the ball into the basket" with full knowledge that to be successful, the student must get under the ball.

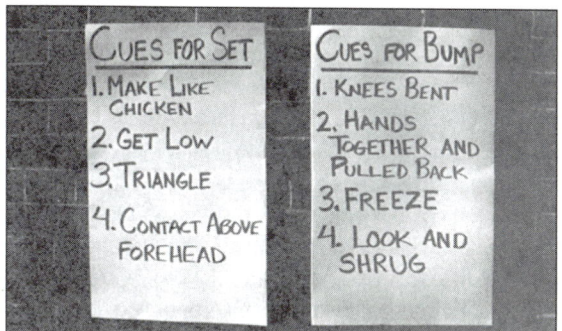

Cues facilitate cognitive understanding of a skill.

In these examples the cues do not focus the learner on how to do the movement. Rather, the learner's attention is focused on the intent of the movement, under the assumption that to be effective, the learner must also do the skill correctly.

Good Cues Are Appropriate to the Learner's Skill Level and Age

Selecting cues to present to learners involves making judgments about the ages and ability levels of the learners. Both of these learner characteristics significantly affect the types of cues selected and how they are communicated.

Skill level of the learner. Although most young learners are beginners, some are not; although some older students are advanced, most are not. Thus, teachers in physical education will be working primarily with beginners in their classes. As learners become more proficient in their movement skills, they can profit from a different kind of learning cue. Teachers must learn to adjust their cues to the proficiency levels of the learner.

Beginning learners. Beginning learners are at a cognitive stage of learning a motor skill. The intent in selecting cues is to give the learner the "whole idea" of the skill or the "gross action" of the skill in as few words as possible. It is not until after the learner has had some experience with the skill that he or she can use more specific information on how to do it. In one

sense, that is why environmental design (designing the environment of the task to elicit the movement) for many skills is effective for the beginning learner. Too much analysis destroys the response. An example of the whole action would be when the teacher says, "squash" to get a soft landing from a jump. Demonstration at this level is also critical to communicate the whole idea.

Advanced learners. Once learners have passed the initial cognitive stage of learning, they move into the associative stage. At this stage they are expected to be able to concentrate on more specific aspects of the skill. However, the details, like the original cues, should be kept selective and ordered by importance. As always, the cues should be appropriate for the level of proficiency of the learner. When working with more-advanced learners, teachers should avoid the temptation of trying to correct everything that is wrong at one time. Even an advanced learner cannot attend to large numbers of cues at one time. With the advanced learner, process-oriented cues are used rather than "gross framework" cues, but the cues must be limited in number all the same. To get a soft landing with a more advanced learner, the teacher might say "Reach with your toes and bend at the hips, knees and ankles."

Age of the learner. Students of different ages have different learning characteristics that should be considered in the selection and organization of learning cues. Although great differences exist between individual students of the same age, recognizing the age characteristics of learners in terms of their ability to profit from different types of cues can guide the teacher's efforts. For example, "transfer your weight to your right foot" would not be a good cue for young children and "use your Superman speed" would not be a good cue for older learners.

Young learners. Two problems should be remembered when working with young learners. The first is that they have less movement experience to bring to a new skill and therefore cannot call up large chains of previously established prerequisite motor responses. It is possible that a young learner will be putting together most of the parts of a complex chain for the first time instead of just combining them in a new way, as an older learner would. The second problem associated with young learners is their undeveloped verbal skills. Most of the terms used in physical education textbooks to analyze skills have little meaning for young learners. The abstract nature of most language used for movement description is not appropriate for learners functioning at concrete levels of abstraction.

Cue selection for young learners at the beginning stages in learning a skill, particularly a complex skill, can take several forms. Young learners are adept at mimicking behavior; that is, they are able to reproduce whole actions with surprising accuracy merely by seeing the action. Therefore, demonstrations that are accurate and overemphasize the critical cues often are useful. Freezing a movement at its critical points to create a visual picture also is helpful.

A second strategy useful with young learners is focusing the learner initially on the whole action and what it should produce, rather than presenting a process analysis of what is happening in the action. Teachers who want to emphasize getting power in a jump can focus learners on "jump as high as you can" rather than on "bending at the hips, knees, and ankles and using the arms to drive up to full extension." Another way to elicit the jump might be to use the cue "jump to a complete stretch in the air." The cues used in these examples help the learner to form a visual picture of the whole action.

Environmental design is particularly useful for the young learner. Responses can be elicited by creating an environment requiring the correct response. Overhand throwing patterns are better elicited using the cue "throw as hard as you can" in conjunction with a high target placed just within maximal throwing distance of the student. Tight forward rolls are elicited by short spaces between equipment, by the cue "roll as slowly as you can," or "how many rolls can you do on the mat before coming to the end of the mat?" Young volleyball players are encouraged to "get under the ball" by a high net rather than a low one.

Young learners can focus on refining cues after experience with the gross action. At this point, the whole response does not need their attention and they are able to attend to more specific cues in future performance. If students are still not performing the gross action with consistency, the teacher must go back and find cues that will communicate to learners the intent of the task. If some consistency in performance has been attained, the teacher can move on to focus the learners on what is happening in different aspects of performance to refine the learner's response. However, the number of cues given to the learner must always be few, accurate, and at a next stage in refinement. Observation of many effective teachers with young children has shown that the focus of follow-up refining tasks is narrow.

Older learners. Many times older learners already have an idea of their ability to succeed or fail with a task based on their past performance with the same or a related task. If the learner has not been successful with the task in the past, motivation to learn it again in the present may be decreased. Additionally, movement responses needed for successful performance may have been learned and practiced incorrectly for a long time. Changing established patterns is difficult.

However, older learners have increased ability to profit from verbal communication. Many words meaningless to young learners may be used with older learners. An older learner can call up chains of motor responses without paying attention to every aspect of the response. Previous experiences with similar motor responses help the older learner select the right cues from a movement environment.

Many teachers continue to "overload" the information-processing system, particularly of older learners, by presenting far too many cues to performance. The phrase "paralysis by analysis" rings true. A useful exercise for teachers is to reduce the number of initial cues they present to a maximum of four and then see if they can list which cues they think are going to be needed at higher levels of task refinement. Older learners in many school situations may not have acquired fundamental skills; therefore, the teacher cannot count on these being present. For students who have not been successful in the past, the teacher must take care to design tasks that ensure success in a reasonable amount of time. Although it is possible to learn even rather complex skills through a completely random process of trial and error, one of the teacher's jobs is to shorten the time it takes to learn. Teachers can do this if they select cues wisely and attend to the limited information-processing abilities of students. Older learners have different problems and different resources, but a beginning learner, whether young or old, is still a beginning learner. Many of the approaches described previously for the younger learner are appropriate for an older learner who is a beginner.

Good Cues Are Appropriate for Different Types of Content

The type of learning cues the teacher uses should vary with the kind of content being presented and the specific task. Motor content may be a closed skill, an open skill, or a movement concept. When establishing progressions for each of these content areas, the teacher will use a variety of tasks requiring different types of cues. Three types of cues are presented in box 4.5.

These three types of cues are largely representative of the different types of motor content we teach in physical education. Discussion of cues for closed skills, open skills, and movement concepts follows.

Cues for closed skills. Most people's mental image of teaching physical education is usually that of a teacher explaining and/or demonstrating a movement to be reproduced by the learner. The teacher's role in such situations is to translate movement into verbal and visual pictures for the learner in ways that organize cues and facilitate the student's development of a motor plan. The student's role is to reproduce the desired response.

The selection of cues for closed skills consists largely of cues for the response that create visual pictures of the critical elements of the skill. When working with closed skills, many effective teachers demonstrate a movement by freezing critical spatial aspects of the movement and drawing attention to body-space relationships and to the movement processes that move the body from one position to the next. The phrase "scratch your back" is an effective

---

BOX 4.5

Cues for Different Kinds of Content

Cue for the response

Gives the learner information on the process of the movement.
Task: Chest pass to a stationary partner.
Example: Place your feet in a forward stride position.

Cue for *adjustment* of the response

Gives the learner information on how to adjust a movement response to a different condition.
Task: Dribbling a basketball against a defensive player.
Example: When being closely guarded, keep the dribble close to your body.

Cue for the *use* of a response

Gives the learner information on how to use a movement in a particular situation.
Task: Passing a basketball to a player on the move against defense.
Example: Pass the ball ahead of the moving receiver; get rid of the ball quickly; pass the ball from the level at which it is received.

---

cue, used to describe the position of the racket head before the forward swing in the tennis serve.

Teachers can facilitate the accurate reproduction of closed skills by vividly sequencing the action of the skill with a few descriptive terms. If the teacher can use these cues in a way that also communicates the dynamic qualities of the movement (including the rhythmic quality of the movement), the motor plan of the student is likely to be more accurate. An example of rhythmic sequences is the cue "hand-hand-foot-foot" used for the cartwheel. Many skills can be sequenced rhythmically to provide another dimension that adds accuracy to the learner's motor plan.

Cues for open skills. The specific type of response for an open skill changes with the environment in which the skill is performed (e.g., dribbling a soccer ball is never the same in all conditions). Most teachers begin by teaching an open skill in a closed way. Teachers will often reduce the complexity of the environment for the beginning learner almost to the point of that necessary in practicing a closed skill (e.g., demonstrating how a skill will be performed without using the ball; practicing batting using a batting tee; practicing a layup shot from the same spot without any interference). When practice of an open skill approximates closed skill practice, cues can be similar to those given for closed skills. However, practice should not remain in closed skill conditions for a long period.

When an open skill is practiced in a changing environment or a closed skill is practiced in a different environment, the type of cues needed changes from cues about the performance of the response to cues concerned with adjusting the response to meet changes in the environment. The cues used should reflect the specific environmental conditions to which the learner is being introduced.

EXAMPLE:
The throw pattern in a baseball game changes according to how the throw needs to be mad e, how quickly

the throw needs to be made, and the direction of the throw relative to receiving the ball.

EXAMPLE:
The golf swing changes when using a wedge to get the ball out of a sand trap.

As each of the conditions mentioned is introduced, the learner should be focused on how to appropriately make the change in the throw pattern or golf swing to be successful.

Perceptual cues are critical to open skills—cues that guide the learner not in the performance of the movement action, but in the appropriate selection of an action for the given situation. The ability to perform the action required as an appropriate response is assumed by the time learners get to complex environments.

The changes in the type of cue that becomes useful in complex environments are illustrated in table 4.1, which describes the development of the basketball dribble through four stages of skill development. If the cues used for the sample task provided are

---

T A B L E   4 · 1

Changes in the Appropriateness of Cues for the Basketball Dribble

Stages in games play development	Sample task	Appropriate cues
One	Dribble the ball at different levels in your own space. Travel with the ball in different directions.	Use pads of fingers and push ball down to produce force. Change contact point on ball to produce different directions.
Two	Dribble the ball to a wall, pass it, receive it, and continue dribbling to a new wall; stay moving the whole time.	Pass at an angle to a wall to lead the ball so that it can be received on the move. Make smooth transitions between dribbling and passing, passing and receiving, and receiving and dribbling.
Three	Play one-on-one offense against defense with offense dribbling and defense trying to touch the ball.	Keep body between ball and the receiver. Change hands. Maintain eye contact with the defense.
Four	Play four-on-four full court basketball.	Do not dribble if a teammate is open ahead. Use the dribble to allow a teammate to get open.

studied, a change from cues for how to execute the dribble to cues for how to use the dribble in increasingly complex game situations can be seen.

The information learners receive in the form of cues should be the content of teacher feedback to learners on their performance. If teachers must continually focus students on cues more appropriate to earlier stages of skill development, the lesson they are currently teaching may be too difficult. In such cases, it would be wise to return to earlier stages of skill development.

EXAMPLE:

If students are playing two-on-two in basketball and the teacher's feedback is still on how to execute the dribble or how to execute the pass, students are probably not ready for two-on-two basketball. The cues for two-on-two basketball should primarily involve strategies and what to do in offensive and defensive relationships.

Cues for movement concepts. The types of tasks presented in the development of movement concepts are so varied that precise guidelines are difficult to specify. Two common types of tasks used in developing concepts are illustrated in box 4.6.

When teachers ask students to choose a response within a concept, they usually attach limitations to the students' choices. These limitations serve as cues to guide the students in selecting appropriate responses. In the examples given for choosing a response, the limitation in the first task is "three parts of your body." In the second task the limitation is "changing your direction." The limitations that the learner must attend to as cues when selecting a sequence must be few in number. It is not uncommon to hear elementary physical education teachers ask students to change their level, direction, and speed as they travel. Students, even adults, cannot attend to this number of cues.

When teachers ask students to apply principles to a movement response or to discover principles from their movement responses, cues should function to give the learner a strategy for solving the problem. In the examples given for applying a concept, the

---

BOX 4·6

Common Tasks Used in Developing Concepts

Choose a movement response within a concept

Example tasks:

Balance on three parts of your body
Travel in different ways, changing your direction
Design three exercises for developing hamstring flexibility

Problem solving to determine movement principles

Movement tasks:

Where should the weight be when you finish the forehand stroke?
Design a strategy for defending the goal rather than the player.
Determine the best stance for a ready position in a sport.
Determine where to contact a ball to put different spins on the ball.

---

teacher has asked students to focus on the transfer of weight from the back foot to the front foot in the tennis forehand. A useful cue for the students might be to "focus on where your weight is after you have finished your swing." In the second task, a useful strategy for designing a defense might be to "try placing your defensive players at different spots under the goal."

In both examples it is necessary for students to know the concept words being used before being asked to work with them. Ideas such as balance, travel, weight, and strategy for defense must be clearly defined.

Cues Are More Effective If They Are Sequentially Organized and Learners Have the Opportunity to Rehearse Them

Students are more likely to be able to use cues if the cues are organized sequentially for them and if they have the opportunity to rehearse the order in which the cues will be performed. Complex tasks that require more description are presented more clearly if the teacher takes as a cue a descriptive phrase, reduces it to a single word, sequences the cue words for the learner, and then gives the learner an opportunity to rehearse the learning cues. When teachers do this, they are using summary cues. The following examples of the sequencing of summary cues for different kinds of tasks illustrate their use:

Bowling: "push away-extend-swing back"
Rising and sinking: "rise turning-sink twisting"
Traveling and balancing: "travel-balance-travel"
Floater serve: "toss-back-extend-stop"

The use of summary cues allows the learner to practice the order of complex skills without having to remember lengthy descriptions of how each phase of the movement should be done. Most teachers learn through trial and error which words are most effective in eliciting desired movement responses from students. Perhaps someday, experienced and effective teachers can share in more formal ways what has worked for them. Meanwhile, inexperienced teachers should spend time preparing and designing word cues for students and putting them into a summary sequence.

A teacher trying to get young children to achieve flight off a piece of apparatus and land with a soft landing might have several alternative word cues. Initially, the teacher might consider action words such as *jump* and *land*. These words sequence the action, but they do not cue the learner to the quality of the movement desired. They are hollow in their communication abilities. Alternative cues to "jump" and "land" are "spring-extend-squash." These cues, put in sequence, communicate a great deal more.

Summary cues do several things for learners and the teacher. They highlight the significant aspects of a movement, which helps learners remember and form visual pictures of what they are trying to do. They sequence actions for learners and can also provide a rhythmic cue if chosen carefully and expressed dynamically. Summary cues can serve also as observation cues for the teacher and establish a common language for teacher feedback.

Summary cues summarize information presented to the learner at another time. The cues are effective only if they are meaningful to the learner and have the same meaning for both learner and teacher.

Box 4.7 provides the teacher a checklist of the characteristics of a good task presentation. Good teachers cannot always be as clear as they want to be. However, with practice, teachers can make clarity in task presentation a part of their teaching repertoire.

BOX 4·7

Teacher Checklist for Task Presentation

1. Do I have the *attention* of the students?
2. Have I included a *set induction* for the beginning of the class?
3. Is my presentation *sequenced in logical order?*
4. Have I presented both *examples and nonexamples?*
5. Have I *personalized* my remarks?
6. Have I *repeated* things that are difficult to understand?
7. Have I related new material to *previous experience?*
8. Have I *checked for student understanding?*
9. Is my presentation *dynamic?*
10. Does my *demonstration:*
    Reflect accuracy?
    Use students?
    Use proper organizational aspects of practice?
    Emphasize important information?
    Provide information on why a skill is performed a certain way?
11. If I am using *media,* have I *prepared in advance?*
12. Are my *learning cues:*
    Accurate?
    Appropriate for the content?
    Appropriate for the age and ability of the learner?
    Condensed to effective word cues?
    Summarized and sequenced?
13. Have I *separated the organization and content* aspects of my presentation?

SUMMARY

1. Students must be attentive if they are to profit from a task presentation.
2. Clarity of communication is assisted by attending to the factors that aid communication between people.
3. Verbal communication, demonstration, and the use of media materials are the most common forms of task communication. Each has its advantages and should be used with attention to guidelines for its effectiveness.
4. Critical features of a skill are selected to be the most important information on how to do a skill.
5. A learning cue is a word or phrase given to a performer that identifies and communicates the critical feature of a movement skill or task. Good cues are accurate, critical to the task being presented, few in number, and appropriate to the age of the learner and the stage of learning.
6. Cues that sequence the action and communicate not only the action but also the movement quality of the action assist the learner in developing a more accurate plan for the task.
7. Organizational aspects of a task should be separated from the content dimensions of a task.

CHECKING YOUR UNDERSTANDING

1. What are some major causes of student inattention? How can the teacher best prevent inattention?
2. What are some things teachers can do to improve communication with learners in task presentation?
3. What are guidelines for using demonstration effectively?
4. What are the advantages and disadvantages of media materials?
5. What are the characteristics of good learning cues? Design a set of learning cues you would use with young beginning learners and then for older advanced learners for a closed skill, open skill, and movement concept.
6. What focus can be used if young students doing a vertical jump are not obtaining adequate flexion, are not using their arms as much as they could, and are not getting full extension? Why would this focus be effective?
7. What are organizational signals? Where are they most necessary in a physical education class?

REFERENCE

Werner, P., & Rink, J. (1989). Case studies of teacher effectiveness in physical education. *Journal of Teaching in Physical Education, 4*, 280–297.

SUGGESTED READINGS

Belka, D. (2002). A strategy for improvement of learning-task presentations. *Journal of Physical Education, Recreation and Dance, 73*(6), 32–35.

Briggs, L. J., et al. (Eds.). (1991). *Instructional design: Principles and applications* (2nd ed.). Englewood Cliffs, NJ: Educational Technology Publications.

Gassner, G. (1999). Using metaphors for high-performance teaching and coaching. *Journal of Physical Education, Recreation and Dance, 70*(3), 33–35.

Landers, D. M. (1978). How, when, and where to use demonstrations. *Journal of Physical Education and Recreation, 49*(1), 65–67.

Levin, T., & Long, R. (1981). *Effective instruction.* Washington, DC: Association for Supervision and Curriculum Development.

Magill, R. (1994). Communicating information to enhance skill learning [Monograph]. *Quest 46*(3).

McBride, R., & Carillo, D. (2000). Incorporating critical thinking into a secondary-school wellness unit. *Journal of Physical Education, Recreation and Dance, 71*(9), 20–24.

McKethan, R., & Turner, E. (1999). Using multi-media programming to teach sport skills. *Journal of Physical Education, Recreation and Dance, 40*(3), 22–25.

Mitchell, D., & Hutchinson, C. (2003). Using graphic organizers to develop the cognitive domain in physical education. *Journal of Physical Education, Recreation and Dance, 74*(9), 42–47.

Rink, J. (1994). Task presentation in pedagogy. *Quest 46*(3), 270–280.

Rink, J., & Werner, P. (1989). Qualitative measures of teaching performance scale (QMTPS). In P. Darst, D. Zakrajsek, & V. Mancini (Eds.), *Analyzing physical education and sport instruction* (2nd ed.). Champaign, IL: Human Kinetics.

5 Content Analysis and Development

O V E R V I E W

One characteristic that distinguishes the expert from the novice teacher is the ability of the expert to relate and transform the content for the learner. To do this, the teacher needs a knowledge of the content and a knowledge of general pedagogical skills, but the teacher also needs a knowledge of how to best teach particular content. This is called content pedagogical knowledge (Shulman, 1987), and this work emphasizes the critical role that content and knowing how to best teach content plays in the teaching-learning process. This chapter establishes skills in content analysis and development as essential content pedagogical skills of the teacher.

Standard 3: Planning and Implementation

Physical education teacher candidates plan and implement a variety of developmentally appropriate learning experiences and content aligned with local, state, and national standards to develop physically educated individuals.
NASPE Beginning Teaching Standards, 2008

O U T L I N E

- **The process of content development—Overview**
  Establish a progression (extension)
  Demonstrate a concern for quality
    of performance (refinement)
  Give students an opportunity to
    apply/assess their skills (application)

- **Planning for content development: The developmental analysis**
  Developing extension tasks—The teacher's
    progression
  Adding the qualities of refinement
  Designing application/assessment
    experiences for content

What content development looks like in
a real lesson

■ **Guidelines for developing different types
of content**

Developing closed skills
Developing closed skills performed in
different environments
Developing open skills

■ THE PROCESS OF CONTENT DEVELOPMENT—OVERVIEW

One of the essential content pedagogical skills is the ability of the teacher to break down the content and sequence it into appropriate learning experiences. Chapter 1 establishes the movement task and the student response to that task as the primary interactive unit in physical education classes; chapter 4 describes how tasks can be presented to learners. However, movement tasks are not delivered unrelated to each other. Teachers use progressions of tasks to lead the learner from beginning levels to more-advanced levels with the content. Teachers establish progressions of content based on their instructional objectives, their knowledge of the nature of content and ability to analyze that content, and their assessment of student needs in relation to the content. *Sequencing movement tasks in a manner that has the potential to facilitate learning is the nature of content development.* Consider the scenario presented in box 5.1.

You will notice that this lesson contains many movement task–student response units. You will also notice that the tasks used in this lesson have some relationship to one another. The lesson content is taught through a *process* that takes the learner from one level of performance to another level of performance through a carefully designed sequence of tasks. This process is called *content development.* The way in which teachers develop content can best be described in terms of teacher content decisions from the beginning of a lesson to the end of a lesson. Good content development has the following characteristics:

It sequences learning experiences from simple to complex or from easy to hard.

It focuses the learner on achieving good performance.

It provides opportunities to apply skills.

Establish a Progression (Extension)

Sequencing learning experiences from simple to complex or from easy to hard is sometimes called *progression.* Teachers do this through a series of **extension tasks.** Teachers start at a less difficult or less complex point and gradually add complexity and difficulty. Sometimes the teacher does not add difficulty or complexity but merely finds another way to practice the same task. Sometimes the teacher must reduce complexity even more. A few of the ideas Fred used in the lesson on fielding a softball described in box 5.1 (see p. 84) follow:

From no ball to ball
From close distance to far distance
From a ball coming directly to the receiver to one in which the receiver had to move
From no emphasis on speed to an emphasis on speed

This development of content is called **intratask development** because the skill the teacher was working on was the same. Fred was sequencing the conditions of the softball fielding task. Sometimes teachers change skills altogether in a lesson that includes more than one skill, such as fielding and batting. This kind of development is called **intertask development** because the skills are different and not related except in a large sense. Teachers establish lessons, units, and yearly program plans based on their knowledge of both intertask and intratask development. The tasks that manipulate the level of complexity or difficulty to previous tasks are called *extension tasks.*

BOX 5·1

Sequencing Movement Tasks in a Softball Lesson

Fred is a third-grade physical education teacher beginning a unit on softball and will focus the lesson on fielding skills. After he orients his class to the day's lesson, Fred presents the following task to the group:

"Stand about 20 feet from your partner and slowly roll the ball to your partner. Show me what you think would be the best way to field the ball and send it back."

After the students have had sufficient time to try different ways, Fred calls the group back in and asks for volunteers to resolve the problem. Several students who have played Little League baseball identify a standard fielding position. Fred remarks that these students have had some experience in baseball and thanks them for their demonstration. He asks the class, "Why do you think this is the best way?" and students respond that it prevents balls from going through the legs.

Fred presents appropriate cues for the fielding position and then has the entire class practice the appropriate position without the ball. He then asks them to quickly move up to a "pretend ball" and get in position on his command; then he asks the students to do it in their own time.

Fred notices that although many of the students are getting their body into position, many of them are neglecting to get their glove down on the ground. He stops the class and says, "You are doing a super job of getting your body into position; now let's focus on getting that glove all the way down." He demonstrates the skill again, emphasizing in the demonstration getting his glove down.

Fred follows these initial experiences with the following tasks:

"Send the ball to your partner's right or left so that he has to move a few steps."

"What is the best way to move your feet to get to your right or left quickly? Let's work on that."

"When you feel that you are ready, move back a few steps from your partner so that the ball can come a little faster."

"See how many you and your partner can field in a minute without letting the ball get past you."

"This time I want you to watch your partners as they field the ball. You are looking for two things: Does your partner get into position, and does your partner get the glove down? I want you to stop practice the minute you see that your partner needs to know that he or she is not doing it right and see if you can help."

Demonstrate a Concern for Quality of Performance (Refinement)

The second characteristic of good teacher development of motor skills content is the communication to students of a concern for the quality of student performance. Concern for quality of student performance can be exhibited by teacher feedback to the class or individual students about how they are performing. It is also exhibited very clearly by teachers when they stop student practice and focus students on achieving particular movement qualities. The intent is that students resume their practice with a focus to improve how they are doing the task. When Fred called the class in because he observed that the students were not getting their gloves on the ground to field the ground balls

and when he focused the class to go off and practice getting the glove on the ground, he was demonstrating a concern for quality. He was refining performance. These types of tasks will be known as **refining tasks.** The following are other examples of refining tasks:

"Now work to get your landing as soft as you can."

"Make sure your weight is transferred to that forward foot after your stroke."

Refining tasks can have a powerful impact on student performance when the teacher keeps the focus of improvement narrow and when students are held accountable for working within the focus of the refining task. Accountability in this case means that if the teacher does not see students working with the focus of the task, the teacher calls the students in once more and reemphasizes that focus. If the teacher asks students to improve some aspect of performance, then the teacher should see an intent to improve that aspect of the student's work in the subsequent practice.

Give Students an Opportunity to Apply/Assess Their Skills (Application)

The third characteristic of good content development involves the way in which teachers integrate opportunities for students to apply their skills. In most skill learning, students are asked to focus their attention on how they are moving. This is the efficiency component of motor skills. Although the teacher may be interested in good form, students are largely interested in doing something with a movement, that is, accomplishing some purpose. Eventually, students will be asked to apply their skills to experiences in which they will be focused on factors other than how they are moving. This is the effectiveness component of motor skills. A competitive game, for instance, focuses on the goal of the game (i.e., how to score, not how to move to score). Dance experiences focus on the expression of the movement. Teachers can also ask students to apply their skills by assessing the form used in performance (e.g., "Rate yourself on your use of the cue").

In our example lesson, Fred used an application task when he asked the students to see how many times they could field the ball in a minute without letting the ball get by them. Beginning basketball dribblers can test their ability to keep the ball going without losing control or their ability to keep the ball from their partner. The skill is not being used in the basketball game, but it is being applied. Fred also used an application task when he had one partner assess the form of another partner. Application experiences are added when students are both confident and competent with a particular level of a skill.

Effective progressions provide opportunities for students to use their developing skills in application experiences throughout the development of their skills. Teachers do not wait until all the skills of basketball are "learned" and then have the students play a full game of basketball. The teachers include basketball-like games and self-testing and assessment experiences throughout skill learning.

Reducing the complexity of tasks helps beginning learners.

Students can test their skill effectiveness at almost any stage of the progression if the application experiences use the level of skills that students have learned and not more-advanced skills. We will call tasks that provide students with opportunities to apply and assess their skills **application/assessment tasks.**

In an actual lesson, the teacher's development of content can be seen through an analysis of the type of tasks presented. The teacher begins with an initial task, which we will call the **informing task.** An *informing task is the initial task in a sequence of development for a skill in a lesson.* From that initial task the teacher develops the content. The development of content is achieved through the integration of all three of the teacher moves described: (1) *extension*—the gradual progression of difficulty and complexity; (2) *refinement*—a concern for the quality of student performance; and (3) *application/assessment*—the integration of application experiences. Together, the three teacher moves describing the type of task constitute the progression through which the teacher develops the content. They have been labeled and defined for discussion purposes as follows:

- **Informing.** The initial task in the progression of a skill.
- **Extension.** A teacher move that communicates a concern for changing the complexity or difficulty of student performance.
- **Refinement.** A teacher move that communicates a concern for the quality of student performance.
- **Application/Assessment.** A teacher move that communicates a concern for moving the student focus from how to do the movement to how to use the movement or an assessment of form.

Although all teacher content behaviors contribute to these processes, the movement task the teacher gives the student (e.g., "Bounce the ball ten consecutive times in the same spot without moving" or "Today we are going to play softball") is the most obvious and most critical way in which progression is established. There is growing research support (see chapter 2) for teachers' use of extension, refinement, and application/assessment tasks in their progressions. Only practicing "the game" is not sufficient for student skill learning. Box 5.2 (see p. 87) describes two progressions used to teach the overhead set in volleyball. The progression that includes both extension and refinement and application/assessment tasks at less than a full game level of application for beginning learners has the greatest potential to improve learning.

Content development is important. At a general level, it is a measure of the clarity of teacher goals and an intent to teach for student learning. It distinguishes the intent to merely provide activity for students and the intent for students to learn. At a more specific level, it is a measure of the teacher's ability to blend concerns for the progression of conditions of practice, the quality of performance, and the integration of application experiences. The presence of extension indicates a desire on the part of the teacher to sequence experiences—to build toward more complex and difficult forms. The presence of refinement indicates a concern for quality; the teacher does not just let students get through a movement experience but insists that the skill is done well. The presence of application indicates a desire to help the students use the skills they develop while learning how to perform the skills well.

■ PLANNING FOR CONTENT DEVELOPMENT: THE DEVELOPMENTAL ANALYSIS

Adequate development of content during the teaching process can be facilitated by teacher planning. In the past, teachers learned to develop appropriate sequences of experiences for learners primarily through a process of trial and error and through insightful perspective on the content. The process of selecting sequences of experiences is facilitated if teachers in their planning do a **developmental analysis** of the content they are teaching. A developmental analysis of the content is a chart of content development that uses three columns (extension, refinement, and application), as presented in table 5.1. Developmental analyses for the tennis serve and basketball dribble are presented at the end of this chapter and are referred to during the chapter discussion. Included are a developmental analysis for the tennis serve (box 5.6, p. 102), a developmental analysis for the basketball dribble (box 5.7, p. 103),

---

TABLE 5·1

Developmental Analysis of Content

Informing task: Teacher describes the initial skill to be learned.

Extension	Refinement	Application/assessment
A task that adds complexity or difficulty to the prior task	Qualitative aspect of the extension task	A competitive, self-testing, or performance focus

BOX 5.2

Appropriate and Inappropriate Progressions for the Overhead Set

In each lesson the teacher has explained and demonstrated the overhead set and begun practice with having students set the ball back to a partner from a short toss. The students have practiced the forearm pass before the set in a previous lesson.

Teacher A—Inappropriate progression

Task One: Toss the ball to your partner with a high toss from about ten feet. Your partner sets the ball back to you and you catch it.

Task Two: Now let's use the overhead set in a game. You must use two hands to set the ball to another person to forearm pass before you can send the ball back over the net.

How this progression looks when graphed:

Informing Task
Extending Task
Refining Task
Application/Assessment Task

                           1.   2.
                      Task number

Teacher B—Appropriate progression

Task One: Toss the ball to your partner with a high toss from about ten feet. Your partner sets the ball back to you and you catch it.

Task Two: This time as you practice, try and get yourself in the "get set" position before you hit the ball. Get there and get ready.

Task Three: If your trajectory isn't high on the ball after you set it, what does that mean for where you are hitting it? How can you get a high trajectory? Okay, this time get under it more.

Task Four: When you and your partner can both set the ball five times in a row with a high and accurate trajectory, take two or three steps back and make your toss higher and try it.

Task Five: Now let's try the set from a forearm pass. Toss the ball to your partner. Your partner will forearm pass the ball to you; you will set it back to them, and they will catch it. The sequence becomes toss-forearm pass-overhead set and catch. (toss-pass-set-and-catch).

Tasks Six: When you can do this five times in a row, move farther away from each other and see if you can still make it work.

Task Seven: In groups of three, one person serves the ball, one does a forearm pass, and one sets the ball. Start with an easy serve and make the serve more difficult as you are ready.

How this progression looks when graphed:

Informing Task

Extending Task
Refining Task
Application/Assessment Task

          1.   2.   3.   4.   5.   6.   7.
                 Task number

and a developmental analysis for the concept of force reduction applied to manipulative objects (box 5.8, p. 104). Once you have finished reading this chapter, the sequence of these analyses should be clear.

The developmental analysis breaks the content down into its component parts—extension, refinement, and application. The developmental analysis gives structure to the teacher's ability to provide appropriate, progressive sequences of experiences. It helps the teacher to identify the characteristics of good performance for an experience and to integrate appropriate application experiences. The developmental analysis begins with identifying the extension aspects of skill development.

Developing Extension Tasks— The Teacher's Progression

A developmental analysis of content begins with the extension column. At this point the teacher decides how to (1) reduce the complexity and difficulty of content for learners and (2) order the parts that will be added to create a sequence, or chain, of experiences. The teacher must first think through factors that add complexity and difficulty to a learning experience and then sequence experiences in a progressive order. Many factors can be manipulated to change the complexity or difficulty of motor performance. The following factors have been selected for discussion and are summarized in box 5.3 (see p. 89):

- Practice of parts
- Modification of equipment
- Spatial arrangements for practice
- Focus of intent of performance
- Number of people involved in performance
- Conditions of performance
- Changing the rules
- Number of combined skills or actions
- Expansion of number of different responses

Practice of parts. Teachers can often reduce the difficulty of beginning stages of learning skills by breaking a whole action into parts and practicing the parts before the whole is put together. Most instruction in square or folk dance is done this way. The teacher begins with a small part of the dance and then adds other parts of the dance, combining parts until the whole dance is learned. Similarly, the tennis serve can be learned after the whole skill is presented by first practicing the toss of the ball without the racket, then the swing of the racket without the ball, and then both the toss and the swing together with or without the ball. Unless there is a safety or other reason not to practice the whole first, students should have some experience with the whole before practicing parts.

When skills are complex, there is a real advantage to reducing the skill to its parts after some practice of the whole. When skills are not complex or when breaking the skill into parts would destroy the rhythm of the skill, practice of parts in beginning stages is contraindicated.

Teachers will also want to consider the idea of *backward chaining* (introduced in chapter 4), or beginning the practice of parts with the last part in the chain. Backward chaining is useful for many complex skills. Practicing the main action first, before the preliminary action of a skill, can give more meaning to the parts leading to the main action. Examples of backward chaining include the tennis serve progression that begins with the last part of the striking action (hitting the ball from a racket position behind the back); the bowling or basketball layup progression that eliminates the approach; the folk dance progression that begins with the chorus; and the shot put progression that begins with putting action (rather than the steps into the action).

When teachers choose to present a skill to learners in parts, it is critical that students first have an opportunity to practice the whole skill if possible, or when not possible, to see the whole skill performed. Many teachers who break down skills for students neglect to give students a feel for the whole action before they break down the skill. Practice of parts is not meaningful if there is not some idea of the whole skill.

Modification of equipment. One of the most useful ways to reduce the difficulty or complexity of performance in learning skills is to modify the equipment or its arrangement. Skills that directly manipulate objects, such as putting the shot, throwing a football, or passing a volleyball, are many times more easily learned with equipment of reduced size or weight. Skills that use implements are likewise more easily learned when skis, clubs, or rackets are shorter or

BOX 5·3

Summary of Extension: Common Methods of Extending the Movement Task

Breaking down a skill into parts

Example:

- Practice the takeoff and placement of the ball in the layup shot in basketball.
- Practice dropping the ball for a courtesy serve in tennis or racket skills.

Modifying equipment

Example:

- Begin with a light ball and increase the weight of the ball in volleyball.
- Reduce the size of rackets initially and then increase the size and weight of the rackets for racket sports.

Making the space larger or smaller

Example:

- In a chasing game, decrease the space to make it easier for the tagger.
- In two-on-one soccer, increase the space to make it easier for the offense.
- Increase the force requirements for a throwing or striking skill by increasing the distance.

Changing the goal (intent) of practice

Example:

- Practice the tennis serve to get a feel for the rhythm and then practice to get the ball in the court.
- Practice batting to get a hit and then practice to place the ball in different locations.

Adding or decreasing the number of people

Example:

- Practice dance steps first by yourself and then with a partner.

- Practice two-on-one in soccer and then two-on-two. (Note two offense vs. one defense is usually easier than two-on-two.)

Changing the conditions of performance

Example:

- The defender is trying to stay with the offensive player—you are not yet trying to get the ball away.
- If you are having trouble getting the ball over the net, take a few steps in front of the service line.
- Practice playing basketball without the dribble.

Changing the rules

Example:

- You can use as many hits as you need to get the ball over the net.
- We are not going to call the traveling rule today very strictly.

Combining two skills

Example:

- Practice shooting in basketball and then practice dribbling and shooting.
- Practice a forward roll and then practice a forward roll into a headstand.

Expanding the number of different examples of a concept

Example:

- From task of "Show me what a balance is" to "Show me three different ways to balance."
- Design three exercises to improve back flexibility.

lighter. This is particularly true for younger learners, who may not be able to learn an efficient movement pattern with equipment disproportionate to their size. It is also helpful for beginners of any age to use equipment that permits earlier efficiency of performance. As discussed in chapter 2, students will choose an appropriate response for the conditions and their abilities. A good rule to follow is that *if the* when space is reduced. When establishing progressions, the effects of reducing or expanding the spatial arrangements for experiences throughout the progression must be considered.

When planning progressions for the development of sport skills, it is also helpful to consider game requirements. The forearm pass in volleyball must eventually be done from a serve that comes from the other side of the court. Practicing the forearm pass from a short toss of a partner may be helpful initially, but unless the teacher increases the space between the partners and eventually uses a thrown or hit ball from a distance, the student cannot be expected to be able to use a forearm pass from the volleyball serve. With large numbers of students there is a tendency to reduce the space allocated for practice. Progressions must be designed to increase the amount of space and the amount of force required because the amount of space that objects cover and the force of the objects are so integrally related and because the goal is for students eventually to be able to either produce or receive objects with force.

If the equipment encourages less than mature and efficient patterns, teachers must consider changing the equipment.

equipment encourages less than mature and efficient patterns, changing the equipment should be seriously considered.

Equipment arrangements that can be modified in a learning environment include lowering or raising volleyball nets to encourage particular skills, lowering baskets for younger learners, and increasing the size of targets or goal areas to encourage success at beginning levels of development. Gymnastics equipment can be modified in height, and in educational gymnastics the arrangement of groups of equipment in relation to each other can be manipulated to control difficulty.

Spatial arrangements for practice. Teachers can establish a progression of difficulty through spatial arrangements. The level of difficulty in skills involving throwing, catching, or striking projectiles is increased or decreased by manipulating the distance, and therefore the force requirements, of the skills. Skills involving moving with others in space, such as dribbling a basketball, are increased in difficulty

Focus of intent of performance. At any point in a progression of experiences, difficulty can be extended or reduced by manipulating the instructions for the intent of performance. This was referred to as the *goal orientation* of the task in chapter 4. The goal orientation of the task can have a significant effect on how a learner performs a skill. The practice of batting, for example, changes considerably when the focus shifts from only hitting the ball to placing the ball in a specified area or to hitting balls so that the trajectory is different. Running for practice of form changes considerably when running for speed becomes the intent. Throwing in track and field changes when distance becomes the intent. Teachers can manipulate student intent in the design of experiences and their progressions.

Number of people involved in performance. Many skills initially are practiced by individuals but eventually will be used with others in a more complex activity. Practicing a skill individually is almost always easier than practicing it with others. As soon as other participants are added, the skill is out of the complete control of the individual, and individuals must begin to adapt to one another. For example, practicing tennis strokes alone by using a ball machine to serve the ball eliminates the variation that comes when another person serves the ball. Practicing a dance step first without a partner eliminates the need to relate the movement to the partner while the step pattern is being learned.

Many skills are difficult to practice individually, such as catching at the beginning stages. For this skill, learners eventually need balls coming to them, and walls create too much force. In cases such as this, partners are necessary for individual practice.

In most progressions, other people are added to develop relationship skills (both cooperative and competitive) in the use of a motor skill. Most team sports involve both competitive and cooperative relationships with others. These relationships are built gradually by adding people one by one to a progression. Volleyball or most net activities can begin with relationships between two people and advance very gradually to relationships of two-on-two, three-on-three, four-on-four, and so on. Basketball and field activities can be developed by using similar progressions. Spatial arrangements must increase to accommodate greater numbers of participants. The idea of gradually adding people to whom the individual must relate should also be considered in gymnastics. Educational gymnastics and traditional stunts and tumbling units use group work, but working with others in these areas is difficult and should progress gradually.

Conditions of performance. Conditions of performance that increase or decrease the level of difficulty of content are largely content specific. The teacher will have to think through ways to make the content more and less difficult. In most manipulative patterns (e.g., throwing, catching, striking), the following conditions of performance can be modified to increase or decrease the difficulty of practice:

Less difficult

- Low speed
- Low force
- Stationary sender
- Stationary receiver
- Movement forward
- Medium level of trajectory

More difficult

- High speed
- High force
- Moving sender
- Moving receiver
- Movement backward or sideways
- High or low level of trajectory

The Real World box below provides a situation in which the conditions of performance are *not* anticipated adequately.

Music is a condition of performance that plays a critical role in dance progressions. The decision to add music and the choice of speed of the music are important decisions that affect progression. Skills are more easily learned initially without music, and in the case of fast rhythms, they are more easily learned at slower speeds. Music added to any activity can facilitate or hamper performance depending on the extent to which the tempo of the music is consistent with the natural tempo of the movement.

Changing the rules. The difficulty of an experience can be increased or decreased by manipulating the *rules* of many sport activities. Rules are conditions of practice that limit performance. They limit how individual skills are performed and how people

---

Example of Poor Progression

The teacher begins class with a demonstration of the overhead set in volleyball. After practicing the hand position while seated, students are divided into groups of six. Each group is asked to form a circle. Students are told to practice setting the ball to the person next to them around the circle. The students do not experience any degree of success in this skill. They are unable to pass the ball to the person next to them because they have to receive the ball from one direction and then pass it in another direction. The condition of practice is too difficult because students have not had an opportunity to first send the ball in the same direction from which it is received.

interact with each other. Rules that are safety considerations (e.g., the height of the hockey stick after a swing) should be included from the beginning. Teachers should also ask themselves if not applying a rule will cause bad practice habits that cannot be easily changed. When safety or practice habits are not problems, it can be helpful not to apply a rule that complicates initial learning. When and to what degree the traveling rule is added to basketball dribbling or illegal hits are called in volleyball can be manipulated as part of a progression.

Game rules most certainly can be adapted and should be modified. *A good rule to follow is that if a rule or other aspect of a game destroys the continuous nature of play, modifying that element should be considered.* Good examples of this are eliminating the serve in beginning tennis or volleyball and making other arrangements for foul shots in basketball.

Number of combined skills or actions. Many perspectives on progressions of skills stop with the individual skill and move directly into competitive uses of the skill in complex situations. The full development of a skill must include combining that skill with other skills with which it will be used. Students do not just shoot baskets in basketball; they dribble and shoot, or they receive a pass and shoot. Students do not just set a volleyball; they receive a pass, set a volleyball, and move into another defensive or offensive position. Teachers must consider how skills will be used and prepare learners for the variety of ways in which the skill will be performed with other skills. If students will have to dribble and shoot or receive a pass, dribble, and pass, they should have the opportunity to practice all possible combinations of skills in less complex environments before they are expected to combine these skills in complex situations.

Expansion of number of different responses. In progressions of concept teaching, or divergent inquiry (chapter 8), an eventual goal is for the students to transfer their knowledge of a concept to new experiences. Progression of experiences will move from experiences that help students to define the concept to experiences that expand the number of appropriate responses and ask students to apply what they have learned. Initial experiences must help the student

define the concept (e.g., what is a balance?), and later experiences in a progression must expand the number of ways in which the concept is applied. (e.g., find three ways to balance on three parts of your body). Still later experiences will ask the students to select and refine their responses (e.g., choose one of these ways and make it a really good balance). When the teacher asks for different responses, the complexity of response is increased. A teacher who first defines for students what the word *balance* means, has them work on a balance, and then asks students to find as many different balances as they can is expanding the concept for students. A teacher who defines for students the type of exercise necessary to produce cardiorespiratory endurance and then asks students to find two types of exercise to achieve cardiovascular endurance is expanding the concept for students. Guidelines for these types of progressions are discussed in chapter 12.

Establishment of sequences of experiences. Sequencing experiences for students is not easy. Teachers must think through the content and make decisions about how the content can best be sequenced for a particular group of learners. The extension column of a developmental analysis describes the sequence the teacher has chosen to use with a particular group of learners. Examples of sequences of extension for the tennis serve and the basketball dribble are presented in the developmental analyses for the tennis serve and basketball dribble at the end of this chapter (pp. 102–104). Inherent in each of these sequences are many of the ideas for gradually building in complexity and difficulty that have been discussed. In the development of these skills you will notice many examples of ways to build in progressions. You will also notice many examples of both intratask and intertask development.

Once the teacher has established a sequence building in complexity and difficulty, he or she must give some thought to identifying the qualities of good performance for each of the extensions of tasks provided. This is the refinement aspect of the developmental analysis and is discussed next.

Adding the Qualities of Refinement

The refinement column of the developmental analysis answers the question "What does it mean to perform the task well?" For each experience listed in the extension column of a developmental analysis of content, a dimension of quality is described in the refinement column. The teacher in the tennis serve developmental analysis (pp. 102) identified what is important about the movement characteristics of the performer of each of the extension experiences provided: The teacher has established *cues* for each task identified as an extension task. The refinement column is concerned primarily with cues for how to do the skill (form characteristics). In many cases this will be so, but there are times when cues for the response (execution of the movement) are not what is most important. Consider the example from the basketball dribble developmental analysis (pp. 103–104). At the end of the progression, the refinement column is not concerned with how the basketball dribble is performed but with how the player adjusts the dribble to the conditions of a defensive player. As discussed in chapter 4, this is a cue for an adjustment of the response. Because this is a later stage in the progression, the technique of dribbling is assumed to have been developed; the attention thus is put on how to *use* the dribble.

The refinement column serves the following purposes in planning progressions for students. The refinement column

- identifies cues the teacher can use for the presentation of tasks,
- focuses the teacher on what to observe in performance, and
- provides information to use in teacher feedback to students.

In an actual lesson, after the teacher presents a task to the class, he or she observes the students for information in the refinement column. If the teacher does not see good performance as identified by the cues in the refinement column, the teacher has several choices:

- Correct performance individually if problems are not widespread.
- Make the task easier if it is too difficult.
- Stop the class and focus the entire class on a cue that will improve performance (the refinement task).

It is not easy to complete the refinement column of a developmental analysis because most physical educators cannot know everything they need to

about every skill that they teach. However, excellent resources are available that describe how skills are performed, and these can be useful to both beginning and experienced teachers. It is helpful, but not sufficient, for physical educators to be able to perform skills themselves. Teachers must also be able to describe good performance at different stages of the development of content. Teachers must prepare. As you teach skills to students, you will improve at sequencing tasks and focusing students on what is important if you will evaluate your success.

When teachers have filled in the extension and refinement columns of the analysis, they are ready to consider planning for ways in which experiences can be provided to help the learner apply skills. Application is discussed in the next section.

Designing Application/Assessment Experiences for Content

The application assessment column of the developmental analysis describes experiences that can help the students apply their developed skills to situations that shift the focus from *how to move* to *using* the skill or *assessing* the skill. The application column completes the developmental analysis (pp. 102–104) for the tennis serve and basketball dribble.

Application assessment experiences are usually, but not necessarily, competitive or assessment experiences. Application tasks redirect the learner's focus from *how to do the skill* to *accomplishing a goal using the skill. Application tasks can also provide the student with information on performance characteristics of the task.* The following are examples of application tasks:

- Self-testing (individual or partner)
  Learners are encouraged to test their mastery of a skill (e.g., see how many, how quick, how far).

EXAMPLE:
"How many times can you toss and catch without dropping it?"
"How far can you stand from the wall and still hit the wall?"
"Check off which of the cues for this skill you have mastered and which ones you are still working on."

Self-testing activities motivate competent learners.
(Courtesy SIUE photo.)

■ Self-testing (group)
A group of learners are encouraged to test their mastery of a skill.

EXAMPLE:
"How long can you keep the volleyball up in the air without letting it hit the floor?"
"How many times can your court pass the volleyball over the net using at least two passes on each side?"

■ Competitive
Activities are played against others with varying degrees of complexity.

EXAMPLE:
One vs. one basketball
Eleven vs. eleven soccer

■ Assess performance using criteria
Provide objective feedback on performance, either process or product of performance.

EXAMPLE:
"Take your checklist of cues for this activity and your videotape and assess the degree to which your play is consistent with the cues we have been using for game play."
"One partner is an observer and you are going to look to see if your partner holds his or her balance for six seconds before moving into the next action in the sequence."

Application experiences are a powerful focus. *No matter what additional focuses teachers may give an*

experience, the application focus will dominate most of the time. Application experiences change the learner's focus from *how the movement is performed* to *the goal of the skill* or to a focus *of meeting the assessment criteria.* For this reason, students should be competent and confident with the content before their abilities are tested. When beginners who have been working on dribbling skills in basketball are asked to use that skill in a relay race for speed, ball control decreases significantly, no matter how much the teacher reminds the students to control what they are doing. The students are not yet competent in the skill. Competitive focuses can improve the performance of students who have achieved a degree of competence and confidence with content. They can decrease the level of performance of students who have not. For these latter students, competitive focuses are likely to be discouraging rather than motivating.

Application experiences should be congruent with the level of extension and refinement in a progression. The following example illustrates a progression of experiences for students that uses an application task that is not appropriate for the level of extension or refinement developed:

■ Practice forearm volleyball pass with a partner from an easy toss.
■ Without a net, practice forearm pass from a partner's toss, moving forward, backward, or sideways to receive it.
■ Practice forearm pass to set up overhead set for the partner from a toss.
■ Use the forearm pass in a game of volleyball.

The teacher who planned this progression began by considering the conditions that made the forearm pass difficult. The teacher decided that the initial toss should be easy and that the performer should not have to move. The second experience encourages the performer to move, and the third experience focuses on what to do with the forearm pass. These are important considerations in developing this skill, but the progression does not go far enough. Because several critical elements are left out of the practice of the forearm pass before a full game is played, it can be predicted that students will not be able to use the pass successfully in the full game situation. Most critically, students will be given no experience with receiving balls coming forcefully over the net. This experience could have been gained if the ball had been served or tossed over the net. Even if all other game conditions (e.g., number of people on a court; choosing the bump or overhead set) are practiced, this single condition will prohibit success with the use of the skill.

The developmental analysis can serve as a check to see if the application experiences in the progression are appropriate for the level of development of the content. Application experiences in sport activities should be spaced throughout a progression of experiences and not be reserved for the end of a progression. They should also use the level of skill development that the learner has experienced in a noncompetitive focus. Teachers can consider achievement level when designing these experiences for students and can also transfer some of that responsibility and choice to students.

What Content Development Looks Like in a Real Lesson

This chapter began with a scenario describing a teacher named Fred teaching fielding skills. It might be useful to go back to Fred's lesson (box 5.1, p. 84) to see if you can determine what you think Fred's developmental analysis of the fielding skill might look like. In his lesson Fred used extending tasks, refining tasks, and application assessment tasks. It is unlikely that Fred used all the extension tasks or application tasks he had listed or that he shared with the students all of the cues he had identified in the refinement column for each of the tasks. Because teachers base what they do in an actual lesson on the needs of learners at the time, several ideas regarding content development and the use of the developmental analysis in teaching should be kept in mind.

There is no set sequence of extending, refining, and application assessment tasks. After teachers do a developmental analysis of the content and present the initial task, they decide what to do based on what they see. Possible actions are presented in box 5.4.

Teachers skilled at developing motor skills with students blend these "teacher moves" into their lesson appropriately. At times, beginning teachers who gain some insight into the complexity of the process used

---

B O X   5 · 4

Options for Teachers Based on Observed Learner Needs

Restate the task
> When it is obvious that the learners did not understand or choose not to work within the limits of the task.

Skip steps in the progression
> When the task is too easy.

Reduce the difficulty or complexity of the original task
> When learners are having little success.

Use a refining task
> When learners are not exhibiting the performance cues identified in the refinement column for a task.

Use an extending task, planned or unplanned
> When learners are ready to increase or decrease the complexity of the skill.

Use an application task
> When learners are confident and competent enough with the task presented.

---

to develop content have remarked, "Well, that's coaching!" The point is that good coaching is good teaching. Good coaches are actually good teachers.

■ GUIDELINES FOR DEVELOPING DIFFERENT TYPES OF CONTENT

The preceding sections developed general concepts for use across content areas. The examples given were for a closed skill (tennis serve) and an open skill (basketball dribble). In the next section, ideas for the development of different types of content are more specifically explored. Chapter 3 identifies a classification for three different kinds of motor skill content: (1) closed skills, (2) closed skills in differing environments, and (3) open skills. Each of these categories is unique in its learning intent and therefore requires a different approach to the development of learning outcomes. In this part of the chapter, some implications of the unique nature of the content for the design of a development analysis are discussed.

Developing Closed Skills

The intent of the development of closed skills is to produce consistent and efficient performance in a defined environment. However, skills can rarely be practiced at the beginning stages of learning the way they will eventually be used. Thus, teachers must make many decisions regarding progression and development of a skill.

Prerequisites to learning

- *Establish prerequisites.*
- *Modify the skill or equipment to ensure success.*

Prerequisites for learning closed skills usually include both physical abilities (e.g., strength, flexibility) and motor abilities. Physical abilities are important factors in gymnastics skills. Students who do not have the abdominal strength or arm strength necessary for a hip circle on the uneven bars or a swing on the parallel bars will not be successful to any degree with these skills until their physical abilities are developed.

Motor ability is an important factor in manipulative patterns with objects. Students who have developed strong throwing patterns are in a better position to learn striking patterns than those who have not. Students who have developed strong locomotor patterns will be able to call on these patterns when needed to move to or with objects. Motor ability is a function of experience and maturation.

Teachers who have to teach closed skills to students who do not have the prerequisite abilities must establish these abilities, modify the skill or equipment to permit success, make provisions to teach a different skill, or provide different experiences. Teachers should ask themselves if learning the skill at that particular time is important. Programs for young children and handicapped students should be carefully selected for skills important at a particular stage of learning. Although it probably is possible to eventually teach any skill to any student, teachers must consider a particular student's stage of development. Teachers must decide whether the skill learned warrants the time spent and whether the time can be best spent on other skills that can be learned more efficiently or on other experiences that provide a developmental base for motor learning.

Whole-part question

- *Teach the whole whenever possible.*
- *Break down the skill into parts after providing students an opportunity to see or practice the whole.*

As discussed previously, teachers of closed skills must decide whether to teach a skill as a whole action or to break it into parts. This decision is often called the *whole-part dilemma.* Closed skills should be taught as a whole if possible. The rhythm of the movement performed in parts is often not the same as the rhythm of the whole. One part of a movement is preparation for another part. There is no guarantee that a student who can perform each part separately will be successful with the whole. A golf swing is a good example of a highly rhythmic skill that is destroyed if broken into parts.

Nevertheless, it may be desirable to teach complex skills, such as the tennis serve, in parts. Even under these conditions, however, many learning theorists recommend that the student be given an opportunity to work with the whole action before working with parts. The progression then becomes a whole-part-whole progression.

Teaching a skill as a whole does not preclude teachers from focusing students on parts. The refinement column of the developmental analysis in this case becomes a critical aspect of progression. Because learners will not be able to attend to all that they should at one time, the teacher orders what the students will be asked to focus on in the refinement column, even though the practice conditions remain the same. A good example of this is in practicing the golf swing. Although the students may be doing the whole swing, the teacher can establish a progression of what is important to focus on first, such as the role of the hips and left arm, head, and so on.

There are no set answers to the whole-part question. Each skill is in a way unique. The complexity and rhythmic nature of the skill should help serve as guidelines for when to break the skill apart and when to teach it as a whole.

Modifying equipment

- *When it is the equipment making success difficult, modify the equipment.*

When teaching closed skills, if the conditions of performance are reduced, teachers must decide whether learning can occur more rapidly and more successfully by modifying the equipment. In most cases, students will profit from modified equipment when it is the equipment making success difficult. Clubs or rackets that are too long or too heavy; balls that are too hard, too heavy, too small, or too large; or goals that are too small, too high, or too far all make success difficult for the beginning learner.

If the learner must modify the pattern of the skill to be effective with regulation equipment, the equipment should be modified. Such is the case with young students who must shoot underhand to do a free throw with high baskets or who must use two hands on a projectile when the skill calls for only one hand. The equipment should be modified in these cases, because it is not suitable for the age or level of skill of the student.

Many beginning students do not have the prerequisite physical abilities to manipulate or use regulation-size equipment. Beginners can profit from shots that are light, bowling balls that are light, bows with a low pull weight, or hurdles that are low. Equipment can also be modified to eliminate the fear aspects of regulation equipment for beginners (e.g., a rope can be added to the high bar; rope hurdles can be used instead of wood; soft balls can replace hard balls).

Changing conditions of practice

- *Change the conditions of practice to ensure success and build difficulty gradually.*
- *When working on the form of the movement, remove knowledge of results.*

Closed skills will eventually be performed in stable conditions, and extensive practice in the "real" environment will ultimately have to occur. Teachers can reduce initial practice conditions to ensure success or can focus the practice on efficiency rather than effectiveness.

As long as the conditions of practice do not destroy the integrity of the skill, they may be changed to ensure success. Serving lines in volleyball, tennis, or other target skills can be moved up initially to decrease the force production needed for success.

Teachers should also consider removing student knowledge of results from the environment in initial practices. Removing knowledge of results means not letting students see whether their action was effective. If students are not permitted access to knowledge of results, it is easier to get them to refine their performance and to focus on the critical kinesthetic cues aspect of closed skills. Bowling pins can be removed and golf swings or archery shots can be aimed into a net to eliminate knowledge of results.

Establishing a progression of intent

- *Modify the goal (intent) of performance to ensure success.*

Most closed skills have a definite performance goal. Manipulative skills (e.g., bowling, golf, archery) usually are target oriented. Nonmanipulative skills (e.g., dance, swimming, diving, gymnastics) have a form goal. Self-testing skills (e.g., high jump, javelin, hurdles) have an effectiveness goal.

Beginners should not be held to the same standards of accuracy, form, or effectiveness that surround the performance of the skill at advanced levels. Goals for effectiveness and efficiency should be reduced for the beginner and gradually increased as ability increases. These goals should be part of the teacher's planning and should be included when the developmental analysis of the content is done. Beginning bowlers can strive initially to keep the ball in the alley. Beginning tennis servers can attempt to get the ball over the net or can hit into the fence. The skill is performed as a whole, but the goal of practice changes with ability, thus allowing success to be built into the progression.

Accuracy versus force production

- *High degrees of accuracy should be required only after force production abilities have been established.*

Many closed skills of a manipulative nature are accuracy oriented (e.g., basketball free throws, tennis serves, bowling, archery, golf). In such a progression, teachers must decide when to stress accuracy and when to stress force production. Motor-learning work in this area suggests that force production should be emphasized first. High degrees of accuracy should become the focus of practice only after some degree of consistency of form has been established. Teachers who stress accuracy too soon force students to modify their form, because the students have not reached high enough levels of control to experience success at being accurate. An example of this occurs frequently in the tennis serve. Many students can accurately serve the ball with a "chop" stroke instead of the full tennis serve. Students will use a "chop" stroke if they are asked for high degrees of accuracy, because they cannot be accurate with the full tennis serve.

Teachers are often reluctant to allow students to practice skills with maximum force production. This is because of managerial and organizational difficulties involved in giving students enough space to let objects fly out of control. However, there is little transfer from skills practiced with little force to those practiced using maximum force. If the skill requires force production, it is unlikely to be learned without having opportunities to use maximum force.

Environmental design

■ *Design the environment to elicit a response when possible.*

Environmental design is a useful way to establish progression for learners at beginning stages, because verbal communication is not as critical. Equipment or a learning environment can be arranged to promote learning. This is called *environmental design.* An example of environmental design is putting a stick out in front of a student practicing the front dive to encourage the student to jump *up* first, not *down*. Another example is placing targets on a tennis fence at the height where the ball is to be hit to provide a guide for learning. A tennis teacher can use environmental design to teach the rhythm of the serve by having students swing a sock with a ball in it. If students break the rhythm, the ball loses its centrifugal force. Teachers can encourage tight forward rolls by asking students to do three consecutive rolls on a small mat.

There are many ways to encourage learning difficult skills through environmental design. Teachers can develop the ability to design environments to promote skill learning by asking themselves, "How can I put students in a situation that will *bring out* a particular movement or movement quality?"

Developing Closed Skills Performed in Different Environments

■ *Introduce the skill in the simplest environment and extend practice into all types of the environment used in the activity.*

■ *Alert the learners to the types of modifications they may need to make in their performance for different environments.*

Closed skills in different environments are developed in ways similar to those used for closed skills. Skills used in different environments will eventually have to be practiced in those different environments. The basic pattern of the skill, such as bowling, a golf swing, or a forward roll in Olympic gymnastics, is modified when the environment changes. These patterns should be established with some consistency under simpler conditions before more complex conditions are introduced, such as bowling for spares, hitting a golf ball out of a sand trap, or doing a forward roll on the balance beam.

When planning for later progressions in skills that will be used in different environments, teachers should include many different practice environments. The specific modifications the learner will need to make in the basic pattern should be part of the refinement column of the developmental analysis. Differences between these modifications and the basic pattern will need to be communicated to the learner through teacher cues (e.g., instructing a student to descend on the ball for a golf shot in tall grass) or through problem-solving experiences that help the learner identify how the pattern changes under new conditions. Box 5.5 presents an example of a developmental analysis for a closed skill used in different environments.

Developing Open Skills

Progressions of experiences for open skills should be developed with the intent of helping performers adapt skills to the complex changing environment in which the skills will be performed. To develop useful progressions of experiences for open skills, teachers must do a thorough analysis of the ways in which these skills will be used in the open environment.

BOX 5.5

The Golf Swing in Different Environments (Right-Handed Performer)

Extension	Refinement	Application/Assessment

Individual

Get the ball out of tall grass and sand.

Use a descending, punchlike blow, not a long takeaway.
Open iron a few degrees at address.
Maintain firm grip.
In sand do not contact ball but contact sand behind ball.
Skim club head through sand and float the ball out.
Close the club face to knife through heavy sand.
Position ball opposite left hand.
Pull left side back from target line.
Use a short backswing (down and through).

Place the ball in sand and grass; attempt to get the ball (1) a short distance from the hole in one stroke or (2) a long distance from the lie in one stroke.

Partners

Place the ball in grass and sand; see who can get the ball to a target area in the least number of strokes.

Play balls on a slope. Play a downhill lie.

Use open stance perpendicular to the slope; play ball near right foot with right knee flexed.
Backswing first pickup with striking action down the slope.
Use well-lofted clubs.
Aim to the left of the target.

Play an uphill lie.

Swing parallel to the slope.
Aim to the right of the target.
Use more club to increase height.

Play a ball higher than the feet.

Use erect address.
Use flatter swing.
Aim to the right of the target.
Use shorter club.
Open stance slightly.

Play a ball lower than the feet.

Bend over to address ball.
Stand closer to ball.
Swing in an upright plane.
Use longer club.
Aim to the left of the target.

Group

Use three balls for each of four positions (downhill lie, uphill lie, ball higher than feet, and ball lower than feet); use same target area for each group of players and each condition; record number of strokes it takes players to get all twelve balls into the target.

Discussion: The teacher has anticipated the different environments the students will have to adjust to. The teacher has provided experience in those different environments and cues that change the way the basic stroke is performed in those environments.

Cues used for this analysis were taken from B. L. Seidel, et al., *A Conceptual Approach to Meaningful Movements,* 2d edition, 1975, 1980, Wm. C. Brown Publishers, Dubuque, Iowa.

Note: A major assumption in this progression is that the students have developed some degree of consistency with wood and iron shots under ideal conditions.

Most open skills used in physical education are skills used in game situations. Thus the teacher must be able to identify specifically how a skill is used in a game. Analyses of what learners must be able to do to use both the volleyball overhead set and the tennis forehand in a game situation follow.

Volleyball Overhead Set

- The player must be able to set a ball:
  Coming from different directions
  To different directions
  Coming to and from different force levels and trajectories
  By moving in different directions
  From a stationary position
  Coming from a serve or a forearm pass
- The player must be able to decide:
  When the appropriate time is to use the set in relation to the forearm pass
  When the ball is his or her responsibility
  Where to set the ball

Tennis Forehand

- The player must be able to strike the ball with a forehand stroke:
  Coming from different directions
  To different directions
  Coming from different levels
  To different levels
  Coming with different amounts of force
  Coming with different amounts of spin
  By moving in different directions to contact the ball
  From any position on the court
  To any position on the court
- The player must be able to decide:
  Where spatially to place the ball in the opponent's court
  When it is appropriate to use the forehand stroke
  When to put different kinds of spin on the ball

This analysis forms the basis for establishing a progression of experiences that moves from less complex to more complex conditions (extension).

Doing a developmental analysis of open skills is more difficult than doing a developmental analysis of closed skills, because the learner must be prepared to adapt the skill to rapidly changing conditions. Students who can perform the skill under one set of conditions may not be able to perform appropriately under other conditions unless prepared to do so. In the volleyball and learner example above, you will notice extensive **intratask development** to prepare the learner for the responses they will need in an open environment.

Many of the same concerns that guide the development of closed skills are concerns in the development of open skills. Decisions regarding modifying conditions, choosing between whole and part progressions, changing practice conditions, and encouraging force production before accuracy are based on criteria similar to those discussed for closed skills. However, some decisions are unique to the development of open skills.

Teaching open skills initially as closed skills

- *Practice of open skills in closed environments should be limited.*

A critical controversy among physical educators is whether an open skill should be taught first as a closed skill. A typical example of teaching an open skill first as a closed skill is to have the student bat off a tee before swinging at a moving ball. Batting off a tee is a closed skill because the batter does not have to adjust the skill to the speed, level, or direction of an oncoming ball. Most theorists and practicing teachers agree that there is merit in reducing the complexity of the open skill for the beginning learner to the extent that the skill becomes more closed in its characteristics. Teaching open skills in closed conditions, however, does pose problems.

If teachers think in terms of two separate abilities involved in the development of open skills, decisions about progressions become easier. The first is the ability to respond with the proper movement pattern. In batting, this first ability is to swing the bat with the proper form (efficiency). The second is the ability to adapt the skill to the situation. In batting, the batter has to time the swing properly and at a level appropriate to the oncoming ball, an element of the situation over which the batter has no control. A skill cannot be performed effectively unless the student has acquired skill in both the *response* and the *selection of the response* (adjustment). Skilled performers not only execute well, but they also select an appropriate response.

Initially, it may be desirable to practice a response (particularly complex patterns) without having to adjust the skill to a changing environment. There is, however, a danger in practicing open skills in closed environments for too long. If the skill becomes highly developed as a closed skill, the performer may not be able to adapt the skill to the appropriate environmental cues. The environment of the closed skill is predictable, whereas the environment of the open skill is not. Preparation for unpredictable environments requires variability of practice and practice in changing environments.

Practicing the execution (response) and use of response

- *Progressions for open skills should include opportunities to practice the execution of a response and to practice selecting the appropriate response.*

There are two aspects to skill development in open skills. The first aspect develops the ability to execute a response by moving in a particular way (intratask development). The second aspect prepares the learner for selecting the proper response. Both are necessary for the complete development of skillfulness.

In the game of basketball, the basketball dribbler must be able to do the following:

- Dribble at different speeds.
- Dribble the ball at different levels.
- Use different locomotor patterns with the dribble.
- Change direction while dribbling.
- Dribble and pass.
- Dribble and shoot a basket.
- Dribble and stop while maintaining possession.

These abilities are responses that the basketball dribbler must have available to be successful at dribbling the ball in a game situation. These are

abilities to execute a response. The basketball dribbler must also be able to choose the appropriate response to any given situation. The skilled dribbler chooses the appropriate time to dribble fast, slow, or at different levels; to change direction; to pass or shoot from the dribble; or to stop. The ability is related to the use of the response. The appropriate response depends on the conditions of the game at any particular point.

In progressions for open skills, practicing not only the execution of the movement but also the selection of the response must be considered and planned for in any developmental analysis of content. Practicing the selection of the response adds *perceptual complexity* to the environment and helps the learner decide how to respond. It is easier to develop progressions for responses alone than it is to develop progressions that help the learner respond correctly to the perceptual cues of the environment. The more choices the learner has to make, the more difficult the response.

An example of practicing the selection of the response in basketball dribbling is teaching students how to respond to a defensive player trying to get the ball away. In this situation the cues for selection of the response become the following:

- Defend the ball by placing the body between the ball and the defense.
- Keep the dribble low.
- Change direction quickly.
- Keep an eye on the defense.

The student should be able to dribble close and at a low level and protect the ball with the body. In volleyball the concern in a progression for teaching the overhead set is not how to do the overhead set, but when to select it and where to direct it. In a badminton progression of the drop shot the concern no longer is how to do a drop shot, but when to choose a drop shot. The development of response selection follows the development of a reasonable amount of control with skill. When students reach the point of choosing responses in a complex environment, the responses should be already developed to a reasonable level of consistency.

See boxes 5.6 through 5.8 for further information about open skills.

B O X   5 · 6

The Tennis Serve (Right-Handed Player)

Extension	Refinement	Application
Practice grip.	Hold racket head like a knife and use continental grip (halfway between eastern forehand and backhand). Spread fingers. Hold racket firmly.	Close eyes and attempt to pick up racket and assume proper grip.
Practice stance.	Stand 2 to 4 feet from center mark. Use throwing stance. Keep front toe 2 inches behind service line at 45-degree angle. Check shoulder width.	Assume proper stance from all four serving positions. Practice until five tosses in a row land consistently in proper place on the court.
Practice toss.	Push ball into air. Check height above extended racket. Ball should drop 1 foot to right of front toe.	
Toss and strike ball with an open hand from "scratch your back" position; stand a few feet from net and serve over net.	Keep elbow parallel to ground. Hand should brush over head. Use pads of fingers, not palm.	Practice until three hits clear the net in a row.
Toss and strike ball with a racket from "scratch your back" position; choke up on racket; stand at midcourt and serve ball over net.	Loosen grip on racket. Maintain grip. Contact ball at full extension.	Practice until three hits in a row clear the net and ball lands within service court.
Change sides of court.	Maintain form.	Same as above.
Stand farther back; slide grip down; strike ball from "scratch your back" position; serve ball over net.	Hit out on ball, not down.	Same as above.
Stand at baseline; add backswing; use normal grip; serve ball over net.	Break wrist. Maintain grip. Keep continuity of backswing and striking action.	Same as above.

Discussion: The teacher in this skill has identified the following variables to manipulate the complexity and difficulty of the serve:

    Racket or no racket
    Length of grip on racket
    Whole striking action and parts
    Distance served over net
    Target of serve
    Right or left court target

Each of these variables is manipulated in the progression. Each level of experience in the extension column also has associated qualitative cues, which appear in the refinement column, and appropriate application experiences.

B O X   5 · 7

The Basketball Dribble

Extension	Refinement	Application
Dribble a ball in personal space.	Flex knees.	Dribble the ball as many times in a
Dribble continuously without losing control.	Maintain low body position.	row as possible while (1) looking at ball, (2) changing hands, and (3) not
Change level.	Keep head up.	looking at ball.
Move the ball to different parts of personal space.	Keep ball toward dribbling side.	
Change hands.	Push ball to the floor with fingers.	
Dribble while looking someplace else.		
Travel with the ball in general space.	Change angle of rebound with speed.	Move as fast as possible without
Travel slowly.	Keep ball out in front of body with speed.	losing control of the ball.
Change direction (forward, backward, and sideways).	Change angle of body to upright with speed.	Touch as many different lines in the gym with the ball as possible in 30 seconds.
Change speed.	Be aware of others (eye contact off ball).	Play frozen taggers game (half the class is spaced out as frozen
Stop and start quickly.	Look for spaces to move into.	obstacles trying to tag ball).
Change levels.		
Keep ball close and then far away.		
Travel in smaller shared space while increasing speed.		
Dribble and pass the ball.	Make smooth transition from dribble pass and pass to dribble.	Go to as many different walls as possible in 1 minute without losing
Dribble, send ball to the wall, pick up the ball, and continue dribbling.	Send ball to the wall at an angle and speed that will allow continuous	control.
Dribble and pass to a partner.	traveling.	
Dribble and pass while moving in same direction at slow speed.	Pass ahead of moving partner.	
Dribble and pass while moving in same direction at increased speed.	Maintain awareness of partner during dribble.	
Dribble and pass while traveling in different directions in a confined area.	Use the pivot to change direction in stopped position.	
Maintain possession against a defensive player.	Place body between ball and defense.	Maintain possession as long as possible without stopping the
Another student tries to force a loss of control.	Keep ball low and close.	dribble or losing control.
	Anticipate move of defensive player.	
Another student tries to gain possession of the ball.	Change speed when appropriate.	Give defense a point every time they touch the ball in 1 minute.
Maintain possession with a partner against one defensive player.	Dribble when defense is in a position to block pass and pass when pass is	Keep control of the ball with partner as long as possible.
Play with no line of direction (keep-away situation).	open.	Start at one end of a space and try
Add directional goal.	Make quick passes.	to move the ball down to the
Add traveling rule.	Move into empty spaces to receive pass.	opposite side to score a point (minimum of three passes without
	Defensively force a bad pass.	loss of control).

(continued)

The Basketball Dribble—cont'd

Discussion: The teacher in this analysis has identified three phases of skill development for the dribble. The first phase is practice of ball control responses. The second phase is practice using the dribble with another skill, with other players. The third phase uses the dribble in competitive relationships with others. The following variables were established as being part of the complexity and difficulty of the skill and are part of intratask development of the task:

Weight and size of ball
Level of dribble
Direction of ball around personal space
Dominant or nondominant hand
Stationary or moving player
Relationship to another offensive player
Relationship to a single defensive player
Relationship to offensive and defensive players at same time

Directional or nondirectional goal
Direction of locomotion
Speed of movement
Distance of ball from the body
Number of people active in one space
Combinations with other skills
Traveling rule

Note: There is a choice of ball size and weight.

BOX 5·8

Force Reduction: Manipulative Objects

Extension	Refinement	Application
Toss a ball into the air and receive it so that it makes no noise in the hands.	Reach to receive. Move down with object until the force is reduced.	Toss ball as high as possible and still receive it with "soft hands."
Identify concept (force is reduced by giving with it).	Create maximal distance to receive the force.	Come as close to the floor as possible before stopping the ball.
Receive thrown balls of different types (e.g., footballs, basketballs, softballs).	Place body parts directly behind object to receive the force.	Go as long as possible with partner without any sounds being made by hands.
Receive self-tossed balls.	Adjust hand placement to the level of the ball and shape of object.	Go as far away as possible from partner and still maintain quality of catch.
Receive balls from different directions.	Move to get behind object.	
Receive balls from increasing distances and force levels.		
Receive balls while both stationary and moving.	Anticipate where ball will land.	
Receive manipulatable objects with implements (e.g., scoops, lacrosse sticks, hockey sticks, bats).	Same as all of above with the adjustment of an implement.	Same as all of above with the adjustment of an implement.
Receive objects at increasing distances and force levels from a partner.		
Receive objects both while stationary and moving.		

SUMMARY

1. Content development is the progression of tasks teachers use to take the learner from one level of learning to another.
2. Different types of content (closed skills, closed skills in different conditions, open skills, movement concepts) require an emphasis on different aspects of skilled performance and therefore an emphasis on different types of development.
3. In a lesson, the teacher develops the content through a process using extending tasks, refining tasks, and application tasks:
   - Extension tasks change the complexity or difficulty of the prior task.
   - Extending tasks focus the learner on a qualitative aspect of performance.
   - Application/assessment tasks ask the learner to use the prior task with a competitive, performance, or self-testing or assessment focus.
4. The teacher can plan for different aspects of development by doing a developmental analysis of the content.
5. Open skills must ultimately be developed to the level of complexity that is part of the way the skill will be used. This means that complex conditions must be gradually added to practice.
6. Closed skills and closed skills in different environments may be initially practiced by reducing the complexity and difficulty, but they should be practiced primarily in the conditions in which the skill will be used.

CHECKING YOUR UNDERSTANDING

1. Identify and describe the three different content moves that establish progression and represent the way the teacher develops lesson content.
2. What are six aspects of a movement task that can be manipulated by the teacher to increase or decrease the complexity or difficulties of practicing a motor skill?

3. How should the progression established for an open skill differ from that of a closed skill?
4. What purpose does the refinement column of a developmental analysis serve in helping the teacher in instruction?
5. Develop the extension column for a closed skill and open skill, attending to the unique aspects of progression established in the chapter.
6. For the progressions established in the previous question, fill in the refining aspects and possibilities for application.
7. Why are application tasks such a powerful focus for student work? What guidelines should the teacher follow in deciding to move to an application task?
8. When the teacher does a developmental analysis and uses it as a guide to plan a lesson, how does the teacher know when to give a refining task or when to extend the task?
9. What is the difference between practicing the response and practicing the selection of the response in an open skill?

REFERENCE

Shulman, L. (1987). Knowledge and teaching: Foundations of the new reform. *Harvard Educational Review, 57*(1), 1–22.

SUGGESTED READINGS

Adams, D. (1999). Develop better motor skill progressions with Gentile's Taxonomy of Tasks. *Journal of Physical Education, Recreation and Dance, 70*(8), 35–42.

Chase, M., Ewing, M., Lirgg, C., & George, T. (1994). The effects of equipment modification on children's self-efficacy and basketball shooting performance. *Research Quarterly for Exercise and Sport, 65,* 159–168.

Doering, N. (2006). Using stories to teach flow in educational gymnastics. *JOPERD, 77*(1), 38–44.

French, K. E., et al. (1991). The effects of practice progressions on learning two volleyball skills. *Journal of Teaching in Physical Education, 10*(3), 261–275.

French, K. E., Rink, J. E., & Werner, P. H. (1990). Effects of contextual interference on retention of three volleyball skills. *Perceptual and Motor Skills, 71,* 179–186.

Harrison, J., Pellet, T., & Buck, M. (1993). The effect of drill, game, and equipment modifications on achievement by low skilled learners. *Research Quarterly for Exercise and Sport, 64 (Suppl.), A-83.*

Masser, L. (1985). The effect of refinement on student achievement in a fundamental motor skill in grades K-6. *Journal of Teaching Physical Education, 6*(2), 174–182.

Nilges, L. (1999). Refining skill in educational gymnastics. *Journal of Physical Education, Recreation and Dance, 70*(3), 43–48.

Pellett, T., & Harrison, J. (1995). The influence of refinement on female junior high school student's volleyball practice success and achievement. *Journal of Teaching in Physical Education, 15*(1), 41–52.

Pellett, T., Henschell-Pellett, H., & Harrison, J. (1994). Influence of ball weight on junior high school girls' performance. *Perceptual and Motor Skills, 78,* 1179–1384.

Peterson, S., & Cruz, L. (2000) Using small-sided games in traditional activities. *Strategies, 14*(2), 19–21.

Rink, J., et al. (1992). The influence of content development on the effectiveness of instruction. *Journal of Teaching in Physical Education, 11,* 139.

Sawicki, T. (2000). Developmentally appropriate activities using games modification. *Strategies, 14*(2), 19–21.

Developing and Maintaining a Learning Environment

6

O V E R V I E W

One of the most difficult functions of teaching for beginning teachers is management. Teachers must elicit the cooperation of students to engage in learning and must develop and maintain a learning environment that supports learning. This chapter is meant to help you design and maintain a learning environment and to help you move students from teacher control to student self-control. The goal of a good management system should be to establish student responsibility for their behavior. The chapter presents the interrelationships between a management system and the teaching of content. Ideas for establishing and maintaining rules, as well as routines and strategies for developing self-control and handling student discipline problems, are presented.

Standard 4: Instructional Delivery and Management

Physical education teacher candidates use effective communication and pedagogical skills and strategies to enhance student engagement and learning.

NASPE Beginning Teaching Standards, 2008

O U T L I N E

- **The ecology of the gymnasium**
- **Establishing and maintaining a management system**
  Establishing routines
  Establishing class rules
  Gaining and maintaining the cooperation of students

- **Strategies for developing student self-control and responsibility**
  Hellison's levels of responsibility
  Behavior modification
  Authoritative orientations to management
  Group process strategies for developing self-direction
  Conflict resolution

107

- **Discipline: What to do if it does not work**
  Deterring problems before they become
  problems

Continued inappropriate behavior
Handling students who continually
misbehave

■ THE ECOLOGY OF THE GYMNASIUM

Physical education classes should be characterized by an environment conducive to learning. Gymnasiums should be places where all students can have positive experiences and where students are both physically and psychologically safe. Teachers and students should enjoy being there. Gymnasiums should be places where teachers want to work and have something to teach students and where students want to learn. Teachers have a responsibility to (1) provide students with content to learn that is appropriate and challenging, (2) develop and maintain an environment conducive to learning that content, and (3) cultivate increasing levels of student responsibility. When teachers fail to use their authority, knowledge, and skills to develop these abilities, they are abdicating their responsibility.

We usually think about teaching in terms of both management functions of teaching and content functions of teaching:

- **Management:** Arranging the environment for learning and maintaining and developing student-appropriate behavior and engagement in the content
- **Content:** The substance of a curriculum area— what is to be learned

Good management skills of the teacher are essential for effective teaching. They alone are not sufficient to make you an effective teacher, but you cannot be an effective teacher without them. Although it is helpful to talk about teaching in terms of management functions and content functions of teaching, recognize that these two functions are connected. They interact with each other in the context of a class that has unique characteristics. As was described, the teacher may have designed a suitable learning experience but may not be able to obtain or maintain student cooperation to engage in that learning experience. Likewise, a teacher may have good basic management skills but may have nothing valuable to teach students; therefore, student cooperation is lost, regardless of good management techniques.

The teaching-learning process is often referred to as an ecological system, because the idea of an ecological system implies an interdependence of many systems working at the same time. The content and management systems that you establish with your class are two such interdependent systems. Because management and content are interdependent systems of instruction, they should share the same curriculum objectives. It is incongruent to expect learners to work with content at advanced levels and be independent learners within a management system that aspires to student obedience (McCaslin & Good, 1992). An example from physical education illustrates the strong relationship between content and management.

EXAMPLE: Kevin is a high school teacher taking a course in teaching strategies for his master's degree. The faculty at Kevin's high school has been working on ways to help students to be more motivated and to be engaged in learning experiences at a higher level. Kevin has begun to think about the potential of physical education to contribute to student independence, interdependence, and higher-order thinking skills. Kevin's teaching is direct. Kevin believes that he needs to keep students in control at all times and that the student's role should be primarily one of obedience. Kevin rejects every strategy mentioned in his graduate class because his perspective on using that strategy is that students will be out of his control and not engaged in the content without his direct involvement in everything they do. Because Kevin has not worked on helping students to be more self-directed in their learning, Kevin's options for how to teach the content are limited. Kevin has limited not only *how* students will learn but also *what* students will learn.

Educators have come to think about management as a problem of obtaining and maintaining order (Doyle, 1984). *Order in an educational setting means high levels of engagement in what the student is supposed to be doing and low levels of inappropriate and disruptive behavior.* Remember that a student technically "on task" may not be engaged in the content in a meaningful way—that is, at a level of engagement that has the potential to effect learning. Remember also that students interacting with each other may be engaged in the content in an appropriate way. It does not necessarily follow that because students are being "good," they are learning, or because classes appear to be disorganized or students appear to be off task, they are.

Student compliance alone is a limited goal for an educational program. Student compliance suggests that the students are able to do what the teacher says—they are willing to cooperate with the teacher. In most settings, teachers should have higher expectations for student behavior. A better measure of effective teaching is the degree to which the teacher has been able to develop *high levels of student engagement* in the content. Engagement in the content is a necessary condition for learning and is a minimum expectation for effective teaching.

To achieve high levels of student engagement in the content, the teacher should be able to use a variety of teaching strategies with the assurance that the students will be able to function within these strategies. (Alternative teaching strategies will be discussed in chapter 8.) From a managerial perspective, this means that students must be able to act responsibly without much teacher direction or monitoring and must be able to interact with each other in positive and supportive ways. In some gymnasiums, students work independently of the teacher on a variety of tasks. In other gymnasiums, students can work in groups productively and supportively of each other. The teachers have established expectations for much more than just control with their classes. In still other gymnasiums, there seems to be a constant battle between the teacher and students for control. Even minimal levels of compliance have not been established.

This chapter is designed to help you establish and develop a management system with your classes. In many schools today, schools have established management systems that clearly define school rules, school procedures, and the consequences of students not complying with those rules and procedures. Teachers will want to be consistent with the established school management system but will have to interpret the rules and procedures established for the physical education environment. Teachers will also

need to establish a management system for the unique physical education setting.

In this chapter we will consider strategies for both obtaining and maintaining control, as well as teaching for more-advanced levels of student engagement with the content and self-directed behavior. Remember that you cannot get to the higher levels of student self-directed behavior without first establishing minimal levels of control in your classes. Also, the manner in which you establish this control will affect your ability to move students to more-advanced levels of self-direction.

■ ESTABLISHING AND MAINTAINING A MANAGEMENT SYSTEM

One of the first steps in establishing good management in your classes is to establish class routines and rules that you teach and hold students accountable for on a day-to-day basis.

Establishing Routines

Routines are a customary way of handling a situation and are an essential ingredient of good management in the gymnasium. Teachers should establish routines with students for frequently occurring events in the gymnasium so that more time can be devoted to substantive parts of a lesson. Many events occur over and over, like taking attendance, getting equipment, changing clothes, and so on. When teachers have routines for handling these events, students know what the expected behavior is and are more likely to behave appropriately. Many teachers in physical education have established customary ways of handling the following events:

Locker room routines

When to enter

Where to put clothes and what they bring with them.

Permitted social behavior

Amount of time for dressing before and after class

Leaving the locker room, where to wait, when to leave

Permission to enter locker room during class

What to do if you don't remember your locker combination

Before-class routines

What to do when leaving the locker room before class starts

For elementary, how to enter gymnasium and where to go first

Attendance procedures

Lesson-related routines

What areas of the gymnasium are "out of bounds"

How to obtain and put away different types of equipment

What signal you will use to stop and start activity

When you want to talk to students, should they stay where they are or gather in an area of the gymnasium; should they stop work on command or finish their movement; should they put their equipment down; should they sit off the mats

How students will get a partner; small group; large group

What to do when your equipment invades the working space of others

How to distribute space for practice among individuals or groups

How students should get your attention for help

How to get out and return student journals

How to obtain a pencil and scoring sheet for self- or peer assessment

End-of-lesson routines

How a lesson should be ended

If students take less time to dress, can they continue to practice

Other considerations

How to handle late arrivals

How to deal with students who are not dressed out

How to handle water breaks

How to handle going to the bathroom

How to handle fire alarms

What to do in case of an injured student

You should be able to describe exactly how you want students to handle these events. Routines should be designed to make events run more smoothly and to maximize the opportunity to engage in the content.

Routines should be taught to students, practiced, and reinforced. Guidelines for each of the routines mentioned are described in the Real World box (pp. 111–112). Some basic principles regarding establishing and maintaining routines follow.

Teaching routines. Routines can be taught to students in different ways. Usually teachers will spend time at the beginning of the year explaining and in some cases practicing routines. Young learners will need practice of many routines and constant

Fitness routines are often used to begin longer classes.

Guidelines for Establishing Routines

Locker room routines

The objective in establishing locker room routines is to make changing clothes a safe, sensitive, and efficient process. Locker rooms must be monitored by the teacher initially and in some cases every time a group of students is in the locker room. Students should have sufficient time and space to dress and should have a safe place to hang their clothes so that coming to physical education is not a hassle.

Many secondary programs allow five to seven minutes before and after class for dressing. If students need showers, more time must be allotted. Absolutely no horseplay should be permitted in the locker room, and all students should come into the locker room and leave at the same time to prevent any problems with theft. If locker rooms are crowded, students should be allowed to wait for the next class elsewhere after dressing. Most schools request that students not be allowed into the hall to go to their next class until the bell ending a class has rung.

Before-class routines

Elementary

Elementary students usually enter the gymnasium as a class. It is helpful for the teacher to greet the students at the door and then move them right into the beginning of class. If this is not possible because of back-to-back classes, often the case in the elementary school, a routine should be established to have the students quietly come into the gymnasium to a designated location (center circle or line on the side of the gymnasium) to sit and wait for the teacher.

Secondary

After students finish dressing, they will come into the gymnasium. If possible, equipment and a supervising teacher should be in the gymnasium so that students will have an opportunity for more practice while waiting for others. Generally students will dress more quickly if they know there is something for them to do when they get into the gymnasium.

Attendance

It is not necessary to check attendance in most elementary school settings in self-contained units. Who is absent for the day is information easily obtained from students or the teacher as students come into the gymnasium. In secondary school, the objective should be to check attendance in the most efficient way. There are many good ways to check attendance that do not waste time having the teacher call out the names of every student.

Each student has a spot to go to; the teacher scans for empty spots.

Each student has a squad; the squad leader (this position should rotate) checks attendance for a squad and hands an attendance card back to the teacher.

The teacher checks attendance during a beginning warm-up routine.

Lesson-related routines

Distributing equipment

Teachers should have several access points for distributing and putting away equipment. In the elementary school this prevents a "rush" to get the equipment. At all levels this saves time.

Out-of-bounds

Early on, teachers should designate where it is and is not appropriate for students to find a "working space." For elementary children, having a working area several feet from the wall eliminates "wall huggers." In the secondary school, large equipment is often placed in some areas of the gymnasium, which presents a safety problem.

Signals

The use of signals is context specific. Signals are essential to start and stop work in the elementary school, because as soon as an activity is mentioned, young children want to do it before the teacher finishes giving all the instructions. Teachers often must use the phrase, "When I say 'go,' I want you to. . . ." If this is not a problem in the secondary school, teachers can be more informal about the communication to "go."

(continued)

Guidelines for Establishing Routines—cont.

In large spaces or outside, most teachers must use a whistle or a drum to get students to stop what they are doing and listen to further directions. In smaller spaces, usually a voice command is sufficient. If you do not need to use a whistle, it is more desirable not to use one.

Instead of demanding an immediate halt to activity, the "stop" signal should mean to "bring to a close what you are doing." This helps avoid the risk of students endangering themselves if they are in the middle of a movement.

If you do not have to bring students "in" to change the activity or change the task, it is better not to do so. However, if attention, hearing, or seeing is a problem, teachers should gather students closer to them for transitions.

Grouping

Alternatives for grouping are described in chapter 3. Generally students should be taught to group themselves unless the teacher wants to use other criteria for putting students into groups.

End-of lesson routines

Closure

Before students leave the gymnasium to go back to their class or to the locker room, it is usually recommended that they gather for a summary of the lesson and preparation by the teacher for the next lesson.

Dismissal

Elementary children need a procedure for lining up to go back to their class. It is helpful for teachers to establish a consistent location for students to line up that does not interfere with the class coming in.

Students should know that when they are dismissed, they will go to this location to line up. Secondary students can go into the locker room after being dismissed.

Other needed routines

Late arrivals

Late students usually come into a class when the teacher is occupied giving directions to students. The teacher should not stop the whole class to deal with a late arrival but should establish a procedure to have that student wait until a more opportune time for the teacher to move them into the class activity.

Water and bathroom breaks

If a water fountain and bathroom are available in the gymnasium, the teacher should allow students to get a drink of water and go to the bathroom at any time. Sometimes elementary students make a "game" of going to the water fountain. This is one of those areas in which the teacher may have to have specific rules that become more flexible as students demonstrate that they can handle the responsibility. When an entire class lines up for water, a great deal of time is taken out of class. In many secondary schools, water and bathrooms are located in the locker room and locker rooms have to be locked.

Injured students

If a student is not badly injured, generally the teacher can allow other students to continue with what they are doing while the teacher attends the injured student. Usually a teacher can send the injured student to the nurse's office with another student. If the student needs a great deal of help, the teacher should have the class stop and sit while the teacher sends for help.

reinforcement. The teacher may have to practice routines for several weeks before a routine becomes well established in a class. Older learners usually have established routines that the teacher may want to modify. In either case, the teacher must share expectations with students for a routine and the appropriate behavior that is expected in carrying out a routine. Students

will learn what is expected if both positive and negative examples of appropriate behavior are used and if students understand the need for appropriate behavior. The most significant factor affecting the establishment of routines in a class is the degree to which the teacher consistently reinforces those routines. If teacher teaches a routine and then does nothing whe routines are not followed, it is unlikely that the routine will be established.

Degree of structure. Highly structured situations are characterized by step-by-step teacher directions and student responses. The more structure, the smaller the steps. In less-structured situations, the learner is asked to respond to more than a simple direction without being cued by the teacher. These examples that follow of a highly structured and a less-structured routine for getting practice started with partners in a manipulative task illustrate this point:

EXAMPLE: *Highly structured:* "Sit next to a partner in a good space. One partner go get a ball and sit back down in your space to show me you are ready to begin. When everyone is ready, I will give the signal to get started."

Less structured: "Sit next to a partner. When I say go, I want one partner to go get a ball, and then both of you find a space and begin practicing."

The ultimate goal should be for the teacher to work toward less structure as students can manage and be responsible for their behavior. Less-structured routines assume students will respond appropriately and encourage student responsibility and decision making about appropriate behavior. Less structure does not mean less appropriate behavior; it means more appropriate behavior that permits more time to be spent on the lesson content. Effective teachers add structure when needed and begin removing it as students are ready to become more independent. Different groups of learners need different degrees of structure in routines. Young learners and groups of learners who cannot handle less formal ways of doing things need more structure. For instance, some secondary students can come into a gymnasium from the locker room and work productively practicing with equipment before the rest of the class is ready to begin the lesson. Other groups of secondary students may need to come into the gymnasium and wait for other students and the official beginning of a lesson before they can practice because they are not able to use that time productively. Helping students to work in more-unstructured ways can be taught.

EXAMPLE (ELEMENTARY): "Let's see if you and your partner can find a place to work and begin working without me having to give you a signal to begin. What am I going to be looking for as you try to do this without a signal?"

EXAMPLE (HIGH SCHOOL): "Some of you have asked to be able to play badminton when you come out of the locker room and before we officially start class. I think that would be great but it means that you will need to act responsibly during this time. What do I not want to see?"

Reinforcing routines. Once a routine has been taught, it must be reinforced. Many teachers think because they have taught students how to do something, they will not have to deal with that idea again. However, even after routines are taught, student behavior can begin to drift without reminders, class discussions, and occasional reteaching. This is particularly true as the school year progresses, after vacations, and toward the end of the year. Effective teachers continuously reinforce routines established throughout the year.

EXAMPLE: "I called you back here today because as I asked you to begin working on the task I saw that several people were not able to handle this yet. What is it that we should be doing when you move to your area of work?"

EXAMPLE: "Your team is supposed to be working on a defense for your game today. Some of the teams are working very hard and getting a lot done. A few of the teams are having trouble focusing their efforts. How can I help you get started?"

Establishing Class Rules

Whereas **routines** should be established for customary ways to perform regularly occurring activities in classes, rules should be established that make clear expectations for appropriate conduct in class. **Rules** are general expectations for behavior in a setting. Children who have been in school for a number of years already have been exposed to many "going-to-school rules." When you work with very young children, you will find that ideas such as raising the hand, lining up,

> ### BOX 6·1
>
> ### Basic Rules in Physical Education
>
> The following rules are generally accepted as those basic to a positive and safe learning environment in physical education:
> - When others are talking, we try not to talk.
> - Be supportive of our classmates' efforts.
> - We respect the rights of others.
> - We take care of equipment.
> - We try our best.

- developed cooperatively with students when possible.
- stated positively.
- made explicit to learners (posted if necessary).
- reinforced consistently and fairly.
- few in number.

Teachers may consider more specific rules for particular lessons or content areas. For instance, a teacher may make a rule, "no resting on the gymnastics equipment" or "no resting on a mat" to eliminate attention problems that can occur when students are in contact with equipment in gymnastics. A teacher may make a rule that when asked to stop work in a ball-handling class, students may need to put their ball down on the floor in front of them to prevent problems with students bouncing the ball and trying to listen.

Gaining and Maintaining the Cooperation of Students

A large part of teacher management is spent in processes designed to gain and maintain the cooperation of students to follow routines and rules, to behave in appropriate ways, and to engage in the content at a high level. Several strategies for gaining and maintaining the cooperation of students are presented in this chapter. As you move through this material and begin to think about the management system you will establish for your classes, several ideas should be remembered relative to establishing a management system.

Plan a progression of experiences toward your learning environment goal. Students at different ages need different emphases in management. Brophy and Evertson (1978) developed four stages of development that can help teachers direct their efforts in establishing and maintaining a learning environment in the gymnasium (see box 6.2).

Although this developmental perspective is helpful, it must be remembered that a new teacher in a new situation must establish his or her management system; that system may be different from what the students are accustomed to and therefore must be taught.

Student management behavior is learned. Many beginning teachers talk about "good" students and

calling out, and following directions that have not been targeted specifically to the child may not be demonstrated by the child. Physical education classes share many of the rules established by the faculty and administration for a particular school. In addition, the unique setting of physical education requires additional rules to make the time spent in the gymnasium both a positive and a safe learning experience (see box 6.1).

Rules are basically concepts. As concepts they are not specific to any one situation and can be applied to many situations. Because rules are concepts, their meaning is often implicit rather than explicit in a situation. Teachers will have to teach what rules mean in a variety of situations by using both positive and negative examples of appropriate behavior. For instance, teachers may find students work independently without interfering with each other in a manipulative skill lesson, but when they are in a gymnastics lesson, they tend to socialize and create dangerous situations by trying to help each other through a movement. The rule of not interfering with others who are practicing may need to be taught for a particular situation. Teaching may imply sharing expectations or the problem, and students and teacher cooperatively deciding on solutions to the problem. Rules, like other concepts, are learned through continuous examples of what is an appropriate response to a rule and what is not appropriate. The younger the child, the more examples of appropriate and inappropriate behavior are necessary to develop and communicate a rule. Generally, rules should be

Stages of Development Relative to Learning Environment in Gymnasium

Stage One: Kindergarten through Grades 2, 3

Students are compliant and want mostly to please adults. They need to be socialized into "going-to-school roles." They require a great deal of formal instruction in rules, procedures, and expectations in the gymnasium.

Stage Two: Grades 2, 3 through Grades 5, 6

Most students still want to obey and cooperate with the teacher. Less time needs to be spent in management.

Stage Three: Grades 5, 6 through Grades 9, 10

Peer group relationships become extremely important. Students tend to question authority and seek ways to get attention through humorous, disruptive remarks and horseplay. The management task becomes one of motivating and controlling students to do what they know they should be doing. Working with individual students becomes more important.

Stage Four: After Grades 9, 10

A return to an academic orientation toward school usually develops. Student social development and emotional development are more stable. Management generally takes less time.

Source: J. Brophy and C. Evertson, "Context Variables in Teaching" in *Educational Psychologist,* 12:310–316, 1978.

"bad" students as though students are born with these characteristics. As a teacher you will need to think about teaching student behavior in your classes in much the same way as you will consider teaching your students a new motor skill. Students are starting at different points, and taking a student from one level to another requires that you plan experiences at an appropriate level. It would be foolish to expect students who have difficulty working independently in learning tasks without a great deal of supervision to work independently with a small group in an unstructured learning activity. It is not that the goal is not worthwhile; it is that the teacher must first teach students to become more independent of teacher supervision if they do not already have those skills. The teacher needs a progression to teach independent working skills and productive group skills.

Positive is more effective than negative. Positive approaches to engaging students and maintaining their cooperation are more effective than negative ones. Teachers should not be in adversarial roles with students and spend class time primarily as police trying to catch students misbehaving. Positive environments are more easily established and maintained when teachers teach expectations and the reasons for rules and expectations in advance and address problems constructively and cooperatively with students. Maintaining a positive approach to behavior and management is easier if teachers view inappropriate behavior as they would an incorrect answer to an academic question or incorrect form in a motor skill.

Teachers should not see inappropriate behavior as a personally threatening student response. Teachers should be willing to understand and work with students who have special problems and, in general, should have respect for the individuality of each of their students. Teachers can be caring and concerned and still have high expectations for student behavior and respond in a firm manner. Effective managers rely on instruction and persuasion rather than power and assertion (Brophy, 1983).

EXAMPLE: Elwardo had great expectations for his beginning year of teaching. The first couple of weeks, students did everything he asked and things went very well. Then students started to test him. Elwardo asked a student, in a nice manner, not to do something. Elwardo turned and walked away from the student and out of the corner of his eye watched the student do exactly what he had just asked the student not to do. Elwardo "saw red" and felt personally threatened by the student's behavior. Before he turned around, however, he took a deep breath and decided that he was going to handle the matter in a firm professional manner and not respond in a manner that would communicate to the student that he was personally threatened.

Know what you expect. Before you can institute a management system, you must decide what constitutes order and engagement and what constitutes inappropriate behavior for both management and content tasks. This is often the most important part of establishing control in a class and the most often neglected. Because beginning teachers find it difficult to deal in advance with expectations for student behavior, they often are *inconsistent* in what they expect from students and have to regain control after losing it. *Consistency is a critical aspect of good management, and you cannot be consistent unless you have decided ahead of time what your expectations are for student behavior.* Observing good teachers and the expectations they have for student behavior can help you make decisions about what you want in your classes. After you have decided what you expect, you can decide how to get there.

Decide what your ultimate goal is for student behavior. Students may not be ready for many of the ideas you may have, but you should have a long-term goal. Where would you like your students to be at the end of the year? At the end of two years? Are you willing to take the time to teach students these behaviors? Do you think the goals for students (self-direction and control) are important enough?

Share with students ahead of time your expectations for behavior. Although class procedures and rules can help in establishing a baseline

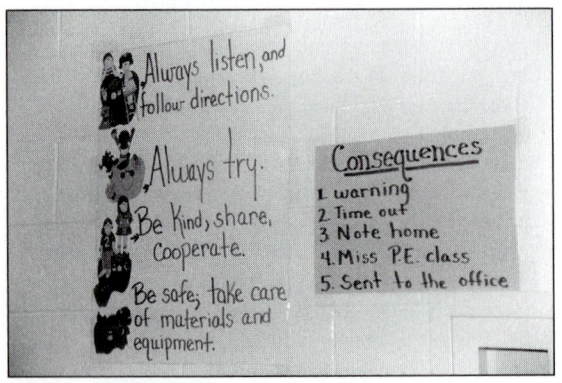

Teachers should share expectations for behavior with students ahead of time.

of appropriate behavior, they cannot prepare you or students for all events that take place in your classes. *Students should not learn what is expected by doing it "wrong."* Unfortunately, because teachers have not made their expectations clear to students in advance, students often learn what the teacher really expects only by engaging in inappropriate behavior. A primary characteristic of a good management system is that expectations are made clear ahead of time—not after students have misbehaved.

Strive to help students internalize appropriate behavior. Students will internalize appropriate behavior more if they are helped to understand why particular responses are appropriate. Teachers want students to choose to behave in appropriate ways, not because there will be negative consequences if they do not, but because the students value appropriate behavior. Students can be helped to value appropriate behavior and internalize expectations if they are given reasons why particular behaviors are appropriate and others are not and if they participate in the decisions to establish public expectations for behavior.

EXAMPLES: "If everyone calls out at one time, no one will be able to hear anyone."
"How can we have everyone working at one time without worrying about getting hit with a ball?"
"Why do you think I am concerned with what I see?"

Expectations for appropriate engagement in learning experiences must also be established. Most often teachers have taken the time to teach students rules and procedures for organizational tasks, such as taking out equipment, dressing for activity, lining up, and taking attendance, but they have failed to teach students what is expected in terms of participation in learning tasks. Teaching rules for social participation and expectations for participation in learning experiences reduces inappropriate behavior in the content of your lesson. What is expected when practicing by yourself? How should you work with a partner or small group? What should you do if your ball moves into another person's practice area? What does it really mean to practice a skill to try and get better at it? What do you do if you need help? These ideas are critical to the quality of the learning experience and must be considered by teachers and taught and reinforced to students.

Management is an ongoing process. Management goals are really never achieved. Once the teacher has established a learning environment characterized by control, he or she must maintain it. Once the teacher establishes a learning environment with minimal levels of student control, he or she should be working toward helping students to greater and greater levels of self-control.

■ STRATEGIES FOR DEVELOPING STUDENT SELF-CONTROL AND RESPONSIBILITY

Most of this chapter to this point has addressed minimal expectations for control in the physical education class. Establishing basic routines and rules will help classes run smoother and will help make the physical education class a positive and productive learning experience. Students cannot learn unless teachers have been able to elicit the cooperation of students to this minimal level. The role of the teacher in this context is to teach and persuade students to comply with procedures and class rules that have been developed cooperatively or established solely by the teacher. The need for control and compliance should in no way be underestimated. It is a first step to creating an environment where more important types of learning can take place.

Physical education settings have a great deal of potential to contribute to student attitudes about themselves, others, and the interdependent world in which they live. The affective goals that are part of the national standards for physical education (see chapter 1, p. 3) clearly define values and attitudes toward self, others, and the content of physical education that are affective in their orientation. The recent emphasis on conflict resolution and teaching character confirms the importance of the affective goals of physical education. The nature of what we teach and how we teach it is a laboratory of important life skills. The active, social nature of the physical education environment offers the educator a powerful setting for teaching human values and relationships and for helping young people find a place and meaning in their world.

The idea of going beyond mere compliance in our classes necessitates an understanding of what is minimal and what is the desired direction. Minimal levels of control that permit instruction to take place in the gymnasium require primarily that students do what the teacher says. This critical idea is essential for student learning to take place but provides the students little they can take with them to real-life settings and limits the types of learning experiences the teacher can provide.

Children today, as well as adults, have an unprecedented amount of freedom and choice in their lives. They will need to learn how to choose what they do and what is important to them based on a set of developing values that will help them lead happy, productive, and meaningful lives. Students will eventually leave the control of the teacher and other people who control their lives. Making the transition from external to internal control of behavior must begin in school. Unfortunately, many kindergarten students have more opportunity to practice and exercise self-control than many high school students.

Many physical education teachers assume that their classes are going well if students do not give them any trouble and comply with the "rules." To aspire to such a minimal level of personal and social responsibility is to disregard the great potential of our field to move students to much higher levels of functioning. To move students to higher levels of functioning, teachers must be willing to aspire to more than control. They must be willing to take time to teach students how to function at higher levels and to share their power and control. You may encounter students who are operating with no control. What is important is that you do not leave them there.

There are many approaches for developing values and higher-level behaviors with students. The effective teacher will use different strategies for different purposes and different contexts. Helping students to become more self-directed, responsible, and caring people takes time and will initially cut down on content time in your classes. In the long run, however, a learning environment will be established that will support learning the objectives you have for motor skill learning and fitness and will make a valuable contribution to developing a physically active lifestyle. When your students become more self-directed in your classes, you not only will save time, but will open up many opportunities to work with students in ways not possible without self-management skills. Each of the strategies described in the following discussion is based on certain assumptions about human behavior and what controls it.

Hellison's Levels of Responsibility

Don Hellison (2003) described five developmental levels en route to acquiring values and a lifestyle that would help students make wise choices and lead them to a personally satisfying lifestyle. These developmental stages of responsibility are described in box 6.3. The manner in which Hellison described each stage is not as important as the implications of what is happening from the zero level of control to the more-advanced stages. The first four stages described by Hellison trace development from behavior that shows no control to behavior that accepts a more self-directed sense of responsibility for behavior and decisions. The fourth level takes the student beyond the self to feeling some sense of responsibility for others, and the fifth level talks about transfer of behavior to situations outside the gymnasium.

Hellison's work describes a system of teaching strategies designed to move students from lower to higher levels of responsibility. Teaching strategies are designed to create an awareness of appropriate behavior and goals, provide students with opportunities to reflect on their behavior in relation to behavior goals, provide students opportunities to set personal goals for behavior change, establish consequences for both positive and negative behavior to encourage positive growth, include students in group processes designed to share teacher "power," and help teachers to interact with students in growth-producing ways. In Hellison's work these strategies can be used to move students to higher levels of responsibility. Teachers looking for good concrete ways to develop a systematic way to help move students to higher levels of responsibility are encouraged to consult Hellison's original work.

BOX 6·3

Hellison's Developmental Levels

Level 0: Irresponsibility

Characteristics: Unmotivated; undisciplined; denies personal responsibility; verbally or physically abusive of others; interrupts; off task on a continuous basis; needs constant supervision

Level I: Self-control

Characteristics: Not highly engaged in the lesson, but not disruptive; does not need constant supervision; goes through the motions of compliance

Level II: Involvement

Characteristics: Demonstrates self-control and an enthusiasm for the subject matter; willing to try new things and has a personal definition of success

Level III: Self-responsibility

Characteristics: Ability to work without direct supervision; can identify own needs and interests and is independent in his or her pursuit of them

Level IV: Caring

Characteristics: Cooperative, supportive, and caring about others; willing to help others

Level V: Outside the gym

Characteristics: Transfers responsible behavior to life settings outside the gym

Adapted by permission from D. Hellison, 2003, *Teaching Responsibility Through Physical Activity* (Champaign, IL: Human Kinetics Publishers), pp. 10–21.

Behavior Modification

Strategies related to behavior modification have their roots in behavioral psychology. Behaviorists believe that human behavior is primarily the result of conditions and that if the conditions can be changed, the behavior can be changed. Although it is impossible to be aware of the specific behavior of all their students, teachers can look primarily for reasons students are responding the way they are that possibly can be changed in the instructional environment. The key to a behavioral approach to changing behavior is the idea of *reinforcement*. A major assumption of **behaviorism** is that people respond in certain ways because they are reinforced by those responses. The job of the teacher is essentially to reward students for responding in positive ways and to not reward students for responding in ways that are not positive behaviors. Box 6.4 describes

consequences that both reward and deter behavior as is appropriate. These ideas are organized on a continuum related to the amount of effort and preparation the teacher must use in their implementation. If students do not respond to the ideas that require little preparation and attention, then the teacher must move up the continuum to be effective in changing behavior.

Teachers who use behaviorism are specific about what is appropriate behavior and take time to help

---

BOX 6·4

Consequences for Rewards and Deterrents

Consequences that function as rewards

Simple consequences requiring little preparation and effort

Giving feedback (i.e., telling students or a class what is specifically liked about their work or behavior)
Giving a smile, a thumbs-up, or a wink
Giving applause
Giving a pat on the back
Allowing student to line up first to leave class
Allowing student to serve as a teacher's aide

Consequences requiring some preparation and effort

Giving an individual award certificate
Awarding a happy face or a star
Putting student on a superstar list on the bulletin board
Sending a positive note to parents
Allowing student to use special equipment during free time
Allowing a time for special games or free play
Arranging a visit from a local coach
Allowing best class or squad to have special time in the gym before or after school or at lunch
Awarding special prizes (e.g., a balloon, a ball, jacks, a rope, or a Frisbee)

Consequences requiring extensive preparation and effort (use with caution)

Awarding tokens that students can collect and "cash in" for privileges
Arranging a trip to see a local game or to a dance

Consequences that deter students from undesirable Behavior

Simple consequences requiring little preparation and effort

Ordering student to desist (i.e., telling student to stop the behavior)
Having student state the rule being broken
Telling student the expected behavior
Maintaining eye contact until the behavior stops
Moving nearer to the student
Giving students a chance to choose a place to work where they will not be tempted to misbehave
Ordering a time-out (i.e., forbidding student from participating for a designated time)
Making student be last in taking a turn

Consequences requiring some preparation and effort

Having a conference with the student
Isolating student in a hall or away from class
Sending a negative note to parents
Calling parents
Keeping student after school
Denying student a privilege
Assigning student detention

Consequences requiring extensive preparation and effort (use with caution)

Sending student on a trip to the principal's office
Denying student a special class treat such as an assembly or a field trip
Establishing a behavior contract
Using a behavior modification program
Removing student from class

students clearly understand the meaning of what that behavior might be. Lower-level expectations usually take the form of rules or stated teacher objectives for student behavior that are taught, posted, and shared. Objectives for more complex and higher-order behaviors are shared explicitly and taught to students as the students are ready.

Suggestions for using behavioral techniques

Define the behavior explicitly. Before you attempt to teach students to behave in any particular way, make a list of what you consider appropriate behavior and inappropriate behavior. The more important the behavior, the more complex it is likely to be and the more important it is that you can give enough examples to get the message across. Do not make your expectations trivial, but make the examples of those expectations specific. Know why the behavior is important and share this with students. The example that follows was selected to demonstrate how a complex behavior can be taught using behavioral principles.

> EXAMPLE: You want students to be supportive of others in the class. You make a list of appropriate and inappropriate responses. Some of the behaviors you list are as follows:

Appropriate

Willing to work with all students in the class

When another student tries hard but still makes a mistake or has difficulty, encourages that person for his or her efforts, even if that student is an opponent in a game situation

Catches another person's ball when it comes into own space and hands it to that person

Inappropriate

Complains when has to work with a girl, a boy, a student who is unskilled, or any student who might be considered by others as "undesirable"

Ridicules, laughs at, or otherwise makes another feel inferior about his or her effort

Kicks another person's ball when it comes into own space

Take time to teach and communicate the behavior. Although rules and procedures can be easily communicated by the teacher or designed by a class without much effort, important and complex behaviors are probably best shared in an interactive discussion with students. The teacher can help students to know the concept of the behavior by the following:

- Developing consensus for the importance of the behavior
- Describing situations where students have choices of how to respond and are helped to understand what the significance of the choices might be
- Developing enough examples of both appropriate examples of the behavior and inappropriate responses

In some cases it may be necessary to emphasize what you are trying to teach by having students practice the behavior or role-play situations where the choice of response is most likely to occur.

> EXAMPLES: "Johnny, I want you to help me out here. Sally's ball has rolled into your space. Show me what you think you might do to help Sally."
>
> "Freddie is on your team and has just served the ball into the net. Every time Freddie serves the ball, it goes into the net. How do you think players on Freddie's team should react to Freddie? Who would like to pretend to be Freddie? Who would like to react to Freddie?"

Reinforce positive responses. When teachers are working on a behavior, they can reinforce that behavior by calling attention to the behavior either publicly or privately. Because young primary children are still at a stage in which adult approval is important, public praise is often helpful. However, it may not be reinforcing to have the teacher praise older students, and alternative ways to communicate your support may need to be sought. Initially, immediate and frequent praise helps to define the behavior and make clear the expectations. The teacher should gradually withdraw both the immediacy and frequency of praise.

You can also reinforce positive responses immediately when they are very low frequency behaviors by stopping the class and sharing with the class that you have seen an appropriate response (like the kind of behavior we have been talking about). You can also privately reinforce a behavior with a student. Or you can talk about what you have seen at the end of class.

In cases where teachers are working with students operating at low levels of control, many teachers resort to more tangible rewards as reinforcers other than teacher praise. For example, placing student names on a board who were observed behaving appropriately, setting up a system of points or rewards, or using free time or some other special arrangement as a reinforcer does work to initially create compliance and a heightened awareness of appropriate behavior. The teacher's goal is to help students internalize appropriate behavior and gain a sense of self-control. The teacher must adopt a long-term plan for removing the external reinforcers he or she uses to create compliance. Continued and extensive use of external rewards makes the transition to self-control more difficult. External rewards should be used when necessary, but they should be gradually withdrawn.

Teachers should encourage reflective behavior in students.

Ignore inappropriate behavior in some cases if it is not disruptive to others. Some children behave inappropriately so that they can get the attention of the teacher or other students. If you determine that students are doing this, it is appropriate to ignore their inappropriate behavior and reward their appropriate behavior as long as the inappropriate behavior is not disruptive to others and as long as the behavior does not escalate to higher levels of disruptiveness to get your attention.

Exhibit appropriate behavior yourself. Students cannot be expected to behave in particular ways unless the teacher also behaves in those ways. Students learn a great deal more from what you do than from what you say. Teachers have a responsibility to act as an adult and interact with others in positive and professional ways at all times.

Develop reflective skills on the part of learners. Ask students to evaluate their own behavior and responses either in writing or verbally at the end of a class or week.

> EXAMPLE: "Write down in your journal today one thing you did that showed support for another person in the class and one task you worked on with a great effort today."

One of the problems with behavioral orientations to management and student discipline is that although behavioral methods are effective in producing student compliance and obedience, they are often used in a way that does not help the student to internalize appropriate behavior, develop self-discipline, or learn to be a risk taker. Student compliance is not a sufficient goal for educational programs that seek to develop self-discipline. Part of the problem is how behavioral approaches have been used, and part of the problem is the goal to which teachers aspire.

It has been difficult for behavioral orientations to management to help students make the transition from teacher control to student control. The overuse of external rewards and failure to withdraw them; a lack of flexibility in rules, regulations, and expected behavior for changes in context; and a complacency on the part of teachers to be content with what is called in physical education "the busy-happy-good" syndrome (Placek, 1983) have all contributed to ineffective management systems.

Authoritative Orientations to Management

In response to the poor management of the schools, McCaslin and Good (1992) suggest that teachers should think in terms of an **authoritative management system,** the goal of which is self-discipline. Authoritarian management is discussed in the next section, not as a total management system but as a perspective on making management appropriate for the situation and changing needs of students toward self-discipline. The following ideas are inherent in establishing an authoritative orientation to management.

Teachers should take a firm but flexible perspective on management. Authoritative managers have clear expectations for students, but these expectations remain flexible. This means that the rules, procedures, and expectations are considered flexible and context specific. Expectations change from one group of students to another, one content area to another, one learning experience to another, and one student to another.

Teachers should take time to teach students self-directed behavior. Authoritative managers discuss with students why particular behaviors are important and how students might meet the expectations teachers have for them. Internal control and self-discipline are valued, and it is made clear that they are valued.

Teacher control is released as students are ready to accept more responsibility for own behavior. One of the problems with how behavioral systems have been implemented is that rules, procedures, and expectations for behavior do not change. Teachers tend to maintain the same level of expectations for students, and for the most part, in physical education this level of expectation has been low in terms of students' responsibility for their own behavior. Sixth graders should be capable of more independent behavior than first graders, and tenth graders should be capable of more independent behavior than sixth graders. The focus of authoritative discipline is on transferring the responsibility for behavior to students as students are ready. As students are ready to handle more of the responsibility for their behavior and are ready to be put in situations that demand more self-responsibility, the teacher's management system should change with the emerging capabilities of students. Rigid, highly specific gymnasium rules are not flexible enough to encourage students with different abilities to be more responsible.

Group Process Strategies for Developing Self-Direction

In most classes, teachers find that group process strategies are effective ways of working with groups of learners to establish higher expectations for behavior and to solve problems that occur in relation to behavior. Group process strategies stress the group and social context of the school environment. Some of the basic strategies used in this approach follow.

Involve students in decision making. Using this strategy means that many rules and procedures, as well as more content-oriented decisions, can be made with student input. The teacher poses a problem (even if it is only a problem for the teacher) that needs a rule or procedure, and the students help establish the rules or procedures. Using this strategy well means that the teacher must be willing to take the time to work through solutions with students. It means that you may want to let students try solutions you feel may not work and then let them evaluate and reformulate their solutions. When students have made decisions regarding rules, it is still necessary for teachers to reinforce those rules and remind students of their decisions.

Students are more likely to behave in ways consistent with rules, procedures, and goals if they have had a part in designing them. However, the teacher must be willing to take the time to bring problems back to the students when compliance is not acceptable.

Resolve conflicts through discussion. When conflicts arise, teachers stop what they are doing and make students aware that there is a problem. They then lead a discussion with students on how to resolve the conflict. The goals of the discussion are to help students gain a sense of responsibility for their behavior and to help them recognize their responsibility toward others and to themselves.

Use role playing to communicate concepts. Role playing was previously discussed as a strategy in behavioral modification It is used here in a similar way—to help students come to know a desired behavior in a meaningful way. Role playing involves allowing students to put themselves in the position of another person and act out that role in a situation. The goal of role playing is to help students see other perspectives on a problem. Usually the teacher structures the role-playing situation by framing the problem or conflict and describing how people representing each of the parts feel about the problem. Potential learning in role playing is increased if the teacher makes explicit what is happening in the acting out and summarizes the lesson to be learned.

Understanding and accepting. Understanding why a student may be acting inappropriately is important. However, do not confuse understanding with accepting. You can understand why a student may be behaving in a particular way but you do not have to accept it and, in fact, should not.

Conflict Resolution

One approach to helping students find appropriate ways of behaving in group settings is conflict resolution (Johnson & Johnson, 1995). Although conflict resolution strategies have grown primarily out of efforts to deal with violence in the schools, they are used as preventative programs to change schools from environments in which the role of the teacher and school is primarily that of the authority handing out punishments and rewards to students to places where students learn self-regulation and cooperation skills. A major thrust of these programs is to organize a great deal of the instruction in cooperative learning groups of students under the assumption that student conflict and misbehavior arise primarily out of competitive learning environments. Cooperative learning is discussed in detail as a teaching strategy in chapter 8.

In schools that adapt conflict resolution programs, students are taught strategies for dealing with conflicts that arise between them. In some cases individual students are selected and trained as negotiators. The role of the negotiator is to

- describe and make clear the *positions* and *feelings* of each party in the conflict;
- help students in conflict understand the perspective of the other person;
- invent mutually beneficial options for resolving the conflict; and,
- help students in conflict come to a "wise" agreement.

In many cases the teacher will be the negotiator of conflict and is expected to help students resolve conflicts that arise between students as well as conflicts that arise between the teacher and the student. The resolution should be presented in a manner that leads the student through the process just described. Only if the role of the negotiator fails does the teacher or another student become the arbitrator who makes the final decision in the conflict.

■ DISCIPLINE: WHAT TO DO IF IT DOES NOT WORK

Discipline is what you do when, despite your best efforts, students do not cooperate and choose to behave in inappropriate ways. Not all students will choose to cooperate when you have been positive about

Guidelines to Prevent Discipline Problems

- Establish an effective management system.
- Have a positive attitude toward all students.
- Share your expectations clearly and in advance.
- Involve students in rules and procedures.
- Have an appropriate and challenging curriculum.
- Display enthusiasm toward what you are teaching.

establishing the learning environment you desire, and many of these students will have to be treated by the teacher on an individual basis. Not all students will respond to any one management or discipline system, nor will all students respond in the same way to your efforts at discipline. Teachers will have fewer discipline problems if they follow the guidelines presented in box 6.5, but most teachers will have to deal with the individual problems of students who exhibit inappropriate behavior and sometimes disruptive and problem behavior.

Deterring Problems Before They Become Problems

If the teacher has made expectations clear to students and has provided enough structure and reasonable expectations for behavior, most infractions of rules or behavior expectations will be short term and easily handled with some simple techniques. This is where Kounin's (1970) ideas of *withitness* (the ability to be aware at all times of what is going on regardless of what you are doing) and *overlappingness* (the ability to do many things at one time and do them well) become important. Teachers must work to prevent problems before they become major discipline problems.

Maintaining eye contact. Generally, if the teacher catches a student behaving inappropriately and briefly maintains eye contact with that student, the student will eventually stop the behavior. Sometimes it is necessary for the teacher to stop what he or she is doing and saying to emphasize the point.

Proximity control. When teachers use **proximity control,** they move physically closer to the student to make known that they are aware that inappropriate behavior is taking place. They do not have to say anything, and usually students will stop the inappropriate behavior.

Asking students to stop what they are doing. This is the most fundamental and sometimes forgotten technique a teacher has to eliminate inappropriate behavior. It is called a *desist*. Desists work only if they are not overused. If a teacher has to continually remind the same student or if a class of students is behaving inappropriately, desists are *not working* and it is time to move on to other techniques that address the issue more seriously. When possible, desists should be private communications with the student, although it is not always possible to do this.

Clarifying appropriate behavior. Instead of just asking students to stop misbehaving, sometimes it is helpful to clarify for students what they should be doing. This focuses the student on appropriate rather than inappropriate responses. Two examples of teacher clarification of appropriate behavior follow.

EXAMPLES: "How are we supposed to get the equipment out?"
  "What is good partner behavior?"

Removing the student physically from the problem. If a student is having difficulty behaving appropriately because of the equipment or working close to an area that presents problems (e.g., water fountains, baskets, other equipment) or if he or she is close to other students who encourage misbehavior, the teacher can ask the student to work in another location or assign him or her to a different partner or group.

Continued Inappropriate Behavior

Generally speaking, if the techniques just discussed do not eliminate inappropriate behavior for more than a short time, the teacher must increase the level of response. The following ideas are useful.

Widespread class misbehavior. If you find that more than one or two students are engaging in inappropriate behavior, working with individual children may not be appropriate. You will need to stop the class and address the problem specifically. Consider the following teacher/student interaction:

"Would everyone come in here for a minute. I don't know what the problem is today, but for some reason we are having trouble attending to what we are supposed to be doing. There must be some kind of a crazy bug going around or something. Who can tell me why you think I am having trouble with what is going on?

"What is it that we are supposed to be doing?

"Let's go back to work and see if we can try this again."

In the conversation, the teacher is calling attention to the problem, making it clear that what has occurred is inappropriate, and focusing the students on what they should be doing. The important issue is that at this level the approach is still positive. It is more like a class desist and will normally eliminate most problems. If the problems continue, the teacher may need to continue with the following remarks:

"Some of you are obviously not ready to work today. Let's just sit here for a minute. When you think you are ready to continue and work appropriately, stand up and begin. If you are not, you may sit here until you are ready. If you go out to work and you are still having problems, I may need to sit you over on the side to think about what you should be doing."

Time-out. Time-out is a useful technique to handle disruptive and inappropriate behavior for young children and for students who want to participate in class. It is not appropriate for students who would rather not be participating, because it reinforces inappropriate behavior for these students.

The teacher who uses time-out asks a student to sit out of activity in a designated area. Sometimes teachers ask students to sit out for a designated time, for example, five minutes. Sometimes, teachers may say, "When you think you are ready to participate again, come tell me." Other times the teacher will leave students in time-out until the teacher comes and tells them they can rejoin the activity. Time-out works best if students are not left the entire period. For older students, a consequence at this level may be to take away a privilege like a choice of activity, but more effectively to make arrangements to see the student after class or school, or use the school discipline system to "write a student up" for misbehavior.

Negotiation/confrontation. When teachers use negotiation/confrontation to solve problems either between themselves and students or between students, they are attempting to get students to accept responsibility for their behavior and to design a plan of action to improve their behavior. It is important when using this strategy to help the students recognize and own the behavior and then to work through a plan of action to improve the behavior. A description of a simple interaction of this type follows:

Teacher: "What do you think is the problem here?"
Student: "We were hitting balls over the fence."
Teacher: "Why do you think we don't want balls over the fence?"
Student: "Because we waste time going to get them."
Teacher: "How are we going to change what you are doing?"
Student: "We are not going to hit the balls over the fence anymore."

When water breaks become a problem during class, structure may be necessary.

Teacher: "What do you think I should do if it happens again?"

Student: "Not let us use the balls."

Handling Students Who Continually Misbehave

Most schools have discipline programs in place that clearly define what a teacher should do when faced with continued inappropriate behavior. The physical education teacher should be a part of establishing that discipline program and should respond to student misbehavior in a manner consistent with that policy. Most of these programs are designed so that the consequences for misbehavior continuously increase as the level of the misbehavior or the consistency of the misbehavior increases.

Students who misbehave on a continuous basis in your class are most likely doing the same in other classes in the school. The most effective solutions to continuous misbehavior problems are those reached with the cooperation of all teachers in the school so that the student is confronted with consistent expectations and responses. Individual students who continually misbehave in class are not easily handled without one-on-one attention of the teacher. Initially you should focus on this student and get a sense of what exactly the student is doing during class and under what conditions.

Generally, you should single this student out for extra positive attention to show him or her that you care, but do not reinforce misbehavior. Doing this during class time is sometimes difficult because the rest of the class is then left on their own. Individual conferences are best held when the teacher has time either before or after class or before or after school. If misbehavior continues, you will have to begin to plan on spending time with this student individually and prepare consequences that require more effort on your part. Box 6.4 (p. 119) describes increasing levels of consequences for student misbehavior. At the far end of the scale are those interventions that require a great deal of teacher involvement in the individual case. Teachers may need to become involved at these levels to effectively change student behavior.

Several ideas should be considered when dealing with individual behavior problems.

- *What you do with the group must not affect the child negatively, and, conversely, what you do for the child must not affect the group negatively.* This means that you cannot allow the individual student to disrupt the learning experiences of the rest of the students in your class. You must act. Second, you should not for the sake of the rest of the class respond to individual students in a way that can harm them (e.g., using students for a negative example).

- *Try to understand the cause of the behavior.* Students usually misbehave because of either personal or social adjustment problems they are having. Sometimes they misbehave because they are seeking attention, control, or power or because they have low self-esteem. There may be ways that you can help the student meet his or her needs in this area in positive, constructive ways. These kinds of solutions are usually long term and may not solve the immediate need for behavior change. Examples are (1) giving students the attention they need for positive behavior and (2) putting them in charge of something for the class or something they can do outside of class.

- *Respond negatively to the behavior, not the person.* One of the most useful ideas that teachers should maintain when dealing with inappropriate behavior is to separate their response to the misbehavior from their response to the person misbehaving. Teachers should maintain a concerned, caring attitude toward students and approach misbehavior positively. This does not mean that teachers should not be firm about the expectations for changing behavior.

EXAMPLE: You did not come into class ready to work today and that was a problem for me and your classmates. I know you can do better. Next class I want to see a real change. I want to see you before class so we can make sure we are both tuned in to what that means.

- *Focus interactions with students on a resolution of the problem.* For emotionally charged problems with students, the teacher should initially be an active listener. You should allow the student to vent anger if necessary, help him or her to understand where the anger may be coming from, and then begin to focus the student on defining the problem and coming up with solutions to the problem. You should explore possible solutions and come to some agreement on implementation of those solutions. Follow up on whether those solutions are working, and revise the plan if necessary.

- *If less formal methods of changing behavior do not work, explore the idea of contingency contracts with students.* If you have talked with students and set goals for changing behavior, only to learn that students are not complying with expectations for behavior change, you may have to begin more formal procedures for changing behavior. Contingency contracts are one such technique. Contingency contracts set goals for student behavior that are achievable (one step at a time) and reward students extrinsically for demonstrating that they have reached their goals. Rewards can be something as simple as a star; a small token; candy; time to do special things in class; and, in general, anything that is positively reinforcing for a particular individual. The teacher establishes a contract with the student and specifies what the student must do to meet the goals set for a particular period. At the conclusion of the period, the student is rewarded for meeting the goal and a new goal is established that leads the student closer to the desired behavior. Usually rewards will be sufficient to change behavior. If not, the teacher may want to build into the contract negative consequences for not meeting the goals, such as having to spend time after school or being denied a privilege. Monitoring of the contract should be done for each class and can be done by the student through self-evaluation or done initially by the teacher and later by the student. The long-term goal of contingency contracting should be to bring the student to self-directed behavior. To do this, the periods for rewards and the expectations for rewards will increase until the student is responding appropriately without the rewards. Box 6.6 presents some guidelines for discipline.

B O X   6 · 6

Some Dos and Don'ts of Discipline

Do

Use student names
Expect students to behave
Ask yourself why
Be firm and consistent

Don't

Publicly reprimand
Downgrade students
Engage in confrontation
Give threats

Involving others in your efforts with problem students. If you have done all that you can with many of the ideas just expressed, it may be necessary to enlist the help of others.

Involving parents. Schools usually have policies for calling parents about behavior problems in class. You will need to know what these policies are before enlisting the help of parents. Most parents are concerned about their child's progress and behavior in your class. If you call them, you should clearly explain what the problem is and what you are doing about it. What you do not want is for the parents to overreact to the child's problem or to take a defensive posture toward the problem; you want to have them support you in your efforts by communicating their concern to the student and maintaining communication with the parents.

Involving the principal. Most schools have policies regarding teachers sending students to the office or a designated place when they present behavior problems the teacher cannot handle within the class. Teachers should use the threat of the principal or detention center as a last resort, only when they cannot handle the problems themselves. Many secondary schools have behavior management systems that include "writing students up" and detention arrangements. Unfortunately, the overuse of these systems often results in increased school misbehavior. School administrators are primarily responsible for making decisions about what to do with students who continuously misbehave in all their classes. Punishment, detention, suspension, and involvement of school counselors are alternatives.

SUMMARY

1. Good management skills are essential for good teaching.
2. Content and management are interdependent systems of instruction.
3. The objective of a good management system is a high level of engagement in what the student is supposed to be doing.
4. Teachers must teach students what is expected and then maintain the environment they establish.
5. Routines are events that occur frequently in the teaching-learning environment that are handled in a similar manner.
6. Class rules should be few in number, taught as concepts, and reinforced consistently.
7. Behavior modification primarily uses clear expectations and reinforcement to establish student control.
8. Authoritative discipline establishes student understanding of appropriate behavior and remains firm but flexible to teach students self-direction.
9. Group process strategies stress the group and social context of the school environment and focus on involving students as a group in decision making.
10. The best approach to discipline is a preventive one.
11. Teachers should attempt to solve minor discipline problems before they become major ones.
12. If despite the teacher's best efforts, a student does not choose to cooperate, the teacher should solicit the help of others within the school.
13. Continued discipline problems require more involvement and more preparation to change student behavior on an individual basis.

CHECKING YOUR UNDERSTANDING

1. What is meant by the idea that instruction and management are part of an interdependent ecological system?
2. What is the major purpose of a management system?
3. List five key ideas important to establishing a management system.
4. Describe how you would establish a routine for taking attendance with high school students.
5. How are self-management skills developed? How would you begin to develop self-management skills for the attendance-taking routine you established in the preceding question?
6. Describe the similarities and differences among behavioral modification, authoritative discipline, and group process orientations to developing student control.
7. List five things you can do to prevent small incidences of misbehavior from becoming large ones.
8. What should you do with a student who, despite your best efforts, is disruptive on a continuous basis and chooses not to cooperate?

REFERENCES

Brophy, J. E. (1983). Classroom organization and management. *Elementary School Journal, 83*(4), 265–286.

Brophy, J., & Evertson, C. (1978). Context variables in teaching. *Educational Psychology, 12,* 310–316.

Doyle, W. (1984). Classroom organization and management. In M. Wittrock (Ed.), *Handbook of research on teaching* (3rd ed.). New York: Macmillan.

Hellison, D. (2003). *Teaching responsibility through physical activity.* Champaign, IL: Human Kinetics.

Johnson, D., & Johnson, R. (1995). *Reducing school violence through conflict resolution.* Alexandria, VA: ASCD.

Kounin, J. (1970). *Discipline and group management in classrooms.* New York: Holt, Rinehart & Winston.

McCaslin, M., & Good, T. (1992). Compliant cognition: The misalliance of management and instructional goals in current school reform. *Educational Researcher, 21,* 3.

Placek, J. (1983). Conceptions of success in teaching: Busy, happy, and good? In T. Templin & J. Olson (Eds.). *Teaching in physical education.* Champaign, IL: Human Kinetics.

SUGGESTED READINGS

Anderson, A. (2002). Engaging student learning in physical education. *Journal of Physical Education, Recreation and Dance, 73*(7), 35–39.

Beighle, A., & Pangrazi R. (2002). The seven habits of highly effective physical education teachers. *Teaching Elementary Physical Education, 13*(4), 6–9.

Conkle, T. (1999). Roll-call with a purpose. *Journal of Physical Education, Recreation and Dance, 70*(6), 14–15.

Curwin, R., & Mendler, A. (1988). *Discipline with dignity.* Alexandria, VA: ASCD.

Du Bois, S. (2002). Lessons in leadership: Empower the children. *Teaching Elementary Physical Education, 13*(1), 27–29.

Henderson, H., French, R., Fritsch, R., & Lerner, B. (2000). Time-out and over-correction: A comparison of their application in physical education. *Journal of Physical Education, Recreation and Dance, 71*(3), 31–35.

Landy, G. (2003). Signals—The management tools of physical education. *Teaching Elementary Physical Education, 14*(1), 28–29.

Lynn, S. (1994). Create an effective learning environment. *Strategies, 7*(4), 14–17.

Markos, N., & Boye, A. (1999). What is your class management IQ? *Strategies, 12*(6), 20–22.

Spickelmeir, D., Sharpe, T., Deible, C., Golden, C., & Kruger, B. (1995). Use positive discipline for middle school students. *Strategies, 8*(8), 5–8.

Townsend, S., & Rairigh, R. (2001). Behavior assessment: A sports tracking system. *Teaching Elementary Physical Education, 12*(5), 25–29.

Willis, C. (1995). Creative dance education—establishing a positive learning environment. *Journal of Physical Education, Recreation and Dance, 66*(6), 16–20.

7

Teacher Functions During Activity

O V E R V I E W

Teachers can perform many functions while students are engaged in a movement task. Some of these functions contribute directly to lesson objectives, some make only an indirect contribution to lesson objectives, and others make no contribution to lesson objectives. Effective teachers are active teachers who are actively engaged in promoting learning. Active teachers minimize the time they spend on activities that cannot contribute to lesson objectives and maximize the time they spend on those activities that can contribute to lesson objectives. This chapter describes the many different instructional functions that teachers engage in during the time students are working on the task and helps the teacher learn how to arrange them in order of priority.

Standard 4: Instructional Delivery and Management

Physical education teacher candidates use effective communication and pedagogical skills and strategies to enhance student engagement and learning.
NASPE Beginning Teaching Standards, 2008

O U T L I N E

- **I've sent the students off to practice—Now what?**
- **Setting priorities of what to do first**
- **Maintaining a safe learning environment**
- **Clarifying and reinforcing tasks for learners**
- **Maintaining a productive learning environment**

- **Observing and analyzing student responses**
  Positioning of the teacher
  Determining a plan for observing large groups
  Knowing what to look for

- **Providing feedback to learners**
  Evaluative and corrective feedback
  Congruency of feedback
  General versus specific feedback
  Negative versus positive feedback
  The target of feedback
  Timing of feedback
  Use of feedback to promote student
    understanding
- **Changing and modifying tasks for
  individuals and small groups**
  Extending the task for individuals

Designing applying/assessment task for
    individuals
Changing the task completely for individuals
Refining the task for individuals
- **Indirectly contributing behaviors**
  Attending to injured students
  Engaging in off-topic discussions
  Dealing with the personal needs of students
  Participating with students and officiating
- **Noncontributing behaviors**

■ I'VE SENT THE STUDENTS OFF TO PRACTICE—NOW WHAT?

Beginning teachers quickly acquire the skills of task presentation because that is the role of the teacher most common to our perspective on what it means to teach: Teaching means telling people what to do. Few beginning teachers give much thought to what happens after they ask learners to engage in a movement task or learning experience. This is an uncomfortable period in the instructional process for beginning teachers because what they do as teachers depends greatly on what the students do in relation to what the teachers asked them to do.

Teachers are as active during this time as they are at all other lesson times. This is the time, more than all other times, that teachers must function in many different ways. Teachers must be able to handle the many different things going on in the gymnasium while maintaining an awareness of exactly what every student is doing. Kounin (1970) called this *withitness:* the ability to be aware at all times of what is going on regardless of what you are doing. He also coined the term *overlappingness,* the ability of the teacher to do many things at one time and do them well. Effective teachers demonstrate both withitness and overlappingness. The Real World box (p. 132) illustrates the point with actual lessons.

Box 7.1 identifies some common teacher functions from the examples presented in the Real World box,

---

BOX 7·1

Common Teacher Functions During Activity

Group 1: Directly contributing behaviors

- Maintaining a safe learning environment
- Clarifying and reinforcing tasks for learners
- Observing and analyzing student responses
- Providing feedback to learners
- Changing or modifying tasks for individuals and small groups
- Maintaining a productive learning environment

Group 2: Indirectly contributing behaviors

- Participating with students and officiating
- Dealing with the personal needs of students
- Engaging in off-topic discussions
- Attending to injured students

---

as well as other lesson observations. The functions in group 1 are those related to working directly with the lesson content. These functions contribute the most to lesson objectives and student learning. The functions in group 2 are an important part of teaching but can contribute only indirectly to lesson objectives. It is important for teachers to know how to handle all of these.

This chapter discusses the teaching functions that contribute the most to student learning. These

THE REAL WORLD

Teaching: Doing Many Things at the Same Time

Example: Elementary

Ms. S meets the class of 27 first graders at the door of the all-purpose room and asks them to put their tennis shoes on if they have brought them. Tommy cannot get the knots out of his laces, so the teacher helps Tommy. Sally comes up to say that she got new tennis shoes last night and they really run fast. The class gradually gathers in the center of the room, and the teacher explains that they will be working with tossing and throwing beanbags. During the explanation of the day's activities, the classroom teacher comes into the room with two additional students, who had arrived late for school. Ms. S asks them to join the class.

Ms. S asks the students to pick up a beanbag from those scattered on the floor, to find a space in the room, and to start tossing and catching the beanbag without letting it hit the floor or going outside their own space. Ms. S picks up the extra beanbags as the students begin their work and puts them into a basket. She comments to the whole class that their work is quiet and controlled because she has heard no voices and has heard no beanbags touch the floor. She helps Mary direct her beanbag to remain in front of her and asks Kevin to reduce the level of his toss so that he can maintain better control.

Ms. S asks the class to begin tossing the beanbag to different levels while still maintaining control and to try catching the beanbag so that it makes no noise in their hands. She moves over to Brian, who has lost his beanbag on a light fixture on the ceiling, and asks him to get another one from the basket. Sheila comes up to the teacher to say that she has to go to the bathroom. Ms. S gives her permission and resumes her observation of the class.

Now compare the actions of the first-grade teacher with those of a ninth-grade teacher during the following episode.

Example: Secondary

A coed ninth-grade class is working on covering space in fielding in a modified softball game. Three fields are set up, with ten students at each field. One student is "up at bat" and throws the ball into the field, trying to advance as far as possible without being put out. Players rotate into the nine fielding positions and keep scores.

Mr. T is moving from one field to another, providing assistance to individuals and feedback to the whole group. Jeff, a rather heavy boy, has let a simple catch pass him without making any attempt to receive it. Other students in Jeff's group are yelling at him. Mr. T moves out to Jeff and asks another player to cover Jeff's position. He pulls Jeff aside to ask what the problem is. Jeff relates to Mr. T that if he tried, he would miss it anyway, so he doesn't want to try. Mr. T asks Kevin to come over to the side and asks him to work with Jeff until Jeff feels secure with fielding balls. Mr. T explains to Kevin that Jeff should start with slow balls coming right to him and then should try balls coming faster that force him to move. Darlene comes over to tell Mr. T that her glove is broken. Mr. T motions to Darlene to take another.

Mr. T moves to another group and asks how many have scored beyond first base. Nobody raises a hand, and Mr. T comments that their fielding must be getting better. He blows his whistle and calls all the students to one spot. He explains to the group that they are now going to try to prevent any runner from getting to first base. Any fielder who touches a ball that results in an out before first base will get one point. Any runner who scores will double his or her points.

---

functions are referred to as **directly contributing behaviors** because they have the potential to directly contribute to the content of the lesson. Teachers also must deal with the situations listed in group 2 in box 7.1, which are a part of some lessons. These behaviors of the teacher will be referred to as **indirectly contributing behaviors.** They are a necessary and important part of teaching but are not actually lesson related and only *indirectly* contribute to the lesson content. The chapter ends with a discussion of behaviors teachers should avoid that make *no contribution* to the lesson.

■ SETTING PRIORITIES OF WHAT TO DO FIRST

Work with experienced and successful teachers has identified the idea that teachers do have a strategy for dealing with what their role is during the time students are active. What these teachers do is to identify some priorities for what to do first. Whereas beginning teachers are likely to move into the group when they first start to practice to offer individual students help, experienced teachers first stand back in a position to observe the whole group and ensure that the learning environment is a safe and productive one. The teacher then focuses on student responses to determine how the class as a whole is handling the task. What follows is a chronological list that describes what experienced teachers are likely to do first as they send students off to practice a task. Each of these ideas will then be discussed separately in terms of suggestions for how to do it.

Priorities for what to do first

1. Make sure the environment is a safe one.
2. Make sure students understand the task and are engaged in the task as it was designed.
3. Observe to determine the specific responses of the class as a whole to the task in terms of the learning objective. Adjust the task as needed.
4. Recheck continuously that student work is productive.
5. Observe individual performance and assist as possible.
6. Maintain awareness of the whole group. Be alert for task pacing needs and task engagement.

Several ideas should be obvious from the activities just listed. First, successfully performing all of these functions depends on the teacher's ability to observe and analyze what the students are doing. Second, all of these functions are interrelated; they affect each other. When task environments are safe and when tasks are clear to learners and appropriate for both the group and individuals, learners are likely to be engaged in the task. A teacher actively engaged in giving feedback to learners potentially maintains

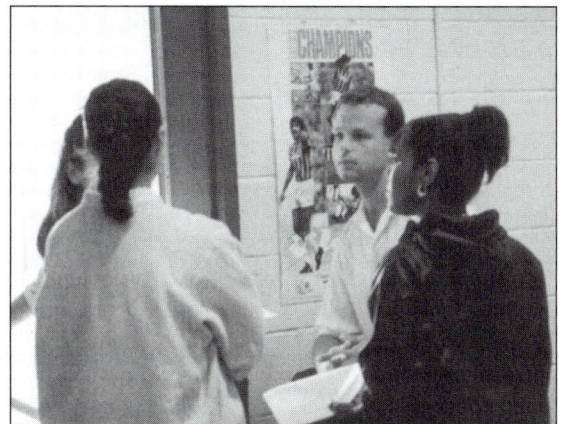

Sometimes the best way to handle problems that arise during class is to take a few minutes before or after class to interact with students.

a productive and usually safe learning environment. Teachers who modify tasks for individuals or small groups within a class also make the environment safer and more productive. All behaviors that have the potential to contribute directly to student content learning communicate to the student the teacher's interest in the student learning. Communicating the intent that learning should occur is essential to effective teaching.

During this scenario the teacher is always alert to the needs of both the group and individuals within the group. However, unlike many beginning teachers, experienced teachers are likely to recognize the importance of maintaining contact with the group and meeting the needs of the group. Only when the group is engaged appropriately and productively can the teacher attend to individuals or individual groups of students. The teacher does not neglect individuals but must put them on "hold" until group needs are met.

The priorities just discussed are those that directly contribute to lesson content. It is likely that during this time the teacher must also effectively handle many indirectly contributing episodes and perhaps some that make no contribution to the lesson.

■ MAINTAINING A SAFE LEARNING ENVIRONMENT

Safe learning environments can almost always be prepared for in advance. Experienced teachers learn to anticipate safety problems and to arrange equipment, space, and people so that the environment both is safe and facilitates learning (see chapters 3 and 6). Experienced teachers also learn to build safety into the tasks they give learners (e.g., coming down on the feet softly from a handstand; making sure no one is around before swinging a racket, stick, or club). Experienced teachers teach for safety and student responsibility for safety.

In situations where advance preparation has not been adequate, the teacher's first priority during activity is to make the environment safe. The Real World box describes common situations that could potentially lead to safety problems/injuries. Safety

takes precedence over all other concerns. Regardless of the cause, unsafe conditions must be changed either by stopping the activity of the entire class or of the individuals involved or by removing the unsafe conditions in a less obtrusive way.

■ CLARIFYING AND REINFORCING TASKS FOR LEARNERS

Many teachers find it necessary to clarify or restate the task for learners shortly after students begin work on a task. Sometimes this is necessary because the teacher observes that students are not responding to the task in the way intended, and sometimes a teacher restates the task to reinforce on-task behavior and hold students accountable for the task as it was presented.

Teachers working with students not accustomed to working within the limits of a task or with a more narrow focus on tasks may need to clarify tasks on a more continuous basis until students recognize that they must attend to task directions because they will be held accountable for them in their work.

> EXAMPLE: The teacher has asked students to focus on stepping into a tennis swing. Although the students are working on their swing, the teacher sees no evidence that students are attending to stepping into their swing. The teacher stops the group and restates the task.

> EXAMPLE: The teacher has asked the students to shoot the basketball at the wall so that they can practice rebounds with a partner. After the students begin working, it is clear that the height of the tape the teacher put on the wall does not allow the ball to bounce off the wall in a way that would allow the students to get a "gamelike" feel for rebounding. The teacher stops the class and asks students to focus their shots considerably higher than the tape on the wall.

The ideal situation is to avoid the need for clarifying, redesigning, or restating a task by presenting an appropriate task with clarity the first time. However, if the teacher observes that students are not responding quickly or correctly to the task presented, clarification and reinforcement are necessary. Teachers who continuously find it necessary to reinforce or clarify the task should reexamine their original presentations. Inexperienced teachers tend to blame off-task behavior

---

THE REAL WORLD

Common Safety Problems Created by Teachers

1. Students are trying to perform skills they are not yet capable of doing, such as vaults on apparatus or catching hard batted balls from a close distance.
2. Students are working too closely together with striking equipment such as rackets, sticks, or bats.
3. Activities that require students to move fast do not have enough room to help the student slow down (e.g., putting the finish line of a race too close to the wall).
4. Choosing activities that put students at risk unnecessarily (e.g., murder ball).
5. Students have not been taught how to work with an awareness of others and space, such as moving to catch a ball in shared space.
6. Students have not been taught to work with control or the teacher does not insist on control (e.g., placing body parts on the floor in gymnastics rather than throwing body parts on the floor and receiving the weight of the body softly).
7. Large pieces of apparatus and other equipment surrounding the gym make an "attractive nuisance."

on "bad" students, when the fault actually lies in how the teacher prepared the students for the task.

Teachers can clarify or reinforce the task without stopping the class by restating the task while students are preparing for or engaged in activity. If confusion is not widespread, a few individuals who are not on task can be redirected. This can be accomplished by positively reinforcing those students who are on task. For example, during a tennis lesson the teacher might say, "Most of us are practicing sending the ball to the wall with one bounce in between."

Nevertheless, there are times when, after realizing that students are not responding to the task as the teacher originally intended, the entire class must be stopped and directions explained. Teachers should not be afraid to do this. If the teacher selected the original task because it was appropriate, it is important that students work with this task. If students do not respond to a task in the way teachers intended them to respond, it usually is because the students do not know what they are supposed to be doing. Sometimes this is because the teacher is not clear to begin with, and sometimes it is because students are not listening or are accustomed to not attending to the specifics of what a teacher has said. No matter what the cause, teachers should not hesitate to stop and get what they want in student responses. Inexperienced teachers have a tendency to accept any response of students rather than reinforcing only the desired response.

■ MAINTAINING A PRODUCTIVE LEARNING ENVIRONMENT

The idea of clarifying and reinforcing the task for the learners during an activity is closely related to the idea of maintaining a productive learning environment. Choosing to clarify and reinforce the task usually indicates that the teacher has decided that off-task responses are occurring because the students did not understand or were not attending to the directives involved in a task. This is usually the case when off-task behavior occurs shortly after the task has begun. However, when teachers find a productive learning environment slipping away from them as the activity progresses, they should look for other causes for the off-task behavior and respond differently. For example, a sudden increase in

noise directly outside the classroom may be preventing students from properly concentrating on the task.

Off-task behavior is difficult to deal with because of the many different causes. A more complete discussion of how to handle off-task behavior is presented in chapter 6 and will not be duplicated here. A primary cause of off-task behavior with students is that the task is inappropriate for either the group or individuals, either because of the content of the task or how the task is organized.

EXAMPLES:
- The teacher has asked students to work on a backward roll. Students who cannot do a backward roll are likely to find something else to do. Students lose interest quickly when the task is not appropriate because it is too difficult or too easy. Again, the teacher should strive to design a task that is challenging but not frustrating for the student.
- The teacher has lined up students to wait for a turn to practice a skill. Students waiting for a turn are likely to find something else to do.
- The teacher has grouped students and has put students together who cannot work productively together. The teacher has not focused students on working together before sending them off to practice.
- The teacher has sent students off without much structure to practice a skill for which they have little experience. The teacher may need to initially add structure to the practice before students are sent off on their own.

Sometimes the task needs more structure to maintain interest. Structure, as previously discussed, can be added by (1) giving the students a certain time in which to accomplish specific goals, (2) having students perform on signal, (3) putting students in an organizational arrangement that is easier for the teacher to directly monitor, or (4) narrowing the focus of the task. More task structure creates more accountability for performance. Students who cannot work in self-directed ways will need more task structure.

To make a judgment about what to do, a teacher must first decide why students are off task. The examples just given describe situations that are the result of the task and the arrangements the teacher has made for organizing students to work on the task. *If students begin to work on the task but gradually lose interest in the task, the problem is most likely related to task pacing.* Task pacing has to do with the amount of time teachers give students to work on a task before changing the focus of the task, providing some kind of a break from the task, or changing to a new task. Task pacing is a significant concept in motor skill learning because to learn motor skills, students will need much practice and teachers must acquire strategies to help students maintain interest in that practice. The following ideas will help maintain student interest and on-task behavior for longer periods:

- *Provide feedback to students on performance.* When teachers are actively engaged in providing both individual and group feedback during instruction, student interest in the task is maintained for longer periods.
- *Provide a break from practice.* Often students need a break from practice. The teacher can call students in and have some students demonstrate what they have done. The teacher can keep the same focus when practice is resumed or can change the focus to an aspect of practice that needs work.
- *Reorganize the practice.* Teachers can redesign the organizational arrangements for tasks by changing the manner in which students are grouped (different partners), the equipment, or the space students will use. Because each of these ideas provides a change, it is likely to increase productive practice for longer periods.
- *Extend the task with a lateral extension task.* Teachers can design another task that does not change the difficulty of the skill students are working on but requires the students to practice that skill in a different way (e.g., setting a volleyball into a basketball hoop rather than to a partner).

When individual students are having difficulty attending to the lesson and the teacher has decided that the task is appropriate for these students, the teacher must act to stop or change off-task behavior before it becomes a problem. A complete discussion of management and discipline is provided in chapter 6. What follows are some actions that teachers can take during the time students are working on a task that will usually solve most problems.

EXAMPLE: The student knows what is expected but has made the decision not to respond appropriately. The teacher has the following alternatives:

- Move the student to another location.
- Redirect the student to the task.
- Inform the student that the conditions of participation are that the student respond with appropriate behavior.
- Remove the student from the situation on the condition that the student may return when ready to accept responsibility for proper behavior.

Sometimes, despite all efforts to keep students productive, teachers have a few students who make the decision not to respond appropriately. If this type of behavior involves more than a few students, the cause of this lack of appropriate response should be looked for in teacher behavior.

■ OBSERVING AND ANALYZING STUDENT RESPONSES

Observation of student responses is an essential skill for teachers. You cannot provide students with feedback, assess their performance, or make decisions about what to do next unless you can observe and accurately determine what it is students are doing. In recent years physical educators have begun to look at the processes of observation and analysis as separate learned skills that do not come naturally to most teachers.

Your skill in observing depends on many factors, including your knowledge of what you are teaching, whom you are teaching, and the context of the specific class you are teaching, as well as the complexity of the environment and the content you are observing. Teachers who have many students, who are observing unfamiliar skills, or who are not comfortable in the teaching role will not be as good at observation of movement responses as teachers who have smaller classes, who are dealing with familiar content, and who are comfortable in a teaching role. Problems with some skills are also more difficult to see. Skills like the overhand throw pattern or the long jump occur so quickly that it is difficult to do an accurate analysis of problems without being able to slow down the skill.

The following key points from the work of Barrett (1979, 1983), Biscan and Hoffman (1976), and Craft (1977) provide some guidelines for teachers who want to improve their observation of student responses:

- The position that the teacher observes from is critical.
- Teachers do better if they know in advance specifically what they will be looking for.
- Observation of large groups of learners seems to be enhanced if teachers have a strategy for observing a large group.

The following section considers the implications of each of these statements for the teacher during activity time.

Positioning of the Teacher

The position of the teacher during activity time is critical from three perspectives. First, teachers responsible for a whole group of learners should never remove themselves for long periods of time from a position that allows them to constantly view the whole group. Second, teachers may need to change positions to get a new observation perspective when looking for different aspects of performance. Third, where teachers stand affects the performance of students.

Teachers of large groups learn early that moving throughout the group and getting to all parts of the available space increases on-task behavior and tends to keep students more productive. Teachers should try not to get caught in the center for any length of time. The center does not allow the teacher to remain visually in contact with the whole group. Furthermore, students will not use the space a teacher has reserved for the teaching position. Teachers who do not make any place in the work area a home base avoid these problems.

Where teachers position themselves is critical to their ability to judge particular aspects of performance. Different motor skills and different parts of a motor skill require different views of performance. For example, teachers cannot discriminate lateral movement in the run if they are observing from the side. Similarly, teachers are probably in a better position to judge some aspects of the overhand throw pattern from the front and others from the side. All teachers,

but particularly inexperienced teachers, need to consciously select an observation position based on the specific aspect of the skill they are trying to observe. When teachers send students off to work in groups for any length of time, they continue to have a responsibility to observe and work with the students in these groups. They will need to continually check what is going on in all the groups when they decide to spend time with one group.

Determining a Plan for Observing Large Groups

In studying observation skills, Barrett (1979, 1983) found that if teachers of large groups have a plan for observing individuals, they are more likely to use their observation time effectively. The observation plan may be (1) to scan the whole group for one particular movement aspect, (2) to select a few individuals known to be of different skill levels, or (3) to observe only a few students at one time, selecting different students at another time. A plan for observation helps the teacher avoid the problem of looking but not really seeing. This problem can occur easily when the teacher is confronted with a sea of performers.

Closely related to the idea of whom to observe and what to look for is the decision of how long to stay with one student or one group. The length of time a teacher observes one student or one group depends largely on what the teacher is looking for. Although some judgments about performance and on-task behavior can be made quickly, many cannot, thus requiring the teacher to see more than one trial of the same skill or spend time observing what a group is doing. The teacher must determine how many students to observe and what is most important to observe. In observing a skill such as the tennis forehand, critical aspects such as arm extension can probably be observed rather quickly with a scanning strategy. If the important cues are determined before instruction by using a developmental analysis of the content, the teacher's selection is easier. However, the teacher still must order sequentially what the initial focuses of observation will be and what can be delayed.

Knowing What to Look For

If a teacher presents the following tennis task to a group of learners, what should be looked for?

EXAMPLE: The student and a partner should send the ball back and forth to each other with forehand strokes, concentrating on getting the arm extended.

The first observation cue in this task is an obvious one: The teacher should be looking for arm extension. Where should the teacher stand to observe arm extension? What levels of feedback statements would be congruent with this task? Arm extension can probably be observed best from the front. To be congruent, teacher feedback should be related to arm extension. What is most important to remember in this example is that the teacher has to make a decision about what to look for.

Deciding what to look for is complicated by tasks that ask students to focus on many aspects of performance at the same time and by tasks that have no specific focus. If students are asked to focus on so many specifics that the teacher cannot determine an observation focus, it can probably be assumed that students are being overloaded with cues on which to focus their work.

At times a task has no specific stated focus that provides the teacher with a clear cue of what to focus on. An example of this situation is when students, primarily beginners, are simply given the idea of a movement and then asked to try it. As previously stated, the teacher in this case should first observe to make sure students are trying to perform in a way consistent with how the skill is grossly performed. For example, if the teacher has asked students (1) to support their weight on their hands by raising their feet in the air and (2) to bring their feet down softly and close to their hands, the teacher probably should be assessing their intent to come down softly and close to their hands. Knowing that students who do not initiate their movement by raising their hips will have difficulty bringing their feet down close to their hands helps the teacher to assess causes of feet not landing close to the hands. Next, the teacher probably should assess the gross aspects of performance and mentally note them to provide further cues after students have had an opportunity to practice.

In the case of the handstand task, the gross aspects might be the position of the head and hips and the push off the floor with the foot. There probably are critical features of movements more important to observe than others. It is not enough to be able to analyze a movement. Teachers must be able to select cues according to their objectives and the stage of the learner.

If the tennis forehand is being presented for the first time, what gross observation cues are most important for the teacher to observe? There is no set answer to this question, but rather a range of correct answers that experienced and successful teachers have discovered through trial and error and much educated guessing. When presenting tasks to beginning learners, teachers should select a limited number of critical features of the task to communicate. The cues the teacher gives to the learner should also serve as the observation cues for the teacher. For the tennis forehand, a teacher of beginners would probably want to observe first whether the student's side is toward the net and then the path of the racket head through space.

Perhaps there will be a time when the study of teaching physical education will involve learning critical observation cues for teaching different skills at different levels. Until such time, teachers will need to do much skill analysis and put much effort into consciously and deliberately selecting observation cues for the tasks they give. Many of these decisions should be made in planning and should be identified specifically on the lesson plan for beginning teachers.

Physical educators will find themselves giving tasks to groups of students and having to observe what groups are doing because of the recent emphasis in education on the value of students working together in cooperative learning environments. Examples of learning tasks that are partner- and group-centered are as follows:

EXAMPLE:
With your partner develop a dance that uses at least three of the skills that we have been working on during this week. A list of those skills is on the wall. Your movements and transitions must be smooth. You may choose to synchronize the movements with your partner or to establish a lead/follow relationship with your partner. Work on your dance until you can do it two times in a row in the same way.

EXAMPLE:

Your team will have ten minutes today to practice the skill you identified in the last lesson as needing the most work. Each captain was asked to go home and work on a good way to practice the skill from the team skill practice handbook. After that practice you will have two things to do. The first thing you must do is to decide who from your team is going to be the referee and the scorekeeper for today's game and who is going to be in charge of equipment for the rest of this week. You must write down these decisions in your team folder. You will then have about seven minutes to plan your strategy for today's game and to get your team ready to play. I have been really pleased with the responsibility that each captain has taken to make these practices go well, and all of the teams for the last class period were ready to go when their games were supposed to start.

We can use the same strategy for observation with groups of learners, as we discussed, for individual performance. Our first task as an observer is to make sure that students understand the expectations for the learning experiences and are working productively on the task given to them. In the case of the partner task, are the students working cooperatively and with a strategy that would allow them to complete the task as defined by the teacher? The cues for the partner task were that the dance as designed uses three of the skills specified by the teacher, the relationship between the partners is either to produce synchronized movements or a lead/follow relationship, and the dance is repeatable. We want to make sure that students are using the cues in their work. Likewise, the learning experience for the team example is equally explicit in expectations for students. Students are expected to be productively engaged in the practice of a skill identified by them in the last class period. They are expected to choose a referee, a scorekeeper, and someone to be responsible for equipment and to write these things in their team folder for the day. They are also expected to get themselves ready for their game on time. An assumption of group learning experiences is that the interaction between members of the group will be positive and inclusive. All members of the group must have a part in the decision making and completion of the tasks assigned to a group. The teacher will want to observe the interactive process in each group and make sure that this is occurring and to intervene to suggest ways in which it may occur if it is not. The teacher would need to observe to make sure that the group process was not only positive and inclusive but also that the work of the group was focused on the tasks that they were given. Sometimes this means that the teacher may need to be a silent observer of the process for periods longer than would be required to observe motor skill performance.

■ PROVIDING FEEDBACK TO LEARNERS

The teacher functions and behaviors that have been discussed so far are necessary to maintain an on-task, safe, and productive learning environment. However, none of the behaviors communicates the content of the task to students. Instead, the behaviors establish and maintain the conditions for learning.

Feedback is information learners receive about their performance. The teacher of motor skills does not have permanent products of student motor performance (unless he or she uses a video or DVD recorder), such as examinations or written assignments, that can be taken home and carefully evaluated. A large percentage of feedback students get on motor performance occurs during or immediately after performance. Although the specific relationship between teacher feedback and student learning in physical education classes has not been demonstrated, teacher feedback plays many other roles in group instruction, other than just providing individual students with information on their performance.

Teacher feedback maintains student focus on the learning task and serves to motivate and monitor student responses. When the teacher gives attention to the student, that student (and others as well) is likely to be more motivated and also to remain on task. Specifically content-related feedback communicates the teacher's intent to help students improve the quality of their responses and therefore is likely to contribute to a task-oriented and productive learning environment.

The need to react immediately to student responses places a heavy burden on the observation and analysis skills of the teacher. Providing appropriate feedback

TABLE 7·1

Evaluative and Corrective Examples of the Different Classifications of Feedback

Classification	Evaluative	Corrective
General	"Good job."	"Don't do it that way."
Specific	"You really got your legs extended that time."	"Point your toes."
Negative	"First graders play better than you."	"Try not to bend your knees."
Positive	"Tommy has got his ball in the target every time."	"Keep your knees locked."
Class	"This class has improved 100%."	"Don't forget to get back to home base position after you hit the ball."
Group	"This group is not working as well as I know you can."	"Play your own position."
Individual	"You're not stepping into the ball."	"Step into the ball."
Congruent*	"Your pass made the receiver stop."	"Lead the receiver a little more."
Incongruent	"Don't dribble the ball until you look to see if someone is open."	"You are not passing to everyone in your group."

*Assuming the task is to work on getting the pass ahead of the receiver so that the receiver does not have to stop to receive it.

is perhaps the behavior that most taxes a teacher's knowledge and observational skills.

Types of feedback can be classified in many ways. Each type of feedback serves a different purpose in the instructional setting and therefore should be used with a specific intent. Table 7.1 illustrates the classifications of feedback discussed in this chapter.

Evaluative and Corrective Feedback

Evaluative feedback occurs when a value judgment concerning how well or poorly a task was performed is directly communicated to the learner. Evaluative feedback is a judgment made about the **past** performance of the student. **Corrective feedback,** sometimes called prescriptive feedback when it is specific, gives the learner information on what to do or what not to do in future performances. Teachers will often couple evaluative and corrective feedback together, such as, "You really got your feet into position that time; now let's try

and follow through on your stroke." In the first part of the feedback, the teacher was making a judgment about previous performance, and in the second part of the feedback statement, the teacher was giving the student information on how to correct future performance.

Evaluative and corrective feedback can be (1) congruent with the focus of the task or incongruent with the focus of the task; (2) general or specific; (3) negative or positive; and (4) directed to the class, a group within the class, or an individual.

Congruency of Feedback

Congruency refers to the relationships between the content of feedback, the focus of the task, and the cues that teachers give for the task. Congruent feedback gives information on performance or results *directly related* to what the learners have been asked to focus on. Some examples of congruent feedback for the task of dribbling a soccer ball while concentrating on using the inside of the foot are the following:

- "You're still using the outside of your foot occasionally."
- "Not the front of your toes, John."
- "That's it, Betty, the inside of the foot each time."
- "Stay with the inside of your foot, Susan."

Each of these feedback statements refers directly to the inside characteristic of the foot dribble.

Incongruent feedback gives information to the learner that may be important to the skill but is not specifically related to the task focus. Some examples of incongruent feedback for the task just described are the following:

- "Keep the ball closer to you."
- "Watch where you're going."
- "Get those feet around when you're changing direction."

The feedback is incongruent because it does not focus on dribbling using the inside of the foot. When teachers give a high percentage of congruent feedback, their teaching becomes more narrow and more focused. Student effort can also become more narrow and more focused. Congruent feedback reinforces the task focus. The usual approach to feedback is to use what is called the *shotgun approach*. The shotgun approach involves asking the learner to focus on a task and then giving feedback on everything the teacher knows or observes related to that skill. Physical education teaching would be more effective if teachers narrowed the number of cues they give students related to a movement task and tried to keep their feedback related to those cues. Students can focus on only a limited number of cues. These cues should be carefully selected by the teacher, and the feedback the teacher gives should reinforce the cues given. Student focuses are hard to maintain when the teacher continuously uses feedback to switch focuses within short periods. This is particularly true in situations using an interactive strategy, where all students are working on the same task.

Teacher feedback is a powerful agent in focusing student responses. It is a great help when it reinforces the desired intent of the task, but it can be just as powerful in changing the intent of students' work. Consider the situation where a teacher asks students

to balance on a variety of body parts. The teacher observes a student doing a headstand and cries out, "Johnny is doing a headstand." Within seconds the entire class is doing headstands. The headstand, however, was not the intent of the task—the intent was a variety of ways of balancing on three parts. The teacher in this instance has changed the intent through the feedback provided. A better approach would be either to positively praise the idea of the headstand and challenge students to seek other responses as well or to make sure that a variety of student responses is praised.

The teacher who asks students to focus on the quality of performance and then does nothing but reinforce winning, losing, or scoring in games probably will not see quality. A competitive situation is a student focus difficult to orient in another direction. The more that competition becomes part of the feedback structure of the teacher, the more intense the focus becomes in the minds and work of the students. All feedback cannot always be congruent. Students need individual help, and sometimes this means asking for higher or lower levels of refinement from individuals within a class. The first observation cue the teacher should use, however, is to look at performance in relation to the focus of the task. The teacher should then provide appropriate congruent feedback before moving on to other cues.

General versus Specific Feedback

The use of **general feedback** versus **specific feedback** has been the subject of much research in motor learning and in teaching. Theoretically, specific information should be more valuable to the learner. Specific feedback has the potential to contribute to student learning a great deal more than general feedback. Specific feedback also serves a major role in maintaining student attention to the task and in developing accountability for tasks. Most teachers are trained to be specific in their feedback.

For specific feedback to be helpful to the learner, it must be related to an aspect or a result of performance that is fairly consistent. At the beginning stages, learners who do not make the same response consistently probably cannot use feedback related to inconsistent errors. Young children and beginners probably should be given general information that clarifies the *intent* of the performance rather than the details of the performance. Experienced teachers who work with students with low self-concepts probably will agree also that sometimes more general positive feedback that helps to increase student motivation is more critical than specific feedback on incorrect performance. In any case, the concepts used in verbal feedback should be those understood by the learner.

There are many levels of general and specific feedback. Consider the following statements:

- "Good."
- "Good hit."
- "Good follow-through on the hit."

The word *good* is the most general of the three statements. Teachers use general feedback statements like "good" primarily to increase student motivation. What is being evaluated with the word *good* is sometimes difficult to determine. Teachers may use "good" to mean "good effort," "good, you're on task," or "good hit" in the content of a hitting task. The learner will probably be confused. The word *good* should be used to reinforce good performance by helping students understand *what* was good about performance.

The ability to give accurate and appropriate specific feedback depends on clear skill goals, knowledge of how skills are performed, and good observation and analysis skills. When teachers realize that they are giving mostly general feedback on performance, they should train themselves to follow up the feedback by questioning *what* was good about the performance.

Some real differences appear to occur in the frequency with which teachers give feedback on skill and other student behaviors at different age levels (Rink, 1979). Elementary teachers give more feedback, college teachers rank second, and secondary teachers provide the least feedback to their students. A great percentage of that feedback is general, however, which seems to indicate that the teachers are using the feedback more as a motivating and monitoring tool than as specific information to learners on their performance.

Negative versus Positive Feedback

Descriptive studies in physical education have shown that feedback in gymnasiums tends to be more negative than positive. This is unfortunate but probably attributable to the notion that the physical educator's job is to correct errors. Actually, students can be helped to correct errors in positive ways. Information about what is good in a performance is as valuable as information about what is wrong. Consider the following statements:

- "You're putting too much force on the ball."
- "Use less force on the ball."

The difference between these two statements is a subtle one. The first is a perspective on past performance (evaluative) and the second a perspective on future performance (corrective). Teachers often assume that students know what to do when told what not to do. This may be a false assumption.

Clarity of feedback can be enhanced by helping students to understand the difference between their performance and the desired performance. For example, this can be achieved if both of the statements just given are used in conjunction with each other when the teacher feels the need to provide corrective feedback. The student then benefits from examples of both what to do and what not to do. This type of feedback becomes even more effective if the teacher can spend time with the student (or group) until the student has had an opportunity to use the information provided. The student's understanding of the feedback then can be checked. Teachers not needed by the whole class can afford to do this.

Some recent interpretations of research have overemphasized the idea of negative versus positive feedback and implied that teachers should not even tell students when the students are doing something wrong. This research has been misinterpreted. What is implied in the research is that negative criticism is to be avoided, particularly criticism attached to the person rather than the behavior. Information on performance that tells the students the response is not correct is valuable and does not need to be harsh or critical in its delivery. Teachers can correct errors without appraising the individual and should make the distinction between the *behavior* of the person and the *person* when providing feedback (e.g., the teacher should say "Get the snap in the wrist quicker" rather than "You're not doing it right, John"). Teachers who are sensitive to the student's need to be successful, particularly in the eyes of the teacher, will sensitively communicate error to students and give students information on how to perform correctly.

The Target of Feedback

Teachers will want to direct their responses to different units of learners at different times during a lesson. The following categories describe the targets of teachers' feedback:

- *Class:* Feedback is directed to all the learners in the class.
- *Group:* Feedback is directed to a part of the learners in a class.

For individual feedback to be effective, teachers must have time to work with students. *(Courtesy SIUE Photo.)*

- *Individual (Class):* Feedback is directed to one individual so that the whole class benefits from the comment.
- *Individual (Private):* Feedback is directed to one individual in a private way.

A typical model of instruction in physical education describes the teacher giving a task and then frantically running from student to student to correct errors. If students can work independently and productively for long periods, individual private communications may allow the teacher opportunities to be more specific and to individualize. However, one problem with this model is that there usually is not time to get to every student. Teachers who try earnestly to get to every student at least once during the class period frequently fail. Better ways exist to provide more information on performance to more learners.

Many times in physical education classes, particularly with beginners, the majority of learners can profit from the same feedback. In these instances teachers should consider directing their comments to the whole class. Comments directed to an individual so that the whole class can hear or comments directed to the class as a whole also serve a strong monitoring function in group instruction. Where active monitoring is necessary, such as in elementary schools, feedback directed in this way can be especially helpful. However, singling out a secondary school student for public feedback may have strong social consequences for this age student and should be avoided.

The following examples of feedback directed to the class and feedback directed to an individual, so that the whole class can hear, illustrate the use of these types of feedback:

- **Feedback directed to the class**

    Situation: The teacher has given high school tennis students the task of tossing the ball in the air continuously until it consistently falls in front of the toe. The teacher observes that many of the students are gripping the ball incorrectly for the toss.

    Feedback: The teacher stops the whole class and says, "Many of you are tossing the ball from the palm of your hand. Toss the ball from the pads of your fingers." The teacher then demonstrates the proper toss and sends students off to practice.

- **Feedback directed to a student so that the whole class can hear**
  Situation: The teacher has asked a class of second-grade students to jump off benches softly so that their landing cannot be heard. The teacher notices that a few students continue to land hard from these jumps.
  Feedback: The teacher selects a student who is landing quietly and says so that the whole class can hear, "Johnny's landings are so soft that I can't even hear them."

Timing of Feedback

The sooner feedback is given after performance, the more potential it has to help the learner. Feedback can immediately follow performance, or it can be delayed. A teacher moving from student to student most often provides feedback immediately after performance, as does a teacher who stops a group of students who have similar problems.

Teachers who give students time to practice and then provide evaluative and corrective feedback as a task focus delay feedback but provide a future focus that is valuable. Delayed feedback with a new task focused on improvement may increase the quality of performance in large instructional groups, particularly beginners. Delayed feedback with no opportunity to improve performance does little to help students improve performance.

Use of Feedback to Promote Student Understanding

Teacher feedback is a useful tool to help students understand cognitively what they are doing, what they should be doing, and why adjustments should be made. If teachers have time to spend with individuals, they can promote cognitive understanding of movement information on why it is important to perform in particular ways. The national content standards in physical education (NASPE, 2004) put a great deal of emphasis on students understanding how to improve performance. Consider the following episode:

EXAMPLE: Teacher A observes a student not transferring weight to the forward foot on a tennis backhand. Teacher A goes up to the student and says, "Where is your weight when you finish your stroke?" The student replies, "I don't know." Teacher A tells the student, "Do it again and tell me." The student follows the teacher's instructions and replies, "On my back foot." Teacher A asks, "Where should it be?" and the student replies, "On my forward foot." Asked "Why?" the student says, "Because I can hit harder." Teacher A confirms the student's discovery and says, "Yes, because you are then using the momentum of your body weight to help you get more power, and you're able to hit the ball harder."

The problem of weight transfer could have been handled easily with a simple "Step forward into your swing as you come through." The teacher might have been successful in correcting student error in this case. The teacher chose to take a less efficient route to change, hoping more understanding would develop on the part of the student.

Understanding is largely a cognitive goal. Its influence on skill development is not clear. Like movement concepts, the intent is not only immediate change in the single skill, but also transfer to other skills.

■ CHANGING AND MODIFYING TASKS FOR INDIVIDUALS AND SMALL GROUPS

Another major role of the teacher during activity is to change and modify tasks to make them more appropriate for individuals. No matter how much effort a teacher has put into individualizing tasks, there always seems to be a need to make tasks more appropriate for individuals or small groups within a class. Increased opportunities for participation outside the school setting have increased, not decreased, the range of abilities within physical education classes. Teachers can modify tasks to make them more appropriate for individual learners in much the same way that they develop tasks for an entire class. They can do the following:

- Change the content of the task entirely by asking individual students to work on something the whole class is not working on.

- Extend the task for individuals by reducing the complexity, expanding the complexity, or seeking a variety of responses from the same individual or group.
- Move students into or out of competitive situations.
- Extend the task laterally (another way to practice the same task at the same level of difficulty) for individual students.
- Prescribe levels of refinement or correct errors on an individual basis.

For example, if the task is for partners to strike a ball back and forth across the net continuously without losing control, the task can be modified in numerous ways for individuals or small groups of learners. (It is assumed that each student has a paddle or racket and that each set of partners has a whiffle ball, sponge ball, or tennis ball and a net or some other barrier to send the ball over.) Using the example, the following discussion explores the possibilities for making the task appropriate for different individuals within the class. These possibilities are described in the constructs of extending, refining, and applying/ assessments that are used for the analysis and development of content.

Extending the Task for Individuals

The first modification considered is how the teacher may have to change the conditions of the task. Based on individual needs, the teacher in this example may need to do the following:

- Move students having difficulty controlling the ball closer to each other.
- Move students back who are not getting a powerful enough hit on the ball and are just tapping it.
- Create boundaries for students not controlling the direction of the hit.
- Ask students to start placing the ball away from their partners when the students have achieved a high level of control and continuous hits with the task the way it is.
- Move some students back to hitting the ball against the wall by themselves.

- Change the whiffle ball, sponge ball, or tennis ball to an object that is easier to control.

These are adjustments the teacher can make in the conditions of the task based on the observed needs of individuals within a group. Many lessons need some modification for individual students, either because the students are working above their level of ability and are not successful at the task or because they are successful every time and are not being challenged.

The concept of error rate is again a useful concept for many of the tasks teachers give in physical education. If students are successful with a task almost every time, the teacher should consider challenging the students above the conditions of the task. If students fail more often than they succeed, the teacher probably should assume that the conditions of the task are too difficult. Even in situations that allow students to choose a level of response, the teacher should help them work at the appropriate level of response.

Designing Applying/Assessment Task for Individuals

A second way the teacher can modify tasks for individuals is to move them into or out of a competitive setting or ask students to assess their performance. Unfortunately, it is the applying task that is most often inappropriate for individuals and groups within a class. This is also a task that teachers are reluctant to modify for students.

The teacher in the sample task can move students into a competitive situation by asking students who are ready for the challenge to keep track of the number of times they can send the ball back and forth to their partner without missing. The teacher can also ask some students to design a game using the skills they have been practicing. Students who have competence and confidence in these skills will be highly motivated by the opportunity to test/assess them under more gamelike conditions.

When a large portion of the class is not ready for a competitive experience, the teacher may have to meet the needs of students who are ready by changing the task to an application/assessment task on an individual basis. In situations where a large portion of the class is ready for a competitive experience and a small portion is not, the teacher may have to remove individual students from the competitive task.

Changing the Task Completely for Individuals

A third alternative for making the task appropriate for individuals or small groups is to change the task completely. To completely change rather than modify the sample task, the teacher must change it from a striking task to a nonstriking task. In classes involving mainstreamed handicapped students, changing the task becomes a critical need. In the sample task this can be done by having students toss a ball to a bounce rather than strike it at each other.

Complete changes of tasks for individuals or small groups are most appropriate in situations where teachers have chosen to introduce specialized skills. Asking students who cannot place any weight on their hands to do a cartwheel is not only a waste of time but inexcusable from the standpoint of both safety and the students' motivation. Asking students to serve a volleyball overhead when they cannot contact the ball with an underhand serve is equally unacceptable. The teacher who has chosen to give highly specialized tasks that offer little room for varied responses must be willing to change the task appropriately for students who are not ready for these skills and to move advanced students beyond the skill given.

Refining the Task for Individuals

An alternative to modifying tasks on an individual or small-group basis is to provide a focus with a greater or lesser degree of quality. The refining task asks students to perform some aspect of the original task with better quality but also enables teachers to reduce overall expectations. In the striking with paddles example, typical refining tasks might be the following:

- "Get your side to the net."
- "Contact the ball farther from your body."
- "Control the ball within your own space."
- "Follow through with your weight on the forward foot."

Refining tasks that ask students to improve some aspect of their response are the most common attempts to individualize tasks for different learners, as discussed in the previous section on feedback. Refining tasks also serve to reinforce what is important and hold students accountable for good performance.

■ INDIRECTLY CONTRIBUTING BEHAVIORS

Indirectly contributing behaviors focus the teacher's attention on the students and the learning environment but do not make a direct contribution to the content of the lesson. Some examples of behaviors that do not serve a content function are attending to an ill or injured student, engaging in off-topic discussions with students, or repairing equipment that breaks during a lesson. As is the case with noncontributing behaviors, teachers do not always have a choice in performing these functions. The following discussion of some of the most common events in this category, however, focuses on those situations where teachers do have a choice of actions.

Attending to Injured Students

Injured students must be attended to. Once again, the goal is to handle the problem in the least disruptive way. Most schools have standard procedures for handling the problem of injured students, and teachers are obliged to follow this policy. The teacher must decide whether to allow the rest of the class to continue or, in the case of a serious injury, to stop class activity. Minor injuries can be handled by older students with direction from the teacher, except in situations where blood has spilled. In today's school environment, to protect themselves and other students from HIV and AIDS-related diseases (Sutliff & Bomgardner, 1994), teachers have specific procedures for handling bodily fluids that have spilled. Almost all schools have someone designated for first aid. The teacher should quickly dispatch students with minor injuries to this person and resume work with the rest of the class. Under *no* conditions should the class be left unattended. Seriously injured students should not be moved until qualified personnel arrive.

The personal problems of students should be handled quickly so that the teacher can attend to the needs of the group.

Engaging in Off-Topic Discussions

Discussions with students about intramurals, favorite professional sports teams, new tennis shoes, or baby brothers may enhance relationships between the teacher and the students but contribute little to the content of a lesson. Physical education lessons are almost always structured by time and have a clear beginning and end. Off-topic conversations are probably best left for times before the official beginning of the lesson content or immediately after. This is particularly true if the conversation involves more than one interaction with a student. Saying "Let's talk about it after class" and then following up after class usually helps to keep students on task, allows teachers to resume their obligation to the rest of the class, and meets the need for personal interaction between teachers and students.

There are also critical times during a lesson when the teacher is needed by the whole group, such as at the beginning of a task. At these times a personal conversation with one student can have a disastrous effect on the productive work of the group.

This stance may seem like a harsh, unfeeling, and antiaffective approach to student-teacher personal

interaction. Teachers should not ignore or turn off a student who wants to talk. However, off-topic discussions should be handled graciously but quickly and then picked up again by the teacher at a more opportune time.

Dealing with the Personal Needs of Students

During activity is the time when teachers are most often forced to deal with the essential and often nonessential bathroom needs of students. Inexperienced teachers often are frustrated by the intrusion of such earthy requests into their well-planned lesson. These intrusions are, however, facts of life in the gymnasium, and teachers should be prepared in advance to deal with their occurrence.

The ideal situation is to have students leave and take care of these needs without having to request permission of the teacher. All teachers should work toward this goal, even though it may still be necessary to know when a student is leaving the room.

The beginning teacher should be aware of potential problems with these situations. In the elementary school and middle-school environments, getting a drink and leaving the gymnasium can become a contagious game with as much importance to the elementary school child as being first or last in line. Many teachers handle this situation effectively by discriminating between real needs and requests that are part of a game. When the request is part of a game, the teacher does not grant the request. Some teachers also challenge students to make the decision involved in this situation and help them to choose wisely. Students should be reminded to take care of their needs before coming to the gymnasium. Teachers who have resorted to "water at the end of class" procedures have decided that the time needed to help students make wise decisions in this area is not worth the time needed for other objectives.

Although most secondary students are capable of taking care of such needs before class, the teacher must be prepared for emergency requests. The problems connected with these requests are different from those identified at the elementary and middle-school levels. Increased vandalism, drug problems, and theft in many situations prevent teachers from allowing students unsupervised freedom. Many locker rooms, where toilet facilities are usually located, must be locked during class to protect the personal items of students and to ensure teacher supervision of the facilities. Again, it should be stated that this is not a desirable situation and teachers should carefully consider ways in which more responsible student behavior can be supported and encouraged.

Participating with Students and Officiating

In most instances, teachers who participate in an activity with students, officiate student play, or merely supervise student activity remove themselves from teaching behaviors that might have a more direct effect on student performance. A teacher might participate for short periods to illustrate a point or motivate student performance. When the teacher participates with only a small part of the class, however, the remaining members of the class do not have a teacher.

Teachers who put themselves solely in the role of an official make it difficult to play more of a direct role with students. The rationale the teacher has when doing this is usually that the students need uninterrupted play and "no coaching." This rationale is difficult to accept, because even most professional players are continuously coached during game play.

Teachers who see themselves primarily as supervisors of activity usually give as their rationale the need of students for more unstructured free play. Whether the instructional period is the proper place to meet this need is arguable. When time is limited, the need for guidance in the learning process would seem to be greater. Quality instruction increases student learning. Indirectly contributing teacher behaviors are often necessary to maintain a productive learning environment. The teacher must, however, guard against becoming so engrossed in participating, officiating, and supervising that no time is left for the directly contributing behaviors discussed in the previous section.

■ NONCONTRIBUTING BEHAVIORS

Noncontributing behaviors add nothing to lesson content. Fire drills, announcements over a public address system, and conversations with principals who enter the classroom and immediately want to talk to the teacher are events that occur during real instructional situations. Teachers have little control over these situations, but the teacher can minimize disruption in these and similar situations in two ways. First, the teacher should prepare students to respond to events like announcements and fire drills with behaviors structured ahead of time. Second, the teacher must respond in a consistent manner to these events. For example, the disruptive effect of visitors can be minimized by asking students to continue to work independently when possible. Even principals and supervising teachers can be asked to talk with the teacher later and should respect the teacher's desire to attend to the class. As a routine procedure, students should be asked to stop work and remain still during public address announcements without direction from the teacher. They should be asked to stop work and await teacher directions for a fire drill.

Unfortunately, some teachers remove themselves from an instructional situation by choice. Teachers who line the field for another class, physically leave the room, or attend to any activity not related to the students and the lesson are not functioning as teachers and make an unwise and legally liable choice.

In summary, noncontributing behaviors have a negative effect on instruction. They are to be avoided when possible and handled in the least disruptive way when unavoidable.

SUMMARY

1. Teachers perform many functions during the time students are engaged in a movement task.
2. Six major teacher functions have the potential to directly contribute to lesson content:
   Maintaining a safe learning environment
   Clarifying and reinforcing tasks for learners
   Maintaining a productive learning environment
   Observing and analyzing student responses

Providing feedback to learners

Changing and modifying tasks for individuals and small groups

3. Active teachers are continuously engaged in directly contributing behaviors.

4. Each of the directly contributing teacher functions during activity is interrelated.

5. Indirectly contributing behaviors focus the teacher's attention on the students and the learning environment but do not make a direct contribution to lesson content. Injured students, off-topic discussions, and equipment breakdowns are some examples of indirectly contributing behaviors. These events must be dealt with in ways that do not unnecessarily remove teachers from more directly contributing behaviors.

6. Noncontributing teacher behaviors have no potential to contribute to lesson content. These behaviors include events such as fire drills; public address announcements; teacher conversations with those outside the class; and the removal of the teacher, either physically or psychologically, from the students. Noncontributing behaviors should be avoided when possible and their disruptive influence minimized when avoidance is not possible.

7. Write an example for each of the following types of feedback: (1) general, positive, directed to the class, and evaluative; (2) specific, negative, directed to a group, incongruent, and corrective; and (3) specific, positive, directed to the individual, corrective, and congruent.

8. Listen to an audiotape of teaching and categorize the feedback of the teacher as being (1) congruent or incongruent; (2) general or specific; (3) negative or positive; and (4) addressed to an individual, group, or class. Evaluate the teacher's responses for each of these categories.

9. Design two movement tasks and show how they might be modified during activity (either up or down) for students by extending, applying, refining, or completely changing the task.

10. Watch a video of a physical education lesson and identify from the tape students who should have the task modified for them.

11. List three different tasks from different motor skills and indicate where the teacher should be located to best observe performance.

12. For the tasks chosen for the preceding question, determine what the focus of teacher observation should be.

CHECKING YOUR UNDERSTANDING

1. How can a teacher best handle a visit by a parent or principal that occurs during class time?

2. What is the best way to respond to a student who wants to engage the teacher in an off-topic discussion during a critical part of the lesson?

3. Why is the role of the participant or official not usually a wise choice for the teacher during activity?

4. List six behaviors teachers can engage in during activity that have the potential to directly contribute to lesson objectives.

5. Why should the teacher not hesitate to clarify a task when student responses are not what is expected?

6. How can a teacher get off-task students on task?

REFERENCES

Barrett, K. (1979). Observation of movement for teachers: A synthesis and implications. *Motor Skills: Theory into Practice, 3*(2), 67–76.

Barrett, K. (1983). Observing as a teaching skill. *Journal of Teaching in Physical Education, 3*(1), 22–31.

Biscan, D., & Hoffman, S. (1976). Movement analysis as a generic ability of physical education teachers and students. *Research Quarterly for Exercise and Sport, 47*(1), 161–163.

Craft, A. (1977). The teaching of skills for the observation of movement: Inquiry into a model. *Dissertation Abstracts International, 38*(4), 1975A. (University Microfilms No. 77-21, 745)

Kounin, J. S. (1970). *Discipline and group management in classrooms.* New York: Holt, Rinehart & Winston.

NASPE. (2004). *Moving into the future: National standards for physical education* (2nd ed.). Reston, VA: NASPE.

Rink, J. (1979). *Development of an observation system for content development in physical education.* Unpublished doctoral dissertation, Ohio State University, Columbus.

Sutliff, M., & Bomgardner, R. (1994). HIV/AIDS—How to maintain a safe environment. *Journal of Physical Education, Recreation and Dance, 65*(5), 53–56.

SUGGESTED READINGS

Boyce, A., Markos, N., Jenkins, D., & Loftus, J. (1996). How should feedback be delivered. *Journal of Physical Education, Recreation and Dance, 67*(1), 18–22.

Chen, D. (2001). Trends in augmented feedback research and tips for the practitioner. *Journal of Physical Education, Recreation and Dance, 72*(1), 32–36.

James, R., & Dufek, J. (1993). Performance excellence: Movement observation: What to watch and why. *Strategies, 7*(2), 17–19.

Pellett, T., & Henschel-Pellett, H., & Harrison, J. (1994). Feedback effects: Field-based findings. *Journal of Physical Education, Recreation and Dance 65*(9), 75–78.

Silverman, S., Tyson, L., & Krampitz, J. (1992). Teacher feedback and achievement in physical education: Interaction with student practice. *Teaching and Teacher Education, 8,* 333–344.

Teaching Strategies

8

OVERVIEW

Teaching functions are usually performed within an instructional framework—a delivery system for getting the content to the learner. This instructional framework is called a teaching strategy, and in group instruction it organizes both student and teacher roles. Each teaching strategy assigns different roles to the learner and the teacher for one or more teaching functions. When teaching strategies are combined with specific objectives and particular content, they are sometimes called instructional models. Teachers select an instructional strategy based on the nature of the content, the objectives of the teacher, and the characteristics of the learner.

This chapter compares and contrasts direct instruction and indirect instruction and then describes seven major teaching strategies and how they provide for specific instructional functions. Their advantages and disadvantages for use in a group instructional setting are explored.

Standard 4: Instructional Delivery and Management

Physical education teacher candidates use effective communication and pedagogical skills and strategies to enhance student engagement and learning.
NASPE Beginning Teaching Standards, 2008

OUTLINE

- **Direct and indirect instruction**
- **The teaching strategy as a delivery system**
  Selection of content
  Communication of tasks

  Progression of content
  Provision for feedback and evaluation
- **The teaching strategies described**
  Interactive teaching

Station teaching
Peer teaching
Cooperative learning
Self-instructional strategies

Cognitive strategies
Team teaching
■   **Selecting a teaching strategy**

Chapter 3 discusses different ways in which the teacher can design learning experiences and movement tasks to achieve different learning outcomes. In a large-group instructional setting, teachers can organize these experiences in different ways: (1) by varying the level of responsibility and engagement of the learner with the content and (2) by organizing the experiences so that both the student and the teacher function in different ways in the instructional setting.

Deciding what teaching strategy to employ and how much responsibility to assign to the learner does not only include questions about the involvement of the learner in the learning process. Teachers can choose specialized approaches for cognitive processes to encourage positive social interaction among students or to use space and equipment more efficiently. They can choose to design lessons with different organizational formats (e.g., individual, group, partners, whole class). They can also choose different ways of communicating tasks to learners and providing for content progression, student feedback, and evaluation.

No one schema for or description of method can address all of these issues in the gymnasium. The type of cognitive learner involvement, the organizational format for instruction, and the degree of student decision making can be combined in many different ways.

■ DIRECT AND INDIRECT INSTRUCTION

One of the major decisions teachers have to make in regard to the selection of a teaching strategy is the extent to which the lesson should be approached using direct instruction or indirect instruction. The teacher effectiveness research of the 1970s led educators to the realization that students are more likely to learn specific content when teachers teach that content directly. Direct teaching involves the following:

- A task-oriented but relaxed environment with a clear focus on academic goals
- The selection of clear instructional goals and materials and highly active monitoring of student progress toward these goals
- Structured learning activities
- Immediate academically oriented feedback

Highly active teaching, focused learning, and student accountability are inherent in the idea of direct instruction. In physical education, direct instruction usually implies that the teacher is in total control of what the students are learning and how they are learning it. Physical educators who use direct instruction do the following:

- Break down skills into manageable, success-oriented parts
- Clearly describe and demonstrate exactly what the learner is supposed to do
- Design structured tasks for students to practice what is to be learned
- Hold students accountable for the tasks they present through active teaching and specific feedback
- Evaluate students and their own teaching on what the student has learned

As instruction moves to more indirect methods of teaching, teacher control of the learning process becomes shared with the learner. Indirect instruction is not as easily described as direct instruction but usually involves one or more of the following descriptors:

- Content is presented more holistically. Instead of breaking down what is to be learned into many subskills, chunks of content more meaningful to the learner are used.
- The student's role in the process of learning is usually expanded so that student thinking, feeling, or interaction skills are built into learning experiences designed by the teacher.

■ The individual nature of student abilities, interests, and needs receives more consideration.

A basketball lesson presented using direct instruction and indirect instruction is described in box 8.1. A lesson on a movement concept is presented in box 8.2 (see p. 154). In the direct instruction example, the role of the student is largely to do what the teacher says and to match the demonstration of the teacher. In the indirect instruction example, the teacher is concerned with the process of learning and individualizing the practice.

Direct instruction is the best way to teach when content has a hierarchical structure and is primarily basic-skill oriented and when efficiency of learning is a concern. When teacher objectives and goals require more complex learning and when teachers have lesson objectives that involve other learning domains (cognitive, affective), direct instruction may not be the best choice despite its efficiency. In physical education, the decision of whether to teach material with direct or indirect instruction is complicated by the idea that motor skills are learned primarily through practice and cognitive processing of that practice, but not through complex cognitive processes. Teachers who involve students at higher levels of cognitive functioning, however, may have a better chance of ensuring that the student is processing what they are doing motorically. They may also have a better chance of teaching motor content for transfer of learning to other applicable skills or tactics of game play.

Maximum practice in limited program time is often attained through direct instruction. Advocates of indirect instruction are concerned with the relevance and meaningfulness of what is to be learned. Too often direct instruction results in learning out of context with little meaning to the learner and little attention to engaging the learner at a more holistic and higher level. The National Standards for Physical Education (NASPE, 2004) clearly identify outcomes usually taught with more indirect teaching styles, such as learning how to learn, values, feelings, independence, and social skills. These same standards identify those outcomes, such as competency in motor skills, usually taught more effectively with more direct teaching styles.

At different points in the development of educational theory, education has moved closer to direct

---

BOX 8·1

Basketball Lesson: Direct and Indirect Instruction

Direct instruction: Basketball chest pass

1. Teacher demonstrates a chest pass with clear cues and organizes students in groups of two to practice the chest pass from a stationary position.
2. After observing the students, the teacher refines the chest pass with the following tasks: Demonstrates the step into the throw and asks students to "Do five more chest passes and step into your throw this time."
3. Teacher extends the task with "When I give you and your partner the signal, take two steps back and see if you can maintain a good crisp pass."
4. "Now let's try sending the chest pass to a moving receiver."

Indirect instruction: Basketball chest pass

1. "Today we are going to work on getting the ball to a receiver a short distance away as quickly as possible. Let's look at this tape of professional players and see if we can identify the really good short and quick passes and how the players seem to do it."
2. "You and your partner find a place to practice, and see if you can identify at least three things that are important to doing this skill well from a stationary position."
3. Students come back in and share their responses. Teacher summarizes what a good short, quick chest pass should look like.
4. Students attempt to use the cues defined by the group to practice the chest pass from a stationary position. Teacher refines individually and through tasks as necessary.
5. The teacher moves around the room and asks students who are ready to move back and try the skill from an increased distance.
6. "When you feel that you are ready, try the pass with the receiver moving into a space to the left or right of you."

---

or indirect instruction in a cyclical way. Educational literature of today has embraced more indirect teaching styles that promote more meaningful

---

BOX 8·2

Movement Concept Lesson: Direct and Indirect Teaching—Absorbing Force by "Giving"

Direct teaching

1. The teacher presents the concept of giving formally as reaching and then giving with the force over a great distance.
2. The teacher demonstrates reaching and giving with a landing from a jump and asks students to try it. The teacher refines performance and extends the difficulty as is applicable.
3. The teacher demonstrates giving with a ball from a self-toss and partner throw and asks students to see if they can use the cues reaching and giving as they catch the ball. The teacher refines performance and extends the difficulty as is applicable.
4. The teacher demonstrates the giving action with a hockey stick and then asks students to use the cues to reach or meet and give to receive the hockey puck or ball from a partner.

Indirect teaching

1. The teacher explains that the focus of today's lesson is going to be how to absorb force and asks students to jump into the air and see if they can figure out how they might land so that the force is easily absorbed and makes no "noise" on the floor. The students identify several ideas that the teacher explores with the group, asking the students to try the individual ideas. The students identify what they consider the "cues" for absorbing force from a jump, and the teacher puts them on the board.
2. The teacher explains to students that there are different sizes and shapes of balls, bats, and sticks that they might use. Students identify which piece of equipment they might want to use, and the teacher groups the students by the piece of equipment they have chosen. The group task is to identify the cues that describe how to catch or receive the ball or how to use the stick or bat to receive an object so that the force is absorbed. Students are sent off to work in different groups.
3. When the groups have finished, they write their cues on the board for their piece of equipment and the class comes together.
4. The teacher asks the students to review all of the cues on the board and to identify the similarities and differences in the cues. Students are then asked to see if they can identify one set of cues that might be useful for most situations in which you might have to absorb force.

---

learning and more student involvement in the learning process. The perspective of this text is that good teachers can and do use both direct and indirect teaching strategies—often within the same lesson. The decision of whether to use direct or indirect instruction should be based on teacher goals and objectives and the nature of what is to be learned in the context of a specific situation. Effective teachers do not make a decision to operate at one end of this continuum or another based on beliefs about which method is better. Different outcomes are likely to be produced by each orientation (Wubbels, Levy, & Brekelmans, 1997). Effective teachers choose direct instruction when it is important for learners to master basic skills efficiently. They choose more indirect methods appropriately for other objectives and goals. Effective teachers should have available to them a broad spectrum of teaching strategies that they can use effectively.

The teacher must remember also that the selection of a teaching strategy depends on the level of self-direction teachers have developed with their students. Although many teaching strategies can be designed to use more direct or indirect methods of teaching, others require that students be able to function independently of a high degree of teacher monitoring. *Teachers who have not created an appropriate learning environment and who have not developed self-direction skills with students are limited in the teaching strategies they can use effectively.*

Direct instruction and indirect instruction are holistic concepts depicting two poles of a continuum primarily representing an approach to organizing content. Therefore, many instructional factors can be varied by the teacher that can support either direct or indirect instruction. In other words, you can use a variety of teaching strategies to deliver either direct or indirect instruction. Many of the teaching strategies described in this chapter can be used to present content either directly or indirectly.

In 1966 Mosston made a monumental contribution to the methodology of teaching physical education with his description of teaching styles, which ranged from command to discovery. The spectrum of teaching styles was largely based on the amount of decision making students were given in the learning process. Some of the styles were very much direct teaching, and some more indirect teaching styles. Since that time, the spectrum of teaching styles has been developed to include ten different styles, which give the learner different responsibilities in the teaching learning process (Mosston & Ashworth, 2002). These style are described in Box 8.3. The original work talked about lessons taught in a style. Pedagogues have come to recognize that rarely does a teacher teach a whole lesson using one style, but rather the teacher chooses different styles to meet different objectives. Likewise, the issue of teaching style is not one versus the other. Good teachers will use a variety of styles throughout a lesson.

This text treats different pedagogical approaches to teaching as teaching strategies that are organized by teaching functions.

■ THE TEACHING STRATEGY AS A DELIVERY SYSTEM

A **teaching strategy** is designed to arrange an instructional environment for group instruction. A key point is that *groups do not learn—individuals do.* This means that group instructional environments must be arranged to facilitate the learning of individuals. Individual learners in physical education must still be provided with appropriate content that is clearly communicated. They must be provided with the opportunity to practice accurately and to progress appropriately, and they must be provided with feedback on their performance. When teachers organize students in groups, the role of each member of the group must be clear, and the need for clarity of task, progression, and feedback is no less important.

Teaching strategies organize instruction so that teaching functions are performed in different ways in the instructional process and give the teacher and learner

BOX 8·3

Spectrum of Teaching Styles

Style A	Command	Teacher makes all decisions.
Style B	Practice	Students work in pairs; one performs while the other provides feedback.
Style C	Reciprocal	Students work in pairs; one performs while the other provides feedback.
Style D	Self-Check	Students assess their own performance against criteria.
Style E	Inclusion	Teacher planned, students monitor their own work.
Style F	Guided Discovery	Students solve teacher-set movement problems with assistance.
Style G	Divergent	Students solve problems without assistance from the teacher.
Style H	Individual	Teacher determines the content. Students plan own program with teacher as the advisor.
Style I	Learner Initiated	Students plan own program with teacher as the advisor.
Style J	Self-Teaching	Students take full responsibility for the learning process.

Source: Mosston, M., & Ashworth, S. (2002). *Teaching Physical Education.* (5th ed.). San Francisco: Benjamin Cummings.

different roles. The major teacher functions important to discriminating teaching strategies are the following:

- Selection of content
- Communication of tasks
- Progression of content
- Provision for feedback and evaluation

The decisions teachers make in regard to these functions significantly affect the potential of instruction to accomplish intended objectives. The nature of these decisions is described in the following section.

Selection of Content

A major problem in group instruction is that students function at different levels of ability in most tasks. The selected content must meet the needs of individuals within a group setting. In large-group instruction this involves decisions such as the following:

- How can content be made appropriate for many learners with different content needs?
- Should each student be doing the same thing at the same time?
- Should content be different for different students?
- Who makes decisions relative to content, the teacher or the student?
- What level of student engagement should the content seek to develop?

Communication of Tasks

In a learning experience, students must be told what they are expected to do. This instructional function describes the way tasks are communicated to groups of learners. It involves decisions on how to communicate the learning task to students. Possibilities include verbal communication of the teacher or student, demonstrations, written handouts, posters, task cards, computer programs, and other audiovisual materials.

Progression of Content

In an instructional setting, arrangements must be made for students to progress from skill to skill and from one level of performance of a skill to another. Progression from one skill to another is called *intertask development* (e.g., going from forehand to backhand in a racket skill) and progression from one level of performance of a skill to another is called *intratask development* (e.g., going from practicing the forehand from a toss to practicing the forehand from a fence) (see chapter 5).

Progression of content focuses on the arrangements for both skill-to-skill progression (intertask development) and within-skill progression (intratask development) in a learning experience. A teaching strategy must build in the extension; refinement; and, where appropriate, application/assessment aspects of the development of content. Progression of content involves answering questions such as the following:

- Who decides when a student advances in difficulty or to another skill?
- Should criteria be established for performance?
- Should those criteria be established ahead of time?
- Should the criteria be communicated to students? If so, how should they be communicated?

Provision for Feedback and Evaluation

Providing feedback to learners and evaluating student responses is a critical teaching function in instruction. Group instructional settings make giving individual feedback and evaluating performance difficult. To give individual feedback and evaluate performance, the teacher can consider some of the following alternatives:

- Teacher observation and feedback
- Peer feedback
- Self-assessment
- Environmental design
- Formal testing
- Videotaping

■ THE TEACHING STRATEGIES DESCRIBED

Seven basic teaching strategies for the design of learning experiences in physical education have been identified:

- Interactive teaching
- Station teaching
- Peer teaching
- Cooperative learning
- Self-instructional strategies

- Cognitive strategies
- Team teaching

The strategies described are by no means inclusive, nor do they always appear in a pure form as a strategy for an entire lesson in a real situation. Many of these strategies can be and are used in combination with each other for different learning experiences throughout a lesson.

Each of these strategies will be discussed relative to the way it arranges the instructional environment. You will find as you read about each of the strategies that each focuses and highlights one aspect of instruction but may say little about other instructional functions. Although the arrangement of conditions for one instructional function affects possibilities for arranging other functions, it is also possible to use several teaching strategies simultaneously.

Interactive Teaching

By far the most common strategy for the design of learning experiences in physical education is an interactive strategy. Most people will have no trouble conceptualizing the interactive strategy. The word *teaching* often implies a teacher telling, showing, or directing a group of students on what to do; students doing it; and a teacher evaluating how well it is done and developing the content further. This is a type of interactive strategy. In **interactive teaching** the instructional process is teacher controlled. Like an orchestra without a conductor, instruction cannot continue without the teacher.

In interactive teaching, a teacher move, a teacher's decision of what to do next, is based on the response of students to a previous teacher move. Teacher planning facilitates the process, but teachers' next moves are based on student responses. The teacher is dominant in this strategy and is most often responsible for all four teaching functions. Usually an entire class of students works on the same task or within the same task framework.

An interactive teaching strategy can be used to teach any content. Examples of teachers using interactive teaching to teach the open skill of the tennis forehand and a movement concept related to balance are given in boxes 8.4 and 8.5. The discussion now focuses on how each instructional component is arranged when an interactive teaching strategy is used.

B O X 8 · 4

Interactive Teaching of Tennis Forehand (Middle School)

The teacher is in the first days of a tennis unit with eighth-grade students. A few of the students play tennis outside of school, but most students have no tennis experience.

Before class begins, the teacher asks to speak with the experienced students. He tells them that during the first part of the period they are to go baseline to baseline, alternating forehand and backhand strokes, and see if they can begin placing the ball closer to the corners as they are successful.

The teacher then reviews the cues of the forehand with the rest of the class by walking the students through the skill without the ball. He paces the practice the first few times and then asks the students to practice the action faster on their own. The teacher breaks down the group into partners (their choice) and explains that each set of partners will have six balls. One partner tosses the ball from a few feet away so that it bounces to the forehand side of the hitter. The hitter then strikes the ball with a forehand stroke. The teacher demonstrates by tossing the ball to a class member, emphasizing where the toss should be placed and the contact point where the ball should hit the racket. He asks the students to put two hitters on each side of each court, and practice begins.

During practice, the teacher reminds several tossers to try to place the ball so that it bounces to the hitter about waist high. He gives specific feedback to several hitters on "swinging through the ball." The teacher stops the class and asks students how far away from the ball they should be when hitting it. Several students give different answers. Students are again asked to swing their rackets without the ball and to freeze the action when they think contact occurs. Students respond, and the teacher asks them to go back to what they were doing and try to make sure they are extended at the contact point by judging the distance from the ball. The teacher moves to the advanced group to give feedback and to change the task to practicing serving.

BOX 8·5

Interactive Teaching of Balance (Upper Elementary School)

The students are met at the door by the teacher. They are asked to warm up on the mats scattered throughout the all-purpose room by taking their weight on different parts of their body and getting good extension. The teacher moves throughout the group while the students are warming up. She asks individuals to get more extension and clarity in the body shape they are assuming and positively reinforces those students who have clarity of shape and extension.

The teacher begins the lesson by asking students to select an inverted balance that they can hold for at least six seconds. She then asks students to find at least three ways they can get out of this balanced position to a new base of support. While the students are working, the teacher moves through the group, helping individuals with the balances they have chosen. She stops the group and asks several students to demonstrate the way that they have chosen to move out of their balances. The teacher comments that she has seen rolls, twists, steplike actions, and slides. She asks students to go back and continue to explore possibilities for moving out of their balances and tells them that they may choose a new balance if they want to.

While the students are working, the teacher asks some of them to try some specific way of moving out of their balances, such as a transfer of weight onto another body part, a roll, or a twist. As students work, the teacher reminds them that they can try moving forward, backward, or sideways out of their balances.

The teacher stops the whole class. She asks them to put together a sequence that includes a balance, a transfer of weight out of their balance, and a new balance. She tells them that they may include traveling if they wish. Students are reminded that the balances must be still for at least six seconds and have a clear shape and that weight must be transferred in a logical and controlled way.

Selection of content—Interactive teaching.

Interactive teaching uses the movement task directed to an entire group. Content can be individualized or not individualized, depending on the design of the task. The following examples of alternative tasks for a lesson in basketball shooting illustrate the flexibility of the movement task for selecting appropriate content for individuals within a group:

- "Everyone do ten layups from each direction and ten foul shots."
- "Decide whether you need to work on layups or foul shots, and do ten of what you need the most work on."
- "We will be working on foul shots today. Choose a distance from the basket where you can be successful. As you become more consistent in getting the ball into the basket, move back toward the foul line."

Each of these tasks gives students a greater or lesser degree of freedom to choose appropriate content. As the tasks allow more student decision making, they become more indirect in their nature. The tasks involve open and closed skills of a specialized sport. When concepts are the content, the same degrees of freedom are present also, as illustrated by the following tasks within the concept of balance for the elementary school and high school:

Elementary School

- "Balance on your head and two hands."
- "Balance on three parts of your body."
- "Find a balance you can hold for six seconds."

High School

- "Apply the 2–3 defense we used in class."
- "Develop a way to protect the space of the basket without person-to-person defense."
- "Develop a 2–3 zone defense."

The first task in each case offers students little freedom of choice, whereas the second task offers more choice. The third offers even more choice and allows the content to be most individualized.

When teachers use an interactive teaching strategy, the appropriateness of the movement task determines the ability of the strategy to meet the needs of individuals within the group. Students should be given different amounts of freedom to respond, depending on the learning objectives and the variance in ability levels within the group. A task that allows little freedom of response can be given only when it can be assumed that the task is appropriate for all students. If the teacher asks students to skip and some children cannot skip, students are put in a difficult position. If the teacher asks students to gallop or skip and all students can gallop, students are better served. When it cannot be assumed that one single response is appropriate for all, the task must be structured to permit the potential for success for all students.

When the teacher gives students little freedom in what to do or how to do it, interactive teaching is sometimes referred to as *command teaching* (Mosston & Ashworth, 1994), such as when a teacher is leading exercises, karate drills, or pacing cues for a folk dance and students are asked to respond to a signal on command. When students have an opportunity to self-pace their practice of a teacher-presented task, the amount of teacher control is decreased and is sometimes known as *practice style* (Mosston & Ashworth, 1994).

At the other end of the continuum is much of what has been called *movement education*. In movement education the teacher is likely to give students a task (usually related to a concept) that has potentially more than one correct response (e.g., "Balance on four parts of your body"). Both command teaching (usually one potential response) and movement education (more than one potential response) tend to be interactive teaching strategies in that the teacher is primarily responsible for the selection of task, the communication of the task, the progression, and feedback and evaluation. In movement education, the student is given the option to select content within a framework set by the teacher. In command teaching the student is given no options for content selection. Although small-group and other organizational patterns can be used, the teacher largely directs his or her efforts to the whole class.

Communication of tasks—Interactive teaching. When an interactive strategy is used to teach a specific skill, the teacher usually takes complete responsibility for communicating tasks. This does not mean the teacher cannot be assisted by students or materials. It means that the teacher is always responsible for the communication of the task and never entirely gives up the role of task communication to other sources. The selection of cues and the clarity of presentation become critical components of task communication.

In interactive teaching, the teacher plays the dominant role in task communication because tasks are largely the result of an interactive process. Tasks are based on previous student responses, and content cannot be locked into a predesigned progression. Teachers do not know exactly what the next task will be until they see students respond to a previous task. Sometimes the next task will ask for quality (refinement), sometimes it will expand or reduce complexity or difficulty (extension), and sometimes it will test the effectiveness of student responses in an applied setting (application/ assessment).

Progression of content—Interactive teaching. In interactive teaching, the teacher usually takes complete responsibility for progression but may share this responsibility with students. One of the advantages of interactive teaching is that progression can be appropriately selected and paced based on teacher observation of the performance of students. Astute observers know when to ask for quality and know what kind of quality to expect (refinement). They also know when to increase the level of difficulty of a task and when to decrease the level of difficulty (extension). When the next task is based on the observed performance of a previous task rather than the passage of time, the interactive teaching strategy is being used effectively. Without this interactive process between student responses and the teacher's next move, an interactive strategy loses its advantage over more managerial and predetermined progressions. With experience, teachers become more able to anticipate student responses and make better judgments about what to do next in a lesson.

Provision for feedback and evaluation— Interactive teaching. In a purely interactive strategy, the teacher takes primary responsibility for feedback and evaluation. In interactive teaching, the teacher should be free during activity to provide students with feedback; thus the teacher should give serious thought before doing anything other than attending to this role (e.g., being a partner to an odd student, participating, arranging equipment for the next task).

Feedback can be given to individuals or to the group as a whole while the students are active or after activity has stopped. By pacing performance to the extent that students must rely on teacher cues to start, continue, and stop performance (command teaching), the teacher limits the amount of feedback, particularly individual help, that can be provided to students. A teacher who sends students off to practice on their own is in a better position to provide feedback but assumes students know what to do and can work independent of specific cues.

Strengths and weaknesses of strategy— Interactive teaching. The strength of interactive teaching as a strategy for the design of learning experiences is that it *is* interactive. Teachers can establish progression and provide for the individualization of content through the movement task by delivering it at an appropriate time. The control of progression and the development of content are flexible and based on the observed needs of learners. Because the teacher usually addresses the whole group when communicating the content, student understanding can be determined and communication immediately adjusted. Feedback and evaluation are more difficult in interactive teaching with large groups because the teacher is actively involved in task selection, communication, and progression.

Interactive teaching puts a premium on the observation and decision-making skills of the teacher, who must quickly make decisions about what to do next. Some teachers have trouble designing movement tasks that actually do individualize the selection of content and progression or have not developed independent working skills with students that would make working on different tasks or different levels of tasks productive. In this case interactive teaching may turn into a situation where the content is not appropriate for all learners.

Station Teaching

Station teaching arranges the environment so that two or more tasks are going on in a class simultaneously in different places. Usually, each separate task is assigned an area or a *station* in the gymnasium, and students rotate from one station to another. Sometimes **station teaching** is called *task teaching.*

Station teaching has become a popular teaching strategy in physical education. When used effectively, it can provide a framework for learning experiences that satisfies all instructional functions. However, there are times when station teaching, like all other strategies, is not a wise selection. These situations will be pointed out as station teaching is explained. An example of a station-teaching lesson is provided in box 8.6.

BOX 8·6

Station Teaching of Volleyball (High School)

The teacher begins the lesson by explaining that from now on the first 15 minutes of each class in the unit will be devoted to the stations arranged in the gymnasium. He describes the following stations:
- Set against the wall
- Serve against the wall
- Bump with a partner
- Spike against the wall from a set
- Dive

The teacher reviews each task and tells the students to do each task ten times. Students work with partners and record their progress each day on an individual progress sheet. Each group of two has one ball that is taken with them from station to station. Partners move to another station when they finish.

Selection of content—Station teaching. In station teaching, the teacher decides on the tasks ahead of time. There are many reasons teachers may want different tasks going on at the same time.

- Equipment problems—When there is not enough equipment, the teacher may feel it is important for all students to use this equipment.
- Space problems—It may be advantageous to mix tasks that require more space with those that do not require as much space.
- Individualizing content—A learning experience might be individualized by assigning students to stations based on their ability or interests and by not having students rotate to all of the stations.
- Motivation—Teachers may also want to keep students motivated by practicing many similar tasks for short periods in different ways at different stations (parallel tasks).

Communication of tasks—Station teaching. One of the most difficult aspects of station teaching is arranging for the communication of tasks. Usually, several tasks must be presented at the same time. The problem is to get everyone going quickly without losing students in a sea of directions for tasks that do not immediately concern them.

Teachers using station teaching have tried to solve the problem of task presentation in many ways. Large posters, task cards, audio, video, or computer programs can be used to communicate tasks. Older students or peers can be assigned task communication at a station. Each student can also have written directions for a station before going to that station. More often, the teacher attempts to give directions for each station at the beginning of the learning experience.

To be effective, tasks must be simple and clearly stated. With younger students a demonstration at each station is almost a necessity. It is difficult to use station teaching to introduce new skills to students that require extended description because of the limited task presentation time available. It is also critical that the tasks selected take about

the same amount of time and are self-motivating. When one task is over quickly and others take more time, students are left waiting at one station until everyone finishes, or if they are permitted to move on, a disproportionate number of students are at one station.

Sometimes station teaching can be used to work with advanced students or students needing more help with a task. By getting the majority of students productively engaged in a self-motivating task, the teacher becomes free to establish another station for more individualized help or to introduce a skill that needs close teacher involvement. This strategy is often effective in a gymnastics lesson or track and field lesson. Students can practice skills previously introduced without the teacher while the teacher establishes another group to introduce new tasks or to give individual help.

Progression of content—Station teaching. Station teaching works best with skills at each station that are unrelated to each other in terms of progression, tasks that are at the same level, or skills that have already been introduced to the students by the teacher. That is because task progression in station teaching is difficult to design.

To make task progression work the teacher must describe the criteria to be used to move from one level of a progression to another, and it is difficult to establish easily understood criteria. It is difficult to put criteria into words or pictures that communicate form or qualitative cues. Establishing quantitative criteria, such as "*When* you can do this two times in a row without losing control, move on to the next task," is easier.

Teachers must also take care to design stations with equivalent tasks in terms of time for completion. When one station is a prerequisite to another, often too many students are stalled at one of the stations. Teachers can have students choose a level of participation and not have them change stations.

Provision for feedback and evaluation— Station teaching. In station teaching, many different tasks are going on at the same time. The teacher in this situation most often plays the role of a manager, maintaining productive work and pacing the work from one station to another. Provision for feedback and evaluation should be a teaching function that station teaching handles well, because the teacher is freed from other teaching functions once the assignment at a station is made. The teacher has more freedom to (1) move from one station to another to provide feedback or (2) remain at one station to present a new task to students or provide specific help. Students must be able to maintain a productive level of engagement for the teacher to be freed to perform these functions.

Many beginning teachers who have not established independent working skills with students find that they will be needed as managers and must therefore make other arrangements for feedback and evaluation. Tasks in most content areas can be designed so that students receive information on their performance from the task (e.g., throwing at a target). Self-testing activities are usually successful and can be made even more so if students are required to record their scores and later their progress when tasks are repeated. Tasks structured with minimal numbers of repetitions for a skill, such as ten overhead passes or ten smashes over the net, also provide feedback and the potential to help students remain productive. Students have more difficulty with qualitative tasks that focus on form without some accountability for form, but many successful teachers have used peer assessment at stations. Teachers provide students with criteria to be assessed in partners or small groups.

Strengths and weaknesses of strategy— Station teaching. Many teachers chose station teaching as a teaching strategy because it offers flexibility in content selection and allows students to work in small groups with varying degrees of co-operation. All students can be active doing different things. The exact nature of the content and the arrangements for time at each station can be decided by the teacher or the student.

Independent working skills must be taught and established before station teaching can be used effectively. When students can work independently without close teacher monitoring, the teacher is free to provide feedback, evaluate student progress, or work with a small group at a single station.

Some types of content work better than others in station teaching. In most school situations, limited provisions for task communication make new or complex skills difficult to work with in a station-teaching format. New process-oriented tasks, such as those emphasizing form, are difficult to communicate and to establish accountability systems for. Individual self-testing, environmentally designed tasks, product-oriented tasks, and the practice of skills already learned that do not need a great deal of teacher refinement or development are usually the most successful.

The most difficult part of station teaching is maintaining quality of performance in student responses. It is not uncommon to see students racing through gymnastic skills or exercises or manipulating tasks with no attention to how they are completing a skill. If quality of performance is important to the task, teachers must find ways to hold students accountable for quality. Writing process criteria on the task card usually is not an adequate way to communicate qualitative concerns or to hold students accountable for quality. Teachers must clearly communicate the qualitative goal orientation of the task in their task presentation and stop the work of students when the quality of the work is not being attended to.

Peer Teaching

Peer teaching is an instructional strategy that transfers the teacher's responsibility for instructional functions to the student. It generally is used in conjunction with other strategies but is worth exploring as a separate option. A peer-teaching strategy can be used with any teaching function defined in this chapter. Examples of the use of peer teaching, both in a complete lesson and in parts of a lesson, are provided in boxes 8.7 and 8.8.

Peers can present tasks when the experience is carefully structured by the teacher.

Peer Teaching (Whole Lesson)

Gymnastics (high school)

The teacher divides students in a gymnastics class into ability groups of four socially compatible students each. The students had been working on apparatus and floor exercise routines. Each student in the group now teaches her or his routine to the other members of the group.

The teacher explains that the student teaching the routines (the peer teacher) is responsible for the quality of performance of the learners and that groups will not be evaluated on the level of difficulty but on the following criteria:

- Clarity of body shape throughout the routine
- Smoothness of transition throughout the routine
- Control of movement
- Dynamic quality of execution (use of shape, speed, level, force, etc.)

The peer teacher is encouraged to first demonstrate and explain how each part of the routine is done and then to give students practice on parts. When students can do each part with quality, the peer teacher moves to put the parts together. Groups move at their own pace but are encouraged to practice one routine until it is done well before moving on to another routine.

The experience takes three class periods. On the last day each group demonstrates what it has done.

Peer Teaching (Part of a Lesson)

Dance (high school)

The teacher teaches a complex dance step to a large group of students. All but a few students are ready to move on to a more-advanced use of the step. The teacher appoints several students who have mastered the step to work with those who have not. He encourages the peer teacher to use the proper cue words and to slow down the step pattern until it is attained by the learners.

Dance (elementary school)

A third-grade class is divided into groups of four learners. Each group choreographs its own dance to simple folk dance music. The teacher selects two of the groups to teach their dances to the whole class. Each group demonstrates its dance to the whole class. The teacher then asks each member of the group to teach a part of the dance to the whole class by explaining how it is done and then helping the rest of the class perform.

Volleyball (middle school)

The teacher works with the whole class on the volleyball underhand serve. She then divides the class into groups of four. One student serves the ball on one side of the net, and one student serves the ball on the other side of the net. One student on each side coaches the server. The coach's job is to check for the following teaching cues that have been given for the underhand serve:

- Using up and back stance with body lean
- Hitting ball out of hand with no toss
- Finishing with weight on forward foot

Each group has a skill card with the cues listed. Coaches are told to look for only one cue each time the ball is served and to tell the server whether that cue has been observed.

Selection of content—Peer teaching. The teacher usually selects the content in a peer-teaching strategy, but sometimes a movement idea, concept, or project developed by a student or group of students is taught by students to other students. For example, elementary school students might design sequences of locomotor patterns and then teach these patterns to other students, thus choosing the task within a framework set by the teacher. Secondary school students might participate in the same type of experience by sharing their designs for game play, dances, or exercise routines.

Communication of tasks—Peer teaching. In peer teaching, one student is often used to show or, more literally, teach a skill to another. Skilled or experienced students can be matched with students who are having difficulty or who are inexperienced. Students can be asked to communicate a task to the whole class or to part of a class (in conjunction with station teaching). When a student is used as an auxiliary teacher at a separate station from the teacher, it must be remembered that students acting as teachers also have needs—not only personal skill needs, but also needs for support and guidance in their teaching efforts. Peer teachers need to be taught how to do a good job as a teacher. Peer teaching is most successful in classroom work when older students help younger students. Peers many times have a communication advantage that the teacher does not. Thus even if peers serve no other function within an instructional experience, they often communicate tasks well.

Progression of content—Peer teaching. Progression of content is almost always a teacher function even when peer teaching is used. Skill-to-skill or within-task progression should be clearly communicated when the peer teacher has responsibility for progression. This progression can be verbally communicated to the whole group and is usually planned ahead of time with the peer teacher. The qualitative criteria must also be clear to the peer teacher.

Provision for feedback and evaluation—Peer teaching. Of all the instructional functions most appropriately assigned to peer teaching, the function of feedback and evaluation is one of the most appropriate. Teachers of large groups have difficulty performing this necessary function because of large classes and limited time. The recent emphasis in physical

Students can be taught to provide feedback to each other. (*Courtesy SIUE Photo.*)

education on teacher accountability for student performance has put an increased emphasis on student assessment. When students receive good feedback on their performance throughout the instructional process, they are more likely to focus more on improving their performance during the instructional process and more likely to learn and perform better at the end of the instructional process. Students who are trained to be good observers and who are given guidance on what to look for in providing feedback can help each other a great deal and can assess each other's performance.

Partner work is often used effectively to establish a peer relationship for feedback and evaluation. When peer feedback and peer assessment do not work, it is often because the teacher has not given the observer *clear and limited criteria for observation* and because a clear expectation for improved performance has not been communicated. The teacher will need to hold the peer responsible for good and accurate feedback and assessment.

Peers are often used successfully to assess performance (1) when the product of performance is easily measured, such as the number of trials out of ten throws that hit a target or (2) when students are given one aspect of performance to look at, such as "*Tell* your partner whether he stepped into his swing." Students are capable of observing in more-complicated ways and helping each other in more-sophisticated ways if the teacher is willing to teach

THE REAL WORLD

Establishing the Peer Relationship

Chang is a first-year teacher working with his students (eighth grade) for the first time to establish a peer relationship for teaching. He has asked students to score trials in a peer assessment experience and they were able to act responsibly in that situation, but he has been reluctant to give students more responsibility. What follows are his efforts at gradually introducing students to a peer "teaching role." Chang has decided to use students to provide feedback to each other on their performance.

1. Students are working on a two-on-two basketball task with no goals. The students have been working on quick passes and passing ahead of the moving receiver on offense and on moving into an open space (cutting) when they do not have the ball. Chang works first with the class as a total group. He asks for four volunteers to do the two-on-two task so that the rest of the class can be the observers and provide feedback. Each student has a clipboard, pencil, and sheet that describes the cues and has a place to list the students' names. Chang directs the class to observe the offensive players. He stops the play and then asks the observers how they would rate the use

of each of the cues by each of the players. He spends time asking them why they would give the score that they have given so they know what they are looking for in good performance. He then leads the group through a discussion of what they might say to each of the players to help them improve their performance and makes sure that students understand how important it is to describe what the players did well as well as what they might do to improve. The effect of negative feedback is fully explored from a personal perspective.

2. Students are then organized into small groups of five (four players and an observer). Each student will get an opportunity to play offense and defense and also to be an observer. They are given time to work with the task and to share their observer's comments with each other.

3. Chang then leads the class through a discussion of how they "felt" getting feedback from their observer and what kind of feedback was helpful to them. They are then asked to give feedback to the person who gave them feedback on the helpfulness of the information they were provided.

peers how to observe and how to help each other. The Real World box describes the efforts of one teacher to develop peer observation skills. Productive peer relationships take time to develop, and teachers should not expect students to function well in these situations without clear guidance or expectations and without practice.

Strengths and weaknesses of strategy—Peer teaching. As a teaching strategy, peer teaching can be used for all instructional functions or only one. Like all teaching strategies, it can be used for part of a lesson or for a whole lesson. The key to peer teaching is the peer relationship. The teacher must be careful not to put a peer teacher in a threatening social relationship with his or her peers. The teacher must be sure that students will work together in a productive way. A productive relationship between

peers will not occur unless the expectations of the relationship are clear and students are held accountable for specific criteria and responsibilities. In other words, the peer relationship and responsibilities must be structured. Teachers who put students together to teach or observe each other with no guidance as to how to teach or what to observe will be disappointed by the results.

When peer-teaching experiences are used well for one or more instructional functions, more individualized work can be done. The teacher's attention in peer teaching should shift from the performance of the learner to guiding the peer relationship.

Peer-teaching experiences have the potential to develop in the peer teacher important skills of observation and analysis and a more thorough understanding of both motor and social skills. Both the learner and the peer teacher can profit from such experiences.

Cooperative Learning

Cooperative learning is a popular teaching strategy (Johnson, Johnson, & Johnson-Hulebec, 1994, 2002; Kagen, 1990; Slavin, 1988, 1990; Smith, 1987) developed by Johnson and Johnson (1975). Academic areas, particularly in many middle schools, currently emphasize cooperative learning strategies of teaching. Cooperative learning has grown out of a recognition that adults need to be able to appreciate diversity and work with others in a diverse society to lead productive and happy lives and therefore students need to learn how to work with others productively. Advocates of cooperative learning also focus on the "socially constructed" nature of learning. Cooperative learning has the potential to increase student learning, as well as to contribute to social and personal development. Box 8.9 illustrates a lesson where the teacher is using cooperative learning. There is some support for the notion that many children, particularly those students in some minority groups, learn better in a cooperative learning setting.

In cooperative learning, groups of learners are assigned a learning task or project to complete as a team. Students are grouped heterogeneously according to different factors such as race, ability, or social needs. Groups, as well as individuals, are evaluated according to how well they complete the task or project, in addition to the manner in which they work together to complete the tasks. Like all teaching strategies, these gains are not automatic. Students must be well prepared for the expectations involved in working together for a common goal. Positive results are attained only if the goals students are given are meaningful, students are taught how to cooperate, and accountability for the process and the product of the learning experience are evident to the student.

Selection of content—Cooperative learning. Usually the teacher selects the task or project to be completed by the students in cooperative learning, although students may have a choice or role in defining the goal to be achieved. To produce meaningful interaction with both the content and each other, tasks must be selected that have the potential

---

B O X   8 · 9

Cooperative Learning Lessons: Folk Dance Unit

This is a lesson the author has used with middle-school students very successfully. The objective of the lesson is for all of the students to be able to perform five different folk dances skillfully.

1. Students are divided into five different groups that will be their home groups. They are told that each member of their home group will learn a dance that they will be responsible for teaching. Their home group will be assessed as a team at the end of the three lessons to determine how well each member in their group performs each of the folk dances. A videotape of all five dances is shown to the entire class, and each group assigns one member of their team to learn one of the dances.

2. Students from each group learning the same dance meet in a part of the gym. They are given a video instructional tape for the dance and written directions. During this first experience their role is to help each other learn the dance using the materials provided. Each member of the "learning group" must know and be able to do the dance well before any member can go back to their home group.

3. When students return to their home group, they are each given taped music for their dance and instructions to teach the dance to their home group until every member of their home group knows the dance.

4. As part of the third lesson all groups perform each dance. The teacher videotapes the performance and assesses each group's performance of each dance. The teacher shares the assessment of the dances with the students in the next lesson and they get to do each of them "for fun" several times.

---

for teaching something meaningful and at the same time requiring the cooperation and skills of the group. If a task can be solved immediately by one member of the group, the task was not a good choice for cooperative learning. The goal in task selection should be to design an experience that develops the interdependency of all the members of the group.

Cooperative learning experiences in physical education are becoming more common. The very nature of our content has great potential for its use as a teaching strategy. It is possible to design cooperative student experiences that are fun and do achieve some social and affective goals in physical education without contributing to student learning in the content of physical education. Many cooperative games of this nature have been designed, such as working as a team to get through a pretend swamp. The skills needed in activities such as this are cooperative but contribute little to the unique content goals of our field. Cooperative learning experiences should be designed to contribute in some way to the psychomotor goals of physical education, as well as the social and emotional development of students.

Four different cooperative learning formats have been used extensively in the classroom in physical education. The reading list at the end of this chapter provides additional examples of the use of many of these formats as they are used in physical education. Brief descriptions of these follow:

JIGSAW (Aronson et al., 1978). In the jigsaw approach to cooperative learning, a project is designed that has the potential to be divided into components. The project is divided into component parts essential for its completion. Each student in the group is given a part of a project. All the students responsible for a particular component form an initial group and are given resources to learn their part. In a modification of Jigsaw I, Jigsaw II does not require that each student be given separate materials on a subject, but all students are exposed to the same materials and one member assumes responsibility for a part of the materials. Each student then has an essential part of the project, which he or she must share with the group. The jigsaw creates interdependency because each student has a unique part of the project.

Potential PE Jigsaw. Every member of a team or group is responsible for a different component of fitness in building a warm-up routine.

Each member of a group is responsible for a different skill in a sport in a sport unit or a different folk dance in a folk dance unit.

■   ■   ■

TEAMS-GAMES TOURNAMENT (TGT) (Slavin, 1983). In TGT, heterogeneously grouped teams work together to master content for competition against other teams. For the tournament and competition, students are grouped homogeneously according to ability. Both individual scores and cooperative team scores are kept.

Potential PE TGT. TGT has great potential for physical education, particularly in individual sports. Teams are formed heterogeneously for practice and homogeneously for competition. Practice groups must be taught how to facilitate the improvement of all members. NOTE: Sport education is a variation of this model that does not regroup teams homogeneously. Sport education is described in more detail in chapter 12 (Siedentop, Hastie, & van der Mars, 2004).

■   ■   ■

PAIRS-CHECK. In the pairs-check, two groups of two students work together. Each pair is set up as a peer-teaching group, as described in the previous section. In pairs-check, two groups of pairs come back together as a group of four to check, evaluate, and revise what they have done.

Potential PE Pairs-Check. Peer-teaching groups are established to learn a skill. The pairs then form a group of four with another two students to help each other learn the skill and assess the skill. Peers are used to develop a "double stunt" in tumbling or a movement sequence; pairs-check is used to teach what one group has developed to another group.

■   ■   ■

CO-OP. In co-op, a project is designed that has many components. The group decides for which components members will be responsible. Individual students are evaluated on the extent to which they fulfill their specific responsibility to the group.

Potential PE Co-op. Teams balanced in ability are developed for a sport. Each team is responsible for equipment, warm-up, officials, a ten-minute practice schedule each day, scoring, and coaching during play. Students are assigned roles, which may change each week (similar to the sport education model developed by Siedentop, 2000, and described in chapter 12).

Groups are responsible for designing an aerobic dance routine that balances the components of fitness.

You will notice that the experiences just described are broader than most tasks used in other strategies. More responsibility is given the learners to not only resolve a problem but also design a process to resolve the problem. The solution to a problem as well as the process that is used is assessed. More effective cooperative learning experiences have the potential for students to have *different* interdependent roles.

Communication of tasks—Cooperative learning. Teachers will want to communicate a cooperative learning task after groups have been selected to work on the task. Group selection is one of the most important aspects of cooperative learning. *Although there are times when teachers will want to form homogeneous groups, most of the time groups should be selected that are heterogeneous in relation to gender, skill ability, ethnic orientation, or race.* The social interaction skills of all of the learners are a strong consideration in group membership.

Teachers have several options for communicating cooperative learning tasks. Usually teachers will communicate the task to all the groups at the same time. Task communication must involve both the expectation the teacher has for the goal of the learning experience and expectations for how the goal should be reached as a group. The more independent the groups of learners, the more open the teacher can be about the process to be used. Students just beginning to work cooperatively will need more structure by the teacher as to how the task is to be solved. They may need to have the teacher give the directions for getting organized, give students some time to complete the organizational responsibilities, and then have the students report what they intend to do before they move on with a project. Likewise, students can be held accountable for each step of the process before they are permitted to move on to the next step. The amount of step-by-step structure students need depends on their ability to work together productively and independently of the teacher. Students who have learned to work more independently of the teacher may not need to be monitored by the teacher as closely.

Clarity of expectations is critical to a well-designed cooperative learning task, both for the group and for the individual. Written materials are often used to summarize the task for students. These materials can describe the following:

- Finished product—what the finished product should look like and the criteria for assessing the finished product.
- Steps to be completed en route to the finished product—exactly how students are to get to the finished product in terms of what needs to be done and in what order.
- Roles for each of the participants in a group.
- Project components—a specific listing of all of the components of the project including the process and product.
- Resources available to students.
- Time frame for completing the project.
- "Rules" for how the project is to be completed.
- Evaluation procedures for the group and individuals in the group.

Progression of content—Cooperative learning. Progression of content in cooperative learning experiences is either built into the task or left to the learners. When teachers are just beginning to work with students in cooperative learning experiences, they may want to structure the task to include a progression such as the following:

1. Elect a leader.
2. Divide your group into three teams of two people.
3. Formulate three different possible defenses.
4. Try all three defenses, and evaluate them according to the criteria listed.
5. Choose one defense you think is the best.
6. Work on the defense until everyone can do it well.
7. Prepare to present your defense to the class as a whole.
8. Assess your participation in this project as well as the participation of others in the group.

Each step of the progression can initially be checked by the teacher. Students more experienced with working in groups may not need as much structure in process and should be allowed to design strategies for arriving at solutions to the task and work at their own pace. The teacher should intervene with groups having trouble getting started and should suggest an approach.

Provision for feedback and evaluation—Cooperative learning. Once a task has been presented, the teacher should be free to provide feedback to groups on how they are working and how well they are completing the assigned task. One of the advantages of cooperative learning is that the teacher is free to stay with a group for as long as needed, under the assumption that other students are productively engaged in their own work. The teacher should be an astute observer of group process to be effective in this role. Teachers can suggest alternative strategies for completing the task and resources. Students should be allowed to work out their own problems and false starts without a great deal of teacher interference. However, *groups should not be permitted to flounder for long periods without teacher help.* If some groups need direction and structure, it should be provided.

Because it is likely that different groups not only will arrive at a different solution to the problem, but also will use a different process, all groups can usually benefit from "sharing" sessions, in which groups have the opportunity to present to other groups what they developed and how they developed it. The teacher can use these opportunities to emphasize group process skills and to make students aware of the advantages of diverse talents and abilities. The teacher can also use these opportunities to talk about strengths and weaknesses of the products produced by the groups, such as "*What* did you like about the solution this group developed?" or "*How* do you think this group could improve what they did?"

More formal evaluation sessions that provide feedback to individual groups on the "product" and the process are helpful. Feedback and evaluation are easier if the teacher establishes *clear criteria* in advance when communicating expectations to students. One of the primary goals in using cooperative learning is to help students understand (1) how to work with others so that everyone benefits and (2) the advantages in working with others to accomplish a task in a cooperative way. Feedback and evaluation must be concerned with the product of the group as well as the process that was used because group process is so important to this strategy. If the teacher is going to do an evaluation of group process and not share this evaluation with the students, much is lost.

Teachers will have to individualize their progressions for learners because students will most likely not finish their projects at the same time. Teachers will need to have additional tasks or extensions of the same task available for those students who complete their projects before other groups.

Strengths and weaknesses of strategy—Cooperative Learning. Cooperative learning is an investment in time. Teachers use cooperative learning because they think the time spent in helping students to learn how to work together and to deal with content at a higher level is a good investment. Not all group work or partner work is cooperative learning. Cooperative learning experiences are structured specifically to accomplish cooperative learning goals and improve the interaction among students. If the teacher is not willing to take the time to help students interact in positive ways with each other, cooperative learning often falls short of its goals. If the content the students are working with in their groups does not contribute to the curriculum goals of the physical education program, then the cooperative learning experience is likewise inappropriate.

Self-Instructional Strategies

In the simplest sense, **self-instructional strategies** involve a preestablished program for learning that may involve the teacher in a tutorial or managerial role but basically eliminates the teacher from more traditional instructional functions during the instructional process. Self-instructional strategies rely heavily on preestablished written materials, computer programs, media, and evaluative procedures. They may be used to fulfill one or more, and sometimes all, of the functions of instruction. One of the clear goals of the National Standards for Physical Education (NASPE, 2004) is that students become independent learners. Self-instructional strategies for teaching can help students in this area.

In addition to being used for single lessons or parts of lessons, self-instructional models can be designed for an entire course (see e.g., Poole, Sebolt, & Metzler, 2004; Sebolt & Metzler, 1994). Students can work either within the confines of a class or independent of a structured class period. Materials that include progressions of tasks, instructions for task performance, practice recommendations, and evaluative tools are provided. The student and/or the teacher decides where the student enters the progression and where the student ends the progression. *Mastery learning* usually involves a preconceived exit point. The amount of time a student takes to reach this point is flexible. *Contract teaching* and most other forms of individualized program instruction evaluate the student with agreed-on exit criteria. The important aspect of self-instructional strategies is that all the necessary ingredients for student learning must be included in the materials.

It should be clear that students who are to profit from self-instructional strategies must be highly motivated; self-directed; and, to some extent, knowledgeable in how to make the best use of time and the materials provided. Motivation, self-direction, and skill in using instructional materials take time to develop. A teacher would be unwise to move completely to a self-instructional model until these skills are developed. An example of a secondary lesson using a self-instructional strategy is presented in box 8.10, and an example of self-instructional materials that might be used in an elementary school setting is presented in box 8.11.

Selection of content—Self-instructional strategies. The content in self-instructional strategies is usually established beforehand through a list of progressive tasks that are criterion referenced (i.e., they have attached evaluative criteria). Sometimes skills for entire sports are sequenced from beginning to advanced levels with small gradations in between. Students (or teachers) thus can decide to enter the progression at any point. Students are permitted to advance quickly from one level to another through competency testing.

Communication of tasks—Self-instructional strategies. Tasks are usually defined and communicated in written form through charts, printed materials, or task cards. For complex tasks, other media are needed

---

BOX 8·10

Self-Instructional Strategies for Gymnastics (High School)

A teacher is using a partial self-instructional model to teach high school gymnastics skills. Each student is pretested on basic gymnastics skills and selects an area of concentration, either floor exercise or a piece of apparatus. The teacher develops an individual program for each student, which tests basic skills on several pieces of equipment, and a more extensive list of objectives for the student's area of specialization, which indicates a self-designed routine.

The teacher sets up several kinds of media at each station that explain how each skill is performed and the criteria for performance. Sometimes the task is communicated with a large visual poster depicting difficult phases of the skill. Sometimes a loop film or a videotape is set up at a station. In previous years the teacher taught students how to use media materials on a less extensive basis.

The class is organized for three days per week. Students are free to move to any piece of equipment they would like to at any time. The teacher spends a half day at each piece of equipment to provide help at that piece or to evaluate student performance. Students may be evaluated only twice on each skill.

Lists are posted of students who have successfully completed skills at a high level and who are willing to help others.

(e.g., loop films, charts, videotape, DVDs, and computer-generated programs). The increasing use of computers in physical education facilities has a great deal of potential for task communication and interactive programs that are individualized. When students are ready to do a task, they seek direction or descriptions on how to do it.

Students must know how to use materials effectively to learn a skill. In addition, enough materials must be available and convenient for the chosen method of task communication to be effective.

It is possible for teachers to perform task communication in an otherwise self-instructional strategy. In this case students are told that a certain task will be presented at a particular time for those students who

BOX 8·11

Self-Instructional Strategies for Gymnastics (Elementary School)

Learning center

Make sequences on a piece of equipment.

Objective

When you have completed these activities, you will be able to perform a sequence of movements on the equipment provided.

Equipment

This learning center can be used on any of the equipment in the activity area, such as a box or a balance beam.

Tasks

1. Find a piece of equipment where there is room for you to work.
2. Try several different ways of *getting* on the equipment safely. If you always use your hands and feet, try to get on the equipment backward or sideways.
3. When you have chosen the way you like best to get on the equipment, balance two body parts in a twisted shape. Practice the getting on and balancing in the twisted shape until it is easy. Hold the balance while you say your name twice.
4. Change your shape to a wide, stretched shape, balancing on body parts different from before.
5. Now find a way to get off the equipment safely. If you use a jump to get off, land as softly as you can.
6. Practice the whole sequence: getting on, balancing in a twisted shape, and changing to a stretched shape and getting off. Keep doing the sequence until it is easy and then go on to the checklist.

Checklist (check off each thing after it is accomplished)

—Is your sequence difficult enough for you, or have you chosen movements that are very easy for you to do? If it is too easy, make one part of it more difficult for yourself.

—Are your balance shapes really held still, or do they wobble around? Practice the balance until you can hold very still.

—Is your sequence smooth when you do it, or are there some jerky parts in it that do not seem to go well? You might want to change some of the movements if there are.

Other possibilities

Try changing the speed of the sequence. Start very quickly and end slowly, or start slowly and end quickly.

Change the place to get on the equipment. Approach it from the other side or one end.

Add another balanced shape to the two on the apparatus.

Finish your sequence with a roll and balance *after* you have landed from the equipment.

Change the speed as you move in the sequence. Begin very slowly and then speed up.

Begin with a quick movement and end very slowly.

Put a turning movement in between two of the shapes.

Start the sequence very high and finish it very low to the ground.

Find a vocal sound that you can make as you do your sequence. If you cannot think of one, try saying "sh-h-h-h-h" in different ways as you move.

Find a partner and see how you can put your sequences together so that you have a duet.

Remember that you *do not* have to do the *same thing* as your partner.

Watch a dance program on television and draw some of the *shapes* the dancers make when they balance in different positions.

Make up a chant that you can say as you do your sequence. Post your chant on the bulletin board.

Write a letter to some aliens on Mars telling them why we dance on earth.

Source: H. Hoffman, et al., *Meaningful Movement for Children: A Developmental Theme Approach in Physical Education*, 1981, Allyn & Bacon, Needham Heights, MA.

are ready to learn it. The rest of the students in the class can remain with their practice programs. Variations of station teaching can be used also, with different tasks presented at different stations.

Progression of content—Self-instructional strategies. One of the advantages of a self-instructional model is that each student can start, progress, and end work in content at an appropriate level. A disadvantage is that the progression is preestablished and may not be appropriate for all students. The example in box 8.11 (see p. 171) individualizes the content by using a movement concept from which the student may choose an appropriate response. Some preestablished programs allow for remedial loops and horizontal development of materials. In these instances, practice materials are provided that permit practice of the same level of an experience in different ways. More-sophisticated materials can be designed so that students can work on specific problems in different ways, as the example in box 8.11 (see p. 171) illustrates.

Criteria for the quality of performance must be built into the instructional and evaluation materials. The two examples provided here do this in different ways.

Provision for feedback and evaluation—Self-instructional strategies. Feedback is essential for learning. Knowledge of results can be built into instructional materials, primarily through self-assessment or teacher assessment, but knowledge of performance is more difficult to obtain through self-instructional means.

Some self-instructional models in psychomotor skills depend heavily on videotape or peer feedback. Ideally, the teacher in a class instructional situation should be available to provide feedback. The teacher's role in a self-instructional strategy, however, is complicated by the teacher's role as a manager. Because of the need to evaluate students and help students use the materials, the teacher may find it difficult to provide adequate feedback.

Self-instructional strategies depend heavily on evaluation. In computer-assisted instructional models used in the classroom for cognitive learning, the computer provides the necessary feedback and evaluation to the learner as part of a program. In physical education, motor skills cannot be evaluated with paper-and-pencil tests or computer responses. Students are most often expected to meet criteria before going on to a new skill or a new level of the same skill. Often the teacher must judge proficiency and thus spends much time evaluating. Teachers who have designed alternative ways to meet this need including the use of peer assessment or designating particular times during a class or on particular days for checking students' progress are usually more successful in fulfilling other roles.

Strengths and weaknesses of strategy—Self-instructional strategies. Self-instructional strategies should probably be the goal of well-developed physical education programs. When students leave school programs, it is a great advantage for them to have the ability (1) to use available materials, equipment, and facilities to facilitate their learning; (2) to use readily available self-instructional books and other resources; and (3) to direct their instruction. Students do not start at this point, however, and teachers should decide whether they want to use program time to teach students how to function in this environment. This is a curricular decision.

Self-instructional models involve predicted progressions. The more specific the progression, the more appropriately a student may be placed in that progression. Progressions may be designed with alternative loops that anticipate a less-than-linear advancement of skill. Such a design aids individualization.

A disadvantage of self-instructional models is the time required to prepare materials. Once materials are developed, planning time is considerably reduced. Good progressions, media materials, and evaluative materials require much time to prepare. Commercially developed materials are available but expensive. In addition, teachers usually spend most of their time teaching students how to use the materials and evaluating progress.

Cognitive Strategies

Cognitive strategies is a label given to a group of teaching strategies designed to engage the learner cognitively in the content through the presentation of tasks. The terms *problem solving, guided discovery, divergent style* (Mosston & Ashworth, 1994), *teaching through questions* (Siedentop, 2000), *inquiry learning* (Harrison, Buck, & Blakemore, 2001), and other terms have been used to describe approaches to the content that engage the learner in formulating responses rather than duplicating the response they have been shown by the teacher. Teachers use a cognitive strategy because they support one or more of the following ideas:

- The process of learning is as important as what is to be learned.
- Students are more likely to be engaged at a higher level with the content when their role in the learning process is more extensive.
- Cognitive strategies allow the content to be individualized.
- Cognitive strategies are a good way to teach concepts to students, and concepts have the potential to transfer to other similar content.
- Cognitive strategies involve the learner cognitively, and cognitive processing for motor skill learning is essential.

The teacher has s everal alternatives if the objective is to cognitively involve the learner. Cognitive strategies usually involve some type of problem-solving process on the part of the learner or groups of learners initiated through the presentation of a task. Problems can be as simple as "Is it better to bend your knees when landing or keep your knees straight?" or as complicated as "Design a sequence of exercises that can be used for a warm-up in volleyball." The level of involvement of the learner varies with the level of cognitive response. When the teacher is looking for a single correct response, problem solving is usually called **guided discovery** (Mosston & Ashworth, 1994) or *convergent inquiry*. The teacher knows the answer to the problem but leads the learner to discover the answer for himself or herself. When the problem is open and there is not one best response but many good responses, problem solving is usually called a *divergent style* or *divergent inquiry*. Although not every response is as good as any other response, there is no single response. In the examples just given, the task related to bending the knees on landing is termed *guided discovery* or *convergent inquiry* and the task related to designing a warm-up routine is called *divergent style*. Examples of both guided discovery and divergent style are presented in box 8.12.

BOX 8·12

Guided Discovery and Divergent Tasks

Guided discovery: Lead the learner to a correct solu tion

Task one: When you are practicing your tennis forehand, try it a few times with your weight staying on your trailing foot and then with your weight transferring to your lead foot. See if you can come to some conclusion as to which is more helpful to you. *(The teacher presents the task—either to individuals or to partners—has students work on it, and then brings the group back to make a decision.)*

Task two: You have several tasks on your task card related to the production of force. One of these tasks asks you to throw, another to jump, and another to strike a ball with a bat. These tasks require that you produce force. Each of your three-member group is responsible for leading the group through one of these skills—first with little force so that you don't throw hard, jump high, or hit far. Then I want you to do the opposite—I want you to do it as hard as you can. What you are trying to do is to see if you can tell me what you do differently in these skills when you want to produce force. Then see if you can come up with a rule that might be used for these skills.

Divergent tasks: Ask the learner to provide a solution where many are possible

Task one: Design a sequence of movements that incorporates traveling and balancing. You must start in a clear and still position and end in a clear and still position. Your transitions must be smooth and your balance held stretched and still for at least six seconds.

Task two: Your team must decide which is the skill you need the most work on and must develop a practice drill that practices that skill the way you think it should be used.

Cognitive strategies focus on the nature of the task presented to the learner and not the organization of instruction. Therefore, cognitive strategies can be used with any of the strategies previously discussed in this chapter that organize instruction. Interactive teaching, peer teaching, cooperative learning strategies, and self-instruction strategies can all be used as a framework for involving the learner cognitively in the process of instruction. Movement education, used extensively in many elementary physical education programs, uses an interactive strategy of teaching that presents to learners both divergent movement tasks and guided discovery tasks, often with a direct instruction approach. Teaching balance as an interactive teaching strategy (presented in box 8.5) is an example of such an approach. Examples of convergent inquiry are presented in boxes 8.13 and 8.14.

B O X   8 · 1 3

Convergent Inquiry—Secondary

A volleyball class has been learning the overhand serve and has developed enough command of the basic mechanics of the skill to begin learning how to direct and control the ball. The teacher wants students to understand that they can control the direction and type of spin on the ball by where they contact the ball.

The first task the teacher gives the students is to ask them to determine where they have to contact the ball if they want it to go left or right into the opponents' court. When the students can identify right of center for a left placement and left of center for a right placement, the teacher asks them to practice getting the ball to different parts of the court with different placements on the ball.

The second task the teacher gives is to ask the students to identify what happens to the ball when they contact the ball with a flat hand on the top or bottom of the ball. Students hit the ball to a wall so that they can get maximum practice. Initially students identify that the ball goes up or down. The teacher then asks the students to pair up. One student observes what kind of spin the ball takes in flight. When students can identify backspin or topspin as the correct responses, the teacher asks the students why they might want to use this type of serve in a game. Students then practice putting spin on their serves over a net until they can control what happens to the ball.

B O X   8 · 1 4

Convergent Inquiry—Elementary

Students are working on jumping for distance. The teacher wants them to understand how to make their jumps more forceful. Half the class is asked to jump as far as they can while the other half of the class observes. The teacher asks the observers to identify the students they think jumped the farthest. Students then reverse observer and performer roles, and the teacher asks several of the students identified as having a forceful jump to demonstrate again for the class. This time the teacher asks the students to identify what the demonstrators did to make their jump forceful. When several key aspects of the preparation and takeoff are identified, the teacher asks all the students to try to make their jumps more forceful by using the identified cues. As students are ready the teacher then proceeds to help them identify important aspects of the flight and landing phases of the jump.

The emphases on cooperative learning, instructional processes that involve the learner in the process of assessment (see chapter 11), and the process of learning make cognitive strategies an appropriate choice for the design of learning experiences. Cognitive strategies have a great deal of potential to increase the level of involvement of the learner. The disadvantage is that cognitive strategies designed to lead the learner to knowledge usually take more time than those in which the teacher shares the knowledge directly with students.

Cognitive strategies can be used for one task (e.g., Where should your head be at contact with the ball [golf lesson]?) or they can be used as an entire lesson (e.g., identifying an appropriate ready position for activities that require a fast response in many directions). Sometimes the teacher can "dump" a large and involved task on the learner (e.g., develop a gymnastics routine of three balances with a partner), and sometimes the teachers must provide more structure to the process (e.g., develop a balance with a partner, link it to a second balance, then add the third balance).

Team Teaching

Team teaching is a teaching strategy in which more than one teacher is responsible for delivering instruction to a group of learners. When physical education classes became coeducational, many educators looked toward team teaching as a way to meet the needs of both boys and girls heterogeneously grouped by having both a male teacher and a female teacher responsible for a larger group of learners. Team teaching as a strategy has a great potential to meet this need, as well as to deliver effective instruction. Unfortunately, team teaching in practice in many situations has not lived up to its potential. Many teachers are not trained in how to use team teaching and are not able to develop the interactive relationship needed between teachers to make team teaching work. In most situations, team teaching is nothing more than *turn teaching*. Instead of forty students having two teachers, in many cases, forty students now have one teacher.

Team teaching is included in this chapter because, despite its abuse, team teaching presents some unique opportunities to solve instructional problems in gymnasiums shared by several groups of learners and several teachers. When used appropriately, team teaching has the potential to be a "best" solution to many situations that prohibit or make difficult self-contained classes. Even when self-contained classes are a possibility, teachers should seriously consider the following advantages of team teaching.

- **Flexible grouping:** A primary advantage of team teaching is flexible grouping. Team teaching can use any of the previous instructional strategies. The advantage of team teaching is that students can be divided differently each class period or part of a class period to individualize instruction, based on skill level, interest, social needs, or whatever criteria the teachers feel are important. One teacher usually becomes the lead teacher in team teaching and the second teacher the support teacher. Group size can remain flexible so that sometimes the support teacher may have only a small group that may need extra help or may need to move faster than the rest of the class. Teacher roles can change so that the same teacher is not always the support teacher or the lead teacher for instruction. Many effective teachers who use team teaching change roles at the unit level, based on expertise and interest in a content area.

- **Individual help:** The support teacher can be used in instruction to identify students who need help and give help to these students without having the responsibility for the whole class. Feedback and evaluation is difficult in group instruction with only one teacher but is a lot easier when the support teacher is freed from the primary responsibility of the whole class. The support teacher is free to perform any teaching function either with individual students or with small groups of students. Meeting the needs of individuals is a primary potential strength of team teaching.

Strengths and weaknesses of strategy—Team teaching. If team teaching is to be used effectively, teachers must establish a relationship with each other that allows them to feel comfortable teaching "in front of" another professional. For teachers who are not comfortable working in front of their peers, this initially can be threatening, but it is well worth the risk. Teachers must also be willing to plan together and evaluate what they have done together. In some situations this much togetherness is difficult because of personality difficulties or differences in professional goals. As in all relationships, there must be some compromise. Teachers who can establish a real team-teaching relationship tend to learn a great deal from each other. A productive interactive relationship with another professional tends to be growth producing and highly motivating. Productive interactive relationships with another teacher are developed more easily when one teacher does not feel he or she owns "good teaching" and when both teachers are willing to accept that there are different ways to accomplish similar purposes. Often one teacher is stronger than another, but both will grow more if they work hard

TABLE 8·1

Summary of the Strengths and Weaknesses of Seven Teaching Strategies

Teaching strategy	Teacher function	Strengths	Weaknesses
Interactive teaching	Selection of content	Teaching can be individualized by giving learners alternative responses.	Strategy is often abused by selecting one task that is inappropriate for all learners.
	Communication of tasks	New content can be presented. Communication can be adjusted in midstream if students do not understand.	Teacher plays a dominant role in task communication, thereby minimizing the role of the learner.
	Progression of content	Progression is based on previous responses of students and can therefore be appropriate.*	Strategy requires highly developed teacher analysis and observation skills to adjust progression while teaching.
	Provision for feedback and evaluation	Teacher is free to give feedback during activity.	Teacher cannot get to all students.
Station teaching	Selection of content	Many tasks can be given at one time to individualize content or better use space or equipment.*	Strategy requires that students have independent working skills and some familiarity with the tasks.
	Communication of tasks	Materials can be preplanned and established.	Media to communicate tasks are often not used well by students, and teachers cannot take the time needed to explain many different tasks at one time.
	Progression of content	Progression appropriate for students can be built into materials.	Quality of response is difficult to attain, thus limiting tasks to those that do not have a *form* focus.
	Provision for feedback and evaluation	Feedback must be built into task materials; teacher can spend time providing feedback if not needed as a manager or task presenter.	Feedback is hard to provide on a group basis because of the variety of different tasks being performed and management concerns.
Peer teaching	Selection of content	When content is selected by peer teacher, then peer teacher profits from the process.	Peer teachers may be put in a difficult social relationship with their peers. Peer teachers are not qualified to select appropriate content for their peers.
	Communication of tasks	Many different tasks and levels of tasks can be presented because of the number of "teachers." Peer teachers often use simpler language to communicate tasks.	Peer-teaching role requires a lot of teacher structuring. Peer teachers do not have the experience to select appropriate teaching cues.

*Indicates major strength of the teaching strategy.

(continued)

TABLE 8·1

Summary of the Strengths and Weaknesses of Seven Teaching Strategies—Cont'd

Teaching strategy	Teacher function	Strengths	Weaknesses
Peer teaching	Progression of content	—	Progression is usually determined by the teacher or must be guided by the teacher.
	Provision for feedback and evaluation	Immediate feedback can be given to many students at one time; many students can be evaluated in a short period.*	Feedback must be guided by the teacher.
Cooperative learning	Selection of content	Content can be selected to be meaningful to learners. Content is more holistic.*	It is difficult to select content appropriate for heterogeneous groups. More time is required to prepare task and materials ahead of time. More student independent learning skills are required.
	Communication of tasks	Tasks can be communicated using a variety of methods ranging from totally teacher directed to student directed.	Most cooperative learning tasks are broader in scope and therefore require more time to present to learners.
	Progression of content	Teacher can build progression into tasks and materials. Teacher is freed once activity on the task begins to individualize.	Students left to their own progression may not always select an appropriate one.
	Provision for feedback and evaluation	Teachers can provide feedback during independent work of students. Project usually has a culmination that can be evaluated.	It is not always easy to separate individual contributions from the group effort.
Self-instruction	Selection of content	Content can be made completely appropriate for the individual.*	The amount of time it takes to prepare materials necessitates self-motivated learners able to use materials.
	Communication of tasks	Learner can refer to materials when there is a question.	It is difficult to communicate what is important in movement through written materials, which makes media important.
	Progression of content	Progression can be built into materials in gradual steps.	Because progression is preestablished, it may not be appropriate for all individuals.
	Provision for feedback and evaluation	—	Feedback must be built into materials; teachers usually spend most of their time evaluating.

*Indicates major strength of the teaching strategy.

(continued)

TABLE 8·1

Summary of the Strengths and Weaknesses of Seven Teaching Strategies—Cont'd

Teaching strategy	Teacher function	Strengths	Weaknesses
Cognitive strategies	Selection of content	Content can involve the learner more holistically and at any level of student responsibility.*	Time spent in the cognitive is time spent away from psychomotor practice.
	Communication of tasks	Tasks can be presented using any organizational strategy (e.g., media, task cards).	Tasks requiring more student involvement usually take longer to prepare and present.
	Progression of content	Full range of teacher directed to student directed can be used by this strategy.	It depends on how the teacher decides to develop and communicate the progression.
	Provision for feedback and evaluation	If used with more indirect teaching styles, the teacher is free to provide feedback during the time students are working on the task.	If used with direct instruction, feedback is limited as in interactive teaching
Team teaching	Selection of content	The expertise of two teachers making the decision as to appropriate content is usually better than a teacher working in isolation. Any teaching strategy can be used. The second teacher is free to individualize content or to take students in a special group for whom the task is not appropriate.	It requires more planning time and for the teachers working together to have a good working relationship.
	Communication of tasks	Task can be presented using any method or strategy by one or both teachers. Teacher not responsible for task presentation can assist or play different role during task presentation.	It is difficult to establish a relationship between two teachers that permits responsibility for the communication of the task to shift appropriately during instruction. A lead teacher usually has to be established who takes the responsibility for task presentation.
	Progression of content	The second teacher is free to individualize progressions.*	It is always more difficult when several different progressions are occurring within the same class.
	Provision for feedback and evaluation	Feedback and evaluation can be assigned to the free teacher.	When one teacher is doing feedback and evaluation, the lead teacher has to cope with a large group.

*Indicates major strength of the teaching strategy.

THE REAL WORLD

Team Teaching That Works—An Example

Debbie and Mark have been teaching a tennis/pickle ball unit together for their sixth-grade classes. They planned the unit together and have set up the gym so that there is a small court for every four students. During the basic skill instruction phase they took turns presenting the skills. The "free" teacher worked with individual students and "refined" the skill as both teachers saw appropriate. Some of the students need to continue to work on contact, control, and being able to keep the ball going with a partner, and some students are ready to begin working on some tactics related to "making their partner move side to side on the court." At the start of the lesson, Debbie takes the students who are ready to move on and places them on several courts to run a separate lesson on side-to-side and up-the-back tactics. After several days, the more-advanced group is then "mixed" with the less-advanced group for "peer-teaching" experiences. Teams of six players reflecting all ability levels are formed to play games for part of every period while instruction continues in basic skills and strategies.

at developing a supportive relationship with each other. The accompanying Real World box gives a good example of team teaching.

■ SELECTING A TEACHING STRATEGY

As discussed early in the chapter, teachers do not select a teaching strategy and then decide what to teach. The selection of a teaching strategy is based on what teachers hope to accomplish in terms of their goals and objectives. Teachers should be able to appropriately use all of the instructional strategies described in this chapter for different lessons and even for different parts of a lesson.

Many factors influence the choice of a teaching strategy, including the content, the characteristics of the learner, and the objectives and preferences of the teacher. It is the blend of these factors that ultimately causes a teacher to choose one strategy over another. Table 8.1 summarizes the use of the seven different strategies discussed.

SUMMARY

1. Teaching strategies provide an instructional framework for the delivery of instruction.
2. As instruction moves from direct teaching to more indirect teaching, teacher control of the learning process becomes shared with the learner.
3. Most teaching strategies can be used for either direct or indirect instruction.
4. Each of the seven teaching strategies discussed arranges the instructional environment differently for the selection of content, the communication of tasks, the progression of content, and the provision for feedback and evaluation.
5. Each strategy has its advantages and disadvantages. The selection of a strategy depends on the objectives of the teacher for instruction, the content to be learned, and the characteristics of the learners.

CHECKING YOUR UNDERSTANDING

1. Describe the differences between direct and indirect instruction.
2. Describe the advantages and disadvantages of each teaching strategy.
3. Give an example of a lesson best taught with each of the teaching strategies.
4. Produce a developmental analysis of content for the example of a self-instructional strategy for teaching gymnastics presented in box 8.11 (see p. 171). (The extension and refinement is clear in this example.)

REFERENCES

Aronson, E., et al. (1978). *The jigsaw classroom.* Beverly Hills, CA: Sage Publications.

Harrison, J., Buck, M., & Blakemore, C. (2001). *Instructional strategies for secondary school physical education.* St. Louis: McGraw-Hill.

SUGGESTED READINGS

Betchel, P., O'Sullivan, M., & Oliver, R. (2001). Implementing sport education: Staying sane when making change. *Strategies, 15*(2), 19–24.

Bieber, A. (1994). Circuits that work. *Strategies, 8*(1), 21–22.

Block, M. (1995). Use peer tutors and task sheets. *Strategies, 8*(7), 9–11.

Byra, M. (2004). Applying a task progression to the reciprocal style of teaching. *Journal of Physical Education, Recreation and Dance, 75*(2), 42–46.

Chatoupis, C., & Emmanual, C. (2003). Teaching physical education with the inclusion style: The case of a Greek elementary school. *Journal of Physical Education, Recreation and Dance, 74*(8), 33–38.

Cooperative learning that includes students with disabilities. (2005). *JOPERD, 76*(6), 29–35.

Dunn, S., & Wilson, R. (1991). Cooperative learning in the physical education classroom. *Journal of Physical Education, Recreation and Dance, 62*(6), 22–28.

Dyson, B. (2001). Using cooperative learning structures in physical education. *Journal of Physical Education, Recreation and Dance, 72*(2), 28–31.

Dyson, B., & Grineski, S. (2001). Using cooperative learning structures to achieve quality physical education. *JOPERD, 72*(2), 28–31.

Dyson, B., & Rubin, A. (2003). How to implement cooperative learning in your elementary physical education program. *JOPERD, 74*(1), 48–55.

Ellery, P. (1995). Peer tutors work. *Strategies, 8*(7), 12–14.

Graes, M., & Townsend, J. (2000). Applying the sport education curriculum model to dance. *Journal of Physical Education, Recreation and Dance, 71*(8), 50–54.

Griffin, L. (1996). Improving net/wall games. *Journal of Physical Education, Recreation and Dance, 67*(2), 34–37.

Grineski, S. (1996). *Cooperative Learning In Physical Education.* Champaign, IL: Human Kinetics.

Hubball, H., & Robertson, S. (2004). Using problem-based learning to enhance team and player development in youth soccer. *Journal of Physical Education, Recreation and Dance, 75*(4), 38–43.

McBride, R. (1995). Critical thinking in physical education—an idea whose time has come. *Journal of Physical Education, Recreation and Dance, 66*(6), 21–52.

Mitchell, S. (1996). Tactical approaches to teaching games: Improving invasion game performance. *Journal of Physical Education, Recreation and Dance, 67*(2), 30–34.

Siedentop, D. (1998). What is sport education and how does it work? *Journal of Physical Education, Recreation and Dance, 69*(4), 18–20.

Zakrajsek, D., & Carnes, L. (1986). *Individualizing physical education* (2nd ed.). Champaign, IL: Human Kinetics.

Student Motivation, Personal Growth, and Inclusion

9

O V E R V I E W

Motivation and concerns for student personal growth are critical and integral parts of teaching. All educational programs share a concern for the personal growth of students. From a learning perspective, students not motivated to learn most likely will not learn. When personal needs for growth are not met, students have difficulty learning and growing as happy, productive, and contributing members of society. Teachers must create a supportive environment for learning and personal growth inclusive of all students regardless of their "differentness." This chapter discusses the role of student motivation and teacher concerns for student personal growth in teaching and describes how teachers can attend to these needs for all students through their teaching.

Standard 4: Instructional Delivery and Management
Physical education teacher candidates use effective communication and pedagogical skills and strategies to enhance student engagement and learning.
NASPE Beginning Teaching Standards, 2008

O U T L I N E

- **Motivation in learning**
- **Theories of motivation—The why of behavior**
  Behaviorism
  Social learning theory
  Self-determination theory
  Achievement goal and social goals theory

Interest theories
Designing experiences to develop personal and situational interest
Implications of theories of motivation
- **Promoting personal growth through personal interaction**

- **Motivation and personal growth through instructional decision making**
  Planning
  Selection of tasks and design of learning experiences
  Presentation of units and tasks
  Organizational arrangements
  Teacher functions during activity
  Pacing of lessons
  Assessment of tasks, units, and lessons
- **Teaching affective goals as a lesson focus**
  The unique and shared affective goals of physical education

  Instructional strategies for teaching affect
- **Physical education for inclusion**
  Becoming aware
  Developing a climate for inclusion
- **Building equity**
  Gender equity
  Ethnic and cultural differences
  Disadvantaged students
  Students with disabilities
- **Discussion of affective goals for physical education**

Affect is described in chapter 1 as that aspect of development that relates to student feelings, attitudes, and values. Student affect always plays a role in teaching, whether the teacher chooses to focus on student affect in interactions with students or instructional decisions and whether the teacher chooses to work with affective concerns explicitly as part of the curriculum. Student feelings, perceptions, attitudes, and values influence how students respond to themselves, the teacher, each other, and the learning experiences teachers plan.

Educators have focused on the role of affect in learning primarily in terms of issues related to motivating students to learn that which has been decided to be important to learn. Motivation to learn is an essential ingredient of learning. Teachers need methods to help increase student motivation *extrinsically,* as well as methods to develop students' *intrinsic* motivation toward what the teachers are teaching.

Educators have also focused on student affect as it relates to the personal growth of students. Student personal growth has always been an expectation of the schools to some degree. Changes in societal expectations of the role of the school and differences in school and teacher philosophy usually affect the balance between the emphasis on subject matter mastery and the emphasis given to student personal growth. Personal growth is usually associated with the development of positive feelings of self, the acquisition of a value system

internally driven, and a tolerance and respect for others. Some educators say that personal growth involves a responsibility for the needs and welfare of others as well.

As a teacher, you must learn how to increase the potential for student motivation and you should know how best to contribute to the personal growth of each child. Many of you have chosen teaching as a career because you want to play a major role in the personal growth of young people, and you want to use the skills and knowledge associated with physical education to facilitate this growth. In many respects it is the successes teachers have in the development of student motivation and student affect that provide the greatest rewards in teaching.

What makes concerns for the development of student motivation and personal growth so difficult to apply is the uniqueness of the needs of individuals. What motivates one student may not necessarily motivate another. What one student needs for personal growth is not necessarily what another student needs. The art of teaching will always involve the ability to reach individuals while meeting the needs of the group.

The chapter begins with a discussion of student motivation and is followed by sections on teacher-student interaction, building affect into instruction, and teaching values and affect directly and explicitly. The chapter concludes with a discussion of teaching physical education for inclusion and issues of equity in the gym.

■ MOTIVATION IN LEARNING

Although students who are not highly motivated can learn, it is certainly easier for a teacher to facilitate learning if students are motivated. In the simplest sense, motivation is a construct developed to explain *the degree of attraction the learner has to a particular behavior or learning task.* We say that students who persist at a task, spend a long time on a task, or choose to do a task are motivated. Likewise, students who show little persistence, intensity, or initiative toward a particular task are unmotivated. Student motivation is continuously cited by teachers as a major problem in teaching, particularly in secondary physical education.

■ THEORIES OF MOTIVATION—THE WHY OF BEHAVIOR

The manner in which a teacher designs and conducts learning experiences will, in part, determine students' motivation to engage in a learning experience. Teachers want all students to be engaged at a high level with the learning experiences they present. They want them to be intrinsically motivated to participate in the activities and, more important, to develop a personal interest in the activity strong enough to continue to be a participant outside of school and after graduation. Currently the most popular theories to explain motivation are behaviorism, social learning theory, and self-determination theory and its related achievement goal theory. Each of these will be briefly explained with their implications.

Behaviorism

Behaviorism is a theory that emphasizes the role of the environment in shaping behavior. According to behavioral theory, when the consequences of what we do are positive, that behavior is reinforced. This is why positive reinforcement plays such a major role in the educational process. When we are reinforced for what we do, the likelihood of both learning a desired behavior and repeating a desired behavior is increased. While negative reinforcement can decrease undesired behavior (punishment or negative consequences of an act), positive reinforcement for desired behaviors is clearly more powerful a motivator in an educational setting.

Teachers use reinforcement when they give positive feedback or rewards to students for desired behavior. Teachers use negative reinforcement when they express their displeasure in what students do or apply negative consequences to an act. One of the problems with the continuous use of reinforcement to control student behavior is that the objective of an educational program is for students to adopt an internal control of what they do rather than external control. External rewards perceived as "controlling" by the student can also have a negative effect on learning and the chances of the student choosing to exhibit that behavior. Behaviorism used correctly gradually withdraws the external control (shaping) so that students can develop an internal control of behavior.

Social Learning Theory

Social learning theory emphasizes the role that our interactions with other people play in our behavior. We learn through the observation of what others do, we learn when we are reinforced by others for what we do, and we learn by comparing ourselves to what others do. In chapter 4, we focused on the role of demonstrations in presenting tasks to learners. Demonstrations are a form of modeling that is a formal model of what we want students to do. Social learning theorists remind us that students are always learning from what they see us do, whether we intend for them to do so or not. Like behaviorists, social learning theorists stress the importance of being socially "rewarded" for behavior that we want students to eventually "own." Like attribution theory (later in the chapter), they emphasize the role that social comparison (comparing what we do to what others do) plays in determining our motivation to do something. As will be true with all theories that recognize the power of external influences, the role of the educator is to design experiences that lead learners to internal control of what they do.

Self-Determination Theory

Briefly, self determination theory states that students are more likely to engage in behaviors when they are acting out of their own volition (Bryan & Solmon; Deci & Ryan, 2000). People who want to do something are more likely to do it than people who do not want to do something. Likewise, people have shared psychological needs that influence the extent to which they are willing to engage in an activity. In self-determination theory, these are called nutriments and are described as **competence, autonomy,** and **relatedness**. The level of motivation is influence by the extent to which these nutriments are present in a learning experience.

Several levels of motivation are described in self-determination theory, including:

Amotovation: The student has no stimulation to engage, either because of feelings of incompetence or failure to value the activity.

Extrinsic motivation: External motivation is the lowest form of extrinsic motivation. Students participate to attain an external award or avoid the negative consequences of not participating (I'll get something if I do or the teacher will make me sit out if I don't). Students may also be externally motivated to participate because they feel obligated to participate or because they might feel guilty if they don't participate (I said I would do this). Likewise, they may participate because they feel that the activity has value (This is good for me). Many students participate because they want to be "a good student" or, in the case of physical activity, being a participant has positive health consequences (value). Nevertheless, all of these are forms of external motivation. When you look at the previous examples, you will recognize that external motivation is not always "bad" and sometimes is necessary for us to do things we know we should do but are not necessarily intrinsically motivated to do.

Intrinsic motivation: Students who are intrinsically motivated participate for the sake of the activity as an end in itself. The activity may help them feel a sense of personal growth or learning and the opportunity to feel a sense of accomplishment or success. It may also allow them to experience stimulation, joy, delight, thrill, or the aesthetics of an experience. The development of intrinsic motivation should be the goal of what we do as educators.

Supporting student competence, autonomy, and relatedness needs. The need for competence, autonomy, and relatedness can be influenced by how teachers design the motivational climate for learning. Nutriments are fulfilled in social circumstances leading to motivation and accomplishment. Therefore, the nutriments mediate motivation; they do not directly influence it.

Competence can be nurtured by establishing a student focus on task mastery and personal improvement. Greater levels of perceived competence increase self-determination and intrinsic motivation. Past experience influences perceived competence. When students have been successful in the past, they will approach new tasks in that area with a high perceived competence and, therefore, will be more highly motivated participants. In competitive environments, an overemphasis on winning can decrease the motivation of the losers.

Student autonomy is a critical aspect of self-determination and is believed to be more influential than even student perceived competence. Student autonomy is related to the degree to which students feel in control of their participation. It is not to be confused with the idea of giving students total independence and free choice, but is more related to the idea of students having the opportunity to have choices. The teacher's task is to assure that students are engaged in learning experiences that will help them learn appropriate content in a way that is not controlling and gives students opportunities for choices.

The nutriment of relatedness is the third aspect of self-determination theory and concerns our need to love and care for others and be loved and cared for by others. It does not play as influential a role in student motivation as competence and autonomy, but plays a significant role in intrinsic motivation. The social environment in the physical education class can influence the degree to which the student need for relatedness is achieved and, therefore, the intrinsic motivation with which a student participates in physical education activities.

Achievement Goal and Social Goals Theory

Achievement goal theory has been used extensively in educational literature as a guideline for creating motivational climates conducive to developing the intrinsic motivation of students (Guan, Xiang, McBride, & Bruene, 2006). According to achievement goal theory, learners can take two perspectives toward a task. Students who take a **mastery goal (task) orientation** to a task believe that their success is achieved through intrinsic interest, high effort, and cooperation. Those who take a **performance goal (ego) orientation** toward a task believe that success is achieved by being better than others (social comparison). These ideas are related to a characteristic identified as locus of control and to what students attribute their success and failure. Students become more performance goal-oriented as they progress through school. Students who take a mastery goal orientation are likely to be more intrinsically motivated, persist at a task longer, and show more effort. Higher levels of competence are more related to a task-orientated, rather than an ego-oriented, motivation climate.

Students in physical education are also motivated by social goals of participation, which are the desire to form and maintain peer relationships and the desire to adhere to social rules and expectations. The social goals of participation are estimated to have as much influence on participation as the achievement goals.

Creating a mastery-oriented climate Teachers want students to attribute their success and failures to factors within their own control. Therefore, it will be important to try to establish a mastery goal (task) orientation to a task. Students need to believe that their success is achieved through intrinsic interest, high effort, and cooperation, rather than genetics, chance, the equipment, the way the task was designed, or someone else. In order to do this, teachers will need to personalize tasks and expectations to make them appropriate for all students and establish an environment that focuses on effort and improvement rather than performance. One of the best ways to do this is to think about how to give students choices so they can function with the content at an appropriate level to be successful and to reinforce the role of effort in achievement.

Competitive experiences must put winning and losing in perspective. For competition to be a valuable experience, all students must have an equal chance of winning. Competition is not valuable for either winners or losers when the outcome of the experience is established before the competition and when the same participants always win and the same participants always lose.

Creating positive social environments Although the middle school student is particularly dependent upon peer approval and the elementary student more dependent upon adult approval, all students want to be perceived by the teacher, as well as their peers, positively. For the most part, they also want to follow the "rules" in terms of expected social behavior, and they want to achieve. The public nature of performance in physical education makes it very important in our content area not to put students in a position of failure in front of their peers. Students who are put in this position on a regular basis learn not to participate. All students must feel psychologically safe in class. In order to create these environments, students may have to be sensitized to appropriate interactive behavior with their peers and positively reinforced for appropriate behavior. Students who are not perceived positively by their peers may need help in establishing positive relationships, and those who interact with these students may need help on how to be supportive of students who are not socially accepted. Many times, students who are not socially accepted have no chance of becoming socially accepted without the teacher's help.

Interest Theories

Interest motivation theories explore the role of student interest in participation (Krapp, Hidi, & Renninger, 1992). Two kinds of interest have been identified: personal and situational. Personal interest is an inherent desire to participate in the activity, while situational interest deals more with the characteristics of the task. Personal interest is developed over time through a person's experience with the activity, while situational interest is a more immediate characteristic of the task (novelty, fun, excitement). Teachers can develop personal interest through positive experiences that stimulate situational interest (Xiang, Chen, & Bruene, 2005).

Designing Experiences to Develop Personal and Situational Interest

Novelty and challenge are two of the strongest characteristics of situational interest. All of us enjoy something "new" or new ways of doing something we have done before. Well-planned curriculums will assure that students are introduced to new activities and new material in the curriculum each year. Situational interest is often destroyed when students perceive that they have "done this before." Tasks designed to be different and novel will have a better chance of motivating students to want to participate. Novelty may be something as simple as finding a new way to organize students into partners or groups or as complex as designing a new game using the skills that have been learned. Students should not be able to come into class and be able to predict what the teacher is going to do for every aspect of the lesson.

Implications of Theories of Motivation

Several basic principles are common to all of the theories just discussed and are useful to keep in mind when creating a climate for learning for all students. These principles for practice are summarized in box 9.1.

Teachers must find ways for students to meet their needs in positive ways. Often misbehavior can be attributed to the need for attention and power. If students can meet this need in more positive ways, they will not have to resort to negative behaviors.

EXAMPLES:
- "Karen, you are really good at taking weight on your hands. Would you like to demonstrate how you do it?"
- "Frank, as we begin class today, I would like to hear you say two nice things to somebody in your class before the end of the class."
- "Yesterday was not a good day for you, Nicole. Today I know that you can be on task the whole class."

Students must perceive what is to be learned as meaningful. Teachers must find ways to help students see the importance of what they

---

BOX 9·1

Motivating Students in Physical Education

Teachers must find ways for students to meet their needs in positive ways.

Students must perceive what is to be learned as meaningful.

Use a variety of teaching strategies.

Tasks should be designed to permit each student to function at an optimal level of challenge.

Tasks should be designed to allow the student to function with autonomy.

Use external forms of motivation with care.

Variety in learning activities and novel and interesting tasks tend to increase motivation.

Help students to see the purpose for what you are doing, and attach a personal meaning to what you are doing from the students' perspective.

Use culminating activities that permit students to demonstrate efforts of extended and motivated practice.

Help students to understand that all of us are beginners at some point and to understand what it means to be a beginner.

Help students to set goals for physical education that are those of the participant, not the professional.

Use humor.

Help students to attribute their success and failure to a cause controllable by the students.

Develop a task-oriented motivational environment.

---

are doing. Teachers also must take care to ensure that what they are doing has meaning. Pointless and repetitious drills for skills never used in a game are usually perceived by students as meaningless. If students know they will get to use the skills or if skills are applied in game situations as the skills are developed, students are likely to be more motivated. If students have some say in determining their need for practice, they are likely to be even more motivated.

EXAMPLES:
- "Let's look at this videotape of the Olympics and see if we can identify what it is that these people are doing when they run. What do you think we should work on first?"

■ *(Teacher begins a unit with the game rather than skills. After the first day of games, the teacher has an evaluation session.)* "After your games today, what can you identify as what you need to work on? We will try and work on an area of game play and skills and then put it back in the game. After each game we will evaluate what we are doing and choose another area of work."

Use a variety of teaching strategies. Even the best strategies used on a continuous basis are likely to lose their motivating effect. Teachers must continuously search for new ways to do things. Novelty is a factor in student interest. Student interest and motivation are increased also through the use of fantasy, imagination (even older students), and group activities.

EXAMPLES:
■ The teacher plans the unit in detail ahead of time by building in the use of as many different teaching strategies as possible and matching the strategy to the appropriate unit objective.
■ "Let's pretend we are going on a safari today through the jungles. The stations are set up to be different challenges. For example, there will be trees to climb, mountains to get over, and chases with wild animals."
■ "We're going to set up our tournament as the real Olympics."
■ "Today we are going to conduct class as a society that has no tensions among people. In our society everyone is supportive and polite and sensitive to each other's needs. Today is going to be an other-centered day."

Tasks should be designed to permit each student to function at an optimal level of challenge. For most students this means that the student should be able to be successful with a reasonable effort. Tasks that are too simple or too difficult are likely to result in decreased motivation. Continued failure is likely to result in poor achievement motivation and poor self-esteem.

EXAMPLES: The teacher sits down with her lesson plan and, for each task designed, redesigns that task to permit different students to operate at different levels within the task. (See p. 193–194 for specific ways to do this.)

Tasks should be designed to allow the student to function with autonomy. Although it is not always possible to have each student intrinsically motivated to do every task the teacher has planned, teachers should attempt to work toward providing all students with tasks that are meaningful and permit choice and autonomy. Tasks should be presented to create personal interest, dissonance (conflicts that need to be resolved), and curiosity. External control of all learning tasks leads to decreased motivation and a decreased sense of competency.

EXAMPLES:
■ "Today we are going to be working on building a personal warm-up routine for our volleyball unit. The components of the routine are listed on the sheet that you have. You may work to design exercises in one of these components. Each group will be responsible for a different component and for teaching the exercises they have selected to the rest of the class."
■ "I have decided that we need to work on combining dribbling and passing on the move in our games. Why are dribbling and passing important? What is it that gives some of you trouble when you are doing this?"

Use external forms of motivation with care. When teachers use external methods of motivation, the student is motivated by the value of the consequence and not the value of the activity. There are times when teachers must use external motivators to increase student effort; however, external motivators can be used more effectively if the following occur:

1. Rewards are used primarily for mastery of basic tasks rather than learning experiences involving the student at a higher level.

    EXAMPLE: "Yesterday I asked you to keep your score at each station of practice. You got one point for each of ten successful trials at each station. We will do this at the end of each week of classes. At the end of the unit there will be prizes for those students who make the most progress from the beginning to the end. Why do you think I have decided that prizes would be awarded for improvement rather than for the highest score?"

2. Teachers use rewards to link behavior to the internal rewards of being successful at the activity.

EXAMPLE: "The following students will get their names on the list of students who were good sports this week in physical education. I would like each of these students to come up and tell you what they did that they think showed that they were a good sport and to tell you how it made them feel when they were supportive of another person."

3. Competition should ensure that all students have an equal chance of being successful and that winning and losing are depersonalized (not attributed to internal causes). Competition is an ego-involved activity, and therefore students tend to have more at risk in participating.

EXAMPLES:
■ "We will play a round-robin tournament at three levels. Each level will have different rules and will involve a different level of competition. You may choose the level of competition you feel is appropriate for you."
■ "The winners of today's games really worked hard and showed us good performance. How many of you really enjoyed today's games? I could tell all of you were having a good time. We'll see who gets to be the winner tomorrow."

4. Teachers work toward removing external motivators and replace them with methods to increase internal motivation.

EXAMPLES:
■ "I would like to point out something I saw today that really pleased me. I didn't say that any kind of points would be given for people who really worked hard today, and what I noticed was that many of you worked really hard at the lesson even though today was not a point day. How many of you think you could work really hard tomorrow even if we do not give awards?"
■ "Part of learning to be an adult is to do things because they are the right thing to do and not because you think you will get something if you do them. What do you think we can do today that is the right thing to do that we will not be rewarded for?"

5. Use self-testing activities with a focus on personal improvement rather than comparison with others.

EXAMPLES:
■ "See if you can do one more this time than you did last time."
■ "How many of you feel like you were able to pass quicker than in that first game?"

Use a variety of learning activities and novel and interesting tasks to increase motivation. Teachers should strive to provide a variety of tasks. Teachers need not change an objective but need to find different ways to accomplish the same objective to sustain interest (parallel development).

EXAMPLES:
■ The volleyball set can be practiced (1) against a wall, (2) with a partner toss, (3) over the net to a target, or (4) into a basket.
■ Instead of spending a full day or days developing one skill, distribute the practice of skills over a unit and spend less time on each skill per day (distributed practice).

Help students to see the purpose for what you are doing and attach a personal meaning to what you are doing from the students' perspective. Most students identify with sport-related and health-related fitness. Personalizing means to find ways to attach the importance of what you are doing to a particular student or group of students.

Teachers must work to help students attach personal meaning to learning experiences.

EXAMPLES:

- "Who are your favorite basketball players? What do you like about the way they are playing?"
- "How many of you see joggers on the streets when you are coming to school? Why do you think they are doing this?"

Use culminating activities that permit students to demonstrate efforts of extended and motivated practice. Motivation is increased if students are working toward something that is in the more immediate future than a life skill. Most physical education units can have culminating activities. Although tournaments are used frequently, the nature of culminating activities and how they are conducted can be changed and modified to add variety and interest.

EXAMPLES:

- "At the end of this unit we are going to have each of you present a routine that is your best effort. It does not make any difference how hard the skills are. What we are interested in is if you put your routine together smoothly and with good form. We will invite the other class to come see what you have done."
- "The tournament for this unit will also have a value focus. Each team will select one value that they think is an important characteristic to have in life that is often a part of doing well in sports as well. The names of your teams will reflect these values. During game play we expect your team to really demonstrate those values. At the end of the tournament there will be a tournament winner for the group that most demonstrated their value, as well as a winner for competition."

Help students to understand that all of us are beginners at some point and to understand what it means to be a beginner. Many students (and many teachers) attribute success in motor skills to innate ability; they downplay the role of effort, a good strategy for learning, and experience. Motor skill acquisition takes time, effort, and a good strategy for learning. Teachers must help students to appreciate the idea that we are all beginners at some time and beginners make mistakes and cannot perform as well as people who have had experience. Teachers can discuss with students what it means to be a beginner at motor skills and help them feel secure that it is all right to be a beginner. When individuals stop wanting to do things because they are beginners, they stop learning and growing.

EXAMPLE: "We are going to begin a tennis unit today. How many of you have never played tennis before? Some of you have played a lot of tennis, and some of you have not had any experience playing tennis. If you haven't played before, initially you won't be as good as those who have played tennis before. Why not? What do beginners look like? What would happen if we never wanted to try anything because we were afraid of looking like a beginner? How can those of you who have played before help those who are beginners?"

Help students to set goals for physical education that are those of the participant, not the professional. Television and other forms of communication have given us immediate access to the best performances, not only in sports but in all of the performing arts. One of the negative results of this type of access is that many of us no longer can appreciate an amateur performance and choose not to be participants because we cannot be world-class performers. The goal of physical education should be to develop participants. Students need to be helped to understand the value of participation, not just the value of superior performance.

EXAMPLE: "Why do people play sports? How many of you enjoy playing basketball? Why do you enjoy playing basketball? Do you have to be a Michael Jordan to enjoy playing? What can sports do for you?"

Use humor. Teachers should be able to laugh at events and to create humorous situations to develop interest and motivation.

EXAMPLES:

- The teacher makes a point about lack of control in movement by playing the clown.
- The teacher makes a point about being supportive of others' efforts by role-playing an exaggerated unsupportive student.

Help students to attribute their success and failure to a cause that is controllable by the student. Students are likely to protect themselves from failure by not trying if they do not perceive themselves as able to master a task or perceive control of success outside themselves. The teacher can help students to attribute success to their efforts and therefore to increase the likelihood that students will risk failure by (1) giving students criteria on which to judge their success, (2) helping them to set reasonable goals for themselves, and (3) helping them to develop an effective strategy for learning. For low-achievement students, teachers can focus their efforts on the students' efforts and the level at which the students are engaged in the task. Teachers should help all students understand that learning in physical education, particularly motor skills, is an investment in time.

EXAMPLES:

- "Tommie, I am really excited about what you have done today. Yesterday you were having trouble bringing those feet down softly from your weight on hands. Today I could hardly hear them. You must be really concentrating on what you are doing."
- "If you can do one more today than you did yesterday, you are really making good progress."

■ PROMOTING PERSONAL GROWTH THROUGH PERSONAL INTERACTION

One of the most difficult aspects of teaching for a beginning teacher is to find the best way to interact with students. Some beginning teachers err in the direction of trying to make students *like* them. The role of the teacher is *not* that of a "friend." Teachers should act in a student's best interest from the perspective of an adult. At the other extreme, some beginning teachers are so concerned with losing control in their classes, they are often reluctant to communicate their *humanness* to students. Students want a relationship with an adult that is supportive and guiding. They want to know that the teacher cares about them and about what they do. This does not mean that they want a relationship with a teacher who lets them do whatever they want to do. Throw-out-the-ball programs and those designed to just have fun in physical

activity don't win the respect of any students. Teaching is largely about affect: adults who are caring and concerned professionals have a responsibility to (1) help students learn and (2) promote students' personal growth as individuals and as responsible, self-directed members of society.

Through the manner in which they interact with students, teachers can communicate a professional and supportive relationship with students that says, "I care." Although each of you as a unique individual will find your own way of sharing yourself with young people to promote their growth, the following ideas should be considered:

1. *Learn students' names and use them.* Physical education teachers often have many students in each class. Nonetheless, an essential and minimal form of recognition for students is that you know and are able to use their names. Use your role book after each class to identify students you have yet to make some kind of personal contact with. Make learning names at the beginning of school a number one priority. If you have difficulty with names, ask students to wear name tags until you know the names, take a Polaroid picture of the students so that you can learn the names outside of class, or videotape the students giving their names and something special about themselves.

2. *Be enthusiastic and positive about what you are doing.* Enthusiasm is catching. Many people assume that enthusiasm is a personality trait of outgoing and "bubbly" people. Enthusiasm does not necessarily always have to be such high-energy behavior. Students will know by the tone of the teachers' voice and the manner in which they approach a lesson how enthusiastic they are about what they are doing.

3. *Project a caring attitude toward all students.* Caring is projected by the teacher primarily through a genuine interest and recognition of each child. If you go through your student list and you cannot identify in a positive and meaningful way a particular child's needs for growth, it is probably a good indication that you have yet to tune into that child as a growing person. Caring is projected by

the teacher through a sensitivity to the feelings of students and the meaning and significance students attach to events and their interactions with you. Caring teachers tune in to the child as a feeling human being—no matter what behavior the student is demonstrating. Caring teachers do not condone misbehavior, but in dealing with misbehavior they do not undermine the integrity of the child as a person.

4. *Reinforce basic and shared beliefs of honesty, tolerance, respect, risk taking, and effort by modeling these behaviors, as well as reinforcing them when they occur in the class.* Recent societal problems have emphasized not only the need for student personal growth (a return to values that make a democratic and interdependent society and world work) but also a responsibility for developing prosocial behaviors of students (Good & Brophy, 1990). Prosocial behaviors are those behaviors exhibited by students that demonstrate a responsibility for helping other people without being prompted by external rewards.

   Many of the messages students receive from their families and the society outside of school teach them to fear and to interact in destructive ways with those who are different, whether these differences are race, culture, socioeconomic, gender, or physical conditions. Schools and teachers have a responsibility to make students aware of the destructiveness of these attitudes and behaviors and to act positively to change them.

5. *Do not reinforce behavior destructive to self or others by doing nothing about it.* Students learn acceptable ways of interacting with each other not only by what you do, but also by what you do not do. Values, tolerance, and respect for others are learned. Teachers must find ways of communicating what is acceptable and what is not acceptable. Develop an awareness for the effects of your unintended behavior. When you permit students to act in inappropriate ways (name calling, fighting), you give your approval to these behaviors by not doing anything about them.

6. *Do not allow yourself to become threatened by student misbehavior.* Many beginning teachers consider misbehavior of students a personal threat, and they respond to student misbehavior emotionally. This negative emotional behavior can take the form of anger, threats, personal criticism of students, and sometimes even physical abuse. As soon as teachers put themselves in this position, they lose the ability to positively affect student behavior and, in the case of physical abuse, leave themselves open to being dismissed for inappropriate conduct. Teachers can avoid putting themselves in this position by not allowing themselves to be personally threatened by student misbehavior. Professional teachers treat misbehavior as they would an incorrect answer or response in a lesson. They accept that as where the student is at the time and take steps to move the student forward. They do not allow themselves to be personally threatened by a student—they act as a professional.

7. *Make it a practice to intentionally treat all students equitably. Develop an awareness of your patterns of communication to different students.* It is easy for teachers to gravitate to the more-skilled students or the students who the teacher believes will threaten their class control. The research shows many students get lost in the everyday interaction of classes unless the teacher makes a conscious effort to recognize and interact with all the students equally. This is difficult for physical education teachers, who see students infrequently, but attention to all students can be facilitated if teachers will periodically review class lists, consider each student, and make it a point to give attention to students they have been slighting (see pages 199–207 for more help in this area).

8. *Learn to be a good listener and observer of student responses.* You can become attuned to your students by listening to and observing the subtle meanings of their messages communicated by the manner in which they interact with you, with each other, and learning tasks. Listen for motivation and feeling. Give students an opportunity to voice opinions and approach problems constructively with a shared responsibility for solving them.

9. *Chart your life for personal growth.* Teachers who have the most to contribute to young people are those who have met their own basic needs and are working on their own higher-order needs for esteem and self-actualization. Set goals to actualize your potential, both as a teacher and as a multidimensional individual.

■ MOTIVATION AND PERSONAL GROWTH THROUGH INSTRUCTIONAL DECISION MAKING

At one time, planning for student motivation and concerns about student personal growth were not considered necessary. These ideas were inherent in what it meant to *teach.* More recent emphases on subject matter competence and the difficulties in motivating some students make it necessary for teachers to think through and make explicit how they are going to incorporate both motivation and student personal growth into their teaching. Each function the teacher performs has the capability to be designed for different purposes. Moreover, it is possible to integrate into every decision concerns for subject matter competency, motivation, and personal growth. What follows is a discussion of considerations for motivating and developing the personal growth of students through different instructional functions. The unique objectives of physical education are not neglected, but made richer in their development.

Planning

Integrating concerns for student motivation and student personal growth into your teaching requires planning. Box 9.2 describes the efforts of one teacher committed to the personal growth of her students. Although affective goals are cited most often by physical education teachers as primary goals of their program, they receive the least attention as explicit objectives and even less attention in their planning. Integrating concerns for affect and motivation means that these objectives should be an explicit part of the lesson. It is not sufficient to say that you want students to work cooperatively as partners. Unless you have discussed with students what it means to work

---

BOX 9·2

Planning for Student Motivation and Personal Growth

Polly is a high school teacher working in an AB schedule (90-minute periods) who was sitting down to plan a unit on golf for her students. Most of the students had little experience with golf. She wanted to turn them "on" to golf so that they would have a lifetime activity they could enjoy that would keep them physically active. Polly planned the progressions to develop skill and then began to think about how to build in motivation and personal growth objectives into her unit. When she was finished, the following ideas emerged:

1. She would videotape facilities in the community that were available for playing golf and do personal profiles and interviews of "ordinary people" and teenagers who play golf on a regular basis. She would choose people with a variety of skill levels who play regularly and ask them why they play.
2. She would have students keep reflective journals of their thoughts about learning how to play golf. The questions would change with the lessons in the unit and would include ideas such as: Why do I want to learn? Am I getting better? What is fun and not so much fun about this experience and why? What do I like about being out on a golf course?
3. Sometime in the middle of the unit students would go to a golf course to play and to become familiar with the etiquette of golf. They would also be required to play at least eighteen holes of golf on their own before the end of the unit.
4. After most of the clubs were introduced, students would have time each period to select a club that they wanted to work with.
5. Periodically throughout the unit, students would be involved in using videotape for peer and self-assessment of strokes.
6. Variety would be added to each lesson with at least one opportunity each lesson for self-testing or application experiences.

cooperatively as partners, it is unlikely that much will be learned about cooperation.

Physical education offers many opportunities to develop personal growth skills of students, but it is not sufficient to put students into situations that have the potential for personal growth. A primary example of this is the use of team sports by teachers to develop sportsmanship. Team sports have the potential to develop sportsmanship, but they have the potential to develop the opposite as well. Unless teachers make clear their expectations for what sportsmanship is and unless they reinforce sportsmanship in their classes, it is unlikely that merely playing a team sport will result in sportsmanship. In your planning you should do the following:

- Consider not only content, but student motivation—how you can build in a consideration for student motivation into each phase of the lesson and unit.

- Do more long-term planning. Teachers who plan only lessons miss opportunities to build in variety, long-term goals, and those factors that affect student motivation.

- Make goals for student conduct and values explicit in your yearly, unit, and lesson plans as progressive content. Identify what you want to work on, and integrate it with your units and lesson plans.

- If you have to motivate students using external motivation, build in progressive efforts to remove external motivation and replace it with internal motivation.

Selection of Tasks and Design of Learning Experiences

The learning experiences and tasks teachers design are the primary mechanism for subject matter competence as well as motivation and work on student personal growth. It is not enough to be able to identify that students need to work on a two-on-two offense or defensive strategy. How that task is designed in group instruction is critical to its potential to motivate or contribute to student growth. The following ideas should be considered in the design of learning experiences and tasks.

Tasks should be selected that are at an appropriate level of difficulty for all students. It is reasonable to assume that all students are not at the same level of ability in our classes. To make tasks appropriate for all students, teachers must do one of the following:

Provide alternative tasks, such as: "If you can get the underhand serve over the net from half court eight of ten times, move back to the end line."

Design tasks that inherently allow each student to operate within his or her ability, such as: "Find a comfortable distance for you and your partner to practice fielding ground balls" or "Choose an inverted balance you can hold for at least 6 seconds."

Give students a choice in the level they wish to play, such as: "You can choose to be on a team of two-on-two or five-on-five" or "Each group gets to decide what the rules are for their games."

Manipulate the conditions of tasks that the whole class is working on, for example, by changing distances, equipment, rules, targets, or force levels required.

Use self-testing activities that permit students to test their ability within a framework of self-improvement, such as: "How many times in a row can you toss and catch without the ball leaving the ground" or "How many times can your group keep the ball up in the air using either a forearm or overhead pass?" Tasks should be designed to create student interest and maintain student motivation.

Tasks that involve competition should be used appropriately. Consider the following:

Design experiences where all students have an equal chance of winning. If the same students always win and the same students always lose, competition loses its value for both groups and can be detrimental to personal growth.

Focus students on external and controllable aspects of competition, such as practice and effort, and not internal factors, such as innate ability.

Eliminate as much ego involvement as is possible. Attribute winning to effort.

Group students homogeneously by skill level for competition. There is some merit for practice to be in heterogeneous groups, but competition should be with students of the same ability.

Evaluate students on improvement. Students have control of how much they learn. They do not have control of ability or experience coming into a setting.

Use self-testing activities and assessment activities that focus on personal improvement where possible.

Give students a choice of competing and a choice of the level of competition. Competition can enhance performance for skilled students and may decrease performance for unskilled students and beginners.

Use group self-testing tasks, such as: "See how long your group (or you and your partner) can keep the ball going."

Downplay winning and losing in your presentation of the activity and your responses after competition.

Find different ways to practice the same thing. Often the teacher identifies a critical skill that students must master before they can move on in a progression. There are many things the teacher can do to ensure the needed practice of a skill without making the practice boring and repetitious. Teachers can:

Find alternative tasks that require the same skills (parallel development).

Distribute practice of the same task over days in a unit.

Design the curriculum so that the use of some pieces of equipment is reserved for older students.

Involve students in projects and more long-term goals. Link lessons. Students are more likely to work on parts of a whole they feel is meaningful.

Attractive bulletin boards can help motivate students.

Use a variety of teaching strategies throughout the unit of work. (See chapter 8.)

Presentation of Units and Tasks

How students perceive a content area before you begin a lesson or a unit in that content area plays a major role in the motivation they are likely to have for fully engaging in that content. An enthusiastic teacher who is well prepared to motivate a group of students in a lesson can sometimes change the mind of even the student most determined not to like what is coming. The following techniques should be considered.

Use advance organizers for units and lessons. Advance organizers share with students what is to come in the lesson and the unit. It is also important when possible to share with students why you have decided to do something a certain way and why what you have decided to do is important.

EXAMPLE: "Today we are going to start a unit in soccer. You have a check sheet of skills and abilities in soccer in front of you. I know you have played soccer before, and I would like for you to check those skills you do very well with a *check plus;* those skills you do fairly well with a *check;* and those skills you think you really do not do well at all with a *check minus.* That will help me in my planning to make the experiences meaningful to you. We will start off today with three-on-three games and spend some time at the end of the period talking about what we have done. By the end of the unit we should get to play at least seven-on-seven games with a class tournament."

Use motivating introductions to lessons and units that will stimulate interest and curiosity.

EXAMPLE: One teacher wrote a poem about how much fun the unit was going to be. One male teacher began a hockey unit dressed in a kilt. Other teachers have brought in high school or community athletes.

When beginning a unit in an activity that is relatively unfamiliar to students, find a way to give them a sense of the whole (what they are working toward). Many students are learning volleyball for the first time who have never seen volleyball played as a team sport. Many elementary children have never focused in on what many sports look like played well.

EXAMPLE: Short segments of videotape and film of sports and activities are available and will help give students some idea of what they are working toward.

Personalize introductions to units and lessons. Use your experiences or those of members of the class to help students understand that what you are teaching may be relevant to them.

EXAMPLE: "When I leave school a few afternoons a week, I play on a softball team. How many of you have parents or know someone who plays on a softball team as an adult?"

Organizational Arrangements

The manner in which teachers organize equipment, students, and space for instruction is as important as the content they select to teach. **Organizational arrangements** for instruction should be intentionally designed to accomplish specific purposes and not be so routinized by the teacher that the potential for contributing to motivation and the personal growth of students is lost.

Use individual, group, and other organizations to make the practice of a skill interesting. Individual practice, partner practice, and group practice of the same skill add variety and interest to a lesson.

Group students with a purpose. Assignment to work with others or partners depends on the task and the needs of a particular group.

Use homogeneous and heterogeneous grouping with a purpose. There are times when students need to work with others of their ability. When given a choice, students will generally choose someone with whom they are compatible and who is of their ability. Unless some students are always "left out" of the selection process, this system is efficient and normally works well. Heterogeneous groups should be chosen by the teacher to encourage the development of tolerance and understanding among students or to improve the skill ability of students who can profit from working with another of higher ability. Heterogeneous groups should never be used without attention to assigning different roles to students and ensuring that each student can contribute.

Provide opportunity to maintain a group membership. At times there is value in maintaining group membership through a longer period so that students have the opportunity to work through problems. In yearly planning, vary group membership and the time spent with a particular group. Give students within a group different responsibilities and be explicit about what those responsibilities might be. Learn to distinguish productive group interaction from nonproductive group interaction that deteriorates the task orientation of the group.

Use novel types of equipment or novel types of arrangements of equipment to add variety and interest to lessons. Human beings are motivated by novelty. Teachers need to be alert to designing lessons that use different types of equipment and different uses and arrangements of equipment to add novelty to lessons.

EXAMPLES:
- Have students throw or shoot archery at balloons.
- Put instructions on videotape/computers for group work.
- Create obstacles for locomotor lessons with a variety of gymnastics equipment.

Teacher Functions During Activity

Depending on the nature of the task and the nature of the self-management skills of the student, the teacher in physical education should be free to observe and offer individualized help to students during the time the students are engaged in the learning task. This time, when used wisely, can significantly impact the appropriateness of the learning experience for individuals within the class and the effectiveness of the learning experience. Consider the following:

- When students are sent off to work on a task and you are assured that work is safe and focused, use this time to begin to zero in on individual children, particularly those who tend to get lost in the group because they may not necessarily do anything to draw your attention to them. Be alert to subtle hidden messages in student behavior regarding participation and social interactions taking place within the group.

- Use instructional time freed of presenting information and directing students to individualize both the affective goals that you have, as well as the content objectives of a lesson.

- Attend to the guidelines presented for feedback in chapter 7, paying particular attention to providing more support for insecure students. Begin to withdraw adult support for achievement-oriented students. Encourage effort, and attempt to attribute the success of students to their effort.

- Use this time when needed for "off-task" interactions with students you need to communicate with when no other time seems to be available.

Pacing of Lessons

One of the arts of teaching is knowing when to let students continue to practice a particular task and when to call them in to refocus their efforts or to change the task on which they are working. Student motivation can be affected by teachers who do not allow enough time to practice before calling students in, as well as teachers who let a practice deteriorate because student motivation has waned. Consider the following:

- When students are involved in game play, they often resent having their games stopped on a continuous basis. Alert students to the idea that some games will be scrimmages that you will stop when you see the need to. If games are

focused on working on a particular aspect of skill or strategy, make clear your expectations ahead of time and make clear that you will stop them when there is a problem on this particular aspect. Try not to stop the play in a shotgun array of "coaching tips."

- Often it is the teacher, not the students, bored with a particular task. Learn to distinguish between students who just need a physical reprieve and students unmotivated and off task.

Assessment of Tasks, Units, and Lessons

Assessment of learning is probably the most neglected function in teaching physical education. Generally this is because teachers believe that they do not have the time to do any kind of assessment. However, assessment is a critical aspect of learning and an important dimension of motivation to learn. Chapter 11 of this text will deal with issues related to assessment. From a motivational perspective, teachers should consider the following:

- Take time for assessment, even if it means reducing the amount of material taught.

- Assessment begins with setting clear expectations for students and providing feedback to students on performance throughout their work.

- Provide opportunities for students to establish criteria for their work and opportunities for self- and peer assessment through a unit of work, as well as culminating a unit of work. Hold students to the criteria they establish, either as a group or as individuals.

- Take a few minutes after every lesson to review, on an individual basis, what students have done.

■ TEACHING AFFECTIVE GOALS AS A LESSON FOCUS

Affective goals have always been a part of the explicit, as well as the implicit, goals of teaching. Affective goals have not been an explicit part of most educational curricula, however, and therefore have not always received the attention that subject matter competence and other areas of development have received. This is probably for several reasons, including (1) the difficulty of measuring change and growth in affective objectives, (2) the idea that because affective objectives are an implicit aspect of the idea of teaching, it is often assumed that they will be automatic in the teaching-learning environment, and (3) a concern that values are cultural and not shared in a pluralistic society.

Previous sections of this chapter have identified ways in which teachers can implement a concern for affect in their instruction. In these discussions affect is built into a primarily content-oriented instructional perspective. Developing a learning climate for teaching (chapter 6) is certainly largely an affective process. Affect can also be taught as a primary objective of a lesson and the central focus around which all other concerns are built. Goals and objectives for affective outcomes in physical education come from many sources but primarily from the affective dimensions of the content of physical education and the identified goals of education in general or schooling.

The Unique and Shared Affective Goals of Physical Education

The National Standards for Physical Education (NASPE, 2004) identify two affective standards:

Standard 5: Exhibits responsible personal and social behavior that respects self and others in physical activity settings.

Standard 6: Values physical activity for health, enjoyment, challenge, self-expression, and/or social interaction.

These standards are the unique responsibility of physical education and are to be taught not as something to be "caught" by students as a result of their participation in activity but as explicit program goals and lesson objectives. To do this the teacher must plan learning experiences that specifically address the development of these outcomes as well as those we share with other educational programs.

Physical educators have always assumed that participation in sport and physical education was "character building." This is because participation in sport has the *potential* to provide real experiences in such areas as social skills, honesty, integrity, working hard to achieve goals, and handling winning and losing. The mistake that physical educators make is to assume that merely participating in sport will teach these values. In reality, sport participation can teach all of these ideas, but sport and participation in physical activity can also teach students the opposite of these values.

It is possible to make affective goals the framework on which physical education curriculum is designed. An example of an approach to physical education focusing on affective goals is the work of Hellison (1996), discussed in chapter 6. In Hellison's work, a student moves developmentally through five levels of affect, from no control to caring. Lessons are designed to facilitate student growth toward higher levels.

Instructional Strategies for Teaching Affect

Attitudes and values can be taught (Hellison, 2003). A variety of theories describe how values are learned. Likewise, a variety of programs are designed and packaged specifically to teach values. Most of these ideas work because they focus the learner on developing

- an awareness of value positions,
- the importance of different value positions, and,
- the implications of values for behavior.

Values are like other important learning—they usually develop slowly. Ownership of values, the point where you act on a value consistently, takes time. Students who do not share a value and indeed may even act in contradiction to it can be helped to own that value but may not immediately incorporate it into their actions.

Incorporating values into self-initiated action is the goal and not necessarily an en route behavior. Because changes in values and attitudes take a long time to develop, *building affective objectives into instruction and reinforcing affective objectives on a daily basis are the most effective ways to teach affect.*

You can build affective objectives into your teaching in many ways, including the following:

1. Modeling the affective objectives you wish students to acquire.

EXAMPLE: "I'm sorry, Selena, that I interrupted you. I should not have done that."

2. Making clear your expectations for personal and social behavior by the following:

- *Designing learning experiences that have multiple objectives, including affective objectives (rich experiences).*

EXAMPLE: "We will be working on trying to get our feet in the air in a handstandlike position. Some of you will be able to get off the floor only a little bit and then bring your feet back down safely. This is okay, because I know that if you go a little bit higher each time, in a few weeks you will be getting your feet up all the way. What you have to do is learn to be patient with yourself and still work safely and in control. That's what I am really looking for. Can you work hard, be patient with yourself, and be in control?"

- *Helping students to see the value of the behavior through discussion, role playing, and examples.*

EXAMPLE: "When we choose partners, all of you have different reasons for choosing a partner. Can you tell me why you choose a partner? Can you tell me what kinds of things good partners do?"

EXAMPLE: Bring in a videotape of early morning joggers in different parts of the community, the corporate facilities for exercise in neighboring workplaces, and community facilities for recreation. Discuss why these adults are doing what they are doing.

- *Putting the application of that value into concrete examples and behaviors specific to the learning experience of the day.*

EXAMPLE: "What we are going to learn to do today takes a lot of practice to be good. We will practice today for a while, and we may practice this skill a little bit each day. To learn from practice, you have to pay attention to what you are doing. I am going to look for hard workers today—people who want to get better and therefore are thinking about what they are doing as they practice."

- *Positively reinforcing the affective objectives and goals of your program.*

EXAMPLE: "I would like to share something I observed today as you were practicing. When Elaine first started

today, she couldn't do this skill very well. I would like for Elaine to share with you how much she has learned. Is there someone else that you observed that you think worked very hard today and got better?"

3. Making learning experiences positive experiences for all students. The potential for positive experiences in physical education largely depends on the appropriateness of the content for the class and for individuals and a supportive environment for all the students. Teacher support is not sufficient; the social environment created by other students is as critical as the interactions teachers have with classes and individual students. Teachers can teach positive social environment in situations where individuals feel threatened.

4. Helping students to be receptive to new ideas and different perspectives.

EXAMPLE: "George has a very different way of accomplishing this task. George, can you show us your idea?"

EXAMPLE: "I know that some of you may have felt uncomfortable with the dance we did today. Can you put into words how you felt? Why do you think we did the dance? Who got some really good feelings about what we did? Can you tell me what you were feeling? You are going to have to be a little patient with yourself if you had some problems today. I think if you give it a real try, you will learn to enjoy what we are doing."

5. Helping students to appreciate and celebrate diversity.

EXAMPLE: All of you will not be as good at everything we do or may not like everything we do to the same degree as others. That's okay. Isn't it wonderful that we are not all the same!"

6. Helping students to begin to take responsibility for their actions and to become independent.

EXAMPLE: "When you watch sports on TV, sometimes players are not always honest about the fouls they commit. When we play, I am going to ask you to take responsibility for your fouls by raising your hands. I am doing this for two reasons: first, because I cannot officiate all of your games; and second, because I think that learning how to do the 'right thing,' even when we may not get caught doing something wrong, is important. How do you feel about it?"

7. Focusing your assessment and the learning experiences you design in assessment of students on affective as well as other objectives.

EXAMPLE: Use a videotape of your class or reflect on the class as soon after it is over as possible to determine the extent to which students are behaving in ways consistent with your affective objectives.

EXAMPLE: "Over the last semester you have participated in several different activities. In your journals describe to me which of these activities you like best and for each activity how you 'feel' when you participate in that activity."

■ PHYSICAL EDUCATION FOR INCLUSION

In the United States in recent times struggles for power have emerged between special interest and minority groups. Many of these groups of people and the individuals who constitute these groups have suffered in silence for years as their differentness has created conditions that have made it difficult for them to fully develop their potential. Students who are different because of their socioeconomic status, gender, class, race, or physical and mental impairments have struggled to be treated equitably. Equitable treatment of all students is not only a moral imperative but also an investment in the future.

Many people in society tend to be threatened by people different from themselves. The teacher's role is to help all students to see diversity in society as a strength. The moral foundation of this country is based on the idea that this diversity contributes to, not diminishes, who we are and what we are. Unfortunately, placing the battle for equity on power issues, rather than larger moral issues, has created disconnected struggles for power by separate groups. In many cases, the result has created confrontation and defensiveness. Establishing equity as a moral issue has the potential to create understanding, personal growth, and tolerance.

Physical education is a laboratory for social development.

Tolerance is the ability to respect the integrity of others who are different. The development of tolerance as a characteristic of an educated individual should be a major goal of all teachers—not because people are part of a different culture, or gender, or race or because they have particular physical characteristics, but because they are people who have the same rights, dreams, needs, and aspirations as all other people. Just as hate, bigotry, injustice, and intolerance are learned, so are tolerance and sensitivity to the feelings of others. These characteristics are learned in physical education and are taught by physical education teachers.

As a teacher you are part of society. You have developed many of the beliefs, attitudes, and values of your culture. You communicate the values you have through what you say, what you do, and how you do it. We know from research that most teachers tend to sort students into good and bad categories and that usually these categories are highly influenced by student gender, culture, and physical characteristics. Most teachers are unaware that they are making these judgments, but the results are the same. Students tend to be prejudged, avoided, and receive disparate amounts of attention based on teacher perceptions. The student receives these messages loud and clear and responds accordingly, generally with behaviors characteristic of students with low esteem and low achievement orientation, described in the first part of this chapter. Equally important, other students in the class pick up the messages you send and respond to these students in a similar fashion.

This section is divided into several important parts. In the first part you are encouraged to become aware of your values, attitudes, and behaviors—you cannot teach others to be tolerant and to be sensitive to others if you are not. The second part deals with ways in which you can teach tolerance, sensitivity, and inclusion to others. The third part deals with specific needs of students in our classes who are different.

Becoming Aware

Teachers are models. Because physical education is the social laboratory that it is, physical education teachers tend to have a great influence on the formation of values and attitudes students develop toward others. One of the most critical incidences quoted nationally by speakers in both professional and nonprofessional circles is the negative effect on students selected last for a team in their physical education classes. Such practices have had a devastating influence on these students and have ensured that the goal of our programs—participation in activity—will be avoided at all costs. Consider the messages teachers of physical education send with the following practices:

- The student with a disability is left to sit on the side because the teacher has not found a way to include him or her in the day's lesson.
- When students choose partners, they consistently choose those of their own race, culture, or gender. The teacher says and does nothing.
- Students within the class use ethnic and racial degrading comments and remarks to each other. The teacher does nothing.
- The teacher organizes students by gender (for practice, to line up, to go back to their classroom) or chooses teams by gender.
- The teacher acts on the assumption that all Asian students are good academically, but poor in physical skills; all black students are good in physical skills, but poor academically; and girls cannot throw.
- The teacher assumes that a black student who will not look at him or her when being disciplined is being disrespectful.

These incidences are examples of teachers who have not developed the skills and attitudes needed for a physical education program of inclusion.

A first step toward teaching physical education for inclusion is to develop an awareness of your values and attitudes toward students who represent different cultures, races, genders, socioeconomic classes, and so on. The following are suggestions for becoming aware of your values and attitudes and developing a sensitivity for the needs of those students who may be different from you:

- Watch for stereotyping in language, roles, media, and practices in your school and community.
- Make a list of the things you do, as well as the school and community you serve. Become sensitized to issues of social justice.

- Recognize that equal does not always mean fair. Some students need to be treated differently and in a more supportive manner.
- Avoid the tendency to lump all people into a single group. See people as individuals, not as members of a group.
- Become familiar with the worldviews of different cultures. Try not to put a value judgment on these ideas. Recognize them as different, not wrong. Provide a forum for discussing differences when there is conflict.
- Take some risks. Attend events and activities sponsored by individuals and groups outside your own. Participate in workshops, conferences, and classes that deal with race and culture.
- Involve representatives from different cultures in the planning of your program.
- Videotape or audiotape your teaching. Do an analysis of whom you are interacting with and how you are interacting with them in terms of gender, culture, race, physical ability, and so on. Observe the responses of your students to each other. Note how they are treating each other.

Developing a Climate for Inclusion

Despite any moral imperative they may feel toward inclusionary practices, many teachers are in environments where they must cope with not only their values and attitudes toward differentness, but also the values and attitudes of other students in their classes. The lack of social acceptance by peers influences all aspects of students' lives and perceptions of themselves. In these cases, doing nothing is not an option. Ideas relative to socially integrating students who are different can provide some help.

Model attitudes toward differences. Teachers can make a major contribution to the development of positive attitudes toward self and others by how they treat students and respond to them. It is easy to like those students who fit in, who are skilled, and who relate positively to both the teacher and other students. By responding to all students in a more positive, supportive manner, even when disciplining a child, the teacher sends powerful messages

about what is appropriate and what is not appropriate interaction between people. Teachers who abuse their power by threatening students send the wrong messages.

> EXAMPLE: "Tommy, I asked you not to shoot baskets when you were supposed to be working on dribbling the basketball. You will have to take time out for a few minutes. When you think you can come back and join the group and follow directions, let me know and we will discuss it."

Teach students to respect the person and property of others. Let students know that it is not appropriate to hurt others or to make them feel bad. Help students build a sensitivity to the feelings of others.

> EXAMPLE: The teacher has observed that a small group of students has excluded a black child from participation by not ever giving the student a turn. The teacher asks the black child to join another group temporarily and then sits down with the group and talks about how that child must feel in their group. The teacher tries to help them understand how they would feel if they were being excluded because they were different. The teacher makes it clear that such behavior is unacceptable and asks them to try again. After observing the students, the teacher asks those students to stay a minute at the end of the class and positively reinforces their appropriate behavior.

When students demonstrate disrespectful behavior toward you, do not respond in kind. Teach students to ignore the disrespectful behavior of others and to rise above it.

> EXAMPLES:
> - A minority student uses a racial slur when addressing the teacher. The teacher comments, "I know that you are feeling angry at me at this time, but it hurts me when you feel the need to degrade me in this way. I want you to think about what you just did. Let's talk about it after the class is over."
> - The teacher hears comments in the class that represent racial or cultural tension. The teacher stops the class and takes time to talk about that type of behavior: why it is unproductive and how to respond to it.

Positively reinforce appropriate behavior.

EXAMPLE: A team of students includes a mainstreamed student. Some of the students are adjusting what they do based on the ability of this mainstreamed student, and some of the students are not. The teacher comments, "I saw some of you making a decision in what to do with the ball based on the ability of your teammates. I want to thank and support those of you reacting sensitively to the needs of others you were working with."

Facilitate but do not force interaction between students who demonstrate unfriendly behavior toward each other.

EXAMPLE: "When you select a partner or small group to work with, I have noticed that somehow we get all the black students on one team and all the white students on another team. This concerns me because from my perspective you are making the decision of whom to work with on the basis of skin color—which to me is the wrong reason to be chosen for anything. I can choose the groups myself, but I would rather you begin to think about what you are doing. When we come in tomorrow, I would like to see if all of you can be sensitive to this issue. I would like to see groups that do not represent two races in my classes. For some of you this will be difficult. I am asking that you try."

Use cooperative learning strategies. Cooperative learning as a teaching strategy has the advantage of making students within a group interdependent for achievement of the learning task. Cooperative learning as a teaching strategy is described in chapter 8.

Build into your program opportunities to teach students about different cultures.

EXAMPLES:

- The student population of a class consists of a large number of Mexican Americans and those of Latino descent. The teacher has selected activities common to these cultures for a unit in rhythms and dance.
- The student population of a class consists of several students of Asian descent. The teacher has decided that she will take several minutes out of the beginning of each class to help students understand their cultural differences in terms of social interaction, world beliefs, and popular leisure-time activities.

■ BUILDING EQUITY
Gender Equity

Gender is an issue in physical education classes because of some major assumptions our society makes about participation in sport and physical activity. Primarily boys are "supposed" to be skilled and interested in aggressive sport activities, and girls are not. Girls are "supposed" to be interested in gymnastics and dance activities, and boys are not. Fortunately, many of the social stigmas attached to participation or lack of participation are changing. Teachers can facilitate this change and help all students actualize their potential and interests in physical activity by attending to the stereotypes inherent in the sport culture and common practice in physical education.

Teachers can help students feel good about themselves as participants in an active lifestyle by becoming aware of the powerful culture attached to gender-related sport participation and by trying not to attach interest in or successful participation in sport or physical activity to gender. Consider the following teacher comments and their effect on stereotyping participation by gender:

- "You throw like a girl."
- "Get in there and get the ball—be a man."
- "The girls may not want to do this."
- "The boys will do touch football, and the girls dance."
- "You don't want to lose to a girl."
- "You guys . . . "

Consider the effect of gender identification of the following practices:

- Lining students up by girls and boys
- Using male professional sport models on a continuous basis
- Having a gymnasium filled with pictures of male sport figures and no female sport figures
- Excluding dance from the boys' curriculum
- Always asking a boy to demonstrate
- Continuously using gender-specific language

Not all boys like football; not all girls do not. Not all boys are aggressive or highly skilled; not all girls are nonaggressive or unskilled. If physical education is to meet the needs of all students, sport and gender must begin to be disassociated and programs must begin to offer a wide range of options for participation to all students.

Ethnic and Cultural Differences

Research has begun to explore the problems of communication inherent in classrooms, including between students and teachers from different races (Peshkin, 1992). Students from different ethnic and cultural origins (1) may attach different meanings to language, (2) may hold differing perspectives on events, and (3) are taught to value different behaviors and interrelate socially in different ways. What may be perceived by the teacher as a social or learning problem may be a cultural difference. Unfortunately, it is sometimes only in schools where children get to interact with others from a different culture. For minority students, the problems of going to school are increased because of cultural conflicts encountered between the home and the school. The typical classroom values are such things as being on time and turn taking, but some students from different cultures do not share these values. Teachers who work in multicultural environments must resolve these differences in positive ways.

The issue of cultural differences and what should be done in the schools to accommodate these differences is largely a political one. For the student the problem is an immediate one, and it is real. Many of the ideas on developing a climate for inclusion in the previous section are appropriate general guidelines for working in positive ways in multicultural environments. In addition, the following thoughts are provided.

Do not stereotype students into a cultural group. Treat students as individuals. For example, do not assume that all Mexican Americans are late because they do not value time.

Learn about the culture of the students with whom you are working. If you are employed in a school district that serves a large multicultural student body, you will need to do all you can to learn about their cultures by attending community events, reading, and being a good observer of behavior.

Find out why a student is behaving in a particular way—do not assume it is always a cultural difference. If you observe a particular behavior on the part of the student that you do not value, try and find out from the student why he or she is behaving in that way. Sometimes the reason may have little to do with cultural differences, but more with another matter that needs attention.

Treat conflicts in culture as independent decisions. If the conflict is over an idea you deem critical for the child's learning, explain why you are asking the students to conform even though it may be inconsistent with their way of doing things or seeing things. Some cultural practices cannot and should not be accommodated by schools because those behaviors are not accepted by the society as a whole (e.g., physical aggression to resolve issues).

Modify your instruction for non-English-speaking students. Teachers are likely to have students in their classes who do not speak English, or who speak it as a second language with some difficulty. Teachers can help these students profit from instruction by making sure that demonstrations can stand alone as much as possible without verbal language (exaggerated gestures), using written directions (in their native language as well), and using a peer student to guide the non-English-speaking students individually in what they are expected to do. Teachers can help teach English to the non-English-speaking student and a different language to the English-speaking students by asking the non-English-speaking student to identify the equivalent word in his or her own language.

Disadvantaged Students

Students who come from families in low socioeconomic brackets of society are often disadvantaged in school settings. They are disadvantaged not because they do not have material things, but because often their parents are unable to give them the life skills, cognitive development, and social skills necessary to function effectively in the schools. Teachers who work with disadvantaged students and teachers who have disadvantaged students in their classes must make some adjustments for these students.

Recommendations for teaching disadvantaged students are no different from those for all students. The difference is that disadvantaged students are not likely to learn unless the teacher accommodates their needs, and advantaged students often will learn despite what the teacher does. The following ideas are helpful.

Establish a positive personal relationship with the disadvantaged student. Unless teachers can break down communication barriers with students, they are unlikely to be effective in teaching disadvantaged students. However, a warm personal level of communication and support is not used to excuse students' inappropriate behavior or lack of learning. Effective teachers of disadvantaged students have high expectations for students and hold them accountable for learning and behavior. Teachers should not allow students to negotiate lack of learning and performance for behavioral compliance.

Teach social and academic skills necessary for learning. Many disadvantaged students do not have the tools for learning or the social skills needed to function in school settings. These must be taught before real learning can take place. Skills such as listening and paying attention to the teacher, working with a partner, and practicing independent of a high amount of teacher supervision should be taught.

Work on ways to positively increase motivation and self-esteem. The ideas in this chapter relative to increasing motivation and self-esteem are relevant for disadvantaged students. Many disadvantaged students are from minority cultures, may not have high self-esteem, and may not be highly motivated to learn. Tasks should be designed to be challenging but should ensure success. These students will need much positive reinforcement from the teacher, as well as their peers. Achievement not earned through effort should not be reinforced just to build esteem.

Use positive models from their culture. In the case of sport figures, select not only those figures who have achieved in professional sports, but those who are good role models in their personal life and academic life.

Work with other teachers and support personnel in the school, community, and home to meet the needs of the disadvantaged student. Often the physical education teacher operates in the gymnasium as a "Lone Ranger" with students who need consistent and integrated help throughout the school. The physical education teacher should join planning teams to focus on the needs of individual students and to develop comprehensive approaches to disadvantaged students within the school. Teachers should not be afraid to elicit the help of parents and other school personnel in working with students with problems. Do not allow problems to build. Act to correct problems when you can identify them.

Be alert to the idea that many of the disadvantaged students may not share your life experiences and so the examples you may use in your language and explanations may not be understood. In these cases you must explain and give examples. Continuously check for student understanding. Observe insightfully for how a student might be interpreting what you say.

Be alert for the possibility that disadvantaged students may have improper diets and health care problems that may need attention of school and community services.

Direct instruction and teacher-directed learning seem to be the most effective teaching strategies with the disadvantaged students. Although direct instruction is found to be the most effective teaching strategy with disadvantaged students, it is again a question of weaning the students from such high dependency on teacher control (see chapter 8).

Students with Disabilities

Because many students with disabilities are mainstreamed into regular classes, it is likely that physical education teachers will have to find ways to meet the needs of these students within regular physical education classes. There is always a danger in classifying students and suggesting teaching techniques appropriate for students with particular characteristics. Although disabled students may share a disabling condition, it is possible that they share little else with those with the same condition (Schloss, 1992). It is critical that teachers maintain an individual perspective with these students that focuses primarily on what they can do and not what they cannot do. Because most professional preparation programs have a specific course that addresses the needs of specific disability conditions in physical education, this material is not duplicated in this text. The following general guidelines reinforce the needs of these students.

Prepare the rest of the class. Teachers who successfully integrate students with disabling conditions into their classes prepare the rest of the class for their arrival. All of us tend to be afraid of those things we do not understand. Teachers should first help other students in their classes understand the disabling condition and how they can help.

Adapt the activity to the ability of the student. Good teachers individualize the expectations for all students in a class. It is even more critical that teachers individualize the expectations for students with disabilities. Some of the following suggestions are examples of the ways in which teachers can do this.

- *Change the rules of the game on an individual basis.* For example, students having difficulty can play with two bounces of the ball rather than one in tennis, can shoot free throws or serve a ball from a closer distance, can play without the traveling rule in basketball.
- *Modify the equipment.* Students with disabilities can play with lighter balls, smaller rackets, bigger balls, or smaller courts. Specialized equipment for the visually impaired may include balls with a bell or objects strung from a rope so that it doesn't get too far away.

- *Modify the expectations.* Student goal setting should be individualized. Expectations should be modified to meet the needs of students. Fitness exercises and skills requiring physical abilities (strength, speed) should be adjusted to be realistic goals for the individual student.

Make specific adjustments in your task presentations and instruction for specific needs of students with disabilities. Each student with a disability has unique needs that the teacher must consider in his or her instruction. The following examples illustrate some of these instructional needs.

- *Students with a visual impairment.* When delivering instruction, place the student close to you or the visual demonstration or presentation you want him or her to see. Make sure to use clear visual demonstrations that overemphasize points you want to make. Physically manipulate the student through a movement if necessary.
- *Students with a hearing impairment.* Move the student as close as possible to the source of the sound. Use good visual demonstrations and written material (task cards or other directions). If needed, use a microphone at a level that is appropriate for the student. Hand gestures and signals with verbal directions are extremely valuable for this student.

Use peer tutors. The use of peer tutors has been one of the most effective ways to meet the needs of students with disabling conditions. The peer tutor should be selected carefully so that the experience is a positive one for both the disabled student and the peer tutor. The peer tutor must be skilled at the lesson material, dependable, and sensitive to the needs of others. It is helpful to meet with students who are going to be tutors and teach them how to be tutors. In individual lessons the peer tutor should be given specific directions on how to help and adapt what is going on for the student with the disability.

Facilitate—do not force—interaction. It may take some time for a student with a disability to be integrated into your class. Do not force students who are uncomfortable working with a disabled student to work with this student—give it time. If you need to meet with the whole class not in the presence of the disabled student after the disabled student has been introduced into your class, arrange to do this. Do not let negative experiences for either the student or the rest of the class continue without intervention.

Help the student to socially integrate with peers. Teach the disabled student the skills he or she will need to make integration into the regular class work. There are many "going to physical education class" skills that your students have learned over time. A student with a disability who has not been part of regular physical education has not had the opportunity to learn these skills. When you see this child is perplexed and not responding, ask yourself if there are any needed skills that this child has not had the opportunity to learn.

If the disabled student has a problem socially with the other students, it may be because he or she does not know how to socialize with peers in positive ways. Do not be afraid to help this student directly with these problems. The other students must make allowances, but students with disabilities need these skills to be fully integrated into a class.

Focus on what the students can do. It is unfortunate for the child with a disabling condition that most of the attention the child receives is for what he or she cannot do. Teachers need to help these students discover the limits of what they *can* do, not what they *cannot* do. One of the most exciting experiences I observed was to watch a student with full leg braces take a full run and "ditch" his crutches before going over a vaulting box and lowering himself into a roll. When teachers put the emphasis on what students can do and encourage students to extend their abilities in a supportive environment, student motivation, effort, and success increase.

Participate in multidisciplinary planning. Physical education teachers need to have input into and be part of the planning meetings for students with disabling conditions. This is sometimes difficult

The teacher's attitude can help students socially integrate.

when so many students are involved, but it is necessary if the child's physical education experiences are to be positive ones. If you cannot meet with each committee member, make it a point to find out what was discussed.

Focus on lifetime activity skills. Because many students with disabilities have not had the opportunities of able-bodied students, students with disabilities will need your help to make physical activity a part of their lifestyle. It is important to give these students the skills and attitudes essential to be participants rather than to encourage them to use their disabling condition as an excuse not to participate. One way, but by no means the only way, to do this is to encourage and facilitate participation in Special Olympics and other community programs specifically designed for students with disabilities.

■ DISCUSSION OF AFFECTIVE GOALS FOR PHYSICAL EDUCATION

Many of the guidelines discussed in this chapter attend to motivation and personal growth of students by transferring instructional decision making from the teacher to the student. Many teachers make the mistake of assuming that student freedom and student choice always result in positive experiences for students and that teacher control is to be avoided if positive affect is to be developed. As discussed in chapter 6, self-direction and students who respond from an internal sense of control are the goals. The amount of freedom, the amount of choice, and the degree to which motivation efforts focus on internal rather than external control depend on where students are in their development of internal control. It is appropriate for the teacher to act where students are at the time. It is inappropriate to leave them there.

SUMMARY

1. Motivation is an essential part of learning.
2. Students cannot work on fulfilling higher needs until more basic needs are satisfied.
3. The motivation of people toward a particular goal is both a function of their desire to reach the goal and their tendency to want to avoid failure.
4. We tend to attribute success and failure to our ability, our effort, luck, or the difficulty of the task.
5. High-achievement students attribute success to effort and are more motivated by failure. Low-achievement students tend to attribute success to external factors and failure to internal factors. They are therefore not motivated by failure.
6. Teachers can motivate students by attending to principles of motivation in their teaching.
7. The manner in which a teacher interacts with students in a class, as well as on a personal level, impacts the manner in which students are motivated to learn and achieve personal growth.
8. Teachers can build into all aspects of their lessons specific strategies for promoting motivation and the personal growth of students.
9. Affective goals are a specific part of the content of physical education, as well as a shared concern with all education programs.
10. Effective teachers balance students' needs for structure with those for more student control of learning experiences.
11. One of the first steps toward developing a climate for inclusion in your class is to become sensitized to the things that you do that might impact students different from you or society has not treated in an equitable fashion.
12. Teachers can act to develop a climate for inclusion in their classes.

CHECKING YOUR UNDERSTANDING

1. Describe why students may not be motivated to learn from the perspective of need theory, intrinsic motivation, and cognitive theory.
2. State at least five general principles that are implications for teaching from motivation theory.
3. Describe nine ways teachers can promote the personal growth of students through personal interaction.
4. Describe how teachers can integrate motivation and personal growth into their teaching through the following functions:
   Planning
   Selection and design of learning experiences
   Presentation of units and tasks
   Organizational arrangements
   Teacher functions during activity
   Lesson pacing
   Evaluation
5. What are the unique affective goals of physical education? What goals does education share with other educational programs?
6. How can the teacher teach values and affect?
7. Are needs for student choice and more responsibility in the educational process at odds with student needs for structure and teacher control? Why?
8. What are some things teachers can do to bring to an awareness level what they might be doing that may negatively impact students who are "different"?
9. What can teachers do to develop a climate of inclusion in their classes?
10. How can students with disabilities be best handled in your classes?

REFERENCES

Deci, E., & Ryan, R. (1985). *Intrinsic motivation and self-determination in human behavior.* New York: Plenum.

Good, T., & Brophy, J. (1990). *Educational psychology: A realistic approach.* New York: Longman.

Hellison, D. (1996). Teaching personal and social responsibility in physical education. In S. Silverman & C. Ennis (Eds.), *Student learning in physical education: Applying Research to enhance instruction* (pp. 269–286). Champaign, IL: Human Kinetics.

Hellison, D. (2003). *Teaching responsibility through physical activity.* Champaign, IL: Human Kinetics.

Lee, A. (1997). Contributions of research on student thinking in physical education. *Journal of Teaching Physical Education, 16,* 262–277.

National Association for Sport and Physical Education. (2004). *Moving into the future: Content standards for physical education—physical education outcomes.* Reston, VA: NASPE.

Nicholls, J. (1976). Effort is virtuous, but it's better to have ability. *Journal of Research in Personality, 10,* 306–315.

Peshkin, A. (1992). The relationship between culture and curriculum: A many fitting thing. In P. Jackson (Ed.), *Handbook of research on curriculum* (pp. 248–267). New York: Macmillan.

Schloss, P. (Ed.). (1992). Integrating learners with disabilities in regular education programs [Special issue]. *The Elementary School Journal, 92,* 3.

SUGGESTED READINGS

Best, C., Lieberman, L., & Arndt, K. (2002). Effective use of interpreters in general physical education. *Journal of Physical Education, Recreation and Dance, 73*(8), 45–50.

Beveridge, S., & Scruggs, P. (2000). TLC for better PE: Girls and elementary physical education. *Journal of Physical Education, Recreation and Dance, 71*(8), 22–25.

Block, M. (1995). Use peer tutors and task sheets. *Strategies, 8*(7), 9–11.

Compagnone, N. (1995). Teaching responsibility to rural elementary youth: Going beyond the urban at-risk boundaries. *Journal of Physical Education, Recreation and Dance, 66*(6), 58–63.

Driver, S., Harmon, M., & Block, M. (2003). Devising a safe and successful physical education program for children with a brain injury. *Journal of Physical Education, Recreation and Dance, 74*(7), 41–48.

Horton, M. (2001). Utilizing paraprofessionals in the general physical education setting. *Journal of Physical Education, Recreation and Dance, 12*(6), 22–25.

Houton-Wilson, C., & Lieberman, L. (2003). Strategies for teaching children with autism in physical education. *Journal of Physical Education, Recreation and Dance, 74*(6), 40–44.

Johnson, D., & Johnson, R. (1995). *Reducing school violence through conflict resolution.* Alexandria, VA: ASCD.

Krueger, K. (2003). Strengthening character. *Strategies, 16*(5), 17–20.

Latham, A. (1997). Responding to cultural learning styles. *Educational Leadership, 54*(7), 88–89.

Lieberman, L., James, A., & Ludwa, N. (2004). The impact of inclusion in general physical education for all students. *Journal of Physical Education, Recreation and Dance, 75*(5), 42–46.

McHugh, E. (1995). Going beyond the physical: Social skills and physical education. *Journal of Physical Education, Recreation and Dance, 66*(4), 18–21.

Mitchell, C. (Ed.). (1995). *Gender equity through physical education and sport.* Reston, VA: AAHPERD.

Morris, G. (Ed.). (1993). Becoming responsible for our actions: What's possible in physical education. *Journal of Physical Education, Recreation and Dance, 64*(5), 36–75.

Randell, L., Oakland, D., & Taylor, A. (2003). Increasing physical activity in girls and woman: Lessons learned from the DAMET Project. *Journal of Physical Education, Recreation and Dance, 74*(1), 37–44.

Rizzo, T., & Lavay, B. (2000). Inclusion: Why the confusion? *Journal of Physical Education, Recreation and Dance, 71*(4), 32–36.

Roberts, G. (1993). Cooperative learning: Guidelines for choosing games. *Strategies, 6*(5), 12–14.

Schultz, F. (Ed.). (1998). *Multicultural education 98/99* (5th ed.). Guildord, CO: Duschkin/McGraw-Hill.

Smith, N., & Owens, A. (2000). Multicultural games: Embracing technology and diversity. *Strategies, 13*(5), 18–21.

Stuart, M. (2003). Moral issues in sport: The child's perspective. *Research Quarterly for Exercise and Sport, 74*(4), 445–449.

Sutliff, M., & Perry, J. (2000). Multiculturalism: Developing connections in elementary physical education. *Strategies, 13*(5), 33–36.

Tjeersdma, B. (1995). How to motivate students . . . without standing on your head. *Journal of Physical Education, Recreation and Dance, 66*(5), 36.

Webb, D., & Pope, C. (1999). Including within an inclusive context: Going beyond labels and categories. *Journal of Physical Education, Recreation and Dance, 70*(7), 41–47.

Weiller, K., & Doyle, E. (2000). Teacher-student interaction: An exploration of gender differences in elementary physical education. *Journal of Physical Education, Recreation and Dance, 71*(3), 43–45.

Wlodkowski, R., & Ginsberg, M. (1995). A framework for culturally responsive teaching. *Educational Leadership, 53*(1), 17–21.

Wright, P., White, K., & Geabler-Spira, D. (2004). Exploring the relevance of the personal and social responsibility model in adapted physical activity: A collective case study. *Journal of Teaching in Physical Education, 23,* 71, 87.

Xiang, P., McBride, R., & Guan, J. (2004). Children motivation in elementary physical education. *Research Quarterly for Exercise and Sport, 75*(1) 71–80.

Yun, J., Shapiro, D., & Kennedy, J. (2000). Reaching IEP goals in the general physical education class. *Journal of Physical Education, Recreation and Dance 71*(8), 33–37.

Planning

O V E R V I E W

Instruction is a process involving preactive, active, and postactive decision making. Preactive decisions are those involved in planning curriculum, units, and lessons; active decisions are those made during the conduct of the lesson; and postactive decisions are those made as a result of reflecting on and evaluating the processes and products of instruction. Planning is a critical part of the teaching process. The products of planning explicitly describe the teacher's intent for student outcomes and the teacher's strategy for how to bring students to those outcomes. This chapter focuses on planning procedures used in the instructional process. Because many programs have established coursework in curriculum in physical education, a comprehensive discussion of these areas is not attempted in a single chapter. They are described only in terms of their importance to planning the instructional process. The emphasis of the chapter is on lesson and unit planning.

Standard 3: Planning and Implementation

Physical education teacher candidates plan and implement a variety of developmentally appropriate learning experiences and content aligned with local, state, and national standards to develop physically educated individuals.

NASPE Beginning Teaching Standards, 2008

O U T L I N E

- **Establishing goals and objectives for learning**
  Writing objectives in terms of what students will learn

  Levels of specificity in educational objectives
  Objectives in the three learning domains

- **Writing objectives consistent with content standards**
- **Planning physical education experiences**
- **Planning the lesson**
  Beginning the lesson
  Developing the lesson
  Ending the lesson—closure

Format for lesson planning
Planning the curriculum
Developing curriculum from a set of standards
Planning for units of instruction
Considerations in planning unit
Developing the unit
The unit plan

The major focus of this text has been the instructional process—the time students and teachers spend together in the physical education class. To make the instructional process effective in accomplishing program goals, teachers must plan for and evaluate the process. Planning takes place before instruction; evaluation takes place during and after instruction. Evaluation guides future teaching as described in figure 10.1.

Educators plan and evaluate educational experiences at many levels of specificity. National task force groups plan for and evaluate schooling in the country as a whole. National task forces in all content areas, including physical education, have established voluntary content standards describing what all students should know and be able to do in K–12 school programs. States, to which the Constitution has delegated responsibility for education, establish statewide goals, standards, and evaluative procedures for their programs. Local school districts develop standards, or adopt national or state standards; develop curriculums; and monitor student performance in those curricular areas to which they attach greatest importance. Teachers plan, implement, and evaluate curriculums

on a long-term basis and units of instruction and lessons on a short-term basis.

There is evidence that more accountability is being established for what students learn in physical education. Several states and local districts have established ways in which to evaluate physical education school programs and to hold schools and teachers accountable for student outcomes. However, many physical educators, unlike classroom teachers, have not had to design their programs to conform to district, state, or national standards. Most physical educators have complete autonomy regarding curriculum. This is both a professional advantage and disadvantage. The creative teacher is not limited because the curriculum can reflect local student needs. However, the lack of accountability for program goals more often than not leads to programs without goals or programs without any chance of meeting those goals that have been established.

One of the reasons many physical education programs are not effective is that little long-term or short-term planning takes place. The publication *Moving into the Future: National Standards for Physical Education* by the National Association for Sport and Physical Education (NASPE, 2004) should help states, districts, and individual teachers more carefully plan appropriate experiences for students in physical education. Many states and local districts have used this material as a jumping-off point from which to establish their standards for student achievement.

The processes of planning and evaluation are integrally related. Planning establishes goals and specific procedures for reaching those goals. Evaluation discovers the extent to which those goals have been reached and whether those procedures have been effective. Chapter 11 addresses issues related to assessment and evaluation. *Beginning teachers will not really begin to*

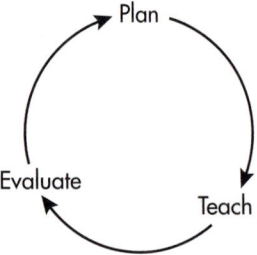

FIGURE 10.1
Evaluation is used as a guide to future teaching.

think as educators until they can establish goals for what they want to do, select what they do in light of those goals, and evaluate what they do based on those goals. Although more experienced teachers can probably reduce some of the detail with which they write short-term lesson plans and still be effective, more extensive planning has a positive effect on the quality of programs. Long-term planning of curriculum and units of instruction is essential for all teachers at any level of experience. Planning is not easy for the teacher to do—the process can be a painful and frustrating one. Although this essential function in teaching requires less effort with experience, it is never easy.

This chapter is divided into two major sections: The first section is designed to help teachers establish goals and objectives for learning, and the second section treats planning at the lesson, unit, and curriculum level.

■ ESTABLISHING GOALS AND OBJECTIVES FOR LEARNING

Learning outcomes are usually written as educational objectives for students at different levels of specificity and for different areas of human development. Inherent in this idea are the following important points:

- Objectives are written in terms of *what students are expected to learn,* not what teachers or students do, during instruction.
- Objectives can be written broadly (e.g., Students will learn how to shoot a basketball) or specifically (e.g., Students will be able to get eight of ten foul shots in the basket).
- Objectives are written for psychomotor, affective, and cognitive learning outcomes.

Each of these points is critical to planning and evaluating instruction. They will be considered separately in the following discussion.

Writing Objectives in Terms of What Students Will Learn

Learning outcomes should be specified for educational programs at all levels of planning in terms of what students will learn from the educational experience. The national standards (NASPE, 2004) are written in terms of what students should know and

be able to do. These standards converted to state, district, and local school standards may be more specific but are still written in terms of student outcomes. In contrast to this, educational goals and objectives are sometimes written in terms of what the teacher or the student will do (describe the process rather than the outcome of that process). The following examples illustrate the difference between specifying objectives as a teacher activity, a student activity, and a student outcome.

> *Teacher activity.* Demonstrate for students how to do a volleyball set/teach the volleyball set.
>
> *Student activity.* Practice the overhead set.
>
> *Student outcome.* Set the volleyball effectively to a frontline player from a toss.

The teacher will want to write both instructional and curricular outcomes in terms of *student outcomes.* Student objectives are usually prefaced with the phrase *"Students will be able to."* This helps the planner focus on a learning product rather than on a learning process. The following objectives are written appropriately in terms of what the learner will be able to do as a result of instruction:

- Pass a ball to a teammate on the move ahead of the receiver without having to stop.
- Demonstrate support for a partner by using an appropriate force level on passes and verbally supporting a partner's effort.

To make explicit a desired learning outcome, objectives are usually written in three parts:

- *Behavior* expected of the student (e.g., strike, hit, show support, pass)
- *Condition* or *situation* under which the behavior is to be exhibited (e.g., work with a partner from 10 feet)
- *Criterion* to be met or *performance level* expected (e.g., use accurate form; be 90 percent accurate)

In the following examples the three parts of an objective are specified:

- Objective 1: The student will be able to travel in general space, using the feet in at least three different ways, without touching anyone else.

  Behavior: Travel

  Condition: In general space on the feet

Criterion: Use three different ways of traveling without touching anyone else

- Objective 2: The student will be able to pass the volleyball effectively to a frontline player from the back line using a legal forearm pass from a ball tossed over the net (the receiver should not have to take more than one step).
  Behavior: Use a forearm pass
  Condition: From a toss over the net, from the back line to a frontline player
  Criterion: Use a legal, effective pass
- Objective 3: The student will be able to shift positions in a basketball game in relation to the location of the ball using the 2-1-2 zone defense.
  Behavior: Shift defensive position
  Condition: Use the 2-1-2 zone defense in game play
  Criterion: Shift appropriately in relation to the position of the ball
- Objective 4: The student will be able to demonstrate responsibility for the partner relationship by passing the ball at a level of difficulty appropriate to challenge the student's partner.
  Behavior: Pass the ball
  Condition: To a partner
  Criterion: Use an appropriate level to challenge partner

The *behavior* component of an instructional objective is written as a verb that describes what the student is to do. It is almost always an action verb and should be written in terms that specify the same thing to anyone who might refer to the term. The following examples illustrate verbs from the three domains that communicate a behavior:

Psychomotor	Affective	Cognitive
Put the shot	Attends to	Remember
Kick	Accepts	Understand
Defend	Expresses	Apply
Do	Values	Analyze
Roll	Enjoys	Evaluate
		Create

The *condition* component of an instructional objective describes the situation under which the action

will be performed. The specification of conditions in physical education objectives is critical. Reviewing the discussion on conditions in chapter 2 will help you understand the implications of conditions for designing appropriate objectives for a particular group of students. For example, a student successful at returning a tennis ball across a net with a forehand drive from an easy toss might not be as successful when the ball is hit to the student, especially if the student has to move to get it. A student who can demonstrate good form in a forearm pass in volleyball from a partner toss may not be able to even contact a ball served over the net. A student who can control a basketball dribble moving forward at a slow speed may not be able to change direction or control the dribble at a faster speed. Conditions, therefore, are crucial.

Conditions for affective and cognitive objectives are likewise important. If I have the objective that "the student will work cooperatively with a partner," I do not know much about this objective unless the conditions are specified, such as "in sharing equipment for a gymnastics lesson" or "using a checklist for a skill assessment." If I have a cognitive objective for students to "identify" the cues of a particular skill, unless I specify the conditions under which the knowledge is exhibited, I have not been clear in defining the outcomes I expect. A student could demonstrate knowledge: when asked by the teacher; on a written test; by using that knowledge in performance; or by sharing that knowledge with a peer.

The *criterion* component of an objective describes minimal levels of performance for the action specified. The criteria are evaluative criteria that indicate when success has been achieved. Criteria are usually specified in two ways: (1) as quantitative (sometimes called product) criteria, which usually deal with the effectiveness of a movement response or other behavior, such as how many, how long, how high, how far, how many correct; or (2) as qualitative (sometimes called process) criteria, which deal with the process characteristics of the movement, such as the form of the movement, the degree of understanding of knowledge, or the extent to which an affective behavior is exhibited.

Writing objectives is not simple. Writing good instructional objectives takes practice.

Levels of Specificity in Educational Objectives

In writing an objective, teachers are forced to consider the level of specificity of the objective. Teachers must determine to what extent it is necessary to spell out the terms of the behavior they want to describe. The degree of specificity of an objective is based initially on the level of planning. However, degree of specificity of educational objectives is an issue widely debated in education circles.

Box 10.1 describes several levels of specificity in educational objectives that might be used in a physical education program at four different levels of planning. At the *standards level,* outcomes for a content area are specified. At a *curricular level,* objectives are broad enough to include the total curricular program; that is, they describe what students should be able to do when they leave a particular program (in this case, an elementary and secondary

school program at a particular school). At the *unit level,* objectives are exit criteria for the completion of a unit; that is, they describe what students should be able to do after completing a unit of instruction. At the *lesson level,* objectives are statements reflecting what students should be able to do at the end of a single lesson.

Sometimes the terms *aims* or *goals* distinguish broad curricular objectives from more specific learning outcomes used in lesson planning (instructional or educational objectives). In more recent times, the use of student standards at the national, state, and district levels provides direction for the development of specific curricular outcomes. Content standards describe behavior at a rather specific level but stop short of identifying the performance criteria for that behavior that could be used for assessment. Outcomes can be described differently at all levels of learning.

The question "How specific is specific?" will continue to be a source of educational debate for a long time. Proponents of outcomes written at a specific level would have educators spell out precise behaviors for all learning outcomes. "Precise" in this sense means describing the behavior and the exact way in which the behavior is measured. The current standards and assessment movement has increased the need to increase the level of specificity of educational objectives. You can't measure general objectives.

An explicit (or precise) behavioral outcome for a physical education class in softball might be the following:

- *Each student should be able to field a batted medium-speed infield grounder that falls within the student's space responsibilities and then throw the ball to the appropriate infielder in time to put the runner out eight of ten times.*

In this example, all conditions and criteria are spelled out to leave no question about what the learner should be able to do on the completion of the lesson. Learning outcomes specified in this way help the teacher plan appropriate instruction and also help the teacher evaluate what students have learned. What would a lesson for the stated objective look like? How would the teacher evaluate the degree to which students had accomplished the objective?

BOX 10·1

Objectives at Different Levels of Planning

Standards level

Demonstrates understanding of movement concepts, principles, strategies, and tactics as they apply to the learning and performance of physical activities

Curricular level

Can apply the concept of force reduction to performance in gymnastics, manipulative, and dance skills

Unit level—softball/baseball

Can apply the concept of force reduction to catch a thrown or batted ball
Can bunt a ball successfully

Lesson level

Can meet and absorb the force of a tossed ball with a bat

Compare the responses to these questions with the lesson the teacher would have to design for the following objective:

- *The student will be able to field balls.*

It is obvious which of the two preceding learning objectives provides more help to the teacher in both conducting and evaluating a lesson.

The assumption underlying the use of precise and explicit educational objectives is that all learning outcomes can be explicitly described and are measurable at all levels of planning. It is also assumed that learning is enhanced when teachers do this. Obviously, not all educators value the use of precise educational objectives. Some teachers assert that not all learning outcomes are measurable or even should be measured. They feel that forcing educators to identify behavior at measurable levels trivializes learning.

Much of the criticism surrounding the use of precise educational objectives centers on the idea that much more is involved in a learning experience than a single measurable objective or a group of measurable objectives. Different students will gain different skills or knowledge from the same experience, and teachers have more than a single measurable experience in mind when they think about learning outcomes. This is particularly true in physical education at the instructional level of planning content. Learning motor skills is a slow process, and describing what students should be able to do in a measurable form after a single lesson is often difficult. Measurable outcomes often address what can be quantified (e.g., how much, how many) and leave out those elements more difficult to measure (e.g., game play, student form in skills, strategies, affective concerns). Teachers who use precise educational objectives to guide planning, particularly at the instructional level, may tend to restrict and narrow learning experiences only to the measurable. Learning experiences thus become flattened and in some cases trivialized in their focus. Skilled teachers have learned to describe learning outcomes at useful levels of specificity and to choose appropriate ways to assess those objectives.

At the other end of the spectrum are teachers who have not thought through learning outcomes or who

deal with them so broadly that the objective provides no direction for the design or evaluation of educational experiences. The following objective for a lesson in soccer will serve as a case in point:

- *The student will be able to dribble the soccer ball.*

No conditions that describe the level of the experience and no criteria for performance are specified at any level in this example. The objective is basically useless for anything beyond saying that the lesson will have something to do with soccer dribbling.

A more common position in education regarding educational objectives is to say that educational objectives should be specified to the degree that they provide direction for the design and evaluation of educational experiences without narrowing those experiences to what is most easily measured. Objectives still include the components of behavior, conditions, and criteria, but in cases where explicit statements describing the criteria are not appropriate, these components are written in such a way that learning outcomes are more implicit than explicit. Following are examples of implicit objectives:

- *The student will be able to accurately use the appropriate fielding strategy for grounders, line drives, and fly balls in a game situation.*
- *The student will be able to demonstrate independence in working on a movement task.*

Implicit in the first objective is the idea that the student will be taught fielding strategies for grounders, line drives, and fly balls and will be given an opportunity to practice these strategies. The words *appropriate* and *accurate* are criteria that are not explicitly defined but are assumed to be part of instruction. *Teachers who do not clearly understand what the words* accurate *and* appropriate *mean are ill served by implicit objectives.* Teachers who have done a developmental analysis of the content they are teaching (in this case, softball fielding) will have specified in their planning what these criteria mean. Learning how to be a teacher is facilitated by making intended learning outcomes clear and explicit. In the second example, the assumption is that the teacher has talked with students and taught students what independent work looks like in a specific task.

Objectives in the Three Learning Domains

The primary and unique contribution physical education makes to the development of students is the development of physical skills and abilities. As an educational program, physical education also has responsibilities to the cognitive (intellect) and affective (attitude, values, and interests) development of students. There is a tendency in physical education to assume that cognitive and affective concerns will be developed automatically as a result of participating in physical education programs. Yet little that is not purposely designed occurs as a specific learning outcome. Students do not learn the rules of games unless the rules are taught; they do not learn to identify concepts unless they are taught to do so; and they will not learn how to interact positively with each other in cooperative or competitive activities unless they are helped to interact appropriately.

Learning outcomes in the affective and cognitive domains can be specified in much the same way as psychomotor outcomes are specified. The two volumes of *A Taxonomy of Educational Objectives* (Bloom et al., 1956; Krathwohl, Bloom, & Masia, 1964) were written to establish a hierarchy of learning levels within these two domains. The cognitive domain establishes skills with cognitive material that require increasingly difficult intellectual ability. The affective hierarchy progresses from the point at which students become aware of their attitudes toward affective concepts to the point at which their values have a direct influence on what they choose to do. These levels are described in box 10.2 (p. 216).

These cognitive and affective hierarchies are important because they remind the lesson planner that a decision about where students are regarding cognitive or affective material must be made *before* determining expectations for performance in these areas. Just as students cannot be expected to use a basketball dribble in a game before they have developed skills under less complex conditions, students cannot

be expected to use cognitive information in complex ways until they have been able to use it at less complicated levels. Students cannot be expected to respond affectively on an internalized level unless they have had opportunities to develop value positions at lower levels of expectation.

■ WRITING OBJECTIVES CONSISTENT WITH CONTENT STANDARDS

Today's educational programs are guided by content standards at either the national or state level. Many teachers are required to indicate the standard they are addressing with their planning materials and objectives. Although there is value in indicating the more holistic standard, there is greater value in teachers indicating the grade level outcomes identified with the standards (Rink, 2009). Most states have begun to identify the outcomes that should accompany each standard for each grade level. The national standard tends to be too broad to provide the direction needed for work at the lesson level. Grade level outcomes can be used as follows:

Example One:

Lesson Objective: The student should be able to maintain possession of the basketball against a passive defender (NASPE Standard 1, GLO 3).

Grade Level Outcome: Demonstrate basic offensive and defensive tactics in simple conditions.

National Standard: Demonstrates competency in motor skills and movement patterns needed to perform a variety of activities.

Example Two:

Lesson Objective: The student should be able to provide accurate and positive feedback to a partner on the basic cues of the volleyball underhand serve (NASPE Standard 2, GLO 2).

Grade Level Outcome: Identify the cues of the basic skills of volleyball.

National Standard: Demonstrates understanding of movement concepts, principles, strategies, and tactics as they apply to the learning and performance of physical activities.

BOX 10·2

Defined Levels of the Cognitive and Affective Domains

Cognitive domain

Remembering. Recalling information

EXAMPLE: The student will list the cues for the basketball set shot.

BEHAVIORIAL TERMS: Recognizing, listing, describing, retrieving, naming, finding

Understanding. Explaining ideas or concepts

EXAMPLE: The student will explain how to decrease force in catching activities.

BEHAVIORIAL TERMS: Interpreting, summarizing, paraphrasing, classifying, explaining

Applying. Using information in another familiar situation

EXAMPLE: The student will describe where the person who does not have the ball should move to receive a pass in a 2 vs. 1 situation.

BEHAVIORIAL TERMS: Implementing, carrying out, using, executing

Analyzing. Breaking information into parts to explore understandings and relationships

EXAMPLE: The student will be able to determine why his/her arrows are all missing the target in one direction.

BEHAVIORIAL TERMS: Comparing, organizing, interrogating, finding

Evaluating. Justifying a decision or course of action

EXAMPLE: The student will be able to determine his/her own personal fitness level and plan a personal fitness program.

BEHAVIORIAL TERMS: Checking, hypothesizing, critiquing, experimenting, judging

Create. Generate newer ideas, products, or ways of viewing things

EXAMPLE: The student will be able to work with a group of four to design a game that uses striking skills.

BEHAVIORIAL TERMS: Designing, constructing, planning, producing, investing

Affective domain

Reception. Student is willing to attend to an idea, phenomenon, or stimulus.

EXAMPLE: The student will be able to attend to teacher directions while holding equipment in the hand.

BEHAVIORIAL TERMS: Student follows directions, replies, uses names.

Response. Student chooses to act in some way to an idea, phenomenon, or stimulus.

EXAMPLE: The student will stop work on a task and follow directions at the teacher's signal.

BEHAVIORIAL TERMS: Student assists, complies, conforms, helps, practices.

Valuation. Student accepts or assumes responsibility for a value.

EXAMPLE: The student will demonstrate responsibility for a safe and productive class environment by working quietly, independently, and with concern for controlled movement.

BEHAVIORIAL TERMS: Student differentiates, initiates, joins.

Organization. Student synthesizes and resolves conflicts between value positions.

EXAMPLE: The student will be able to describe what a supportive team member is expected to do in a game situation.

BEHAVIORIAL TERMS: Student integrates, defends, explains, identifies, alters.

Internalization. Student uses a value to control behavior in a consistent way.

EXAMPLE: The student will be able to work on a task, independent of teacher monitoring, in a productive way.

BEHAVIORIAL TERMS: Students acts, discriminates solves, displays.

▪ PLANNING PHYSICAL EDUCATION EXPERIENCES

Planning for physical education experiences occurs on three levels. At the broadest level, teachers plan **curriculums** (programs of study) for an entire program, specifying the scope and sequence of work for each year and each grade at a school level. At the next level, teachers divide curriculums into units of instruction that pertain to major topics or themes of study within the curriculum. The lesson is the most narrowly focused unit and the smallest period of time for which teachers plan.

All levels of planning are interrelated. The teacher uses the national, state, or district student standards or local curriculum guide to plan units and uses the unit plan as a guide to plan lessons. Much of this text is devoted to decision making at the learning experience and task levels under the assumption that it is at these levels that the student experiences the curriculum. However, there must be consistency among all levels of planning. Goals identified in curriculums must be reflected in units, lessons, and what students actually experience.

Affective and cognitive objectives receive much attention from curriculum and unit planners, but few lesson plans show evidence of affective or cognitive planning. If asked what students should learn from a good program in physical education, many teachers would respond with a long list of affective concerns.

Organizing students, equipment, and space for a safe learning environment takes planning.

If next asked what could be done in a lesson to achieve those goals, many teachers would have difficulty coming up with specific ideas. Although practicing teachers will begin the planning process at the curriculum and unit level, preservice teachers often are called on to begin their experiences with planning at the lesson level. Therefore, lesson planning begins our discussion.

▪ PLANNING THE LESSON

The lesson plan is a guide for the process of instruction for a single lesson and is based on unit objectives. The lesson plan must translate broader aims and goals into specific learning experiences for the student. Good lesson plans are difficult to write, because the more specific that teachers are asked to be in describing their intentions, the more difficult planning becomes. For example, few would question a goal such as "Students should understand how force is produced in the throw pattern." But what does this goal look like as a learning experience? What does teamwork look like, or positive social interaction, or good defense, and, more important, how do you help students progress from where they are to where you want them to be? Expertise in teaching is the ability to understand the content at a high level and the ability to translate that content into learning experiences for students. The lesson plan must translate broad goals and objectives into experiences for particular learners.

The lesson plan is in one sense a teacher's best guess at how to produce student learning for particular objectives and particular students (Good & Brophy, 1990). In the lesson plan the teacher describes the learning that is expected and the learning experiences he or she will use to produce that learning. The lesson plan is a tentative hypothesis. Good teachers will reflect on the effectiveness of what they have done during the lesson and after teaching and make some judgment about how successful they were so that they may learn from each teaching experience.

Each lesson, however, is more than a piece of a bigger objective, unit, or curriculum. Each lesson must by itself have *integrity* and represent a holistic experience that is more than merely the continuation of the lesson before. *Lessons have beginnings, middles, and ends that give structure and meaning to learning experiences.* A description of these aspects of the lesson follows.

Beginning the Lesson

The beginning of a lesson is one of the most important aspects of the lesson. Often teachers are so eager to get students into the activity of the day, they fail to spend a few minutes to help induct students into the lesson. The following ideas are part of beginning lessons. They do not have to be present in all lessons but should be considered in planning all lessons.

Set induction. *Set induction* (sometimes called anticipatory set) is a fancy term for orienting the learners with whom you are working to what they will be doing, how they will be doing it, and why it is important. A teacher's set induction acclimates students to what they can expect in the lesson and should motivate learners to full engagement in what is to come. Adults, as well as children, are more secure if they know what is going to happen before it happens. They find more meaning in what they are asked to do if they are helped to understand why it is important.

> EXAMPLE: "Yesterday when I was observing what you were doing in the two-on-two games at the end of class, I noticed that the persons on the offense without the ball didn't have a clear idea of where they were supposed to go or what they were supposed to do. Today we are going to work on what to do when you don't have the ball. We will start off with a passing warm-up and then try to come up with some ideas on what to do when you don't have the ball. Then we will see if you can put these ideas into your games."

All-class activity. Lessons are usually helped to get off to a good start if the teacher has planned an all-class vigorous activity at the beginning of the class. This is particularly true for young children but just as applicable for older students. An all-class activity tends to focus the students and get them involved vigorously. Vigorous warm-ups can be related to fitness objectives or the content of the day's lesson. The warm-up can precede or follow the set induction for the lesson.

> EXAMPLE (ELEMENTARY): The teacher asks the students to find a space in the general work area and to begin traveling in general space in different directions. Students are then asked to add jumps and turns to their traveling and to stop at the signal and freeze. Each time they freeze, they must stop for about six seconds and then take weight on their hands in a handstand action two times. This is repeated several times.

> EXAMPLE (SECONDARY): The class is in the middle of a basketball unit. Each student is given a ball and asked to begin to dribble in general space. Two students do not have a ball and are "It." "It" tries to tag the balls of other players as they are dribbling. Anyone whose ball is tagged puts his or her ball down and becomes "It" as well. The game continues until no one has a ball. This is repeated several times.

Developing the Lesson

Each lesson is unique, and therefore specific guidelines for how to develop each particular lesson cannot be given. However, some aspects of lessons should be considered regardless of the content.

Use a variety of teaching strategies. As is explained in chapter 9, motivation is increased when teachers use a variety of teaching strategies. Variety does not need to occur in the same lesson but should be reflected over several lessons.

Change the practice conditions for variety. Individual work, partner work, group work; refinement tasks, extension tasks, application assessment tasks; and different equipment and different arrangements and use of equipment can all be used to change the task and still work on the same objectives (intratask development). The use of variety does not have to change the objective. Teachers can practice the same objective in many ways to add interest to a lesson.

Use common sense about the physical demands of a lesson. Seldom should a teacher spend an entire lesson on one skill, particularly in the same conditions. It is difficult to turn upside down and practice rolling for an entire class period. It is also difficult to do just about any single skill (especially when the conditions cannot be changed) for an entire period. Teachers should use common sense when determining lesson objectives for an entire class period. It is better to practice two skills for two days than one skill each of two days. This is particularly true with the scheduling practices in the high school where one class period can be ninety minutes or more, which provides time for teachers to plan work in fitness gamelike opportunities and skill learning opportunities in the same period. The longer the length of the period, the more important it is to combine vigorous work with less vigorous practice and to provide a variety of different types of learning experiences.

Ending the Lesson—Closure

Although it is not always possible because of time constraints and the manner in which a lesson proceeds, there should be a culmination to a lesson. Too often lessons stop in the middle of a task because time is up. Secondary students are sent quickly to the locker room, and the classroom teacher is at the door waiting for the elementary class. The class ends with no real ending. A lesson closing completes a lesson. Often this culmination should take the form of a review of what was learned, an opportunity for teachers to check for understanding, and an opportunity to orient the students to what may come in the next lesson. Sometimes teachers use this culmination time for students to reflect on what they have done in terms of the objectives for the lesson and to write down important points in journals. This closing does not have to take a great deal of time. Verbalizing what was learned often helps give meaning to what was done and prepares the learner for what is to come.

EXAMPLES:

- "Today we worked on trying to keep the ball away from a defensive player. Who can tell me several things you can do to accomplish this? I'm going to write these ideas on the board, and you write them in your journal as we list them."
- "I have put five different ideas on this chart that represent the amount of effort different students put into the class today. I didn't see anyone in this

The physical demands of an experience will vary by students.

lowest category. I would like for you to think for a minute about where you would be on this chart. The next time you come into the gym, I will ask each one of you to write down where you would like to be on this chart and we're going to see if we can accomplish getting everyone to where they should be in the next lesson."

Format for Lesson Planning

As a preservice teacher you will spend more time planning for and evaluating teaching than you will spend teaching. The written lesson plan is designed to help you think through every step of the teaching process. The more detail you can supply about your lesson, the more prepared you will be to teach that lesson.

Many different formats for lesson plans have been proposed. The plan that you are requested to use at your school may differ from the format suggested here, but most plans have similar requirements. The lesson plan format suggested here is an extensive one. Beginning teachers and teachers teaching content new to them will have to plan in greater detail than teachers who have experience teaching particular content. Planning is difficult and tedious, but it is essential if appropriate instruction with clear goals is to be provided to students. An example of a lesson plan is presented in tables 10.1, 10.2 (p. 221), and 10.3 (p. 222–223). You may want to refer to this plan as different aspects of the lesson plan form are discussed.

Heading material. The heading material example in table 10.1 helps identify the purpose of the lesson. The unit to which the lesson is a part and the specific focus of the lesson within that unit are described. The

specific class for which the lesson is designed and the equipment needed for the lesson are also provided in the heading for quick reference.

As a beginning teacher you will probably be tempted to decide what you want to teach and then to write an objective for what you want to teach. *You will not really begin to think as a teacher until you can begin planning by writing down what you expect students to be able to do and then thinking about how to do it.* The advantage of planning by writing an objective first is that the objective forces you to begin to think about *different* ways to accomplish the same goal. The objective of a lesson is rarely the task or the activity. Many different tasks and activities can accomplish the same objective. To check your understanding of the use of objectives, it will be helpful for you to consider an objective and see if you can design several different lesson plans to accomplish the same objective.

TABLE 10·1

Sample Lesson Plan: Heading Material and Objectives

High school folk dance

Class:	Ninth Grade	Lesson Focus:	The schottische step
Unit:	Folk dance	Equipment:	Variable speed record player and record (such as *Happy Folk Dances*. RCA LPM 1620)

Student objectives

Each student should be able to do the following:
  Accurately perform the schottische step alone and with a partner to the rhythm of the music (psychomotor domain).
  Identify the cues to the schottische step (cognitive domain).
  Work productively with a partner to perform the buggy schottische and later to create a new dance (affective domain).
  Use a variety of different spatial dynamics and step variations to design a dance with a partner (psychomotor domain), using the schottische step.

Teacher objectives

The teacher should be able to do the following:
  Give appropriate and specific comments to students on their performance of the schottische step and their self-designed dances.
  Design learning experiences with different amounts of structures appropriate for different lesson objectives within the lesson.

TABLE 10·2

Sample Lesson Plan: The Developmental Analysis of Content

Major task	Extension	Refinement	Application/assessment
The basic schottische step	Move in forward direction alone with no music.	Take small steps.	
	Do part one of step (step, step—step, hop—step, step—step, hop).	Have slight elevation.	
	Do part two of step (step, hop—step, hop—step, hop).		
	Combine parts one and two.		
	Add music to above.	Keep rhythm with music.	
	Play music at reduced speed.		
	Play music at normal speed.		
	Add turns and changes in direction.	Maintain order of steps.	
	Add partner.	Adjust steps to need.	
	Hold two hands facing.		
	Move in forward and backward direction.		
	Move in sideways direction and turn.	Decide where to make turn in the pattern.	
	Comb ine all of the above.	Adjust to partner.	
	Experiment with different partner relationships.	Establish lead.	Use minimum of three different relationships.
		Adjust to partner.	
The buggy schottische	Do part one of buggy schottische (sets of two couples with hands joined face line of direction and follow one lead couple).	Accurately reproduce pattern while synchronized with. group	
	Do two schottische steps (no music and teacher paced).		
	Take four step hops forward.		
	Do part two of buggy schottische.		
	Do two schottische steps (no music and teacher paced).		
	Take four step hops with lead couple dropping hands and casting off (no music and teacher paced).	Drop hands and cast off in line of direction.	
	Join hands and repeat dance (student paced).		
	Combine parts one and two with the music	.	Combine parts one and two with no break. Dance accurately with the music.
Self-designed dances	Using music just worked with, create a dance using the schottische step in groups of four that shows (1) a change in pathway, (2) a change in direction, and (3) at least two different relationships with others.	Be consistent with task criteria. Use phrases and measures. Involve entire group in planning. Make smooth transitions between parts of the dance.	
	Observe half of the class and select one dance that is choreographed and performed well.		Identify what makes good choreography and what makes good performance.

T A B L E   1 0 · 3

Sample Lesson Plan: Instructional Plan

Anticipated progression of tasks	Anticipated time	How task will be communicated	Organizational arrangements	Goal orientation
Introduce schottische step.	2 min.	Demonstration with music.		
Do part one of schottische step. Step is teacher paced. Step is self-paced.	2 min.	Demonstration with cue words (step, step—step, hop—step, step—step, hop).	Individual students are scattered, facing teacher; dance is teacher paced with cues. Dance is self-paced; students move forward within own area.	Perform part one with proper rhythm.
Do part two of schottische step. Practice repeatedly. Step is teacher paced. Step is self-paced.	4 min.	Demonstration with cue words (step, hop—step, hop—step, hop—step, hop).	Individual students are scattered, facing teacher; dance is teacher paced with cues. Dance is self-paced; students move forward in own area.	Perform accurate step pattern.
Combine parts one and two. Practice repeatedly.	5 min.	Walk-through with teacher cueing.	Same as above.	Make smooth transition from part one to part two. Have ability to repeat pattern.
Do schottische step with music. Listen to music first. Perform to music at slow speed.	5 min.	Teacher explanation only.	Individual students are scattered, facing teacher; students move anywhere within the group; dance is paced by music.	Adjust to music.
Use direction changes. Alternate forward and backward movement. Add turns, sideways movement, and music when ready. Design a pattern using directional turns.	7 min.	Teacher explanation and demonstration.	Individual students are scattered.	Make changes without interrupting the flow of the pattern. Decide on what step to make the turn.

(continued)

TABLE 10·3

Sample Lesson Plan: Instructional Plan—cont'd

Anticipated progression of tasks	Anticipated time	How task will be communicated	Organizational arrangements	Goal orientation
Do the step with a partner (step is initially teacher paced and then self-paced). Go forward. Go backward. Combine forward and backward. Add sideways movement and turns. Add different partner relationships.	7 min.	Teacher explanation and demonstration.	Partners are scattered.	Start fast and lead partner. Develop versatility to perform step in a variety of ways.
Do the buggy schottische. Do part one (no music). Do part two (no music). Combine parts one and two (no music).	4 min.	Listen to music demonstration. Teacher explanation only.	Partners are scattered. Sets of two partners are scattered; students have choice of partners.	Accurately reproduce dance.
Do self-designed dances. Create a dance sequence in sets of two partners using the schottische criteria (change in pathway; change in direction; at least two different relationships with others).	10 min.	Teacher explanation and demonstration of an example.	Sets of two partners are scattered.	Develop versatility in use of schottische. Understand phrasing and dynamics of choreography.

Two types of objectives are presented in the lesson material example in table 10.1 (p. 220). *Student objectives* describe what students should be able to do as a result of the lesson. *Teacher objectives* describe specifically what the teacher is working to achieve in the lesson in terms of instructional skills. Listing teaching objectives helps the teacher focus more specifically on instructional behavior that the teacher wants to improve. The same rules regarding specifying behavior, conditions, and criteria that apply to the design of student objectives apply to teacher objectives.

EXAMPLES:
- The teacher will be able to call students by name.
- The teacher will be able to keep the voice tone positive when reacting to off-task students.

Developmental analysis of content. The developmental analysis of the lesson content in table 10.2 (p. 221) describes the *major tasks* of the lesson and explains how these tasks can be extended and how each extension can be refined or applied. Teachers experienced with content may not have to complete this section of the lesson plan. Inexperienced teachers should make sure that they have thought through the content.

Specific procedures for doing a developmental analysis are described in chapter 5. The developmental analysis of content can also be done at the unit level. Teachers who have done a developmental analysis of content as part of their unit plan will not have to prepare one for each lesson. Good developmental analyses of content should be modified and saved for future use. The developmental analysis of the content will assure that the teacher is secure with the content.

Instructional plan. After the teacher has decided on the objectives for the lesson and has thought through the content by doing a developmental analysis, the teacher must put together a plan for instruction (table 10.3). Again, beginning teachers should think through each step and plan in detail exactly what they will do, how they will do it, and the purpose for which they are designing each task. The specificity of planning for more experienced teachers does not have to be as great. The sample instructional plan is written at a medium level of specificity. Task design, presentation, and arrangements are the specific focus of other chapters in this text. The parts of the instructional plan are described in the following discussion.

Column 1—anticipated progression of tasks.
In the first column of the plan, teachers should describe the specific tasks that will be assigned the students. Inexperienced teachers should specify *exactly* what they will say to students to present the task (in almost a script form).

EXAMPLES:
- "Find a partner, go to a space, and begin passing the soccer ball to your partner as quickly as you can."
- "If you can pass five times in a row without losing control of the ball at a high speed, take two steps back from your partner."

You should also make sure that you have built into your plan learning experiences for not only the psychomotor objective but also the affective and cognitive objectives. It cannot be assumed that these objectives will be learned unless the teacher attends to them explicitly in the lesson. As a beginning teacher you should identify specifically where you are going to attend to these objectives.

EXAMPLE:
"Demonstrate cooperative work with your partner by sending the ball to him or her at a challenging but achievable speed and force level."

Column 2—anticipated time.
In the second section of the instructional plan, teachers should identify how much time they expect to spend on each of the tasks specified. The objective in teaching is that students learn what you intend them to learn and not that you finish your lesson plan or a task in the time specified. Specifying time will help you think through how much time you plan to spend on each part of your lesson and will help you give your lesson more integrity. It will also help you realize when your use of time is inappropriate (e.g., too long for a task presentation; too much practice on one part of lesson; not enough or too much planned for the time you have).

Column 3—how task will be communicated.
In the third column the teacher should describe how the task will be communicated for each task specified. Simpler tasks can be communicated verbally, but more complex tasks will need more complicated task presentation (e.g., demonstrations, specific cues, films, handouts).

EXAMPLES:
- Walk-through cues with students
- Teacher explanation/demonstration
- Film with teacher describing cues

Column 4—organizational arrangements.
In the plan's fourth column, specific organizational arrangements for people, time, equipment, and space should be described for each task. Included in organizational arrangement should be how the teacher

will get students into these arrangements. These organizational transitions are often the most difficult for beginning teachers and will need to be planned. Remember that the organizational arrangements that you make for a task are critical decisions and ones that should not be taken lightly. You should organize for safety and maximum activity and with appropriate task conditions for the objective and group of learners with whom you are working.

EXAMPLES:
- Student-selected partners in general space
- Students in two lines facing each other (teacher divides class to stand on each line)

Column 5—goal orientation. Each task should be oriented toward a clear goal, described in the last column. Goal orientation should describe specifically what the teacher is working for in each task. Goal orientation is not the objective for the lesson, but what the teacher hopes to accomplish with the specific task described. The goal orientation the teacher has for a task is really critical and should be shared with students. When first presenting a task, most teachers expect students to get a "feel" for the task. They do not expect students to be highly skilled at what they do; otherwise the task would not be challenging. Many times teacher perceptions of what is good performance and student perceptions of what is good performance differ. Sometimes teachers have higher expectations, and sometimes students have higher expectations than other students. Teachers should plan to share the goal orientation of a task with the students. Sharing expectations with students helps them to know what is expected in their performance. The following examples will illustrate this point:

EXAMPLES:
- "Work to get the whole idea of the skill."
- "Practice until toss is accurate."
- "Just contact the ball with no concern for accuracy."
- "Think about and demonstrate concern for the needs of your partner."

Planning the Curriculum

Many attempts have been made at national and state levels to provide direction for what should be taught in schools. At the national level each program area including physical education has developed a set of national standards that specify what students should know and be able to do as a result of a physical education program. Many states have developed curriculum frameworks that not only specify standards of achievement for different grade levels but also establish a framework for organizing what is to be taught. Local districts must then take these frameworks for curriculum and establish curriculum guides that also specify standards of what each student should know and be able to do.

A key to each of these levels is the establishment of content standards that specify what students should know and be able to do at each level. Content standards are not just directional guidelines for program that teachers should "aim" for. Teachers are expected to get each student to the level of the standard. Curriculum planning for many districts in today's educational climate starts with a set of established standards developed at either the national, state level, or local level. The six national standards developed for physical education (NASPE, 2004) are reproduced in chapter 1 (p. 3). These six expectations for student achievement at the end of the school program are further broken down into grade level outcomes, which are, in effect, expectations for students at each grade level.

Work in setting standards or developing curriculum is a process of *prioritizing* what are felt to be the most important outcomes of a content area. Physical education can accomplish many good things with students. To establish standards and develop effective curriculum to meet those standards, choices have to be made as to what is most important as well as what can be reasonably accomplished given the time constraints of most programs. Standards designed for each grade level also developmentally sequence that standard in terms of what students at each grade level should accomplish relative to that standard.

Having a set of standards is not enough to guide teachers in developing a program. Curriculum guides usually establish a content framework (conceptual scheme for content) and scope and sequence material at a more specific level to guide teachers

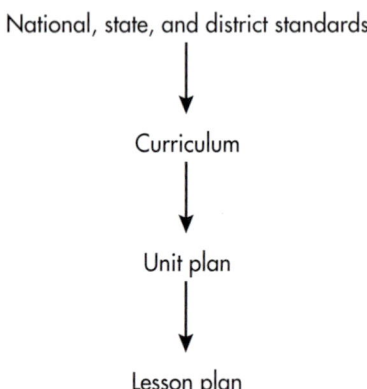

National, state, and district standards

↓

Curriculum

↓

Unit plan

↓

Lesson plan

FIGURE 10.2
The relationship between standards, curriculum, and unit and lesson plans.

in developing units and lessons. The relationship between standards, curriculum, unit, and lesson planning is described in figure 10.2.

Because programs of preparation in physical education include complete courses in curriculum planning, no attempt is made in this chapter to prepare you for the entire process of curriculum planning, but rather to help you to get started and understand the relationship between curriculum planning and unit and lesson planning.

Developing Curriculum from a Set of Standards

Many states and local districts have developed a set of standards that describe what they believe students should know and be able to do in physical education. Many of the state and local standards have been adopted from or adapted from the national standards. The six broad statements that are the national standards can form an overall framework for planning but are not written at a specific enough level to provide the beginning teacher with enough help as to what should be taught. The next level of a standard is sometimes called a grade level outcome. At this level the critical behaviors for that standard for a grade level are described. Box 10.3 (p. 227) lists content outcomes for the second grade. When planning curriculum, teachers will want to establish a yearly scope and sequence for a grade and

make sure that each of the emphases listed under a standard for a grade level is included in their yearly sequence as a learning outcome that is to be achieved.

The outcomes you list for a standard provide the teacher with a lot of choices about what content to teach and how to teach it. NASPE is further developing the standards to include selected performance indicators and assessment material for critical content in each of the standards (Pemetrics, 2008). This addition will continue the trend to define more specifically what students should know and be able to do. However, the teacher will continue to have major decisions to make about what is taught.

The most desirable curriculum plan is that which encompasses an elementary through secondary school program. This is because experiences can be sequenced and continuity can be established among schools and teachers for any particular student. Knowing the curriculum framework that is used for a program and the priorities set by that curriculum is essential for planning units within that curriculum.

Planning for Units of Instruction

Planning units of instruction requires that teachers have a framework for developing scope and sequence. Most readers probably have come from programs at the secondary level that were organized into units using a *movement form* framework. With this format, the curriculum and its units are organized primarily by sport/activity forms and fitness (e.g., volleyball, weight training, dance). This is the most common conceptual scheme for a secondary school physical education program, and it is unlikely that major change will occur in this design. Standard 1 becomes the major framework for the curriculum, and fitness and lifestyle physical activity units are added to the framework. Different frameworks exist to classify movement forms. One system divides sport/activities into the categories of aquatics, team sports, individual and dual sports, outdoor pursuits, self-defense, dance, and gymnastics. Because not all students enjoy the same type of sport/activity, good high school programs give students choices within types of movement forms, and good elementary and middle-school programs will prepare students for a wide range of activities.

B O X   1 0 · 3

Grade-Level Outcomes from Standards

Standard 1

Demonstrate mature form in skipping, hopping, galloping, and sliding.

Demonstrate mature motor patterns in simple combinations (e.g., dribbling while running).

Demonstrate smooth transitions between sequential motor skills (e.g., running into a jump).

Exhibit the ability to adapt and adjust movement skills to uncomplicated yet changing conditions and expectations.

Demonstrate control in traveling activities and weight-bearing and balance activities on a variety of body parts.

Standard 2

Identify the critical elements of basic movement patterns.

Apply movement concepts to a variety of basic skills.

Use feedback to improve performance.

Standard 3

Experience and express pleasure from participation in physical activity.

Engage in moderate to vigorous physical activity outside of physical education class.

Identify at least one activity associated with each component of health-related physical activity.

Standard 4

Engage in sustained physical activity that causes an increased heart rate and heavy breathing.

Recognize the physiological indicators that accompany moderate to vigorous physical activity.

Identify the components of health-related physical fitness.

Standard 5

Apply rules, procedures, and safe practices with little or no reinforcement.

Follow directions.

Work cooperatively with another to complete an assigned task.

Play and cooperate with others regardless of personal differences (e.g., gender, ethnicity, disability).

Treat others with respect during play.

Resolve conflicts in socially acceptable ways.

Standard 6

Gain competence to provide increased enjoyment in movement.

Try new activities.

Express feelings about and during physical activity.

Enjoy interaction with friends through physical activity.

At the elementary level, many curriculums are organized around movement concepts or movement themes, such as striking, throwing, traveling, and balancing, also part of standard 1. An example program for elementary and secondary listing the units for the year is described in box 10.4 (p. 228).

What should be immediately evident in box 10.4 is that the units clearly define standard 1 but do not describe what is going to be done with the other five content standards. It is possible to design units around each of the other five standards. In this case the second grade might have a unit on cooperating with a partner or applying movement concepts to basic skills. The ninth grade might have a unit on the role of sport, games, and dance in modern culture or the recognition of peer pressure as an influence on behavior. More often, when teachers choose to organize the content around standard 1, they must indicate how the other five standards are going to be integrated (threaded) into the planned units. Too often the other five standards are left out of program planning because teachers neglect to include them in their planning.

Units are not always taught on successive days. The unit plan defines the scope and sequence of a theme but does not identify how lessons will be arranged within a program. Units can be taught in sequential class periods, on alternate class days, or in any arrangement the teacher finds desirable. Many

BOX 10·4

Block Plan for a Year of Instruction

Week	Elementary—Second Grade	Week	Secondary—Ninth Grade
1	Traveling (feet only)	1	Students have a choice of soccer,
2	Traveling (other body parts)	2	beginning tennis, aerobic activities, or
3	Weight bearing	3	outdoor pursuits
4	Throwing and catching	4	
5	Throwing and catching	5	
6	Jumping	6	
7	Fitness	7	
8	Creative dance (body awareness)	8	
9	Creative dance (body awareness)	9	Comprehensive fitness unit required
10	Throwing and catching	10	Activity choice of two of the following:
11	Throwing and catching	11	aerobic dance, weight lifting, jogging,
12	Kicking	12	interval training, aerobic volleyball
13	Balancing	13	
14	Traveling and balancing	14	
15	Striking (body parts)	15	Students have a choice of team
16	Striking (body parts)	16	handball, track and field, dance, or
17	Creative dance (spatial awareness)	17	outdoor pursuits
18	Creative dance (spatial awareness)	18	
19	Traveling and rolling	19	
20	Traveling and balancing	20	
21	Fitness	21	
22	Throwing and catching	22	
23	Throwing and catching	23	Students have a choice of archery,
24	Folk dance and rhythmics	24	Frisbee, golf, table tennis
25	Folk dance and rhythmics	25	
26	Self-testing events	26	
27	Self-testing events	27	
28	Traveling and balancing	28	
29	Traveling and balancing	29	Miniunits in archery, golf, table
30	Creative dance (temporal awareness)	30	tennis, Frisbee
31	Creative dance (temporal awareness)	31	
32	Throwing and catching	32	

programs run several units at one time. Some programs space a particular unit of instruction throughout a school year or teach a unit on rainy days only. Teachers can begin a unit, drop it for a while, and then continue the unit.

You will notice in box 10.4 that units tend to be shorter in the elementary school and rotate throughout the year. Elementary units are often cycled and returned to in slightly different forms. It would be foolish, for instance, to run a three-week unit on throwing and catching in the primary grades in the fall and then not return to it until the following year. It might make more sense to run a throwing unit over twelve weeks for the first ten minutes of each class period. Elementary children are involved primarily in learning basic skills, which need a great deal of repetition and practice.

The secondary units in box 10.4 are designed to be long enough for meaningful learning to occur and at the ninth grade to give students a choice of activities so that they can become competent at that activity. Secondary programs usually begin and complete units at one time and do not return to them in the same year.

There is a great deal of flexibility in deciding when and how units are taught throughout a program. Most programs have not exploited this potential flexibility to enhance student learning and interest. Potential alternative ways to block units are provided in box 10.5. Many high schools have moved to block scheduling. In block scheduling a student might have physical education for three days a week one week and two days the next week for a *double period*

Units should be planned and taught with the goal of developing a physically active lifestyle.

(AB scheduling), or the student might have physical education every day for a double period for a semester rather than a whole year (4 × 4). The double period, particularly the AB model (ninety-minute class periods every other day for the year), tends to be ideal for physical education because less time is spent dressing and more time is available for instruction.

Considerations in Planning Units

Once the teacher has decided on the units to be taught in a year's program, individual units should be planned. Objectives for the unit should be clearly specified in terms of what students will learn from the unit. Consideration must be given to how to achieve the goals and objectives of that unit, how to organize the time spent in that unit, and how to evaluate student learning. Just as a lesson has an integrity of its own, so does the unit.

BOX 10·5

Possible Organization of Secondary Units

5-day-a-week normal scheduling

M/W/F   Students have a choice of sport skill units run in six 9-week blocks
       Examples: soccer, tennis, golf
T/TH   Students work with a fitness unit
       Examples: fitness concepts, aerobic dance, weight lifting, jogging

5-day-a-week 4 × 4 block scheduling— double period

$4^1/_2$-week unit in a sport or fitness or alternating units by MWF/TTH
   Example 1: MWF self-defense; TTH golf
9-week units splitting the 90-minute period into two separate units
   Example 2: first half of the period fitness concepts, and the second half of the period a dance unit

AB scheduling—double period (3 days a week one week and 2 days a week the next week for a double period)

9-week unit in a sport or activity
   Example 1: MWF the first week and TTH the second week in Ultimate Frisbee
   Example 2: same as above except 18-week unit with the first half of the class in one activity and the second half of the class in the second activity

Identify all program emphases for a grade level to be included in the unit. Each unit should clearly reflect the specific learning experiences to be used to develop each of the content standards that have been assigned to that unit for that grade level. For instance, if cooperation with a partner is going to be part of a second-grade unit in traveling and balancing, then the unit should have objectives designed to specifically accomplish this purpose.

Amount of time. Blocking time for units is a curriculum decision, but one that has a crucial effect on instruction. The amount of time devoted to a unit is a critical decision, particularly because when more time is spent in one area of the program, there is less time for other areas of the program. The amount of time spent depends on the age of the students, whether that content area is going to be taught again in the same year or different years, and the amount of time required to help students to be able to meaningfully use the information and skills taught.

The length of a unit depends on how many times classes meet each week and the length of a lesson. Traditional secondary lessons of about forty to fifty minutes meeting every day require units of at least six to nine weeks to produce any meaningful student learning in most of our complex sport activities. Elementary school units can vary from several periods to several weeks on a theme, depending on the theme and whether that theme is to be taught again in the school year.

One thing that the national standards have helped do is to focus physical educators on teaching so that students learn content rather than just participate in physical activity. Many students at all levels are participating in the same units with the same beginning point, the same progressions, and the same ending point year after year in their physical education programs because they did not have enough time in any single unit to really learn the skills. Longer units give the teacher the opportunity to teach for learning that includes all of the standards and, more important, to get the students to a level in an activity where participation can be

meaningful. Longer units and teaching so that students learn what they are expected to learn at each grade level may mean that the amount of content the students are exposed to may decrease but the amount they learn should increase.

Beginning a unit. Plan the unit so that it has an integrity of its own. Units should have a clear beginning, development, and ending that culminates work in an area. How a teacher begins a unit of work in physical education can determine the extent to which students are motivated and the extent to which what they learn is meaningful to them.

Orient students to a unit. Units should have their own set induction in which the teacher shares with students expectations for learning, what they will be doing, how they will be doing it, and why it is important. If students have not had a great deal of experience with an activity, teachers should consider showing students what the final product will look like so that they will have some idea of what they are working toward. Often teachers assume every student knows what a volleyball or soccer game looks like, and in actuality most of the class have never seen one. The use of videotape, even tapes of previous students at the end of a unit, can help orient the learners to what it is they are working toward. Consider the following examples of an elementary and secondary unit orientation.

EXAMPLE (ELEMENTARY): The teacher is beginning an educational gymnastics unit with the fourth grade. The focus of the unit will be on combining traveling, rolling, and balancing actions into smooth sequences. The teacher has videotaped Olympic performers in free exercise and also fifth graders from the same school and uses these tapes to focus the students on what is common to both (extended and held balances, clear beginning and ending, and smooth transitions). The teacher comments that each student may not be able to perform all of the skills they see but that the teacher will be looking for how the students put together and execute the skills they do select. The teacher then communicates how they will go about learning to do this over the unit.

EXAMPLE (SECONDARY): The teacher is beginning a unit on team handball, relatively unfamiliar to most of the students. The teacher has videotaped some material from the Olympics to begin a discussion of the idea of the game and an analysis of the skills needed for the game. The teacher then divides the students into teams and lets them play team handball. After the games, each team makes a list of those skills they will need to practice and the rules they do not know that they feel they will need for their games. The teacher suggests that the students will practice a little every day and play a little every day.

Where to begin. Although units usually begin with a simple to complex development of skills and abilities, as was just described in the secondary example, the beginning of a unit does not always have to start with basic skills. Sometimes students will better understand the importance of practicing skills if the teacher begins with game play, works backward, and then uses this experience to help the students see the importance of what they are doing. Chapter 12 describes an approach to teaching games that does not emphasize the teaching of fundamental skills, but rather the fundamental tactics of the activity, as a beginning point.

Pretesting. If teachers do not have a clear idea of where students are at the beginning of a unit, it is often helpful to pretest students on the objectives to be attained in the unit. The teacher might do this informally through an observation check sheet, but more formal testing allows the teacher to share information with individual students so that they may participate in goal setting. Pretesting has the advantage of helping students to set goals and to evaluate their progress through a unit. It also has the advantage of helping the teacher to plan more appropriate experiences for both the class and individual students. For teachers to evaluate students on their progress, pretesting is critical. Otherwise there is no real basis on which to measure progress. In situations where students have had a previous unit in an area and posttesting has been done, pretesting is not necessary.

Developing the Unit

Although much of the development for units takes place when the teacher plans individual lessons, certain ideas should receive the teacher's attention as the unit is planned.

Integrate game play with practice in sport units. Even if the unit objective is that students do not play more than two-on-two in a game situation, it is important to integrate game play through a unit. The practice of teaching all skills the first days of a unit and all game play the last days of a unit cannot be justified. Practice is more meaningful when it is related to game play. Game play does not necessarily mean to play the full game. It means that students should have an opportunity to use the skills they have in a gamelike situation or application task. Likewise, game play is more meaningful if an opportunity to practice between games is provided.

Plan for repetition. Skills are learned through practice. Spaced practice throughout a unit is better than all practice of one skill on one or two days, never to be returned to again. Teachers should also consider that once students have learned a game, a dance, or another activity, opportunities should be provided throughout the year for students to use these skills and to enjoy participating.

Integrate your affective and cognitive objectives. If you are planning your units using a psychomotor framework (e.g., throwing and catching; aerobic dance), you should identify those cognitive and affective skills and knowledge that you are going to include in your unit. How and where the affective and cognitive objectives will be addressed must be identified in your planning. Likewise, if you are using a cognitive or affective framework for your unit, such as developing cardiovascular endurance, you should indicate how your psychomotor content will be included.

Vary the individual lessons. Try not to spend the entire day on one skill. After skills have been introduced, include short practices of more than one skill each day. Find alternative ways to practice the same skill at the same level if necessary, and continuously add complexity toward gamelike conditions as student skill increases.

Vary the type of learning experiences. Build in opportunities for cognitive, affective, group, individual, and self-testing focuses throughout the unit, as well as the use of different teaching strategies to maintain interest and motivation.

Give students a role in the progress of the unit. Student interest and motivation are maintained in units if students are given choices and decisions about the experiences they have.

Build in opportunities for assessment throughout the unit. Assessment should be part of the instructional process throughout the unit. Self-assessment, peer assessment, and teacher assessment should be a continuous process throughout the unit (see chapter 11). Assessment should take place for all unit objectives and not merely the psychomotor objectives.

Ending the unit. Units should have a meaningful end. The culmination of a unit should provide an opportunity for students to use what they have learned and an opportunity for students, as well as teachers, to evaluate student progress.

Because a large part of physical education is concerned with directly observable performance, students should be asked at culminations of units to demonstrate through performance what they have learned. Sport units typically end with some type of tournament. Dance and gymnastic units typically end with some type of demonstration of what has been practiced over time. When conducted as learning opportunities, these opportunities provide the student a meaningful experience with the content.

Assessment. Assessment of units can be either formal or informal but should provide both the teacher and the student the opportunity to determine to what extent unit objectives were met. As is dis-

cussed in the next chapter, too often assessment is used for grading purposes only. Grading is only one use for evaluation. Evaluation also helps the student and teacher determine how much was learned over a unit.

The Unit Plan

Written unit plans are often neglected in planning in physical education. Often teachers plan lessons one at a time, missing opportunities to do long-term planning that could have a significant effect on the meaningfulness, motivation, and learning involved in a unit of instruction. Doing a written unit plan helps the teacher think through what the unit hopes to accomplish and helps the teacher view the organization of learning experiences more holistically.

There is no best way to format a written unit plan. Generally a unit plan includes the following components:

- Clearly stated objectives for the unit that are aspects of all the standards identified for that grade level and that unit
- An identification of the scope and sequence of content
- A block time plan for the unit
- Evaluation procedures

Although different teacher preparation programs require different formats for unit plans, the basic elements are usually similar.

Unit plan objectives. At the unit level, teachers should be able to write meaningful objectives with a high level of specificity. Unlike the lesson plan, which has time constraints for measurable skill objectives, the unit of instruction should permit skill and behavior changes measurable in all three domains. Examples of measurable unit objectives are described in box 10.6 (p. 233).

Scope and sequence of content. It is at the unit level of planning that a teacher can fully use the developmental analysis of content. As described in chapter 5, the developmental analysis of content is concerned with the **scope and sequence**

Example Unit Objectives

Elementary: locomotion

Psychomotor: Students will be able to combine locomotor patterns into short sequences with smooth transitions.

Cognitive: Students will be able to describe what makes a good sequence and good transitions between movements.

Affective: Students will be able to work to refine their responses independently.

Secondary: flag football

Psychomotor: Students will be able to pass a ball accurately from at least 15 yards to a moving player in a game situation.

Cognitive: Students will be able to develop a defense for several basic offensive plays.

Affective: Students will be able to work with a team in an inclusive and supportive way for all team members.

of instructional content in the psychomotor domain. Chapter 5 describes a developmental analysis for single skills or small groups of skills. Inherent in any large unit of instruction are progressions within skills and progressions from skill to skill that must be considered. Complex games and activities are more than the use of separate, isolated skills. Teachers will need to plan for the development of combined skills, as well as transitions into game play. A good developmental analysis of the content will help the teacher sequence material in ways congruent with learning. Strategies for teaching sport and games, as well as other content areas, are described in detail in chapter 12.

Block time plan for a unit. After the teacher has done a developmental analysis of the content to be taught, he or she should begin to lay out the content in the time frame of the unit. Boxes 10.7, 10.8 (pp. 234, 235), and 10.9 (pp. 236–237) illustrate blocked time frames for secondary and elementary

school units. Some teachers use flexible unit times. Thus they can vary the time rather than the content as the unit progresses and adjustments have to be made. What is to be avoided in using a time-frame format is the stubborn insistence on finishing a unit or moving to later stages of the progression regardless of how the students are learning.

Time frames are flexible. If the teacher has assigned several lessons to the development of a particular skill and students have not learned that skill to a consistent level, it makes no sense to move on. Unit plans are flexible guides. The job of the teacher is to see that the students learn, not simply to cover content at all costs.

The more specificity a teacher can include in a blocked time frame for each day of the unit, the more valuable blocked time frames become. It is not useful just to list the name of the skill for each day without giving any indication of the level or type of learning experiences to be included on that day. The examples given in boxes 10.7, 10.8, and 10.9 provide a useful level of specificity without losing the ability to see the total picture of the progression of the unit.

Evaluation procedures for unit. If the teacher has specified unit objectives with an appropriate level of specificity, evaluating the unit of instruction will be easier. The unit plan should describe the tools and procedures used to evaluate a unit.

EXAMPLE: VOLLEYBALL UNIT EVALUATION
- NASPE PE-Metrics volleyball
- Knowledge test on the rules
- Student self-evaluation of skill/game play
- Students' evaluation of what they liked and disliked about the unit

Evaluation procedures should determine the extent to which unit objectives have been achieved for each student and should be described before the unit is taught. Evaluation procedures should include all objectives in all domains of development and should be specified in the unit plan. Evaluation procedures are described in the next chapter.

BOX 10·7

Blocked Time Frame for a Middle-School Volleyball Unit

1. Show volleyball film
   Introduce set
   Individual practice
   Wall practice
   Partner toss

2. Practice set
   Individual practice
   Wall practice
   (self-test)
   Moving partner toss
   Consecutive sets with
   partner
   Direction change
   Introduce forearm pass
   Stationary partner toss

3. Practice set
   Wall practice (timed)
   Consecutive sets with
   partner (10 sets in a
   row)
   Practice forearm pass
   Moving partner toss
   Direction change
   Wall practice

4. Practice set
   Consecutive sets with
   partner (self-test)
   Consecutive sets with
   groups of four
   players (self-test)
   Practice forearm pass
   Consecutive sets with
   partner

5. Combine set and pass
   Toss-pass-set and
   catch with partner
   Pass-set-catch with
   partner
   Consecutive passes
   and sets with
   partner

6. Practice set and pass
   Individual practice of
   pass and alternate set
   Self-test
   Passes and alternate
   sets with partner
   Keep-it-up game with
   small group

7. Play one-on-one
   game (start with toss;
   make partner miss to
   score; use limited
   boundaries; emphasize
   maintaining same
   position)
   Play two-on-two
   game (play side by
   side; emphasize
   cooperation, sharing
   space, passing to
   partner, and returning
   to cover space)

8. Warm up
   Individual practice of
   20 sets
   Wall practice of
   20 sets
   20 sets with partner
   Wall practice of 20
   passes
   Play two-on-two
   game (play side by
   side; place com-
   petitive emphasis on
   offensive strategy
   and opening up)

9. Warm up
   Individual practice of
   wall practice
   of 20 sets
   Wall practice of
   20 passes
   Play two-on-two
   game (play side
   by side)
   Cooperative game
   (self-test)
   Competitive game
   (10-minute game)

10. Warm up
    Same as previous
    block
    Play two-on-two
    game (play up and
    back; emphasize
    adjustments to up-
    and-back position)

11. Warm up
    Same as previous
    block
    Introduce serve (use
    modified distance;
    emphasize
    consistency over net)

12. Warm up
    20 sets with partner
    20 passes with
    partner
    10 serves with
    partner
    Play four-on-four
    game (use no serve;
    allow unlimited hits;
    require three passes
    on a side; emphasize
    spatial relationships
    and rotation)

(continued)

BOX 10·7

Blocked Time Frame for a Middle-School Volleyball Unit—cont'd

13. Warm up
    Same as previous
    block
    Play four-on-four game
    (serve from any point
    or toss; give extra point
    for three hits on a side;
    emphasize offensive
    relationships)

14. Warm up
    Choice of warm-up
    activities
    Have class
    tournament of four-
    on-four games
    Use team evaluation of
    game play as focus
    of next lesson

15. Same as previous
    block

16. Same as previous
    block

BOX 10·8

Blocked Time Frame for an Elementary School Educational Gymnastics Unit (Third Grade)

1. Review traveling on the feet
    Practice of floor work
    Practice on small apparatus
    Practice of sequences
    Review traveling on the hands
    and feet (emphasize clear
    placement, floor work, and
    work on small apparatus)

2. Practice traveling on the hands
    and feet on large apparatus
    Practice of arriving
    Practice of traveling along
    Practice of moving off and on

3. Practice traveling on the hands
    and feet on large apparatus
    Practice of sequences
    Partner work

4. Review traveling on the hands
    only or feet only
    Practice of floor work
    Practice on small apparatus
    Combine traveling on the hands
    and feet with hands only and
    feet only
    Practice on small apparatus

5. Combine traveling on the hands
    and feet with rolling actions
    Practice of floor work
    Practice on large apparatus

6. Practice traveling on the hands
    and feet with rolling actions
    Practice of sequence
    Partner work

BOX 10•9

High School Tennis Unit—4 × 4 Schedule (9 weeks)

	Sunday	Monday	Tuesday	Wednesday	Thursday	Friday	Saturday
Week 1		• Course expectations • View video of professionals, children, and local players • Play singles games for preassessment	Fitness Tennis fitness	Grip • Forehand stroke—without ball and from a toss. Keep moving back to increase distance • Four students at a time use DVD to self-assess and set personal goals • Rally with a partner	Fitness Tennis fitness	• Ready position and foot work side-to-side drill, fly drill • Look at DVD of forehand • Forehand baseline to baseline • Introduce backhand • Teacher review self-assessment projects	
Week 2		• Review backhand • Partner toss/hit to backhand with partner assessment of form • Cooperative game—# of consecutive hits using forehand and backhand at different distances from net	Fitness	• Introduce forehand warm-up drill (10 min.) (FWUD) • Introduce backhand warm-up drill (10 min) (BWUD) • Introduce serve • Introduce beginning rules—(enough to play without the serve)	Fitness	• FWUD; BWUD • Review serve; practice serve • Look at DVD of serve • Practice serve • Review rules • Play game without serve	
Week 3		• FWUD; BWUD • Skill test—fore/backhand • Peer assessment of serve • Serve practice for force • Five-point mini-tournament	Fitness	• FWUD; BWUD; 10 serves in each box (SWUD) • Discuss results of skill tests—set personal goals • Five-point mini-tournament	Fitness	• FWUD; BWUD • Introduce serve warm-up drill • Introduce lob • Practice lob • Test on rules	
Week 4		FWUD; BWUD; SWUD • Review lob-drop and hit; run and hit lob drill • Serve drills • Singles strategy • Groundstroke games	Fitness	• Introduce new drills for forehand/backhand—self-testing • See film on singles strategy • Practice baseline game • Introduce mini-tournament	Fitness	• New FWUD; BWUD; SWUD • Play mini-tournament single game • Teacher assessment of F/B/S during mini-tournament	
Week 5		• New FWUD; BWUD; SWUD • Smash • Smash and lob combination • Net play strategy/volley	Fitness	• Smash and lob drill • Groudstroke, lob and smash comb. • Volley practice • Minigame emphasizing net play	Fitness	• Volley/lob and smash drills • Minigames emphasizing net play • Assignment: Visit community tennis facilities to report their programs	

BOX 10•9 (cont'd)

Sunday	Monday	Tuesday	Wednesday	Thursday	Friday	Saturday
Week 6	• Test on rules • Lob, smash, volley skill tests • Doubles strategy • Class tournament—(two skill levels–round robin) (videotape several games). Divide into teams—team scores	Fitness	• Student choice of skill practice in teams • Doubles strategy • Feedback on skill tests—Setting personal goals • Class tournament—Monitor heart rate during game	Fitness • Assess heart monitor data for game play	• Student choice of skill practice in teams • Analyze strategy from videotaped games (1 each team) • Class tournament—Teacher game analysis by student	
Week 7	• Reports on community resources • Tennis pro—How to become a good player/opportunities for play	Fitness	• Student choice of skill practice by teams • Teacher coaching of players who request help • Class tournament—Teacher game analysis by student	Fitness	• Written test on rules, strategies, fitness, and skill • Class tournament—Teacher game analysis by student	
Week 8	• Teacher choice of skill practice by teams • Feedback on game play • Practice game strategy identified • Class tournament—Teacher game analysis by student	Fitness	• Feedback on written test (review for those students not meeting minimum grade) • Student choice of skill practice • Class tournament—Teacher game analysis by student	Fitness	• Student choice of skill practice • Teacher introduction of useful materials available for tennis. • Class tournament—Teacher game analysis by student	
Week 9	• Final skill test in serve and ground strokes • Teacher feedback on games play—setting goals for final week • Class tournament—Teacher game analysis by student	Fitness	• Class tournament—Teacher game analysis by student • Students failing written test retake	Fitness	• Class tournament—Teacher game analysis by student	

SUMMARY

1. Learning objectives at all levels of planning should be written as student learning outcomes.
2. Criterion-referenced objectives specify the behavior expected of the student, the condition or situation under which the behavior is to be exhibited, and the criterion or performance level expected.
3. Objectives in the three learning domains should take into consideration the level of the student before instruction and be written in terms of an expected level after instruction.
4. The lesson plan is a guide for the process of instruction for a single lesson and is based on unit objectives. The lesson plan includes heading material, student and teacher objectives, the developmental analysis of content, the instructional plan, and evaluative procedures.
5. A curriculum guide is a plan for a program of study and is usually organized conceptually using an organizing element. The organizing element used to structure a curriculum determines the units of instruction.
6. The unit plan consists of clearly stated terminal objectives, an identification of the scope and sequence of content material, a block time plan for the unit, and evaluation procedures.

CHECKING YOUR UNDERSTANDING

1. What is the relationship between planning and evaluating instruction?
2. What are the advantages and disadvantages of writing objectives at a high level of specificity?
3. Write an instructional objective for a beginning learner in softball. Check to ensure that all three components are included.

4. Write two instructional objectives for each of the three learning domains and underline the behavior, the conditions, and the criteria in each.
5. Write a lesson plan for an age level and content area of your choice that conforms to the guidelines established in the chapter.
6. Write a curriculum goal that is affectively oriented. Write an affective instructional objective that is consistent with that goal.
7. Write a unit plan for an age level and content area of your choice that involves a sequence of fifteen lessons and conforms to the guidelines established in the chapter.

REFERENCES

Bloom, B., et al. (Eds.). (1956). *A taxonomy of educational objectives: Handbook 1—cognitive domain.* New York: David McKay.

Good, T., & Brophy, J. (1990). *Educational psychology: A realistic approach.* New York: Longman.

Krathwohl, D., Bloom, B., & Masia, B. (1964). *Taxonomy of educational objectives: Handbook 2—affective domain.* New York: David McKay.

National Association for Sport and Physical Education. (2004). *Moving into the future—national standards for physical education* (2nd ed.). Reston, VA: NASPE.

National Association for Sport and Physical Education. (2008). PE Metrics: Assessing the National Standards. Reston, UA: NASPE.

Rink, J. (2009) *Designing the Physical Education Curriculum Promoting Active Lifestyle.* Boston: McGraw-Hill.

SUGGESTED READING

Jewett, A., Bain, L., & Ennis, C. (1995). *The curriculum process in physical education* (2nd ed.). Madison, WI: Brown and Benchmark.

Smith, S. (2005). Beyond games, gadgets and gimmicks: Differentiating instruction across domains I physical education. *JOPERD, 76*(8), 38–45.

Assessment in the Instructional Process

11

O V E R V I E W

Although assessment has always been part of the instructional process, it has in recent years taken its place with planning as an essential part of the process. The recent focus on assessment in the instructional process integrates assessment into the learning process and emphasizes more authentic and meaningful assessment materials. The increased use of the standards as part of student, teacher, and program accountability by states, districts, and schools has also increased the need for teachers to be skilled in the design and use of assessment materials. This chapter focuses on assessment that teachers and students use in the teaching-learning process to improve performance.

Standard 5: Impact on Student Learning

Physical education teacher candidates utilize assessments and reflection to foster student learning and inform instructional decisions.
NASPE Beginning Teaching Standards, 2008

O U T L I N E

- **The role of assessment in physical education programs**
- **Formative and summative assessment**
  Formative assessment
  Summative assessment
- **Validity and reliability issues of assessment**
  Validity of assessment measures
  Reliability of assessment measures
- **Collecting information: Formal and informal evaluation**

- **Alternative assessment**
  Checklists
  Rating scales
  Scoring rubrics
- **Types of student assessment**
  Observation
  Event tasks
  Student journals
  Portfolio
  Written test

Skill tests

Student/group projects and reports

Student logs

Student interviews, surveys, and questionnaires

Parental reports

■ **Making assessment a practical and important part of your program**

Establish criteria

Use self-testing tasks frequently

Use simple check sheets and rating scales

Use peer assessment

Use thirty-second wonders

Use DVD/computers

Sample student behavior

Get comfortable with technology

■ **Preparing for formal and high-stakes assessment**

■ **Student grading**

Student achievement

Student improvement

Student effort

Student conduct

■ THE ROLE OF ASSESSMENT IN PHYSICAL EDUCATION PROGRAMS

Assessment has always been part of the theoretic model of the instructional process in a model of "Plan–Teach–Evaluate," but it has not received a great deal of attention on the part of practicing teachers in physical education. Physical educators have not valued the contribution assessment makes to the process. Probably the biggest reason teachers in physical education have not attended to assessment and evaluation to the extent that they should is that they have not had to provide information on student performance to anyone. Even the grading process is to a large extent void of "data" in many programs. The failure of teachers to use assessment in the instructional process and to evaluate their programs can also be attributed to the relevance of the assessment materials teachers have been encouraged to use, the practicality of such materials, and the time that assessment is perceived to "take out of" the more important parts of teaching. Teachers have perceived many "tests" as having little relationship to what they are teaching.

Another factor contributing to the lack of assessment in physical education is that teachers in physical education have not had to define learning outcomes for students in specific terms. Assessment determines where students are at a particular time in relation to an intended outcome. If you do not have an intended outcome, or if you haven't defined specific enough learning outcomes for students, then you have no need to determine what students have learned.

Two recent changes in education have increased the need for teachers to assess students. The first is an increased emphasis on providing states, districts, and administrators with information on student performance. We call this accountability. Teachers are being held accountable for what students learn in their programs and will need to assess students to determine what they have learned. When there are positive consequences for doing well and/or negative consequences for doing poorly, we call it *high-stakes assessment.* No Child Left Behind legislation has made high-stakes assessment in the academic subjects a reality. Several states are moving to state assessment for physical education programs. Administrators and parents are provided information on how well students in particular programs are doing, often in relation to a set of content standards identified by the state or district.

Although the need to provide information on student performance to concerned parties outside of the physical education setting is important to the accountability that physical education programs should share with other content areas, there has also been an increased use of assessment to guide the instructional process. Emphases on *alternative* and *authentic* (related to real-world abilities) assessment and the use of assessment as part of the instructional process rather than *apart from* the instructional process have made assessment a major topic at professional meetings in all fields, including physical education. Assessment in the instructional process is important because it provides both students and teachers with objective evidence with which to make decisions. Teachers should teach with clear objectives, assess what they do in terms of those objectives, and provide opportunities for students to assess their progress. Their work becomes focused and accountable, and the work of students becomes focused and accountable.

Assessment is the process of gathering information to make a judgment about the products and processes of instruction (Safrit & Wood, 1995). The use of information to make a judgment about the products and processes of the instructional process is usually referred to as *evaluation*. These terms are used in conjunction with each other—to assess and to evaluate. As a teacher I may collect information that tells me that a student has mastered all but the "forearm lag" in the overarm throw pattern. The information doesn't tell me whether the performance of that student is good or not good. For a first grader that assessment might be excellent. For a player on the baseball team it would not be. Until information is translated into a judgment it is assessment and not evaluation. When teachers use information to make a judgment, they are *evaluating*.

The type of assessment used depends on the purpose for which the information is being gathered and the type of information desired. Assessment in physical education is legitimately used for the following purposes:

- To provide students with information on their progress and status
- To motivate students to improve their performance
- To make a judgment about the effectiveness of teaching
- To provide the teacher with information on the current status of students in relation to objectives so that instruction can be adjusted
- To evaluate the curriculum or program
- To place students in an appropriate instructional group
- To provide the teacher with objective information on students' status for grading purposes

For assessment to directly affect the instructional process, both the teacher *and* the student should receive information that results from an assessment. This is not always the case. Students, teachers, other school personnel, parents, and educational decision-making bodies can receive information from assessment independently and not always share that information with other concerned parties. Sometimes the student is the only one who receives the information (such as a self-testing activity), sometimes the teacher is the only one who receives the information (a final exam not returned to the student), and sometimes students are tested by outside groups and the teacher and the students are not made aware of the results.

■ FORMATIVE AND SUMMATIVE ASSESSMENT

Assessment in the instructional process is often classified in terms of whether that assessment is *formative* or *summative* evaluation. Ideas related to formative and summative evaluation can be best understood in relation to when assessment is done and for what purpose assessment is done. When assessment occurs *during* the unit or program with the intent that work on what is being assessed will continue, the evaluation is said to be **formative evaluation**. When the evaluation takes place at the end of a program or unit, the evaluation is said to be **summative evaluation**. Assessment data submitted to school, district, or state administrators is almost always summative. Teachers use both formative and summative assessment for different reasons. From the list in the previous section, which of the purposes for using assessment would be most associated with formative assessment, which of the purposes would be most associated with summative assessment, and which might be associated with both formative and summative assessment?

Formative Assessment

Formative assessment is assessment that attempts to assess progress toward a goal. Formative assessment procedures are used to make adjustments in the learning process. Teachers often use formative assessment to do the following:

- Involve the students in the process of assessment and goal setting

- Motivate students to improve their performance
- Make a judgment about the effectiveness of teaching
- Provide the teacher with information on the current status of students in relation to objectives so that instruction can be adjusted
- Place students in an appropriate instructional group
- Provide the teacher with objective information on students' status for grading purposes

Although these reasons are important reasons for using formative assessment, perhaps the most important reasons are those concerned with making assessment a learning experience for students. In chapter 5 we talked about the use of the application/assessment task as an important part of content development in establishing progressions. The application/assessment task that provides data or information on performance is formative assessment. The assessment is part of the learning process the teacher uses to develop the content with the learner.

EXAMPLES:
- Students assess their progress on the wall volley on a daily basis and record their score in their journals.
- Students work in partners to assess their use of critical cues on the overhand throw pattern.
- Students write in their journals how they would characterize their independent working skills for the day.

In the preceding examples the students are receiving information on their performance. At the same time what is important in performance is being reinforced and they are learning how to reflect on their performance. Instruction becomes more meaningful and more personalized for learners when they are involved in both goal setting and assessment. When assessment is used on a regular basis, students are more motivated to achieve and are more focused in their learning.

EXAMPLE: The class has been working on setting personal fitness goals for the semester. Students are asked to assess their performance in several areas of fitness and to set personal goals for improvement relative to those goals. At periodic intervals, progress is assessed and students are free to reformulate their goals.

In the fitness example, assessment is used to personalize the fitness objectives, an essential ingredient of the long-term objectives we have for students in this area.

Formative assessment is an ongoing process in instruction and just as important for the teacher as it is for the student. Teachers should continuously assess student progress toward program and unit objectives. Continuous assessment has the advantage of providing guidance to the teacher about where students are so that teaching and objectives can be modified and made more appropriate to where the students are at any one time. If you do not know where they are, then you can't make the needed adjustments.

Teaching should be a process of collecting information on student performance and adjusting the learning process to meet the needs of learners. In this sense the process of teaching by definition includes formative assessment. Teaching is only successful to the extent that (1) teachers clearly define their objectives for lessons, (2) the tasks are goal oriented, and (3) the teacher is capable of both observing and analyzing the student responses in respect to the established goals and objectives. Information collected through observation and analysis is used to make a decision about how to adjust the instructional process for both the whole class and the individual learner.

Summative Assessment

Summative assessment measures the degree to which objectives have been achieved and is conducted at the conclusion of a lesson, unit of instruction, year, or program. Information collected as summative assessment is used primarily to measure achievement and to compare students with others or with a defined standard established by the teacher. Although summative assessment has always been an important aspect of the grading process, teachers are being asked to produce hard data on student achievement. An increased emphasis on holding teachers accountable for student outcomes has made summative assessment an important part of assessing the degree to which programs are doing what they are intended to do for students.

Summative assessment usually takes place at the end of instruction. Most summative assessment in physical education occurs at the end of a unit of instruction or school year. Evaluative information collected at the end of instruction generally is used to determine the relationship between what a student can do and (1) what students of a similar age can do or (2) what has been established as a criterion. Evaluating students in terms of what other students can do is called *norm-referenced* evaluation. National norms are established by testing large numbers of students and determining where most students are in respect to a measure. School norms might be established by testing large numbers of students within a school over time. Norms for tests can change with the group used to establish the norms.

Evaluating students in terms of a stable standard is called *criterion-referenced* evaluation. Students in this case are assessed according to the extent to which they meet a criterion score established ahead of time. The difference between criterion-referenced and norm-referenced evaluation is the standard you want to use to make a comparison. If you compare students with other students (either national or school-based norms), you are using norm-referenced evaluation. If you compare students with a criterion you have set for a class, you are using criterion-referenced evaluation. The national standards for physical education have identified a level of health-related fitness that is criterion based as the standard for all students to achieve. The standard is based on the level necessary to achieve the health-related benefits of physical activity. Technically, 100 percent of the students who take the fitness test could achieve the highest level or the lowest level. If the fitness test were "norm-referenced," as many fitness tests of the past were, a percentage of students would always "pass" the test and a percentage of students would always "fail" the test.

If teachers have support for establishing a standard criterion on which to evaluate students, criterion-referenced evaluation has some advantages. If the teacher has selected the criterion arbitrarily and has done little to help students achieve the criterion, program goals are not well served by criterion-referenced evaluation. Most teachers are familiar with fitness norm-referenced tests. The national standards for physical education use the term *competency* to describe the expected level of performance in movement activities. Because this term is generally described but not specifically applied in the materials, teachers or individual states or districts would have to determine what exactly competency meant applied to a specific activity. In this sense, performance would then be assessed on a criterion. Because not many criterion-referenced tests are available commercially, many teachers will be involved in establishing criterion-referenced assessment materials directly applicable to their situation. The PE-Metrics material developed by NASPE is assessment material for the national standards that can facilitate this process (NASPE, 2008).

Summative evaluation information is used for giving student grades, for classifying future instruction of students, for evaluating the effectiveness of the instructional process, or for measures of accountability at different administrative levels. Evaluative information collected but not used to help with future instruction or shared with students does not represent a wise use of instructional time.

■ VALIDITY AND RELIABILITY ISSUES OF ASSESSMENT

Teachers who collect information on student performance will want to make sure that the information they collect reflects where students are in respect to an intended outcome. The assessment must be a valid measure of that outcome and the assessment, and the procedures used must be reliable. These two characteristics are the acid test of good assessment.

Validity of Assessment Measures

Tests are valid when they measure what you are assessing. A good example of validity would be the extent to which a test of free throws in basketball measures how well a player can play basketball. If it is possible for a player to be good at free throws but not good at playing basketball, then the basketball free throw test might be a valid test for the basketball free throw but not a valid test for how well a player plays the game. Written tests of knowledge are valid when they accurately sample the knowledge base of the learner in a content area. Affective measures are valid when the behavior observed or written reflects the construct or idea. If, for example, you want to assess the extent to which students are able to "cooperate" in your class and you decide to observe student cooperative behavior, what would you count as "cooperative behavior" and what would you not count as "cooperative behavior"? The appropriateness of the behaviors you select to include and not include would reflect the validity of your assessment.

Tests and measurement experts talk about different ways of establishing the validity of an assessment. The most common validity used in measures in physical education is for the teacher to define the critical elements of what is to be measured and then match the measure to the list of critical evidence. This type of validity is usually called *content validity*. An observation checklist for a skill or affective behavior, or the written test, is matched to the defined characteristics for that skill or behavior to determine the "fit," or validity. In establishing more formal tests for use in many content areas, a group of experts is asked to determine the validity of the criteria being used.

A second way to establish the validity of the measures you are using to assess students is criterion-related validity. Criterion-related validity matches the extent to which a score on one test matches the score on another test that has been shown to be valid. Students who do well on one test should do well on the other, and students who do poorly on one test should do poorly on another. For example, you would expect the one-mile run test, the twelve-minute run-walk test, and the pacer test for cardiovascular fitness to be highly correlated. If the best players in basketball (those who win) score well on a test and the players who do not win do not score as well, then the test is a valid measure of basketball playing. If one test has discriminated stronger and weaker players and the test you design discriminates these same players in the same way, then the test you design would also be considered valid. The method you used to establish the validity would be called criterion-related validity because you have matched your test with a measure considered valid.

Reliability of Assessment Measures

The reliability of assessment measures refers to the *consistency* of a measure. If a student takes the same test or does the same assessment task at two different times, will he or she get the same score? A test is reliable if the score received on two different days is the same. The reliability of a measure is usually obtained through a test-retest measure.

When observational data are being collected, a major concern related to reliability is the agreement between observers. This is sometimes called the *objectivity* of the observers and is an important part of the reliability of the collected data. Two people looking at the same performance should score that performance in the same way. Usually when observers do not have a high level of agreement in what they are seeing, it is either because the criteria for one score being different from another are not established clearly or because one observer is more proficient in using those criteria. In either case, the information collected would not be reliable because it was not objective.

EXAMPLE OF OBJECTIVITY:

	Observer One	Observer Two
Observation 1	4	4
Observation 2	3	3
Observation 3	9	8
Observation 4	2	6

In the preceding example, observers one and two agreed on the first and second observations. They were close on observation number 3 but were not close in observation number 4. In this case, you could assume that they were using different criteria to assess the fourth observation. The problem may be in the definitions that were part of the instrument used to observe, or the problem may be in the interpretation of that definition by one or both of the observers.

Many of the new assessment strategies are based on observations of actual student performances. Reliability of these measures is a big issue in decisions involved in how to use information collected with these assessments because of the reliability problems in observing complex behavior. The simpler the behavior, the easier it is to observe reliably. On the other hand, it is the complex behavior of students in an instructional setting that is often most important (e.g., not the skill but the use of the skill in a real-world setting). More current emphases in assessing students in actual game play make establishing clear criteria for observations essential.

The extent to which it is *okay* to use assessment measures that do not have high degrees of reliability depends on the way in which the information obtained is going to be used. The issue becomes mainly one of using the information for informal or formal assessment. You cannot justify failing a student in physical education based on data you collected that are not reliable. If data are going to be used for high-stakes assessment, data must be valid (box 11.1).

BOX 11·1

Making Your Assessment Reliable and Valid

You can help to make your data reliable and valid by attending to the following ideas:

1. Make sure that the assessment task or test that you use is related to your objective and that you have taught to that objective. If the objective is given to you by outside sources, teach to that objective.
2. Clearly define the criteria that you would consider good performance for that assessment task or what you want the students to know or be able to do.
3. Establish specific levels of performance in terms of differences between performance for different abilities.
4. Practice using a tool in as many contexts in which it will be used (different skill levels, different ages, different classes).
5. If it is your tool and you have a choice, revise it, based on need after practice.
6. Check your reliability by scoring a group of the same students at different times.
7. Stay with the criteria used in the tool. Do not use sources of information that you have about a student from other performances.

■ COLLECTING INFORMATION: FORMAL AND INFORMAL EVALUATION

Assessment information on instructional products and processes can be collected using both formal and informal means of collecting data. Formal assessment is usually standardized. Standardized tests have the advantage of established reliability and validity and either norm-referenced or criterion-referenced scoring that enables the teacher to interpret student performance. Teachers who give the AAHPERD volleyball serve test to their students are using a formal means to collect data on student serving ability. Teachers who observe students serving a volleyball and mentally note their ability are using informal means of evaluation. Teachers who use a checklist to evaluate a student's serve every time that student serves during a game are making an informal means of evaluation more authentic. Following are examples of assessment techniques used most often in formal or informal evaluation:

Formal	Informal
Skill tests	Rating scales
Written tests	Description of student performance
Records of performance	Checklist of skills completed
Videotaped formal analysis	Student journal of progress
Win/loss record of a student	Student interviews
	Self-testing with records of performance
Fitnessgram	Peer assessment using checklist

Formal evaluation techniques are used primarily when more complete, valid, and reliable information is required on each student. Designing valid and reliable tests takes a great deal of time and effort, particularly if normative data are to be supplied with the test. Generally teachers do not take advantage of the available tests to evaluate students in all areas of the physical education program. The references and suggested readings listed at the end of the chapter can help the teacher access many already developed instruments. Many of the skill tests used in physical education have an identified positive relationship to being able to play the game.

Most recently the trend has been away from more formal assessment measures to *alternative assessment* techniques. Alternative assessment techniques are more informal and in physical education tend to rely on observation techniques.

■ ALTERNATIVE ASSESSMENT

One of the reasons teachers most commonly give for not using assessment is the time it takes to do it. Because many measurement issues are involved in collecting reliable and valid data when these data are going to be used for research purposes or for more high-stakes assessment, more time is necessary to make sure the assessment is an accurate representation of what a student has done. However, the practicing teacher must balance the need for reliable and valid information against the practical issues involved in limited program time and too many students. Too much concern for the validity and reliability of tools for assessment as part of the instructional process has had the effect of eliminating the use of assessment in many instructional programs.

A reason that alternative assessment techniques have become more popular is that they tend to focus on more meaningful "real-life" learning. Many students who can pass a test cannot *use* what they have learned in a real-life setting (e.g., students can tell you how to take their heart rate but cannot use the information they have collected to make a decision about their level of activity). Authentic assessment focuses on the use of what is learned in real-life settings. This has not been as much of a problem in physical education settings as in other content areas. Most physical educators have used observation of performance as the assessment of choice, although they have not always attended to the reliability and validity of those observations. Alternative assessment techniques can be used for all of the learning domains and are most applicable to using assessment as a "learning experience" that is part of the instructional process rather than something that is "done to" students.

Most alternative assessment relies heavily on the assessor making a judgment about some performance.

Sometimes that performance might be a physical skill or ability; sometimes it might be an affective or cognitive behavior. Often that performance is assessed on more than one dimension (e.g., knows the rules of the game and can use the skills of the game). To assess performance, particularly that which occurs in a real-life setting, the assessor must rely on some way to reliably and validly observe what a student has done. What follows are some practical techniques that the teacher can use to collect information on what the student has done. Most of these techniques are part of the observational literature. The intent is to be practical and to provide the teacher with better information than can be gathered from "eyeballing" a class.

Checklists

Checklists are used when it is important to know whether a particular behavior or characteristic of performance exists. Sometimes checklists are used in physical education for teachers to check off whether a student has done a skill, has handed in something, or has met some other expectation. Most often checklists are established as critical features of performance and the teacher determines whether the student is exhibiting that critical feature in his or her performance or product of performance. Checklists are most associated with live observational performance but can be used for written and other work as well as videotaped performance. The following examples of checklists illustrate their use to assess both a psychomotor as well as an affective learning outcome.

EXAMPLES:

Psychomotor Skill—Volleyball Forearm Pass

_____ Get set position

_____ Shrug shoulders

_____ Contact point

_____ Follow-through

Affective Behavior—Participation

_____ Willingly participates in vigorous behavior

_____ Willingly takes risks

_____ Willingly participates in new activities

_____ Willingly joins others who may be different

Fitness—Outside Participation

Contract for outside of class participation includes at least three times a week:

                At least twenty minutes of moderate to
_____ vigorous activity
_____ Adult contact to verify participation
_____ Contract is completed
_____ Contract is verified by the adult

In each of these examples the teacher must have a clear idea of when the behavior has been exhibited and when it has not been exhibited. Most of the time it is more helpful to know the degree to which a behavior has been exhibited, which is why rating scales tend to be more common than checklists.

Rating Scales

Like checklists, rating scales are most associated with observational data. Whereas checklists determine whether a behavior or characteristic exists, a rating scale usually is used to determine the *degree* to which that characteristic exists. In the preceding examples, the quantity or the quality of each of the behaviors indicated might be assessed using a rating scale.

EXAMPLE: GETS INTO POSITION

_____ Always	_____ Not at all
_____ Most of the time	
_____ Sometimes	_____ Partially
_____ Rarely	
_____ Never	_____ All the way

Rating scales are useful for student self-assessment and peer assessment when the criteria are specifically described (e.g., "most of the time means more often than not"). Often when teachers use checklists, students will usually say that they "have done" or "can do" something. When they are forced to consider the degree to which they can do something and to become more analytical about performance, they are more apt to focus on the quality of that performance. Likewise, teachers who use rating scales for student performance are more apt to collect useful data that can describe where students are in progress toward a goal. This information is more useful in prescribing instructional needs and more useful in giving feedback to learners on how they need to improve.

BOX 11·2

Examples of Rating Scales Used for Assessment

Elementary

Gymnastics Sequence: Rate each of the following characteristics on a three-point scale:

1 = always
2 = sometimes
3 = never

_____ Holds the balance still for at least six seconds
_____ Includes a clear beginning and clear ending (pose)
_____ Transitions between movements are smooth
_____ Includes work at different levels

Secondary

Affective Concerns (8th grade)

1 = characteristic is always present in behavior
2 = characteristic is present in behavior most of the time
3 = characteristic is present in behavior some of the time
4 = characteristic is not present in behavior

_____ Ability to work with a small group on a project
_____ Ability to work independently
_____ Enjoys learning new activities
_____ Willingly joins others in physical activity
_____ Is not unduly influenced by peers in a negative way
_____ Accepts a controversial decision of an official
_____ Participates in a manner safe for others

Additional examples of rating scales are provided in box 11.2.

Scoring Rubrics

Complex behavior usually needs to be assessed on many dimensions. To observe many dimensions of behavior at the same time, the use of scoring rubrics has been established. A scoring rubric is in one sense a multidimensional rating scale used to judge performance. The process of developing a scoring rubric is deceivingly simple. First you decide on the assessment task that you want to assess. You list the criteria that characterize good performance for that assessment task and then establish levels of performance for each of those criteria. All important criteria are defined at the highest level, and then levels of that performance are established. The most important part of designing a scoring rubric is for the teacher to establish ahead of time the important criteria to be assessed. The criteria must be critical to the context of the task. For example, you cannot ask students to throw to a partner ten feet away and assess them on a mature throwing pattern. If assessment is part of instructional planning, then there should be a close match among what the teacher plans, what is taught, and what is assessed. Scoring rubrics should be shared with learners. The following is an example of a scoring rubric designed to assess a student project at four levels.

EXAMPLE: ASSESSING A STUDENT PROJECT

Score 4 points if the student:

Completes all aspects of the project
Communicates information neatly
Organizes information to communicate
Is accurate in all information provided

Score 3 points if the student:

Misses only one aspect of the assignment
Is neat with one or two exceptions
Organizes information well with one or two
  exceptions
Is mostly accurate

Score 2 points if the student:

Misses two aspects of the assignment
Is neat with more than two exceptions
Organizes information well with more than two
  exceptions
Is mostly inaccurate

Score 1 point if the student:

Misses more than one of the assignments
Is neat with more than two exceptions

Does not organize information well
Is mostly inaccurate

Boxes 11.3 and 11.4 (p. 249–254) are examples of scoring rubrics established for both a team and individual sport. These examples are used for formal assessment and illustrate standardized protocols. Scoring rubrics are not only used for psychomotor objectives. Teachers can establish scoring rubrics for written tests, the assessment of student journals or projects, or any time complex and multidimensional performance needs to be assessed. All of the information on scoring rubrics does not have to be done at one time. Teachers might assess one aspect of performance and then come back again another time to assess another aspect of performance.

■ TYPES OF STUDENT ASSESSMENT

Although most of your experiences in assessment as a student were probably the skill test or written test, many types of assessment can be used by teachers to collect information and provide students with a variety of learning experiences in many intended leanings. A few of these are described in the next section.

Observation

As stated earlier, observation is one of the most appropriate and common forms of assessment used in physical education. Observational assessment is a useful form of assessment for the teacher to assess student performance and for students to use to assess themselves or each other. When students assess themselves or each other, the assessment experience becomes a good learning experience for students. Students who have to use a set of criteria to assess their performance or the performance of others learn what is important in what you are trying to teach them and learn to focus their efforts on improvement.

The Real World box (p. 255) describes the efforts of both an elementary and a middle-school teacher to use self-assessment and peer assessment.

BOX 11·3

High School Basketball*

Assessment task

Play half-court basketball three-on-three competently.

Criteria

- Consistent and proficient ball-handling technique (passing, dribbling, receiving a pass)
- Good technique and usual consistency in shooting
- Usually uses offensive strategies (runs patterns, works defenses, pass, catch, and pass-run decisions) with good technique
- Usually uses defensive strategies with good technique
- No observable errors in rules and rare rule violations

Specific protocol–directions to students

You will be asked to play a modified game of basketball with three people on a side using a half court for twenty minutes. You will be assessed on your ability to dribble, pass, and shoot; your ability to play offensively and defensively; and your ability to follow the rules, etiquette, and safety of the game. All the rules of half-court basketball will be used. The game will start and resume after each score by the nonscoring team putting the ball in play outside the circle. You will be asked to call your own out of bounds and rules violations and keep score. Each team will be given five minutes to warm up with a ball any way they would like to.

Facilities, equipment, and supplies

One half court of a basketball court is necessary for each three-on-three game. One basketball per team is necessary for warm-up.

Camera location and operation

The camera can be placed center court with the zoom closed so that the corners of the circle intersect the back line of the court at the edge of the bottom edge of the viewing screen. Once a game starts the cameras can be left on in the above position until it is over.

Testing situation

Randomly assign students to be tested to a team of three students. Randomly assign teams to play each other. Read the testing protocol to students. Give students five minutes to warm up as a team. Start and stop the camera and game at the same time.

High school basketball assessment task scoring rubric

Level 3:

- No observable errors in dribbling and passing
- Shoots proficiently and consistently
- Executes offensive strategies proficiently and consistently (runs patterns, avoids defenders, pass, catch, and pass-run decisions)
- Consistently applies defensive pressure with good technique
- Consistently executes defensive strategies (defensive pressure, defensive positioning) with good technique
- No observable errors in applying rules and rarely commits violations (e.g., walking, fouls)

*Used with permission of the South Carolina Physical Education Assessment Program.

(continued)

BOX 11·3

High School Basketball—cont'd

Level 2:

- Consistently maintains control of ball, dribbling and passing with proficient technique
- Usually shoots with success and good technique
- Usually demonstrates evidence of offensive strategies (runs patterns, avoids defenders, pass, catch, and pass-run decisions) with good technique
- Usually applies defensive pressure with good technique
- Usually demonstrates evidence of defensive strategies (defensive pressure, defensive positioning)
- No observable errors in applying rules and exhibits few violations

Level 1:

- Usually loses control of the ball when dribbling and passing
- Poor technique passing and shooting
- Rarely shows evidence of offensive strategies
- Rarely shows evidence of defensive pressure or rebounds
- Rarely shows evidence of defensive strategies (or poor technique, out of position, few/no rebounds)
- Exhibits little knowledge of rules, commits frequent violations

Level 0:

- Rarely demonstrates basketball skills, strategies, or knowledge of rules

(continued)

Teachers can take a few minutes after class to assess students.

If self-assessment and peer assessment are to work, students must be taught how to assess. Student beginning experiences with self-assessment or peer assessment might be limited to only observing one criterion or recording objective data. As students become more experienced observers and you have developed the expectation with students to do a good job in the assessment process, students can be given more responsibility for the assessment process. First efforts at peer and self-assessment will involve an investment in instructional time. That investment will be returned severalfold as students begin to assume more of the responsibility for the instructional function of feedback (see chapter 8).

Event Tasks

Event tasks are tasks to be assessed that ask students to perform or do something that can be accomplished within a *single instructional period*. Event tasks are often meaningful "culminating" experiences that have some flexibility of student responses. Examples of event tasks in physical education would be:

- Gymnastics routine
- Playing the game
- Dance routine

BOX 11·3

High School Basketball—con't

High School Basketball: Score Sheet

School: _____   Date collected: _____

Coder: _____   Date Coded: _____

Student # and Gender	Ball Control	Offensive Skills			Defensive Skills			Overall
		Patterns	Shoot	Pass	Pressure	Position	Rebound	

B O X   1 1 · 4

High School Tennis*

Assessment task

Demonstrate competence in tennis in two games of singles tennis (or 10 minutes of play).

Criteria

- Interprets and applies game rules and etiquette
- Demonstrates consistent performance with good technique in the forehand, backhand, and serve
- Uses basic offensive tactics (uses force, places ball, moves opponent) consistently
- Uses basic defensive tactics (returns to home base, chooses strokes appropriately) consistently

Specific protocol–directions to students

You will be asked to play two games of singles tennis or play for six minutes, whichever comes first. Each player will serve one game. Both servers will serve from the court nearest the camera. The person serving will call out the score before serving. No one game will be more than three minutes and there will be no more than two deuces per game. You will be assessed on how well you interpret the rules, how well you keep score, how accurate and honest you are, how well you use good game etiquette, how well you execute the forehand and backhand strokes and the serve, and how well you demonstrate offensive and defensive strategy. You will be given five minutes to warm up before the game.

Equipment and facilities

Two regulation courts are preferable. A racket for each player. Two cans of tennis balls.

Camera and operation

It will take one camcorder for each court. Place the camera far enough away to be able to view both sides of court with as large a picture as possible. Keep the camera stationary and recording once play has started. Keep the sound on. Each game should be recorded in full for three minutes.

Testing situation

Students should be paired according to ability by the perspective physical education teacher. Allow students to warm up for five minutes prior to videotaping game play.

High school tennis assessment task scoring rubric

Level 3:

   Consistency in performance and proficient technique is demonstrated in:
   - Interpreting/applying game rules and etiquette
   - The forehand stroke
   - The backhand stroke
   - The service; placed into the opponent's correct service court
   - Offensive tactics (uses force, moves opponent)
   - Defensive tactics (returns to home base, chooses strokes appropriately)

*Used with permission of the South Carolina Physical Education Assessment Program.

(continued)

BOX 11·4

High School Tennis—cont'd

Level 2:

Consistent performance and good technique in:
- Interpreting/applying game rules and etiquette
- The forehand stroke
- The backhand stroke
- The service; placed into the opponent's correct service court
- Offensive tactics (uses force, moves opponent)
- Defensive tactics (returns to home base, chooses strokes appropriately)

Level 1:

Some level of consistency in performance and/or some technique in:
- Interpreting/applying game rules and etiquette
- The forehand stroke
- The backhand stroke
- The service; placed into the opponent's correct service court
- Offensive tactics (uses force, moves opponent)
- Defensive tactics (returns to home base, chooses strokes appropriately)

Level 0:

Little consistency in performance and some/poor technique in:
- Interpreting/applying game rules and etiquette
- The forehand stroke
- The backhand stroke
- The service; placed into the opponent's correct service court
- Offensive tactics (uses force, moves opponent)
- Defensive tactics (returns to home base, chooses strokes appropriately)

(continued)

- Warm-up routine
- Sequences of locomotor skills

The notion of event tasks is related to the idea that students should use what they have learned in meaningful ways. Good event tasks used for assessment have the following characteristics:

- Are specific to the instructional intention
- Enable students to demonstrate their improvement and ability
- Use real-world content
- Integrate knowledge and abilities when possible

Providing opportunities for students to use what they have learned in physical education "performances" is not difficult for the physical education teacher to do at any level. Usually the event task is assessed with a scoring rubric, which means the teacher must make a decision about the dimensions of performance that are important and then establish different levels of performance for each dimension (see the earlier section on scoring rubrics). Teachers can assess the event task at the time it is presented or can videotape the performance for teacher, peer, or self-assessment at another time.

High School Tennis—cont'd

High School Tennis: Score Sheet

School: _____

Coder: _____

Date collected: _____

Date Coded: _____

Student # and Gender	Rules/Etiquette		Skills			Tactics	
	Game Rules	Etiquette	Forehand	Backhand	Serve	Offensive	Defensive

Example of Peer Assessment and Self-Assessment

Elementary—peer instruction

Ms. Galvin is a second-year teacher. She spent her first year with her third-grade students establishing procedures and a management system that would work for her. She has decided that her students were ready to begin to learn how to use peer assessment to improve their skills as well as the skills of others. The students have been working on a striking task with plastic rackets and sponge balls. Ms. Galvin brings the students together and explains what they are going to do. She passes out a simple check sheet that lists three cues important to the striking task and explains how important it is for the students to be "good teachers" and that good teachers know how to observe well. She then proceeds to demonstrate and have several students demonstrate the striking task when the first cue is done correctly and when it is not. She repeats the procedure with the second cue and then the third cue until students are clear when they see the cue being performed and when they do not. Ms. Galvin then passes out pencils to one of the partners in pairs of students and a small clipboard for students to write on. She asks the students to go back to their space with their partner. One partner is to do the striking task two times, and the other is to determine whether the *first* cue was present. She asks the students to write down a yes or a no next to the first cue for their partner. Ms. Galvin waits until everyone is finished and then proceeds with the second and third cue in a like fashion before switching partners. She repeats the procedures with the next partner and asks students to share the information with the partner so that in their next practice they can get better. Students resume practice on the striking task after returning their materials to a designated spot.

The next time the class uses peer assessment Ms. Galvin begins in the same way; she then starts to release the structure so that students become more independent with the procedure each time. She is working toward the goal of students being able to pick up the score sheet that they need, listening to directions about what constitutes each characteristic they are observing, and then proceeding independently with the assessment.

Secondary—self-assessment

Some of the students in Mr. Roberts' ninth-grade class have chosen team handball as one of the movement forms in which they will develop proficiency. They are in their sixth week of a nine-week unit. Mr. Roberts has videotaped at least one game for each of the students in the class. Students have used rating scales and simple checklists before in both peer and self-assessment. This time he goes over with them a scoring rubric for team handball similar to box 11.2 on page 247. One student volunteers to be the subject for the group, and they follow this student through the game. They talk about each aspect of the assessment. Mr. Roberts tells the students that several copies of the taped game are available in the school's media center for their use and can be checked out. Students are expected to turn in a copy of the scoring rubric filled out for their performance and an evaluation of their performance that designates strengths, weaknesses, and two personal goals for the last weeks of class.

Student Journals

Student journals are most often "notebooks" in which students are asked to *reflect* on their performance and/or share their *feelings, perceptions,* and *attitudes* about their experiences in physical education on a regular basis. Student journals provide the opportunity for teachers to personalize physical education. Information that the students write in their journals is usually not graded, although sometimes teachers use the same notebook for class notes, projects, and the student's thoughts and feelings.

Student journals take time from class but many teachers who use student journals feel as though the time is well worth the effort. Student journals provide the

Student journals are an effective way to get students to reflect on their performance and behavior.

teacher the opportunity to bring the values, attitudes, and feelings that are part of the national standards for physical education to an awareness level that gives them an emphasis in the program. Most teachers either ask students to bring their journals with them to class or store them somewhere in the classroom. They can be handed out quickly and collected quickly with clear organizational procedures established by the teacher.

Portfolio

The portfolio is a *representative* collection of a student's work *over time*. A portfolio for a high school physical education student might include different types of evidence that the student has met the standards established for a program, such as fitness scores; DVDs of performance in several different activities representing different movement forms; scores on written tests or student projects demonstrating understanding of concepts; and evidence of participation in physical activity outside of physical education class, such as a student log and a journal of thoughts, feelings, and perceptions related to physical activity. Professionals in creative fields like photography, graphic design, and advertising have used portfolios for a long time. When applying for positions, they bring a prospective employer their portfolio of work representing their best efforts.

Although portfolios can be established for students by teachers, the intent of portfolios is to involve students in the process of assessment and to produce student ownership of what goes into the portfolio. Portfolios can be used to represent several years of work, a year's work, a unit of work, or a single learning goal. Ideally, the teacher establishes the learning goal and the student decides what goes into the portfolio that would provide evidence of the student's work toward that goal. The teacher should also establish clear criteria for how the portfolio will be assessed. Usually the teacher establishes a scoring rubric that provides enough flexibility for students to individualize the type of evidence provided and for students to be creative in their efforts. The teacher may limit the number of items that may be included so that the student has to make choices about what best represents evidence that they meet the learning goal. A sample scoring rubric for a portfolio in a fitness unit is presented in box 11.5.

Written Test

Most students are familiar with the written test as assessment in all content areas. The written test is still one of the best ways for teachers to determine student knowledge. When teachers try to observe knowledge through performance, it is always difficult to determine whether the student has the knowledge and just can't use it or whether he or she can perform but really doesn't have the knowledge. From chapter 2 you have learned that knowledge and execution are two different abilities in motor skill acquisition. Although knowledge can facilitate execution, you can have knowledge but not be able to execute.

Any written test should *sample* student knowledge. You cannot test everything a student knows about a subject but will need to make sure that the test you construct adequately samples the types of information that students should have and you have taught. If you have taught a skill unit and have included knowledge of how to do skills; knowledge of rules; knowledge of strategies; and knowledge of conditioning, safety, and

BOX 11·5

Example of a Fitness Portfolio— 12th Grade

Purpose

The purpose of the portfolio is to demonstrate your ability to assess and evaluate your fitness level, set appropriate personal fitness goals, and design a personal fitness program to meet those goals over the course of the semester.

What is to be included

1. An assessment of personal fitness in all five components of health-related fitness and an identification of which method you used to assess that aspect of fitness
2. A presentation of your judgment about the meaning of the fitness scores you received
3. A presentation of your goals based on the data you have collected
4. Evidence of what you have done to meet those goals and your level of success with those goals

Assessment of the portfolio

Your work will be assessed on the following criteria:
1. The portfolio includes evidence supporting all four dimensions described above.
2. The evidence supplied is accurate.
3. The evidence supplied is adequate to support your ideas.
4. The evidence supplied communicates clearly.

so on for that activity, then the knowledge test you construct should sample these areas in the proportion that you taught them and with the weighting that you have assigned to each area of knowledge. It is also important that test items reflect the level of understanding that was taught. Physical education teachers often teach for high levels of conceptual understanding and design test items at lower levels of understanding (e.g., teach for understanding of why you do something and test for knowledge of what to do).

True/false questions, multiple-choice questions, and other short-answer tests are easy to grade but

more difficult to construct so that they are reliable and valid measures of what students have learned. Essay tests are easy to give but more difficult to grade reliably. Essay tests are often scored with a scoring rubric.

For the younger student, teachers often use pictures (e.g., showing correct and incorrect performance) or symbols (e.g., smiley faces) to construct written tests. Many teacher preparation programs require all graduates to be familiar with the reading level of students of different ages. In constructing test items this is critical. Teachers not familiar with the reading levels of their students should consult a teacher who is.

Written tests do not have to be time consuming. Many successful teachers take a minute or so out of the beginning or end of a class to ask one or two questions about a previous lesson content (formative assessment) rather than take an entire class period at the end of a unit to assess cognitive knowledge.

Skill Tests

Skill tests have been discussed earlier in this chapter as a valid means of determining the skill level of students in motor skills. Teachers can design skill tests that more closely match their objectives or can use those that have been developed as reliable and valid measures of specific abilities. The best skill tests are valid and reliable measures of what they are trying to assess. They are also easy to administer from a practical perspective. Many skill tests can be used for peer or self-assessment learning experiences as formative assessment. Used in this way, tests such as the wall volley test allow the student to chart his or her progress over time. Skill tests used for grading students on their skill development should be administered more formally to ensure the accuracy of the data.

One of the biggest reasons teachers cite for not using skill tests is their difficulty of administration. If the teacher tests each student separately, this is so. Many tests, however, can be given to a whole class in a short time if students are taught how to administer and score the tests for each other or for themselves. When assessment is part of the normal instructional process for students, then the management of test administration is not difficult for teachers and students to accomplish.

Student/Group Projects and Reports

Student and group projects can be designed as learning and assessment experiences in many ways. Most typically, students are asked to investigate, design/construct, and present their work in some form. Projects usually require more extensive time to complete than one class period and often require independent and out of class work on the part of the student or groups of students. The most common form of student project is the written report, but physical education content lends itself to a variety of presentation formats that probably are more closely related to the teacher's objectives in our content. Providing opportunities for students to use what they have learned in physical education "performances" is not difficult for the physical education teacher to do at any level. Students can design performance routines, offensive and defensive strategies, dances, computer programs for activity, warm-up routines, personal fitness programs, games, and other activities. They can present their work in a variety of formats: live, written, videotape, computer programs, plays, role playing, short stories, artwork.

Projects should be carefully structured so that students understand the expectations and criteria for assessment. If groups of students are expected to work together to complete a project, then the teacher must also structure the process students are expected to use to work together. Student projects are usually assessed with a scoring rubric that the teacher shares ahead of time with the students. The following example describes a project in secondary physical education. The scoring rubric for assessment of this project is provided in box 11.6.

> EXAMPLE: Students are asked to investigate the opportunities for participation in their community for a sport/activity of their choice (facilities, cost, qualifications of personnel, location, hours of operation, etc.). They

may present this information to the class through written materials gathered from community facilities, videotape, pictures, and so on.

Student Logs

Student logs usually establish a record of participation or some other behavior or characteristic over time. Students who record how many miles they have walked each day or keep track of weight gain or loss, win-loss records, practice time, or participation in physical activity outside of physical education are keeping a log. Student logs can be a self-assessment or can be used so that a responsible adult or peer must verify that the information recorded is correct (see the upcoming section on parental reports). Student logs are most valuable when students are also asked to do something with the information or to reflect on the meaning of the recorded information. Student logs as assessment and learning experiences are more effective if the period in which students are asked to keep a record is not overly long.

> EXAMPLE: Students are asked to keep a record of their participation in physical activity after school and on weekends for three weeks. At the end of three weeks, students are asked to assess and evaluate their level of activity based on health-related criteria and to set personal goals for the next three weeks.

Student Interviews, Surveys, and Questionnaires

Teachers need to know as much as they can about what students are thinking and feeling in order to teach effectively. One of the most useful ways to gather information on student thinking and feeling is to ask them. Teachers can collect a great deal of information on student perceptions of their program by using surveys, questionnaires, and the student interview. Written surveys and questionnaires are effective when it is important to get information from many students. Student surveys and questionnaires should be as brief as possible, as easy to respond to as possible, and should be

BOX 11·6

Scoring Rubric for Student Project

Students have each chosen a sport/activity to investigate in the community in terms of opportunities for participation and values of the activity.

Purpose of project

To make a presentation to the class on the opportunities for participation for the sport of their choice

What is to be included in the presentation

- Public and commercial facilities available for participation in this activity
- Summary of public and commercial programs available including:

  cost

  qualification of personnel to conduct/lead the activity

  hours of operation

  how popular the activity is at this location
- Value of participation in this activity

Presentation

Each student will have fifteen minutes to present his or her activity and may use videotape, interviews with participants or personnel who operate facilities, brochures and other written material, library resource material, or whatever the student feels is appropriate to present the activity.

Assessment

Level 4

All critical aspects of the value of the activity and opportunities for participation are present and accurate.

The material is communicated in a well-organized and clear fashion.

The material is communicated in a creative and enthusiastic way.

The presentation was on time and ready to go when asked.

Level 3

Most critical aspects of the value of the activity and opportunities for participation are present but not entirely accurate.

The material is communicated clearly.

The presentation lacks enthusiasm.

The presentation was on time and ready to go when asked.

Level 2

The content presented is not complete and not entirely accurate.

The material is communicated with a lack of clarity.

The presentation lacks enthusiasm.

The presentation was not on time and ready to go when asked.

Level 1

The content presented reflects little effort at gathering information or organizing ideas.

The material is communicated with a lack of clarity.

The presentation lacks enthusiasm.

The presentation was not on time and ready to go when asked.

conducted at a time when there is no advantage to finishing early (e.g., If I finish this quickly, I can go over with my friends).

Student questionnaires or surveys can be done with one or two questions at the end of a class period or with more extensive inquiries into student interests in activity or perceptions of their personal experiences in class. Teachers can interview individual

students or small groups of students. A sample interview format for middle-school students is provided in box 11.7 (p. 260).

A few minutes spent with a few students before or after school or on a lunch break can help the teacher gather valuable information on what students are learning, what students are feeling, and how students perceive what is happening in their classes. This information can

Sample Questions for a Middle-School Interview

1. What is it that you most like about physical education? Why?

   Probes: What makes the class fun?

   What are the activities that are the most fun?

   What do your classmates do that makes the class fun for you?

   What do I do that makes the class fun for you?

   How could we change the class to make it even more fun for you?

2. What is it that you do not like about what we do in physical education?

   Probes: What are the activities that you most don't like? Why?

   What do your classmates do that makes the class not fun for you?

   What do I do that makes the class not as much fun for you?

3. Do you think that all the students in the class like/dislike the above in the same way you do?

   Probes: How might other students respond to these same questions?

   Who would agree with you? Why?

serve to guide the teacher in planning future experiences by helping them to understand what is happening in their classes from the student perspective. Older students are more likely *not* to respond with answers they think the teacher wants to hear, whereas younger students are easily led into finding the answer they think the teacher might want.

Parental Reports

Parental reports are records signed by the parent or another adult (guardian, coach, community sport personnel, etc.) used to verify student participation and in some instances the quality or progress of that participation. Getting parents to sign a form that indicates the student has done something is a useful tool

for physical education teachers to help students make the bridge from participation inside physical education to participation outside physical education. For example, national standard 4 is "Achieves and maintains a health-enhancing level of physical fitness." Unless we have ways to verify participation outside of the physical education class, it is difficult to hold students accountable for the "physical fitness" aspect of what we are trying to do.

Boxes 11.8 and 11.9 (p. 261–262) illustrate parental reports for a young child and an older student that might be used to verify participation in physical activity outside of the physical education class. The parental report serves to involve the parent or other adult in the student's learning, but the parental report should be the responsibility of the student. The student may ask an adult to sign the report, but it should be the student who is responsible for asking the adult to participate and getting the signature of the adult. There will be adults who are less than honest in their assessment of the student's participation. Teachers must balance the value of the experience for the large majority of students against the potential for some adults not to be accurate in their assessments. Adult confirmation of participation can be made more effective if adults are asked for home or work numbers and if teachers randomly select adults to call to verify the student participation.

■ MAKING ASSESSMENT A PRACTICAL AND IMPORTANT PART OF YOUR PROGRAM

The number and variety of potential ways in which students can be assessed in physical education can be overwhelming. Practicality is one of the essential characteristics of any assessment program. What follows are some suggestions that describe how to begin to integrate assessment experiences as a regular part of your program.

Establish Criteria

Assessment will be facilitated if you can describe specifically what "good" performance is when you plan a learning outcome. Write these criteria down

BOX 11·8

Example of a Parental Report

Elementary

Name of Child _____   Date _____

Dear Parent: We are working on encouraging students to be physically active in their free time and drawing attention to the value of physical activity to "feeling good." Please help your child fill out the following information at some regular time each day for the next week beginning with Monday, October 4th, and ending with Sunday, October 10th. I will collect the sheets in gym class on Wednesday, October 13th.

> Thank you,
> Mr. Gonzales
> Physical Education Teacher

Levels of activity

Not active (e.g., sitting, standing)
Moderately active (e.g., walking, helping wash car)
Vigorously active (e.g., running, swimming)

Day of the week	What I did today	Circle the level of the activity	How long
Monday		Not active Moderately active Vigorously active	
Tuesday		Not active Moderately active Vigorously active	
Wednesday		Not active Moderately active Vigorously active	
Thursday		Not active Moderately active Vigorously active	
Friday		Not active Moderately active Vigorously active	
Saturday		Not active Moderately active Vigorously active	
Sunday		Not active Moderately active Vigorously active	

BOX 11·9

Example of a Parental Report (Older Student)

Secondary

East Ridge High School
Participation Verification Form

Instructions: Please sign this form next to the activity described only when you have direct information that the student has participated in the activity.

Date	Time	Participation	Signature

and think about how you might go about sharing them with the students you are assessing.

Use Self-Testing Tasks Frequently

Instruction can be designed to include self-testing or other application tasks to assess student progress, such as asking, "How many times can you keep the ball going across the net to a partner?" When the content lends itself to application tasks, such tasks should be spaced frequently throughout the instructional process to provide feedback to both the teacher and the student. Sometimes it is useful to have students record their scores on self-testing activities so that both students and teacher can check student progress. Student progress can be recorded in student journals or notebooks or on sheets available for the student to record data and then hand in to the teacher. Having consistent procedures for handing out and returning journals,

pencils, and recorded sheets efficiently will help the process a great deal.

Use Simple Check Sheets and Rating Scales

Many important objectives in physical education are too complex to be assessed with simple self-testing activities, and the teacher may not want to use more formal tests that take a great deal of time out of the program. As described in the section on rating scales earlier in this chapter, rating scales assign point values to different levels of ability of a skill, component of a skill, or behavioral characteristics. For instance, you might decide to look at the form with which students execute an overhand serve in tennis. At the simplest level you would assign a "1" to students who cannot make contact, a "2" to students who can make contact from a high toss, and a "3" to those students who are showing good beginning form based on their ability to toss and hit the ball in one continuous overhead motion. In a more complex scale you would divide up the serve into its components. The teacher would observe a student during practice and rate each student in the class or do a sample of students of different abilities to make a determination of what needed to be done in the next class period.

Simple rating scales can be used to assess more complex types of behavior as well, such as the ability to work independently, to stay focused, or to play in a game. Rating scales are difficult to use reliably without clear definitions of what each category represents, so they have limited value for research or for summative evaluation. They are useful, however, for the practicing teacher who needs quick and practical ways to collect information that is more than "eyeballing" student progress. Rating scales force the teacher to look at and assess individual students, which is a key to the value of rating scales in instruction.

Use Peer Assessment

Peer teaching is a useful way to collect a great deal of information on student progress in a brief time. Students can be given a rating sheet or asked to score a more formal test. With clear directions from the teacher, good information can be collected on student performance. The rating scale is particularly useful for peer assessment because it provides criteria for making a judgment. Using the rating scale for peer assessment forces the student to consider and focus on the criteria the teacher has presented and begins to develop observation skills on the part of the peer assessor. For peer assessment to be useful, students should be taught how to observe for the criteria that are part of the rating scale and how to do peer assessments. The teacher can collect the data or can use it primarily to provide feedback to the students.

Use Thirty-Second Wonders

When teachers want information from learners that is not necessarily performance related but is related more to students' perceptions, knowledge, attitudes, or feelings, they can use the thirty-second wonder at

Peer assessment can be used effectively to collect good information on student performance.

any point in the lesson (beginning, middle, or end). Students quickly respond to one question or two questions, return their responses, and get on with the rest of the lesson. Teachers have used the thirty-second wonder with questions such as the following:

- How hard did I work today?
- What do I need to work on in this skill?
- What did I like and dislike about class today?
- What did I do today to help someone else?
- What does my team need help with?

Thirty-second wonders can be used in conjunction with student journals or apart from them. The more teachers use this technique and establish student procedures for how to obtain and return writing materials, the less time it should take. Many teachers spread thirty-second wonder forms and pencils against the wall and then have a box or crate to collect the material.

Use DVD/Computers

CDs and DVDs should be used widely by physical education teachers to assess performance. The advantage is that the teacher does not have to take time out of class to do the assessment. These formats can record performance or behavior in a lesson to be evaluated later by the teacher, such as the following:

- Formal tests of students
- Game play to be assessed by the teacher

- Skill practice to be spot-checked by the teacher to determine where students are
- Management or affective concerns and objectives evaluation
- Teacher instructional skills (see chapters 13 and 14)

Sample Student Behavior

Most teachers think that every student has to be evaluated on every objective. If an evaluation is going to be used for student grades, this is true. If, however, the teacher is using evaluation to collect information on program objectives or teaching, this is not true. Teachers can sample classes or students, perhaps assessing different things with different students.

EXAMPLE: You have three volleyball classes, and you want to assess the extent to which students have acquired game skills, as well as other skills. The teacher can videotape only one representative class and assess the extent to which students are able to use skills and strategies in a game situation. The teacher might also assess a different skill in each class more formally. The teacher would use this information to determine the percentage of students who have accomplished the intended objectives for a program or unit and to what degree.

Get Comfortable with Technology

Many useful technical instruments and tools for recording and manipulating data useful for student performance are available. Most people are familiar with heart rate monitors and other devices used in the fitness area that are reasonably priced for public school use. Handheld computers for recording data on students can be downloaded into programs that allow the teacher to retrieve that data in different ways. They are a significant improvement over the clipboard. Teachers can then print out reports for parents and students, and they can look at data across classes and across years to do different types of assessment.

All gyms should have visual recording and computer capabilities for both teacher and student use. An increasing number of computer programs and assessment materials for sport and fitness make a computer station in the gym a growing necessity (see Mohnsen, 2004, for resources and ideas on technology).

■ PREPARING FOR FORMAL AND HIGH-STAKES ASSESSMENT

Many teachers find themselves in the position of having to submit data on student performance to administrators and state officials. The nature of formal assessment makes it different from the assessment teachers do every day as a part of their instructional process. Because the information will potentially have consequences for the student, teacher, school, or school district, the information provided must be an accurate assessment of what students do. To make the assessment as accurate as possible, teachers need to attend to the following ideas.

Familiarize yourself with the assessment material and procedures. Formal assessment material will have protocols (directions) for when, how, and under what conditions tests should be administered. Teachers should follow those directions specifically. If a test protocol gives specific directions for how many trials a student gets, how long they have to take a written test, how many students should be tested at a time, and so on, then the teacher needs to follow those directions. Test protocols are designed so that each student takes a test in the same manner.

Familiarize students with what they will be asked to do. In many instances teachers can practice the test with students. Having students practice the test ensures that they are familiar with what they will be asked to do and the criteria upon which their performance will be judged. The test should not be the sole purpose of instruction; on the other hand, if the test is a good measure of what students can do, particularly in motor skills tests, then practicing the test is good instruction. Practicing a test will also enable teachers to iron out any problems they might have in test administration. If, for example, a test requires videotaping of students, the teacher will get an opportunity to practice using the camera and setting it up in a way that allows the best view of student performance.

Technology can help the process of self-evaluation and peer evaluation.

Organize the class so that the class can be tested efficiently. One of the reasons teachers do not like assessment is that they feel as though it takes too much time. One of the reasons that it takes too much time is that they have not thought through ways in which they might administer the test efficiently. All needed materials should be out and ready ahead of time (e.g., equipment, pencils, paper, videotape, boundary lines, etc.). Decide how many students can be tested at a time. If only a few people can be tested at a time, plan to have something for students to do who are not being tested. Use student assistants to help with the testing or videotaping or to help with activities for students not being tested (older students or reliable students in the same class). If need be, train the students ahead of time.

Record and organize data you collect immediately. Data you collect can easily be misplaced or lost in busy schedules. Label and put in a safe place any data that you collect so that you will always know where to find it. Label videotapes and rewind them so that they are ready to go.

Practice using the assessment instrument. If you will be required to score students' written tests, projects, or videotaped performance, practice using the scoring instruments ahead of time with examples of student performance that will not be used in the data you are submitting. Check your scores with a criterion tape (student performance scored by an expert) or another faculty member. Accurate data require that a teacher is able to use scoring instruments accurately and reliably, and developing the skills to do this takes time.

Score student performance. If you are using an observation instrument or scoring rubric to assess student motor performance, written projects, or written tests, you will have to remind yourself to score only what you see and not what you know that student can do from other performances not on the test. If possible, score one part of the test for each student before moving on to another part of the test. If scoring large numbers of students, make sure that you score the last students the same way you scored the first students.

Follow protocols for submitting data. Be clear about when and how and to whom you are to submit data on your students. There should be no errors in following directions. If you are not clear about how to do this, then ask. You must follow directions.

Use tests as a learning experience for students. If possible, students should receive information on their performance on a formal test if the test is to be a learning experience. If teachers do not do the grading of test, then they too should have access to the information if the assessment experience is to be of more value than just holding students and teachers accountable.

■ STUDENT GRADING

The reality is that teachers need to give students grades in most teaching situations despite the number of students and the limited program time too often assigned to physical education. Grades are used by different people for different purposes. They are sent home to inform parents about the progress of their child; they are used by the administration and others who see the grades to determine whether a student is successful in an educational experience; and they are used often by the teacher to inform the students of their progress and create accountability for student effort and achievement. Regardless of the type of assessment used to provide grades, the student should be assessed on *criteria that are consistent with the teacher's program objectives and established ahead of time.*

Debates regarding grading usually center on the question, "What criteria shall be used for grading students?" Usually the following criteria are considered:

- Student achievement
- Student improvement
- Student effort
- Student conduct and compliance

In academic areas in the school curriculum, academic achievement is used almost exclusively as the primary factor considered when giving student grades. Physical educators have been reluctant to use student achievement criteria as a major part of their grading system. The introduction of content standards for physical education and more specific performance indicators established by many states and districts should begin to change the emphasis placed on this factor in our grading systems.

Student Achievement

Student achievement includes an objective assessment of where the student is relative to either a standard the teacher has established or normative data, such as scores on a fitness test, skill test, written tests, evaluation of game play, or what the student can do with fundamental or developmental skills. Grading on student achievement has the advantage of communicating more accurately where the student is relative to the objectives of the program. Parents, for instance, know that their child is good in physical education if the student receives an "A." College admissions personnel know how good a person is in physical education by the grade received.

Student Improvement

Grades based on student improvement are determined by assessing where students begin in an area to be evaluated and then assessing where they are at the completion of a grading period. Students are given credit for improvement. Using student improvement in physical education classes does, however, have problems. More-skilled students and sometimes less-skilled students will not make as much progress as students who have the prerequisites for learning but have not had much experience with skills. For this reason teachers who consider student improvement will often grade on a combination of both student performance and improvement. Considering student improvement in the grading of students seems to most people more "fair" because of the varying potential students have for achievement.

Student Effort

Student effort is usually a subjective judgment by the teacher relative to how hard students try to improve. The assumption is that you cannot expect any more from students than to have them work at their capacity and that if they are working at their capacity, they will learn. Unfortunately, many teachers set their expectations at such low levels in their classes that maximum effort means that the student does not give the teacher any trouble—what Placek (1983) calls "busy, happy, good." In this sense, effort is more a behavioral characteristic than it is real effort to get better at the content of physical education. If students were showing effort and your program is appropriate, then you should see improvement.

Student Conduct

Student conduct usually includes dressing out, coming to class on time, listening to instruction, and the affective behavioral concerns of the program and school (e.g., honesty, courtesy, respect for others). Judgments regarding behavioral characteristics are made with student attendance and dress records, as well as subjective judgments regarding the conduct of the student in class.

Whereas most practitioners in the field tend to grade primarily on student effort and student behavioral characteristics, most leaders in physical education advocate basing student grades on student performance, improvement, or a combination of the two. Teachers cite as reasons for lack of adequate assessment (1) large numbers of students and (2) inadequate amount of program time. Leaders in the field recognize that respect for physical education programs is hindered by a lack of meaningful assessment. Dressing and participation should be a minimal expectation, not a criterion for getting an "A."

The best situation in grading is to be able to report all of the criteria or at least some of the criteria separately. In this way, effort is not confused with ability or behavioral characteristics. If this is not possible, teachers should try to report student improvement and performance apart from effort and behavioral characteristics.

EXAMPLE: "A-1" in which "A" represents a combination of performance and improvement and "1" represents effort and behavioral characteristics.

In the elementary school, grades are used primarily to report to the parents on the progress of their child. The most important information for parents to have is an assessment of where their child is in relation to other children developmentally in basic skills. This is difficult to do with a single grade. Most teachers have developed letters to send home to parents with report cards, with an assessment of where the parents' child is in the basic skills part of the program, fitness data when available, and an assessment of behavioral characteristics, as well as suggestions for parents on how to work with their children in the motor skill area.

Whatever criteria the teacher uses, particularly at the secondary level, these criteria should be shared with students ahead of time. Students should know at all times where they stand in a class. The grades that they receive should not be a surprise.

SUMMARY

1. Assessment is the process of gathering information to make a judgment about the products and processes of instruction.

2. Formative assessment is designed to assess progress toward a goal, and summative assessment measures the degree to which objectives have been achieved.

3. When teachers establish a standard that students must meet, assessment is said to be criterion referenced.

4. Assessment is valid when it measures what you are trying to assess.

5. Assessment is reliable when the measurement process used in the assessment is consistent.

6. Authentic assessment focuses on the use of what is learned in real-life settings.

7. Checklists, rating scales, and scoring rubrics are used to observe a performance.

8. Observation; event tasks; student journals; student portfolios; written tests; skill tests; student/group projects and reports; student logs; interviews, surveys, and questionnaires; and parental reports are assessment techniques that can be used to assess the degree to which students have achieved in the intended outcomes in physical education.

9. Assessment can be used practically in physical education classes if teachers design assessment materials that do not take up a lot of time and are used consistently during each class period.

10. Students should be graded on the intended outcomes of a program in relation to their improvement and performance.

CHECKING YOUR UNDERSTANDING

1. Why is assessment a critical part of the instructional process?
2. Give two examples of formative assessment.
3. Give two examples of summative assessment.
4. How do you determine the validity of an assessment?
5. How do you determine the reliability of an assessment?

6. Describe three alternatives for assessing psychomotor performance.
7. Describe three alternatives for assessing cognitive performance.
8. Describe three alternatives for assessing affective performance.
9. How can assessment be used in a practical way as part of a physical education program?
10. Design a system for grading students in an elementary and secondary physical education program.

REFERENCES

Mohnsen, B. 2004. *Using technology in physical education* (2nd ed.). Champaign, IL: Human Kinetics.

National Association for Sport and Physical Education. (2004). *Moving into the future: National standards for physical education* (2nd ed.). Reston, VA: NASPE.

National Association for Sport and Physical Education. (2008). PE-Metrics. Reston, VA: NASPE.

Placek J. (1983). Conceptions of success in teaching: Busy, happy and good? In T. Templin & J. Olson (Eds.), *Teaching in physical education,* Champaign, IL: Human Kinetics.

Safrit, M., & Wood, T. (1995). *Introduction to measurement in physical education and exercise science* (3rd ed.). St. Louis: Mosby.

SUGGESTED READINGS

Allen, R. (2002). Using assessment data to monitor physical education programs. *Journal of Physical Education, Recreation and Dance, 73*(8), 25–31.

Arbogast G. (2002). Assessment issues and the elementary school-age child. *Journal of Physical Education, Recreation and Dance, 73*(7), 21–34.

Ayers, S. (2003). *ASK-PE: Physical education concepts test.* Reston, VA: AAHPERD.

Barton, G. (2002). A statewide assessment program for physical education? It's a good thing. *Teaching Elementary Physical Education, 13*(5), 6–22.

Boyce, A. (2000). The video final: Testing for the application of knowledge in a context-rich environment. *Journal of Physical Education, Recreation and Dance, 71*(1), 50–52.

Boyce, B. (1990). Grading practices: How do they influence student skill performance? *Journal of Physical Education, Recreation and Dance, 61*(6), 46–48.

Cruz, L., & Peterson, S. (2002). Reporting assessment results to parents. *Journal of Physical Education, Recreation and Dance, 73*(8), 20–24.

Gallo, A., Sheehy, D., Patton, K., & Griffin, L. (2006). Assessment benefits and barriers: What are you committed to? *JOPERD 77*(8), 46–50.

Harvey, S. (2007). Using a generic invasion game form assessment. *JOPERD, 78*(4), 19–25.

Herman, J., Aschbacher P., & Winters, L. (1992). *A practical guide to alternative assessment.* Alexandria, VA: ASCD.

Hichwa, J. (1995). Grading in physical education, *Middle School Physical Education, 1*(3), 15.

Kinchin, G. (2001). Using team portfolios in a sport education program. *Journal of Physical Education, Recreation and Dance, 72*(2), 41–44.

Kozub, F. (2001). Using task cards to help beginner basketball players self-assess. *Strategies, 14*(5), 23–27.

Martin, J., Kulianna, P., & Cothran, D. (2002). Motivating students through assessment. *Journal of Physical Education, Recreation and Dance, 73*(8), 18–19.

Marzano, R. (2000). *Transforming classroom grading.* Alexandria, VA: ASCD.

Melograno, V. (1994). Portfolio assessment: Documenting authentic student learning. *Journal of Physical Education, Recreation and Dance, 65*(8), 50–55.

National Association for Sport and Physical Education. (2000). *Assessment series for K–12 physical education and professional preparation.* Reston, VA: NASPE.

Seeley, M. (1994). The mismatch between assessment and grading, *Educational Leadership, 52*(2), 4–6.

Seidel, K. (2000). *Assessing student learning: A practical guide.* Reston, VA: NASPE.

Tomlinson, C. (2008). Learning to love assessment. *Educational Leadership. 65*(4), 8–13.

Turner, N. (1995). Struggling with assessment issues. *Middle School Physical Education, 1*(3), 1–4.

Veal, M. (1988). Pupil assessment practices and perceptions of secondary school teachers. *Journal of Teaching Physical Education, 12,* 327–342.

Veal, M. L. (1995). Assessment as an instructional tool. *Strategies, 8*(5) 10–15.

Wegis, H., & van der Mars, H. (2006). Integrating assessment and instruction. *JOPERD, 77*(1), 27–34.

Welk, G., & Wood, K. (2000). Physical activity assessments in physical education: A practical review of instruments and their use in the curriculum. *Journal of Physical Education, Recreation and Dance, 71*(1), 30–40.

Content-Specific Pedagogy

12

OVERVIEW

Most methods of teaching texts, as this one, provide descriptions of generic teaching skills—those that can be used across contexts that are likely to be encountered. In reality, these skills become principles that, when applied appropriately to different situations, will help you be effective as a teacher. Skilled teachers are effective at knowing which principles to apply in different situations and how to modify principles for different contexts. These are generic principles of teaching that are useful across contexts. There is another knowledge base that moves beyond this general pedagogy that is content specific. This chapter provides the reader with pedagogical ideas related to several content areas.

The first section of the chapter presents a conceptual model for thinking about the way we teach games and sports. The intent again is to help you think about games more holistically and to help you do long-term planning in this area. The second section identifies typical concepts included in physical education and presents a framework for thinking about how to teach concepts for transfer of learning. The third section presents some basic ideas for thinking about how to teach fitness, dance, gymnastics, and outdoor pursuits as content-specific pedagogy.

Standard 1: Scientific and Theoretical Knowledge

Physical education teacher candidates know and apply discipline-specific scientific and theoretical concepts critical to the development of physically educated individuals.

Standard 3: Planning and Implementation

Physical education teacher candidates plan and implement a variety of developmentally appropriate learning experiences and content aligned with local, state, and national standards to develop physically educated individuals.

Standard 4: Instructional Delivery and Management
Physical education teacher candidates use effective communication and pedagogical skills and strategies to enhance student engagement and learning.
NASPE Beginning Teaching Standards, 2008

O U T L I N E

- **Teaching lifetime physical activity and fitness**
  Teaching lifetime physical activity
  Teaching fitness concepts in the classroom
- **Curricular alternatives to teaching fitness**
- **Teaching games and sports**
  The games stages
  Considerations using the games stages
  Tactical and skill approaches to teaching games and sports

Sport education
Dance
Gymnastics
Outdoor pursuits
- **Movement concepts—Teaching for transfer**
  Learning theory associated with the transfer of learning
  Important concepts in physical education
  Teaching movement concepts

■ TEACHING LIFETIME PHYSICAL ACTIVITY AND FITNESS

Most physical educators support the idea that their major program goal is to get students, and the adults they will become, to lead a physically active lifestyle. An important program goal is the development and maintenance of an active lifestyle and health-related fitness. Two national standards (NASPE, 2004) address this issue:

Standard 3: Participates regularly in physical activity.

Standard 4: Achieves and maintains a health-enhancing level of physical fitness.

What should be clear from the content standards described is that the goals span all three domains. Students should maintain a physically active lifestyle, be fit, maintain fitness, have knowledge related to fitness, and, most of all, value physical activity and fitness in their lives. The ultimate goal of physical education is an active lifestyle that goes beyond narrow perspectives of physical fitness easily attained with conditioning. Preparing students for a lifetime of physical activity is our major goal. It is not difficult to understand how to make students fit from a conditioning perspective. You have had coursework that has taught you the principles involved in developing cardiorespiratory endurance, strength, muscular endurance, and flexibility. What is not as clear is how to incorporate fitness into physical education curriculums and how to ensure that students will engage in an active lifestyle as students and as adults.

Incorporating fitness into programs and teaching fitness and lifetime physical activity goals are two of the most difficult aspects of program design for several reasons:

1. Many programs do not have the time to develop fitness, much less maintain it within the confines of the instructional program.

2. Many older students do not enjoy working hard physically, no matter how much we justify it on the basis of health.
3. Fitness gains are short-lived—unless you maintain a level of activity, you are likely to lose it.
4. Teaching for specific cognitive and affective goals has not been a strong suit of physical education teachers.
5. Helping students to make the transition from what they do in physical education class and what they do outside of physical education class and as adults requires that we focus our efforts on how to teach for transfer and how to change behavior.

Despite the problems associated with fitness and lifetime physical activity in the curriculum, most teachers value its inclusion and most teachers want a balanced program. The recent emphasis in the national media on the obesity epidemic and health problems directly associated with the lack of physical activity have made this a priority in our programs. The national standards document makes specific recommendations for what aspects of fitness should be taught at what grade levels and for student expectations in terms of developing a physically active lifestyle. Although the focus of this text is not a curricular focus, the following curricular alternatives for including fitness in programs are briefly described (Rink, 1993) so that their implications may be discussed.

Teaching Lifetime Physical Activity

There is a great deal of support for the idea that the goal of the physical education program is a physically active lifestyle. In the past, we have assumed that if we made students fit and if we gave them the skills and knowledge to remain physically active, they would. Unfortunately, it has not worked out that way and teachers must find better ways of helping students to transfer what happens in school to what happens outside of school. If we want students to make the transition to what they do outside of our classes, we must teach for this objective directly as well as incorporate this goal into every unit that we teach. The following ideas should be considered when planning to achieve this standard.

Develop awareness of what students do outside of class and reinforce an active lifestyle. Kindergarten students can be helped to develop an awareness of what they do outside of class with inquiries as to "What did you do at recess today?" "How many of you did something that made you breathe hard?" Older students can keep logs of what they do and begin to analyze those logs for lifestyle issues.

Help students to make the transition to outside of class in all teaching units. Regardless of what you are teaching, maintain a focus of the work on helping students to make the transition to outside of class. If you are teaching tennis, then students need to know where they can play tennis in their communities and how to go about getting involved in tennis. Teachers can help students sign up for youth sports leagues, intramurals, or other opportunities to be active in the community. If you are teaching a fitness unit, then students should understand how to develop fitness independently of you and should also receive information on community resources.

Hold students accountable for what they do. If students are to be active adults, then they will need to begin as active youth. There is no reason teachers cannot grade and hold students accountable for doing something outside of the physical education class. Younger students can be required to participate for a minimum amount of time after school in physical activity. Older students can be responsible for developing and conducting a personal program for physical activity for a longer period.

Include organized activity and lifestyle changes. Students should leave our programs not only with an interest in participating in organized physical activity. They should leave our programs willing to make lifestyle choices for physical activity. Younger students are not as in control of these choices but can still be helped to understand that when they choose to walk rather than ride and when they choose to do something physically active rather than to sit with computer games, they are making good decisions. Older students have many more choices, and it may be more difficult to get them out of their cars and into physical activity but it is essential that we do so.

Teaching Fitness Concepts in the Classroom

Many physical education teachers find themselves in the position of having to teach cognitive concepts related to fitness. Students should leave their physical education program with the skill and the knowledge to develop and maintain fitness. This means that they need to know a lot about fitness, what it is, how it is developed, and why it is important to their health. Many high school programs use physical education textbooks and devote a portion of their program time to teaching in the classroom, and many physical education teachers find themselves uncomfortable in this setting.

Teaching in the classroom requires as much planning as teaching a motor skill or activity. The following guidelines will assist you in that effort.

Establish a learning environment. The learning environment of the classroom is in a sense more formal than most teachers have established in the gym. Teachers must have rules and procedures on how to come into class, how and when to be ready for class to start, how to ask a question, when it is permissible to talk to a neighbor, how to turn in assignments, and what to do when the bell rings. Teachers must make class rules explicit and continuously reinforce the rules students are expected to follow. Expectations for the quality of work students are to hand in or do in class should likewise be explicit and be reinforced.

Plan lessons that involve the students. There is a tendency for physical education teachers to think that teaching in the classroom is "telling." Although cognitive material must be communicated, the major job of the teacher is make the material meaningful for students. If fitness material is to be meaningful, students must use it and work with the ideas and apply it to their lives. Teachers can do this most effectively by involving students in both independent and group projects and discussions that require them to use material. Use set induction and lesson summaries similarly in your work in the gym.

Use the blackboard and written handouts. A lot of the cognitive material in the fitness area involves terms and ideas that are unfamiliar to students. Seeing ideas in writing helps students identify terms and understand what you are communicating verbally. Group ideas together (such as components of fitness) so students can conceptually map the ideas and their relationships.

Use audiovisual aids and technology. Physical education teachers need to become skilled in the use of computers, PowerPoint software, and other audiovisual aids available to teach fitness. Price reductions in heart rate monitors, digital pedometers, accelerometers, and other technology have made these tools within reach of most physical education programs.

Hold students accountable for written work and outside work. Students in many situations are not accustomed to "homework" in physical education. Communicating those expectations may require that teachers find ways to ensure that students do the assignments they are given. With time, the number of nonparticipants will decrease.

There are two approaches to fitness. One is an exercise or training approach, and one is a physical activity approach. The assumption of the activity approach is that if teachers can get students active in physical activity, then fitness will follow. An activity approach is recommended for the elementary school level. Likewise, the best approach for most secondary students is an activity approach with the caveat that they also need to know how to assess and develop fitness using both exercise and activity.

■ CURRICULAR ALTERNATIVES TO TEACHING FITNESS

Most programs are faced with the problem of not having enough time in their regularly scheduled classes to actually develop fitness. Alternative curricular approaches to this problem can make fitness a viable option for physical education curriculums.

Choose several grades throughout the curriculum that will focus primarily on fitness. Rather than doing a small amount of work in fitness every year, teachers should target particular grades and do a good job in fully developing work in fitness in all three domains for those years.

> *Planning and instructional implications:* Physical education curriculum would have to be planned on a K–12 basis (e.g., fourth-, eighth-, and tenth-grade fitness emphasis). The knowledges, skills, and attitudes appropriate for each level would be clearly described. Teachers would design an entire year or a large part of the year to meet these objectives. Sport skills would not be ruled out but would be taught with a fitness concept focus, as well as designed to meet primarily fitness objectives. Teachers at all three levels would have to teach skills, knowledges (including concepts), and attitudes. Having a full year to focus on fitness and physical activity would allow the teacher to continuously reinforce concepts and to fully develop ideas, as well as have enough time to expect students to show achievable conditioning behavioral gains and attitude development. In grades not emphasizing fitness, fitness and lifetime fitness objectives would be reinforced.

Use school time other than physical education time. With the growing health concerns of an overweight and obese population of students, more and more physical educators are asked to take on a new role as the physical activity director of the school. Physical education teachers must consider time before school, after school, at recess, and in the classroom as opportunities for students to engage in physical activity. They must also think about developing programs that encourage and in some cases require students to be active when they leave school. There are a limitless number of possibilities to do this. Some examples follow:

1. Establish walking trails/tracks around the school that students can/must use during at least part of their recess time.

2. Open up school facilities during lunch, before school, and after school for students as a "fitness" center.

3. Establish a personal fitness program for students, monitor the program frequently and reinforce the expectations of the program.

4. Facilitate students signing up and becoming involved in community activities.

5. Participate in local marathons/walk to school programs and other events that promote participation in physical activity.

6. In the elementary school work with the classroom teacher to establish an activity period every day.

7. Establish school walking clubs and jogging clubs for lunch, before school, and/or after school.

Approach fitness as a health maintenance behavior. Sometimes this approach is called the "brushing your teeth" approach to fitness. Students may not enjoy sweating and working hard, but it is something that they must learn to include regularly in their lives. Few of us get any particular enjoyment from brushing our teeth, but we do it anyway because we were made to do it as children and value it as adults. Programs of this nature can be conducted as part of class, as part of school requirements, or as independent programs with accountability for student progress (you do not graduate unless you reach your fitness goals). The emphasis is primarily on giving students the skills to view fitness as a health maintenance behavior. Conditioning aspects would be stressed.

> *Planning and instructional implications:* In this model the teacher's role affectively is not necessarily to try to convince all students that they will like what they are doing (develop internal motivation), but that it is critical that they do it. Although the goal remains to internalize the value of fitness for the student, the teacher is not opposed to using external rewards to get students to do what they may not be ready to value. Implementation requires individualized realistic goals for each student and accountability mechanisms for monitoring student progress.

Choose motor skill activities that also have a high fitness value. Using this approach, teachers would select the activities and sport skills they include in their programs primarily on the basis of their contribution to fitness objectives, or students who do not meet their fitness goal have the option to choose activities within the program that have the potential to develop fitness. Activities that have the potential to develop fitness (e.g., soccer or aerobic dance for cardiorespiratory) would be offered and those activities with little conditioning value in the narrow sense, such as football, archery, golf, and table tennis, would not be included. This curricular alternative may meet the immediate needs of students to develop and maintain fitness. It probably would not meet the long-term need to develop interests in lifetime physical activity.

Planning and instructional implications: The teacher who chooses activities for their fitness value must decide either to (1) conduct the activity to help students to be skilled in the activity so they have the skills to want to participate or (2) use the activity for its fitness potential and not necessarily be concerned with skill development (aerobic volleyball or basketball). The choice is between developing and maintaining fitness of the students at the time the activities are offered and building skills that can be used later to maintain and develop fitness. Generally the teacher will do skill development, which is not likely to result in immediate aerobic benefits, and also include in each lesson long periods of aerobic activity.

Design instruction in motor skills to include vigorous activity. In lesson planning, teachers would ensure that at least a part of the instructional lesson, regardless of content, included a significant amount of vigorous activity and also ensure that students make the connection between what they do in class and what they can do with the activity outside of class and in the community.

Planning and instructional implications: Many times teachers trying to engage students in vigorous activity for a part of every lesson believe that they must resort to learning experiences that are different from the lesson content. Teachers who are the most successful in using class time effectively to accomplish both fitness and skill development objectives practice the content of the lesson in a way that also contributes to fitness goals. Remember, even archery and golf can be aerobic activities if that is your aspiration.

Keep fitness days and motor skill days separate in the program. Schools that have five-day-a-week programs have the option of dividing the week into distinct emphases. Most commonly this becomes M/W/F—motor skill and T/Th—fitness throughout the

Fitness is for life.

year. With the popularity of secondary block scheduling, additional options devote part of the class period to fitness and part of the class period to motor skills.

Planning and instructional implications: Planning for both emphases would be primarily separate. Because the fitness program would run for the entire year, the activities and teaching emphasis in the year's program would need to change. Students should not be expected to do the same thing two days a week for the entire year.

Summary of teaching considerations—fitness. Each of the program orientations described has advantages and disadvantages. What these approaches to putting fitness into a program have in common are the following:

- A need for long-term planning
- A need to teach cognitive material for learning and to teach concepts to a level of transfer
- A need to teach values and attitudes
- A need to develop management skills with students to the point where self-direction and independent work are possibilities

The goal of these approaches is for students to value fitness and to have the skills to develop their own fitness programs and habits of physical activity outside of class (to be independent). Learning experiences in fitness must be carefully selected so that they contribute to these goals rather than ensure that the student will not participate when given the choice. The most successful programs have been those that have been personalized (students select personal objectives) and those in which students have been given choices (options in how to achieve goals). Some basic considerations for teaching fitness are presented in box 12.1.

■ TEACHING GAMES AND SPORTS

Most of the discussion throughout this text has been on the development of individual motor skills and singular concepts. For many closed skills, the action of one skill is all that must be considered (e.g., bowling). For complex team sports that use many open skills, such as basketball, tennis, and volleyball, the game is more than the sum of the individual

---

BOX 12·1

Basic Considerations for Teaching Fitness and Lifetime Physical Activity

1. Decide on what your goals are and what approach you will use over a K–12 perspective.
2. Individualize programs by using preassessment to set personal student goals and postassessment to monitor the development of those goals.
3. If program time is limited, find ways to use time outside of class for development and maintenance of conditioning.
4. Help students make the connection between in class and what they do outside of class.
5. Focus on more than one aspect of fitness in a class period (exercise for a whole class period in one component is difficult).
6. Ensure that exercises are being done correctly. Keep up-to-date with the latest information on "best" ways, as well as harmful exercises.
7. Find ways of organizing the class so that there is maximum activity.
8. Teach the "why" as well as the "how" of fitness.
9. Make your goal student independence, as is appropriate for age level.
10. Keep parents and students informed on progress.
11. Redefine your role as a physical educator to include being the physical activity director for the school to utilize out-of-class time.

---

skills of the game. Each game or sport consists of many different motor skills that must be acquired and used in conjunction with each other, and players must learn to use these skills appropriately in offensive and defensive frameworks. Instruction on how to use these skills is different from learning the motor skill. Two discussions follow. The first presents a framework for looking at progression of both skill development and tactical (offensive and defensive strategies) development in the teaching of games and sports. The second discussion considers the order in which students learn to be skillful in the motor skills of the sport as well as the tactics involved in playing the sport.

The Games Stages

Preparation for complex game play requires that the individual be able to combine skills, use skills in more complex ways, and relate to others in both offensive and defensive relationships. This section presents a way to look at developing games players from a more macro perspective that considers both the improvement of skills and tactics in games from a developmental framework. The important aspects of the games stages have emerged from studying how skills are used in games rather than how individual skills are executed. The progression of teaching games gradually increases the level of complexity of practice to gamelike conditions.

The development of games players can be conceived as consisting of four stages, described in box 12.2 and illustrated in table 12.1 (pp. 277–280), for the game of basketball. The stages are described individually in the following discussion.

Stage one—developing control of the object. In stage one the teacher is concerned with the ability to *control* the object or body. Beginning learners are faced with the problem of not knowing what an object will do when they throw, strike, hit, catch, or collect it or how to make the object do what they want it to do. Minimal levels of control are established in this stage of learning to play games. Control means rather specific things for different skills. Generally, control means the following:

- **Sending actions** (e.g., striking, kicking, throwing). The individual can consistently direct the object to a place with the intended force qualities.
- **Receiving actions** (e.g., catching, collecting). The individual can obtain possession/control of an object coming from any level, direction, or speed.
- **Carrying and propelling actions** (e.g., carrying a football, dribbling). The individual can maintain possession of the object while moving in different ways and at different speeds.

The development of skill in stage one involves providing experiences in obtaining control. These experiences are first given in the easiest of

---

> **B O X   1 2 · 2**
>
> ## The Games Stages
>
> **Stage one**
>
> - Concern with individual skills
> - Ability to control an object
>
> Sending actions—direct the object to a place with the intended force qualities, level, and direction in a consistent manner, stationary and on the move.
>
> *Examples*
>
> Simple—forearm pass from a light toss directly back to the tosser.
>
> Complex—forearm pass from a served ball to players on the left and right who catch it.
>
> Receiving actions—can obtain possession of the object coming toward them from any level, direction, or speed, stationary and on the move.
>
> *Examples*
>
> Simple—fielding a ball rolled from a short distance directly to the player.
>
> Complex—fielding a ball thrown hard to the left or right of a player.
>
> **Stage two**
>
> - Using skills in combination with each other
> - Relating movement to others in cooperative ways
>
> *Examples*
>
> Simple—dribbling and doing a set shot in basketball.
>
> Complex—keeping the ball going across a net in tennis with a variety of strokes/keep it up in volleyball.
>
> **Stage three**
>
> - Basic offensive and defensive strategy
>
> *Examples*
>
> Simple—one-on-one basketball; no shooting.
>
> Complex—five-on-five soccer with two goalies.
>
> **Stage four**
>
> - Modified games with changes in the rules, boundaries, number of players, etc.—specialized positions
> - The full game
>
> *Examples*
>
> Simple—introduction of specialized basketball positions.
>
> Complex—the full game with all the rules.

TABLE 12·1

The Four Stages of Games Skills Development: Basketball

Extension	Refinement	Application
Stage one		
Skill: dribbling		
■ *Major task: dribbling in self-space*		
Change levels. Dribble around the body. Step forward, backward, and sideways.	Use pads of fingers on the ball (giving). Work on body position (bend knees and have action at elbow). Use a slide step.	Go as long as possible without losing control of the ball. Change direction as quickly as possible without losing control of the ball.
■ *Major task: dribbling in general space*		
Change direction. Move from slow to increased speeds. Change levels. Take eye contact off the ball occasionally. Increase complexity of environment (more people, smaller space, obstacles).	Be aware of others and appropriately change speed and direction for encounters. Place ball out from body for increased speed. Contact ball behind line of direction for change in direction.	Go as fast as possible and still maintain control of the ball.
Skill: passing and receiving		
■ *Major task: stationary passing to a stationary receiver*		
Stand at different levels. Receive at different levels. Pass the ball from different levels. Receive a ball at full extension from personal space. Pass a ball from the level at which it was received. Use a bounce.	Use body flexion to generate force and step in to the pass. Use two hands to guide the ball. Give with the ball to receive it. Use one continuous action for receiving and passing. Find the point at which the ball will rebound to desired place for a particular force level.	Make as many passes as possible without losing control. Make as many passes as possible in 30 seconds.
■ *Major task: stationary passing to a moving receiver*		
Vary the distances. Vary the levels of the pass. Move away from, toward, and to the side of the passer.	Place the ball ahead of the receiver to where the receiver will be. Use the pivot. Use the pivot to face the line of direction. Choose the appropriate level of the pass for the direction of the receiver.	Make as many passes in a row as possible without losing control. Make as many passes as possible in 1 minute without traveling as a receiver.

Note: No attempt has been made to be inclusive in this analysis. For example, the skill of shooting has been left out of early stages to save space.

(continued)

TABLE 12·1

The Four Stages of Games Skills Development: Basketball—cont'd

Extension	Refinement	Application
■ *Major task: moving passes to a moving receiver*		
Pass to stationary receiver. Pass to moving receiver. Use different levels of pass. Vary distances. Pass to force partner to receive the ball at full extension.	Send the ball so that the receiver does not have to stop (lead pass). Find the point the receiver can catch the ball at full extension. Use appropriate levels of pass for distance from partner. Get rid of the ball before steps are taken.	Make as many passes in a row from as far away as possible without losing control. Make as many passes as possible, using all the spaces available, in 1 minute.
Stage two		
Skill: combining dribbling and passing		
■ *Major task: individual dribbling and passing to a wall on the move*		
Change speed. Increase complexity of the environment. Change direction. Change pathway.	Be aware of others. Receive the ball from the dribble to make the pass a continuous action. Place the ball on the wall so that it returns (angles) ahead of the receiver.	Get to as many different walls as possible in 1 minute.
■ *Major task: dribbling and passing to a partner*		
Dribble and pass moving in the same direction. Dribble and pass moving in different directions. Increase distance between partners.	Make smooth transition from the dribble to the pass (one action). Use minimal number of dribbles before pass. Maintain awareness of location of receiver. Use appropriate pass for relationship to partner (direction and distance).	Make as many continuous passes as possible without losing control of the ball. Make as many passes as possible in 30 seconds without losing control of the ball.
■ *Major task: passing in groups of three or four*		
Have no directional goal. Have directional goal. Use unlimited space. Use limited space. Add the dribble.	Cut into an open space to receive ball. Move behind receiver. Maintain awareness of passes and potential receivers. Use the dribble only to await a potential receiver.	Go as long as possible without losing control of the ball.

(continued)

TABLE 12·1

The Four Stages of Games Skills Development: Basketball—cont'd

Extension	Refinement	Application
Stage three		
Skill: offensive and defensive strategies against the dribble		
■ *Major task: seat tag (two students, using no ball, face each other and try to tag each other's seat)*		
Use unlimited space.	Use quick changes in direction to "fake."	Go as long as possible without having
Use limited space.	Maintain facing relationship in offensive moves.	the seat tagged.
	Use quick slide steps with the feet.	
■ *Major task: individual dribbling with defender trying to touch the ball*		
Use unlimited space.	Offense	Maintain possession of the ball for as
Use limited space.	Use body to protect ball.	long as possible.
Add rule infractions.	Change hands.	Try to get by the defense.
Add line of direction.	Use quick actions to fake defense.	
	Keep body position and level of dribble low.	
	Defense	
	Stay close to dribble.	
	Use fakes to get possession.	
	Maintain eye contact with trunk and upper body of dribbler.	
	Stay between defensive player and desired direction.	
Skill: offensive and defensive strategies using the pass, dribbling and shooting		
■ *Major task: two offense against one defense (traveling violation liberally enforced)*		
Use unlimited space.	Offense	Play keep-away game (change middle
Use limited space.	Use quick passes.	player when play is touched by
Enforce traveling violation.	Use appropriate pass for position	defense).
Have no directional goal.	of defensive player (high for	
Have directional goal.	player in middle, bounce for	
Combine dribbling and passing.	passes closely guarded, chest	
	for open receiver and passes).	
	Move into an open space to receive a pass (cut).	
	Time cut.	
	Use the dribble only when receiver is not free.	
	Defense	
	Choose to stay with one player.	
	Remain between ball and receiver.	
	Make body shape wide and low to receive quickly.	

(continued)

T A B L E   1 2 · 1

The Four Stages of Games Skills Development: Basketball—cont'd

Extension	Refinement	Application
■ *Major task: two offense against two defense (no dribbling)*		
Use unlimited space.	Same as above with more emphasis on quick passes and on defense remaining between ball and intended direction of offense.	Same as previous.
Use limited space.		
Have no directional goal.		
Have directional goal.		
Combine dribbling and passing.	Make quick changes from offensive to defensive role.	
Combine dribbling and passing with shooting to a target.		
■ *Major task: three offense against two (or three) defense (no dribbling)*		
Use unlimited space.	Offense	Play half-court ball.
Use limited space.	Emphasize third offensive player setting up a future play using spatial relationships of offense and defense.	Play full-court ball.
Have no directional goal.		
Have directional goal.		
Combine dribbling and passing.		
Combine dribbling and passing with shooting to a target.	Defense	
Add offensive and defensive fouls.	Practice zone defense possibilities once scoring is added.	
Add out-of-bounds rules.	Make quick changes from offensive to defensive role.	
Stage four		
Skill: modified basketball game		
■ *Major task: four offense against four defense using all skills and major rules*		
Require minimum of three passes before scoring.	Use advanced strategies (plays) for offense and defense.	Play half-court ball.
Use no dribbling.	Discuss specific game situations and establish strategies for specific conditions.	Play full-court ball.
Use no foul shooting.		
Start game with a throw-in.		
Use zone defense only.	Modify games to encourage particular aspects of play that the teacher finds are weaknesses.	
Determine set plays to get into the key.		
Use half court.		
■ *Major task: regulation basketball*		

---

conditions, and gradually the attainment of control is made more difficult by manipulating the level, direction, and force of the object being sent or received. The development in stage one also includes the changes from stationary to moving objects and from stationary to moving receivers. Consider the sequence a young child might follow learning how to catch a ball and contrast that with the sequence you might use to develop the forearm pass in volleyball.

Catching a ball

Intra-task Development

Light toss out of hand
Increase height of toss
Increase distance of toss
Toss to left and right
Receive toss from another
Increase force and distance
Vary levels of throw
Increase force and distance
Catch on the move

Forearm pass

Intra-task Development

Pass from light toss
Increase height of toss
Increase distance of tosser
Receive toss from left and right
Move into toss and pass
Increase force and distance
Vary levels of throw
Pass served ball coming from different directions

In each of these examples a gradual progression is established that will lead the student to increasing levels of mastery and control over the object by changing the conditions. The idea of establishing a gradual level of progression is also illustrated in the basketball example on pp. 277–280. All manipulative tasks can be reduced or increased in complexity by manipulating the force (speed/distance), direction, and level of the object, as well as the idea of stationary or moving players. Catching or throwing on the move is more difficult than catching or throwing from a stationary position. Although skilled players acquire high levels of control of the objects used in games and sports, a minimal level of control is necessary to participate in playing the game or sport.

Stage two—complex control and combinations of skills. Stage two is also concerned with the individual's control of the object, but the practice of the skills becomes more complex. In stage two, skills are *combined* (such as dribbling and passing); *rules* are emphasized that limit the way an action can be performed (such as traveling in basketball); and skills

are practiced in cooperative *relationships* with others (e.g., volleyball keep-it-up; hitting back and forth in tennis).

Practicing skills in combination is a critical and often neglected aspect of learning how to play games. A student who can dribble a ball and can pass or shoot a ball may not easily dribble and shoot or dribble and pass in combination. This is because *the preparation for the second skill takes place during the first skill (transition).* Combined skills have a transition phase that is often neglected by teachers and performers but is critical to skillful performance. Many beginning learners in basketball will dribble—stop—and then pass the ball. The focus on teaching students in stage two activities is on the transition movements between skills. Although many students with practice will come to a smooth transition, many students will not without help from the teacher. In the soccer dribble and shoot, for example, players must place the ball at the end of the dribble in a position where they can shoot or pass the ball—not stop and then move the ball into position to shoot or pass. The following example from the complex game of soccer illustrates some of the possible combinations necessary for full development of stage two.

Soccer stage two combinations

- Receive a pass and dribble
- Dribble and pass
- Dribble and shoot
- Receive a pass, dribble and shoot
- Head a ball and dribble
- Head a ball and pass
- Head a ball and shoot

Even in game situations that involve discrete skills, practicing skills in combination is important. In stage two in volleyball, for example, one student may bump the ball to another, who will set it for a spike or set it to another player, who will set it for a spike. To determine what skills to practice in combination, teachers must analyze a game to determine what skills will be used in combination in a game. Skills should ultimately be practiced the way in which they will be used in a game, even to the point of serving a volleyball and then moving into position.

Stage two also engages students in cooperative practice activities with others, such as the game of keep-it-up in volleyball or keeping the shuttlecock going across the net in badminton. At this stage the object of the game is still mastery and control of the object, not competition against those with whom you are working. Activities are in one sense *group cooperative activities* in which the focus of the activity is mastery of control of the object.

Stage three—beginning offensive and defensive strategies. In stage three the focus is removed from the execution of the skill to simple offensive and defensive roles with the use of the skill. When stage three experiences are introduced, the assumption is that students do not have to devote all of their attention to controlling the object and can focus on the use of the skill in offensive and defensive relationships. Stage three considers the basic tactics (strategies) in sport activities and begins to build these tactics, first in less complex conditions and then in more complex conditions.

Two forms of popular sports have complex strategies. The first is an **invasion game** (sometimes called *keep-away games*) and the second form of popular sport is usually referred to as **net activities**.

Invasion games. Basketball; soccer; speedball; lacrosse; hockey; and, to some extent, football are invasion games. In invasion games players share the same court or field offensively and defensively and roles change according to who has the ball. In this type of game the offensive objective is to maintain possession of the object and score offensively. The defensive objective is to get possession of the object. Stage three in these types of sport activities is concerned with establishing ways to obtain and maintain possession of objects to score. The following examples of beginning strategies from invasion games illustrate the skills and abilities that need to be taught at this stage.

Invasion game strategies

How to maintain possession one-on-one
How to obtain possession one-on-one
How to maintain possession two-on-one
How to obtain possession two-on-one

How to maintain possession two-on-two
How to obtain possession two-on-two
How to maintain possession three-on-two
How to obtain possession three-on-two
How to maintain possession three-on-three
How to obtain possession three-on-three

Each of these ideas has a set of critical cues related to the strategy that is part of each game. Each offensive player (the player with the ball and the player[s] without the ball) has a separate role. Each defensive player (the player with the ball and the player[s] without the ball) likewise has a separate role to play. When these roles are taught before the game gets too complex, students have the foundation for playing the game in more complex forms (whole court or field, all the players, all the rules).

Net activities. The second type of popular sport is net activities. Volleyball, tennis, and badminton are examples of net activities. In net activities players do not share space at the same time. The object in net activities is to score by making the other team miss the ball. Offensive and defensive strategies involve learning how to defend your space and learning how to make the opponents miss the ball. Offensive and defensive strategy for net activities consists largely of the following:

Offensive strategy for net games

Place the ball on the opposite court in a space not defended well by the other team.
Use an offensive difficult-to-return hit (e.g., badminton smash, volleyball spike, tennis smash).
Use a change-off hit (e.g., drop shot, dink) when the other team expects one of the hits just mentioned.
Change the direction or level of the ball.
Play to an opponent's weakness.
Set up several plays in a row to pull the defense out of position.

Defensive strategy for net games

Defend the space.
Anticipate where the ball will be placed.
Block offensive shots.

Students should be able to use offensive and defensive strategies of games in stage three under less complex game situations in which the focus of the activity can be the basic strategies. The simplest condition for most sports activities is a one-on-one situation (two-on-one when the control of the skill action is difficult, as in soccer). It is at this simplest level that strategies are introduced. As is the case with invasion games, the development of skill in net games takes place from simple to complex. Students in one-on-one play in volleyball can begin to develop offensive strategies. As more players are introduced, the students are helped to understand how to relate what they do to additional players and most of the time increased space. In volleyball, for instance, having two people on a court requires that players know how to share space. The frontline player in an up-and-back position must be helped to know how to open up (turn sideways as the ball comes overhead) and how to make the discrimination of what to let pass overhead.

Complexity is developed in stage three by adding people (in both offensive and defensive roles), boundaries, scoring, and rules for the conduct of the activity. As another element of complexity is added, students are helped to adjust their responses to what is added. Complexity is added gradually.

Stage four—complex game play. There is no exact point where stage three experiences end and stage four experiences begin. Stage four experiences are complex. Stage four includes the full game and those experiences modified to help students reach that point. For most games, stage four begins when offensive and defensive players become specialized. Players are added, most skills are used, and the conduct and organization of the game becomes more complex (e.g., rules for starting, procedures for rule infractions, scoring, and out-of-bounds play are added).

When students reach stage four, it is assumed that fairly high levels of individual skills have been established and that students have acquired basic games strategies used in simplified game conditions. For example, it is assumed that students can defend against an offensive player individually and

High levels of skill are attained after careful progressions and successful practice.

with others in basketball or that they can place the ball away from an opponent and defend their space in a net activity.

A key aspect of conducting stage four activities in a meaningful way is the concept of *keeping the game continuous.* If a rule or part of a game performed in a certain way slows down the continuous flow of the game, the game should be modified to keep it continuous. If students cannot use all the players on a team, the number of players should be reduced. Examples of game modifications include eliminating free kicks or foul shots, replacing the serve in volleyball, or batting in baseball with a throw or batting off a tee for some players, starting a game from an out-of-bounds play, and reducing the size of the playing field.

The teacher who chooses to use a stage four game in a lesson does not give up the role of the teacher. The object is to teach students how to play the game well, not merely to let them play when they reach this level. A stage four task is an application task that can be extended by making the play more difficult or less difficult. The teacher should also refine students' performance through the use of refining tasks and a clear focus for their play.

EXAMPLE: "I will be looking for the defensive players to open up the space in your games today. Every time I do not see a good use of space on the part of the defense, I will stop the game."

Sometimes teachers hesitate to modify games or change the rules because the game is sacred. Unskilled soccer players who cannot get the ball to the wing are not playing the game the way it should be played. A tennis game that begins and ends with the serve is not tennis. A basketball game that involves one player dribbling down the court to shoot and others attempting to rebound so that they can do the same is not basketball.

Considerations Using the Games Stages

Like any conceptual framework for teaching, the games stages should be used and not abused. Some key ideas regarding the stages should be considered when planning curriculums and lessons:

1. **Students do not leave one stage when they are ready for another.**

   It is not possible to master a stage. Minimal levels of competency must be obtained before students can be successful with experiences at a higher level, but even varsity basketball practices include experiences at all stages, with an emphasis on stages two and three.

2. **The most neglected stages of development of games skills in physical education programs have been stages two and three.**

   If the skills developed in stages two and three in table 12.1 (p. 277) are examined, it can be seen that the essential aspects of both skills and game strategies are best taught at these levels. It is not uncommon to see units of instruction established

that move directly from stage one to stage four. The result is always the same—play is not continuous, and the skills seem to fall apart. If teachers would analyze the demands of games and then gradually increase the complexity of those demands as students are ready, students would be more successful and would be able to play the game. A volleyball game in which the receiving team backs out of the way of the ball as it comes over the net cannot do much to increase students' approach tendencies toward volleyball.

3. **You can determine the skills students need to play the game by analyzing how skills are used in a game and what strategies are involved.**

   You can determine progressions for developing skills and strategies by gradually adding complexity from the simplest conditions to gamelike conditions. Look at what a player does during the game—describe it and then order learning experiences that will develop these abilities.

Tactical and Skill Approaches to Teaching Games and Sports

The difference between the ability to execute a skill and the ability to use a skill in a game situation is made clear in dialogue focused on which is more important (skill development or tactical skill development) in learning how to play a game or sport. Several physical educators, both in the United States and in England, have suggested that students should start learning how to play games by learning the tactics of those games and sports first rather than beginning with learning the skills. (For a discussion of these issues see Griffin & Butler, 2005; Rink, 1996; Thorpe, Bunker, & Almond, 1986; or Turner & Martinek, 1995.) The assumption is that it is the tactics that are the meaningful part of the game and that students will develop the skills out of a need to know how to execute a skill after they begin to use strategies. For instance, students will learn about moving a badminton opponent around a court and will learn how to use an up-and-back strategy without ever having to know that one shot may be called a *drop* shot and the other a *clear* or *smash*. The teacher intervenes to help students refine skills when the students are ready. Using a games-for-understanding approach, students in soccer will learn the game in simple conditions but will again start with the tactics without an emphasis on how to dribble or how to pass or how to shoot.

The games strategy approach to teaching games has much in common with cognitive strategy approaches to learning and particularly constructivist approaches to learning discussed in chapter 2. Ideas related to the *selection of what to do* are separated from ideas related to *how to do it.* Several orientations can emerge from these ideas.

Teaching an understanding of the basic tactics of a type of game. Teachers who want to give students a basic understanding of a type of game would begin with learning experiences that reduce the game or sport to its essence. Small-sided games are used in this process. In an invasive game such as basketball or soccer, students might begin with two offensive players against one defensive player. In this format learners would begin to understand the need for the specific skills needed for maintaining possession of the ball, those skills needed to move the ball with a teammate, and those skills needed to obtain possession of the object from the other team. The specific motor skills needed to execute the strategy would emerge from the experience and then be refined (e.g., how to do a chest pass would only be taught as students need the chest pass in their play). The teacher would design specific experiences to develop student knowledges of when to pass, when to maintain possession, and where to move on the court or field. Further, the students would be developing an understanding of the game that would transfer to other invasion games. How to execute the motor skills to accomplish the tactics of the game would only come as students begin to try and execute the strategy and need to know "how" to execute the strategy.

To use tactics of any activity, the player must have some level of control of the object (stage one). A teacher has two options. You can reduce the manipulative skills used in the game (e.g., change striking to throwing and catching), or you can stop and give the students some level of control of the object and then put them in tactical experiences.

A games-for-understanding approach to teaching sport and games is inherently motivating to students because what is meaningful to the students is playing the game and not practicing the skills. Advocates of a games-for-understanding approach to teaching games and sport point to the failure of students to be able to use a skill in a game when students are taught a skill approach as support for teaching tactics first. In one sense a games-for-understanding approach starts with stage three of the games stages described in the previous section.

Teaching the tactics/strategies of games more formally. An alternative to the notion that there are general strategies of games is to acknowledge the more explicit strategies inherent not only in types of games but in specific sports. Although general strategies are common to both basketball and soccer, sport-specific tactics are also part of each sport. The number of players, the number of specialized positions, the rules, and so on, make each sport and game unique. These more specific tactics must be taught explicitly in terms of "if-then" relationships. Examples of sport-specific "if-then" relationships are as follows:

- Volleyball: *If* two people come up to block the spike, *then* pass the ball to a different player to spike.
- Soccer: *If* the defensive player moves up to take the ball away, *then* pass it. *If* the defensive player continues to back up, *then* keep the ball in a dribble.

These sport-specific "if-then" relationships are critical for more skillful levels of strategic play and are necessary extensions of the more generic strategies that are common to types of games.

Should I teach skills, or should I teach tactics? The issue is not whether a teacher should teach skills or should teach tactics. Games/sports players need both skill and strategy. Skill development and tactics development are interdependent; that is, the development of one is constrained by development in the other. Players may only be able to advance so far in tactics development before their lack of skill limits what they can choose to do. Likewise players cannot reach advanced levels of skill without also being involved in using that skill strategically.

Skill instruction usually does not transfer to a game because the manner in which the skill is practiced is not related to the way in which the skills are used in a real game. When students are ready to begin to play games at a beginning level of play (stage three), there may be merit in teaching the basic tactics of games forms if students do not already have these basic tactics (net activity and invasion game basic strategies). If students do have the basic tactics for games, then the approach to teaching tactics probably should be for the teacher to specifically identify as learning objectives particular if-then tactics to be learned by students as well as specific levels of skill to be acquired by learners. Whether these skills and these tactics are taught directly or indirectly is in one sense irrelevant to developing skillful games/sports players. The important idea is that the students be able to execute the skill and use the tactics.

Skill development as well as game tactics development should be integrated with game play at the appropriate level of complexity. In other words, students should have opportunities to play the game on a continuous basis, and instruction in skill and strategy should grow out of that play. Skill development out of context for a long time followed by game playing for a long time without additional skill development is an inappropriate approach to teaching games and sports.

Sport Education

Sport education is a relative newcomer to the list of approaches to teaching games and sports. Originally developed by Daryl Siedentop, sport education attempts to take all that is good about the sport experience and provide more authentic sport experiences in the physical education setting (Siedentop, Hastie, & van der Mars, 2004). It is a curriculum and an instructional model for teaching sport. This means that there is not only a specific content to be taught but the manner in which that content should be taught is also specified. According to sport education enthusiasts, the problem with the way in which

sport has been taught in more traditional physical education settings is that it has been decontextualized. Skills and knowledge are taught out of the context of playing the game and being a participant in the game in its fullest sense.

The goals of sport education are to:

Develop skills and fitness specific to particular sports

Appreciate and be able to execute strategic play in sport

Participate at a level appropriate to their stage of development

Share in the planning and administration of sport experiences

Provide responsible leadership

Work effectively within a group toward common goals

Appreciate the rituals and conventions that give particular sports their unique meanings

Develop the capacity to make reasoned decisions about sport issues

Develop and apply knowledge about umpiring, refereeing, and training

Decide voluntarily to become involved in after-school sport (Siedentop et al., 2004)

In sport education long sport seasons replace the common short unit in a sport. This enables the skills, competencies, and processes involved in becoming a player and participant time to be developed. Students are placed as members of a team, and they maintain their team affiliation throughout the unit. Teachers can choose and organize teams using different criteria, but normally teams are chosen to be heterogeneous (mixed abilities and contributions). The number of players on a team depends on the level of play that will ultimately be the goal (5 vs. 5, 8 vs. 8, etc.). Larger teams can be broken down into smaller units at early stages of the sport season. When teachers plan their sport seasons, they plan on formal competition throughout the season, even though the competition may take different forms at different stages of the season and may consume different amounts of time of a class period. There is always a culminating event to the season such as a tournament or performance of some sort.

In sport education, most of the time class work is organized by teams and the role of the teacher is to encourage student leadership and decision making in the process of learning and competing. There are team captains, managers, referees, and scorers, and there may be statisticians, students in charge of publicity, trainers, and so on. The amount of responsibility given to students at any one time depends on the ability of the students to handle that responsibility and more importantly the ability of the teachers to help students learn responsibility. Early parts of the season are spent teaching students their responsibilities and learning the skills, knowledge, and strategy to play the game well. Teams practice, train, plan, and play on a regular basis. Teachers *teach* students to perform all the roles necessary for the system to run smoothly. They establish clear rules and expectations for meeting responsibilities and participating as an ethical and fair-play participant, and they hold students accountable for those expectations.

Sport education is in one sense the ultimate cooperative learning experience for students. While students learn to compete against others, more importantly they learn to work with each other to accomplish group goals. The teacher's role in sport education is different from normal instruction. To teach sport education well, the teacher must do extensive planning and teaching to help students fulfill their roles in the process and to help them work with each other in productive and inclusive ways. Students are not well served by teachers who use sport education as a model to just play the game. It is beyond the scope of this text to fully develop sport education as both a curriculum and an instructional model for teaching. Several excellent references for sport education are included at the end of this chapter.

Dance

Many forms of dance are taught through physical education. At the elementary grades, rhythms, folk and square dance, and creative dance are most popular. At the secondary level, aerobic dance; line and square dance; and modern, jazz, and other forms of contemporary dance are popular. Content-specific

Older students can find dance challenging and enjoyable.

pedagogy is involved for each of these forms. There are also some general ideas relative to teaching dance that teachers should consider in their planning. The suggestions that follow are divided into two sets. The first set describes those ideas most appropriate for direct instruction as seen in box 12.3. The second set is primarily for creative dance forms shown in box 12.4 (p. 289). Many teachers will include aspects of both in the same lesson and unit.

Gymnastics

Gymnastics in physical education is usually taught either as Olympic gymnastics or as educational gymnastics. Because most teachers who teach Olympic gymnastics intend that the student be able to do a demonstrated movement skill, direct instruction is usually the primary way in which instruction is delivered. In educational gymnastics the teacher works with concepts. The teacher intends that the learner apply the concepts to a student-selected appropriate response. For educational gymnastics the section on concept teaching is particularly relevant. General guidelines for teaching gymnastics are presented in box 12.5 (p. 290).

Outdoor Pursuits

Many high school programs include outdoor pursuits. It is not uncommon to see programs that include kayaking, orienteering, skiing, bicycling, canoeing,

BOX 12·3

Teaching Considerations: Dance (Direct Instruction)

1. When teaching a step pattern to students, have all students face the same direction. Give students enough room to move so that if one student makes a mistake, other students are not on top of him or her.

2. Change your teaching position so that the students in the front of the group and closest to you are not always in the front: either have students face where you are but change where you are so that other students have a chance to get closer to you, or rotate the students.

3. Use command teaching to walk students through a dance step with clear cues. Cues can indicate the following:
   Which foot to use (right, left, right, right)
   Which direction to go (back, side, forward)
   How the rhythm is performed (quick, quick slow)
   The numerical beat (1-2-3, 1-2-3)
   A combination of above (side 2,3, back 2,3)

4. When teaching a specific step pattern that you want students to "copy," face the group and mirror the image (you go *right* where the directions say *left*). Tell the students you are going to do this so that some students do not attempt to use the exact foot or hand that you are using.

5. When teaching a dance with steps performed to specific music, if possible, students should see the dance performed to the music. If this is not possible, they should see the steps performed to the music at correct speed before trying to learn the dance. DVDs and tapes are now available for many dances and for many dance forms. These should be used. Learners need to see the whole dance with the music.

6. Teach the steps of the dance individually before putting the steps to organizational patterns of the dance (e.g., alone before partners; partners before

circles). Use the names of the step patterns of dances so that they may transfer to other dances using the same pattern (e.g., grapevine polka).

7. If dances have a chorus or repeatable section, teach that first and then the other parts of the dance.

8. Walk the students through a step pattern at a slow speed, using verbal cues or a rhythmic instrument.

9. For complex step patterns, five students time to self-pace practice (do it in their time without your cues).

10. Repeat patterns until they are really learned and the students are comfortable with them.

11. Do not move on unless almost all of the students have the pattern. Pair up slower students with more-skilled tutors to work on a one-on-one apart from what you are doing.

12. Gradually increase the speed of performing a step pattern until it becomes consistent with the music. Add the music for practice of a part of the dance as soon as students can perform the step pattern with the music. Do not wait to add the music until all the parts of the dance are learned.

13. Use a variable-speed record player to adjust students' first experiences with the music to a slower speed if necessary. Maintain teacher verbal cues through initial practices and gradually withdraw them.

14. Build new parts of the dance on parts already learned. For example, if you start with part A and have practiced it to the music, after learning part B, do parts A and B together.

15. Once students have learned a dance, let them do it enough so that it becomes enjoyable to them. Plan on including the dances students know in other lessons.

16. For young learners, do not insist that partners be composed of one girl and one boy.

---

sailing, ropes courses, and many other types of activities. Students enjoy these activities, and they are activities that can be easily pursued in most areas as adults. Teaching these activities requires training beyond what most of you will receive in your undergraduate programs, and many require certification to

teach them in a safe way. You should not attempt to teach these activities unless you have been properly trained to do so. Many communities have facilities and equipment available that they are willing to loan. Likewise, many adults with expertise will donate their time to help you with classes and trips. See

BOX 12.4

Teaching Considerations: Dance (Creative)

1. For beginning learners, add structure to initial experiences. It is difficult to be creative when students have yet to develop responses. Give the students a movement response and then help them explore variations in use of the body and its parts, spatial dimensions, effort actions, and relationships.

2. Keep movement sequences short, so that fast movement will not be interpreted as running around the gymnasium. Use percussion instruments or paced signals to help students mark time (e.g., you want the students to rise slowly from a low-level position to an extended position at a high level. Give them eight counts to get there so they can begin to understand phrasing of movement; if you want to contrast this with an explosive movement, give a hard beat of the drum to be explosive). Withdraw the help of the percussion instrument after students have explored the sequence enough to self-pace the movements.

3. Do not call on students to demonstrate unless you are absolutely sure that their efforts will be received positively by other students and will not destroy the involvement of the student who is doing well.

4. Encourage exploration and variety in responses by helping students to vary the body parts they use;

the actions; the levels of the movement; and the force (weight), speed, and direction of the movement.

5. Early on, teach beginners to sequence their movements with a clear beginning and clear ending.

6. Do not be reluctant to demonstrate examples of what you mean.

7. Make lessons more relevant to learners by mixing work with pure movement concepts (body, space, effort, relationships) with more concrete ideas and expressions, such as action words, poetry, sport skills, conflict, art.

8. Give lessons an identity with material to explore and an opportunity to practice and perfect a response.

9. Do not hesitate to suggest ways in which students might improve their responses by making what they do more clear, by using smoother transitions, and by presenting more interesting use of the body and movement quality.

10. Ensure positive reinforcement to learners for uncommon responses. Positively reinforcing a particular response is likely to send the message that it is the particular response that is good and not necessarily the uniqueness of it.

---

box 12.6 (p. 291) for guidelines to follow when teaching outdoor pursuits.

■ MOVEMENT CONCEPTS—TEACHING FOR TRANSFER

The national standards for physical education (NASPE, 2004) clearly emphasize the importance of teaching movement concepts and principles as a part of every physical education program—*Standard 2: Demonstrates understanding of movement concepts, principles, strategies, and tactics as they apply to the learning and performance of physical activities.*

Concepts are cognitive ideas. Often teachers choose to teach content they hope will transfer to other similar situations. Teachers hope that if they teach the overhand throw pattern, what is learned will transfer

to skills such as the volleyball serve, overhead smash, or javelin. Teachers hope that if students understand how to receive force in one situation, they will be able to use that information in other situations requiring receiving force, such as catching, collecting a soccer ball, or landing from height. The ability to transfer learning from one situation to another is essential to both independence in learning and problem solving.

Many concepts related to movement would be valuable to the learner if taught to the level of transfer. The term **movement concept** is used in this text to refer to ideas that have transfer value. Movement concepts in physical education can be a label for a group of motor responses, such as catching, throwing, or traveling, that are a label for motor skills that can be done in different **contexts.** For example, throwing can be baseball, softball, whiffle ball, or bowling.

BOX 12·5

Educational Gymnastics

1. Gymnastics is primarily a safety problem when students are asked to try to perform skills that they should not be working with. Many students do not have the prerequisite physical abilities for Olympic gymnastic skills, which require high degrees of upper body strength, abdominal strength, and flexibility. The teacher can choose to develop the prerequisites or modify downward the expectations for performance.

2. Students should be taught early how to manage and control the weight of their bodies for safety. Students should be taught how to place body parts on equipment and mats and should not be permitted to throw body parts down on a mat. Crashing is not acceptable. Students can be taught how to come down safely from inverted positions.

3. Gymnastics units must be individualized so that there are different expectations for different students. Students should not be put in the position of trying skills that they are not ready to perform.

4. Students should be encouraged to demonstrate good form in what they do. It is not sufficient to get through a movement. It is better to do a simpler skill with good form than to move unsafely through a skill they cannot control.

5. Station teaching is useful for large apparatus work when skills have already been introduced on different pieces.

6. The use of spotters depends primarily on the age of the student and the difficulty of the skills being performed. Teachers should plan on spotting all aerial movements. Spotting is a skill, and spotters are not always necessary if students have been taught how to manage and control their bodies and are not put in positions where they are asked or feel pressured to do skills that they are not yet ready to do.

7. Young students should be requested to rest off the equipment and mats when the teacher is talking. The temptation to be off task on mats or equipment is more than most young children can handle.

8. Students should be encouraged to bring their movements to a close when the teacher asks them to stop. Some movements are dangerous if abruptly stopped in the middle.

9. For Olympic gymnastics it is sometimes helpful to provide students with checklists of skills in progressive order of difficulty. The teacher may want to evaluate students' success in a skill before they can move on to another skill.

10. Teachers should take advantage of DVDs, videotape, and other visual means of giving students the idea of skills and evaluating students' progress.

11. Teachers should build gymnastics units to a culminating experience even if the culminating experience is a class videotape of what the students have been able to accomplish. Gymnastics is performance oriented, and students will be more highly motivated if they are working toward something.

Movement concepts can also be movement-related ideas and principles that are cognitive and can be applied to a variety of contexts. Six categories of movement concepts useful in physical education are considered in this text as follows. These concepts are listed with examples in table 12.2 (p. 292):

- Action words
- Movement qualities
- Movement principles
- Movement strategies/tactics
- Movement effects
- Movement affects

Learning Theory Associated with the Transfer of Learning

Concepts are taught appropriately when students can discriminate when to transfer the idea to a new situation and when not to (Merrill, 1971). Movement concepts are used to a greater or lesser extent as the content of physical education, depending on the curricular and philosophic orientation of the program. Movement concepts as content in physical education have the potential to deal more broadly with the subject matter of physical education and achieve long-term curricular goals.

BOX 12·6

Guidelines for Teaching Outdoor Pursuits

1. Plan on spending at least the first instructional period in the classroom with many visual aids to teach safety. Do not waste time going out to a lake, course, or other area only to sit students down and talk to them for the entire period.
2. Beginning lessons are difficult because safety is such a strong aspect of most of these activities. Be creative about ways to involve students actively while they are learning how to be safe.
3. Do not tolerate any breach of safety rules for any reason.
4. Keep the numbers small in these classes. It is better to have a small group for a shorter time than a larger group for a longer time. This is because it is difficult to keep large groups safely involved.
5. Teach the basic concepts of these activities and reinforce them as the progression moves from simple to complex.
6. Encourage students to become involved in community opportunities in the activity.
7. Include at least one trip to a nearby site. Spend some time acquainting students with what is available to them in their area, as well as the surrounding area.
8. Bring in adults from the community to talk to the students about what they have done with the activity.

Learning theory related to teaching for transfer has been explicit about what learning is likely to transfer and what learning is not likely to transfer. Chapter 2 discusses what we know about transfer of learning from one motor skill to another. Generally, the ideas related to transferring cognitive information are similar. The more a new situation has in common with a situation already experienced, the more likely transfer will be. Researchers who take a cognitive perspective on transfer stress the role that cognitive memory structures play in transfer. Past learning is organized into memory structures, retrieved when the individual is faced with new learning situations. Knowledge learned in one context can be retrieved for use in another context when the individual sees relationships between information already stored and new experiences. Using this perspective, a primary role of the teacher is to help the learner organize and structure experiences so that information can be retrieved for new situations. This means the teacher must relate new experiences to previous ones and try to help the learner see more holistic perspectives on what is learned (how it is useful and in what contexts it is useful).

Important Concepts in Physical Education

Teaching for appropriate transfer of skills, attitudes, and knowledge requires different types of processes than teaching for the specific instance. It also requires a high integration of curricular and instructional planning. Every instructional lesson must be viewed as a part of an integrated whole. Teaching for transfer of a concept from one situation to another takes time—time to plan both curriculum and instruction in a carefully integrated manner and time to teach students. *Concepts and Principles of Physical Education: What Every Student Needs to Know* (Mohnsen, 2003) identifies the important concepts and principles students should know at each grade level and provides teachers with suggestions for how to teach those concepts to students.

Movement concepts as content in physical education are most likely not as familiar as physical fitness or motor skills. For this reason, six types of movement concepts have been identified and are explained next with a description of the intent of instruction in that concept. The division between these content areas is not always clear in a real teaching situation. Instructional goals are complex, often multifaceted, and interrelated. This section is followed by a discussion of how to teach movement concepts.

Action words. Action words are broad categories of movements that include many different specific responses. The terms *balancing, traveling, striking, rising, receiving,* and *turning* are action words that are concepts because the action can be performed in many different ways and in many different contexts. A person can balance on one foot, two feet, or a head and two feet. A person can travel

T A B L E   1 2 · 2

Movement Concepts

Concept type	Content area	Specific example of a concept
Action words	Traveling, balancing, sending, striking, throwing, turning, rising	Balance: Increasing the size of the base stabilizes a movement.
Movement qualities	Quickness, directness, levels, directions, bound movements, pathways, body awareness, sudden and sustained movements	Sudden and sustained movements: Contrasting types of movement are part of expressive experiences. An appropriate effort quality must be selected for skill movement.
Movement principles	Follow-through, weight transference, spin, stability, force production, force reduction	Force production: The more body parts involved in an action, the greater the force.
Movement strategies	Offensive strategies, defensive strategies, cooperative strategies, adjustments to relationships with others	Lead pass: A ball should be passed ahead of a moving receiver.
Movement effects	Relationships of exercise to heart, muscular strength, endurance, flexibility	Strength: Muscular strength increases with increases in the workload or the duration of activity.
Movement affects	Relationships of participation in experiences to feelings, expression, social behavior, teamwork, fair play	Feelings: People perform better when teammates are supportive.

by skipping or running using the feet or by rolling or cartwheeling using other body parts. We give specific names to some responses within a concept, such as a headstand or a forehand tennis stroke. Some responses we do not have names for, such as a balance on one hand and two feet. As concepts, action words include not only the responses for which there are names, but also all responses possible that fit the definition of the concept.

Teachers who use action words that are concepts as the content rather than only the specific responses that constitute that concept do so for several reasons. First, they assume that there is value in performing the action in a variety of ways, including ways for which there may not be labels. Second, teachers who use action

words teach for *the set of ideas that are common and important in the concept.* For example, what is common and important in all types of jumping actions is the flexion and the powerful, force-producing extension that follows. As the teacher expands the number of ways in which students jump and produce elevation, the focus on flexion and extension remains constant. The teacher wants this ability to transfer to any jumping situation the student encounters (e.g., high jump, long jump, hurdle).

The process in teaching action words requires that the teacher continuously expand the number of ways students experience the action while holding constant the focus on what is important in skillful performance.

EXAMPLE: Mike has decided to teach the concept of striking. He gives his students many experiences striking objects with different parts of the body and with different implements (e.g., rackets, bats, sticks). He teaches his students what is important to all striking activities, such as where force is applied to direct the object and the speed of the striking implement prior to contact. He provides new experiences and asks students to apply what they have learned. He continuously reinforces major ideas related to striking in all student striking experiences throughout his program.

Movement qualities. Another way of looking at movement responses is to organize them by the quality of the movement they share. Movement qualities are classes of movement responses that share a movement quality. Words that describe the spatial aspects (level, direction, pathway, plane), effort aspects (time, weight, space, flow), or relationship aspects (matching, leading, cooperating) of movement are movement concepts that in a broad sense are qualities of movement. Most of the more current movement quality concepts used in programs come from the descriptive analysis system of movement developed by Rudolf Laban (see, for instances, Graham, Holt-Hale, & Parker, 2004). Content in physical education classes can be levels of movement, sudden and sustained movement, or leading and following relationships. The broader categories of body awareness, space awareness, effort, and relationships can also be categorizing concepts to be taught as content.

Most teachers who teach content organized as movement qualities believe that a physically educated person should have a broad range of experience with these qualities and should be able to transfer the use of the quality to new, appropriate situations. For example, if students have had experiences stretching, they should be able to reproduce the feeling of the stretch for skills such as the handstand or tennis serve. Students who have experience with light touch should be able to understand what is required in a basketball layup, badminton drop shot, or a volleyball dink. Teaching movement qualities develops both a cognitive and psychomotor movement vocabulary

that students can draw on in future learning as they experience the effect of the quality studied on their movement and develop kinesthetic awareness for the quality.

Movement qualities are used extensively in dance instruction, in which the teacher is likely to see students working on slow, sustained movement or quick, sudden movement as the content. The process of development is similar to action words in that the teacher continuously expands the number of ways the student experiences the movement quality. What remains constant is the emphasis on the student accurately producing the quality as the type of action changes.

EXAMPLE: Margo has organized her lesson around spatial relationship concepts. Students explore the different directions they can move and contrast that with the idea of pathways, levels of movement, and actions of single body parts. Margo wants to help the students build a vocabulary for describing how movement uses space and also wants the children to become aware and proficient in using space.

Movement principles. Movement principles are a broad category of concepts that include principles governing the efficiency and effectiveness of movement. Ideas such as (1) the relationship of weight transfer or follow-through to force production and (2) the effect of top spin on the flight of a projectile, as well as ideas related to stability and balance, are movement principles that can become the content of a lesson rather than a by-product of other lesson focuses. Movement tactics for games include ideas related to how and when to gain possession of the object in invasion games and how and when to obtain possession as well as tactics related to offensive and defensive play in net games. The intent in teaching movement principles is to have the students generalize to new experiences where the principles are useful in assisting the beginning stages of the learning process.

The process involved in teaching movement principles can vary from one situation to another. What is most often common in all good teaching of principles is the process of defining the principle, providing examples and negative examples, and providing opportunities for students to apply the principle. It is possible to teach an entire lesson on a movement principle, which allows time for full development. Usually, however, principles are integrated into lessons with other objectives, which makes full development difficult and the need for constant reinforcement through other applicable experiences critical. Teaching that leaves learning at a cognitive level is not sufficient.

EXAMPLE: Terry is teaching a lesson in which the primary focus is balance. She wants students to understand what makes a balance more stable (e.g., having a low or wide base of support; keeping the center of gravity over the base of support). Students explore a variety of balances in gymnastics and other sport settings, trying to increase and decrease stability in different ways. Terry wants the students to be able to make themselves more stable when they need to be and less stable when quick movement is desired. Terry will reinforce the experiences students have in balance throughout her program.

Movement strategies. Movement strategies are ideas related to how movement is used in cooperative and competitive relationships with others. The section on teaching game strategies and tactics has specifically addressed this issue. Movement strategies involve such ideas as passing ahead of a moving receiver, adjusting dance steps as a leader or follower, and defensively placing oneself between the goal and the ball. Movement strategies are adjustments individuals must make in their movement when they are engaged in experiences with others.

As discussed in the section on the games stages, all keep-away activities share common strategies, as do all net activities. Teachers who teach strategies as concepts do so with the intent that the strategies will transfer to different experiences. Teachers who teach strategies as concepts common to many game forms rather than one specific sport do so with the intent that students will be able to transfer these strategies appropriately (e.g., hitting the tennis ball to an open space just as one hits the volleyball to an open space; zone defense in soccer, basketball, and football). Transfer will occur more easily if the concept is defined and if students are given many different opportunities to apply the concept appropriately.

EXAMPLE: Dee is teaching a unit on net activities. Dee hopes to teach (1) offensively placing the ball or shuttlecock in the opponent's open space, (2) defensively returning to the center of one's space after each play, and (3) offensively changing the direction and force levels of placements in the opponent's court. Students begin a one-on-one situation with an easy striking skill (paddles and a foam ball) in a limited space. Students experience the strategies with and without implements and gradually move into specialized sport forms. The strategies are kept consistent as students experience different sport forms through the curriculum.

Movement effects. Movement effects are concepts related to the effect of movement experiences on the performer. The effect of vigorous exercise on the heart and the types of exercise that produce muscle endurance, strength, and flexibility are all movement effects concepts. Ideas related to exercise physiology are primary sources of movement effects concepts. These ideas are essential for students to know and to be able to use if they are to be able to achieve and maintain appropriate levels of fitness independently.

When a movement effect is the concept to be learned, the intent is that students are able to apply the concept to new experiences. If students fully understand the effects of vigorous activity on heart rate, they should be able to describe and design activities that have the potential to decrease resting heart rates. Students who think that jogging is the only exercise that can be used in a training regimen to improve cardiovascular endurance have undergeneralized the concept. Complete concept development means that students can discriminate those experiences that have the potential to improve heart-lung functioning from those that do not.

The process involved in teaching principles of movement effects is again one that begins by defining the concept and helping students to understand the principles involved. It is followed by helping the students to generalize that principle to all applicable situations.

> EXAMPLE: Kevin has decided to teach the concept of flexibility. He wants students to be able to apply the principles of flexibility to a variety of joints. He brings in a visual aid of the shoulder joint and points out opposing muscle groups. Kevin then talks about how flexibility is developed over a joint and the result of flexibility exercises on the muscles and tendons. Initially, several exercises for several joints are given to the class to illustrate how best to increase flexibility in a joint. Then students assess their levels of flexibility and are asked to design two exercises for each joint identified by the student as needing an increased range of motion. Kevin assesses the accuracy of the students' choices of exercises, and students begin a personal program to improve flexibility.

Movement affects. Movement affects are a special classification of concepts that focus exclusively on the affective area of human development. Movement affects concepts are related to expressiveness, the joy of moving, fair play, teamwork, feelings that describe why people move, and the effects of movement on affect. They are most closely related to National Standard 6, which indicates that students should *value physical activity for health, enjoyment, challenge, self-expression, and/or social interaction* (NASPE, 2004). When movement affect is a primary goal of instruction, the intent of the teacher is to develop some aspect of feelings, attitudes, or social relationships that will transfer to other movement experiences and, most of the time, to student behavior in general. A continuous goal of physical education programs is a positive attitude toward activity. Movement affects as a specific content focus go beyond making learning motor skills a positive, successful experience. The major content focus of lessons is affective rather than psychomotor.

Teachers may want to teach expressiveness or fair play specifically. They may want to put students in tune with how they feel as a mover in different situations, such as winning and losing in risk-taking activities; in movement that demands light, sensitive movement responses; and in movements that use much space. When an affective concept is taught,

experiences are designed specifically to develop affective behaviors.

Teaching concepts related to movement affects requires that students understand and, more important, feel or have an attitude toward that concept. Teaching affective concepts directly means that student feelings, attitudes, and social relationships—not just behavior—must receive attention.

> EXAMPLE: Chang has decided that he wants his students to get in touch with their feelings about themselves in different movement qualities. He chooses to teach a dance lesson that focuses on contrasting light and indirect movement with direct and strong movement. He knows that some students will have difficulty with the feelings elicited in moving lightly and indirectly (floating-like movements). He also knows that some students will have difficulty moving with strong, direct movements (punching movements). He begins his lesson by describing and defining these ideas by taking students through examples of both types of movements. He then asks them in a variety of tasks to explore ways in which they can use these qualities with other actions and with other body parts. He then works on having the students build sequences that will contrast the two qualities. At the end of the lesson Chang takes time to discuss with the students their feelings in this experience and their preferences for one or the other quality.

Teaching Movement Concepts

The choice to teach movement concepts generally means that the learner will be involved at higher levels of cognitive processing, the degree to which depends on the intent of the learning objective. Although the primary value of teaching concepts is their transfer to different contexts, teachers can have different intentions in teaching concepts. Some of these objectives are:

1. They can intend that a student *know* a concept and be able to reproduce it on a test when asked (e.g., knowing that it is necessary to step forward on the opposite foot).

2. They can intend that a student comprehend the concept and thus be able to use it in the specific context in which it is introduced (e.g., producing force in throwing).

3. They can intend that a student be able to apply the concept to a given situation (e.g., giving an example of how force can be produced in the tennis forehand).

4. They can intend that a student be able to apply information to new movement experiences when not focused on the concept (e.g., stepping forward when learning a new skill without being told to do so).

You will recognize that each of these intentions is a different level of cognitive learning (from chapter 10, "Planning") and that defining the concept in example number 1 is the easiest level to attain. Using the information in new contexts when not cued to do so is the most advanced level of concept learning. However, many levels of intent probably are missing from this list. The important point is to recognize that there is a real shift from knowing a concept in a cognitive sense to being able to use a concept behaviorally.

Concepts can be taught at any of these levels and many other levels in between. The word *concept* is cognitively oriented, and in many cases physical educators have intentionally designed programs to develop cognitive abilities in relation to these concepts. In some cases, however, physical educators have taken a cognitive idea whose value is its effect on performance and left it at the cognitive level. The value of a cognitive idea in physical education rests with its ability to be applied by the student to a psychomotor concern. The value of concept teaching in physical education is the effect the concept has on what the student *does* rather than on what the student *knows*.

At one level, the process involved in teaching a concept is easy. All that is required are the following actions:

- Define the concept for learners.
- Teach the critical features of the concept.
- Apply the concept to many examples (examples both where the concept is applied appropriately and where it is not).
- Give the student many opportunities to use the concept appropriately in different contexts.
- Reinforce the use of the concept throughout the program when appropriate.

Concept learning is not that easy, and we have only best guesses about how to help students learn a concept to the point at which they can apply that concept to all applicable situations on a regular basis. What follows is a discussion of how this might occur.

Defining the concept with students. Because concepts are ideas and not a label for a single concrete response, students must be given a clear idea of what is and what is not the concept. The idea of the concept of "truck" will illustrate the point. Children learning about differences among trucks, cars, vans, and buses often confuse them because whether something is a truck or a van or a car depends on more than one criterion. They learn to distinguish differences through many examples that allow them to discriminate the critical features of a concept. Although the concepts that you will teach will be more difficult than merely learning how to discriminate the idea of a truck, the process is the same. The first step for a teacher is to be clear about the critical features of the concept. Table 12.3 (pp. 297–298) defines several examples of concepts from each category of concepts and their critical aspects.

Once teachers are clear about the concept, they can begin to help define it for students. Teachers can verbally define the concept for students and ask students to provide examples of the concept to check their understanding.

EXAMPLE: "We make our bodies move in two ways: (1) by flexing our muscles and then extending them and (2) through a process of rotation. This is flexion and extension of the legs. This is flexion and extension of the arms. This is rotation. If I want to produce more force in a skill that needs force, I will have to increase the degree to which I flex and then extend and/or rotate. I will need to make the movement bigger. Who can name a movement that needs a lot of force? Okay, everyone stand up and show me how you might do that movement with a little force. Now show me how you might increase the force used in that movement? How did you make it bigger?"

Students can also be asked to give examples first and then to define the concept more specifically.

T A B L E 1 2 · 3

Identifying Critical Aspects of Concepts

Concept	Definition	Examples	Nonexamples	Critical aspects
Force reduction (movement principles)*	Force is reduced by receiving force over a greater distance.	Bunt a baseball. Catch a ball. Roll. Bend knees when landing from height.	Allow caught ball to bounce out of the hand. Strike a ball rather than bunting. Land from height with the knees straight.	Reach with a body part to absorb force. Move with object in line of direction until force is reduced. Create maximal distance to receive force.
Strong movement (movement quality)	Strong movement is movement that has an inner quality of strength and tension; it is more isometric.	Perform any action of the body or its parts, at any speed, whether stationary or traveling, that has an inner tension. Take a firm action or assume firm position.	Perform any action or assume any position of the body or its parts, at any speed, whether stationary or traveling, that has a light, loose, buoyant tension.	Be aware that inner tension can be experienced without the action accomplishing forcefulness. Use strong movement as preparation for forceful application of force. Be aware that strong movement is important to the forceful application of force.
Productive partner relationships in manipulative skills (movement affect)	Partners are responsible for challenging each other within personal limits, and the task is set by the teacher.	If the teacher asks students to receive the ball at different levels, the throwing partner sends the ball to challenging levels within the ability of the receiver.	If the teacher asks students to receive the ball at different levels, the throwing partner sends the ball to levels that are too easy or too difficult for the receiver.	Each partner is responsible for working with the other partner at an appropriate level of work. Each partner must make a decision about appropriateness and work within those limits.

*See pp. 301 for a developmental analysis of this movement principle.

(continued)

TABLE 12·3

Identifying Critical Aspects of Concepts—cont'd

Concept	Definition	Examples	Nonexamples	Critical aspects
Rolling (action word)	Rolling is transferring weight to adjacent parts of the body excessively to reduce force by rounding those parts.	Do forward rolls. Do shoulder rolls. Do rolls initiated with any part of the body.	Allow the body to go flat. Use step actions. Slide.	Round parts and take weight successively. Guard action with the hands. Assume rounded body shape.
Offensive strategies in net activities (movement strategy)	Offensive play in net activities consists of (1) placing the ball in a space in the opponent's court where the player is not, (2) changing the direction of the oncoming object to make opponent move maximal distance, and (3) changing the force of the oncoming object.	Place to corners when defensive player is in center. Use a drop shot or a smash in tennis or badminton effectively.	Return the object (1) from the same direction, (2) to the opponent, or (3) with anticipated force level.	Anticipate where opponent will be on court. Look for the largest and most distant space to place object. Use changes in force level as unanticipated moves.
Development of muscular strength (movement effect)	Muscular strength is developed using the principle of work overload by increasing either the number of repetitions over time or the intensity of workload.	Lift weights (gradually increasing repetitions or size of weight). Do push-ups (increasing number of repetitions).	Lift weights (keeping repetitions and size of weight constant). Do push-ups (keeping number of repetitions constant).	Identify duration and workload and gradually increase them.

EXAMPLES:

- "Who can tell me how to make your heart beat faster?"
- "What is a locomotor movement?"
- "How do we make a ball go farther when we are throwing?"

Verbal definition alone without concrete examples is appropriate for concepts students have already experienced. It is usually not effective with young children who are still in the concrete stages of cognitive development or for any learner who lacks experience in the concept to be discussed.

Most teachers find that concepts must be defined in an experiential way. Students can be led through an example of the concept or a use of the concept (e.g., striking, traveling, cardiorespiratory exercise, flexibility), and then the teacher can talk about the experience in terms of the definition and critical ideas of the concept. Frequently, more than one example is necessary. In the examples given, the teacher would lead the group through many examples of increasing force in a movement, such as throwing, jumping, striking, and skipping. Examples of what is *not* the concept often help to define the concept by providing contrast, as illustrated in the following examples.

EXAMPLES:
- The teacher wants children to understand the concept of general space as defined by the basketball court lines in the gymnasium. She describes the boundaries and then asks the students to find a place to stand in general space. She calls this "personal space." Students are then asked several times to find a different space. Finally, the students are asked to find a space not in the defined area.
- The teacher defines the concept of zone defense as guarding *space* rather than the *person*. He places students on a basketball court around the key and demonstrates areas for which students are responsible. Students are then instructed to shift with the position of the ball. Next, the teacher arranges the group in a different spatial pattern and asks the students to apply the same idea to the new situation.

The examples a teacher uses in concept definition are critical to student understanding. They must be a representative sample of possibilities. If the teacher selects examples that share another similar characteristic in addition to the concept characteristics, students are likely to *undergeneralize* the concept (e.g., if every example of a fruit is red, children will think all fruit has to be red). If the teacher in the first example chose for demonstration purposes students who responded correctly inside the line but who were all on one side of the basketball court, students would be apt to think that general space meant being in a space on that one side of the court. If the teacher in the second example had used only one arrangement of people, students would probably think that zone

defense was that single arrangement of people. As it is, the teacher in the second example has narrowed the application of the concept to basketball, and it is unlikely that students will be able to transfer the idea of zone defense to other appropriate activities, such as soccer, field hockey, or football, without additional help. What should be clear from this discussion is that teachers may narrow the applicability of a concept or the chance of transfer of the concept to a wider representation of contexts by the examples they choose. If teachers limit the examples, then students are likely to limit the application of the concept. The more examples and the wider the representation of those examples, the more likely the concept is to transfer.

Often, using an example of the opposite of a concept can help students to define concepts, particularly broadly applied concepts. Students can be helped to understand what traveling is if they know what traveling is not. They can be helped to understand teamwork if they understand what teamwork is not. These examples should be well selected and few in number so as to critically define the concept for students.

Expanding responses of students. Often teachers will want to expand or extend the applicability of a concept that is learned in one context to another. The intent is to help students apply the concept to a representative sampling of the experiences to which the concept is to be transferred. If traveling is to be defined as any action that moves the body from one place to another by using the feet or other body parts (including such motions as rolling, swinging, and sliding), a wide range of sample experiences must be provided. If cardiorespiratory endurance can be increased by manipulating the load, intensity, and duration of many different kinds of exercise, students must have an opportunity to apply these critical ideas to a representative sampling of activities (not only jogging).

The teacher can choose either to guide or to direct the exploration and application of experiences. As a teacher, I can give students the experiences and ask them to apply the principles, or I can ask students to select the experiences and then apply the principles. In teaching the concept of striking, for example, the teacher can lead students through striking with each part of the body or the teacher can ask the students to strike balls using different parts of their bodies. You will recognize that the choice the teacher is making in this instance is one of teaching strategy—whether to guide the exploration or to give students responsibility for selection of responses. The same choice is open to teachers when working with action word concepts (e.g., striking, throwing, spinning), more cognitively oriented concepts (e.g., flexibility development, force production), or affectively oriented concepts (e.g., teamwork, leadership, positive social interaction).

> EXAMPLE: The teacher has worked with students on the concept of flexibility and has given the students several critical aspects of the development of flexibility for a particular joint. The teacher can then either go through several joints with the students to ensure they can apply the concept or ask the students to take the critical features of the concept and apply them to a joint of their selection.

The process of expansion is often assisted by narrowing choices initially and then expanding them later. This statement seems contradictory, but consider the results when a teacher says, "Write a composition on anything you want," and the idea of restricting or narrowing choices can be appreciated. Choices can be narrowed by such directives as the following:

- Balance on three parts of your body, rather than choose a balance.
- Select activities you would do every day to set up your own cardiorespiratory endurance program, rather than select an activity.
- Let's work on being supportive to our classmates when they are having difficulty, rather than work well with others.
- Choose a throwing action to show that you understand how weight can be transferred to produce force, rather than choose an action.

Narrowing choices ensures experience with a representative sample of behaviors and also assists students with the process of application.

A word about quality. As discussed in the beginning of this section, the value of teaching concepts is their application to behavior. Sometimes teachers become so absorbed in expanding responses, they neglect the quality of the response. Exercises done incorrectly, balances not held, movement responses that apply principles inefficiently, or strategies performed incorrectly are not useful and defeat the purpose of development. It is not enough to "know" concepts in a cognitive sense; their value is their skilled application to experience.

To refine the responses of students, the teacher must establish criteria for good performance and hold students accountable for the criteria established. Teaching concepts is easier if the teacher establishes criteria in advance through planning. An example of a developmental analysis for a lesson on the concept of force reduction is provided in table 12.4 (p. 301).

If good balance is defined as holding an extended position still for six seconds, student responses should be still and extended regardless of whether the balance is on two feet or two hands. If a good spot in general space is away from equipment, students should be held accountable for selecting a good spot. Even when responses are varied and are chosen by students (e.g., "Choose a throwing pattern you can use to demonstrate transfer of weight"), students still need to be helped to throw well in whatever patterns they choose. The cognitive idea is not enough.

Critical ideas are inherent in many concepts transferred from one experience to another. These critical aspects are almost always part of concepts that belong to action words categories, movement principles, movement strategies, and movement affects. Sometimes a single critical idea, such as increasing the base of support increases stability, is all that the teacher wants to develop. As described in table 12.4, however, several critical aspects are inherent in most concepts.

In one sense, critical aspects (features) are the "how to do" concept being taught. If the concept is how to improve cardiorespiratory endurance, the critical aspect is the information that is used to improve cardiorespiratory endurance (e.g., overload). Thus, the critical aspects are subconcepts or principles that govern how the concept is used. They are what the teacher hopes will transfer when students decide how

TABLE 12·4

Force Reduction: Manipulative Objects

Extension	Refinement	Application
Toss a ball into the air and receive it so that it makes no noise in the hands.	Reach to receive. Move down with object until the force is reduced.	Toss ball as high as possible and still receive it with "soft hands."
Identify concept (force is reduced by giving with it).	Create maximal distance to receive the force.	Come as close to the floor as possible before stopping the ball.
Receive thrown balls of different types (e.g., footballs, basketballs, softballs).	Place body parts directly behind object to receive the force.	Go as long as possible with partner without any sounds being made by hands.
Receive self-tossed balls.	Adjust hand placement to the level of the ball and shape of object.	Go as far away as possible from partner and still maintain quality of catch.
	Move to get behind object.	
Receive balls from different directions.	Anticipate where ball will land.	Same as all of above with the adjustment of an implement.
Receive balls from increasing distances and force levels.		
Receive ball both while stationary and moving.		
Receive manipulatable objects with implements (e.g., scoops, lacrosse sticks, hockey sticks, bats).	Same as all of above with the adjustment of an implement.	
Receive objects at increasing distances and force levels from a partner.		
Receive objects while both stationary and moving.		

to approach a new striking skill, how to receive force, or how to select experiences that will improve cardio-respiratory endurance.

Critical ideas, or aspects, are determined by the teacher before deciding how to develop the material for students. Along with the definition of the concept to be learned and the examples, identification of the critical ideas inherent in a concept prepares the teacher to do a developmental analysis of the concept for teaching.

Concepts to be transferred to a more limited range of context (e.g., zone defense to basketball; weight transfer to tennis) require only that the teacher have the students apply that concept to a particular setting.

Concepts to be transferred to new and unidentified experiences require a lengthy process of development. Concepts used in this way must be taught for transfer and to become automatic in the student's behavior. Because concept teaching developed to this level is lengthy and time consuming, teachers must carefully select the concepts they want to teach in this manner.

SUMMARY

1. Teaching fitness and lifetime physical activity requires specific planning in the curriculum and specific instructional procedures.

2. A major goal of our programs should be to develop physically active lifestyles. Teachers can teach for a physically active lifestyle.

3. Teachers have curriculum alternatives for organizing both fitness and lifetime fitness into their curriculums.

4. When the content to be taught is a complex game, with many different skills used in offensive and defensive relationships with others, the complexity of interrelationships between skills and the use of those skills must be considered. There are four stages in the development of a complex game, which progress from the development of mastery and control of the object to the use of skills in complex offensive and defensive arrangements.

5. At stage one, players acquire the ability to control an object.

6. At stage two, players acquire the ability to use skills in more complex contexts and to combine skills together skillfully.

7. At stage three, students acquire basic offensive and defensive strategies (tactics) for game play.

8. At stage four, players can play the game in complex environments.

9. Two common forms of games are invasion games and net games.

10. A games-for-understanding approach to teaching games and sports assumes that the tactics of the sport should be taught first.

11. A movement concept is a label for a group or class of motor responses or movement ideas that share similar relationships.

12. The intent in teaching movement concepts is transfer of learning from one situation to a new situation.

13. Movement concepts can be action words, movement qualities, movement principles, movement strategies, movement effects, and movement affects.

14. Movement concepts are taught by defining the concept for learners, providing many examples and opportunities to use the concept, and reinforcing the use of the concept in new situations.

15. Teachers who want to include fitness in their programs must first do long-term planning to decide what they want to teach and the best way to teach fitness in a K–12 program.

16. Teaching dance, gymnastics, and outdoor pursuits requires context-specific pedagogy that should be considered when approaching these content areas.

CHECKING YOUR UNDERSTANDING

1. Choose a team sport and make a list of four major tasks that might be included under each of the games stages.

2. Choose two skills from a team sport and describe how these skills are used in a game situation.

3. Describe how you might begin to teach tennis using a games-for-understanding approach.

4. List two different concepts under each of the major kinds of concepts typically included as content in physical education.

5. For one of the concepts listed in number four, describe the procedures you would use to teach that concept for transfer to a unique situation.

6. Describe five different ways a teacher might include fitness in a physical education curriculum.

7. List eight ideas that the teacher should consider when teaching each of the following:
   Folk dance
   Creative dance
   Gymnastics
   Outdoor pursuits

REFERENCES

Graham, G., Holt-Hale, S., & Parker, M. (2004). *Children moving: A reflective approach to teaching physical education* (6th ed.). Boston: McGraw-Hill.

Griffin, L., & Butler, J. (2005). (Eds.). *Teaching games for understanding: Theory, research and practice.* Champaign, IL: Human Kinetics.

Merrill, D. M. (Ed.). (1971). *Instructional design: Readings.* Englewood Cliffs, NJ: Prentice-Hall.

Mohnsen, B. (Ed.). (2003). *Concepts and principles of physical education: What every student needs to know.* Reston, VA: AAHPERD.

National Association for Sport and Physical Education (2004). *Moving into the future: National standards for physical education.* Reston, VA: NASPE.

Rink, J. (1993). Fitting into the curriculum. In D. Hohn, R. Pate, (Eds.), *Fitness in physical education.* Champaign, IL: Human Kinetics.

Rink, J. (Ed.). (1996). Tactical and skill approaches to teaching sport and games [Summer Monograph]. *Journal of Teaching in Physical Education, 14,* 4.

Siedentop, D., Hastie, P., & van der Mars, M. (2004). *Complete guide to sport education.* Champaign, IL: Human Kinetics.

Thorpe, R., Bunker, D., & Almond, L. (1986). *Rethinking games teaching.* Loughborough, UK: University of Technology, Department of Physical Education and Sport Science.

Turner, A., & Martinek, T. (1995). Teaching for understanding: A model for improving decision making during game play. *Quest, 47,* 44–63.

SUGGESTED READINGS

Cardinal, B., Cardinal, M., & Burger, M. (2005). Lifetime fitness for health course assessment. *JOPERD 76*(8), 48–52.

Consolo, K. (2007). Maximizing safety, social support and participation in walking/jogging/running classes. *JOPERD, 78*(8), 20–24.

Foley, J., Tindall, D., Lieberman, L., & Kim, S. (2007). How to develop disability awareness using the sport education model. *JOPERD, 78*(2), 32–37.

Kulinna, P., Zhu, W., Behnke, M., Johnson, R., McMullem, D., Turner, M., & Wolff, G. (1999). Six steps in developing and using fitness portfolios. *Teaching Elementary Physical Education, 10,* 15–17.

Lynn, S. (2002). Content specific pedagogy for teachers (feature). *Teaching Elementary Physical Education, 12*(3), 6–20.

McNamee, J. Brueker, S., Murray, T., & Speich, C. (2007). High-activity skills progression: A method for increasing MVPA. *JOPERD, 78*(7), 17–21.

McNamee, J., & Steffen, J. (2001). Getting off the ground with rock climbing. *Journal of Physical Education, Recreation and Dance, 12*(6), 26–30.

Morgan, C., Pangrazi, R., & Beighle, A. (2003). Using pedometers to promote physical activity in physical education. *Journal of Physical Education, Recreation and Dance, 74*(7), 33–38.

Pritchard, T., & McCollum, S. (2008). Bowling for a lifetime using sport education. *JOPERD, 79*(3), 17–23.

13 The Professional Teacher and the Continuous Learner

O V E R V I E W

Most preservice students in physical education have not thought much about what happens as they make the transition from being a full-time student to a full-time teacher. Like most transitions in life, the passage from student to teacher is an exciting time with high expectations. It is also a time that can be filled with a lot of self-doubt and uncertainty. This chapter will help to prepare you for the transition from student to teacher and to launch a rewarding professional career. The chapter emphasizes developing the commitment and skills to be a self-directed learner who accepts the responsibility for continued professional growth.

Standard 6: Professionalism

Physical education teacher candidates demonstrate dispositions essential to becoming effective professionals.
NASPE Beginning Teaching Standards, 2008

O U T L I N E

- **Teaching as a profession**
- **What does it mean to act professionally?**
  Professional teachers acquire the skills for best practice
  Professional teachers are continuous learners
- **Collecting information on your teaching**
  Maintaining a teaching portfolio
  Collecting data on the products and processes of teaching

- **Observing and analyzing your teaching**
  Deciding what to look for
  Choosing an observational method or tool to collect information
  Collecting data
  Analyzing and interpreting the meaning of data
  Making changes in the instructional process
  Monitoring change in teaching

■ TEACHING AS A PROFESSION

When you made the decision to go into teaching, you made the decision to join a profession. Professions in a society are awarded special status with accompanying privileges and responsibilities. Not all occupations are considered professions. Professions are usually characterized by the following:

The occupation requires extensive preparation and expertise.

Professionals in a field have a shared language not common to the general public.

The occupation provides an essential service.

Members share a strong service motivation; they are dedicated and committed to the service they provide.

The occupation is characterized by a high level of public trust.

There are agreed-upon technical and ethical standards that monitor entrance into the profession.

Members are socialized into and share a perspective on what constitutes "best practice," normally defined by professional organizations and a historical set of ethics and values.

Accountability for performance comes from within the profession.

Occupational practice is rooted in a discipline.

Practice of the occupation is free from direct on-the-job supervision of individual performance.

If you think about some of the ideas expressed in the preceding list, you will begin to realize that the world of work is different for professionals and nonprofessionals. Not only do professionals perform an essential service that not just anybody can do, but also there is an assumption by the public that individuals who practice the profession will act professionally. The public trust accorded to a profession might be considered directly proportional to the number of individuals within the profession who do act professionally.

■ WHAT DOES IT MEAN TO ACT PROFESSIONALLY?

To act professionally is to provide "state-of-the-art" service and to maintain your commitment to doing this throughout your career. Professionals in a field who do not act professionally and do not provide their clients with best practice reduce the trust the public confers on the profession. Each member of the profession has an obligation to preserve and develop public trust by doing a good job. There are many ways teachers can ensure that they will contribute to the profession and do a good job of teaching.

Professional Teachers Acquire the Skills for Best Practice

Professionals should be prepared at the start of their careers to provide best practice. Table 13.1 lists the beginning teaching standards developed by the National Association for Sport and Physical Education (2008). These are expectations that the profession has for the beginning teacher. Be aware of the expectations for best practice for this stage of your career. These standards are used to assess teacher preparation programs in physical education. A good teacher preparation program should give you the opportunity to develop these abilities and technically should not let you graduate unless you have acquired the expected skills, knowledge, and dispositions. It is up to you to take advantage of the opportunities provided to you. For many college students this requires a change in perspective from an *other-directedness* to a *self-directedness*. You will mature as a professional as you begin to want to do the best job that you can because of your commitment to providing students with the best possible experience and not because someone else is requiring you to do something.

As you finish your teacher preparation program, you might want to do a self-check to determine if you have the abilities described by these standards. If you do not, you will want to develop a plan to acquire these skills. Although it is reasonable for beginning teachers to learn a lot during their first few years from experience, it is not reasonable to expect that you will acquire these skills independently by practice alone. The college and university setting has the resources to help you acquire these skills, and during your initial preparation to be a teacher is the time that you should be working hard to develop these skills.

TABLE 13·1

National Standards for Beginning Teachers

Standard 1: Scientific and Theoretical Knowledge

Physical education teacher candidates know and apply discipline-specific scientific and theoretical concepts critical to the development of physically educated individuals.

Outcomes—Teacher candidates will:

1.1 Describe and apply physiological and biomechanical concepts related to skillful movement, physical activity, and fitness.

1.2 Describe and apply motor learning, psychological, and behavioral theory related to skillful movement, physical activity, and fitness.

1.3 Describe and apply motor development theory and principles related to skillful movement, physical activity, and fitness.

1.4 Identify historical, philosophical, and social perspectives of physical education issues and legislation.

1.5 Analyze and correct critical elements of motor skills and performance concepts.

Standard 2: Skill and Fitness Based Competence*

Physical education teacher candidates are physically educated individuals with the knowledge and skills necessary to demonstrate competent movement performance and health enhancing fitness as delineated in the NASPE K–12 Standards.

Outcomes—Teacher candidates will:

2.1 Demonstrate personal competence in motor skill performance for a variety of physical activities and movement patterns.

2.2 Achieve and maintain a health-enhancing level of fitness.

2.3 Demonstrate performance concepts related to skillful movement in a variety of physical activities.

Standard 3: Planning and Implementation

Physical education teacher candidates plan and implement a variety of developmentally appropriate learning experiences and content aligned with local, state, and national standards to develop physically educated individuals.

Outcomes—Teacher candidates will:

3.1 Design and implement short- and long-term plans that are linked to program and instructional goals as well as a variety of student needs.

3.2 Develop appropriate (e.g., measurable, developmentally appropriate, performance based) goals and objectives aligned with local, state, and/or national standards that lead to student learning.

3.3 Design and implement content that is aligned with lesson objectives.

3.4 Plan and implement effective demonstrations, explanations, instructional cues, and prompts to link physical activity concepts to appropriate learning experiences.

3.5 Plan for the management of resources to provide active, fair, and equitable learning experiences.

3.6 Adapt instruction to diverse student needs, adding specific accommodations and/or modifications for student exceptionalities.

3.7 Plan and implement progressive and sequential instruction that addresses the diverse needs of all students.

3.8 Design and implement student learning experiences that integrate technology.

Standard 4: Instructional Delivery and Management

Physical education teacher candidates use effective communication and pedagogical skills and strategies to enhance student engagement and learning.

Outcomes—Teacher candidates will:

4.1 Demonstrate effective verbal and nonverbal communication skills across a variety of instructional formats.

4.2 Provide instructional feedback that results in skill acquisition, student learning, and motivation.

4.3 Recognize the changing dynamics of the environment and adjust instructional tasks based on student responses.

4.4 Utilize managerial rules, routines, and transitions to create and maintain an effective learning environment.

4.5 Implement strategies to help students demonstrate responsible personal and social behaviors in a productive learning environment.

*Physical education teacher candidates with special needs are allowed and encouraged to utilize a variety of accommodations and/or modifications to demonstrate competency and performance concepts (modified/adapted equipment, augmentative communication devices, multimedia devices, etc.) and fitness (weight programs, exercise logs, etc.).

(continued)

TABLE 13·1

National Standards for Beginning Teachers—con't

Standard 5: Impact on Student Learning

Physical education teacher candidates utilize assessments and reflection to foster student learning and inform instructional decisions.

Outcomes—Teacher candidates will:

5.1 Select or create appropriate assessments that will measure student achievement of goals and objectives.

5.2 Use a variety of appropriate assessments to evaluate student learning before, during, and after instruction.

5.3 Utilize the reflective cycle to implement change in teacher performance, student learning, and instructional goals and decisions.

Standard 6: Professionalism

Physical education teacher candidates demonstrate dispositions essential to becoming effective professionals.

Outcomes—Teacher candidates will:

6.1 Demonstrate behaviors that are consistent with the belief that all students can become physically educated individuals.

6.2 Participate in activities that enhance collaboration and lead to professional growth and development.

6.3 Demonstrate behaviors that are consistent with the professional ethics of highly qualified teachers.

6.4 Communicate in ways that convey respect and sensitivity.

Source: National Association for Sport and Physical Education (2008).

Professional Teachers Are Continuous Learners

The practice of teaching is driven by a desire to nurture and direct the growth and learning of students. Teachers committed to their profession measure their success by their ability to facilitate student growth and learning. Your teacher preparation program can give you the skills described as beginning teacher skills (NASPE, 2008), but it will be up to you to be a continuous learner. Continuous learners in the teaching profession stay current in their field, take responsibility for continued growth, and are reflective in their practice.

Stay current in your field. Even the most-prepared teachers can lose their ability to provide students with state-of-the-art teaching when they do not stay current in their field. Like other professions, the knowledge base for how best to teach and what to teach grows with each year. Accountability for staying current comes primarily from a teacher's commitment. Rarely are teachers dismissed because they are not current. Teachers have been given a lot of flexibility in their work hours and the extent to which they are monitored. The public assumes that the lack

of direct supervision is necessary for professionals to use their time to stay current and to contribute to the profession. Unless you take advantage of the professional opportunities available to you, you will quickly become outdated.

One of the best ways to stay current in a field is to read professional journals and books and to attend professional workshops, meetings, and conferences—to be involved. Opportunities for professional development will come in many forms, including an increasing number of Internet services and dialogues directly related to teaching physical education. Box 13.1 describes opportunities for joining professional organizations and their advantages. Box 13.2 describes the professional journals most popular for the practicing physical educator. Box 13.3 describes the most popular websites for physical educators. With today's Internet search tools, physical educators can find information from credible sources on almost any sport or activity.

A profession is usually responsible for ensuring that the public receives best practice through maintaining continuing education programs for practitioners. Many local school districts provide opportunities for physical education teachers in the

BOX 13·1

Professional Organizations for the Practicing Physical Education Teacher

How professional organizations serve you

1. Professional organizations play a major role in representing your interests politically. They allow teachers to speak as one voice in the political environment that creates policy directly impacting you and your students.
2. Professional organizations educate the public as to the purpose and importance of the profession.
3. Professional organizations are committed to providing service to their members to disseminate "best practice." Journals, newsletters, and other publications keep you abreast of what is going on in your field. Conventions and workshops provide opportunities for teachers to share and interact with each other as well as learn new skills and become more knowledgeable.

Generic education organizations

National Education Association (NEA)
Association for Supervision and Curriculum Development (ASCD)

Organizations for physical education teachers

National Level

National Association for Sport and Physical Education (NASPE) (a national association in the larger organization of the American Alliance for Health, Physical Education, Recreation and Dance [AAHPERD]).

State Level

The state level of the alliance is usually designated with the state initials preceding AHPERD (e.g., SCAHPERD for South Carolina).

Why do I have to pay?

Professionals who join professional organizations must pay membership dues, usually on a yearly basis. Professional organizations cost money to operate and cannot function without the support of their members. The more members a professional organization has, the greater the potential impact the professional organization can have in educating the public and, perhaps more important, the policymakers who directly impact the practice of the profession. The more members an organization has, the greater the service to the organization's membership.

BOX 13·2

Professional Journals for Physical Education

Subscribing to professional journals is one of the easiest and least expensive ways for professionals to stay current in their field. The most popular professional journals in physical education that directly serve the practitioner are listed here with the name of the publisher.

The Journal of Physical Education, Recreation and Dance (AAHPERD)
Strategies (AAHPERD)
Teaching Elementary Physical Education (Human Kinetics Publishers)
The Physical Educator Phi Epsilon Kappa Fraternity
Journal for Teaching Physical Education (Human Kinetics Publishers)

district to hold in-service workshops specifically designed to meet your needs. Teachers should look at these days as opportunities to learn and to grow professionally. They should play a major role in ensuring that their district provides them with meaningful opportunities to grow and to develop by suggesting programs that would be beneficial, putting on programs for other teachers, and visiting other teachers in the district and other districts to learn from them.

More in-depth opportunities for you to grow professionally and personally are provided by coursework offered by most colleges and universities. Some coursework will provide you with an increased knowledge about the content or the learners you are working with, and some coursework will be more directly

BOX 13·3

Popular Websites and Listservs for Physical Education

AAHPERD   *www.aahperd.org*

NASPE (link from AAHPERD)

NASPE-TALK (link from NASPE)

NASPE-FORUM (link from NASPE)

U.S. Department of Education   *www.ed.gov*

Fitness Link   *fitnesslink.com*

FITNESSGRAM   *www.cooperinst.org/5.html*

PE Central: lesson plans, activities   *pecentral.org*

National Coalition for Promoting Physical Activity
   www.ncppa.org

President's Council on Physical Fitness and Sport
   www.fitness.gov

National Association of Governor's Councils on Physical
   Fitness and Sport   *fitnesslink.com/govcounc.htm*

PE Links 4 U   *www.pelinks4u.org*

ESPN: in-depth sports rules, etc.   *espn.sportzone.com*

American Heart Association   *www.americanheart.org*

Walking   *www.walkingabout.com*

Student social responsibility   *www.hellison.com*

Fitness   *www.fitnesstutor.com*

Aerobic dance   *www.turnstep.com*

National Strength and Conditining Association
   www.lift.org

Links to many sports
   www.yahoo.com/Sports_and_ Recreation

Technology   *www.PEsoftware.com*

related to the teaching process. Many states require teachers to go back to school on a regular basis, and most teacher pay scales reward teachers for the accumulation of college credits and advanced degrees. Teachers who find it difficult to both work and go to school usually use the summer months when school is out to return to school.

Take responsibility for your growth. Although staying current in terms of defining best

practice is a major task of the teacher as a continuous learner, professional teachers also know how to use experience as a vehicle for professional growth. Teachers can learn a great deal about teaching through experience alone. There are problems, however, with a learn-through-experience model of improving teaching skills. First, many teachers do not learn through experience—if this were the case, every teacher with ten years of experience would be a good teacher, and this is not so. Second, by changing what they are doing on a trial-and-error basis, many teachers make the wrong change for the wrong reason. For example, a beginning teacher might conclude, "Students responsible for independently setting out apparatus and working in small groups fight with each other." As a result of this conclusion, the teacher might then decide to take the responsibility for setting out the equipment. The problem, however, is not in the students but in the way in which the teacher taught students to take responsibility. When trial and error is used, teachers often make decisions based on insufficient information and with less than a total perspective.

Teachers who have strategies to help them improve their teaching are more likely to grow as teachers and be able to use their experience for professional growth. You will be observed and analyzed by others while student teaching and throughout your teaching career. Sometimes this supervision will involve more subjective analyses of your teaching and sometimes more objective analyses. Your growth as a teacher is not likely to come as much from others as it is from your ability to take the responsibility for your growth. Continuing growth as a teacher depends largely on your ability to do the following:

- Reflect on relationships between what you do as a teacher, why you do it, and the effects of what you do on students in relation to your teaching goals.

- Collect information on the teaching-learning process that will help you make judgments about what is occurring and use information that you collect to make changes in what you do.

National Board Certification. After three years of teaching, certified teachers can apply for National Board Certification. This program was designed to reward excellence in teaching, and in many states teachers are rewarded financially for seeking and obtaining National Board Certification. The National Board for Professional Teaching Standards has identified five core propositions for what teachers should know and be able to do, around which the criteria for certification are built:

- Teachers are committed to students and their learning.
- Teachers know the subjects they teach and how to teach those subjects to students.
- Teachers are responsible for managing and monitoring student learning.
- Teachers think systematically about their practice and learn from experience.
- Teachers are members of learning communities (NBTPS, 2008).

The process to become a board-certified teacher is an extensive one, and most people who have participated in the process view it as a valuable experience. The NBTPS.org website provides all the information needed on how to apply and what is involved in the process.

Become a reflective practitioner. To grow as a teacher you will have to learn to be a reflective practitioner. The reflective practitioner takes time to *think* about what he or she is doing and why. Reflective practitioners are willing to ask good questions about the goals and practices of their teaching and to keep an open mind about the meaning of their experiences. Reflective practitioners are willing to tie the big ideas about teaching (e.g., fostering in each child a positive sense of self) with a routine teaching act (e.g., choosing teams) and see the connection. Some of the questions you will want to ask yourself about your experiences are the following:

- What happened in this experience, and why did it happen?
- What am I doing/not doing that contributes to my long-term as well as short-term goals?
- How do I feel about what I am doing as a teacher?

The ability to observe teaching and student learning is an essential skill for all teachers.

- Did anything important happen to the students today? To me, the teacher?
- What made what I taught important to the students?
- Which students did I "connect" with today? Not "connect" with?
- Did my teaching work? Why did what happened work/not work? What did I do better today?

One way to give structure to the reflective experience is to use a reflective journal similar to what was suggested for students in chapter 11. The Real World box on p. 311 presents the entry of an experienced teacher in a reflective journal. Excellence in teaching is a journey, not a destination. The journey on the road to excellence involves reflection on not only the appropriateness of the big ideas that surround what we do (e.g., our goals and objectives) and the beliefs that

THE REAL WORLD

Journal Entry for a Reflective Journal

Today was a disaster. I wanted the students to begin to use the video camera set up to do some self-assessment, and I was not prepared for how much structure they would need to do this without interrupting the normal flow of the class. Students were lined up in back of the camera waiting to tape their performance and half of them did not know how to run the camera so they were interrupting the rest of the class on a continuing basis. For the next lesson I am going to have to spend some time and teach the students how this all can be done without interfering with the rest of the class.

BOX 13·4

The Reflective Process at Work

Kathy came into teaching because she had positive personal experiences in physical education and athletics. Kathy had a teacher/coach who took a personal interest in her and always seemed to know what to say and do to help Kathy be the best athlete she could be and also be the best person she could be. Kathy's coach helped her to be supportive of others and to be a positive leader. Kathy's coach also helped her to sort out what was important in life and to put athletics in perspective.

Kathy's beginning teaching experiences were in a low-socioeconomic community. She began her school year wanting to make a contribution to her students, who she believed needed a positive role model and someone to help them build their self-esteem. Within a short time Kathy's classes were out of control—chaos prevailed. Kathy spent several months convinced that she had made a mistake going into teaching and questioned her vision of a better world. When she returned for her second year, Kathy began a new strategy. She decided that her vision was not wrong but that her methods of getting to her vision were inappropriate. Kathy began assessing the effect of her teaching on students. She did this both formally, by videotaping what was happening in her classes and collecting some objective data, and informally, by judging what was working and what was not working. She did this during her classes, as well as after her classes, sometimes just pulling herself away from what was going on in her class to take thirty seconds to ask herself what was happening and why. When she found things that did not work, she asked why and remained open to the idea that she was largely responsible for this. Kathy did not lose her vision, but she decided to make her behavior more appropriate for where the students were in relation to that vision. She gained patience. She stayed at the same school for seven more years and in that time was able to move her classes to many aspects of self-control that were part of her vision. Although she was not able to reach all students, she made a major impact on the lives of many.

govern our actions (e.g., I think physical education should . . .), but also the effectiveness and viability of the most basic instructional skills (e.g., our selection of cues). All of these levels of practice come together in the teaching act, which becomes the "impact" level for what we do. You cannot sort out one without also considering the other.

The process of reflection can help you clarify your goals as a teacher and decide how to best accomplish those goals. Consider the experience of Kathy presented in box 13.4. Kathy needed to gain control of her classes. To do this, she realized that she was going to have to be much more structured in her teaching than she wanted to be. Kathy had the skill to add and remove structure as needed. Because Kathy had a vision of her potential contribution to a "bigger picture," she was not satisfied with just having control and was able to gradually remove the structure.

Teachers can learn to be more reflective about their teaching if they will set aside time to reflect on their teaching. Sometimes this means that you may have to put aside some time after a class to think about what went on. Sometimes you may need to design some questions that will guide your reflection, and sometimes you may want to structure the process of reflection even more by forcing yourself to take a few minutes out of every day to write in a journal about your teaching and about learning how to be a teacher. The process of reflection can be facilitated through the use of videotapes or audiotapes of lessons, which allows you to appraise what went on from the comfort of your living room or office.

■ COLLECTING INFORMATION ON YOUR TEACHING

One of the best ways to grow as a teacher is to look directly and specifically at the products and processes of your teaching. Two approaches to do this are to maintain a teaching portfolio and to collect objective data on student learning and the teaching process.

Maintaining a Teaching Portfolio

Chapter 11 talks about the use of the portfolio to document student performance over time. The electronic portfolio makes collecting and saving the products of your teaching easier. The portfolio is also useful for teachers to document their teaching performance. The portfolio provides a useful vehicle for you to look comprehensively at how your students have changed over time in terms of your goals for them as well as how you have changed over time in terms of your teaching. One of the most useful aspects of portfolios is the process of collecting what is to go into the portfolio. When you have to make a decision about what is important to go into the portfolio, you are engaging in a process of reflection and engagement about what you are doing that is growth producing. Developing a portfolio and deciding what should go into it encourages you to reflect on what you think you should be doing and how well you are doing it. Examples of items teachers might include in the portfolio are as follows:

- Examples of student progress in your class
- Assessments of student performance on standards
- Examples of lesson plans and curriculum and unit plans that show your improvement over time

- Material that documents the development of assessment material
- Videotapes/DVDs of what you consider to be evidence of teaching that matches your goals
- Self-evaluation of your teaching
- Observational data on your teaching
- Your reflective journal
- Documentation of attendance at professional meetings
- Reflections on the meaning of books or articles you have read or meetings you have attended
- Evaluations of teaching done by others (administrators, students, peers)

Collecting Data on the Products and Processes of Teaching

As valuable as reflection may be to you as a developing teacher, there will be times when you will want to collect objective data on your teaching. Teachers' perceptions of what has occurred in their classes are often not accurate. Teachers heavily involved in the process of teaching are often not able to observe what is happening in their classes with the detail needed to make good judgments about what may be contributing to their success or problems.

Direct observation of students and the teacher can provide more accurate information on some aspects of the teaching-learning process. Although you can put information on student products into your portfolio, you will also be concerned about what you do as a teacher; therefore, you will want to collect observational data on the instructional process.

Direct **systematic observation and analysis** of instruction is a process that allows you to collect objective information on the instructional process and analyze that information in a meaningful way. This information is usually collected by a live observer or by using audiotapes or videotapes in the form of data on the instructional process. Direct observation is useful to collect information on what students did in a class as well as the instructional skills used by the teacher. Unlike reflection, direct observation is designed to provide objective information on the instructional process. Though direct observation cannot tell you what to value about what is happening in your teaching, it can provide you with information from which you can make judgments about what is happening.

Most beginning teachers are still in the process of refining their basic instructional skills. Direct observation is particularly useful to collect data in this area. Some of the most common concerns of beginning teachers relative to the development of their basic instructional skills for which data are usually collected using systematic observation are the following:

- The amount of instructional time spent organizing a class and/or how this is done
- The amount of appropriate practice time students have
- The progressive sequence of the teacher's tasks
- The amount of decision making permitted students
- The teacher's primary role during activity time
- Student off-task behavior
- The type and quality of teacher feedback
- Student social interaction with each other
- The task presentation of the teacher

Direct observation is a process usually described in the following steps:

1. Deciding what to look for
2. Choosing an observational method or tool to collect information
3. Collecting data
4. Analyzing and interpreting the meaning of data

Of the steps listed, perhaps the most difficult one to do is the first one. Many times teachers know that something is not going well, but they are not sure what it is and why it is not going well. Events often have many alternative explanations. Box 13.5 (p. 314) describes some of the questions that teachers might ask about their teaching and some instructional factors that might be related to their questions. After asking a question, the teacher would choose a way to look at some of the factors that might be related to that question, would choose an observational tool or technique to collect information, collect data, and then interpret the meaning of the data.

Although teachers are free to design an observational tool, many useful tools have already been developed that the teacher might want to consider. The last chapter of this book describes basic observational techniques and tools for looking at the following:

- Student motor activity
- Student use of time
- Content development
- Teacher feedback
- Student conduct
- Task presentation
- Teacher movement and location

No one expects you to be a master teacher your first year as a teacher. You are expected, however, to look at your skills and abilities as a master teacher "in process." This means that you should be able to set goals for your professional growth and be able to work toward meeting those goals. Professional goals can include one or more of the following:

- Learn to teach new content.
- Improve some aspect of your teaching.
- Set up a research project to answer a question you have had regarding the teaching-learning process.
- Share your skills with others.

Many of the previous chapters have included material that will help you with developing a strategy to meet these goals.

◼ OBSERVING AND ANALYZING YOUR TEACHING
Deciding What to Look For

When teachers are preparing for the profession, their instructors and supervisors, to a large extent, select what they are to observe in their teaching and help them to analyze what is good and what requires change. Practicing teachers, however, must make these judgments based on their knowledge of effective teaching and their instructional goals in a particular teaching setting. The selection of what to look at in teaching depends on where teachers think they may need improvement based on their observations of the outcomes of their teaching. The analysis begins with defining the problem and seeking possible solutions, as was described in box 13.5.

BOX 13·5

Questions About Outcomes and Possible Related Dimensions

Question	Possible related dimensions
Is the teacher getting the kind of quality being sought for student responses?	Inappropriate task; lack of practice time; inappropriate development of material; inappropriate quantity and quality of feedback; inappropriate cue selection; low student motivation
Is the teacher spending a lot of time managing after students begin working on a task?	Poor task clarity; inappropriate environmental arrangements; inappropriate tasks
Does the teacher's feedback tend to be general?	Lack of knowledge of the subject matter; failure to plan specifically; inappropriate teaching roles during activity; poor observation skills
Do students fail to work within the dimensions of the task?	Poor task clarity and cue selection; inappropriate tasks; inconsistent monitoring; inappropriate degree of task structure
Do some students fail to become involved?	Need for task modification; inappropriate environmental arrangements; unclear teacher expectations; poor class social interaction
Is the teacher's practice time limited?	Inappropriate use of student time; inappropriate use of teacher time; inappropriate practice organization
Do management transitions consume more time than they should?	Unnecessarily divided management tasks; student inattention; overly complex organization relative to practice time; failure to teach frequently used routines
Does student on-task behavior decrease with time spent on task?	Unchanging task focus; inappropriate tasks; inappropriate teaching roles during activity
Does the teacher feel like a police officer in the classroom?	Unclear teaching expectations; inappropriate degree of structure; inconsistent monitoring; inappropriate content
Are students not successful with the task?	Inappropriate tasks; inappropriate task presentation; inappropriate feedback; lack of practice time
Do students fail to respond creatively when asked to?	Poorly defined concept; feedback inconsistent with creativity; nonsupportive environmental arrangements; poor class social interaction

This list is by no means complete, but it should help teachers begin the analytic process. Teachers may want to verify the problem through observation that specifically focuses on the dimension identified. Determining possible causes of problems is not easy and requires a great deal of reflection on the part of the teacher. Few of the causes listed are directly attributable to students. The teacher is in control of the instructional process and should be able to adjust that process to students, needs. Comments such as the following may be true but offer little help in solving the problem:

- "The students weren't listening."
- "Students don't have the arm strength."
- "The students in this class never do what they're told."

Teachers should think in terms of how their teaching can change student behavior in a positive direction. Teaching decisions must be based on their appropriateness for specific teaching conditions. Once possible causes are identified, data are systematically collected to determine whether a particular cause is contributing to the problem in any way. This is the developing-an-awareness stage.

Once the data have been collected, teachers can decide whether the teaching behavior is appropriate for the group of students with whom the teacher is working. Before data on problems, causes, and possible solutions can be collected, however, a tool or technique to observe what is happening in your class must be chosen.

Choosing an Observational Method or Tool to Collect Information

Once the teacher has decided what to look for, a method of collecting data must be selected. Similar types of information can be collected in different ways, as described in chapter 14. The decision of what method to use or what tool to use depends primarily on what type of data the teacher is looking for and the practicality, reliability, and validity of the instrument.

It is possible to collect information on an informal basis by looking at a videotaped lesson or listening to an audiotaped lesson and making a few notes on the instructional behavior or instructional event being examined. This procedure is valuable, particularly if time is important and if teachers are not sure exactly what behavior they are interested in focusing on. For example, a teacher trying to determine causes of off-task behavior might isolate an incident of off-task behavior in some students and begin zeroing in on the possible causes by reviewing the events leading up to that behavior. Although this analysis is not aided by specific instrumentation, it is systematic. The teacher might identify several plausible causes, including teacher clarity of task presentation, organizational clarity, and teacher positioning. Next, the teacher might choose a specific instrument to isolate these causes and study them in more detail.

Most instructional analysis is aided by using a specific tool to look at specific instructional events. These tools must be selected with care if the information recorded is to be useful. *Observational tools* are valuable to the extent that they do the following:

- Provide information important to the question being asked
- Are practical
- Provide objectivity by inferring as little as possible about the behavior being studied
- Can be used reliably
- Collect valid data

High-inference tools require much more observer judgment than do **low-inference tools.** Tools that require observers to infer little from the behavior they are recording produce the most accurate data. Observers looking for the occurrence or nonoccurrence of demonstration in a lesson do not have to make many inferences based on what they see. Observers looking for accurate demonstrations must use their judgment a great deal more. To define *accurate,* criteria must be established that can be judged through observation, and observers must be consistent in using the established criteria. Criteria for accuracy of demonstrations might include the following:

- Uses the whole action
- Uses accurate speed
- Uses accurate flow of the movement
- Includes implements or objects appropriately
- Ensures that conditions of demonstration reflect conditions in which the skill will be used

The purpose of this discussion is not to discourage teachers from looking at behaviors that are hard to make judgments about, but to encourage them to establish criteria for what they are looking at. The criteria teachers select must be put in directly observable terms so that difficult judgments are made as low inference as possible. Teachers want the information they collect to be useful. It can be useful only if they can be reasonably sure that the information reflects what happened.

Reliability of the observational tool. The term *reliability,* when used in conjunction with observational tools, can have several meanings. First, it refers to whether the tool can be used to observe in a consistent way. To observe accurately, the observer must code or record a behavior, such as positive feedback, each time it appears and not when it does not appear. Reliability is usually determined by comparing the observations of one observer with those of another observer considered to be an expert. When no expert is available, reliability is usually determined by *agreement* between more than one observer on the same event. Agreement between observers is usually called **interobserver agreement.** Reliability also depends on the observer's ability to be *consistent* (i.e., to code the same behavior in the same way more than once). Would an observer code the same lesson the same way on different days? Agreement of one observer with himself or herself is usually called **intraobserver agreement.**

Reliability is a function of an observational measure and not an observational tool in its entirety. In other words, a particular observational tool may enable the teacher to observe some events reliably and not others.

To use observational tools to collect information, teachers should test themselves to see if they can observe reliably what they are looking at. Many sophisticated means of testing reliability are available for research purposes. For a teacher seeking improvement in teaching skills, one of the easiest ways to compute reliability is through the use of simple percentage of agreement. Simple percentage of agreement is computed with the formula presented in box 13.6.

Researchers use varying criteria for reliability, depending on the sophistication of the tool. For purposes of self-improvement, the reliability of the tools teachers use should be at least 70 percent.

Validity of the observational tool.   The term *validity* refers to the degree to which an observational tool measures what it purports to measure. Validity is critical in choosing an observational tool. For example, to look at the amount of *personalizing* a teacher did with students, personalization might be defined using the following behaviors:

- Teacher calls students by name.
- Teacher touches students.
- Teacher refers to experiences students have inside and outside of class.

A system could be designed that counted the number of times teachers exhibited these behaviors. It could then be said that teachers who exhibited more of these behaviors personalized more with students than teachers who engaged in these behaviors less frequently. However, is this necessarily true? Are there other ways teachers personalize? Is every time a teacher calls a student by name a valid example of personalizing?

Validity is difficult to measure. Validity could be added to the behaviors described by attaching some conditions to the behaviors (e.g., teacher touches student with *intent* to personalize). Another category could be added to record unpredicted incidents of teacher personalization. Attaching conditions to the behaviors and allowing observers to make judgments about events could add to the validity of what is described. In many cases, however, these changes would also decrease the reliability of the information collected.

It is difficult to design instrumentation that is valid and reliable. Reliability is a major factor in validity. If the data are reliable but do not validly reflect what is being looked at, the data are not useful. On the other hand, valid data that are not reliable are of no use either. Sometimes it is worth sacrificing some reliability if this enables the observer to look at events in teaching that are difficult to observe. Nevertheless, *observers should strive for valid and reliable data.*

To collect reliable and valid information about their teaching, teachers must be skilled in the use of the instrument they choose. If the data are to be used exclusively for a teacher's personal improvement, it is not as critical that the teacher agree with other observers on what is and what is not a described behavior (interobserver agreement). What *is* critical is that the teacher agree with himself or herself (intraobserver agreement).

Before teachers begin using an observational tool, they must define the instructional events they want to collect information on and be able to give numerous examples of these events. For example, assume a teacher wants to observe the off-task behavior of students practicing throwing ground-level and high fly balls to a partner. Which of the following events would be considered off-task behavior?

- Partners are standing next to each other chatting.
- Partners are using high fly balls only.

BOX 13·6

Formula to Compute Simple Percentage of Agreement

$$\text{Percentage of agreement} = \frac{\text{Number of agreements}}{\text{Number of agreements} + \text{Disagreements}} \times 100$$

In simple observational systems, such as determining the time spent in activity, the agreement between two observers might be computed in the following way:

Observer 1 = Activity time of 35 minutes
Observer 2 = Activity time of 45 minutes
Agreement = 35
Disagreement = 10
Percentage of agreement = $\frac{35}{45} \times 100 = 77.7\%$

If working with a ten-category system, the scores for two observers would be described as follows:

Category	Observer 1 Number of behaviors	Percentage of behaviors	Observer 2 Number of behaviors	Percentage of behaviors
1	28	18	15	10
2	18	11	16	11
3	3	2	7	5
4	30	19	29	20
5	18	11	16	10
6	16	10	13	9
7	18	11	22	15
8	18	11	22	15
9	6	4	3	2
10	4	3	4	3
Totals	159	100	147	100

The column labeled "Number of behaviors" represents the number of times each observer recorded a behavior in each of the categories. The column labeled "Percentage of behaviors" gives the percentage of the total number of behaviors represented by each category.

To compute percentage of agreement for a system such as this, the difference in percentages between the two observers for each category is recorded. For this example the computation would be as follows:

Category	Percentage difference between observers
1	8
2	0
3	3
4	1
5	0
6	1
7	4
8	3
9	2
10	0
	22% Disagreement

Percentage of agreement is computed by subtracting total disagreement from 100:
Percentage of agreement = $100 - 22 = 78\%$

- One partner makes no attempt to catch the ball but backs out of the way.
- Partners are too far from each other to catch the ball before it bounces.

Whether the teacher considers these events off-task behaviors is determined by the teacher's definition of off-task behavior and by the specific ground rules chosen for applying that definition. There are few absolutely clear, black-and-white instructional events. The difficulty of observation is to decide which events, out of all those events that fall into the gray area of decision making, the teacher will focus on.

Teachers can improve their reliability in the use of an instrument by anticipating gray areas in advance and designing a set of ground rules for making decisions about these events. Throughout the data collection, they will need to revise their definitions or reexamine the instrument definitions to observe reliably and accurately.

Once teachers have defined the behavior they want to observe and have chosen the events they will collect data on, they must practice using the observational tool. There is no substitute for practice. After teachers begin to get some consistency in their observations, they must check their reliability. This can be done by using the instrument on a representative sample of their teaching or on another's teaching in a similar environment. The same lesson should be coded twice, and the reliability should then be computed using the percentage-of-agreement formula described in box 13.6 (p. 317). At least one full lesson should be used to determine reliability. Teachers should work with the tool until they have achieved a percentage of agreement of at least 70 percent.

Collecting Data

One problem teachers face in the schools is how to collect information on their teaching while they are teaching. Several alternatives exist for the teacher interested in self-improvement:

- Audiotape lessons
- Video lessons
- Ask colleagues for help
- Ask students for help

Audiotape lessons. Many teaching behaviors can be observed through the use of audiotape alone. *Audiotape* offers several advantages over other ways of collecting information. The teacher does not have to depend on anyone else, and the equipment is readily available and inexpensive and can be used over and over for different purposes.

It is recommended that the teacher wear the tape recorder when recording. It is possible to place a recorder somewhere in the gymnasium and record much of what is going on, but the quality of the recording is not satisfactory. Knapsacks, jackets with large pockets, or belts to which recorders can be attached can be used to hold recorders if more specialized equipment is not available. Microphones can be clipped or pinned to clothing, but most built-in microphones also do a good job.

Audiotape is useful for many instructional events at which it is not necessary to collect visual data. Even when videotape or other tools are used to collect data, it is highly recommended that teachers use audiotape on a continuous basis to listen to their teaching.

Video lessons. Some instructional events require the visual observation of the activities of students and teachers. For example, data on teacher positioning, accuracy of teacher feedback, or student movement responses to tasks cannot be obtained by audiotape. *Video* is extremely useful because the teacher can observe the results of behavior on student work and can replay the video to look at many different dimensions of teaching.

Camcorders that record digital data have made collecting video much more convenient. Most schools have video equipment available, and all teachers should be familiar with the operation of this valuable tool. Some schools have personnel assigned to help teachers use the equipment or to do the recording. If no other assistance is available, an older student who is not participating can be asked to run the camera, or teachers can leave the camera set up in a corner of the gymnasium with the lens on wide angle.

One word of caution on the use of video—the microphones on some cameras are not sensitive enough for large gymnasiums, particularly when the gymnasium is noisy. Whenever possible, cordless microphones, which have also become much less expensive, should be used with the video equipment.

Ask colleagues for help. It is possible for teachers to improve their teaching without the assistance of others, but it does help to have others interested in what the teachers are doing. Data collection is easier when more than one teacher is interested in improving teaching skills through systematic means. Working with other teachers also provides a needed support system and another set of eyes for analysis.

Teachers tend to be defensive about their teaching, and this inhibits shared work to improve teaching. Defensive positions stem primarily from a feeling that one is not as good as one should be. Perhaps it would help to know that all teachers can profit from efforts to improve their teaching skills. Even a teacher's superiors and supervisors (I include myself) are much better at describing what is wrong than they are at doing what should be done.

Ask students to help. Students can be taught to use simple observational systems and to run equipment, and most are delighted to be asked. Students who have free time during the school day or who are not participating can be valuable observers for many behaviors and instructional events. *Students should not be removed from class time,* however, to perform this function.

Analyzing and Interpreting the Meaning of Data

Most of the tools described in this text are non-evaluative tools. They help to describe what occurred but do not tell the teacher if what occurred was good or bad. *Evaluative judgments* must be made using information on the following:

- The conventional wisdom of the field of teaching
- The teacher's instructional goals
- Information on the students
- The specific teaching situation of the lesson

For example, suppose a teacher's analysis shows the class receiving only 30 percent practice time. How would these data be interpreted? There are tolerable limits for some instructional events beyond which no lesson should go. For example, activity time should probably never fall below 50 percent under any circumstances, and in most cases, although not all, it should be higher. If new material is being introduced or the teacher is working on management skills or affective concerns, there is reason to consider lower activity levels appropriate.

Most teaching behaviors have desirable limits for specific situations. The degree to which a teacher is working within these limits must be interpreted by the teacher based on the data collected. For example, a teacher working with students in game strategies should have a high percentage of feedback to students related to the strategy and not the mechanics of the movement. A high percentage of feedback on mechanics may indicate that students are not ready for a stage three games experience.

Interpreting the meaning of the data obtained through observation and deciding on the appropriateness of the behavior described test the analytic skills of even the most competent researcher. The process is an exciting one, however, and provides teachers with valuable insight not only into their teaching, but also into the instructional process as a highly interdependent set of instructional events.

Decisions about the appropriateness of teaching behavior are best made over many lessons. Teachers need the freedom to respond to the day-to-day needs of learners in a class. If, however, patterns of behavior are identified over several lessons that clearly describe teaching behaviors beyond desired limits (i.e., little feedback, little activity time, a great deal of off-task behavior, little demonstration), there is cause for concern.

Making Changes in the Instructional Process

Making a change in teaching is not easy, even when teachers identify the change they want to make and are fully aware of what they are doing. Most likely they have been doing what they are doing for a long time, and the behavior is a natural one for them. New behavior does not feel natural and may even feel awkward at first.

Change can be made easier by initially limiting expectations and setting temporary goals that will help teachers on their way to a larger goal. For instance, if teachers are not accustomed to giving specific feedback, they might begin with a small ratio of specific to general feedback and then gradually increase it.

Change can be expedited if teachers do not try to change more than one process teaching behavior (i.e., one that occurs during instruction). It is difficult to keep track of more than one process variable because teachers must remain conscious of their behavior and teach at the same time. Changing their behavior takes much effort and a willingness to tolerate initial frustration if they are not able to immediately accomplish what they set out to do.

Monitoring Change in Teaching

After teachers decide to change teaching behavior, they should verify that change through additional observations of their teaching. It is possible to think that a change has occurred when, in reality, it has not occurred to any great extent. Teachers who have fully developed an awareness of their behavior usually do know the extent of the changes they have made, but few teachers can remain aware for long periods. New teaching behaviors, like new motor skills, must be practiced until they become automatic. To that end, checking the progress of change is necessary.

SUMMARY

1. Members of a profession have privileges granted to them by the public and responsibilities to the public not given to occupations that are not professional.
2. Teachers who act professionally have acquired the skills of best practice and are continuous learners who stay current in their field, take responsibility for their growth, and develop the skills of a reflective practitioner.

3. Professional organizations are political advocates for the profession, play a role in educating both the public and policymakers about the profession, and directly serve members with educational programs.
4. Teachers are expected to stay current in their field through participating in in-service opportunities and returning to school for graduate-level coursework.
5. Developing and maintaining a teaching portfolio requires that teachers reflect on what they do and collect information on the teaching-learning process.
6. Direct observation of the teaching-learning process allows teachers to collect information on what is happening in their classes and is useful to look at what students are doing as well as what the teacher is doing.
7. Teachers who choose to directly observe their teaching must (1) decide what to look for, (2) decide the observational method or tool they will use, (3) choose a way to collect data, and (4) analyze and interpret the meaning of the information they have collected.

CHECKING YOUR UNDERSTANDING

1. What are the characteristics of a profession?
2. How are professionals treated differently from nonprofessionals in the workforce?
3. What are the privileges and responsibilities of being a member of a profession?
4. How can a teacher act "professionally"?
5. Why should professionals support professional organizations?
6. What opportunities are provided teachers to be continuous learners?
7. What is the reflective practitioner?
8. What is a teaching portfolio, and what might be included in a teaching portfolio?
9. What process might teachers use to collect observational data on their teaching?

10. How might teachers use direct observation to help them sort out why they may be having management problems in their classes?

REFERENCE

National Association for Sport and Physical Education. (2008). *National standards for beginning physical education teachers.* Reston, VA: NASPE.

SUGGESTED READINGS

Cusimano, B., Darst, P., & van der Mars, H. (1993). Improving your instruction through self-evaluation: Part one: Getting started. *Strategies, 7*(2), 26–29.

Cusimano, B., Darst, P., & van der Mars, H. (1993). Improving your instruction through self-evaluation: Part three: Teacher position and active supervision, *Strategies, 7*(4), 26–29.

Cusimano, B., van der Mars, H., & Darst, P. (1993). Improving your instruction through self-evaluation: Part six: Professional growth plans. *Strategies, 7*(7), 26–29.

Darst, P., Cusimano, B., & van der Mars, H. (Eds.). (1989). Improving your instruction through self-evaluation: Part two: Using class time effectively, *Strategies, 7*(3), 26–29.

Darst, P., Zakrajsek, D., & Mancini, V. (Eds.). (1989). *Analyzing physical education and sport instruction.* Champaign, IL: Human Kinetics.

Firestone, W., & Pennell, J. (1993). Teacher commitment, working conditions and differential working policies. *Review of Educational Research, 63*(4), 489–529.

Stiehl, J. (1993). Becoming responsible—Theoretical and practical considerations. *Journal of Physical Education, Recreation and Dance,* May–June, 38–40.

van der Mars, H., Cusimano, B., & Darst, P. (1993). Improving your instruction through self-evaluation: Part five: assessing student behavior. *Strategies, 7*(6), 26–29.

Wolfe, P., & Sharpe, T. (1996). Improve your teaching with student coders. *Strategies, 9*(7), 5–9.

14 Observation Techniques and Tools

O V E R V I E W

In chapter 11 teacher observation was identified as a critical means for collecting assessment data on student performance. Observation for student assessment can be done by teachers, the student, or student peers. Chapter 13 identified teacher observation as an essential skill for collecting information on the teaching-learning process; in this context, observation is being done to assess the teaching process and the performance of the teacher. Regardless of the purpose for which observation is being used, the techniques available are the same and teachers should be knowledgeable about how to use observation to collect valid and reliable information.

This chapter will help you to understand the wide variety of observational assessment techniques and tools available as well as help you to use these techniques and tools in a valid and reliable way to collect information. The first part of this chapter describes alternative methods and techniques for the observation and analysis of instruction. The second part of the chapter describes several tools commonly used to collect information on the basic instructional skills of the teacher.

Standard 5: Impact on Student Learning

Physical education teacher candidates utilize assessments and reflection to foster student learning and inform instructional decisions.
NASPE Beginning Teaching Standards, 2008

O U T L I N E

- **Observational methods**
  Intuitive observation
  Anecdotal records
  Rating scales

  Scoring rubric
  Event recording
  Duration recording
  Time sampling

- **Observational tools for the analysis of teaching**
  Student motor activity: ALT-PE
  Student use of time
  Content development: OSCD-PE

Teacher feedback
Student conduct
Qualitative Measures of Teaching
  Performance Scale (QMTPS)
Teacher movement

■ OBSERVATIONAL METHODS

Different types of observational techniques and methods will give the observer different types of information. An observational technique or other method of collecting data on teaching is like a lens or filter on a camera. In selecting the lens or filter to be used and pointing the camera in a particular direction, the photographer chooses not only what is seen but also what is not seen. A lens pointed in one direction cannot see what is outside the limitations of that lens. Observers can sit down with a blank sheet of paper and record what is interesting to them. They can decide to look for a specific characteristic or set of behaviors (e.g., does the student bend his or her knees when landing; the number of times students support each other's performance in a class) and either count the number of times a behavior occurs or merely record that a behavior did occur. They can use a stopwatch to record how long a particular instructional characteristic (e.g., vigorous activity or activity time) occurred. Observers can also categorize behaviors (e.g., types of feedback; types of passes in a game situation; type of offensive stroke used), relate one behavior to another (e.g., teacher feedback to student response), or use a time-sampling technique to record only at particular intervals or times. These are different methods and techniques available to the teacher and students for recording observational data on teaching.

Each observational method and technique has advantages and disadvantages and is useful for different purposes. The methods and techniques vary in their practicality and in the ease with which both valid and reliable data can be obtained. There is no one best method of recording observational data.

Intuitive Observation

An intuitive method of observation is not a systematic method. The observer does not go into an observation with the intent to look at anything specific or to record what is seen in any formal sense. An observer using an intuitive method of observation makes conclusions without collecting specific information. Most student behavior and teaching is observed in this way.

Use. Observers who use an intuitive method of observation rely on their judgment of what is seen to draw conclusions about what has occurred and the value of what has occurred. A teacher who jots down notes with comments on students such as "uses offensive and defensive strategies well" or comments on teachers such as "organized well" or "needs to circulate more among the students" or "task presentation unclear" is using an intuitive method of observation. Figure 14.1 (p. 324) is an example of an observational record done to assess a teacher using intuitive observation. This information is usually shared with a teacher in verbal or written form.

Strengths and weaknesses. Because intuitive observations are not done systematically, the probability of arriving at invalid and unreliable conclusions is high. The more experienced the observer, the less probability this will occur, but even two experienced observers will rarely come to the same conclusion or select the same behaviors to look at in more detail.

The strength of intuitive observation is that this method can begin to isolate glaring problems in performance and is therefore useful when more specific events have not been identified as being important to look at. The observer is not limited to a set

Teacher _Sally Jones_   Lesson content _Tossing and catching_

Class and grade level _3rd Mrs. Steele_   Date _Nov. 3_

Observer _Mr. Fields_

Teacher strengths
- Delivers tasks clearly
- Tasks are appropriate for group
- Equipment arrangements planned for

Teacher weaknesses
- Doesn't wait for student attention before speaking
- Lets tasks deteriorate into unproductive behavior before refocusing
- Little specific feedback

Student _Shamika Roosevelt_

Tossing and Catching   Date _Nov 3_

Can toss and catch without loss of control in self-space.
Loses the ball at high speeds or when tossing to different directions. A consistent "worker"

FIGURE 14.1
Intuitive observation recording sheets.

of preconceived descriptions of performance. Even when more specific tools are used, much insight into student performance and the instructional process is obtained by observers who are free to view all instructional events in the context in which they occur and who do not go into an observation with tunnel vision.

Intuitive observation requires no formal training in a specific tool or data analysis. This makes it practical and appealing. However, because data are not collected in any systematic way, recording the progress of the student or teacher over time is difficult. For example, if an observer notes that the teacher does not give much specific feedback, it is difficult to determine whether improvement occurs in the next observation because insufficient information was collected.

Application. Intuitive observation is most useful when specific events or behaviors have not been determined as being important to observe. Intuitive observation is extremely useful for teachers to use to initially describe student performance or behavior because writing a description forces you to think through exactly what you are seeing. Intuitive observation is also useful for teachers who have not previously assessed their instructional skills. Many teachers who have not recorded or listened to their teaching should initially listen or view their teaching without looking for specific things. They can then take notes on what they want to view more specifically with a more systematic tool.

Intuitive observation is also useful for generating hypotheses. Teachers who have identified global problems in their teaching (e.g., off-task behavior) may want to view their teaching more globally at first to begin to determine possible causes. Those hypotheses can then be tested with more specific observations using a systematic tool.

Anecdotal Records

The observer doing an anecdotal record establishes broad categories of concern and then takes notes on everything that happens related to those categories. Notes are usually kept in the form of a log into which

nonevaluative statements are made describing what is occurring.

Use. The anecdotal record provides a description of events. In the teaching-learning process the anecdotal record can be used to describe what teachers do, what students do, or the relationship between what teachers do and students do. Figure 14.2 (p. 326) is an example of an observation that focuses on the interaction between the teacher and the individual student. It is important in doing an anecdotal record to record events objectively without evaluating whether what occurred was good or bad. Judgments about events are made only after the anecdotal record is complete.

Strengths and weaknesses. The anecdotal record is useful for collecting a great deal of valid and reliable data on events in the teaching-learning process. Because data are not organized into preconceived categories or lists of occurrences, the data represent what happened and can be analyzed from different perspectives. This eliminates the danger of important context being lost in the recording procedures.

Anecdotal records are not highly systematic. There is the danger of different observers recording different information on an occurrence. However, more highly trained observers learn to record objectively and in great detail. Thus, the method can be a reliable and valid way to collect information.

The major disadvantage of anecdotal records is the amount of information that must be recorded at great length and then analyzed. The usefulness of anecdotal records is the detail. Sorting out the detail into meaningful information after an observation takes time and sensitivity to that data.

Anecdotal records at first appear to be simple. Learning to observe without bias and without being evaluative, however, is more difficult than most people realize.

Application. Anecdotal records are useful for collecting data before hypothesis generation. This means that teachers can view in detail the behavior of a student, their own behavior in a specific situation, or

Student _Vickie S. Age 12_   Lesson content _Gymnastics_

Teacher _Tim C._   Observer _T. Pine_

Date _3/5_   Time _3rd Period_

Vickie waits for the teacher to begin by sitting attentively. At the start of instruction Vickie turns to a neighbor and comments that she can't wait for class to be over. The teacher continues instruction on the handstand and asks students to get a partner. Vickie slides close to Sharon. The teacher asks partners to find a mat. Vickie and Sharon are the last to get up and find a mat on the outskirts of the activity area. They both lie down flat on the mat. The teacher instructs the class to begin. Vickie and Sharon rise slowly. Vickie puts her hands and knees on the mat and stays in that position. The teacher comes over and asks Vickie to see if she can get her legs up. Vickie raises her seat and gets ready to lift one leg. The teacher turns and goes to a new student. Vickie goes back to the hands and knees position and stays there until the next skill is presented.

FIGURE 14.2
Anecdotal record recording sheet.

their interaction with the student to try to generate hypotheses about that behavior. For example, a teacher might ask the following questions:

- What does the single student experience in my class?
- How do my students interact with each other?
- How do my students respond to my individual attention?
- How do I respond to student inattention? Off-task behavior? Student unskilled responses? Student skilled responses?

These and other questions might cause teachers to observe their lessons using an anecdotal record. The question would serve as the focus for what is recorded. The observer would record all the behavior of the student to answer the question of what the single student experiences in the class. The observer would record all, or as much as possible, of the interactive behavior of student to student to answer the question of how the students interact with each other.

After the anecdotal record is complete, the teacher looks at and tries to understand what happened and possible relationships between what occurred. The teacher can test those relationships with a more specific observational tool or can make a judgment that change is needed, with some insight into what needs changing.

Anecdotal records are useful to teachers when the specific behavior important to a question cannot be anticipated in advance. For instance, teachers could try to predict all the things students could possibly experience in a physical education class and make a list of those behaviors. Teachers could then check that list every time a student did something on that list. However, teachers risk not including some important behaviors if they try to anticipate in advance what will occur. The list may not exhaust all possible behaviors. The anecdotal record ensures that this does not occur, because the behaviors are not classified until after they have been recorded. After many anecdotal records on the same question, teachers may then be better prepared to design more specific instruments that cut short recording and analysis time and enable comparison of lessons to be made.

Rating Scales

Of all the observational techniques available to look at teaching or skill performance of students, the reader is probably most familiar with the rating scale. The rating scale divides a phenomenon to be observed into either qualitative or quantitative levels (e.g., always, sometimes, never; poor, fair, good, excellent).

Use. Rating scales are used when specific behaviors have been identified as being important to look at and when specific levels of those behaviors can be described. Rating scales attempt to quantify data. This means that they look at the quality of an event and assign it a level or number. Figure 14.3 (p. 328) is an example of a rating scale used to describe skill performance in volleyball.

Strengths and weaknesses. Rating scales are deceptively simple. They are easy to design but difficult to learn how to use well enough to collect reliable data. For instance, consider the difficulty of learning how to classify student responses into the levels "highly skilled," "skilled," "average," and "poorly skilled" or classifying teacher cues as "appropriate," "somewhat appropriate," or "not appropriate." To use either of these scales reliably, a great deal of effort must be put into definitions and specific criteria for each level. Observers need much training to learn how to use the system reliably.

The problem with rating scales is that they usually are abused. They are often used without the benefit of careful definitions or adequate training in the use of those definitions. In such cases they are nothing more than quantified subjectivity and have little value.

Rating scales are useful for studying qualitative dimensions of behavior that other observational methods do not handle well. If the rating scale is used carefully and with attention to reliability, it can be an extremely useful method.

The teacher who wants to design a rating scale should select the dimension to be studied and the number of levels of that dimension that need to be discriminated. The more levels there are, the more difficult it is

Volleyball Assessment

Name of student	Forearm pass	Overhand pass	Serve	Total
D. Dasilva	2	2	3	
K. Kirtes	1	2	2	
L. Moley	2	3	3	
J. Nelson	3	3	3	
V. Niles	1	1	1	
P. Pope	2	2	3	

Forearm pass
1 — Cannot receive a serve and direct it with any accuracy
2 — Receives a serve most of the time and directs accurately
    sometimes
3 — Receives and directs the serve most of the time

Overhead pass
1 — Cannot convert a ball over the net or a forearm pass to an
    overhead pass and direct it with any accuracy
2 — Can convert a ball to a pass and direct it with accuracy some
    of the time
3 — Converts and directs a pass accurately most of the time

Serve
1 — Cannot get the ball over the net
2 — Gets the ball over the net some of the time
3 — Gets the ball over the net most of the time

FIGURE 14.3
Rating scale.

to discriminate those levels reliably. Each level should have carefully designed definitions that clearly delineate one level from another. The rating scale should be practiced in each setting for which it is going to be used and modified where necessary. Use of the tool should be practiced until it can be used reliably.

Application. Rating scales are useful for qualitative dimensions of behavior (i.e., when it is not sufficient just to know whether a behavior occurred or did not occur). Appropriateness of teacher or student behavior, skill levels of students, creativity of response, quantity of response (e.g., number of student practice attempts), or form characteristics of a skill response are instructional events for which a rating scale could be useful. Rating scales are most useful for discrete, observable behavior. Global evaluations of broad and complex phenomena are not useful. Students can do self-assessment or peer assessment using rating scales if the teacher is willing to take the time to teach the students how to discriminate each level of performance.

The rating scale is useful for monitoring behavior. Averages for each skill or each lesson can be determined, and the progress of the teacher or students can be determined over time. Because rating scales are practical instruments, they have a great deal of appeal to teachers attempting to evaluate large numbers of students quickly. Because teachers must observe each student, although for a limited time, rating scales can be a useful tool, particularly for formative evaluation.

Scoring Rubric

As described in chapter 11, a scoring rubric is in one sense a multidimensional rating scale. Several criteria can be evaluated at one time to determine an overall score. Like a rating scale, the scoring rubric divides a phenomenon into several levels qualitatively. The scoring rubric looks at several criteria at one time.

Use. Scoring rubrics are particularly useful for assessing complex student behavior such as game play (see chapter 11 for specific examples). They are also useful for looking at specific teaching behaviors, but since an overall evaluation of teaching requires the assessment of far too many criteria, they are not useful for this purpose. If we were to take the volleyball rating scale assessment in figure 14.3, we could establish a scoring rubric by making each of the skills assessed a criterion and would be able to evaluate overall performance. We would establish what an overall Level 1, Level 2, and Level 3 performance would be using all three skills.

Scoring rubrics can be used holistically or analytically. Holistic scoring rubrics would have a set of criteria for each level, and the observer would make a decision regarding which level best describes the performance. Analytical scoring rubrics would rate each criterion separately and then give the overall score an arithmetical average to determine the final score.

Application. Scoring rubrics have become the tool of choice for many student assessments in physical education and can be used quite reliably by teachers who know the content they are observing. They are very useful to add a dimension of "objectivity" to the idea of observation because they require the teacher to observe with a set of criteria for performance rather than an intuitive response to what is good and not good. Teachers can design scoring rubrics by establishing a set of criteria for good performance and then making a decision about the number of levels needed to assess and what the criteria look like at each of the different levels.

Event Recording

Event recording is one of the most-used observational methods in teaching. Event recording determines the occurrence or lack of occurrence of the behavior or event being observed. Observers check when a behavior, such as a student skill characteristic or a teacher demonstration, occurs. Usually, the frequency of that event is determined by counting the number of times the behavior occurs in a lesson.

Use. Event recording is used when the occurrence or lack of occurrence of a behavior is important to know or when knowledge of frequency of a behavior is important. Behaviors can be important because they positively influence learning (e.g., feedback) or because they negatively influence learning (e.g., criticism or conduct interactions between the teacher and student).

Usually, several behaviors or different dimensions of the same behavior are recorded at one time. Figure 14.4 (p. 330) is an example of an event recording sheet that not only records the occurrence of feedback but also begins to sort the feedback behavior of the teacher into types of feedback. This information can then be converted into a total number of behavior occurrences or, if comparisons between lessons with different time allotments are needed, into a rate per minute. Teacher or student behaviors can then be

Teacher __H. Shots_____   Lesson content ___Softball_____

Observer __R. O'Hara_____   Date ____5/2_____

Target of feedback	Task number 1	2	3	4	5	6	7	8	9	10	Total	%
Class	✓										____	___
Group											____	___
Individual		✓	✓	✓	✓						____	___
Positive or negative											____	___
Positive	✓			✓							____	___
Negative		✓	✓								____	___
Specificity											____	___
General	✓			✓							____	___
Specific		✓	✓								____	___
Type of feedback											____	___
Evaluative	✓			✓							____	___
Corrective		✓	✓								____	___
Not applicable											____	___
Congruency with cues											____	___
Congruent		✓	✓								____	___
Incongruent											____	___
Not applicable	✓										____	___

Length of lesson in minutes _____

Rate per minute of feedback _____

FIGURE 14.4
Event recording sheet (teacher feedback).

monitored to determine whether they have increased or decreased with each lesson.

Figure 14.5 presents a recording sheet to be used by student peer assessors to look at offensive and defensive play in badminton. The observers can record every time they see a player use the offensive or defensive characteristic or they can record if they see it only once. The teacher who wants to design a system using event recording must carefully define each behavior being observed and practice using that definition reliably over any contexts in which the system applies. Students should be taught what "counts" for a behavior and what does not count. In figure 14.5, for example, students would have to know what returning to home base position looked like and what it did not look like in order to use the checklist appropriately.

Strengths and weaknesses. Event recording is systematic and can result in valid and reliable data. The only observer judgment that needs to be made is whether the behavior occurred. This makes event recording practical to use. The difficulty of obtaining reliable data increases with (1) the number of

different behaviors observed at any one time and (2) the amount of observer inference required to make judgments. Teacher demonstration is a fairly easy behavior to discriminate. Student off-task behavior requires more inference. The appropriateness of the teacher's task requires even more inference.

The reliability of event recording can be increased with careful definitions and much practice in discriminating when the behavior occurs and when it does not. The validity of event recording rests with the appropriateness of the definitions used to discriminate the behavior. For instance, if nonverbal behavior is excluded from teacher feedback, the feedback behavior of a teacher who gives a thumbs-up signal to a student is eliminated. Therefore, the information on teacher feedback does not reflect the reality of the situation and is less valid to any description of feedback.

Application. Event recording is useful to observe any event or behavior for which quantitative information on an occurrence is useful. If the question "How much?" is asked, event recording is a useful choice of methodology. Because event recording does not deal well with context or appropriateness, event recording should be used with care to describe teaching behavior. Knowing that the teacher has a high rate of feedback or uses demonstration frequently may be of little value if the feedback is not appropriate or if the demonstration is not accurate. Likewise, simple event recording does not deal well with relationships between different kinds of behaviors. The sequence of events and the events that preceded or followed a tallied behavior are lost.

Duration Recording

Duration recording is an observational technique that provides information on the use of time. This technique can answer the questions of how time is spent or how much time is used for specific dimensions of the teaching-learning process.

Use. The basic tool in duration recording is a stopwatch. Observers keep track of when an event occurs and when it ends. Time for that event is then summed to get a total for a lesson or unit. Duration

---

Name of Student Observed ———————————

Name of Observer ———————————

Date ——————

Offensive Play

—— Returns the shuttlecock to a side of the court away from an opponent

—— Returns the shuttlecock to the back of the court away from an opponent

—— Returns the shuttlecock to the front of the court away from opponent

Defensive Play

—— Quickly returns to "home base" position after each shot

—— Clears the shuttlecock to the back when put in a defensive position

FIGURE 14.5

Peer assessment checklist for beginning offensive/defensive game play in badminton.

recording has been used successfully to record how students spend their time. Exclusive categories (e.g., listening, waiting, being organized, receiving behavioral instruction, making a skill attempt, playing a game) are part of many tools that have looked at how students spend their time.

Figures 14.6 (p. 333) and 14.7 (p. 334) illustrate two methods of duration recording. The first uses a time line, and the other keeps track of actual time spent. When using a time line, the recorder codes on the time line when an event occurs and when it ends. The advantage of the time line is that the relationship between the sequence of events is preserved.

Sometimes the sequence is unimportant, and the teacher may be interested just in how much time is spent doing what. Figure 14.7 illustrates how the teacher can keep track of time spent on different stages of game play in a unit.

Strengths and weaknesses. Duration recording can result in both valid and reliable data with little effort and training. Most events for which time data are useful are relatively easy to define and to discriminate in an instructional setting. This keeps training time at a minimum.

Duration recording is useful only for large global ideas that occur for long periods. If behavior changes quickly, there is little point in trying to record it using duration recording. The more frequent the changes in behavior being recorded, the more difficult it is to get reliability and the less practical duration recording becomes as a technique. For instance, teacher feedback takes, on the average, five seconds and would not be a good choice for duration recording.

As with other observational methods for looking at specific behavior, definitions must be established for the occurrence or lack of occurrence of an event when duration recording is used. When looking at broad categories of events, it is sometimes difficult to anticipate all cases of occurrence or lack of occurrence (e.g., how many students have to be active for activity time). Practice using the definitions in a variety of situations will help uncover problem areas and will enable the observer to collect valid and reliable data.

Application. Duration recording is most useful for looking at how students or teachers spend their time. How students spend their time, while not of particular interest to students, should be of interest to teachers. Questions on student use of time, particularly those behaviors related to appropriate practice time, maximum vigorous activity in relation to fitness activities, and other student behaviors are appropriately handled by duration recording. Also, such questions as how much time a teacher spends observing, giving directions, dealing with problem behavior, or organizing for activity are handled well by duration recording.

Time Sampling

In time sampling, the observer at a designated interval of time makes a decision on an instructional event. Usually the interval of time is more than a minute and sometimes as long as ten or fifteen minutes.

Use. Time sampling is used to observe instructional events that do not change quickly. For example, it has been used to spot-check the number of students participating in activity at any one time (Dodds, 1973). Every two to three minutes the observer counts the number of students not active or not appropriately engaged in activity. Time sampling is also useful for looking at the amount of time spent in different content areas of a lesson or in determining teacher positioning.

Strengths and weaknesses. Time sampling enables the observer to collect useful information in a short time. Because time sampling uses so little observer time, the observer is free to use other observational methods to look at other instructional events. When definitions are clearly written and appropriate, time sampling can yield highly reliable and valid data.

Time sampling can be used only for behaviors that do not change quickly. For example, it is useless to use time sampling as a method of getting information on teacher feedback. Feedback occurs frequently at certain times in a lesson and not at all at other times. The behavior chosen must overlap the time chosen to sample. Again, the smaller the interval of time, the less likely the results are to reflect a sampling error.

Teacher Use of Time

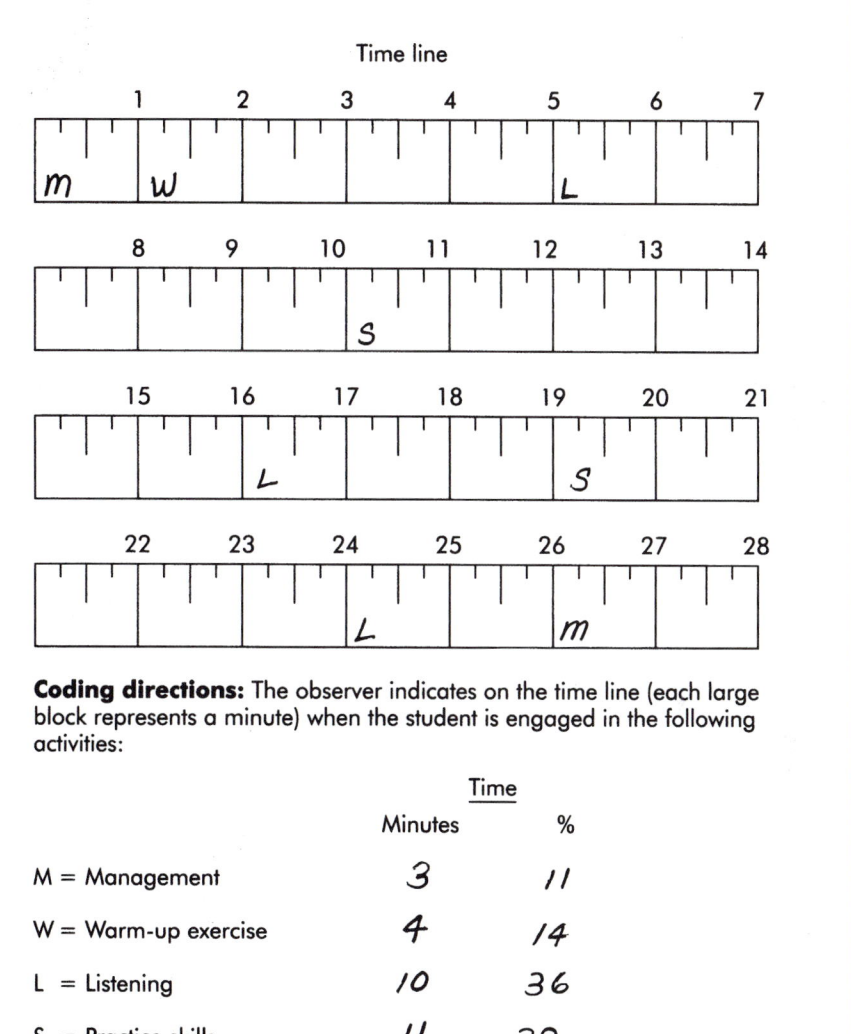

Coding directions: The observer indicates on the time line (each large block represents a minute) when the student is engaged in the following activities:

	Time	
	Minutes	%
M = Management	3	11
W = Warm-up exercise	4	14
L = Listening	10	36
S = Practice skills	11	39
G = Game play	0	

FIGURE 14.6
Duration recording sheet (time line).

Teacher _T. Mand_   Lesson content _Basketball_

Lesson number _6_   Date _1/3_

Observer _R. M._

Time spent in stages of game play   **Total time   %**

Stage one _30", 45", 20"_   _95"_   _5_

Stage two _60", 80", 120", 123"_   _383"_   _21_

Stage three   _0_   ___

Stage four _22"_   _1320"_   _73_

Lesson beginning time _10:45_   Total lesson time _1798"_

Lesson end time _11:30_

Coding directions: The observer starts a stopwatch every time the students begin work in one of the four stages of game play. The watch is stopped when work in that stage concludes. The amount of actual time spent at each stage is recorded on the appropriate line. At the conclusion of the lesson, the amount of time spent at each stage is totaled and divided by the total lesson time to get the percentage of time spent at each stage.

FIGURE 14.7
Duration recording sheet (real time).

Application. Time sampling is a useful method of observation when the information desired is on instructional events or characteristics that appear distributed through a lesson. Because time sampling requires so little observer time, it is a useful technique for teachers while they are teaching to keep track of what students as a whole are doing, as in the spot check, or what individual students are doing. Content of lessons can also be recorded using time sampling. How much time is being spent on different skills or different stages of skill development thus can be determined.

Teachers who want to use time sampling should do the following:

- Determine the instructional event they want information on.
- Decide how they want to discriminate the dimension being studied (e.g., event, category, rating scale).
- Determine the appropriate interval to collect valid data on that dimension. The appropriate interval can be determined by starting with small time units and increasing the time unit only to the point where the sample sheet reflects what occurred in the lesson.

■ OBSERVATIONAL TOOLS FOR THE ANALYSIS OF TEACHING

Many different observational tools already exist that have been used to collect information on different aspects of the teaching-learning process. Many of these tools were designed for research purposes and are not practical for the teacher whose purpose is self-improvement. Seven tools are presented in this section to collect information on the following:

- Student motor activity: ALT-PE
- Student use of time
- Content development: OSCD-PE
- Teacher feedback
- Student conduct
- Task presentation
- Teacher movement and location

These tools were selected to represent both important dimensions of the teaching-learning process and different observational methods. Category definitions are provided for the tools, but in some cases the definitions are not sufficient to fully communicate the intent of that category. Researchers use manuals that give many examples of each category. However, even without more elaborate examples, teachers will be able to use most of these systems with some degree of reliability. It is suggested that teachers keep a *decision*

log of examples they have difficulty with as they are learning to use a system. This will enable teachers to set ground rules for using the instrument in their particular situations.

Student Motor Activity: ALT-PE

Academic Learning Time–Physical Education (ALT-PE) was developed by Siedentop and the graduate students at Ohio State University (Metzler, 1979; Siedentop et al., 1979; Siedentop et al., 1982). The instrument was designed to measure the portion of time in a lesson that a student is involved in motor activity at an appropriate success rate. The total instrument is capable of describing the context of physical education lessons in which the total class is involved and the type of motor involvement of a selected sample of students. Several different types of observational methods can be used with ALT-PE. The small portion of the full instrument presented here provides information on motor activity only. The reader is encouraged to consult the ALT-PE manual for the more complete instrument and other types of methods.

Purpose. The purpose of this instrument is to describe the amount of time students are engaged in motor activity at an appropriate level of difficulty. See box 14.1 for category definitions.

Recording procedures. Four different observational methods are available to collect ALT-PE data on the categories just listed. These procedures follow.

Interval recording. Short intervals (usually six seconds) of alternating observing and recording can be used for one student or an alternating sample of students (typically three students are used). Usually a prerecorded audiotape is employed to signal the beginning and end of an "observe" six seconds and then "record" six seconds format. During the observing interval, the observer watches one student. At the recording interval, the observer decides whether the student is engaged in motor activity. If the student is engaged in motor activity, the observer classifies that engagement as being either MA, MI, or MS. If the student is not engaged in motor activity, the observer

BOX 14·1

Category Definitions for Student Motor Activity: ALT-PE

Motor appropriate (MA). The student is engaged in a subject matter–oriented motor activity in such a way as to produce a high degree of success.

Motor inappropriate (MI). The student is engaged in a subject matter–oriented motor activity, but the activity or task is either too difficult for the individual's capabilities or so easy that practicing it could not contribute to lesson goals.

Motor supporting (MS). The student is engaged in subject matter–oriented motor activity when the purpose of assisting others to learn or perform the activity (e.g., spotting, holding equipment, sending balls to others).

Not motor engaged (NM). The student is not involved in subject matter–oriented motor activity. This category can be further described in terms of what learners are doing when they are not motor engaged as follows:

    Interim (I). The student is involved with a noninstructional aspect of the ongoing activity.

    Waiting (W). The student has completed a task or motor response and is waiting for the next opportunity to respond.

    Off-Task (OF). The students are not doing what they are supposed to be doing at the time.

    On-Task (OT). The student is appropriately engaged but not in a subject matter–related motor response.

    Cognitive (C). The student is appropriately involved in a cognitive activity.

the number of students engaged at an appropriate level of motor activity (MA). Data can be presented as an average for the class.

Duration recording. The observer monitors a single student using a time line to categorize into the four categories what the student is doing the entire period. Another alternative is to measure just MA time—starting a stopwatch when the student is appropriately engaged and stopping the watch when the engagement stops. Total MA time for the lesson can be presented as a percentage of total lesson time.

Event recording. The observer counts the number of practice trials at an appropriate level of difficulty (where discrete trials are inherent in the activity). Data are presented as MA trials per minute or per larger unit of time.

Figure 14.8 describes a typical recording sheet for collecting ALT-PE data on engagement level only using the interval method of recording. In summarizing the data, the teacher counts the number of intervals scored in each category for each student observed. The critical variable is the number of intervals the student is engaged at a motor-appropriate level of involvement. To make this meaningful, the number of motor-appropriate intervals (MA) is expressed as a percentage of the total number of intervals recorded for a student.

Interpreting data. The average ALT-PE motor-appropriate categories for physical education classes lie somewhere between 14 and 25 percent (Parker, 1989). This is not particularly good. If motor-appropriate time is highly related to learning, teachers should strive for the highest possible level of motor-appropriate time.

ALT-PE is considered by some authors to be the single best predictor of teacher effectiveness in physical education (Siedentop et al., 1979). A study done by Silverman (1991) showed a relationship between high levels of student engagement and student learning. It is reasonable to assume that the student engaged more at an appropriate level of difficulty in motor activity will learn more. Although there are problems with the application of this idea to different physical education settings, it has a great deal of logical support and is, at

continues to define the behavior in terms of the categories I, W, OF, OT, and C. Data can be presented as a percentage of each category. A typical recording sheet for this instrument is described in figure 14.8. Only the learner involvement categories are used. Context level is not used.

Alternative Recording Procedures

Group time sampling. Every two minutes the observer scans the group (fifteen seconds) and counts

Academic Learning Time—Physical Education

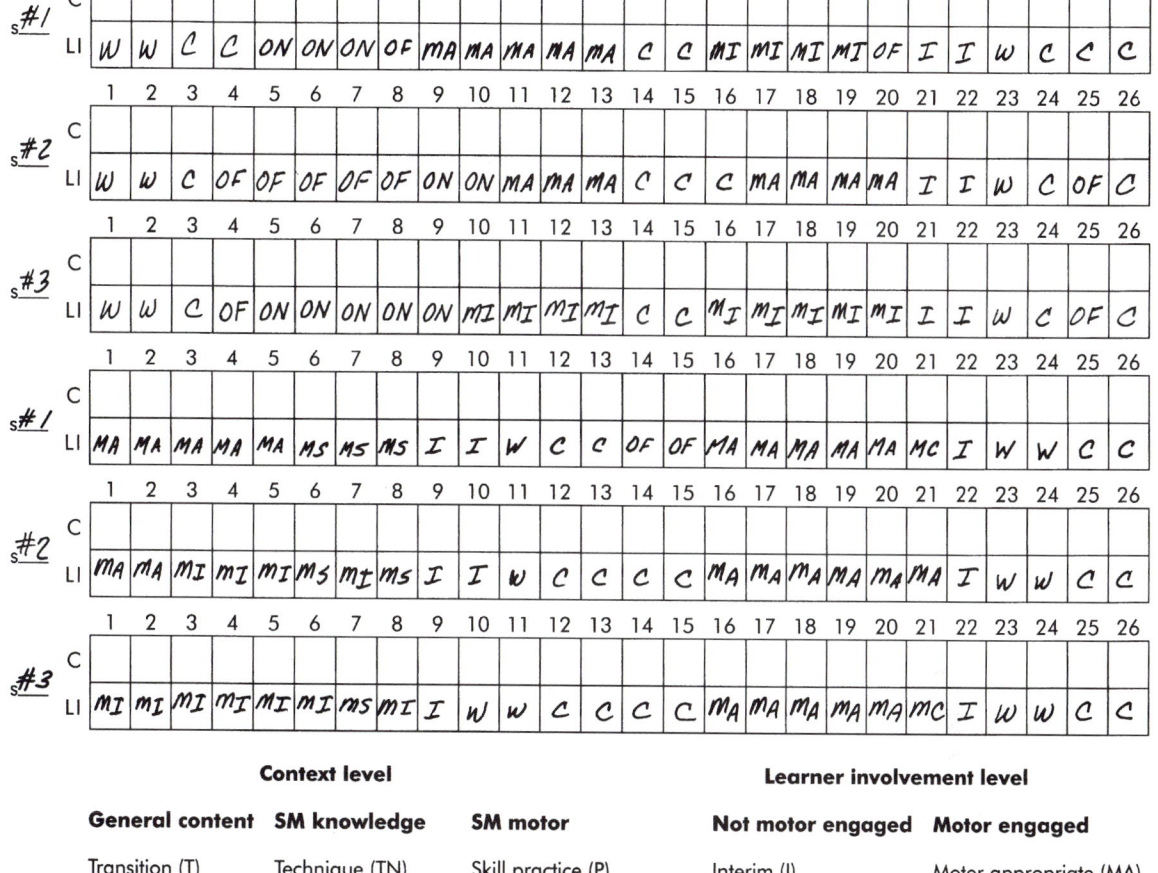

FIGURE 14.8

Example of ALT-PE data using interval recording.

minimum, a necessary but not a sufficient condition for learning.

Student Use of Time

Purpose. The purpose of this instrument is to describe how students spend their time. See box 14.2 for category definitions.

Recording procedures. Several alternatives are available for recording how students spend their time. Duration recording can be used by employing a time line or by placing real time into the appropriate categories. When 51 percent of the students change what they are doing, the observer notes the time and marks a recording sheet. The most common method of using

BOX 14·2

Category Definitions for Student Use of Time

Management organization (MO). Students are engaged through activity or listening with organizational arrangements for people, time, equipment, or space that support lesson content.

Management conduct (MC). Students are engaged through activity or listening with functions that direct or maintain the expectations for conduct.

Activity (A). Students are motorically engaged in the lesson content.

Instruction (I). Students are receiving information on the lesson content.

Off task (OT). Students are not engaged as directed by the teacher.

Student Time

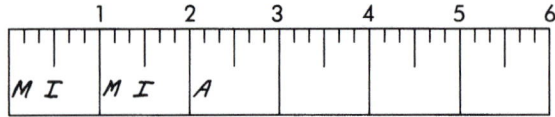

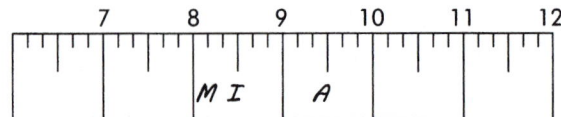

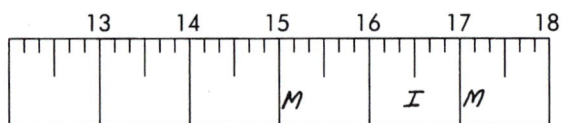

CODING DIRECTIONS: The observer codes either M (management), A (activity), or I (instruction) directly on the time line to indicate what the student is doing. Each block represents 1 minute divided into six 10-second units. It is necessary to indicate a change only from one category to another category.

Total number of 10-second intervals ___*108*___
Total M ___*24*___   % M ___*22*___
Total A ___*63*___   % A ___*58*___
Total I ___*21*___   % I ___*19*___

FIGURE 14.9
Duration recording sheet (student time expenditure).

this type of instrument is to use interval recording (note on the recording sheet what is happening every ten seconds). In either case the total group or a single student can be observed. Data can be analyzed in terms of the percentage of total time devoted to each of the categories.

The simplest form of this instrument is to select three categories of engagement (instruction [I]; activity [A]; and management [M]) and to code one of the three every ten seconds on a time line. If the category changes within the ten-second interval, the observer must make a judgment regarding which category best describes that ten-second interval. An example recording sheet is provided in figure 14.9.

Interpreting data. Although activity time is not as specific a measure of appropriate motor-engaged time as ALT-PE, activity time will give the teacher a measure of a student's opportunity to practice or to learn motor activity. High levels of activity time are desirable, and the level should probably never fall below 50 percent of total time in a physical education class. The use of the other categories will give the teacher an indication of where the time that decreases activity time is being spent. These other areas then

can be decreased if needed. Large blocks of management or instructional time consistently over a period of lessons should be avoided.

Content Development: OSCD-PE

The Observation System for Content Development–Physical Education (OSCD-PE) (Rink, 1979) was developed to look at the way teachers develop the content of their lessons. It is a sophisticated interaction analysis tool with many facets. One of the pieces of information it collects is a description of task sequences in terms of their development focus in a lesson. That small part of the instrument is included here.

BOX 14·3

Category Definitions for Content Development

Refining task. A refining task seeks to qualitatively improve the way in which students are performing a previous task (e.g., "This time work on getting your toes pointed").

Extending task. An extending task seeks a variety of responses or adds complexity or difficulty to a previous task.

Applying/assessment task. An applying task asks students to use their motor skill in an applied, competitive, or assessment setting (e.g., "How many times can you toss the ball up into the air without losing control of it?" or "Today we are going to play softball").

Informing task. An informing task states or presents a motor task that is not an extending, refining, or applying task. This task is usually the first task and merely describes what the students are to do.

Repeat task. A repeat task is the same task as the previous task with no changes.

Purpose. The purpose of this instrument is to describe the way content is developed in a physical education lesson in terms of the focus of the motor task. See box 14.3 for category definitions.

Recording procedures. Several observational methods are available as alternatives for describing content development through the task focus. The first and easiest to use is event recording. When the teacher gives a task, the observer determines the type of task and places a point on the polygraph in sequence (see figure 14.10). If information on how long students work with a task focus is desired, duration recording can be used to record how much time is spent on each task. The observer starts a stopwatch when a task begins and stops the watch when a task ends. This information can be recorded next to the designated category of the task.

Interpreting data. Some teachers are able to develop content with students by refining or changing the task on an individual basis. In large classes

characteristic of most physical education settings, this is not possible and the focus given tasks presented to the entire class becomes important.

There is no ideal sequence in which tasks should be presented. However, if teacher lessons continuously lack refining and extending tasks or if they move quickly from the informing task directly to the applying task, the appropriateness of the way the content is developed is questionable. In the example lesson in figure 14.10 you will notice that the sequence of tasks the teacher developed used refining, extending, and applying tasks. In this particular lesson there are more refining tasks, but all lessons do not have to have such a high percentage of refining tasks.

Teacher Feedback

Teacher feedback has been the focus of many different observational tools. Fishman and Tobey (1978) developed an instrument that describes in relative detail six different dimensions of augmented feedback in physical education lessons. Systems designed for research purposes by students at Ohio State University used simple event recording to classify feedback into different categories (Dodds, 1973; Stewart, 1983). The tool presented is a modification of these event-recording systems. The reader should consult chapter 7 for other possible dimensions of feedback that may need to be included.

Purpose. The purpose of the teacher feedback instrument is to describe the type and frequency of feedback given to students in a physical education lesson. See box 14.4 (p. 341) for category definitions.

Recording procedures. Event recording is the best method of collecting this information. A suggested recording sheet is provided in figure 14.11. In this recording sheet, only the type of feedback, target of feedback, and the positive/negative aspects of feedback are recorded. If other aspects of feedback just described are to be included, they must be added to the recording sheet. Each time a feedback statement is given, the observer puts a slash in the appropriate category. Data are analyzed in terms of the amount of feedback given in a particular lesson (divide the

Content Development

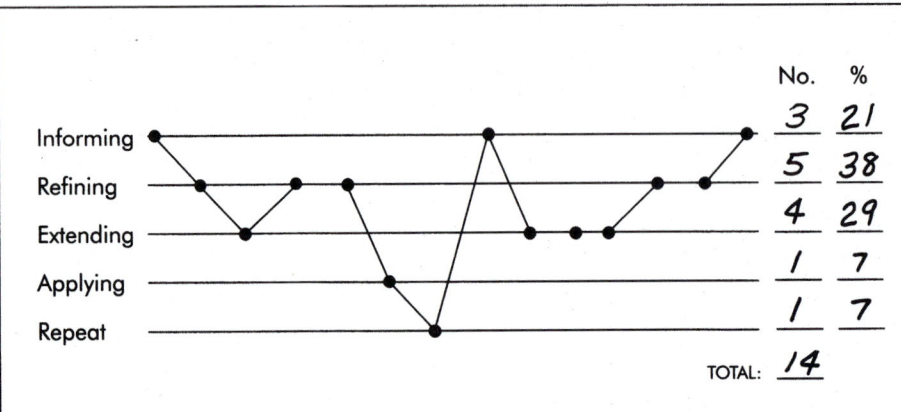

	No.	%
Informing	3	21
Refining	5	38
Extending	4	29
Applying	1	7
Repeat	1	7
	TOTAL:	14

Coding directions: After each task is given, the observer decides whether the task is an informing, refining, extending, or applying task or whether it is the same task repeated. A dot is placed in the row and column of the graph in the sequence the tasks are presented, and then the dots are connected.

FIGURE 14.10
Task focus recording sheet (content development).

number of feedback statements by the number of minutes to produce a rate per minute [RPM] score). Data are also analyzed in terms of a percentage of feedback for each of the concepts of the instrument (e.g., for the target of feedback the percentage of feedback statements falling into individual, group, and class).

Interpreting data. For the most part, it is desirable to have feedback that is more specific than general; more positive than negative; more corrective than evaluative; and more congruent than incongruent. The results of research on the specific role of feedback in learning motor skills in a group instructional setting have not been consistent. This is probably because it is difficult to describe the appropriateness and accuracy of feedback for different learners in different contexts. Value judgments placed on the desirability of feedback stem largely from data generalized from other teaching settings and from theoretic support. Feedback also plays a major role in monitoring student performance and maintaining student focus.

Data must be interpreted in context. For example, it may be inappropriate to give much individual feedback in a creative dance lesson. It may be appropriate to give much individual feedback in a lesson using manipulative skills in which the students are reviewing or practicing what they have already learned and the teacher is free to work with individuals. Collecting data on teacher feedback can describe what the teachers are doing. The teachers must interpret the appropriateness of what they are doing for the lesson they have taught.

BOX 14·4

Category Definitions for Teacher Feedback

Target

Class. Feedback directed to the whole class.
Group. Feedback directed to more than two students.
Individual. Feedback directed to one or two students.

Type

Evaluative. Feedback that makes a judgment about past performance.
Corrective. Feedback that suggests how future performance can be improved.

Level of specificity

General. Feedback that is evaluative but does not include information on why the judgment was made (e.g., "Good job").
Specific. Feedback that is evaluative and includes information on why the evaluation was made.

Positive or negative

Positive. Feedback that is expressed positively in terms of what the student did right or should do correctly.

Negative. Feedback that is expressed negatively in terms of what the student did or should do (e.g., "Don't step into the swing" or "That's not quite right").

Context of feedback

Skill. Feedback is related to the substantive part of the lesson.
Behavior. Feedback is related to management (either organization or conduct of the students).

Congruency

Congruent. Feedback is directly related to the focus the teacher has given a task (e.g., the teacher has asked the students to get under the ball and the feedback statement is "Tommy, you are really getting under the ball").
Incongruent. The feedback statement is not related to the specific focus the teacher has given for a task, no matter how appropriate that feedback statement may be (e.g., the teacher task is to get under the ball; the teacher feedback is "Try to get your elbows out to receive the ball").

Student Conduct

Student conduct is sometimes referred to as *student behavior* ("behavior" meaning the appropriateness of the way students conduct themselves in a setting). This instrument is another modification of information available from OSCD-PE (Rink, 1979). It is based on the assumption that it is important to know how teachers develop and maintain appropriate behavior in their classes.

Purpose. The purpose of this instrument is to describe how teachers structure, direct, and reinforce their expectations for the appropriate behavior of students. See box 14.5 for category definitions.

Recording procedures. The observer records three dimensions of the manner in which the teacher

deals with the conduct of students: the type of language communication; when the teacher's behavior occurred; and whether the behavior is positive or negative. Event recording is the most useful observational method for this system. Every time a conduct-related teacher behavior occurs, it is classified into one of the boxes illustrated in figure 14.12. To do this, the observer must first decide whether the behavior is *structuring* (making clear expectations), *soliciting* (requesting an immediate response), or *appraising* (sharing a value judgment about behavior with students in relation to student conduct). If the teacher behavior occurred before any student conduct behaviors, it is considered *preventive*. If it occurred after student conduct problems, it is considered *corrective*. The third decision is to decide whether the behavior is expressed positively in terms of what students should do or did, or

Teacher **R. Stewart**   Date **4-20**

Observer **T.S.**   Length of period **45**

Grade level **10**   Number in class **30**

Lesson content **tennis-forehand**

	Class	Group	Individual
Evaluative General	Positive **11** / Negative	Positive / Negative	Positive ЖЖ ЖЖ ЖЖ ЖЖ ЖЖ ЖЖ ЖЖ / Negative
Specific	Positive **1** / **11** Negative	Positive / Negative	Positive ЖЖ ЖЖ ЖЖ / Negative
Corrective	Positive / Negative	Positive / Negative	Positive ЖЖ 111 ЖЖ ЖЖ / ЖЖ ЖЖ Negative

Total feedback **88**

Total evaluative **60**   % Evaluative **68**
Total corrective **28**   % Corrective **32**

Total general **42**   % General **70**
Total specific **18**   % Specific **30**

Total negative **42**   % Negative **47**
Rate per minute of feedback _____

FIGURE 14.11
Teacher feedback coding sheet.

negatively, in terms of what students should not do or did. A recording procedure that uses codes for each of these categories and maintains the sequence of events may be useful also.

Interpreting data. Many times students in physical education classes learn how to behave by making mistakes and being corrected on these mistakes. In figure 14.12, the teacher plays primarily a corrective role in handling student conduct. A better way for teachers to communicate their

expectations for behavior is to make those expectations clear ahead of time (structuring and preventive) and positively. Teachers often omit structuring behavior when handling the conduct of students—whether before there is a problem or after there is a problem.

Soliciting directives to students on conduct (most often used to desist behavior) work when they are not overused and abused. Directives are abused when students are not told in advance what the expectations for behavior are and when the same behavior

BOX 14·5

Category Definitions for Student Conduct

Type of communication

Structuring. Structuring is any teacher verbal behavior (except an appraisal) that communicates information on the manner in which students are to conduct themselves but does not expect an immediate response (e.g., "We're going to *walk* over to get our equipment today").

Soliciting. Soliciting is any teacher verbal or nonverbal behavior that communicates information on the manner in which students are to conduct themselves and expects an immediate response (e.g., "Stop fighting" or "Put the balls *inside* the hoop"). Soliciting is a teacher reaction to student behavior. A negative solicitation for students to stop what they are doing is called a *desist* behavior (Kounin, 1977).

Appraising. Appraising is any teacher verbal or nonverbal behavior that makes a judgment about the way students have conducted or are conducting themselves (e.g., "I like the way Sally is sitting quietly waiting to begin").

When the behavior occurred

Preventive. Preventive behaviors are any structuring, soliciting, or appraising conduct comments by the teacher that occur *before* there is evidence of a need for that behavior (e.g., "Before you start, remember you are working quietly and in your space").

Corrective. Corrective behaviors are any structuring, soliciting, or appraising conduct comments by the teacher that occur after there is evidence of a need for that behavior (e.g., "Don't pick at the foam of the balls").

Positive/negative

Positive. Positive behaviors are any structuring, soliciting, or appraising behaviors by the teacher that are not put in a negative framework (e.g., "Tommy, get back in line").

Negative. Negative behaviors are any structuring, soliciting, or appraising behaviors by the teacher that are explicitly put in a negative framework (e.g., "Don't get out of line," or "You're behaving like 2-year-olds").

---

is continuously the content of a directive (i.e., when the teacher nags). Positive directives are usually more appropriate than negatively stated ones and achieve the same purpose.

Appraising behaviors, frequently used with young children to reinforce expectations, are effective. Teachers may also want to include in their description whether the behavior is directed to the class or to individuals. Most teachers structure behavior through the class and deal with problems individually.

In the example data in figure 14.12, the teacher spent much time dealing with behavior problems—primarily telling students not to do something. Unfortunately, most of the time was spent trying to correct problems after they became problems, and little time was spent trying to prevent problems by clarifying expectations for behavior ahead of time.

Qualitative Measures of Teaching Performance Scale (QMTPS)

Purpose. The Qualitative Measures of Teaching Performance Scale (QMTPS) (Rink & Werner, 1989) was designed to collect data on several instructional variables at the same time. The major constructs of the instrument are the following:

- Type of task (informing, refining, extending, repeating, applying)
- Task presentation (clarity, demonstration, appropriate number of cues, accuracy of cues, qualitative cues)
- Student responses appropriate to task focus
- Teacher specific congruent feedback

See box 14.6 for category definitions.

Recording procedures. QMTPS can be used live, but it is easier to do the observation with this

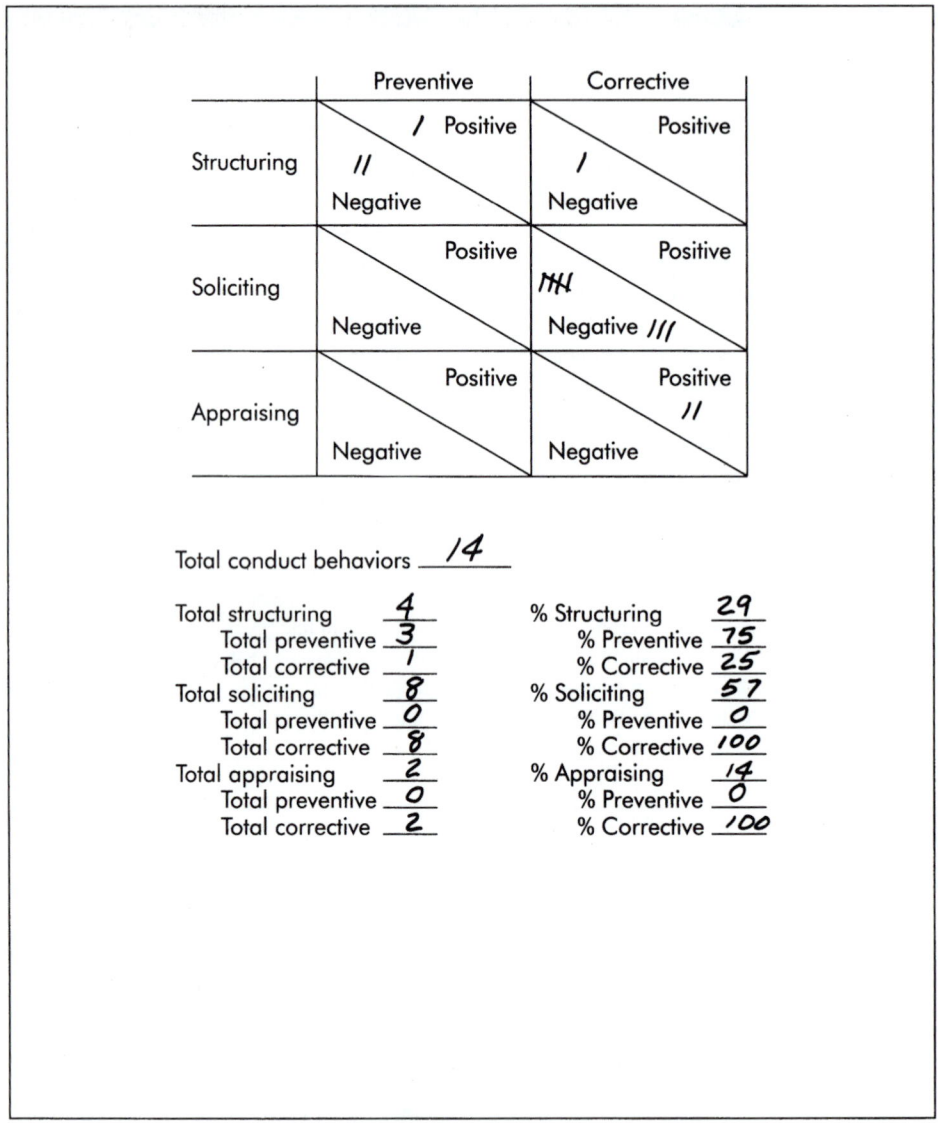

FIGURE 14.12
Student conduct–related teacher behavior recording sheet.

instrument if video is used. A typical recording sheet for this instrument is described in figure 14.13. (p. 346) The observer stops the video after each movement task is given by the teacher. The observer then makes a decision regarding the type of task and all of the task presentation categories. The video is continued and then stopped again after the teacher indicates that time for practice of that task is over. At this time the observer codes the student responses and feedback categories of the instrument.

BOX 14·6

Category Definitions for the Qualitative Measures of Teaching Performance Scale

Type of task

Informing. A task that names, defines, or describes a skill or movement concept with no focus other than just to do it. It usually is the first task in a sequence of tasks.

Refining. A task that qualitatively seeks to improve motor performance. Usually this type of task focuses on improving the mechanics of a skill or tactical/strategic aspects of play.

Extending. A task that quantitatively changes the original task content by manipulating the level of difficulty or complexity of conditions under which the task is performed or that seeks a variety of responses.

Repeating. A simple repetition of the previous task with no changes.

Applying/assessment. A task that focuses the purpose of student performance outside the movement or an assessment of that movement. It is usually competitive or self-testing.

Task presentation

Clarity. Teacher's verbal explanation or directions communicate a clear idea of what to do and how to do it. This judgment is confirmed on the basis of student movement responses to the presentation and is relative to the situation.

Yes – Students proceed to work in a focused way on exactly what the teacher asked them to do.

No – Students exhibited confusion, questions, off-task behavior, or lack of intent to deal with the specifics of the task.

Demonstration. Modeling desired performance executed by teacher, student(s), and/or visual aids.

Yes – Full model of the desired performance.

Partial – Incomplete model of task performance exhibiting only a portion of the desired movement.

No – No attempt to model the movement task.

Appropriate number of cues. The degree to which the teacher presents sufficient information about the movement task without overloading the learner.

Appropriate – Three or fewer new learning cues related to the performance of the movement.

Inappropriate – Either more than three or no new learning cues related to the movement.

None given – No attempt at providing learning cues was made.

Student responses appropriate to the task focus. The degree to which student responses reflect the intent to perform the task as stated by the teacher.

All – No more than two students exhibited inappropriate responses.

Partial – Three or more students exhibited inappropriate responses.

None – No students exhibited appropriate behavior.

Teacher specific congruent feedback. The degree to which teacher feedback during activity is congruent with (matched to) the focus of the task.

Yes – More than two incidences of congruent feedback.

Partial – One or two incidences of congruent feedback.

No – No congruent feedback was given.

Interpreting data. To analyze QMTPS data, the observer adds the number of tasks. Each dimension of the instrument (e.g., type of task, clarity, demonstration) is then analyzed in terms of the percentage of the total tasks categorized a particular way. In the data expressed in figure 14.13, for instance, only two of the fifteen tasks are presented with a full demonstration (13%). In most of the constructs of the instrument, category number one is a more desirable category. A higher percentage of tasks in this category should reflect a more skilled teacher.

As in all instruments, however, the data must be interpreted in the context of the lesson. Studies correlating teacher effectiveness in producing learning with the total average score on the QMTPS indicate that the effective teacher averages a total score of at least 50 percent.

It is also possible to calculate a total QMTPS score by adding the percentage score for the most desirable categories for each concept and dividing by the number of concepts. We have found in our work with teachers that if the total QMTPS

Qualitative Measures of Teaching Performance Scale

Name of teacher **M. Martins**   Name of coder **C. Fry**

Focus of lesson **Throwing - 2**   Lesson number **2**

Task		Presentation of task						
Number	Type of task	Clarity	Demonstration	Number of cues	Accuracy of information	Qualitative information	Student response appropriate to the focus	Specific congruent feedback
1	I	1	1	1	1	2	2	2
2	E	1	2	2	1	2	1	3
3	R	2	2	1	1	1	3	2
4	R	2	3	3	3	2	3	1
5	E	1	3	3	3	2	3	2
6	E	1	1	2	1	2	3	1
7	R	2	2	2	1	1	3	2
8	RE	1	3	1	2	2	3	2
9	A	2	3	2	2	2	3	2
10	RE	1	3	1	1	2	3	2
11	R	1	3	3	3	1	3	2
12	E	1	2	3	3	2	3	2
13	R	1	3	3	3	2	3	1
14	A	1	3	3	3	2	3	1
15	A	1	3	3	3	2	3	1
Totals		1.11 2.4	1.2 2.4 3.9	1.4 2.4 3.7	1.6 2.2 3.7	1.3 2.12	2.1 3.13	1.5 2.9
Percent for each category		1.73 2.27	1.73 2.27 3.60	1.27 2.27 3.60	1.40 2.13 3.47	1.20 2.80	1.7 2.7 3.87	1.34 2.60 3.07
Percent most desirable		73%	13%	27%	7%	26%	7%	34%

Type of task
  I-Informing
  R-Refine-quality
  E-Extend-variety, difficulty
  Re-Repeat-repeat same task
  A-Apply/Assessment

Clarity
  1-Yes
  2-No

Demonstration
  1-Full
  2-Partial
  3-None

Number of cues
  1-Appropriate
  2-Inappropriate
  3-None given

Accuracy of information
  1-Accurate
  2-Inaccurate
  3-None given

Qualitative information
  1-Yes
  2-No

Student responses
  1-All
  2-Partial
  3-None

Specific congruent feedback
  1-Yes
  2-Partial
  3-No

FIGURE 14.13
Qualitative Measures of Teaching Performance Scale.

score falls below 50 percent, a teacher usually has instructional communication problems that need to be addressed. It is not possible, or perhaps even appropriate, for teachers to always score in the most desirable category every time they present information to learners. Teachers should, however, try to attend to these communication indicators in their teaching.

Teacher Movement

Purpose. The purpose of this instrument is to determine teacher movement throughout the class. Teachers who move to different parts of the gymnasium or play space during a class can better monitor and relate to all students than teachers who tend to stay in one area or move to only selected areas of the play space.

Recording procedures. Information on where a teacher moves during a lesson can be recorded in many ways. One of the most useful is described in figure 14.14. To use this recording sheet the observer starts with the box in the top left corner that represents the play space. If the play space in use is shaped differently, it would be appropriate to draw different boxes. Each of these boxes represent five minutes of time. The observer merely draws a connecting line to where the teacher moves in the box as illustrated.

Interpreting data. Although it is sometimes appropriate for a teacher to spend a longer amount of time in one area than another, the overall pattern of the teacher's movement throughout a play area should reflect an attempt to move to all areas of the play space. If teachers consistently fail to get to particular areas

Observation of teacher movement

Teacher _F. Razor_   Date _4/21_

Lesson content _dance_   Observer _Jackie_

Grade level _7_

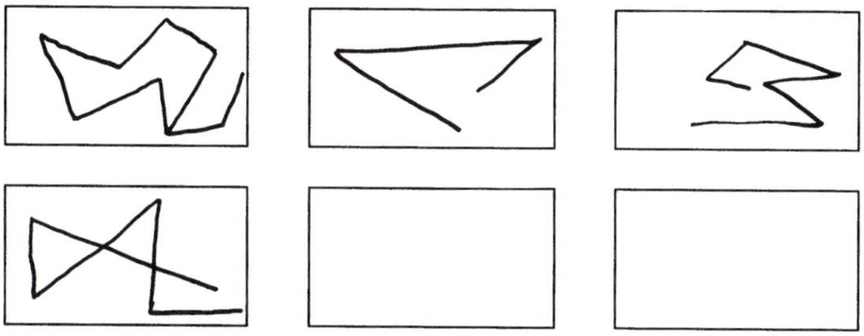

Coding direction: Each box represents 5 minutes of class time. Draw a continuous line indicating the teacher's movement through the area for each 5-minute time interval. Analyze each of the 5-minute time segments to ensure that the teacher is getting to all of the areas of the facility where the students are working.

FIGURE 14.14
Observation of teacher movement.

Teaching Diverse Students
Reflection Assignment *

1. Using your class of students, identify four or five individuals who represent the diversity of your population. In other words, in your opinion, these individuals are somehow very different from each other. Describe the differences that made you place them in this diverse group. Now, thinking about each individual, determine how many similarities they actually have with the students you placed in this group. A thorough reflection is expected, not just a listing.

2. Locate on your recorded lessons an incident where you addressed diversity both in your planning and in your teaching. Identify the *exact time* in the DVD where the incident can be identified. Include the following in your written response:
   - Describe the incident inclusive of the student involvement, your involvement, and the diversity connection.
   - How exactly did you write this in your lesson plan?
   - Reflect on your actions in the incident.

3. Locate on a recorded lesson a point where you observed an incident in which, after viewing it on the DVD, you realized you could have prevented a problem or aided a student better by taking another action. Include the following in your written response:
   - Describe the incident you observed when watching the lesson.
   - What were your thoughts in response to what you could have done differently?
   - If this incident brought something to your attention that motivated you to adjust something in your next lesson, share what you did.

4. We know that learners, regardless of age, have different strengths/weaknesses, have varying needs, have different learning styles, and bring with them a variety of prior experiences. Describe how you were able to meet the learner disparities of your class. Maybe you addressed diversity in learning through the way you developed your objectives, through intratask development, and/or through variety in your task presentations. Provide a different example of how you planned and taught to meet individual differences in each of the three learning domains. These examples must be different from any you have discussed earlier.
   - For cognitive learning to occur, what we teach students has to go beyond short-term memory to long-term memory. Students should be able to demonstrate understanding of movement concepts, principles, strategies, and tactics as they apply to the learning and performance of physical activities.
   - For motor learning in elementary school, we want students to go beyond the cognitive stage to the associative stage, or beyond the precontrol/control level to the utilization level. Ultimately, we want them to be competent in motor skills and movement patterns needed to perform in a variety of physical activities.
   - From an affective domain, physical education students should be learning to exhibit personal and social behaviors that demonstrate respect for self and others in physical activity settings. Additionally, they should be learning to value physical activity for health, enjoyment, challenge, self-expression, and/or social interaction.

5. Evaluate yourself honestly on the following and then set a goal as to how you can improve in two areas identified as unacceptable or needs improvement. If all areas were target, set a goal as to how you can maintain in at least two areas.

FIGURE 14.15
Used with permission of Dr. Tina Mall, University of South Carolina.

		Unacceptable (no evidence)	Needs Improvement (occasional evidence)	Target (consistently evident)
	Diversity Self-Evaluation			
1.	Demonstrates equity in working with students of all races and ethnicity. Does not have racial stereotyped thoughts or make racial stereotyped statements.			
2.	Demonstrates equity in working with students of both genders. Does not use sexist language or gender stereotyped statements. Does not have gender discriminating thoughts.			
3.	Demonstrates the ability to interact with all students and adults without discriminating against race, gender, physical abilities or disabilities, size, sexual orientation, etc.			
4.	Demonstrates compassion for all students and appears to put their needs ahead of own.			
5.	Is open to views of all students.			
6.	Values students as individuals.			
7.	Teaching strategies are used that promote success for all students.			
8.	Lesson plans demonstrate evidence of adaptations needed for students with unique needs.			
9.	Demonstrates evidence of not using put-downs or allowing others to put down their peers. Intervenes in biased interactions among students.			
10.	Selects materials, uses culturally diverse examples, and designs activities in ways that demonstrate appreciation of diversity.			

FIGURE 14.15 *(Continued)*

of the play space, students soon learn where they can go to "hide" should they want to.

Student Diversity Teachers in today's schools are likely to have a large number of students of different races, ethnic origins, and skill levels. It is always difficult when teachers are asked to relate to and work with students different from themselves and classes with a great deal of diversity. Developing an awareness of your own behavior and responses to different students is a first step to being able to meet the needs of all students. Figure 14.15 describes a reflective exercise that will help teachers understand their own behavior.

SUMMARY

1. The same instructional phenomena can be observed with different observational tools and with different observational techniques.
2. An observational tool is like a lens on a camera—it determines what you see, as well as what you do not see.
3. Intuitive observational procedures are not systematic. Observers make judgments without collecting data.
4. Anecdotal records describe in detail what an observer sees in a nonevaluative way. Data are sorted into meaningful information after they are collected.
5. Rating scales divide a phenomenon being observed into quantitative or qualitative levels. Levels must be divided specifically.
6. Event recording determines the occurrence or lack of occurrence of an event. Usually, the frequency of an event is also determined.
7. Duration recording determines the amount of time devoted to a particular behavior or instructional phenomenon. Duration recording can add up real time for an event or use a time line to determine the sequence and duration of events.
8. Time sampling is a technique that allows the observer to sample the occurrence of a behavior that does not change quickly by observing at periodic intervals (e.g., every ten minutes).
9. Many different observational tools have been developed to look at teaching. These tools can be used in a flexible way, both in combination with other tools and with different observational methods. The tools described in this chapter allow the teacher to collect information on the following:
   Student motor activity: ALT-PE
   Student use of time
   Content development: OSCD-PE
   Teacher feedback
   Student conduct
   Task presentation: QMTPS
   Teacher movement and location

CHECKING YOUR UNDERSTANDING

1. Identify the observational techniques or methods you might use to collect data on the following:
   The type of feedback a teacher gives
   The ability of a student to use the cues you have given in a motor skill
   The incidence of a student's off-task behavior
   The ability of a student to keep score in a game
   Time allotted to activity
   The amount of lecturing a teacher does
   The cooperative behavior of a student in a group setting
   What students like/dislike about their physical education class
   The accuracy of a teacher's demonstration
   Causes of off-task student behavior
   The progression the teacher uses in terms of refining, extending, and applying
   Major problems a teacher might be having in a class
   Teacher enthusiasm
   Teacher use of questioning
2. Design an observational system for a student and/or teacher behavior of your choice. Describe the type of observational method you will use, define your categories specifically, and state your coding procedures.
3. Use your observational system on a recorded lesson. Analyze and interpret your data. Evaluate your observational tool.
4. List the advantages and disadvantages of the following techniques and methods of observation:
   Intuitive observation
   Anecdotal records
   Rating scales
   Event recording
   Duration recording
   Time sampling

REFERENCES

Dodds, P. (1973). *A behavioral competency-based peer assessment model for student teacher supervision in elementary physical education.* Unpublished doctoral dissertation, Ohio State University, Columbia.

Fishman, S. E., & Tobey, C. (1978). Augmented feedback. In W. Anderson & G. Barrette (Eds.), What's going on in the gym? *Motor Skills: Theory into Practice* [Monograph 1].

Kounin, J. (1977). *Discipline and group management in classrooms.* Melbourne, FL: RE Krieger Publishing Co., Inc.

Metzler, M. (1979). *The measurement of academic learning time in physical education.* Unpublished doctoral dissertation, Ohio State University, Columbia.

Parker, M. (1989). Academic Learning Time-Physical Education (ALT-PE), 1982 Revision. In P. Darst, D. Zakrajsek, & V. Mancini (Eds.), *Analyzing physical education and sport instruction* (2nd ed.). Champaign, IL: Human Kinetics.

Rink, J. (1979). *The development of an instrument for the observation of content development in physical education.* Unpublished doctoral dissertation, Ohio State University, Columbia.

Rink, J., & Werner, P. (1989). Qualitative Measures of Teaching Performance Scale (QMTPS). In P. Darst, D. Zakrajsek, & V. Mancini (Eds.), *Analyzing physical education and sport instruction.* Champaign, IL: Human Kinetics.

Siedentop, D., Birdwell, D., & Metzler, M. (1979, March). *A process approach to measuring effectiveness in physical education.* Paper presented at the American Alliance for Health, Physical Education, Recreation, and Dance National Convention, New Orleans, LA.

Siedentop, D., Tousignant, M., & Parker, M. (1982). *Academic learning time-physical education: 1982 revision coding manual,* Columbus, OH: Ohio State University, College of Education, School of Health, Physical Education and Recreation.

Silverman, S. (1991). Research on teaching in physical education: review and commentary, *Research Quarterly for Exercise and Sport, 62*(4), 352–364.

Stewart, M. (1983). Observational recording record of physical education's teaching behavior (ORRPETB). In P. Darst, V. Mancini, & D. Zakrajsek (Eds.), *Systematic observation instrumentation for physical education.* West Point, NY: Leisure Press.

SUGGESTED READINGS

Cusimano, B., Darst, P., & van der Mars, H. (1993). Improving your instruction through self-evaluation: Part one: Getting started, *Strategies, 7*(2), 26–29.

Cusimano, B., Darst, P., & van der Mars, H. (1993). Improving your instruction through self-evaluation: Part three: teacher position and active supervision, *Strategies, 7*(4), 26–29.

Cusimano, B., van der Mars, H., & Darst, P. (1993). Improving your instruction through self-evaluation: Part six: Professional growth plans, *Strategies, 7*(7), 26–29.

Darst, P., Cusimano, B., & van der Mars, H. (1993). Improving your instruction through self-evaluation: Part two: Using class time effectively, *Strategies, 7*(3), 26–29.

Darst, P., Zakrajsek, D., & Mancini, V. (Eds.). (1989). *Analyzing physical education and sport instruction* (2nd ed.). Champaign, IL: Human Kinetics.

van der Mars, H., Cusimano, B., & Darst, P. (1993). Improving your instruction through self-evaluation: Part five: Assessing student behavior, *Strategies, 7*(6), 26–29.

Wolfe, P., & Sharpe, T. (1996). Improve your teaching with student coders. *Strategies, 9*(7), 5–9.

Glossary

Academic learning time (ALT)   The time a learner spends with the content at an appropriate level of difficulty.

Achievement theory   A theory of motivation that emphasizes the idea that a person's motivation toward a particular goal is a function of the relative strength of both the desire to achieve and the tendency to avoid failure.

Adaptability of skill performance   A quality related to the degree to which a performer can adjust movement performance to conditions surrounding performance.

Affective objective   An educational outcome specified for the development of feelings, attitudes, values, and/or social skills.

Application/assessment task   A teacher move that communicates a concern for moving the student focus from *how to do the movement to how to use the movement,* or an assessment of form.

Associative phase   The second phase in learning a motor skill, in which the learner can attend more to the dynamics of a skill.

Attention   Alertness in a particular situation to selectively receive and process information.

Attribution theory   A theory of motivation that emphasizes the important role of what people attribute success or failure to as a critical aspect of their approach to achievement-oriented tasks.

Authoritative management   A perspective on classroom management that has as its goal student self-management, but releases control as students are ready.

Automatic phase   The last phase in learning a motor skill, in which processing has been relegated to lower brain functions.

Backward chaining   A progression of parts that starts with the last part of a skill.

Behaviorism   A psychology of human behavior emphasizing environmental contingencies.

Bilateral transfer   Transfer of learning between limbs.

Closed skill   A motor skill performed in a fixed environment.

Cognitive objective   An educational outcome specified for the development of knowledge and thinking-related processes.

Cognitive phase   The initial phase of motor learning, in which the learner is engaged primarily in processing how the movement should be performed.

Cognitive theory   A holistic perspective on learning, emphasizing problem solving, transfer, and creativity.

Cognitive theory of motivation   A theory that emphasizes the subjective experience of the person as an explanation of behavior.

Congruent feedback   Feedback on performance consistent with the immediate task focus and cues.

Content behaviors   Those teaching behaviors that are directly related to the content of the lesson as opposed to the management of the lesson.

Content development   The teaching process that takes the learner from one level of performance in a content area to another.

Context   The specific situational conditions.

Continuous skill   Skill that has arbitrary beginning and ending points, such as dribbling a basketball, swimming, and running.

Cooperative learning   A teaching strategy in which learning tasks or projects are assigned to a heterogeneous group of learners to work cooperatively as a team.

Corrective feedback   Feedback that gives the learner information on what to do or not to do in a future performance.

Cue for the response   A learning cue that gives the learner information on the process/mechanical efficiency of the response.

Cue for use adjustment of the response   A learning cue that gives the learner information on how to adjust the movement response to a different condition.

Cue for use of the response   A learning cue that gives the learner information on how to use a movement in a particular situation.

Curriculums   Plans for programs of study.

Developmental analysis   An analysis of lesson content divided into a progressive assessment of extension, refinement, and application.

Direct instruction   A highly structured, step-by-step, teacher-dominated, active style of teaching.

Discrete skill   A skill performed once, with a clear beginning and end.

Distributed practice   Practice of the same skill over more than one day.

Effectiveness of skill performance   A quality of a movement related to the degree to which the movement accomplishes its intent.

Efficiency of skill performance   A quality of a movement related to the degree to which the movement is mechanically correct for a given performance and situation.

Environmental arrangements   Organizational arrangements for people, time, space, and equipment.

Environmental design   An approach to instruction that attempts to elicit good performance through the design of the task and environmental arrangements for the task.

Evaluative feedback   Feedback that makes a judgment about past performance.

Expectancy effects   The relationship between teacher expectations for behavior, the characteristics of the student, and the achievement of the student.

Extension task   A teacher's move that communicates a concern for changing the complexity or difficulty of student performance.

Feedback   Information an individual receives as a result of a response.

Formative evaluation   Assessment of progress toward a goal.

General feedback   Feedback that acknowledges performance but conveys no specific information on performance.

Goals   Broadly defined outcomes of an educational program.

Guided discovery   A problem-solving teaching strategy in which the teacher leads students to a correct answer.

High-inference tools   Those observation tools that require a great deal of observer judgment to use.

High-stakes assessment   Any assessment linked to accountability for the results.

Humanism   A psychology of human behavior emphasizing personal control.

Implicit curriculum   What students learn or experience in school that is not expressed explicitly.

Indirect instruction   A less-structured learning environment in which the goals may not be explicit and a portion of instructional functions are transferred to the student.

Indirectly contributing behaviors   Teaching behaviors that contribute only indirectly to lesson content by structuring or maintaining the learning environment.

Information processing   As a learning theory, an emphasis on how learners select, interpret, use, and store information.

Informing task   The first task in a progression of content.

Interactive teaching   A teaching strategy in which a teacher move is based on the immediate responses of students.

Interobserver agreement   Agreement between more than one observer on the same event.

Intertask development   A progression from one skill to another (e.g., volleyball underhand serve to volleyball overhand serve).

Intertask transfer   Transfer of learning between skills.

Intraobserver agreement   Agreement of one observer with himself or herself on two observations of the same event.

Intratask development   A progression of experiences related to a single movement skill or idea.

Intratask transfer   Transfer of learning within the same type of skill.

Invasion games   Those activities and sports that involve changing offensive and defensive roles in shared space according to who has the ball.

Knowledge of performance (KP)   Information the learner receives on how the skill is being performed (mechanical or feeling of the skill).

Knowledge of results (KR)   Information the learner receives on the extent to which a movement or skill has accomplished its purpose (e.g., whether the ball went into the basket).

Learning   A relatively permanent change in behavior resulting from experience and training interacting with biological processes.

Learning cue   A word or phrase that identifies or communicates to a performer the critical features of a movement skill or task.

Learning experience   A set of instuctional conditions and events that gives structure to an experience and is related to a particular set of teacher objectives.

Limited task   A movement task that gives little choice to students in their response.

Low-inference tools   Those observation tools that do not require a great deal of observer judgment to use.

Management behaviors   Instructional behaviors related to structuring, directing, or reinforcing appropriate conduct, as well as arranging the learning environment (time, space, people, equipment).

Massed practice   Repetitive practice of the same skill over time.

Motor program   A memory representation for a pattern of movement.

Movement concept   A label for a group of motor responses or movement-related ideas that share particular characteristics.

Movement task   A motor activity assigned to the student that is directly related to the lesson content.

Net activities   Those activities such as volleyball and tennis that involve alternating discrete skills, usually over a net.

Noncontributing   Any teacher behavior that does not contribute to the lesson objectives in a direct way (e.g., talking to a visitor who comes into the gym or getting equipment ready for the next class).

Noncontributing teaching behaviors   Teaching behaviors that make no contribution to lesson content.

Objectives   Specifically identified desired outcomes of an educational program usually specified for affective, cognitive, and psychomotor areas of development.

Open skill   A motor skill performed in an environment that is changing during performance.

Order   In relation to classroom ecology—high levels of engagement in what the student is supposed to be doing and low levels of engagement in inappropriate behavior.

Organizational arrangements   The arrangements teachers make for the organization of people, space, time, and equipment for a particular task or learning experience.

Peer teaching   An instructional strategy that transfers the teacher's responsibility for instructional components to students, who function in the role of the teacher.

Postlesson routines   The routine events that take place in a class after the instructional lesson is concluded.

Prelesson routines   The routine events that take place in a class before the onset of the instructional lesson.

Proximity control   Standing near or touching a student who may be disruptive, expressing a concern in the behavior.

Psychomotor objective   An educational outcome specified for the development of physical abilities or neuromuscular skills of the learner.

Refining task   A teacher move that communicates a concern for the quality of student performance, such as "Work to get your toss a little higher."

Reliability of observational tools   The degree to which an observational tool/construct can be used accurately and consistently to collect data.

Routines   Established and customary ways of handling events that occur with great frequency in a class setting.

Rules   Designated acceptable or unacceptable behaviors.

Scope and sequence of instructional content   What is to be learned and how what is to be learned should be organized for delivery to the learner.

Self-instructional strategies   Teaching strategies designed to permit the student to function with a degree of independence from the teacher.

Serial skills   Several discrete skills put together, such as a handstand into a forward roll.

Set induction   That part of the lesson in which the teacher orients the students to what they will be doing, how they will be doing it, and why they will be doing it.

Specific feedback   Feedback that conveys specific information to the learner on performance.

Station teaching   A teaching strategy that arranges the environment so that two or more tasks are going on at the same time in different places.

Success rate   The degree of success a learner experiences in learning.

Summary cues   Sequenced cue words that summarize the critical features of a task.

Summative evaluation   An assessment of the degree to which program objectives have been received.

Systematic observation and analysis   A process of collecting objective information on the instructional process and analyzing that information in a meaningful way.

Target of feedback   The individual, group, or class to which feedback is directed.

Teaching function   Those critical aspects of teaching that must be attended to regardless of the content or context of a lesson.

Teaching strategy   A framework that arranges an instructional environment for group instruction.

Team teaching   A teaching strategy in which two or more teachers share the responsibility for instructional functions for a given class.

Transfer of learning   The influence on one skill of having learned another skill.

Unlimited task   A movement task that gives students maximum opportunity to respond in different ways.

Validity of an observational tool   The degree to which an observational tool measures what it purports to measure.

Index

AAHPERD (American Alliance for Health, Physical Education, Recreation and Dance), 308
Ability levels
  appropriateness of learning experience, 11, 31, 32–33
  grouping for movement tasks, 47
  learner characteristics, 37–39
  learning cues, 75–77
  motivation of students, 193
Academic Learning Time–Physical Education (ALT-PE) instrument, 335–338
Accountability, 271
Accuracy
  force production versus, 97–98
  of observations, 315 (*See also* Reliability of data)
Achievement theory of motivation, 184–185
ACSD (Association for Supervision and Curriculum Development), 308
Action words, 291–293
Adaptation of skill performance, 55, 58
Advanced learners, learning cues for, 75
Affective goals/objectives, 3, 4–5, 206–207. *See also* Motivation
  defined levels of, 216
  establishing, 212
  integration with psychomotor and cognitive objectives, 11–12, 231
  as lesson focus, 197
  movement concepts, 295
  rating scale for, 247
Age of students, 75–77
Agreement between observers, 316
Alternative assessment, 246–248. *See also* Assessments
ALT-PE (Academic Learning Time–Physical Education) instrument, 335–338
American Alliance for Health, Physical Education, Recreation and Dance (AAHPERD), 308
Amotivation, 184
Analysis by teachers, 136–139. *See also* Observation

Anecdotal records, 325–327
Applications/assessment tasks, 46
  for content development, 84–85, 93–95
  interactive teaching strategies, 160
  OSCD-PE category definitions for, 338–339
  QMTPS category definitions for, 343–347
Appraising behaviors, 341, 343
Aronson, E., 167
Ashworth, S., 173
Assessments, 240–268. *See also* Observation
  alternative, 246–248
  applications/assessment tasks, 46 (*See also* Applications/ assessment tasks)
  formal, 264–265
  formal/informal evaluations, 245–246
  formative, 241–242
  grades/grading, 266–267
  group projects, 258
  integration into program, 260–264
  interviews, surveys, and questionnaires, 258–260
  in lesson plans, 232
  observation, 248–256
  parental reports, 260–262
  peer instruction, 255
  portfolios, 256
  rating scales, 247, 262–263 (*See also* Rating scales)
  skill tests, 257–258
  student journals, 255–256
  student logs, 258
  for student motivation, 196
  summative, 242–243
  of teaching skills, 318–319 (*See also* Teachers)
  validity/reliability issues, 243–245
  worksheets for basketball, 249–251
  worksheets for tennis, 252–254
  written tests, 256–257

Association for Supervision and Curriculum Development (ACSD), 308
Associative stage in motor learning, 25, 26
Attendance-taking, 111
Attention, 64–66, 125. *See also* Behaviors
Attribution theory, 35–36, 183
Audiotaping classes, 318. *See also* Media usage
Authoritative management systems, 122
Automatic stage in motor learning, 25, 26
Autonomy, 187

Backward chaining, 68
Badminton, 71
Balance, 158
Barrett, K., 137
Basketball
 direct/indirect instruction, 153
 dribbling skills, 56, 78, 103–104
 dribbling skills, progression for, 103–104
 passing skills, 58
 skills/stages of learning, 277–280
 worksheets for assessments of skills, 249–251
Bathroom breaks, 112, 147–148
Before-class routines, 110, 111
Beginners, 25, 75, 189
Beginning teachers, 189
 goals of, 210–211
 lesson plans by, 220
 NASPE national standards for, 305–307
Behaviorism, 24, 119
Behaviors
 ALT-PE category definitions, 335
 attention, 64–66
 changing, 319–320
 conduct, grading, 266–267
 conduct, measurement tool for, 341–343
 directly/indirectly contributing, from teachers, 132, 146–148
 discipline, 123–128
 establishing objectives for, 211–212
 event recording, 329–331
 expectations for, 115–116
 misbehaving students, 126–128
 modification of, 118–122
 off-task, 135, 315
 personal growth promoted through, 190–192
 prosocial, 191
 rating scales measuring, 327–329
 sampling student, 264
Beliefs in teaching, 16–17
Bilateral transfer, 36
Biscan, D., 137
Blakemore, C., 173
Bleeding injuries, 146

Bloom, B., 215
Bowling, 55
Boys, 202–203. *See also* Gender
Brekelmans, M., 154
Brophy, J.
 prosocial behaviors, 191
 stages of development, 114
Buck, M., 173
"Busy-happy-good" syndrome, 122

Caring attitudes, 191
Carrying actions, 276
Chance groupings, 48
Changing instructional process, 319–320
Checklists, 246, 262–263
Choice, 206–207
Choosing teams, 47
Clarity in instructions, 134–135
Classroom management. *See also* Management behaviors
 rules/procedures for, 113–114
Closed skills, 29–30, 275
 content development for, 96–98
 design of learning experiences, 56–58
 learning cues for, 77
 open skills practiced as, 77–78
 practice conditions for, 33
Cognition
 defined levels of, 216
 demonstrations for problem-solving, 70–71
 development, intelligence and, 38–39
 establishing objectives for, 212
 integration with psychomotor and affective objectives, 11–12, 231
 motor programs, 27
 movement concepts, 289–301 (*See also* Movement concepts)
 objectives, 3, 4
 orientation to learning motor skills, 24
 strategies for teaching, 172–174, 178
 teacher pacing of movement tasks, 49
Cognitive stage in motor learning, 25
Cognitive theory, 24
Collaboration with colleagues, 308
College education, 305
Combinations of skills, 281–282
Command teaching, 159
Commitment to teaching, 18
Communications
 clarity in instructions, 134–135
 cooperative learning, 168
 expectations for behavior, 120
 goals for movement tasks, 43–46
 peer teaching strategies, 164
 role playing, 123
 self-instructional strategies, 170–172

station teaching strategies, 161
task presentation, 69–72
Competition, 194
Complexity of skills, 96
Computers, 263–264
Concepts
  continuous play, 283
  cues for movement, 79
  demonstrations illustrating, 70–71
  fitness, 272
  movement, 289–301 (*See also* Movement concepts)
  role playing communications, 123
  rules as, 113
Concepts and Principles of Physical Education: What Every Student Needs to Know (Mohnsen), 291
Concrete operational intelligence, 38–39
Conduct, 266–267, 341–343. *See also* Behaviors
Conflict resolution, 123
Confrontations, 125–126
Congruency of feedback, 140–141, 341
Consistency
  in closed skills, 58
  for expectations, 116
  of observations, 316
  of routines, 57
Consistent observable performance, 22
Constructivist instruction, 24
Content. *See also* Content-specific pedagogy
  behaviors, 15–16 (*See also* Behaviors)
  cooperative learning, 166–168 (*See also* Cooperative learning)
  decisions, 8
  development, 14, 83–105 (*See also* Content development)
  developmental analysis of, 223–224
  direct/indirect instruction (*See also* Direct instruction)
  indirect instruction, 153
  interactive teaching strategies, 157–158
  learning cues, 77–79 (*See also* Learning cues)
  of movement tasks, 42–44 (*See also* Movement tasks)
  objectives consistent with, 215
  peer teaching strategies, 163 (*See also* Peer teaching)
  self-instructional strategies, 170
  sequencing for task presentation, 66–67
  station teaching strategies, 161
  teaching strategies and, 152, 154 (*See also* Strategies, for teaching)
  validity, 243–244
Content development, 14, 92–104
  application opportunities for skills, 85, 93–95
  for closed skills, 96–98 (*See also* Closed skills)
  developmental analysis, 88–95
  extension tasks, 88–93 (*See also* Extensions/Extending tasks)
  Observation System for Content Development–Physical Education (OSCD-PE), 338–339

for open skills, 98–104 (*See also* Open skills)
  progressions, establishing, 83, 86 (*See also* Progressions, establishing)
  refinement of tasks, 91–93 (*See also* Refinement of tasks)
  sequencing movement tasks, 84
Content-specific pedagogy, 270–302
  fitness, 270–275 (*See also* Fitness)
  games and sports, 275–286 (*See also* Games)
  movement concepts, 289–301 (*See also* Movement concepts)
Contextual interference, 34
Contingency contracts, 127
Continuous skills, 31
Contract teaching, 170
Control
  of objects, 276
  of objects, force reduction, 300
  of objects affecting strategies, 285
  success/failure, 185, 190
Convergent style/inquiry, 174
Conversations, 146–148
Co-op approach to cooperative learning, 167–168
Cooperation from students, 114–117
Cooperative learning
  combinations of skills, 282
  conflict resolution, 123
  games, 9
  inclusion of all students, 202
  sport education and, 287
  strengths and weaknesses, 177
  as teaching strategy, 166–169
Corrective behaviors, 341, 343
Corrective feedback, 140
Craft, A., 137
Creative dance, 289
Criterion-referenced evaluation, 243
Critical variables in teaching
  academic learning time (ALT) (*See* ALT-PE instrument)
  content/content development (*See* Content; Content development)
  feedback from teachers (*See* Feedback)
  student motivation (*See* Motivation)
Cues for learning, 72–80. *See also* Learning cues
Cultural differences, 203. *See also* Ethnicity
Curriculums, 2, 217
  developing from standards, 226
  in lesson plans, 225–226
  maintaining relationship to instruction, 5
  standards for physical education, 3

Dance, 54
  creative, 289
  movement qualities, 293
  peer teaching strategies for, 163
  teaching considerations for, 287, 288–289

Data
  anecdotal, records providing, 325
  AST-PE, interpreting, 336–338
  formal assessments, 265
  OSCD-PE, interpreting, 339
  QMTPS tool, interpreting, 345–347
  reliability of, 244–245 (*See also* Reliability of data)
  student conduct, interpreting teacher behavior
      for maintaining, 341–343
  student use of time, interpreting, 338
  teacher feedback, interpreting, 339–341
  teacher movement through class, interpreting, 347–349
  validity of, 316 (*See also* Validity of data)
Deci, E., 183
Decision making
  by students, 53–55, 122–123
  by teachers, 161
Defense strategies, 279–280, 283
Delayed feedback, 144
Demonstrations, 69–70
Designing learning experiences, 42–60
Desists, 124
Deterrents, 119
Developmental analysis, 88–95
  of content, in lesson plans, 223–224
Direct instruction
  dance, 288–289
  disadvantaged students, 204
  gymnastics, 287
  as teaching strategy, 152–155
Direct instruction models, 24
Disabilities, students with, 204–206
Disadvantaged students, 203–204
Discipline, 123–128, 341–343
Discrete skills, 31
Distractions, 65
Distributed practice, 35
Divergent style/inquiry, 173
Dodds, P., 332, 339
Duration recording, 331–332, 336
DVD equipment, 72. *See also* Media usage

Educational gymnastics, 287, 290. *See also* Gymnastics
Effectiveness of skill performance, 55
Effects of movement, 294–295
Efficiency of skill performance, 55–56
Effort, student, 266
Elementary school
  assessment of peer instruction, 255
  bathroom/water breaks, 147–148
  convergent inquiry strategy, 174
  defensible and not defensible programs, 4
  interactive teaching strategies, 158
  parental reports, 260–262

peer teaching strategies for dance, 163
rating scale for gymnastics, 247
self-instructional strategies for gymnastics in high school, 170
teaching functions, example of, 132
Emotions, in student journals, 255
Emphasis, in demonstrations, 71
End-of-lesson routines, 112
Engagement in tasks, 109
Enthusiasm, 190
Environmental conditions for learning, 31–32, 108–128
  authoritative management systems, 122
  behavior modification, 118–122
  closed skills and, 58 (*See also* Closed skills)
  conflict resolution, 123
  cooperation of students, 114–117
  discipline, 123–128
  environmental arrangements, 46
  golf swing, 99
  group process strategies, 122–123
  in gymnasiums, 108–109
  inclusion, 201–202
  open skills, 77–78 (*See also* Open skills)
  routines, 109–117
  rules, 113–114
  self-control/responsibility, 117–123
  social, knowledge constructed in, 24
  student decision making for environmental
      arrangements, 53–55
  teaching functions for maintaining, 135–136
  teaching strategies and, 154
Environmental design, 23, 98
Equipment
  arranged for movement tasks, 51
  limitations of, 10
  modification for learning, 88–90, 96–97
  modified for students with disabilities, 205
  routines for use of, 111
  station teaching strategies affected by, 161
  variety of, adding to practice time, 195
  for video- and audiotaping classes, 318
Equity, 202–206
Error rates, 11, 145
Ethnicity
  grouping for movement tasks, 48
  inclusion for, 203
  teaching opportunities about, 202
Evaluations, 240, 245–246. *See also* Assessments
  pretests, 231
  in unit plans, 233
Evaluative feedback, 140. *See also* Feedback
Event recording, 329–331, 336
Evertson, C., 114
Exams, 256–257
Exclusion, awareness of, 200–201

Exercise, 294. *See also* Fitness
Expectations
    disabilities, modifying for students with, 205
    student behavior, 115–116
Experiential teaching, 299
Extensions/Entending tasks, 88–93, 136
    for individuals, 145
    interactive teaching strategies, 159
    OSCD-PE category definitions for, 338–339
External motivation, 187
Externally paced skills, 30
Extracurricular activities, 3
Extrinsic motivation, 184
Eye contact, 124

Failure, 185, 190
Feedback, 28–29, 339–341
    checking for understanding of material, 69
    congruency of, 140–141
    cooperative learning, 169
    general versus specific, 141–142
    interactive teaching strategies, 160
    negative versus positive, 142–143
    peer teaching strategies, 164–165
    self-instructional strategies, 172
    station teaching strategies, 161–162
    targeting, 143–144
    on teaching classes, 319–320 (*See also* Teachers)
    as teaching function, 140–144
    teaching strategies including, 156
Fire drills, 148
Fishman, S. E., 339
Fitness, 270–275
    effects of exercise, 294
    goals for, 6
Fitts, P. M., 29
Flexibility, 295, 300
Folk dancing, 166
Force production, accuracy versus, 97–98
Force reduction, 104, 300
Formal assessments, 264–265. *See also* Assessments
Formal operational intelligence, 38
Formative assessments, 241–242
Freedom, 206–207

Games, 275–286
    complex control and combinations of skills, 281–282
    complex play, 283
    integrating play with practice in, 231
    object control, 276–280
    offensive/defensive strategies, 282–283
    rules of play, 91–92, 205, 283
    stages of learning, 276, 283
    stages of learning basketball, 277–280

Gender
    equity and inclusion, 202–203
    grouping by discouraged, 47
General feedback, 141–142. *See also* Feedback
Gentile, A. M., 29
Girls, 202–203. *See also* Gender
Goal-oriented activity, teaching as, 2–7
Goals
    affective, 197, 206–207 (*See also* Affective goals/objectives)
    of beginning teachers, 210–211
    direct instruction, 153 (*See also* Direct instruction)
    establishing, 211–215
    formative assessment, 241–242
    in lesson plans, 225
    long-term, 194
    as motivation for learning, 35–36
    movement tasks, setting for, 43–46
    nature of motor skills, 29–31
    participant-appropriate, 189
    processes for achieving, 7
    progression of intent for, 97
    realistic, establishing, 5–7
    relation to assessment, 240
    setting for movement tasks, 42
    of sport education, 286–287
    types of, 3–5
Golf, 99, 192
Good, T., 54, 122, 191
Grades and grading, 266–267
Group process strategies for developing self-direction, 122–123
Group time sampling, 336
Grouping of students
    in competition, 194
    movement tasks, design of, 46–48
    observation of teachers, 137
    routines for, 112
    student motivation and, 195
Guided discovery, 173
Gymnastics, 287
    educational, 290
    peer teaching strategies for, 163
    rating scale for elementary school, 247
    safety, 53
    self-instructional strategies for, 170, 171

Harrison, J., 173
Hastie, P., 167, 286
Health, 273. *See also* Fitness
Hearing impairment, 205
Hellison, Don, 118, 197
High school
    bathroom/water breaks, 147–148
    convergent inquiry strategy, 174
    defensible and not defensible programs, 4

High school (*Cont.*)
  fitness portfolio sample, 256
  interactive teaching strategies, 158–159
  parental reports, sample, 260–262
  peer teaching strategies for dance, 163
  rating scale for affective concerns, 247
  self-assessment in, 255
  self-instructional strategies for gymnastics in, 170
  station teaching strategy for volleyball, 160
  teaching functions, example of, 132
  worksheets for assessing basketball skills, 249–251
High-inference tools, 315
High-stakes assessments, 240, 264–265. *See also* Assessments
Hoffman, S., 137
Homework, 272
Human Kinetics Publishers, 308
Humor, 189

Improvement of students, 266
Inclusion, 199–207
  awareness of exclusion, 200–201
  climate for, 201–202
  equity, building, 202–206
  gender and, 202–203
  of students with disabilities, 204–206
  of students with disadvantages, 203–204
Indirect instruction, 24, 152–155. *See also* Direct instruction
Indirectly contributing behaviors, 132, 147
Individualization, 11
Information processing orientation, 24
Informing tasks, 85, 345
Injuries, 112, 146
Inquiry learning, 173
Instructional plans, 224–225
Instructional process, 12–16
  changing, 319–320
  direct/indirect (*See also* Direct instruction; Indirect instruction)
  observing and analyzing, 313–315
  a part of learning process, 22–24
  teachers and, 17–19
Intelligence, 38–39
Intention, 90
Interactions with students, 131, 190–192. *See also* Students
Interactive teaching, 157–160, 176
Internal motivation, 187
Interobserver agreements, 316
Intertask development, 83, 156
Intertask transfer, 36–37
Interval recording procedure for ALT-PE, 335–336
Interviews, 258–260
Intraobserver agreements, 316
Intratask development, 83, 156

Intratask transfer, 36–37
Intrinsic motivation, 184
Intuitive observation, 323–325
Invasion games, 282

Jigsaw approach to cooperative learning, 167
Johnson, D., 123
Johnson, R., 123
The Journal of Physical Education, Recreation and Dance, 308
Journal for Teaching Physical Education, 308
Journals
  by students, 255–256
  by teachers, 311

Keep-away games, 282
Kinesthetics, 293
Knowledge of performance (KP), 28
Knowledge of results (KR), 28, 97
Kounin, J.
  multitasking, 131
  prevention of problems, 124
Krathwohl, D., 215

Laban, Rudolf, 293
Late arrivals, 112
Learning cues, 72–80
  age/skill level appropriate, 75–77
  content appropriate, 77–79
  identifying, 72–73
  organization of, 80
  refinement of tasks, 92–93
Learning environments, 108–128. *See also* Environmental conditions for learning
Learning experiences
  criteria for, 7–12, 42
  designing, 42–60
  establishing goals and objectives for, 211–215
  motor skills, nature of, 55–58
  movement tasks, designing, 42–51
  safety, 52–53
  student decision making, 53–55
  for teachers, 308
Learning factors, 22–40
  critical variables in teaching (*See* Critical variables in teaching)
  learner characteristics, 37–39
  motivation/goal setting, 35–36 (*See also* Goals; Motivation)
  motor skills, 22–29 (*See also* Motor skills)
  practice for motor skills, 33–35 (*See also* Practices/practicing)
  skill development, appropriateness of, 31–32
  transfer of learning, 36–37
Learning theories, 17
Lessons. *See also* Learning experiences
  golf, sample unit plan for, 192

pacing, 196
planning, 217–233
routines related to, 111–112
sample, 12
student involvement with, 270
Levy, J., 154
Lifetime physical activity, 270–272, 275
Listening skills, 191
Locker room routines, 110, 111
Locus of control, 185
Logs, student, 258
Long-term planning, 192, 194
Low-inference tools, 315

Management behaviors, 15–16. *See also* Classroom management
    learning environment, creating, 109–128 (*See also*
        Environmental conditions for learning)
    task presentation directions, 66
Masia, B., 215
Massed practice, 35
Mastery learning, 170
Mastery-oriented climate, 185
Materials, teaching, 172
McCaslin, M., 122
Meaning, 186
Media usage, 72
    as assessment tool, 263–264
    audiotaping lessons, 318
    fitness taught using, 272
    golf facilities, 192
    videotaping classes, 318–319
Merrill, D. M., 290
Metzler, M., 335
Middle school. *See also* High school
    peer teaching strategies for volleyball, 163
    tennis forehand instruction, 157
Minorities, 197–202. *See also* Inclusion
Misbehaving students, 126–128, 191. *See also* Affective goals/
        objectives
Mohnsen, B., 264, 291
Mosston, M., 173
Motivation, 182–207
    affective goals, 197 (*See also* Affective goals/objectives)
    external, 187
    goal setting and, 35–36
    inclusion, 199–207 (*See also* Inclusion)
    intrinsic, 184
    need theory, 186
    personal growth, 190–196 (*See also* Personal growth)
    practical applications for theories of, 186–190
    as requirement for learning motor skills, 28
    station teaching strategies, 161
    theories of, 183–190

Motor programs, 27, 28
Motor skills
    ALT-PE instrument for, 335–338
    breaking into parts, 88
    classification of, 57, 58
    combinations of, 91, 281–282
    communicating goals for, 43–46
    design of learning experiences affected by nature of, 55–58
    efficiency component, 85
    fitness value, 274
    improving, as criteria for learning, 9
    learning factors for, 22–29
    movement tasks, 42–51 (*See also* Movement tasks)
    nature of goals for, 29–31
    practicing, 33–35 (*See also* Practices/practicing)
    requirements for learning, 26–29
    stages of learning, 25–26
    strategies and, 285–286
Movement concepts, 79, 289–301. *See also* Concepts
    action words, 291–293
    affects, 295
    defining, 296–299
    effects, 294–295
    identifying critical aspects of, 297–298
    principles, 293–294
    qualities, 293
    strategies, 294
    teaching of, 295–301
    transfer of learning, 290–291
Movement education style of teaching, 159
Movement tasks, 13, 42–51
    content dimension, 42–44
    contribution of instructional events to, 14
    examples of, 42
    extending, 88–95
    goal-setting, 42, 43–46
    learning cues for, 72–73 (*See also* Learning cues)
    organization of, 42, 46–51
    pacing, 49, 136
    self-testing for, 262
    success rate, 11
    task presentation, 63–81 (*See also* Task presentations)
    varying, 188
*Moving into the Future: National Standards for Physical
      Education* (NASPE), 2, 210
Multitasking, 132

Names, learning, 190
National Association for Sport and Physical Education
      (NASPE), 2
    affective standards of, 197
    goals for learners of, 169
    movement concepts of, 289

National Association for Sport and Physical Education (NASPE), (*Cont.*)
  National Standards for Physical Education by, 23, 153, 210, 211, 226, 308
  standards for promoting fitness of, 270
  standards for teachers of, 17, 305–307
National Board Certification, 310
National Education Association (NEA), 308
Need theory of motivation, 186
Negative approaches, 115
Negative feedback, 142–143, 339
Negotiation, 125–126
Net activities, 282
No Child Left Behind Act, 240
Noncontributing behaviors, 148
Non-English-speaking students, 203
Norm-referenced evaluations, 243
Notebooks, student, 255–256

Object control, 276–280
  affecting strategies, 285
  force reduction for, 300
Objectives
  affective, 206–207 (*See also* Affective goals/objectives)
  establishing, 211–215
  goals compared with (*See* Goals)
  goals distinguished from, 3
  integration of affective and cognitive and psychomotor goals, 11–12
  in lesson plans, 217
Objectivity, 244
Observation, 323–350
  ALT-PE instrument for student motor activity, 335–338
  anecdotal records, 325–327
  as assessment technique, 248–256 (*See also* Assessments)
  duration recording, 331–332
  event recordings, 329–331
  intuitive, 323–325
  Qualitative Measures of Teaching Performance Scale (QMTPS), 343–347
  rating scales, 327–329
  scoring rubrics, 329–331 (*See also* Scoring rubrics)
  skills taught to students, 164–165
  student conduct, 341–343
  student use of time, 337–338
  systematic observation and analysis, 312
  teacher feedback, 339–341
  by teachers, 136–139
  of teachers, 315–320
  time sampling, 332–335
Observation System for Content Development–Physical Education (OSCD-PE), 338–339

Offense strategies, 279, 282
Officiating games/sports, 148
Off-task behaviors, 315. *See also* Behaviors
  causes of, 135–136
Off-topic conversations, 146–148
Ohio State University, 335, 339
Older learners, 76–77
Olympic gymnastics, 287, 290
Open skills, 29–30, 275
  content development for, 98–104
  design of learning experiences, 58
  learning cues for, 77–79
  varying practice conditions for, 33
Organizational arrangements, 13
  in lesson plans, 224–225
  of movement tasks, 42, 46–51
  personal growth enhanced by, 195–196
  sequence of task presentations, 66–67
  task presentations, 66–67
Organizations for professional development, 308
OSCD-PE (Observation System for Content Development–Physical Education), 338–339
Outcomes, 153, 240. *See also* Goals
Outdoor pursuits, 287–289, 291
Outdoor settings, 65
Overlappingness, 132

Pacing, 49, 136, 196. *See also* Time
Pairs-check approach to cooperative learning, 167
Parents, 127, 260–262, 267
Parker, M., 336
Pedagogy, content-specific, 270–302. *See also* Content-specific pedagogy
Peer teaching, 162–165, 176–177
  assessment, 255, 263
  students with disabilities, 205–206
Performance
  adaptation of skill, 55, 58
  consistent and observable, 22
  efficiency of skill, 55–56
  knowledge of, 28
  mature level, 32
Performance-oriented climate, 185
Personal experience, 69
Personal growth, 190–196
  assessment of lessons, 196
  organizational arrangements enhancing, 195–196
  personal interactions promoting, 190–192
  planning lessons for motivating, 192–193
  presentation of tasks, 194–195
  task selection, 193–194
Personalization, 11
Peshkin, A., 203

Phi Epsilon Kappa Fraternity, 308
Physical activity, 270–272
The Physical Educator (journal), 308
Piaget, J., 38–39
Placek, J., 122
Planning, 210–238
  establishing goals and objectives for learning, 211–215
  lessons, 217–233
  of physical education experiences, 217
  unit plans, 232–233
Portfolios, 256, 312
Positive approaches, 115
Positive feedback, 142–143, 339
Poulton, E. C., 29, 56
Practices/practicing
  breaks from, 136
  conditions modified for, 88–90
  as criteria for learning, 10
  integrating game play with, 231
  motivation and, 189
  profiles and success rates, 33–35
  as requirement for learning motor skills, 28
  spaces arranged for, 49–51, 90
  style of teaching, 159
  teaching functions in, 131–132 (*See also* Teaching
    functions)
  variety in, 194
Prelesson routines, 13
Preoperational intelligence, 38
Prerequisites for learning motor skills, 26–27, 96
Prescriptive feedback, 140
Pretesting, 231
Preventive behaviors, 341, 343
Principals, 127–128, 148
Principles, movement, 293–294
Priorities, 133
Problem-solving, 173
Problem-solving tasks, 70–71
Procedures/rules for classroom, 113–114. *See also*
    Classroom management
Professional teachers, 305–320. *See also* Teachers
Progressions, establishing, 8, 86. *See also* Strategies,
    for teaching
  cooperative learning, 168–169
  interactive teaching strategies, 159
  peer teaching strategies, 164
  self-instructional strategies, 172
  station teaching strategies, 161
  teaching strategies and, 156
  whole-part-whole, 96
Propelling actions, 276
Prosocial behaviors, 191
Proximity control, 124

Psychomotor objectives, 3–4, 11–12. *See also* Motor
    skills; Objectives
Public address announcements, 148
Publications for teachers, 308

Qualitative Measures of Teaching Performance Scale
    (QMTPS), 343–347
Qualitative research, rating scales, 327
Quality of movement, 293
Questionnaires, 258–260

Rating scales
  as assessment tool, 247, 262–263
  examples of, 247
  as observational tool, 327–329
Receiving actions, 276
Recording procedures. *See also* Data; Observation
  ALT-PE method, 335–336
  OSCD-PE method, 339
  QMTPS method, 346
  student conduct, 343–344
  teacher feedback, 312
  teacher movement through class, 347
Refinement of tasks, 84, 92–93
  for individuals, 146
  interactive teaching strategies, 160
  OSCD-PE category definitions for, 339
Reflection skills, 121, 310–312
Reinforcement of behavior, 119, 120
Relationships of skills, 281–282
Reliability of data, 315–316
  anecdotal records, 325
  of assessments measures, 244–245
  duration recording, 331–332
  event recording, 329–331
  rating scales, 327
Repetition, 35, 68, 339
Reports, 258
Requirements for learning motor skills, 26–29. *See also*
    Motor skills
Research in physical education. *See* Critical variables
    in teaching
Resources, 308
Respect, 200
Responses
  cues for, 77
  expansion for movement concepts, 299–300
  open skills using, 101
Responsibility, 118, 197, 309
Results, knowledge of, 28, 97
Rewards, 119
Rink, J., 343
Role playing, 123

environment contributing to, 109–117
...sson and postlesson, 13
...s of play, 91–92, 205, 283
...les/procedures for classroom, 113–114. *See also*
    Classroom management
Ryan, R., 183

Safety
  designing teaching experiences, 52–53
  gymnastics, 290
  outdoor pursuits, 291
  teaching functions maintaining, 134
Safrit, M., 241
Scattered formations, 51
Schloss, P., 205
Scoring rubrics, 247–248
  basketball worksheet, 249–251
  in formal assessments, 265
  as observational tool, 327–329
  self-assessment, 255
  student projects, 258
  tennis worksheet, 252–254
Secondary education. *See* High school
Selection of responses, 101
Self determination theory, 183–184
Self-assessments, 255, 262, 312
Self-control, 117–123. *See also* Environmental conditions
    for learning
Self-direction, 122–123
  motivation and autonomy, 187 (*See also* Motivation)
  teaching strategies and, 154 (*See also* Strategies, for teaching)
Self-esteem, 187, 204
Self-instructional strategies for teaching, 169–172, 177
Self-pace skills, 29
Self-testing, 93–94
Sending actions, 279
Sensorimotor intelligence, 38
Sequence/sequencing
  instructions, 25
  movement tasks in content development, 84, 92–93
  task presentations, 66–67
Serial skills, 31
Set induction, 13, 67, 218
Shotgun approach to feedback, 141
Siedentop, D.
  on ALT-PE instrument, 335, 336
  on cognitive strategies for teaching, 173
  on sport education, 167, 286
Silverman, S., 336
Singer, R. N., 56
Skills
  appropriateness of development, 31–32
  basketball, 277–280

content decisions, 8
independence in working on, 162
lifetime activity for students with disabilities, 206
nature and types of, 29–30
performance of, 55
stages of learning motor skills, 25–26
task analysis of, 27
tests of, 257–258
Slavin, R., 167
Social compatibility, 48
Social learning theory, 183
Softball, 84
Soliciting behaviors, 341, 343
Space
  as concept, 299
  for practice, 49–51 (*See also* Practices/practicing)
  for practice, modifying for movement tasks, 88–90
  for practice, station teaching strategies affected by, 161
Specific feedback, 141–142
Sportsmanship, 193
Sports/sports education, 286–287. *See also* Games
Spotting, 290
Standardized tests, 245
Standards. *See* National Association for Sport and
    Physical Education
State organizations for physical education, 308
Station teaching, 160–162, 176
Step patterns, 288–289
Stereotyping, 200, 203. *See also* Inclusion
Strategies for teaching, 155
  in lesson plans, 218
Strategies (journal), 308
Strategies, for games, 282–286
Strategies, for teaching, 152–179
  cognitive, 172–174
  cooperative learning, 166–169
  as delivery system, 155–157
  direct/indirect instruction, 152–155 (*See also* Direct instruction;
    Indirect instruction)
  interactive, 157–160
  movement concepts, 294 (*See also* Movement concepts)
  peer teaching, 162–165 (*See also* Peer teaching)
  self-instructional, 169–172
  strengths and weaknesses of each strategy, 176–178
  team, 175–179
  varying, 187
Structure, 112–113. *See also* Routines
Structuring behaviors, 341, 343
Student responses to instruction, 13–14
Students
  assessments of, 248–260 (*See also* Assessments)
  attention of, 64–66
  conduct (behavior) of, 341–343
  decision making by, 53–55

establishing objectives for, 211–215, 223

feedback to, 28–29 (*See also* Feedback)

grading, 266–267

interactions promoting personal growth, 190–192

misbehaving, 126–128 (*See also* Discipline)

motivation, 182–207 (*See also* Motivation)

paced tasks, 49

peer teaching, 162–165 (*See also* Peer teaching)

projects, 258

Success, attribution of, 185, 190

Success rates, 11

Summary cues, 74, 80

Summative assessment, 242–243

Surveys, 258–260

Systematic observation and analysis, 136–139, 312.
See also Observation

anecdotal records not providing, 325

event recording, 329–331

Tactics for games, 282, 284–286

Task analysis, 27

Task presentation, 63–81

attention of learners, 64–66

checklist for, 80

communicating clearly, 69–72

example of, 64

learning cues, 72–80 (*See also* Learning cues)

modifying tasks, 144–146

personal growth enhanced by, 194–195

QMTPS category definitions for, 345

sequencing content, 66–67

teacher functions, 134–136 (*See also* Teaching functions)

teaching strategies for, 154

Task teaching, 161. *See also* Station teaching

Taxonomy of Educational Objectives, 215

Teachers, 16–19, 305–320

as continuous learners, 307–312

establishing objectives for, 223

functions in teaching-learning process, 15 (*See also*
Teaching functions)

management (*See* Management behaviors)

movement through class, 347–349

organizations for, 308

paced tasks, 49

personal teaching experiences, data collection
of, 312–313

personal teaching process, analysis of, 318–319

professional, characteristics of, 16–19

Qualitative Measures of Teaching Performance
Scale, 343–347

as reflective practitioner, 310–312

standards for, 305–307

Teaching Elementary Physical Education (journal), 308

Teaching functions, 14–15, 131–148

clarification/reinforcement of tasks, 134–135

feedback, 140–144

indirectly contributing behaviors, 147–148

maintaining learning environments, 135–136 (*See also*
Environmental conditions for learning)

maintaining safety, 134

noncontributing behaviors, 148

observation and analysis of students, 13–139

setting priorities, 133

task modification, 144–146

Teaching strategies. *See* Strategies, for teaching

Team teaching, 175–179

Team-Games Tournament (cooperative learning), 167

Technology, 263–264

Tennis, 73, 77

direct instruction for forehand for middle schoolers, 157

forehand, progression of skills, 100

observation of forehand tasks, 137

serving, progression of skills in, 102

worksheets for assessment of skills, 252–254

Tests, 256–257. *See also* Assessments

formal assessments, 264–265

norm- and criterion-referenced, 243

pretests, 231

Thirty-second wonders, 263

Time

arranging for movement tasks, 48–49

duration recording, 331–332

insufficient use of, 65–66

in lesson plans, 224

pacing of lessons, 196

pacing of movement tasks, 48–49, 136

sampling, 332–335

student use of, measuring, 337–338

timing of feedback, 144

in unit plans, 233

Time-outs, 125

Tobey, C., 339

Tolerance, 199–200

Transfer of learning, 36–37, 290–291, 294

Turn teaching, 175

Unit plans, 232–233

University of South Carolina, 73

Validity of data

anecdotal records, 325

assessment measures, 243–245

duration recording, 331–332

event recording, 329, 331

intuitive observation, 323

observation tools, 316

Values, 197

movement concepts, 300

Value, (*Cont.*)
for teachers, 16–17
teachers communicating, 197
Vander Mars, H, 167, 286
Variability, practice, 33–35
Verbal communications, 69, 76, 77. *See also* Communications
versatility, 58
videos, 72. *See also* Media usage
of lessons, 318–319
Visual impairment, 205
Visual materials, 72
Volleyball, 86, 100

peer teaching strategies for, 163
station teaching strategies in, 161

Water breaks, 112, 124, 147–148
Web sites, 309
Werner, P., 343
Whole-part question, 96
Withitness, 124, 131
Wood, T., 241
Written tests and reports, 256–257

Young learners, 75–76